Ethics for Paralegals

ASPEN PARALEGAL SERIES

Ethics for Paralegals

Second Edition

Linda A. Wendling
(formerly Spagnola)

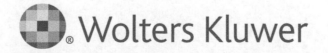

Printed in the United States of America.

1 2 3 4 5 6 7 8 9 0

ISBN 978-1-4548-6914-6

Library of Congress Cataloging-in-Publication Data

Names: Wendling, Linda A., author.
Title: Ethics for paralegals / Linda A. Wendling (formerly Spagnola).
Description: Second edition. | New York : Wolters Kluwer Legal & Regulatory
   U.S./Aspen Publishers, [2018] | Series: Aspen paralegal series | Includes
   index.
Identifiers: LCCN 2017032711 | ISBN 9781454869146
Subjects: LCSH: Legal assistants—United States. | Legal ethics—United
   States. | Legal assistants—United States—Handbooks, manuals, etc.
Classification: LCC KF320.L4 S69 2018 | DDC 174/.30973—dc23
LC record available at https://lccn.loc.gov/2017032711

About Wolters Kluwer Legal & Regulatory U.S.

Wolters Kluwer Legal & Regulatory U.S. delivers expert content and solutions in the areas of law, corporate compliance, health compliance, reimbursement, and legal education. Its practical solutions help customers successfully navigate the demands of a changing environment to drive their daily activities, enhance decision quality and inspire confident outcomes.

Serving customers worldwide, its legal and regulatory portfolio includes products under the Aspen Publishers, CCH Incorporated, Kluwer Law International, ftwilliam.com and MediRegs names. They are regarded as exceptional and trusted resources for general legal and practice-specific knowledge, compliance and risk management, dynamic workflow solutions, and expert commentary.

This book is dedicated to my family, whom I love beyond measure.

To my daughters, Emmelia and Katerina—the lights of my life. I have watched them grow and blossom into beautiful, witty, and intelligent young ladies from the time of the first edition until now. They mean more to me than they will ever know. My heart bursts with pride at their accomplishments and their potential for their future.

To my parents, Susan and Larry Pflum—twin pillars of strength and support. I simply would not be who I am or where I am without them. Every day they find another way to show their love, and I am forever grateful.

To my husband, John Mark Bojanski—my beloved anchor and soulmate. He is always patient, always kind, and always has an open heart. He has brought so much beauty and adventure into my life. He can simultaneously let me soar and hold me safe and close—true magic.

Linda A. Wendling
August 2017

Summary of Contents

ix

Contents

PART TWO   THE ATTORNEY-CLIENT RELATIONSHIP

PART THREE   **THE LEGAL PROFESSIONALS'
ROLES IN THE JUSTICE SYSTEM**

Preface

AN EVOLVING PROFESSION

Welcome to the second edition of "Ethics for Paralegals"! As the years have passed since the first writing, the paralegal profession has undergone some significant changes and grown in importance. Economics has caused a sea change in the way legal service providers market, charge fees, and allocate work. The ABA has taken notice of the significant contributions that paralegals make to the lawyers who employ them, indeed, dedicating an entire webpage to the topic "Information for Lawyers: How Paralegals Can Improve Your Practice." There are two major economic reasons for the increase in the utilization of paralegals, (1) improved profitability to the firm/organization and (2) enhanced client satisfaction due to lower legal bills.

Many people have legal issues and need guidance from a legal professional in order to resolve them; however, the cost of attorney's fees may be prohibitive. Concurrently, legal practices have faced the hard economic choice either to increase fees to meet the financial requirements of running the practice or to turn clients away. The solutions to both needs can be found in the paralegal profession. With the proper education and training, paralegals acquire legal knowledge and skills to perform many tasks previously performed by attorneys. The cost of hiring a paralegal is far less than the cost associated with an attorney. This is the "access to justice" theory. As many potential clients cannot afford the fees and costs associated with obtaining the assistance of an attorney, they are denied access to the justice system. There have been many criticisms that in the justice system, the wealthy can "get away with murder" because they can afford the high cost of legal services and/or pay to drag out the process and drain the other side of resources. Additionally, legal services attorneys are booked beyond their capacity to serve all those who qualify for public legal assistance. As a result, paralegals have become indispensable members of the legal team in both the private and the public sectors. These factors have also led to the development of a licensure system of independent paralegal practitioners in some states called either Legal Document Preparers (LDPs) or Limited License Legal Technician (LLLTs).

Given the economic incentives to increase paralegals workloads with more sophisticated, substantive work, it becomes even more imperative that paralegals understand the complexities of the practice of law in its entirety. While the two professions are distinct from one another, they are inexorably linked. The birth of the practice of law can arguably be traced to the first codifications of enforceable law, the Code of Hammurabi in 1780 BCE. As the legal market and practice becomes ever more complicated—and indeed it has had plenty of time to develop—paralegals need to follow those developments and understand the role they play in ensuring compliance with the standards of ethical practice.

AN ETHICAL PROFESSION

As a society, we have yet to form a concrete picture of a paralegal. Indeed, even attorneys are not clear on what constitutes the practice of a paralegal. In an attempt both to clarify the duties of a paralegal and to educate attorneys, the "patrons" of paralegal services, the ABA has prepared *Model Guidelines for the Utilization of Paralegals*. With these guidelines, the ABA hopes to promote the growth of the paralegal profession by giving attorneys a way to confidently delegate duties for which the paralegals have been trained. As noted above, the effective use of paralegals in the law office increases productivity, billable hours, efficiency, and client satisfaction. Paralegals, working in concert with their supervising attorneys, can find both career and personal satisfaction in knowing that they are a vital part of a team rendering legal services to a broader spectrum of clients and potentially increasing access to justice, with the utmost ethical integrity.

While lawyers are popularly regarded as cunning and dishonest, the profession holds itself to the highest standards of integrity and candor. These high standards apply to paralegals working under lawyers' supervision as well. Indeed, the ABA has created the Model Guidelines for the Utilization of Paralegal Services (MGUPS), which supplement the ethics rules, in that the MGUPS address the relationship between the attorney and the paralegal rather than the attorney and the client. The thrust of the MGUPS is the proper delegation and supervision of tasks to a paralegal and the clarification of the position of paralegal to third parties. While a paralegal performs legal duties, it is the lawyer who remains ultimately responsible for the end product. The lawyer must be sure that the paralegal has the proper skills to competently carry out the task assigned. Furthermore, the paralegal's conduct must be consistent with the lawyer's obligations under the relevant ethical codes; this emphasizes the need for the paralegal student to study the attorney's code of ethics.

The many other organizations involved in the profession have their own definitions and guidelines. However, there are some common elements to all of them. A paralegal is a professional who works under the supervision of an attorney and performs substantive legal work; the time spent on these tasks is billable. In essence, the work performed by paralegals is work that, if the paralegal were not available to perform it, would have to be performed by an attorney. This is the point of this textbook. If a paralegal is performing substantive legal work, that paralegal must also perform that work to the same ethical standards that apply to lawyers. It is imperative that paralegal students learn not only how to perform their jobs well, but also how to perform them ethically. Almost every task performed in the law office, even one not necessarily substantive in nature, has an ethical reason behind the method of performance. Even filing systems conform to ethical standards, by preserving client confidentiality.

As a vital member of the legal team, the paralegal performs tasks that, absent the paralegal, would have to be performed by an attorney. It follows logically, then, that the paralegal, in practicing law under the supervision of an attorney, needs to follow the same rules as an attorney. Otherwise, the delegation of these legal duties to a paralegal would not be proper or ethical. A mantra common in the ethics classroom is this: "A paralegal cannot do that which an attorney cannot do." So it follows that a paralegal must do what an attorney must do—and that is to conform to the ethics rules in every task performed.

The legal profession is self-policing: the rules of professional conduct are written by lawyers and judges and enforced by lawyers and judges. This is different from the situations in almost every other profession, as the latter are governed by rules written by the legislature (of whom about 50 percent hold law degrees). These rules are not a ceiling, but a floor. The standards set forth in the ethics rules are the minimum acceptable actions. Attorneys and paralegals should strive for more—to not only meet, but also exceed these requirements. Ultimately, these ethics rules should be considered alongside your personal moral compass as well.

That being said, why do paralegals and lawyers need a separate and comprehensive set of rules if individual morality is to be considered as well? It is the nature of not only the relationship between the lawyer and the client but also the relationship to the justice system that requires a higher standard of care to be exercised by legal professionals. A client comes to the law office seeking help during an important time in his life. No one seeks out legal advice "for the fun of it." Consulting with a legal professional is expensive and often stressful. A client is in a vulnerable position, and the lawyer is under a special "fiduciary" duty to assist the client to the best of her individual capability. This fiduciary relationship requires that the attorney act with good faith and trust, maintain the confidences of the client, and be truthful and forthright in rendering an opinion regarding the representation of the client.

THIS TEXTBOOK

Ethics can be taught either as a stand-alone course or as an integral part of every legal specialty course—or as a combination of both. The book is divided into three parts. Part One introduces the paralegal student to the basic tenets of legal ethics. Part Two covers the issues, rules, and regulations affecting the paralegal's practice of law and the relationships with clients. Part Three addresses the roles and ethical requirements that legal professionals play in the justice system. Codes of professional responsibility of both NALA (National Association of Legal Assistants) and NFPA (National Federation of Paralegal

Associations) are presented for analysis. In some instances they are very similar, and in others they diverge. This side-by-side comparison provides the paralegal student an opportunity to exercise critical thinking skills.

Additionally, in an effort to make learning legal ethics interesting, comprehensible, and practical, a variety of different learning tools appear in each chapter.

1. **In-Class Discussions** introduce scenarios with potentially diverse or surprising outcomes. This is an opportunity to talk about them with the instructor and other students in class.
2. **Review Questions** of many different kinds address the different learning styles of students. There are "Faulty Phrases" (the statements are false and the student must correct them), Explanations, Multiple Choice questions, and others. The emphasis is on critical thinking and problem-solving skills as they relate to the Rules of Professional Responsibility.
3. **Spot the Issue** is an analytical tool wherein the student must identify the problem in a short fact-scenario.
4. **Research This** attempts to strengthen the student's research skills by providing suggestions for more in-depth study of key issues.
5. **Surf's Up** addresses the current electronic globalization of the practice and problems associated with virtual communications, privacy, and confidentiality. .
6. **Reel to Real** turns the paralegal's critical eye on popular movies portraying the practice of law. The exercise asks the student to scrutinize Hollywood's portrayal of attorneys and ethical dilemmas.
7. **Case in Point** is a section containing the text of a relevant case or ethics opinion, presented for you to read and discuss in class. A summary or case brief, if the students are familiar with that format, should be prepared by the student both to aid the student in active class participation and to reinforce strong writing skills.

NEW FOR THIS EDITION

There have been significant advances in the paralegal profession that are reflected in this second edition. Of course, even as the book was going to press, changes were occurring in the legal field. It is impossible to stay current in print form; however, this text points students to the electronic resources that are most current at any given moment. Further, the exercises are intended to develop this information literacy so that students are practicing this skill throughout their program of study.

Economics

Recognizing the impact that the changing nature of the economics of traditional law firm practice, this second edition addresses those realities. The "unbundling" of legal services has resulted in both the responsible allocation of additional duties to paralegals and the increased potential for the unauthorized practice of law. Access to justice issues have also given rise to an entirely new licensure scheme for what may be termed "independent paralegals," the Limited License Legal Technicians. Those statutes and ethical considerations are discussed in this edition.

Technology in the practice

Economics is not the only factor affecting how law is practiced; technology has had a significant impact on every element of case management. Rules of Professional Responsibility have been changed in this regard. In order for attorneys and paralegals to remain competent and secure client confidentiality, they must have working knowledge of the different technologies available, " including the benefits and risks associated with relevant technology." (See comment 8 to the ABA's Model Rules of Professional Conduct.) Maintaining confidentiality in communicating with the client or securing information is also affected by technologies that demand discretion in using electronic means which can undermine the security of that information.

The Internet & social media

The Internet, its ease of use, and global accessibility has redrawn or eliminated the boundaries of privacy, security, and relationships. The Internet has removed the physical barriers to interactions between people. The practice of law has had to adapt to this new space where disclosures (harmful or not) and conflicts (prejudicial, unintended, or otherwise) are rife. There have been numerous cases of "friending" or "following" that were determined to be inappropriate and/or unethical.

Legal resources

Each development in the legal field has resulted in updates to rules of conduct, case law, ethics opinions, and statutes governing the practice. Each case from the first edition was reviewed for continued relevance. Where there was a more illustrative current case, those changes were made.

About the Author

Linda Wendling (formerly Spagnola) earned her BA in French with a minor in political science from Rutgers College and her JD from Seton Hall School of Law. She is admitted to practice in New Jersey, New York, Massachusetts, and North Carolina, where she now resides.

Upon graduation, she worked for a boutique law firm specializing in construction law. This area of law is its own peculiar creature whose practice requires attention to detail and perseverance to endure years of complex litigation. After leaving active practice in 2001, Dr. Wendling turned to academia. She joined the faculty of Union County College in Cranford, New Jersey. There, she created the Paralegal Program from the ground up and started registering students in 2003. The spring of 2006 saw her first class of graduates earning their associate degrees in Paralegal Studies.

After moving to North Carolina in 2007, Dr. Wendling (or just "W" as her students call her) could not resist the call of the classroom, except this time it was as a student. She pursued a master's degree in constitutional history at North Carolina State University. She also served as the Assistant Dean for Career Services at North Carolina Central University School of Law. The pull of hands-on teaching then led her to South University, where Dr. Wendling served not only as the Legal Studies Program Director, but also as the Chair of the Department serving campuses in ten states.

Learning never ends. Concern for the future led Dr. Wendling to Vermont Law School, where she earned an LL.M. in Environmental Law in January 2016. The culmination of her studies was an appointment to the Paris Climate Change Conference (COP21) as a U.N. delegate to assist Myanmar in preparing their position papers for international negotiation. She currently serves as the co-chair for the pro bono committee for the Environmental Law Section of the North Carolina Bar Association and an appointed member of the board of directors for the Abundance North Carolina Foundation. Dr. Wendling currently serves as the co-chair for the pro bono committee for the Environmental Law Section of the North Carolina Bar Association and an appointed member of the board of directors for the Abundance North Carolina Foundation while managing the Southeastern States of Western Governors University's academic compliance. In this role, she works with a team of professionals ensuring conformity with national, state, and local standards in higher education.

Ethics for Paralegals

Part One

The Practice of Law

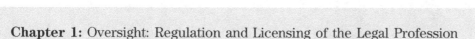

Chapter 1

Oversight: Regulation and Licensing of the Legal Profession

Chapter Objectives

The student will be able to:

- Compare the educational requirements for attorneys and paralegals
- Differentiate among the different types of regulatory plans for the paralegal profession and discuss the pros and cons of each
- Recognize the major associations related to the legal field and identify their mission and role in the paralegal profession
- Identify the various ethical sanctions that can be imposed upon attorneys and the conduct by either the attorney or the paralegal that would warrant those sanctions

This chapter will explore the formal educational requirements and regulations imposed upon the legal profession: *who* may call themselves attorneys or paralegals; *what* steps they must fulfill to achieve that position; *where* they may practice; and *how* they stay current in the field by taking continuing legal education and joining relevant legal organizations.

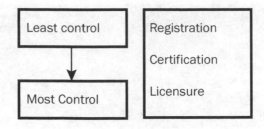

All professionals, those with education and/or experience in a certain field, are responsible to provide the public with the best services they can render. This duty may be imposed by a regulatory body that promulgates codes of conduct or simply by the voluntary observance of "best practices" in an industry. There are varying degrees of control that can be exercised over a particular profession. The least constrictive method is *registration*, as this is a voluntary credential in which a person may choose to become *registered*. The highest degree of control is exercised by a governmental body that issues *licenses* to perform certain services to the public. Between these two extremes lie *certified* professions wherein the characteristics of both registration and licensure are blended in certification. Under the certification method, qualification is completely voluntary (like registration), but there are strict standards that must be complied with in order to use the designation (like licensure). See Figure 1.1 illustrating the relationship between these methods of control.

This text will speak to the generally accepted norms and guidelines regarding attorney and paralegal educational and practice standards across the nation. It will be up to the paralegal student to investigate the particulars of his individual state. This is an exciting time to be a paralegal. Students and professionals have the opportunity to be involved in the process of shaping the future of the paralegal profession, because it still is developing and growing. In order to be best armed for involvement in these issues, it is important for the student to understand the ethical and regulatory models that affect the practice of law for both paralegals and attorneys.

PARALEGALS

Education

There are currently no formal requirements for paralegal education. The local marketplace dictates the extent of education required by the candidate. Generally, the more metropolitan areas and the larger firms look for a four-year degree, while smaller firms may desire a two-year degree (in order to save costs in salary), and some firms are willing to train "in-house" without any formal coursework. Why this range in qualifications? The simple answer lies in the economics of supply and demand. The more qualified candidates there are in an area, the more an employer can demand from them. The best advice to a paralegal student? Know your market and pursue the appropriate level of education.

As a guide, both the American Bar Association (ABA) and the American Association for Paralegal Education (AAfPE) have set forth certain educational standards for paralegals. An institution's decision to comply with these standards and/or to apply for ABA approval is completely voluntary. Along with the ABA and the AAfPE, the International Practice Management Association (IPMA), formerly known as the Legal Assistant Management Association; the National Association of Legal Assistants (NALA); the National Federation of Paralegal Associations (NFPA); and the Association of Legal Administrators (ALA) have recognized that a quality paralegal education consists of at least 18 semester units of paralegal coursework, along with general education requirements earned from an educational institution accredited by a nationally recognized agency.

What is "paralegal coursework?" How does it differ from law school courses? Primarily, a paralegal's education focuses on gaining the **practical skills** needed to enter the workforce as a productive member of the legal team. Much of the coursework is "hands-on" and "how-to." Paralegals are taught not only the substantive and procedural law in various areas of practice, but also what to do with that information. Intricate theory is saved for in-depth law school courses. This is where the difference between law school and paralegal degree programs becomes clear. Many new lawyers enter the workforce having passed multiple grueling exams, certain of their theoretical knowledge base but having no idea either how to prepare a legal document evidencing it or where to file such a document. The hours spent bent over a casebook deciphering court opinions and preparing for a day of Socratic interrogation does not prepare a law school graduate to fill out a HUD statement for a real estate closing. However, since most paralegal curricula do prepare those graduates to do just that, entry-level paralegals must hit the ground running.

practical skills
The ability to put theory into practice by performing the tasks necessary to achieve a desired result.

Regulatory Plans

Just as there are no formal educational requirements in place for paralegals, there is no mandatory authority regarding who may practice as a paralegal.

PORTFOLIO ASSIGNMENT

Write Away

Informal fact gathering is a task normally assigned to paralegals.
Your first assignment is to find all the paralegal education offerings in your state. What are the significant similarities and differences between them? Prepare an internal memorandum to your supervising paralegal manager advising her of your findings.

There have been many attempts in the profession's history and in many parts of the country to somehow control the practice of paralegals. There are generally three means of monitoring and/or controlling a profession: (1) public or private *registration*, (2) private *regulation* and *certification*, and (3) *licensure*. The nomenclature is not nearly as important as the plan and method of controlling the profession, and it will vary from jurisdiction to jurisdiction. The processes may apply to either professionals at the entry level or those of advanced standing, or to both.

Registration

This is the least burdensome and least restrictive of the three main categories of oversight. *Registration* simply results in a list of persons who call themselves paralegals, and the list can be maintained by either a private or public entity. There are no requirements for being able to put your name on the list and registration is voluntary. If your name is not on the list, it has no impact on your right to practice as a paralegal.

Private Regulation and Certification

certification
The recognition of both the successful attainment of a degree of academic and practical knowledge by a professional and subsequent passage of one of the standardized exams.

certificated
Describes a person who has completed a certain course of study and thus earned a certificate from the issuing institution.

First, the distinction between **certification** (or being certified) and being **certificated** must be made clear. Following a course of study may result in earning a certificate of completion from an entity. A person completing the requisites has become *certificated*. This is not the same as taking a comprehensive exam given by a private entity with the purpose of testing the candidate's knowledge base in a given area. Once the candidate has passed the exam, she is considered certified by that private entity. To put this in paralegal terms: There are many, many programs offered that will grant a certificate to a student after he has completed a set of courses. However, there are only a few entities that sponsor a certification exam with an accompanying credentialing designation following the paralegal's name. The organizations that currently have certifications are NALA, NFPA, NALS (the Association for Legal Professionals), and AAPI (American Alliance of Paralegals, Inc.). These certification designations include the following:

- NALA's Certified Legal Assistant/Certified Paralegal (CLA/CP) exam and its newly introduced Advanced Paralegal Certification (APC) exams
- NFPA's Paralegal Core Competency Exam (PCCE) and Paralegal Advanced Competency Exam (PACE), both of which permit those who pass to use the designation "RP©" (Registered Paralegal)
- NALS's Accredited Legal Professional (ALP), which is the entry-level credential; the Professional Legal Secretary (PLS), which is available to those who have worked for three years in the legal field; and the Professional Paralegal (PP), which is available to paralegals who have practiced for five years and met educational criteria

■ AAPI's American Alliance Certified Paralegal (AACP), which is also an advanced certification like the Professional Paralegal (PP). It is available to those professionals who have no less than five years of substantive paralegal experience and meet their educational criteria.

The CLA/CP (Certified Legal Assistant/Certified Paralegal) Exam is an entry-level exam open to recent paralegal graduates that tests basic-level knowledge and skills as well as particulars of legal specialties. NALA has adapted its advanced specialty exams to meet the needs of modern paralegals and reflect the trends in areas of legal specialty. An APC (Advanced Paralegal Certification) provides a curriculum-based measure of a paralegal's competency in a legal specialty. The APC is open only to paralegals already holding the CLA/CP designation. NFPA developed an entry-level or "early career" certification in November of 2011 to complement its well-established advanced designation. The PCCE test focuses on "CORE" skills that entry level paralegals must posses—competency, organization, responsibility, and ethics. Those who pass the PACE exam is are able to use the designation "RP" (Registered Paralegal). It is designed to test the competency level of *experienced* paralegals (two years' experience minimum) who have a certain level of education as well. The test is designed to measure the applicant's ability to apply general knowledge (the test is not practice area-specific) and critical thinking skills to hypothetical situations. The test requires the performance of tasks related to administration and development of client legal matters, factual and legal research and writing, and office administration. Ethics, terminology, and technology are assessed across all the questions. To maintain the credential, the paralegal must also take continuing legal education courses.

Two of NALS's exams are designed for the entry-level and the advanced legal professional. The ALS and PLS are designed for any law office professional; they are not confined to paralegals. The tests are focused on law office procedures and general skills. This is where the PP differs greatly. This new test was created in 2004 and is targeted to the paralegal's knowledge base in substantive and procedural law and the skills to prepare substantive legal work products.

The AAPI exam is designed to credential the experienced paralegal (five years' experience minimum) with certain educational experience as well. The AACP exam requires continuing legal education and adherence to the AAPI Code of Professional Ethics.

The benefit to taking any one of these certification exams is the nationwide recognition of the standards. An employer has an idea of the incoming paralegal's knowledge base. In addition, although the contents of the exams vary, the common thread is the requirement of adherence to the ethical standards of the organization and the commitment to continuing legal education. See Figure 1.2 for NFPA's comparative chart of the major credentials offered by the various paralegal associations.

FIGURE 1.2 ▶ NFPA'S COMPARISON CHART FOR PARALEGAL CERTIFICATIONS

Comparison of National Level Paralegal Certification Exams©

PLEASE NOTE: The content of the chart below is verified only as to the information about the NFPA® Paralegal Advanced Competency Exam (PACE® exam and NFPA's new Paralegal CORE Competency Exam (PCCE™). The information regarding the NALA and NALS exams is unverified, and provided for informational and comparison purposes only. The NALS and NALA information below was obtained from publically available sources about those exams. Please contact NALA and NALS for exact details regarding the CLA/CP or PP exams.

Association	NFPA® Paralegal CORE Competency Exam (PCCE™)	NFPA® Paralegal Advanced Competency Exam (PACE®)	NALA Certified Paralegal/Certified Legal Assistant Exam (CP/CLA)	NALS Professional Paralegal Exam (PP)
Credential	CORE Registered Paralegal (CRP™)	PACE Registered Paralegal® (RP®)	Certified Paralegal (CP); Certified Legal Assistant (CLA)	Professional Paralegal (PP)
Established	2011	1996	1976	2004
Exam Eligibility (Education and/or Experience)	A bachelor's degree in any subject, a paralegal certificate, no experience or continuing legal education (CLE); OR A bachelor's degree in paralegal studies, no experience or CLE; OR A bachelor's degree in any subject, no paralegal certificate, 6 months of experience and 1 hour of ethics taken in the year preceding the exam application date; OR An associate's degree in paralegal studies, no experience or CLE; OR An associate's degree in any subject, a	Associate's degree in paralegal studies obtained from an institutionally accredited and/or ABA approved paralegal program and six (6) years of substantive paralegal experience; OR Bachelor's degree in any course of study obtained from an institutionally accredited school and three (3) years of substantive paralegal experience; OR Bachelor's degree and completion of a paralegal program within an	Graduation from paralegal program approved by ABA or associate degree program or post-baccalaureate certificate program in paralegal studies; or bachelor's degree program in paralegal studies, or paralegal program of 60+ hours, with at least 15 semester hours in substantive legal courses; OR Bachelor's degree in any field plus one year's experience as a paralegal (15 semester hours of substantive legal courses is equivalent to one year's experience as a paralegal); OR	Five years of experience performing paralegal/legal assistant duties. OR Be a graduate from an ABA approved Paralegal Program. OR Hold a Bachelor's degree in paralegal studies. OR Be a graduate from an accredited paralegal program which consists of a minimum of 60 semester hours (of which a minimum of 15 hours is substantive law).

paralegal certificate, no experience or CLE;

OR

An associate's degree in any subject, no paralegal certificate, 1 year of experience and 6 hours of CLE, including 1 hour of ethics taken in the year preceding the exam application date;

OR

Active duty, retired or former military personnel qualified in a military operation specialty as a paralegal and 1.0 hour of Ethics CLE within the year preceding the exam application;

OR

Candidates who are within two months of graduating and registered for the PCC Exam by a Director of a paralegal studies program participating in the PCCE Assurance of Learning (AoL) Program at the Partner level;

OR

A paralegal certificate from a program that meets or exceeds the requirements set forth in NFPA's Short Term Paralegal Program Position Statement, 1 year of experience and 6 hours of CLE, including 1 hour of ethics taken in the year preceding the exam application date;

---

institutionally accredited school (which may be embodied in the bachelor's degree) and a minimum of two (2) years' substantive paralegal experience;

OR

Four (4) years of substantive paralegal experience on or before December 31, 2000.

High School diploma or equivalent plus seven years' experience as a paralegal under the supervision of an attorney, plus a minimum of 20 hours of CLE within the two year period prior to sitting for the exam.

OR

Hold a Bachelor's degree in an unrelated field and have one year of experience performing paralegal/legal assistant duties.

continued

	OR A high school diploma or GED, 5 years of experience and 12 hours of CLE, including 1 hour of ethics taken in the 2 years preceding the exam application date.			
Exam Fees	$215 – Non Refundable	Member: $25 Application Fee; $225 Exam Fee Non Member: $25 Application Fee; $250 Exam Fee	$250 Member Fee; $275 Non-Member Fee; plus testing fees per specific section; *Fees vary by testing center:* One - 1.5 hour session @ each $40 Two - 2 hour sessions @ $40 each Two - 2.5 hour sessions @ $47 each	Member: $200; Non-Member: $250
Testing Dates and Locations	Every day except Sundays and Holidays at Prometric Testing Centers across the United States and Guam, etc. Candidates must take the exam within 90 days of approval of application.	Every day except Sundays and Holidays at Prometric Testing Centers across the United States and Guam etc. Candidates must take the exam within 90 days of approval of application.	January, May and September at ACT Testing Centers in most major cities.	First Saturday of March and last Saturday in September in most major metropolitan areas.
Retest	$215; 6 month waiting period to apply to retest.	$225 Member Fee; Non-Member $250 Fee. 6 month waiting period to apply to retest	$60 fee per section for Member & Non-member; plus applicable testing center fees for the length of session required for the specific section. *Fees vary by testing center*	$50/part Member Fee; $60/part Non-member Fee. No waiting period to retest.

	Two and one-half (2.5) hours	Four (4) hours	Two years to successfully complete 5 major sections and 4 practice area sections. The time begins on the date any section of the exam is first taken.	One Day
Testing Time				
Composition of Exam	**Domain 01: Paralegal Practice** ➤ Paralegal Profession ➤ Ethics and Professional Practice ➤ U.S. Legal System ➤ Legal Research ➤ Legal Writing and Critical Analysis ➤ Communication ➤ Law Office Management and Legal Technology ➤ Civil Litigation **Domain 02: Substantive Areas of Law** ➤ Business Organizations ➤ Contracts ➤ Criminal ➤ Estates, Wills and Trusts ➤ Family ➤ Real Estate ➤ Torts For detailed information please see Appendix A of the PCCE Candidate Handbook available on the NFPA website.	**Domain I** – Administration of Client Legal Matters: conflict checks; develop, organize and maintain client files; develop and maintain calendar/tickler systems; develop and maintain databases; coordinate client services. **Domain II** – Development of Client Legal Matters: client interviews; analyze information; collaborate with counsel; prepare, file and serve legal documents and exhibits; prepare clients and witnesses for legal proceedings. **Domain III** – Factual/Legal Research: obtain factual and legal information; investigate and compile facts; inspect, evaluate and analyze evidence; ascertain and analyze legal authority. **Domain IV** – Factual/Legal Writing: communicate with	Federal law and procedure, major subject areas include communications, ethics, legal research, human relations and interviewing techniques, judgment and analytical ability, and legal terminology Sections of Substantive law include *four mini-examinations* in the areas of: American legal system, civil litigation, business organizations, and contracts.[1]	Part 1 – Written Communications: Grammar and word usage, spelling, punctuation, number usage, capitalization, composition and expression Part 2 – Legal Knowledge and Skills: Legal research, citations, legal terminology, the court system and ADR, and the legal skills of interviewing clients and witnesses, planning and conducting investigations, and docketing Part 3 – Ethics and Judgment: Ethical situations involving contact with clients, the public, coworkers, and subordinates; other ethical considerations for the legal profession; decision making and analytical ability; and ability to recognize priorities Part 4 – All areas of substantive law, including administrative; business organizations and

continued

[1] Information obtained from NALA Website

FIGURE 1.2 ▶ NFPA'S COMPARISON CHART FOR PARALEGAL CERTIFICATIONS (CONTINUED)

		client/counsel; draft legal analytical documents. **Domain V** – Office Administration: personnel management; acquire technology; coordinate and utilize vendor services; create and maintain library and legal resources, develop and maintain billing system.		contracts; civil procedure and litigation; criminal; family; real property; torts; wills, trusts, and estates; admiralty and maritime; antitrust; bankruptcy; environmental; federal civil rights and employment discrimination; immigration; intellectual property; labor; oil and gas; pension and profit sharing; taxation; water; workers' compensation[2]
Review Manual	$75 plus tax and shipping	$82.20 plus tax and shipping	Member $160 plus tax and shipping Non-Member $170 plus tax and shipping Mock Exam Member $45 plus tax and shipping Non-Member $55 plus tax and shipping	
Certification Renewal - CLE	Every two years from anniversary date of exam: 8 hours of CLE, including 1.0 hour of ethics.	Every two years from anniversary date of exam: 12 hours of CLE, including 1.0 hour of ethics.	Every five years – 50 hours of CLE, including 5 hours of legal ethics.	Every five years – 75 hours of CLE, including 5 hours of legal ethics.
Renewal Fees	Member Fee $35 Non-Member Fee $50 Late Fee $50 in addition to renewal fee.	Member Fee $50 Non-Member Fee $75 Late Fee $50 in addition to renewal fee.	$125	$75
Number Certified	169 (3/14)	575 (3/14)	17,711 (11/13)	561 (1/14)

[2] Information obtained from NALS website

Source: Retrieved from https://www.paralegals.org/files/CHART_-_Comparison_of_National_Level_Paralegal_Certification_Exams.pdf. NOTE: NALS has a similar examination comparison chart that can be accessed at: http://c.ymcdn.com/sites/www.nals.org/resource/resmgr/committees/CertificationCompChart2016_F.pdf.

Licensure

The most stringent of all the methods of oversight is **licensure**. Those professions that deal directly with the health, safety, or welfare of the public are generally licensed. The system is designed to provide a safeguard to the public. In professions that are licensed, a governmental entity grants permission for certain persons to practice and use the name of the profession exclusively. Punishments for practicing without a license are also imposed under this scheme. Candidates for licensure must meet certain educational requirements, pass standardized tests, and keep the license current. Each state, via its court system and/or bar association, maintains oversight of all licensed attorneys in its jurisdiction. Each state promulgates its own rules regarding all aspects of the practice of law, although most states have adopted or fashioned their codes on one or more of the ABA models. The ABA has promulgated several sets of models: the 1908 Canons, the 1964 Code, the 1977 Rules of Professional Conduct (formerly "Professional Responsibility"), and most recently, the "Ethics 2000" Recommendations and Rules. Territoriality reigns in the regulation of the practice of law; states are protective of their lawyers, and every state has particulars about education, admission to the bar, continuing legal education, and ethical review. There are many other licensed professions, but paralegal is not currently one of them.

Why are professions licensed? Why do states get involved in the livelihoods of their citizens? States are charged with protecting the welfare of all their citizens, and through licensing certain professions, a state can ensure competency levels in those professions. Additionally, the state can impose penalties on persons practicing without a license. How do states determine what professions they will license? A profession must come in contact with the public, and there must be a potential for harm to occur to the clients of that profession.

It is easy to see why doctors and lawyers are licensed professionals. Doctors hold people's health (sometimes in life-or-death situations) in their hands; lawyers advise the public on matters that affect the legal rights associated with lives and property. What about other professions? Hairdressers and manicurists use volatile chemicals on their clients. Insurance salesmen and brokers deal with planning for the economic well-being of their clients. Nurses, members of a profession that supports doctors, must also be licensed, as they deal with public health issues daily. However, paralegals, members of a profession that supports attorneys, are not licensed—despite the fact that they also deal directly with the public.

The comparison between nurses and paralegals has been made often, and there are many similarities in their supportive roles. However, the licensing issue is the major difference between the two, and this issue has caused a great divide in the legal profession. The national paralegal organizations are not in agreement regarding the necessity for licensure. There are pros and cons to licensing and, so far, the cons are winning. This is evidenced by the fact that no state has enacted a licensing scheme for paralegals, although a growing number have some regulations regarding the practice.

licensure
A program administered by the appropriate governmental supervisory body that permits the practice in a profession by an individual only by and through its regulations and examinations.

under the supervision of an attorney
A term used to describe the work of a paralegal, which must be assigned, reviewed, and approved by a responsible attorney who takes responsibility for the content of the work.

access to justice
The full opportunity of all persons to use all the legal resources available to the public, without regard for their ability to pay or knowledge of the legal system or experience in dealing with lawyers.

The primary argument against licensing is found in the generally accepted definition of a paralegal: a professional who performs substantive legal work **under the supervision of an attorney**. The opponents of licensing advocate that the rules in place for attorneys satisfactorily regulate the paralegals working under their supervision.

The primary argument for licensing is found in the primary reason for the creation of the profession—the need for an economically feasible legal profession that could provide **access to justice**. More information can be found at http://www.atjsupport.org/. A licensed paralegal can perform many of the tasks that would otherwise be performed by a more expensive attorney.

Further arguments on both sides are set forth in Figure 1.3. There are national organizations on both sides of the issue. Their positions will be discussed in the section below dealing with them.

Individual State Regulation

It is each state's prerogative to regulate the practice of any profession within its borders. The practice of law is no exception. The following states have taken official positions by specifically addressing the issue of non-lawyer regulation

FIGURE 1.3 ▶
THE POSITIVES
AND NEGATIVES
OF LICENSURE

Pro-Licensing Arguments	Anti-Licensing Arguments
Standardization of educational requirements—all candidates would have to have similar degrees from approved programs.	Barriers to entry-level paralegals—many paralegals are trained on the job and forcing them to get a certain level of education in order to pass a licensure exam would deter some candidates from entering the field.
Higher salaries for paralegals.	The cost of the salary increase may be transferred to the client.
Possibility for "independent paralegals" to provide a regulated set of services directly to the public.	Limitations on the practice areas or tasks that paralegals could perform. Currently, lawyers may delegate a substantial amount of work without reference to a prescribed set of tasks allowed under regulations.
Recognition of the professional status of the paralegal profession in both the eyes of attorneys and the public.	Practical difficulties in creating and administering a licensing board.
"Quality control" by ensuring both mandates for continuing legal education and sanctions for malpractice and/or ethical violations.	Unnecessary control over an already regulated area—lawyers have discretion and first-hand knowledge as to what their paralegal is capable of doing.
Control over who may use the title of "paralegal."	The use of the title has little impact on who is performing the work and who may engage in the unauthorized practice of law.

of legal practice. This list is not all-inclusive, because the trend towards some sort of state oversight is continuing to grow and interest in it has experienced significant growth in recent years. Many states rely on the national certification programs to provide a credential. By presenting this variety of regulatory schemes, the paralegal student can appreciate the dynamic nature of the profession and its recognition.

Arizona

While it does not have a paralegal regulatory scheme per se, Arizona has enacted a statute defining and certifying "legal document preparers" (LDPs) (*see* Arizona Codes of Judicial Administration §§ 7-208 and 7-201). These legal document preparers must meet certain educational and practice requirements, one of which may be to hold a paralegal degree, and the candidate must pass a test administered by the court. LDPs may provide general legal information and assist in filling out the appropriate forms and documentation where the party is not represented by an attorney. An LDP assists in assuring that all the documents are filled out properly and completely. Under no circumstances can the legal document preparer give specific legal advice or render an opinion or recommendation "about possible legal rights, remedies, defenses, options or strategies." The LDP is subject to sanctions and ethical codes of conduct, including mandatory continuing legal education. This kind of oversight is substantially similar to the kind espoused by the proponents of paralegal licensing. The main difference is that LDPs do not work under the supervision of an attorney, and therefore, the main argument against paralegal licensing—the fact that they are properly supervised and the public is satisfactorily protected—does not apply to LDPs.

California

Preceding enactment in Arizona, California pioneered the concept of legal document preparers. These professionals, as noted above, assist with routine legal tasks, such as typing and filing the paperwork for uncontested divorces, bankruptcies, wills, and similar basic documents. *See* California Business & Professions Code §§ 6402-6407.

California further regulates the practice of nonlawyers by setting legislative standards to define a "paralegal" as a person:

> who is qualified by education, training, or work experience, who either contracts with or is employed by an attorney, law firm, corporation, governmental agency or other entity and who performs substantive legal work under the direction and supervision of an active member of the State Bar of California . . . Tasks performed by a paralegal include, but are not limited to, case planning, development, and management; legal research; interviewing clients; fact gathering and retrieving information; drafting and analyzing legal documents; collecting, compiling, and utilizing technical information to make an independent decision

and recommendation to the supervising attorney; and representing clients before a state or federal administrative agency if that representation is permitted by statute, court rule, or administrative rule or regulation.

Id. § 6450.

This legislation is in addition to the relevant ethical codes, and clearly defines, the differences between California's "legal document preparers" and paralegals. The state also sets minimal educational requirements for entry into the paralegal field, as well as continuing legal educational requirements, including ethical study. Perhaps most significant is the prohibition of anyone who is not directly supervised by an attorney from presenting herself as a paralegal. California paralegals are prohibited from being employed directly by consumers. *Id.* § 6451. Persons doing so can be found guilty of an infraction or misdemeanor punishable by fines starting at $2,500 and possible imprisonment for up to one year. *Id.* § 6455.

Florida

Overcoming the objections of the State's Bar Board of Governors, Florida has a voluntary *registration* program. A candidate must show that he or she possesses either a national certification or meets the education and work experience required to apply for the credential of "FRP" (Florida Registered Paralegal). As of March 1, 2011, the grandfathering of experienced paralegals without the required education is no longer in effect. Experience alone does not form the basis for eligibility for registration. In November 2007, the Supreme Court of Florida approved the Amendments to the Rules Regulating the Florida Bar and instituted the Florida Registered Paralegal Program. This is a voluntary credentialing system that requires certain educational requirements and entrance exam requirements. The Florida Registered Paralegal designation can be acquired in one of three ways:

1. Through education and experience, i.e.:
   a. A bachelor's degree in paralegal studies from an approved paralegal program and a minimum of one year of paralegal work;
   b. A bachelor's degree in any field from an accredited institution and a minimum of three years of paralegal work;
   c. An associate's degree in paralegal studies from an approved paralegal program and a minimum of two years of paralegal work;
   d. An associate's degree in any field from an accredited institution and a minimum of four years of paralegal work; or
   e. A Juris Doctor degree from an ABA accredited school and a minimum of one year of paralegal work.
2. By obtaining a national certification either from NFPA or NALA.
3. Through grandfathering by working five out of the last eight years as a paralegal proven by an attestation of their supervising attorney.

The full text of the new rules can be accessed through the website: http://
www.floridabar.org/TFB/TFBResources.nsf/Attachments/43709F4CEB5E4B9E85
257155005CEBE1/$FILE/Ch%2020%20Paralegal%20Rule.pdf?OpenElement.

New Jersey

New Jersey was one of the very first states to examine the role of paralegals
and the possibility of regulation/licensure. In 1992, the Supreme Court of New
Jersey's Committee on the Unauthorized Practice of Law rendered Opinion 24,
which examined the role of paralegals in the delivery of legal services. The
Committee ultimately recommended that paralegals should be licensed and
function under the direction of the New Jersey Supreme Court. In essence,
the Committee suggested that paralegals should be treated in much in the
same way as attorneys. Opinion 24 was then studied for many years, and in
1999, the New Jersey Supreme Court decided against such a licensure scheme.
"The Court has concluded that paralegal oversight is best conducted by the
supervising attorneys who are responsible for all legal work done by paralegals." New Jersey Supreme Court Committee on Paralegal Education and
Regulation, Administrative Determinations Report, May 18, 1999. However,
the Committee did allow for paralegal associations to create their own system,
so the South Jersey Paralegal Association created the NJCP credential. Visit
http://www.sjpaparalegals.org/njcertifiedparalegal.php. Many states have followed this type of plan in permitting the states' paralegal association to oversee
the certification or registration process.

North Carolina

North Carolina has taken an intermediate position with regard to the control of
the profession. North Carolina, through the Bar Association and approval of the
North Carolina Supreme Court in 2004, has adopted "voluntary certification."
Paralegals who have graduated from a qualified paralegal program can apply to
the State Bar in order to become an N.C. Certified Paralegal. The institutions
that desire to become a "qualified paralegal program" must submit an application demonstrating that are accredited and that they adhere to the relevant
ABA and/or AAfPE standards. The NCCP program sets educational standards
and mandates continuing legal education for paralegals applying for the designation. Candidates must also sit for an exam administered by the State Bar.

Ohio

Ohio has adopted a Bar Certification for Paralegals very similar to the North
Carolina model with a state exam, although it permits paralegals who do not
have formal education in paralegal studies to apply (visit https://www.ohiobar
.org/ForLawyers/Certification/Paralegal/Documents/Paralegal_Standards.pdf).
The Ohio State Bar has the power to grant (or revoke) the OSBA Certified

Paralegal credential. There are different work experience requirements that are dependent on the type of degree earned. Both a post-baccalaureate certificate of at least 20 semester hours and a baccalaureate degree in paralegal studies require one full year of full-time experience as a practicing paralegal, while an associates' degree in paralegal studies of at least 60 semester hours requires a minimum of five years of full-time experience. Any practicing paralegal without a higher degree in paralegal studies must have seven years of full-time experience accrued after December 31, 2006 in order to apply for this credential.

Oregon

The Bar seriously considered granting a Limited License Legal Technician certification. This has not been resolved, but the report is detailed and worth reading. Visit http://bog11.homestead.com/LegalTechTF/Jan2015/Report_22Jan2015.pdf.

South Dakota

South Dakota has a similar statutory approach to those of Arizona and California. It provides oversight to the profession by defining a "paralegal" as a person having a certain education, working under an attorney, and committing to continuing legal education. There is some variation in the actual technical requirements; however, the spirit remains the same as that of the two other states.

Texas

While there is no entry-level certification in Texas, the State Bar certifies its paralegals with experience in the following specialty areas:

- Bankruptcy law
- Civil trial law
- Criminal law
- Estate planning and probate law
- Family law
- Personal injury trial law
- Real estate law

Candidates may have a variety of combinations of experience and education to qualify and must also pass a written examination in their area of specialty.

Washington

The State Bar has fully embraced a licensure scheme for nonlawyers, and although nonlawyers are not necessarily "paralegals," many paralegals will qualify under these programs. There are two categories of licenses: Limited Practice Officer (LPO) and Limited License Legal Technician (LLLT). LPOs are permitted to determine the appropriate forms and prepare and complete them to achieve the clients' objective in closing a loan, extending credit, and selling or transferring an interest in real estate. LLLTs are trained to advise and assist their clients going through a variety of matters in family law such as divorce proceedings and child custody.

Wisconsin

Undaunted by the rejection of the previous attempt to regulate the paralegal profession in 2008, the CLE Committee of the State Bar has put forth a proposal of voluntary certification similar to those in Florida, North Carolina, Ohio, and Texas. The current recommendation includes an educational requirement that a candidate would need to earn at least 18 credits from an ABA-accredited paralegal studies program. There is a provision to permit "grandfathering" acknowledging credit for experience for paralegals currently working at the inception of the program. The proposal mirrors the general requirements for other paralegals under alternate schemes, in that it also imposes ethical obligations, employment by a supervising attorney, and mandatory continuing education. The main difference in licensure is the risk and responsibility that goes along with holding a license. Certain actions (crimes of moral turpitude, criminal activities, malpractice, etc.) can result in revocation of the license and therefore, an elimination of a career path.

From these examples, it is clear that states are using or are contemplating one of these four methods of oversight: (1) no formal oversight procedures for paralegals; rather, leaving the oversight to the employing attorney; (2) statutory definitions, with prohibitions and penalties against others not holding these credentials but using the title "paralegal"; (3) supervised certification or registration through either the State Bar or the State Paralegal Association; and (4) true licensure, mandated and implemented by the highest court of the state. Notably, while Washington comes close, no state has taken this last step with regard to paralegals as of yet to enact a true mandatory licensure scheme, such as the one in place in every state for the oversight of attorneys. To track an individual state's development in this area, the student should consult his state bar and local paralegal association websites. A list of these sites is supplied in Appendix A.

National and Local Organizations

As the profession is developing due to increased demand for cost-conscious legal services, it is also searching for more independence and recognition of its need in providing access to the legal system. While there have been significant steps in recognizing the vital importance of paralegals, there does not appear to be any consensus regarding their status in the delivery of legal services. This is reflected in the above discussion regarding regulation, and the dilemma is further complicated by the fact that there is not a single uniform governing body for the paralegal profession. Contrast that to the highly structured system

SURF'S UP

There are many states that have considered or are currently considering a definition for paralegals or related professions, and/or regulation of the paralegal profession (see NFPA's detailed chart for each state's code regarding the practice of law by non-attorneys: http://www.paralegals.org/associations/2270/files/REGULATION_CHART_02_09.pdf).

Additionally, a list of links for each state's Rules of Professional Conduct and their respective Paralegal Associations can be found in Appendix A.

The links for the states referenced in this section are listed here:

Arizona:
https://www.azcourts.gov/cld/Legal-Document-Preparers

California:
There is a certification for California Advanced Specialists that is available to paralegals who pass NALA's Certified Legal Assistant (CLA) and California Advanced Specialty (CAS) examinations: https://www.nala.org/courses/california-advanced-specialization-discovery http://www.cla-cas.org/.

Denver:
This credential is administered through the state's paralegal association, not the state's bar: http://www.deparalegals.org/dcp-program.php.

Florida:
https://www.floridabar.org/public/consumer/pamphlet014/

Illinois:
This credential is administered through the state's paralegal association (http://www.ipaonline.org/), not the state's bar.

Indiana:
http://www.inbar.org/?RegisteredPara legal

Kentucky:
This credential is administered through the state's paralegal association, not the state's bar: http://www.kypa.org/Certified-Ky-Paralegal.

Louisiana:
This credential is administered through the state's paralegal association, not the state's bar: http://www.la-paralegals.org/lcpcertification/certification information.html.

North Carolina:
http://www.nccertifiedparalegal.org/

Ohio:
https://www.ohiobar.org/ForLawyers/Certification/Paralegal/Pages/StaticPage-785.aspx

Philadelphia:
This credential is administered through the state's paralegal association, not the state's bar: http://keystoneparalegals.org/the-pa-c-p-credential/.

Texas:
http://content.tbls.org/pdf/laspln.pdf

Washington:
A fully functional LLLT (Limited License Legal Technician) and LPO (Limited Practice Officer) program: http://www.wsba.org/Licensing-and-Lawyer-Conduct/Limited-Licenses.

Legal Document Preparer Credential:
For general information on legal document preparers, please visit the National Association of Legal Document Preparers at: http://aldap.org/ethics.htm.

IN-CLASS DISCUSSION

With which state regulatory scheme do you most agree? Why?
What implications does this have for the paralegal profession?

of attorney licensure as overseen by the ABA. There are many diverse paralegal associations, and they each seem to have a slightly different position with regard to the development of the profession. There are currently seven national associations that address the paralegal profession:

AAfPE: The American Association for Paralegal Education recognizes the need to increase and improve access to the legal system by promoting the highest educational standards for paralegals. To this end, the Association encourages professional improvement for paralegal educators, and in collaboration with other paralegal associations promotes professional growth in order to prepare graduates to perform significant roles in the legal community.

AAPI: The American Alliance of Paralegals focuses on the individual paralegal by establishing minimum educational criteria and ethical standards, providing networking opportunities, and serving as a resource center for its members.

ABA: The American Bar Association is the national voluntary bar association for attorneys and oversight body of the legal profession. The ABA serves its members by providing accreditation of law schools and approval procedures for paralegal programs in higher education. Note that seeking approval for paralegal programs is voluntarily sought by universities, colleges, and other institutions. Law schools, by contrast, must be accredited by the ABA in order for their graduates to be eligible to sit for the bar exam. The ABA also supplies and continuing legal education, providing both the legal community and the general population with information about the law and developing initiatives to improve the legal system for the public.

ALP: The Association for Legal Professionals (formerly the National Association of Legal Secretaries) stresses continuing education and offers certifications, information, and training to those choosing any of the occupations in the legal services field. NALS members represent a broad spectrum of legal practice, and the Association offers expertise to make the programs offered valuable to all members of the legal community.

IPMA (formerly **LAMA**): The International Practice Management Association (formerly the Legal Assistant Management Association) "promotes the development, professional standing and visibility of paralegal management professionals." IPMA advocates, through a strong communication network, the paralegal manager's viewpoint and the vital role that these individuals play in the delivery of legal services.

NALA: The National Association of Legal Assistants has a membership of over 18,000 paralegals. Members can have direct membership in the national association or through its 90 state and local affiliated associations. NALA endorses the proper utilization of paralegals in the law office and delivery of high-quality legal services. NALA promotes standards of excellence in paralegal education, training and experience, and ethical responsibility.

NFPA: The National Federation of Paralegal Associations is composed of more than 50 local and state paralegal associations as well as individual members, totaling more than 9,000 paralegal professionals. The goals of the association include promoting the profession, providing leadership, exchanging and disseminating information, and maintaining ethical and educational standards.

Each state has at least one paralegal association for members practicing in that state, and some large urban states have several. Many of these associations are local chapters of either NFPA or NALA. The above list includes only the major national associations, and is not conclusive or definitive in its scope. As a paralegal student, it is important that you explore the resources available to you in your own locality.

This diversity can either be a blessing or a curse. With no unified body, there can be no consensus as to the educational standards, ethical duties, and responsibilities of the position. Indeed, the very definition of "paralegal" remains unsettled. On the other hand, diversity can be celebrated; as the profession matures, it helps to have many viewpoints in order to ensure that the very best of each can be incorporated into the perception of a paralegal. Similar to the "free marketplace of ideas" that founded our nation, the free marketplace of "paralegalism" may shape the profession for the better.

LAWYERS

Here the paralegal student will notice a difference between the educational requirements for an attorney and those for a practicing paralegal. This is due primarily to the great disparity in the lengths of history between the two professions. Attorneys have been around for centuries, whereas the paralegal profession is a relatively recent development in the legal field. The legal profession has had a very long time to develop, hone, and implement the regulations imposed upon attorneys.

Education

In order to become an attorney, a person must meet the following educational criteria:

1. Graduate with a bachelor's degree from a four-year accredited college or university. There is no requirement that a student take any particular course of study. Students from many diverse backgrounds apply to and become successful in law school. The important factor is the development of good writing, comprehension, and analytical skills.
2. Take the LSAT (Law School Admission Test), a standardized test used by all ABA (American Bar Association)-approved schools to assess potential candidates for admission. The test measures comprehension and analytical reading and writing skills. Successful results on the test do not guarantee admission into law school, as the schools use many other criteria for assessing the potential of the applicants.
3. Graduate from an ABA-accredited law school. Law school is a three-year full-time (four-year part-time) endeavor (some may describe it as an ordeal). The standard curriculum for law school includes courses in contracts, constitutional law, torts, property, professional responsibility, legal research and writing, civil procedure, evidence, family law, wills and estates, tax, business organizations, criminal law and procedure, and various electives.

Sitting for the Bar

After all of this academic rigor, the journey is still not over. The J.D. (Juris Doctor) degree does not qualify a person to practice law. More steps still lie ahead. The potential attorney must also do these things:

4. Apply to the State Board of Bar Examiners in each jurisdiction in which she would like to take the bar exam. This is often in the form of a lengthy

REEL TO REAL

The Paper Chase (1973) revolves around a Harvard Law School first-year student's struggle to keep up with the tyrannical professors and intense competition of law school while still maintaining a life. The main character, Hart, begins to question whether he really wants to enter such a high-demand profession. This film portrays the law school ordeal with honesty and accuracy. What do you think of this somewhat cruel process? Does it adequately prepare law students to enter the practice with the aggressiveness needed—or does it simply foster and perpetuate the hostility in our adversarial system?

Compare Hart to the main character, Elle Woods, in *Legally Blonde* (a little bit of a stretch, since the genres are completely opposite). Which student handles law school better? Which one, do you think, is more prepared to enter the legal profession?

written application requiring substantial personal history and letters of recommendation. The Board may chose to accept or deny this application to take the bar exam.

5. Take and pass the state bar(s) of choice. A candidate may usually sit for two bars, if they so choose, within the prescribed test dates. Each state requires two days of examination; one day for writing essays and answering practical assignments specific to that state and one day for the multistate multiple-choice exam.

Character and Fitness

Even though a candidate may prove his or her academic prowess, the Bar requires that the potential attorney demonstrate a level of personal integrity that is necessary in the practice of law.

6. Take and pass the MPRE (Multi-state Professional Responsibility Exam). This Exam is required in all but three jurisdictions in the United States. The purpose of the MPRE is to evaluate the candidate's understanding of the ABA Model Rules. The test requires application of all the rules to factual situations and the candidate must determine if an ethical violation has occurred and what the ramifications might be.

7. Perform other requirements, which may include a character and fitness personal interview and a background check. These requirements examine the candidate's record for evidence indicating that the potential attorney is an upstanding citizen and making a positive contribution to society.

8. Be sworn in before a judge or other designated official and promise to uphold the Constitution and all applicable laws.

Continuing Legal Education

Even after these two significant hurdles have been overcome, the work of an attorney is still not complete. The now-admitted attorney must also:

CLE
Continuing legal education designed to enhance legal services to the public and ensure that the legal professional maintains a certain level of expertise and competence.

9. Attend the required **CLE** (continuing legal education) courses as prescribed by the relevant state judiciary. Generally, this entails more extensive hours for newly admitted attorneys—on average, about 36 hours over a three-year period.

RESEARCH THIS

Find your state bar board of bar examiners' website and find the specific requirements with regard to steps 4-9 above, relating to the application to attain and maintain bar membership.

Ethical Review Boards

After an attorney has navigated this course, she still must bear all the rules in mind in every task she performs, in order to protect her clients' interests and maintain professional integrity. Every ethical board, however designated and controlled by the individual state, is able to hear complaints by persons affected by an attorney's unethical conduct. It is important to note that the grievance procedure does not give a complainant financial compensation for any potential loss. This is due to two factors: (1) the complainant generally does not have to prove any financial harm in order to bring a grievance against an attorney, and (2) the complainant has recourse to the courts for any harm incurred due to the attorney's misconduct as a malpractice claim.

Sanction Powers

If an attorney has been found to have committed a breach of the ethical code of conduct, the review board recommends the appropriate discipline to the state court for action. All of these actions, or **ethical sanctions**, are kept on the attorney's record. In order from least severe to most severe, an attorney can be disciplined in the following ways:

1. **Private reprimand.** A letter from the court is sent to the attorney admonishing him for the inappropriate conduct. In some jurisdictions the term *"censure"* is used in place of reprimand. Ethics boards may consider whether the questionable conduct of the attorney resulted in "any disruption of the legal process" or habitual violations or "hindered the fair and independent administration of justice." *Iowa Supreme Court Attorney Disciplinary Board v. Attorney Doe 792*, 2016 WL 453510, 8. Repeat offenses of behavior that would normally result in a private reprimand may cause the discipline to escalate to a public reprimand or probation.

> *In this case we conclude that the one-year suspension sought by the Board is appropriate. First, the misconduct committed by Attorney Carroll was serious and extensive. In particular, it demonstrated a pattern of deception and misdealing with clients that runs to the very heart of the integrity of the attorney-client relationship. Second, given the number of violations found here, as well as the previous violations for which Attorney Carroll was reprimanded, it is apparent that there is a substantial need for others to be protected from his propensity for misconduct. Third, it is equally apparent, given his three prior reprimands, that Attorney Carroll has a substantial disregard for the rules of professional conduct and likely will commit future violations unless a serious sanction is imposed now. Finally, if we allow this misconduct to pass without a substantial sanction, we will have sent the wrong message to the attorneys of this state with respect to their obligation under the rules.*

> *In the Matter of Disciplinary Proceedings Against Carroll*, 248 Wis. 2d 662, 679 (2001).

ethical sanctions
Methods of disciplining attorneys who commit a breach of the ethical code of conduct.

private reprimand
The minimum censure for an attorney who commits an ethical violation; the attorney is informed privately about a potential violation, but no official entry is made.

public reprimand
A published censure of an
attorney for an ethical
violation.

2. **Public reprimand.** A notice, including the attorney's name and reason(s) for discipline, is posted in the appropriate forum, usually the legal newspaper. A common violation resulting in public reprimand is associated with lawyer advertising. What constitutes "misleading" advertisements will be discussed later in Chapter 6; suffice it to say that attorneys do or should know where to draw the line. This is the reason they are censured more harshly and publicly for such a transgression. All of the following state ethics opinions resulted in public reprimand for the advertising conduct specified. *See, e.g., In the Matter of Naert*, 414 S.C. 181, 184 (2015) ("Respondent agrees [that the] use of opposing counsel's names as keywords in an Internet marketing campaign in a derogatory manner violates provisions of the Lawyer's Oath."); *In re Keller*, 792 N.E.2d 865, 868 (Ind. 2003) (The evidence presented clearly and convincingly establishes that the respondents' advertisements contain a representation or implication regarding the quality of their legal services. Though the respondents' advertisements contain a brief printed disclaimer, "No specific result implied," the advertisements imply that clients represented by the respondents' law firm will achieve favorable results based solely upon the respondents' reputation with insurance companies. The respondents' advertisements create an impression that the claims they handle are settled, not because of the specific facts or legal circumstances of the claims, but merely by the mention of the name of the respondents' firm to insurance companies."); *Office of Disciplinary Counsel v. Shane*, 692 N.E.2d 571, 573 (Ohio 1998), citing *Zauderer v. Office of Disciplinary Counsel*, 471 U.S. 626, 652 (1985) ("The advertisement makes no mention of the distinction between 'legal fees' and 'costs,' and to a layman not aware of the meaning of these terms of art, the advertisement would suggest that employing appellant would be a no-lose proposition in that his representation in a losing cause would come entirely free of charge. Respondents' television commercials suffer from the same deficiency as Zauderer's newspaper advertisements. The commercials do not inform the public that, win or lose, clients who enter into contingent fee contracts are responsible for costs and expenses of their cases.").

3. **Probation.** For a prescribed period of time, the attorney's actions and office procedures can be monitored for compliance with the ethical rules. The court (or other relevant disciplinary body) may also add any terms of probation as may be necessary to ensure ethical compliance. Probation often follows a reinstatement of a suspended attorney; however, the sanction of probation may be properly imposed as the primary penalty. For example, the Supreme Court of Florida sanctioned an attorney for mismanagement of his firm, including permitting a disbarred attorney under his supervision, who was operating in the capacity of a paralegal, to have direct contact with clients. The attorney was placed on probation and was compelled to attend ethics education courses from the state bar and to file quarterly reports establishing that he had not split any fees with

his "paralegal" former lawyer. *See The Florida Bar v. Januschewski*, 2003 WL 23112685 (SCTFL); *State of Florida ex rel. The Florida Bar v. Swidler*, 159 So. 2d 865 (Fla. 1964).

4. **Suspension.** An attorney can be prohibited from practicing law for a specified period of time. This suspension includes a prohibition against performing any legal work, even without receiving compensation. Additionally, the suspended attorney cannot hold herself out as an attorney during that time. The case law suggests that the potential for harm and breach of trust is a driving factor in dispensing this type of sanction. Two common bases for suspension are sexual relationships with clients and neglect of cases—sins of commission and omission, respectively.

> The act of commission, sexual involvement with a client, warrants suspension because it is a violation of the attorney's fiduciary duty to take advantage of the potentially vulnerable position of the client and could compromise the independent judgment of the attorney with respect to the case. See, e.g., PA Eth. Op. 97-100, 1997 WL 671579 (Pa. Bar. Assn. Comm. Leg. Eth. Prof. Resp.); OK Adv. Op. 311, 1998 WL 808034 (Okl. Bar. Assn. Leg. Eth. Comm.); OR Eth. Op. 1991-99, 1991 WL 279201 (Or. St. Bar. Assn.).
>
> The act of omission, neglect of case, has the potential for harm and prejudice to the client in that the entire matter may be lost due to failure to prosecute or running of the Statute of Limitations. "The failure of an attorney to pursue representation on behalf of a client resulting in prejudice to a client's rights is an intolerable breach of trust."

Florida Bar v. Dabold, 2003 WL 23112705, 3 (SCTFL), *citing* 669 So. 2d 1040, 1042 (Fla. 1996).

5. **Disbarment.** An attorney's license can be revoked, and he will be permanently prohibited from practicing law in that state. The decision of the board or committee can provide for reinstatement after a period of time, upon application of the disbarred attorney supported by good cause.

    While attorney advertising seems to fall under one of the least onerous punishments, prohibited in-person solicitation can and will result in disbarment. This "ambulance chasing" is considered horrific for two reasons: (1) It takes advantage of accident victims soon after their injuries, which "presents an opportunity for fraud, undue influence, intimidation, overreaching, and other forms of vexatious conduct" (*In the Matter of Pajerowski*, 156 N.J. 509, 520, 721 A.2d 992, 998 (1998)) and (2) "It is a practice that tends to corrupt the course of justice, and so the more abominable and evil in its incidence" (*In re Frankel*, 20 N.J. 588, 598, 120 A.2d 603, 613 (1955)).

    The second and virtually guaranteed way to disbarment is misappropriation of client funds. There is a "zero-tolerance policy" with regard to the intentional misuse of client money and/or property. The violation does not have to actually cause harm to the client, nor does it have to financially benefit the attorney, to be a sanctionable offense.

suspension
The prohibition of an attorney from practicing law for a specified period of time.

disbarment
Temporary suspension or permanent revocation of an individual's license to practice law.

These are only some of the kinds of ethical violations that will result in these various sanctions. The courts will take every violation seriously and conduct an investigation in order to determine the proper form of discipline to be imposed. There are many interesting situations that do not appear to be a direct breach of the ethical code's language, but have resulted in sometimes severe penalties. The courts keep three goals in mind when determining the degree of sanction to be imposed: (1) fairness to the client and society, (2) fairness to the attorney, and (3) the deterrent effect of the punishment on others. The client and society must feel redressed for the wrongdoing; the attorney must be punished in proportion to the offense; and the punishment must serve as a disincentive to other attorneys, so that they will not be tempted to engage in that type of violation.

Further, the courts will punish a lawyer for any criminal conduct; this should be relatively obvious. However, note that the judicial sanctioning is in addition to the criminal prosecution. Further, any allegation involving **"moral turpitude"** is taken very seriously. "Moral turpitude" has been defined as any conduct that reflects unfavorably upon the attorney's character—his honesty, integrity, and fitness to serve as an officer of the court. Essentially, this is the same examination for character and fitness that a candidate to the bar must pass. This is the way that the judiciary can maintain the character standards once the attorney has been admitted to practice.

moral turpitude
An act or behavior that gravely violates the sentiment or accepted standard of the community.

The guilt of the attorney is not retried in the disciplinary proceeding. The finding of the trial court will be considered conclusive evidence that the attorney committed the conduct in question. *In re Rosen*, 438 A.2d 316 (N.J. 1981). Conduct that is in contravention of any law is considered a sanctionable offense, as the lawyer has been sworn to uphold the rule of law. This can range from the most flagrant offenses to more minor infractions. For example, a lawyer found to have committed vehicular homicide while intoxicated will not only be punished through the criminal justice system, but also be sanctioned by the court.

Having read all this, it is a wonder that anyone goes through this Dantean descent into these levels of Hell (herein referred to as the steps to obtain and maintain a license to practice law). It also should make the paralegal student re-evaluate the common misconceptions about the number of unethical lawyers. The old adage "it only takes one rotten apple to spoil the bunch" is particularly true in the legal profession. Only a small percentage (generally 0.5% nationwide) of practicing lawyers are disciplined each year; most lawyers understand the serious ramifications of violating the rules of ethics.

Since paralegals do not hold a license to practice, they are not subject to the same disciplinary procedures and effectively forced out of practice. However, any paralegal that holds one of the national certifications can lose his membership status and right to use the corresponding credential. Further, serious infractions of professional responsibilities may subject the paralegal to civil or criminal liability. This will be discussed in further detail later in the text.

SPOT THE ISSUE

Larry has been a practicing attorney, duly licensed in the States for 40 years. He has an ongoing business relationship with another attorney, Ruth; they mutually refer clients to each other. Larry practices only worker's compensation law, and Ruth only wills and estates law, and they share a portion of their fees with each other. Ruth was indicted under a Federal fraud charge and was disbarred from practice in the States; however, Ruth continued to refer clients to Larry and Larry continued to pay a portion of the fee collected to Ruth for her referral.

Should Larry be sanctioned for his actions? Why? To what degree? Does the court have this power? Under what premise?

For a hint, see *In re Discipio*, 163 Ill. 2d 515, 645 N.E.2d 906 (1995).

CONTINUING LEGAL EDUCATION FOR PARALEGALS

Professional paralegals and students should understand the importance of continuing legal education (CLE). Just as attorneys must strive to stay up to date in their practice areas, so should the paralegals upon whom the attorneys depend. A paralegal's education does not end after graduation from college or a certificate program, but continues throughout her career. While every day on the job is a learning experience, seminars, online programs, and conferences present the opportunity to expand a paralegal's knowledge and skill base. By participating in continuing legal education, these professionals can both ensure that they are performing to the highest degree of competence and enhance their careers. Both NALA and NFPA have endorsed this ideal in their respective Guidelines and Rules, as shown in Figure 1.4.

There are numerous organizations offering CLE; many state bars offer seminars just for paralegals, and the national and regional paralegal

NALA Guideline 4:

In the supervision of a paralegal, consideration should be given to:

■ Providing continuing education for the paralegal in substantive matters through courses, institutes, workshops, seminars and in-house training.

NFPA EC 1.1(b):

A paralegal shall aspire to participate in a minimum of twelve (12) hours of continuing education, to include at least one (1) hour of ethics education, every two (2) years in order to remain current on developments in the law.

◀ **FIGURE 1.4**
CONTINUING LEGAL EDUCATION REQUIREMENTS OF NALA AND NFPA

organizations not only offer their own CLE courses, but also refer paralegals to independent CLE conference providers that are approved to provide CLE credits. These various organizations provide a diverse array of topics for paralegals at any stage of their careers. Further, many colleges that offer undergraduate or certificate programs also offer CLE courses so that their graduates and other local professionals can further their careers. With the plethora of opportunities to take CLE courses, a paralegal who calls himself a professional would be remiss not to take advantage of them. Moreover, any paralegal holding a certification may be stripped of that designation for failure to comply with that organization's continuing legal education requirement.

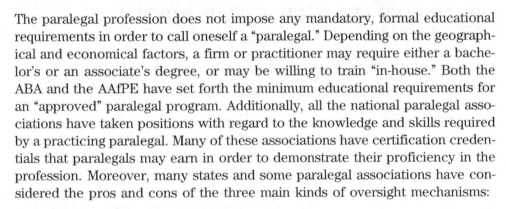

Summary

The paralegal profession does not impose any mandatory, formal educational requirements in order to call oneself a "paralegal." Depending on the geographical and economical factors, a firm or practitioner may require either a bachelor's or an associate's degree, or may be willing to train "in-house." Both the ABA and the AAfPE have set forth the minimum educational requirements for an "approved" paralegal program. Additionally, all the national paralegal associations have taken positions with regard to the knowledge and skills required by a practicing paralegal. Many of these associations have certification credentials that paralegals may earn in order to demonstrate their proficiency in the profession. Moreover, many states and some paralegal associations have considered the pros and cons of the three main kinds of oversight mechanisms:

1. Public or private registration

2. Private regulation and certification

3. Licensure

In an effort to protect the public, the practice of law by attorneys is governed by the court system and/or bar association in their jurisdiction. Attorneys must satisfy several qualifying criteria before they are permitted to practice:

1. Graduating with a four-year degree from an accredited institution

2. Scoring well on the LSAT

3. Graduating with a J.D. degree from an ABA-accredited law school

4. Applying to take the state bar exam

5. Passing the state bar exam

6. Passing the MPRE (Multi-state Professional Responsibility Exam)

7. Performing any other relevant character and fitness reviews in the jurisdiction

8. Taking the oath

9. Attending mandatory CLE sessions

Any violations of the ethical codes applicable to the practicing attorney may result in the imposition of sanctions, which may include any of the following:

1. Private reprimand

2. Public reprimand

3. Probation

4. Suspension

5. Disbarment

Although only attorneys may be sanctioned by an ethical board, both attorneys and paralegals may be subject to criminal or civil suits for their conduct. Further, paralegals who are certified by an association may lose their membership and forfeit their credential.

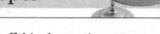

Key Terms and Concepts

American Association for Paralegal Education (AAfPE)
American Alliance of Paralegals (AAPI)
American Bar Association (ABA)
Access to justice
Advanced Paralegal Certification (APC)
The Association for Legal Professionals, formerly National Association of Legal Secretaries (NALS)
Association of Legal Administrators (ALA)
Certificated
Certification
Certified Legal Assistant (CLA)
Certified Paralegal (CP)
Continuing legal education (CLE)
Disbarment

Ethical sanctions
International Practice Management Association (IPMA, formerly LAMA)
Legal Document Preparer (LDP)
Licensure
Moral turpitude
National Association of Legal Assistants (NALA)
National Federation of Paralegal Associations (NFPA)
Practical skills
Private reprimand
Probation
Public reprimand
Registered Paralegal (RP)
Regulation
Suspension
Under the supervision of an attorney

Review Questions

MULTIPLE CHOICE

Choose the best answer(s) and please explain *why* you chose the answer(s).

1. Licensure schemes are designed to:
   a. Collect fees from members
   b. Protect the public from criminals pretending to be something they are not
   c. Ensure that the professionals have and maintain a certain level of education and knowledge about their profession
   d. Permit members to use certain credentials after their names

2. The primary reason for the development of the paralegal profession was:
   a. Attorneys that have too much work to do
   b. To provide low-income citizens with legal services
   c. To increase the salaries of all members of the law office
   d. To enforce educational requirements on all non-attorneys in the law office

3. The worst sanction that can be imposed upon an attorney by the ethics board is:
   a. Imprisonment
   b. Permanent suspension
   c. Disbarment
   d. Fines in excess of one million dollars

EXPLAIN YOURSELF

All answers should be written in complete sentences. A simple yes or no is insufficient.

1. What is *your* primary argument for or against licensure?

2. Which exam sponsored by any of the national paralegal associations do *you* think has the most marketability in employment? Why?

3. How does paralegal coursework differ from that of the law school curriculum?

4. In your own words, describe the differences between regulation and licensure.

5. Why are the ethics boards of all jurisdictions particularly concerned about allegations of "moral turpitude" levied against attorneys?

FAULTY PHRASES

All of the following statements are *false*. State why they are false and then rewrite each one as a true statement. Do not simply make the statement negative by adding the word "not."

1. Once an attorney is disbarred, he can never practice law in any jurisdiction ever again.

2. An attorney should major in a pre-law curriculum when she is going to college so that she is better prepared to go to law school.

3. Once an attorney passes the national MPRE and the "multi-state," he can apply for admission to any bar he likes.

4. An attorney must be convicted of a criminal offense in order to be disbarred.

5. Being certificated and being certified are the same thing, as far as paralegal regulation is concerned.

6. All of the national paralegal associations agree that the paralegal profession should be licensed.

7. Mere accusations of questionable conduct on behalf of an attorney cannot be brought before the ethics board.

Cases in Point
COMPARE and CONTRAST

■ The following contains excerpts from the opinion rendered by the New Jersey Supreme Court Committee on Unauthorized Practice of Law regarding oversight of Independent Paralegals and the Washington State Court Order permitting the establishment of Limited License Professionals.

N.J. Unauth. Prac. Op. 24, 126 N.J. L.J. 1306, 1990 WL 441613 (N.J. Comm. Unauth. Prac.)
New Jersey Supreme Court Committee on Unauthorized Practice
INDEPENDENT LEGAL ASSISTANTS
Opinion Number 24
November 15, 1990

[. . .]

While the ABA definition imposes the requirement that a legal assistant be a person "qualified through education, training or work experience," no law or regulation would prohibit a person lacking that qualification from holding himself out to the Bar as an independent contractor offering to do paralegal work for attorneys. While most of the paralegals who testified do possess education, training or work experience, and many of them recommended that paralegals should have certain minimum amounts of experience or education or a combination thereof,

all of the witnesses recognized that there is no supervisory body which would prevent untrained or otherwise unqualified persons from working as independent paralegals. While it may be suggested that there is no difference in levels of supervision by the attorney in the case of the employed paralegal as against the independent contractor paralegal, common experience and evidence presented to the Committee demonstrate that the contrary is true and, in the case of the independent contractor, the supervision is far less and, unfortunately in all too many cases, non-existent.

Rule of Professional Conduct 5.3 promulgated by the Supreme Court of New Jersey requires attorneys to maintain reasonable efforts to insure that the conduct of non-lawyers (retained or employed) is compatible with the attorney's professional obligations. [FN omitted.] That rule makes the lawyer responsible for the conduct of a retained or employed paralegal that would violate the Rules of Professional Conduct if (i) the conduct is ordered or ratified by the lawyer; (ii) the lawyer has failed to make reasonable investigation that would disclose prior instances of misconduct by the non-lawyer; or (iii) if "the lawyer has direct supervisory authority over the person and knows of the conduct at a time when its consequences can be avoided or mitigated but fails to take reasonable remedial action." It is the view of the Committee that, where there is an employment relationship between the paralegal and the attorney, the attorney will have that direct supervisory authority and will be in a position to take steps to avoid or mitigate the consequences of improper bad actions by the paralegal. If the relationship is one of independent contractor, however, the lawyer cannot have the same direct supervisory authority over the paralegal and is unlikely to learn of conduct in a way that would permit him to avoid or mitigate its consequences. *R.P.C. 5.3*, by limiting the attorney's responsibility to those circumstances wherein he knows of conduct and can avoid it, makes it clear that the protection afforded by the Rule will not extend to the independent paralegal with the same force and effect as it will to the employed paralegal. Since there is no body maintaining files or information with respect to misconduct by paralegals, it is difficult to determine how a lawyer could comply with *R.P.C. 5.3(c)(3)* by making "reasonable investigation" in instances of past misconduct.

As matters presently stand, there is no mechanism that would regulate the conduct of the paralegal other than the supervision of the attorney for whom the work is done, which, more often than not, may be sporadic, uneven or non-existent. That is demonstrated by the following:

1. While there are a number of different associations and organizations with which paralegals may affiliate, there have been no standards or guidelines set down by any body with regulatory authority to control and regulate the activities of independent paralegals.

2. At least one New Jersey college provides an American Bar Association-approved paralegal program and provides a Certificate of Completion to successful candidates. A Bachelor of Arts degree is a prerequisite to the obtaining of the Certificate of Completion. Those requirements are applicable only to matriculating students and it is clear that no law or regulation imposes the requirement of obtaining such a Certificate of Completion on those students who propose to practice.

3. Neither the State of New Jersey, any Bar Association, nor any organization or affiliation of paralegals or legal assistants provides for licensing procedure or any other procedure to regulate and control the identity, training and conduct of those who engage in the work. [FN omitted.]

4. While the ABA definition states that a legal assistant should be "qualified through education, training or work experience" which will serve as a guideline for its members in the use of paralegal assistance, that requirement is not imposed or binding upon a person who desires to engage in independent paralegal practice. Most of the witnesses testified that they believed there should be a requirement of a minimum number of years of training or education to permit one to practice as an independent paralegal. All of them agreed, however, that no such requirement presently exists.

5. There is no paralegal association or organization which functions in a way that can impose any uniform mechanism of standards of ethics, disciplinary proceedings, and rules and regulations to oversee the activities of paralegals. Those who function as paralegals, therefore, do so pursuant to standards and rules either of their own devising or of the devising of the variety of different groups or organizations, none of which have the power to impose adherence to standards or to control or discipline those who do not adhere to standards.

Problems raised by the absence of direct supervision and regulation of the independent paralegal are highlighted by the kind of work being undertaken by some independent paralegals. For example, one of the witnesses testified that she had become an expert in probate matters as a result of experience in the probate field and learned from that experience that many attorneys who do probate work do not specialize in estate work and are generally unfamiliar with the field. Many of those attorneys do not want to refer their matters to attorneys who are specialists, but desire to retain control of their files and clients. Accordingly, those attorneys retain the witness to handle the estates that come into their offices. She testified that she handles matters for approximately forty-five attorneys. She stated that she "ultimately takes full responsibility for making sure that I get done what needs to be done and, believe it or not, that the attorney gets done what he or she needs to get done." She signs correspondence for the attorneys, initialing it to make it clear that she has written the correspondence. She states that she never signs a letter "that contains a legal opinion, legal advice." She does, however, prepare many of those letters for her attorney clients and she has much client contact (Tr. at 24). [FN omitted.] She handles safe deposit box openings, takes clients to motor vehicle departments to transfer vehicles, handles social security matters for them. She charges the attorneys at the rate of $45 per hour. She testified that she accepts work from many attorneys who have no experience or training in estate or probate work. [FN omitted.] Therefore, as a result of her perceived expertise, she does all of the technical estate and probate work for the attorney and the attorney who participated in this practice and collects a fee over and above the charges of the witness faces the possibility of ethical problems. (See, e.g., *R.P.C. 1.5(a)*.)

Another paralegal described a different specialty which permits her to provide a service for attorneys who do not have in-house competence in that specialized area. She stated the following:

On occasion a matter will come into the attorney's office in a very specialized area of law that the in-house staff is unfamiliar with. Rather than send their client away, the attorney can call me to assist. For instance, one of my specialties is bankruptcy law and of late my work in assisting attorneys has been in that area. (Tr. at 69.)

To the extent that paralegals such as the probate specialist and the bankruptcy specialist are providing expertise to attorneys who do not have that expertise in house, their work demonstrates that the concept of direct supervisory control by the attorney is illusory. It seems highly unlikely that an attorney who does not do estate work or bankruptcy work in his office would employ a full-time paralegal to perform that work in the attorney's office. There appears, however, to be some significant group of attorneys who do retain the services of an independent paralegal to fill in that area of specialty and expertise for the attorney that the attorney does not have in house. While the attorney who retains that specialist paralegal may, on the surface, appear to have responsibility for the work of

that paralegal, it is difficult to determine how that attorney can utilize reasonable efforts to insure that the conduct of the paralegal, who is working in a field unfamiliar to the attorney, will be "compatible with the professional obligations of the lawyer" (*R.P.C. 5.3*). Based on the testimony and evidence considered by the Committee, the paralegal admittedly is performing legal services in an area not included within the attorney's range of expertise. It is difficult to see how the lawyer can either order or ratify the paralegal's conduct or provide that direct supervisory authority over the paralegal which would permit the avoidance or mitigation of improper conduct required by *R.P.C. 5.3*. In these areas, the paralegal is becoming a substitute for the attorney, not an assistant to the attorney, and that is a situation which comes about because of the independent nature of the paralegal's work relationship.

The nature of the work of independent paralegals presents other problems. Those paralegals employed in an attorney's office do prepare correspondence that is routinely reviewed and signed by the attorney. The independent paralegals made it clear through their testimony, however, that a much looser arrangement exists in their practices with respect to correspondence and communication. Some of the paralegals keep supplies of the attorneys' letterheads in the paralegals' offices. The paralegals acknowledge that they send out letters, signed in the name of the paralegal, but that they do so without prior review by the attorney. In some instances, the attorneys whose letterheads are used do not receive copies of the letters from the paralegals. The potential for misunderstanding by the public which may receive those letters, and the absence of supervision by the attorney in the use of the attorney's letterhead, is an example of the kind of problem that the practice of the independent paralegal presents.

[. . .]

The Committee is sensitive to the fact that the practice of law becomes ever more complex and that there is a need to provide legal services to the public. Some of the witnesses who appeared before the Committee expressed the view that the work of the independent paralegal would have the result of bringing legal services more extensively to the public and at fee levels that would be more affordable because of the lesser charges involved in the work of the paralegals. It is the view of the Committee that the need to bring services to the public and the need to provide legal services at more affordable rates should not be met by permitting legal services to be performed by non-lawyers who, by virtue of their independent status, cannot be subject to the kind of direct supervision by attorneys that is otherwise required. There certainly are differing levels of complexity in the legal issues and matters to be handled by attorneys and paralegals. When the paralegal is employed by the attorney, the nature of the employment relationship makes it possible for the attorney to make the decisions as to which matters are appropriate for handling by the paralegal and which matters require direct hands-on work by the attorney. When the attorney and the paralegal are separated both by distance and the independent nature of the paralegal's relationship with the attorney, the opportunity for the exercise of that most important judgment by the attorney becomes increasingly difficult.

This is not to say that there are not matters that could be handled by an independent paralegal with appropriate supervision by the attorney contracting with the paralegal. The problem is that the decisions as to what work may be done by the paralegal should be the attorney's to make but the distance between attorney and paralegal mandated by the independent relationship may result in the making of those decisions by the paralegal or by default.

It is the view of the Committee, moreover, that the paralegal practicing in an independent paralegal organization, removed from the attorney both by distance and relationship, presents far too little opportunity for the direct supervision necessary to justify handling those legal issues that might be delegated. Without supervision, the work of the paralegal clearly constitutes the unauthorized practice of law. We found, from the testimony and materials presented to our Committee, that the opportunity for supervision of the independent paralegal diminishes to the point where much of the work of the independent paralegal is, in fact, unsupervised. That being the case, the independent practice by the paralegal must involve the unauthorized practice of law. The fact that some of the work might actually be directly supervised cannot justify the allowance of a system which permits the independent paralegal to work free of attorney supervision and control for such a large part of the time and for such a large part of the work.

Without the direct supervisory control contemplated by *R.P.C. 5.3*, the attorney who utilizes the independent paralegal might not have professional responsibility for the paralegal's misconduct. With the separation of the independent paralegal from the attorney, both by distance and relationship, the ability of the attorney to make reasonable efforts to insure that the paralegal's conduct is compatible with the professional obligations of the lawyer must diminish. The danger of legal work being done without appropriate professional responsibility to the public increases to a point wherein it cannot be condoned.

The attorneys who use independent paralegals are not free of ethical problems. Where the specialized paralegal, for example handling probate matters, charges an hourly fee to the attorney, the attorney may well be put in a position to charge a fee to the probate client which will constitute a percentage of the estate. Most or all of the work will have been done by the paralegal. Since the attorney is not sufficiently skilled in the area to supervise properly the work of the paralegal, the attorney will be compensated for work done by the paralegal that, because of the lack of supervision, will constitute the unauthorized practice of law. That presents a clear ethical dilemma created by the existence of the independent paralegal. [FN omitted.] Where the work of the independent paralegal constitutes the unauthorized practice of law, the attorney retaining that paralegal will be in violation of *R.P.C. 5.3(d)(2)*.

It is suggested that the availability of the independent paralegal makes paralegal services available to the single practitioner who might not be able to employ a full-time paralegal. While there might be merit to making some of the paralegals' time available to the single practitioner, that value does not, in the opinion of this Committee, override the very real problem of lack of supervision inherent in that relationship. There well may be mechanical things to be done by the independent paralegal for the single practitioner. Any part-timer could accomplish that kind of work for the attorney without the risk of unsupervised work that is created by the independent paralegal's distance from the attorney.

We are involved in this inquiry, moreover, with the work of a legal assistant which the ABA defines as being "substantive legal work" which "requires a sufficient knowledge of legal concepts that, absent such assistant, the attorney would perform the task." If the case is beyond the capacity of the single practitioner, whether by virtue of complexity or sheer volume of detail, this Committee does not believe that the problem is properly solved by work done by the independent paralegal who cannot properly be the subject of the kind of supervision that would be required. There are alternatives: The work could be referred to a specialist attorney or to a firm which has, in house, the personnel to handle the volume. This Committee finds, based on the presentation of both documentary and oral materials to it, that the use of the independent paralegal to do the substantive legal work which the attorney would otherwise do, represents an inappropriate level of delegation.

The Committee does not believe that the need for the supply of legal services requires that the Bar utilize independent paralegals whose work is unregulated either by an employment relationship with the attorney or through any systematic body of regulations.

If there is an argument that legal services have not been brought to the consumer over the past years, it is no answer to that argument to permit those legal services to be performed by persons not subject to uniform standards, not subject to training, and who can work independently of the supervision of attorneys which must be the keymark of paralegal work.

The Committee believes that the increasing number of attorneys entering the practice, the availability of legal service programs, and the availability of attorneys to do pro bono work can fill those needs appropriately. It is inappropriate to suggest that there is such a void in the providing of legal services at reasonable rates that independent paralegals should move in to fill that void. At its best, the Committee believes that the remedy of providing legal services through the independent paralegal can create more harm than the perceived ill which it purports to be designed to correct.

The Committee recognizes that the bringing of legal services to the public must be an issue of continuing concern to the Bar. We believe, however, that it is totally inappropriate to suggest that legal services can better be brought to the public by a group that is not subject to any kind of uniform educational, training, professional or ethical standards.

[. . .]

Source: Reprinted from Westlaw with permission from Thomson Reuters.

■ As you have just read, the New Jersey Supreme Court Committee on Unauthorized Practice held that: "The Committee recognizes that the bringing of legal services to the public must be an issue of continuing concern to the Bar. We believe, however, that it is totally inappropriate to suggest that legal services can better be brought to the public by a group that is not subject to any kind of uniform educational, training, professional or ethical standards." How does the Washington State Supreme Court arrive at its conclusion and address the concerns of the New Jersey Committee?

Accessed from http://lawfilesext.leg.wa.gov/law/wsr/2012/14/12-13-063.htm on 4/25/17.

WSR 12-13-063
RULES OF COURT
STATE SUPREME COURT

[June 15, 2012]

IN THE MATTER OF THE ADOPTION OF	)	ORDER
NEW APR 28 – LIMITED PRACTICE	)	NO. 25700-A-1005
RULE FOR LIMITED LICENSE LEGAL	)	
TECHNICIANS	)	

The Practice of Law Board having recommended the adoption of New APR 28 – Limited Practice Rule for Limited License Legal Technicians, and the Court having considered the revised rule and comments submitted thereto, and having determined by majority that the rule will aid in the prompt and orderly administration of justice;

Now, therefore, it is hereby

ORDERED:

That we adopt APR 28, the Limited Practice Rule for Limited License Legal Technicians. It is time. Since this rule was submitted to the Court by the Practice of Law Board in 2008, and revised in 2012, we have reviewed many comments both in support and in opposition to the proposal to establish a limited form of legal practitioner. During this time, we have also witnessed the wide and ever-growing gap in necessary legal and law related services for low and moderate income persons.

[. . .] The Limited License Legal Technician Rule that we adopt today is narrowly tailored to accomplish its stated objectives, includes appropriate training, financial responsibility, regulatory oversight and accountability systems, and incorporates ethical and other requirements designed to ensure competency within the narrow spectrum of the services that Limited License Legal Technicians will be allowed to provide. In adopting this rule we are acutely aware of the unregulated activities of many untrained, unsupervised legal practitioners who daily do harm to "clients" and to the public's interest in having high quality civil legal services provided by qualified practitioners.

The practice of law is a professional calling that requires competence, experience, accountability and oversight. Legal License Legal Technicians are not lawyers. They are prohibited from engaging in most activities that lawyers have been trained to provide. They are, under the rule adopted today, authorized to engage in very discrete, limited scope and limited function activities. Many individuals will need far more help than the limited scope of law related activities that a limited license legal technician will be able to offer. These people must still seek help from an attorney. But there are people who need only limited levels of assistance that can be provided by non-lawyers trained and overseen within the framework of the regulatory system developed by the Practice of Law Board. This

assistance should be available and affordable. Our system of justice requires it.

I. THE RULE

Consistent with GR 25 (the Supreme Court rule establishing the Practice of Law Board), the rule establishes a framework for the licensing and regulation of non-attorneys to engage in discrete activities that currently fall within the definition of the "practice of law" (as defined by GR 24) and which are currently subject to exclusive regulation and oversight by this Court. The rule itself authorizes no one to practice. It simply establishes the regulatory framework for the consideration of proposals to allow non-attorneys to practice. As required by GR 25, the rule establishes certification requirements (age, education, experience, pro bono service, examination, etc.), defines the specific types of activities that a limited license legal technician would be authorized to engage in, the circumstances under which the limited license legal technician would be allowed to engage in authorized activities (office location, personal services required, contract for services with appropriate disclosures, prohibitions on serving individuals who require services beyond the scope of authority of the limited license legal technician to perform), a detailed list of prohibitions, and continuing certification and financial responsibility requirements.

In addition to the rule, we are today acting on the Practice of Law Board's proposal to establish a Limited License Legal Technician Board. This Board will have responsibility for considering and making recommendations to the Supreme Court with respect to specific proposals for the authorization of limited license legal technicians to engage in some or all of the activities authorized under the Limited License Legal Technician Rule, and authority to oversee the activities of and discipline certified limited license legal technicians in the same way the Washington State Bar Association does with respect to attorneys. The Board is authorized to recommend that limited license legal technicians be authorized to engage in specific activities within the framework of—and limited to—those set forth in the rule itself. We reserve the responsibility to review and approve any proposal to authorize limited license legal technicians to engage in specific activities within specific substantive areas of legal and law related practice, and our review is guided by the criteria outlined in GR 25.

[. . .]

II. THE NEED FOR A LIMITED LICENSE LEGAL TECHNICIAN RULE

Our adversarial civil legal system is complex. It is unaffordable not only to low income people but, as the 2003 Civil Legal Needs Study documented, moderate income people as well (defined as families with incomes between 200% and 400% of the Federal Poverty Level). [. . .] Legal practice is required to conform to specific statewide and local procedures, and practitioners are required to use standard forms developed at both the statewide and local levels. Every day across this state, thousands of unrepresented (pro se) individuals seek to resolve important legal matters in our courts. Many of these are low income people who seek but cannot obtain help from an overtaxed, underfunded civil legal aid system. Many others are moderate income people for whom existing market rates for legal services are cost-prohibitive and who, unfortunately, must search for alternatives in the unregulated marketplace.

Recognizing the difficulties that a ballooning population of unrepresented litigants has created, court managers, legal aid programs and others have embraced a range of strategies to provide greater levels of assistance to these unrepresented litigants. Innovations include the establishment of courthouse facilitators in most counties, establishment of courthouse-based self-help resource centers in some counties, establishment of neighborhood legal clinics and other volunteer-based advice and consultation programs, and the creation of a statewide legal aid self-help website. [. . .]

But there are significant limitations in these services and large gaps in the type of services for pro se litigants. Courthouse facilitators serve the courts, not individual litigants. [. . .] They are not subject to confidentiality requirements essential to the practitioner/client relationship. They are strictly limited to engaging in "basic services" defined by GR 21. They have no specific educational/certification requirements, and often find themselves providing assistance to two sides in contested cases. Web-based self-help materials are useful to a point, but many litigants require additional one-on-one help to understand their specific legal rights and prerogatives and make decisions that are best for them under the circumstances.

From the perspective of pro se litigants, the gap places many of these litigants at a substantial legal disadvantage and, for increasing numbers, forces them to seek help from unregulated, untrained, unsupervised "practitioners." We have a duty to ensure that the public can access affordable legal and law related services, and that they are not left to fall prey to the perils of the unregulated market place.

III. SPECIFIC CONCERNS AND RESPONSES

A number of specific issues that have been raised both in support of and in opposition to this rule deserve additional discussion and response.

Proponents have suggested that the establishment and licensing of limited license legal technicians should be a primary strategy to close the Justice Gap for low and moderate income people with family related legal problems. While there will be some benefit to pro se litigants in need of limited levels of legal help, we must be careful not to create expectations that adoption of this rule is not intended to achieve.

By design, limited license legal technicians authorized to engage in discrete legal and law related activities will not be able to meet that portion of the public's need for help in family law matters that requires the provision of individualized legal representation in complex, contested family law matters. Such representation requires the informed professional assistance of attorneys who have met the educational and related requirements necessary to practice law in Washington. Limited purpose practitioners, no matter how well trained within a discrete subject matter, will not have the breadth of substantive legal knowledge or requisite practice skills to apply professional judgment in a manner that can be consistently counted upon to meet the public's need for competent and skilled legal representation in complex legal cases.

On the other hand, and depending upon how it is implemented, the authorization for limited license legal technicians to engage in certain limited legal and law related activities holds promise to help reduce the level of unmet need for low and moderate income people who have relatively uncomplicated family related legal problems and for whom some level of individualized advice, support and guidance would facilitate a timely and effective outcome.

Some opposing the rule believe that limited licensing legal technicians to engage in certain family related legal and law related activities poses a threat to the practicing family law bar.

First, the basis of any regulatory scheme, including our exercise of the exclusive authority to determine who can practice law in this state and under what circumstances, must start and end with the public interest; and any regulatory scheme must be designed to ensure that those who provide legal and law related services have the education, knowledge, skills and abilities to do so. Protecting the monopoly status of attorneys in any practice area is not a legitimate objective.

It is important to observe that members of the family law bar provide high levels of public and pro bono service. In fact, it is fair to say that the demands of pro bono have fallen disproportionately on members of the family law bar. As pointed out in the comments to the Practice of Law Board's proposal, young lawyers and others have been working for years to develop strategies to provide reduced fee services to moderate income clients who cannot afford market-rate legal help. Over the past year, these efforts have been transformed into the Washington State Bar Association's newly established Moderate Means program, an initiative which holds substantial promise to deliver greater access to legal representation for greater numbers of individuals between 200% and 400% of the federal poverty guideline being provided services at affordable rates.

In considering the impact that the limited licensing of legal technicians might have on the practicing family law bar it is important to push past the rhetoric and focus on what limited license legal technicians will be allowed to do, and what they cannot do under the rule. With limited exception, few private attorneys make a living exclusively providing technical legal help to persons in simple family law matters. Most family law attorneys represent clients on matters that require extended levels of personalized legal counsel, advice and representation—including, where necessary, appearing in court—in cases that involve children and/or property.

Stand-alone limited license legal technicians are just what they are described to be—persons who have been trained and authorized to provide technical help (selecting and completing forms, informing clients of applicable procedures and timelines, reviewing and explaining pleadings, identifying additional documents that may be needed, etc.) to clients with fairly simple legal law matters. Under the rule we adopt today, limited license legal technicians would not be able to represent clients in court or contact and negotiate with opposing parties on a client's behalf. For these reasons, the limited licensing of legal technicians is unlikely to have any appreciable impact on attorney practice.

The Practice of Law Board and other proponents argue that the limited licensing of legal technicians will provide a substantially more affordable product than that which is available from attorneys, and that this will make legal help more accessible to the public. Opponents argue that it will be economically impossible for limited license legal technicians to deliver services at less cost than attorneys and thus, there is no market advantage to be achieved by creating this form of limited practitioner.

No one has a crystal ball. It may be that stand-alone limited license legal technicians will not find the practice lucrative and that the cost of establishing and maintaining a practice under this rule will require them to charge rates close to those of attorneys. On the other hand, it may be that economies can be achieved that will allow these very limited services to be offered at a market rate substantially below those of attorneys. There is simply no way to know the answer to this question without trying it.

That said, if market economies can be achieved, the public will have a source of relatively affordable technical legal help with uncomplicated legal matters. This may reduce some of the demand on our state's civil legal aid and pro bono systems and should lead to an increase in the quality and consistency of paperwork presented by pro se litigants.

Further, it may be that non-profit organizations that provide social services with a family law component (e.g., domestic violence shelters; pro bono programs; specialized legal aid programs) will elect to add limited license legal technicians onto their staffs. The cost would be much less than adding an attorney and could enable these programs to add a dimension to their services that will allow for the limited provision of individualized legal help on many cases—especially those involving domestic violence. Relationships might be extended with traditional legal aid programs or private pro bono attorneys so that there might be sufficient attorney supervision of the activities of the limited license legal technicians to enable them to engage in those activities for which "direct and active" attorney supervision is required under the rule.

Some have suggested that there is no need for this rule at all, and that the WSBA's Moderate Means Program will solve the problem that the limited licensing of legal technicians is intended to address. This is highly unlikely. First, there are large rural areas throughout the state where there are few attorneys. In these areas, many attorneys are barely able to scrape by. Doing reduced fee work through the Moderate Means program (like doing pro bono work) will not be a high priority.

Second, limited licensing of legal technicians *complements*, rather than competes with, the efforts WSBA is undertaking through the Moderate Means program. We know that there is a huge need for representation in contested cases where court appearances are required. We know further that pro se litigants are at a decided disadvantage in such cases, especially when the adverse party is represented. Limited license legal technicians are not permitted to provide this level of assistance; they are limited to performing mostly ministerial technical/legal functions. Given the spectrum of unmet legal needs out there, Moderate Means attorneys will be asked to focus their energy on providing the help that is needed most - representing low and moderate income people who cannot secure necessary representation in contested, often complex legal proceedings.

Opponents of the rule argue that the limited licensing of legal technicians presents a threat to clients and the public. To the contrary, the authorization to establish, regulate and oversee the limited practice of legal technicians within the framework of the rule adopted today will serve the public interest and protect the public. The threat of consumer abuse already exists and is, unfortunately, widespread. There are far too many unlicensed, unregulated and unscrupulous "practitioners" preying on those who need legal help but cannot afford an attorney. Establishing a rule for the application, regulation, oversight and discipline of non-attorney practitioners establishes a regulatory framework that reduces the risk that members of the public will fall victim to those who are currently filling the gap in affordable legal services.

Unlike those operating in the unregulated marketplace, limited license legal technicians will practice within a carefully crafted regulatory framework that incorporates a range of safeguards necessary to protect the public. The educational requirements are rigorous. Unlike attorneys, legal technicians are required to demonstrate financial responsibility in ways established by the Board. There is a testing requirement to demonstrate professional competency to practice, contracting and disclosure requirements are significant, and there will be a robust oversight and disciplinary process. This rule protects the public.

Another concern that has been raised is that attorneys will be called upon to underwrite the costs of regulating non-attorney limited license legal technicians against whom they are now in competition for market share. This will not happen. GR 25 requires that any recommendation to authorize the limited practice of law by non-attorneys demonstrate that "[t]he costs of regulation, if any, can be effectively underwritten within the context of the proposed regulatory regime." The Practice of Law Board's rule expressly provides that the ongoing cost of regulation will be borne by the limited license legal technicians themselves, and will be collected through licensing and examination fees. Experience with the Limited Practice Board demonstrates that a self-sustaining system of regulation can be created and sustained. The Court is confident that the WSBA and the Practice of Law Board, in consultation with this Court, will be able to develop a fee-based system that ensures that the licensing and ongoing regulation of limited license legal technicians will be cost-neutral to the WSBA and its membership.

IV. CONCLUSION

Today's adoption of APR 28 is a good start. The licensing of limited license legal technicians will not close the Justice Gap identified in the 2003 Civil Legal Needs Study. Nor will it solve the access to justice crisis for moderate income individuals with legal needs. But it is a limited, narrowly tailored strategy designed to expand the provision of legal and law related services to members of the public in need of individualized legal assistance with non-complex legal problems.

The Limited License Legal Technician Rule is thoughtful and measured. It offers ample protection for members of the public who will purchase or receive services from limited license legal technicians. It offers a sound opportunity to determine whether and, if so, to what degree the involvement of effectively trained, licensed and regulated non-attorneys may help expand access to necessary legal help in ways that serve the justice system and protect the public.

[Footnotes omitted.]

[Dissent to Order filed by Justice Owens omitted.]

[Text of Rule, APR 28 omitted. The full text of APR 28 can be accessed through the Washington State Court Rules website: https://www.courts.wa.gov/court_rules/.]

Source: http://www.wsba.org/~/media/Files/WSBA-wide%20Documents/LLLT/Supreme%20Court/Legal%20Technician%20Rule.ashx

Chapter 2

The Unauthorized Practice of Law

Chapter Objectives

The student will be able to:

- Discuss the development of and necessity for prohibitions against the unauthorized practice of law
- Define the "practice of law"
- Compare the unauthorized practice of law as it relates to attorneys, paralegals, and other support staff
- Identify the various considerations in making a determination as to whether the conduct in question is the unauthorized practice of law

This chapter will focus on *what* tasks may be performed by *whom* in the legal system and *why* there are restrictions on the practice of law. There are certain tasks which have been deemed the practice of law by definition, and are off limits to non-lawyers. Performance of these tasks is considered the "unauthorized practice of law" (UPL). Paralegals are particularly susceptible to overstepping the line during the course of their work, and must understand *how* to avoid UPL.

The dramatics of conducting a trial aside, what kind of work do lawyers do? What is the practice of law? It important for a paralegal to understand the boundaries of the practice by being able to answer these vital questions. Unfortunately, there are not easy, clear-cut answers. The general population, through the *many* television shows and movies made about lawyers, has only a limited consciousness of what lawyers really do. The media limits itself to exposing or lampooning the exciting and/or controversial elements of the practice, usually involving litigation. This is understandable, as the ratings for shows titled *The Research Brigade* and *The Discovery Drudges* would be abysmal.

The boundaries of the practice are far-reaching and their edges are quite fuzzy. Indeed, it is in these border outposts that the practice of law by an attorney overlaps with that by a paralegal. Paralegals *do* engage in the practice of law within their own territories: the law offices where they work. The paralegal's work frees up the attorney's time so that she can concentrate on the core practice—that which only a lawyer can do. The analysis and strategy to be applied in a particular case, the maintenance of the client relationship, and the ultimate responsibility for all the work performed for a client—these tasks make up the heart of the practice of law. A paralegal may take on some of the **substantive legal tasks** that must be performed directly or in support of this core. It is the "core" that is preserved solely for attorneys. Paralegals do not engage in the unauthorized practice of law as long as their work is "of a preparatory nature, such as legal research, investigation, or the composition of legal documents, which enable a licensed attorney-employer to carry a given matter to a conclusion through his own examination, approval or additional effort." *In re Easler*, 272 S.E.2d 32 (S.C. 1980). Substantive legal tasks are duties that take legal analysis and application of specialized knowledge, rather than clerical tasks.

As basic document preparation services have grown in popularity due to the perceived cost-prohibitiveness of attorneys, the courts have more often addressed the issue of the unauthorized practice of law. Companies like Legal-Zoom and Rocket Lawyer have been scrutinized by several bar associations, including the ABA, as those companies have tried to enter the legal services market. North Carolina had a protracted suit with LegalZoom that made headlines across the country. The North Carolina Bar applied its rules regarding "pre-paid legal services" to LegalZoom's application to register as such in the state. After denying the request, the North Carolina Bar adopted further rules regarding these types of services. The provider must both accept payment prior to the immediate legal need of the consumer in order to protect those seeking their services from making a decision about the provision of legal services under pressure and the legal services provided to the consumer must be performed by a licensed attorney in North Carolina. In 2008, the North Carolina Bar sent a "cease and desist" letter to LegalZoom claiming that the company was operating illegally in North Carolina. LegalZoom, using the precedent set by *North Carolina Board of Dental Examiners v. FTC*, 35 U.S. 1101 (2015) defended its activities within the State. In that FTC antitrust matter, the U.S. Supreme Court criticized the Board's control of the non-essential dentist activity (tooth whitening) by the Board's members who were "active market

substantive legal tasks
Duties that take legal analysis and application of specialized knowledge, as opposed to clerical duties.

Proposed State Bill 436:

". . . the parties have settled the dispute and have agreed to the disposition of this action by entry of this agreed Consent Judgment and to comply with the following terms: 1. The parties agree that the definition of the "practice of law" as set forth in N.C.G.S. § 84-2.1 does not encompass LegalZoom's operation of a website that offers consumers access to interactive software that generates a legal document based on the consumer's answers to questions presented by the software so long as LegalZoom complies with the provisions of Paragraph 2 below. 2. LegalZoom agrees that it must continue to ensure, for the shorter of a period of two (2) years after the entry of this Consent Judgment or the enactment of legislation in North Carolina revising the statutory definition of the "practice of law", that: 2 (a) LegalZoom shall provide to any consumer purchasing a North Carolina product (a North Carolina Consumer) a means to see the blank template or the final, completed document before finalizing a purchase of that document; (b) An attorney licensed to practice law in the State of North Carolina has reviewed each blank template offered to North Carolina Consumers, including each and every potential part thereof that may appear in the completed document. The name and address of each reviewing attorney must be kept on file by LegalZoom and provided to the North Carolina Consumer upon written request; (c) LegalZoom must communicate to the North Carolina Consumer that the forms or templates are not a substitute for the advice or services of an attorney; (d) LegalZoom discloses its legal name and physical location and address to the North Carolina Consumer; (e) LegalZoom does not disclaim any warranties or liability and does not limit the recovery of damages or other remedies by the North Carolina Consumer; and (f) LegalZoom does not require any North Carolina Consumer to agree to jurisdiction or venue in any state other than North Carolina for the resolution of disputes between LegalZoom and the North Carolina Consumer."

participants." *Id.* at 1110-1111. The activities of these non-licensed providers were under the control of practitioners who were found to be using the Board regulations to keep competitors out of the market. The key element in this decision as it applies to the professional licensure is the definition of what constitutes the "practice" of a regulated field. The U.S. Supreme Court noted that teeth-whitening was a safe, cosmetic procedure and did not serve to protect the public welfare. North Carolina's dispute with LegalZoom similarly hinges on the definition of the "practice of law" and who may engage in it. On October 22, 2015, the State Bar entered into a consent judgment with Legal-Zoom that would permit the State Legislature to define the "practice of law" in light of new technologies. See Figure 2.1.

HISTORY AND DEVELOPMENT OF THE UNAUTHORIZED PRACTICE OF LAW

The concern of the ethics rules is not the act itself of practicing law; it is the **unauthorized practice of law (UPL)**. Within the four walls of their offices, within their own territories, and given the proper instruction and supervision,

unauthorized practice of law (UPL)
The performance of certain legal tasks by someone other than an attorney, which can result in civil or criminal penalties.

paralegals are practicing law—and are authorized to do so. The authorization comes from the proper delegation of the legal task to the paralegal. It is when a paralegal leaves the supervision of an attorney and/or performs a task that is impermissible that she ventures into the potentially dangerous territory of the unauthorized practice of law. The unauthorized practice of law usually takes one of these three forms:

1. The improper supervision of a paralegal who is performing a legal task
2. Direction by and supervision of the attorney in the paralegal's performance of an improper or unethical task
3. A paralegal failing to recognize their transgression in rendering legal advice

The third is perhaps the most insidious as many paralegals have the knowledge and experience to formulate the correct analysis of the legal matter at hand. When questioned by the client, it is only natural to want to give an answer; however, the response may be in the form of legal advice. A paralegal should refrain and consult the attorney in this case, even when the attorney completely agrees with the paralegal's prior assessment.

Of course, a student, a practicing paralegal, or an attorney would like a clear line of demarcation in the definition of the unauthorized practice. Unfortunately, that is not going to be possible. Numerous courts and ethics committees have been unable to write a concise and thorough definition of the practice of law. As with many questions of law, the answer lies in the facts of the case. In other words, "it depends." As the advice of attorneys grows more and more expensive, the temptation to engage in the unauthorized practice by those not licensed to do so grows.

The unauthorized practice ranges from the obvious, outright behavior of the imposter to behavior that is well-meaning and seemingly harmless (if not downright beneficial). In *Louisiana Claims Adjustment Bureau, Inc. v. State Farm Insurance Co.*, 877 So. 2d 294 (La. App. Cir. 2004), a public insurance adjuster brought an action against a liability insurer to recover for defamation and intentional interference with business relations by telling the adjuster's clients that the adjuster was engaged in unauthorized practice of law. The public adjuster, which negotiated personal injury claims with insurance companies, engaged in the unauthorized practice of law when its representatives evaluated claims and advised clients of their causes of action; evaluating a claim and determining whether it had merit or was frivolous had to be done by a licensed attorney.

Non-lawyer parents, acting solely as a representative of their minor son, lacked authorization to maintain an appeal of their son's libel action against his school. The parents could not proceed *pro se*, although if their son had been of age, he could have done so. The "representation" in this instance required an attorney; the parents were not licensed to practice law as required to act on their son's behalf. *Lowe v. City of Shelton*, 851 A.2d 1183 (Conn. App. Ct. 2004). This outcome was also reached in a similar case of fiduciary representation. The court in *Ellis v. Cohen*, 982 A.2d 1130 (Conn. App. Ct. 2009), refused to make an exception for an executor of an estate to bring a wrongful death/ medical malpractice suit on behalf of the decedent. Clearly, courts have held that the *pro se* exception to the unauthorized practice of law is reserved only for the litigant him/herself. Those who are incapable of representing themselves must engage the services of an attorney.

History

While the above case references are relatively recent, the *regulation* of the practice of law dates back very roughly to the ancient Greeks. As was their style, the Greeks formalized the litigation process, created complex procedural rules, and used legal terminology with aplomb. True to their form, the ancient Romans borrowed, further studied, standardized, and refined their Greek predecessors' work. Through this formalization of the practice of law, a class of professionals that can properly be equated with modern attorneys emerged. The Romans also turned their analytical, scientific eyes on the law and developed the science of jurisprudence, whereas the Greeks had treated it only as a philosophy. Legal professionals in Ancient Rome adhered to extensive rules of procedure that were, prior to their publication by Gnaeus Flavius sometime around 300 B.C., known only to the aristocrats practicing law. Once these "secrets" were revealed, the number of persons practicing and studying the law increased substantially.

It is the same opening of doors, the letting out of "secrets," that has permitted the development of the paralegal profession. Through the impetus of economics and the availability of education, students are able to study and ultimately practice law. Chapter 1 examined the educational qualifications and entry requirements an individual needs in order to be admitted to the practice of law or to be considered qualified to act as a paralegal. This chapter will focus on the definition of the practice of law, identifying those tasks that are fundamental to the profession of attorney and therefore off limits to nonlawyers.

What is it exactly that defines the profession of lawyer and makes it unique and isolated from other professions? The practice of law itself was isolated by the early colonial Americans, who restricted what lawyers could do in response to their general distrust of the traditional English elite. Indeed, the "Massachusetts Body of Liberties" of 1641 prohibited lawyers from receiving a fee for their services. Lawyers were merely to assist the party in preparing the case, and only if the party was unable to carry it on himself. This reflects the ideals of the Pilgrims (a.k.a. English Separatists): Recall the Mayflower, whose passengers felt that their faith would be their guidance and no lawyers would be necessary.

In such a utopian world, this may, indeed, be the case. However, the "melting pot" that became America is a dynamic and diverse group with different ideals and morality. The legal profession grew quickly in response to the need after the Revolution, and continued to grow at a rapid pace. Fortunately, the reputation of the lawyers also flourished.

Necessity

As the reputations and pocketbooks of the attorneys grew, so did the need to protect the profession. Controlling the practice of law can relate either to the cynical view of protectionism toward the livelihood or to the altruistic view that by regulating the practice we can better protect the public. By restricting access to the profession and thereby restricting access to the justice system, lawyers are ensured that they will always have an income. People must pass through the lawyer as "gatekeeper" if they want to accomplish their legal goals.

gatekeeping function
A restriction of entry into a profession to ensure that certain standards are met prior to admission. It serves to protect both the professionals inside and the public at large against unqualified persons performing the tasks associated with that profession.

This **gatekeeping function** may also be described as a "safeguarding" mechanism. By ensuring that only those who are qualified appear before the court, the justice system can also ensure that the parties' interests are protected. Both substantive and procedural laws are very complicated and potentially stringent in their application. It can be a complex and convoluted journey from commencement of suit to final resolution. There are pitfalls along the way that may have serious consequences for the unrepresented party.

Economics

The increasing need for expert legal advice responded also to pure economics; as demand increases, so does the cost of the service. For the most part, the expense is justified; attorneys have received a very expensive education and usually have "paid their dues" on the battleground of legal practice. However, many people simply cannot afford these services. There are some areas of practice in which those in most need of assistance are those least likely to be able to afford it. These areas include, but are not limited to, family issues (divorce, child custody and support, domestic violence, etc.), landlord/tenant matters, bankruptcy, and immigration. How can these citizens access one of the fundamental services provided by the government—having their "day in court"? This is where independent legal service providers entered the scene, using various names: freelance paralegal; independent paralegal; legal document preparer; limited license legal technician (LLLT). The important difference between use of these providers and the traditional means of obtaining legal services is the lack of a supervising attorney. These providers work for themselves, outside of a legal firm headed by an attorney. In response to the demand for affordable and accessible legal services, many states, like those noted in Chapter 1, have developed programs of licensure for these legal document preparers/legal technicians.

There are competing economic forces at play as access to justice increases by these means. As the demand for these services increases, the charges for the services may increase. That is why the paralegal profession developed in the first place—to lower the cost of legal services—but now paralegals have become part of the "elite-in-demand." Additionally, law firms and in-house corporate legal departments have noticed the economic advantages of employing paralegals. A competent paralegal can demand a very high salary. It is a matter of balance. Paralegal professionals, no matter by whom they are employed, want to be paid what they are worth. This is not unreasonable. However, by increasing their worth, they may decrease their accessibility to those members of the public who need less expensive legal services. It's a catch-22. What everyone can agree upon was concisely stated by Robert D. Welden in his article "Defining the Practice of Law—Untying the Gordian Knot," Washington State Bar Association, January 2001:

> All members of society should be able to afford/retain essential legal assistance from individuals who have the requisite skills and competencies and operate subject to an oversight/regulatory scheme that ensures that those whose important rights are at stake can reasonably rely on the quality, skill and ability to perform necessary appropriate tasks.

This statement returns to the issue of UPL. While it is hard to disagree with the access to justice argument, what remains undefined is those "necessary and appropriate tasks" that make up the practice of law, or conversely, those that do not.

DEFINING THE PRACTICE OF LAW

What tasks routinely handled by paralegals may involve the unauthorized practice of law? How can these practicing professionals protect themselves and their supervising attorneys? The practice of law is very, very broad. It is necessary to define that which is solely within the purview of an attorney to perform. Therefore, every task that is not within the particular realm of the attorney should be "fair game" for paralegals to practice within the strictures of the definition of the paralegal profession.

Unfortunately, there is no set definition of the practice of law. Courts have had a tendency to define it in the negative, meaning that they have decided what non-attorneys cannot do, rather than what only attorneys can do. It is important to note that each jurisdiction has its own set of UPL rules; for this reason, the paralegal should research the relevant statutes, case law, and ethics opinions in her jurisdiction. Both NALA and NFPA can only refer the paralegal to the general relevant prohibitions. See Figure 2.2.

The Acquisition of Clients and Establishment of the Attorney-Client Relationship

Taking a chronological approach to the practice of law, the very first step in practicing law is the **acquisition of clients**. This is also the first opportunity to practice law: the determination of whether to take on the particular client, evaluation of the merits of the case and possibility of success, and the establishment of the **attorney-client relationship**. Due to the *fiduciary* nature of the relationship between an attorney and a client, it is significant who establishes its terms. A **fiduciary relationship** is one in which there is, essentially, a "caretaker": one person who agrees to look out for and act in the best interests

acquisition of clients
The approaching of people in need of legal services and the obtaining of their consent to represent them in a legal matter; this may only be done by an attorney.

attorney-client relationship
The legal relationship established between an attorney and client. This relationship has many protective and confidential aspects and is unique in the legal context.

fiduciary relationship
A relationship based on close personal trust that the other party is looking out for the other's best interests using honesty, integrity, and good faith to guide those decisions.

NALA Guideline 2

Paralegals should not:
Establish attorney-client relationships; set legal fees; give legal opinions or advice; or represent a client before a court, unless authorized to do so by said court; nor engage in, encourage, or contribute to any act which could constitute the unauthorized practice law.

NFPA EC 1.8(a)

A paralegal shall comply with the applicable legal authority governing the unauthorized practice of law in the jurisdiction in which the paralegal practices.

About half the states have statutory and/or case law definitions of the "practice of law"; the others have avoided pinning down a definition in favor of a strictly case-by-case approach. There are six generally accepted tasks that are solely attributable to attorneys as the "practice of law":

1. Aquiring clients and establishing the attorney-client relationship
2. Giving legal advice
3. Preparing legal documents
4. Managing a law practice
5. Representing clients in a court of law
6. Negotiating and settling legal claims

of the other. This encompasses the benefactor's duties of good faith, trust, and honesty. Further, the duty of confidentiality attaches at the moment that this fiduciary relationship is created. Clients must trust attorneys with very sensitive information and disclose personal facts; they must be able to rely on a trained professional who is held to ethical standards of practice.

It is important to note that the establishment of the relationship does not rely on the actual signing of retainer agreements. Another aspect of creating the relationship is the setting of legal fees. Fee arrangements are complex enough to warrant their own chapter, and will be discussed later in the text. It is the intent of the client to enter into an attorney-client/fiduciary relationship that actually creates that relationship:

> The existence of an attorney-client relationship does not depend on an express contract or the payment of fees, and may be implied from the parties' conduct. An attorney-client relationship is established when a party seeks and receives advice and assistance from an attorney on matters pertinent to the legal profession. The existence of an attorney-client relationship turns largely on the client's subjective belief it exists and looks to the nature of the work performed and to the circumstances under which confidences are divulged. The existence of an attorney-client relationship is a question of fact.

Moen v. Thomas, 682 N.W.2d 738, 744-745 (N.D. 2004).

The relationship can be created under numerous circumstances, not just the conventional office meeting. An attorney-client relationship may be formed in the local diner over coffee or in the local pub over a pint. The test applied to the determination of whether the relationship is formed is whether the potential client reasonably believed that he was entering into such a relationship. This can be deduced from a positive response to any of the following questions leading to a finding that the relationship was probably formed:

1. Did the attorney volunteer her services in the aid of the prospective client? This may involve identifying oneself as an attorney to the prospective client, thereby appearing to offer one's professional services.
2. Did the attorney agree to investigate the merits of the matter or render any legal advice specific to the facts given by the prospective client?
3. Did the attorney formerly represent the person in another matter? While each matter undertaken by an attorney requires a separate retainer, the fact that the attorney has done work for this person before tends to suggest that the attorney will take on the present matter.
4. Did the attorney accept payment or bill for fees on the work performed regarding the issue presented?
5. Did the prospective client approach the attorney in confidence? The cornerstone of the relationship is the client's reliance on the fiduciary and confidential nature of the relationship.

For example, in *Tormo v. Yormark*, 398 F. Supp. 1159, 1169 (D.N.J. 1975), the attorney told a potential client that he would "see what could be done with regard to settlement." This preliminary contact "was sufficient as a matter of law to impose upon him the duties owed by an attorney to his clients." The potential client was entitled to the same care from the attorney as any other who had formally been taken on as a client. From the moment that a person believes that the attorney is acting in the potential client's interest, the relationship can be found. The Court in *Donahue v. Shughart, Thomson & Kilroy, P.C.*, 900 S.W.2d 624, 629 (Mo. 1995) (en banc), determined that the question of legal duty of attorneys to purported "non-clients" should be determined by weighing the following factors:

(1) the existence of a specific intent by the client that the purpose of the attorney's services were to benefit the plaintiffs.
(2) the foreseeability of the harm to the plaintiffs as a result of the attorney's negligence.
(3) the degree of certainty that the plaintiffs will suffer injury from attorney misconduct.
(4) the closeness of the connection between the attorney's conduct and the injury.
(5) the policy of preventing future harm.
(6) the burden on the profession of recognizing liability under the circumstances.

In *Miller v. Metzinger*, 91 Cal. App. 3d 31, 154 Cal. Rptr. 22 (1979), the attorney's "declaration[s] that his function was purely investigatory and that he did not agree to represent her, charge any fee for his services or secure a retainer agreement do not suffice to eliminate the existence of an attorney-client relationship." Even if the terms of the relationship have not yet been settled upon, the relationship itself may exist. The details can be determined later. "We may agree with [the attorney] that it was merely an accommodation or a pro forma relationship, but we find nevertheless that it was indeed an attorney-client relationship. The duties or specifics of the relationship in this instance might well be disputed, but the fact that an attorney-client relationship existed is clear." *Insurance Co. of North America v. Westergren*, 794 S.W.2d 812 (Tex. App. 1990). The court looks at the conduct of the attorney and the potential client "*in light of the totality of the circumstances*" and may find that there should be, in all fairness, an enforceable agreement for legal services between them. CA Eth. Op. 2003-161, 2003 WL 23146200, 3 (Cal. St. Bar. Comm. Prof. Resp.)

Giving Legal Advice

legal advice
Generally, the provision of guidance regarding the meaning or application of the law or the rendering of an opinion on the possible outcome of a legal matter.

A client comes to the office looking for **legal advice** on how best to proceed in any given circumstance. The rendering of legal advice to the public is the sole domain of an attorney. Clients are expecting to be counseled regarding their rights, potential liabilities, the effect of rules of law and of the court on their case, and the necessary steps to proceed with the matter. These are tasks that "reasonably demand the application of a trained legal mind." *People v. Landlords Professional Services*, 215 Cal. App. 3d 1599, 1605, 264 Cal. Rptr. 548 (Cal. App. 1989) (citing *Agran v. Shapiro*, 127 Cal. App. 2d Supp. 807, 818, 273 P.2d 619 (1954)). Additionally, the determination relates to the strength of the defenses available to the other parties, possible counterclaims, and a potential challenge to the suit based upon failure to state a claim or filing a frivolous suit.

How do courts determine whether the line has been crossed between supplying information relating to the law and rendering legal advice? "Although there may be a 'twilight zone' between those acts that are and those that are not permissible for persons who are not lawyers, it is clear the core element of practicing law is the giving of legal advice to a client. In fact, merely entering into such relationship constitutes the practice of law." *Rhines v. Norlarco Credit Union*, 847 N.E.2d 233, 239 (Ind. App. 2006).

The answer lies in the specificity and expectations of the client. Answering detailed questions about a particular situation forms the base of the trust relationship between attorney and client. The client assumes (correctly or not) that the legal professional to whom she is speaking is knowledgeable and authorized to make legal conclusions. "Because defendant offers counsel in the form of professional guidance to persons seeking to extricate themselves from a legal relationship, the party represented, as well as the public in general, has a right to be assured that these interests are properly represented by members of the bar. To the extent that defendant provides personal advice peculiar to

NALA Guideline 1

Paralegals should:

▪ Disclose their status as paralegals at the outset of any professional relationship with a client, other attorneys, a court or administrative agency or personnel thereof, or members of the general public

NFPA EC – 1.7(a)

A paralegal's title shall clearly indicate the individual's status and shall be disclosed in all business and professional communications to avoid misunderstandings and misconceptions about the paralegal's role and responsibilities.

the dissolution of a specific [situation], she is engaged in the 'unauthorized practice of law.'..." *Landlords* at 1608, citing *State Bar v. Cramer,* 249 N.W.2d 1, 9 (Mich. 1976).

While only an attorney can create the relationship, the client may be unaware of either the paralegal's inability to create this relationship or the fact that the person to whom he is speaking is in fact a paralegal. For this reason, both NALA and NFPA espouse the full disclosure to the public of the paralegal's status. See Figure 2.3.

Preparing Legal Documents

After the determination has been made to take on a particular client, the next step usually involves preparing **legal documents** to initiate or respond to a legal proceeding or to secure the needs of the client in a legally recognizable format. Pleadings, motions, deeds, wills, contracts, briefs, and various other legal documents all secure and potentially affect the legal rights of the client and third parties to the transaction. It is imperative that these writings and instruments are scrutinized by a person trained to perform legal analysis. They are very often initially drafted by paralegals. This is one of the core duties of a paralegal. However, the finalization, ratification, and submission must come by and through the supervising attorney. Independent paralegals or other non-attorneys who do not work under the supervision of an attorney (hereinafter simply referred to as "non-attorneys") cannot perform this last step. This is also the area in which most non-attorneys get into trouble. There are certain professions that do permissibly create documents that are legal in nature, but are so intertwined with and merely tangential to their primary business that the courts do not find that they are engaged in the unauthorized practice of law. For example, realtors prepare sales agreements, mortgage lenders prepare promissory notes, property managers prepare uncontested eviction notices—and the list goes on. There is a fact-sensitive fine line in these situations as to what crosses into the unauthorized practice of law. While there is no prohibition on the preparation of documents incidental to

legal documents
Papers that are filed in furtherance of a court action or secure a legal right or grant legal recourse to a party.

the business, the line is crossed where the employees of the business use their own discretion in selecting which forms to use, and in doing so, affect the legal ramifications of the selected documents.

The preparation of these documents also must not extend past a "form-fill" function on documents that have actually been prepared by an attorney. *Kim v. Desert Document Services, Inc.*, 101 Wash. App. 1043 (2000). It is this reliance of the clients on the representations of the businesses that they would choose the proper legal document for the client's individual situation that gets the document preparers in trouble. This is true even where the document preparers do not make any assertions that they are qualified to make legal decisions or render legal advice. Where is this line that should not be crossed? The court in *State v. Northouse*, 848 N.E.2d 668, 672 (Ind. 2006), stated it best:

> Generally, it can be said that the filling in of blanks in legal instruments, prepared by attorneys, which require only the use of common knowledge regarding the information to be inserted in said blanks, and general knowledge regarding the legal consequences involved, does not constitute the practice of law. However, when the filling in of such blanks involves considerations of significant legal refinement, or the legal consequences of the act are of great significance to the parties involved, such practice may be restricted to members of the legal profession.

A client has a right to expect that her "legal work" will be performed by an attorney or a person qualified to do so under the direct supervision of an attorney. *McMahon v. Advanced Title Services Company of West Virginia*, 607 S.E.2d 519 (W. Va. 2004).

This discernment becomes more complicated in the era of sophisticated software. The owners of an online bankruptcy preparation service were found to have offered its customers "extensive advice" on how to take advantage of so-called loopholes in the bankruptcy code, promised services comparable to those of a "top-notch bankruptcy lawyer," and described its software as "an expert system" that would do more than function as a "customized word processor." *In re Reynoso*, 477 F.3d 1117, 1125 (9th Cir. 2007). Indeed the function of the software itself provided "such personalized guidance" that it was found to have been the practice of law. *Id.* at 1125-1126.

What is important to note is that the preparation of these documents is not (or should not be) the primary goal of these businesses; nor do these businesses presume to act in a role of legal advisor. The clients have no expectation that these businesses have or apply any particular legal knowledge to their situation. Compare this to *Cleveland Bar Assn. v. Sharp Estate Serv., Inc.*, 107 Ohio St. 3d 219, 837 N.E.2d 1183 (2005). The company marketed and sold living trusts and estate plans that they prepared. They also explained the legal consequences of the clients' specific decisions relating to these plans. Although the actual trusts and wills were entered into the company's computer program by "review attorneys" who were under contract with the company, these attorneys did not counsel or come in contact with the clients. The attorneys provided merely a scrivener service rather than a counselor role;

SPOT THE ISSUE

Every person has the right to represent himself in court and to act on his own behalf in legal matters. What, then, can a corporation do on its own behalf? It needs to be represented by a person. Since that person is "representing" the corporation, does she have to be an attorney? Compare these two scenarios:

An investment company apartment manager (who was the company's 99 percent majority interest holder and actually owned the building) filed complaints seeking rent money from tenants in small-claims court. The court provided the proper forms for the manager to fill out and file. The manager then appeared in court and gave testimony; however, he did not engage in cross-examination or legal argument. At no time did the manager hold himself out as an attorney during any of the proceedings.

A director and CEO of a nonprofit organization filed a motion to dismiss a complaint filed against her organization for underpayment of wages to its employees. She also filed other motions relating to this representation of the organization. Her signature indicated she was "Attorney or Agent" of the organization.

Of these two scenarios, what would you characterize as the unauthorized practice of law: the first, the second, both, or neither? Why? What are the aggravating or mitigating factors in your decision? Compare *Cleveland Bar Association v. Pearlman*, 832 N.E.2d 1193 (Ohio 2005), and *Disciplinary Counsel v. Givens*, 832 N.E.2d 1200 (Ohio 2005).

they were restricted to preparing documents as provided by the company. This requirement was a second infraction of the ethical rules. Attorneys must be free to exercise their independent professional judgment in legal situations. Taking direction from a non-lawyer as a result of the agents' unauthorized practice of law was "insult added to injury."

"Independent Paralegals" a.k.a. "Legal Document Preparers"

We have spoken earlier of paralegals who choose to practice as freelancers under term contracts and offer their services to attorneys. There are also

PORTFOLIO ASSIGNMENT

Write Away

In an effort to clarify the role of the paralegals in the firm, the managing partner asks you to write a paralegal job description detailing the duties and responsibilities of the position. The manager wants a narrative of what the paralegals, both employees and freelancers, can and cannot do in order to stay within the UPL statutes of your jurisdiction.

those who are "independent" and offer their services directly to the public without the supervision of an attorney. The freelancers essentially are under the supervision of an attorney; they work for themselves or a "paralegal firm." Their functions are carried out either in the hiring office or in the freelancer's own space. This freelancing offers paralegals a chance to work in many different environments with different attorneys. The only real difference between "traditional" employment and freelancing is who plays the role of "boss." In this type of practice, it is the attorney who is the client of the **freelance paralegal**.

On the other hand, **independent paralegals** do not provide services for use by an attorney; "independent" in this context means freedom from that kind of relationship. This type of practice has a great benefit, as it directly addresses the societal need for access to justice. However, within this type of practice, there are many opportunities to cross the line into questionable territory, as the safety net of an attorney who is ultimately responsible for the work is absent. These independent paralegals are still prohibited from all the activities previously discussed as the unauthorized practice of law. This practice has evolved under another name in order to clarify the services performed by these professionals: "**legal document preparers**" (**LDPs**). Two states that have standardized this profession in the law are California (Business and Professions Code §§ 6400-6415) and Arizona (Code of Judicial Administration § 7-208). Both statutes characterize the career as a self-help service; the client is in control of the decisions that would normally be made by an attorney, thus preventing, in theory, the LDP from exercising legal judgment and rendering legal advice. LDPs primarily provide access to published legal documents from which the client may choose the most appropriate. The LDP may supply general legal information in order to allow the client to make a decision, but may not make any specific recommendations regarding that choice. The LDP can then follow through by completing the selected forms and file them at the direction of the client.

With this delineation of duties also comes responsibility. The statutes provide for legal remedies and penalties to be levied against the LDP who oversteps the bounds of ethical conduct. There is no job description as such for paralegals who practice under the supervision and direction of an attorney; there is merely a proscription against the unauthorized practice of law. In contrast to this "definition in the negative," the LDP statutes are very clear in defining the positive acts that may be taken by those practitioners. Infractions may result in warnings, fines, or, in severe cases, revocation of the right to practice as an LDP. In many ways this reflects the structure of sanctioning for attorneys. Recall that once an industry is regulated, the state has the power to punish the offenders. The state has a substantial interest in protecting its citizens' interests and in ensuring that their legal rights are preserved.

This concern over the protection of the public is so high that it can take precedence over other individual legal protections. The Arizona Supreme Court has found that protecting the public and the integrity of the legal profession is

freelance paralegal
A legal professional who works as an independent contractor under an individual contract with an attorney who provides supervision during a particular time frame or project.

independent paralegals and legal document preparers (LDPs)
A legal professional who offers services directly to the public. LDPs generally restrict their activities to assisting in preparing legal forms based upon the information obtained from their clients and do not and cannot render legal advice or represent their client in legal matters.

paramount to a person's interest in protecting reputation through the tort of defamation. A certified legal document preparer sued an attorney for defamation because the attorney had sent a letter to the state bar association accusing the LDP of the unauthorized practice of law in connection with a divorce proceeding. The Court held that the attorney's communication to the ethics board of the bar was absolutely immune from suit by the LDP. This protection to express even ungrounded fears or accusations is reserved for circumstances where the public interest is so important that the speaker is granted complete freedom of expression that is not dependent on motive or supporting evidence.

> In light of the role now permissibly played by certified legal document preparers in working with the public and providing the public with certain legal services, just as with the legal profession, public policy demands that absolute immunity be extended to members of the public who report alleged unethical conduct by certified legal document preparers. We can conceive of no reason why a person who reports allegedly unethical conduct by a lawyer should be protected by absolute immunity while a person who reports allegedly unethical conduct by a certified legal document preparer should be subjected to the risk of civil liability. Given the public's need for access to legal services and the importance of regulating those who provide such services, there should be no distinction. The proper, fair and efficient administration of justice demands no less.

Sobol v. Alarcon, 131 P.3d 487, 490 (Ariz. Ct. App. 2006).

As could be expected, California leads the pack in the number of businesses formed to supply these legal document preparation services, but as the demand for these services increases, so will the number of businesses. In the same vein, in October 2005 the NALDP (National Association of Legal Document Preparers) was created to address professional, consumer, and regulatory issues related to this new profession. A survey of the cases regarding independent legal service providers highlights the perils of this type of practice; and judging from the most recent cases, it is particularly perilous in Ohio (recall the *Legal Aid State Services* case mentioned previously):

- *Ohio State Bar Assn v. Cohen*, 836 N.E.2d 1219 (Ohio 2005): The office of DocuPrep USA advertised that it could "prepare and file the important documents of life without the services and expense of a lawyer." However, the court found that the office was engaged in the unauthorized practice of law when it selected the forms and causes of action. While the intent of the office may have been honorable (to protect its clients' interests), the clients' reliance on its services to protect their legal rights in court was impermissible and violative of the law.
- *Cleveland Bar Assn v. Para-Legals, Inc.*, 835 N.E.2d 1240 (Ohio 2005): The company's services included legal research, document preparation, and other ancillary legal services. It touted on its letterhead: "We Are Not Attorneys, We Just Do All of the Work!" The particular incident that resulted in the lawsuit was preparation of a petition in the domestic relations court of Ohio without a licensed attorney's oversight.

■ *Ohio State Bar Assn v. Allen*, 837 N.E.2d 762, 763-764 (Ohio 2005): The court was particularly severe in its penalties assessed against the respondent due to his

> repeated transgressions [of UPL] and his demonstrated disrespect for the relator and the board. . . . Respondent flouted our constitutional authority [. . .] to regulate the practice of law and to protect the public from interlopers not subject to the ethical constraints and educational requirements of this profession. Though given ample opportunity, respondent refused to cooperate in this process, flagrantly practiced law without a license, and caused unsuspecting and vulnerable customers harm by taking their money in exchange for providing inferior services with potentially disastrous ramifications.

Four proven instances of UPL resulted in $40,000 in fines ($10,000 per occurrence).

■ *The Florida Bar v. Miravalle*, 761 So. 2d 1049 (Fla. 2000): The operator of a legal form preparation service was found to have engaged in the unauthorized practice of law by rendering services that the public relied upon to properly prepare and file legal documents, not merely providing a "form fill" service. The court also discussed the nature of the company's name ("Express Legal Services, Inc.") and advertisements as misleading, because they gave the impression that the company specialized in certain types of practice and described legal procedures.

■ *Statewide Grievance Committee v. Patton*, 683 A.2d 1359 (Conn. 1996): The Connecticut Supreme Court upheld a very broad interpretation of acts constituting the practice of law. "Doc-U-Prep" provided customers with a questionnaire pertaining to the type of service requested. The Connecticut courts have consistently held that legal document preparation is the type of activity "commonly understood to be the practice of law." *Id.* at 254. "Although such transactions have no direct connection with court proceedings, they are always subject to subsequent involvement in litigation. They require in many aspects a high degree of legal skill and great capacity for adaptation to difficult and complex situations." *Id.* at 254-255, citing *State Bar Ass'n v. Connecticut Bank & Trust Co.*, 145 Conn. 222, 234-235, 140 A.2d 863 (1958).

IN-CLASS DISCUSSION

In light of the fact that legal document preparers/independent paralegals are regulated and must register with or be certified by the state, what is the benefit or detriment to regulating the paralegal profession as a whole? Do you think that "traditional" paralegals have more or less freedom in their practices with regard to the rules of UPL? How would you personally prefer to practice? Why?

Managing a Law Practice

Daily tasks are also performed slightly differently in a law office. There are day-to-day office activities that are common to all businesses, and these can be handled by non-attorney staff. However, the **management of the law practice** must be handled by an attorney. What is the difference between these two realms? The attorney (commonly called the "managing partner") handles the manner in which cases are distributed to the practice areas in the firm, billable hours, client protocol, trust funds, and other issues particular to the practice of law. "Management" also encompasses the ultimate responsibility for all the work that leaves the office and the proper supervision of all employees. This has important ramifications for UPL, as an attorney may not be consistently absent from the office or delegate duties of oversight.

> **management of law practice**
> Oversight of the purely business aspects of the law firm, as well as ensuring that the protocols conform to the ethical requirements placed upon the attorneys and support staff.

While the courts in each jurisdiction determine what constitutes the unauthorized practice and could have differing opinions, it appears that the courts in Ohio have little sympathy for poor office management. An attorney who was bedridden for several months was suspended for six months for relying on his paralegal to help him manage the law practice. *Columbus Bar Association v. Watson*, 834 N.E.2d 809 (Ohio 2005). Even worse, in *Matter of Thonert*, 693 N.E.2d 559, 561 (Ind. 1998), a suspended attorney instructed his staff to keep the lines of communication open with the clients, including advising them of court dates and other matters arising in their cases. Billing was ongoing, as the staff was instructed to send out new statements on accounts receivable. In his absence, the staff was also told to organize the office and close out files. The court concluded that "the conducting of the business management of a law practice, in conjunction with that practice, constitutes the practice of law." *Id* at 563 (citing *Matter of Perrello*, 270 Ind. 390, 398, 386 N.E.2d 174, 179 (1979)). Generally, the courts do not divide the practice of law into practical matters and legal matters. The business elements merge into the legal elements so that there is one cohesive whole. The unique attributes of the law practice make it impossible to conduct the business without knowledge and regard for them. *See Perrello* at 397. The fact that the non-attorney staff members are entirely competent to run the office is insufficient to overcome the mandate that an attorney manage the law practice.

The management of a law firm is distinct from the law office manager/paralegal position in many larger firms and corporations. This position coordinates the activities of the office and the other employees. Strong organizational skills are an essential asset in this field, as the paralegal may also be made a project leader to ensure that certain tasks are performed optimally. Parallel to the managing attorney's role in the law office is the position of **paralegal manager**. Depending upon the structure of the firm or company, paralegal managers generally recruit, interview, and hire new paralegals and help to train them. They also oversee the distribution and progress of paralegal assignments. "In performing these tasks, the Manager plays multiple roles: leader, mentor, advocate, supervisor, trainer, financial watchdog, evaluator, problem solver, and resource manager." *The Value of a Legal Assistant Manager*,

> **paralegal manager**
> A position in a law firm held by a paralegal who generally recruits, interviews, and hires new paralegals and helps to train them.

published by IPMA; this resource is available through their website: http://www.theipma.org/. There are many players in the hierarchical structure of a law firm, not just the managing partner and paralegal manager along with their respective staff. The proper and efficient functioning of the law firm takes many people. Figure 2.4 provides a flowchart of these players.

Appearance before a Court of Law

representation in court
The right to speak and be heard by the court in a legal matter; a duly licensed attorney is the only person other than the defendant or plaintiff who is acknowledged to have this right.

After the matter has been commenced through some sort of legal document preparation, and the attorney has been managing the matter, the next logical step in the progression involves **representation in court** and other tribunals. There are some agencies that permit non-lawyers to represent parties in hearings; however, this is the exception, not the rule. *See Sperry v. Florida*, 373 U.S.

FIGURE 2.4 ▶
STRUCTURE AND FUNCTIONING OF THE LAW OFFICE

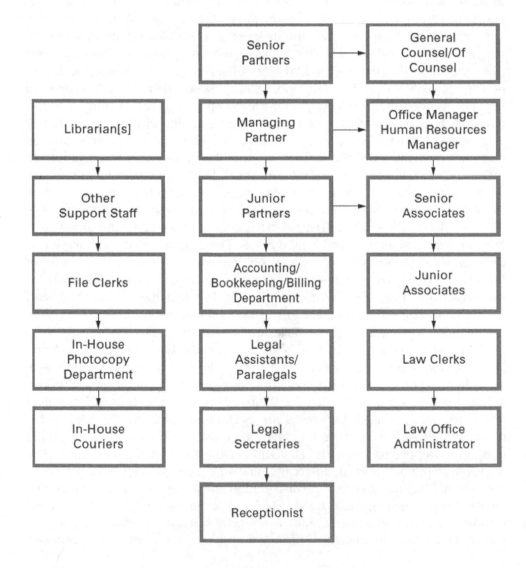

379, 83 S. Ct. 1322, 10 L. Ed. 2d 428 (1963). A non-attorney was engaged in the practice of preparing and prosecuting patent applications in Florida before the United States Patent Office. Under Florida law, this constituted the unauthorized practice of law because the non-attorney was appearing before a tribunal. However, federal statutes and patent regulations authorized practice before this tribunal by non-attorneys. The Federal rules preempted the Florida rules. State rules that are contrary to Federal law are not enforceable. Therefore, the non-attorney practitioner was not guilty of the unauthorized practice of law before the Federal Patent Office.

Paralegals can check their state office of administrative courts for the rules particular to their jurisdiction for non-attorney appearances. The rules will differ from state to state. There are some administrative agencies that perform judicial functions and hold hearings. These agencies can provide for non-attorney representation of the parties before them. In *Caressa Camille, Inc. v. Alcoholic Beverage Control Appeals Bd.*, 99 Cal. App. 4th 1094, 121 Cal. Rptr. 2d 758 (2002), the California Appellate Court concluded that a liquor license revocation proceeding before the administrative agency was not a "court of record." The non-attorney was permitted to represent the corporation that was the subject of the hearing. The New Jersey Office of Administrative Courts states this:

> An attorney may represent a party or a party may present the case him or herself. Additionally, in some cases a non-lawyer may assist a party at the hearing. Some examples are, a paralegal or assistant employed by legal services; a principal of a close corporation; a union representative in a civil service case; and an individual who is permitted by federal law to appear in a Special Education case. In Family Development, Medical Assistance, and Youth and Family Services cases the non-lawyer can ask to be allowed to appear on the day of the hearing. In all other cases, the non-lawyer must complete a Notice of Appearance/Application form and return it to the OAL at least ten days before the hearing.

"Appearance in court" is a term referring to the attorney's right to speak for his client and to be heard on the record. Paralegals often accompany their attorneys to court to assist them at trial, but this presence is not considered an official appearance in court.

The Supreme Court of Ohio found that a paralegal was guilty of committing UPL despite having registered as an "independent paralegal" with the probate court. The paralegal filed the required papers in order to represent a claim in the court; however, a responsible supervising attorney did not sign the registration document. The paralegal crossed out the word "attorney" on the form and inserted "paralegal." The probate court found that while paralegals are permitted to represent claimants, subverting the system by changing the form and acting without the supervision of an attorney was punishable as contempt of court. *Columbus Bar Assn. v. Purnell*, 760 N.E.2d 817 (Ohio 2002).

In all judicial courts, a party may choose to either to represent herself or to have a licensed attorney in that jurisdiction represent her interests. The

Constitutional right to have representation in court does not extend beyond these two classifications of parties. A person who is not an attorney licensed in that jurisdiction cannot represent the party, regardless of how knowledgeable the non-attorney is or how much the party wishes to be represented by that individual. It is well settled that "[t]here is no constitutional right to representation by lay counsel"; that is, a party does not have the right to have a non-attorney represent him. "Any other rule would in effect put this court in the position of sponsoring the unauthorized practice of law." *Rhines* at 239, citing *Terpstra v. Farmers & Merchants Bank*, 483 N.E.2d 749, 760 (Ind. Ct. App. 1985) (citations omitted), *reh'g denied*.

Interestingly, many courts have decided that an attorney, who acts on her own behalf as a *pro se* litigant must follow the ethical rules and avoid contacting the opposing party, even though there is no prohibition against lay litigants from contacting each other. The rationale for this prohibition is grounded in the very concerns over who should be permitted to practice law. Attorneys are permitted exclusive rights to practice law because they have specialized knowledge of the intricate workings of the law and legal system. Using this knowledge when they are a *pro se* litigant against the opposing party, who may not have this degree of knowledge, would potentially give the *pro se* attorney an unfair advantage. Some courts have taken an absolutist position, where no harm needs to be shown from the contact in order to hold that the communication is prohibited by the ethical rules. *See, e.g., Runsvold v. Idaho State Bar*, 925 P.2d 118 (Idaho 1996); *In re Haley*, 126 P.2d 1262 (Wash. 2006); *Sandstrom v. Sandstrom*, 880 P.2d 103 (Wyo. 1994). Other courts will examine the facts of the particular case at hand to determine whether the communication was of a legal nature, or the type of contact that would ordinarily and permissibly take place between lay litigants. *Pinsky v. Statewide Grievance Committee*, 216 Conn. 228, 578 A.2d 1075 (1990). The *Pinsky* court's rationale indicated that contact between litigants is specifically authorized by the relevant professional codes. The restriction on direct communication with the represented opposing party is limited to the situations where the attorney is representing a client. Therefore, an attorney who is representing himself and not a client may communicate with the other litigant directly. ("While the [attorney]'s conduct may have been less than prudent, it did not violate Rule 4.2."). *Pinsky* at 236.

Negotiation and Settlement

negotiation and settlement
The alternative means to terminate a legal matter rather than full trial on the merits. As the settlement has the same force as a final adjudication, an attorney must perform the tasks associated with it.

Finally, negotiating and settling a matter is exclusively an attorney's job. **Negotiation and settlement** takes skill, tenacity, and experience to achieve the proper and just result for the client. Strategy regarding procedural and substantive law must be taken into account during this time. The court has previously held that, when a person who is not an attorney represents another in the negotiation and settlement of a personal injury claim for consideration, pursuant to a contingency fee contract, that person has engaged in the unauthorized practice of law. *Duncan v. Gordon*, 476 So. 2d 896 (La. App.

2d Cir. 1985). It is the unauthorized practice of law because the person must advise the client of issues concerning the redress of a legal wrong. *Id.* Negotiation and settlement are functions solely performable by an attorney. Attorneys are able to analyze the merit of a case's facts in light of the current state of law. For example, a trained, impartial attorney can reliably gauge the value of settlement versus litigation. This is not to say that others who are not licensed could not make that determination, but remember, again, that the courts and clients can hold an attorney accountable for imprudent actions taken in this regard.

Delegation of settlement negotiations to non-attorney staff will result in the finding that the supposedly "supervising" attorney assisted in the unauthorized practice of law. In an extreme case, an attorney completely renounced the essential role of the attorney in settlements. In *In re Sledge*, 859 So. 2d 671 (La. 2003), the attorney was absent from his law practice for approximately half the time, delegating complete control of the management of the law office to his staff. Most shockingly, he

> admitted there were often cases that were handled from the interview stage to the settlement distribution without any involvement on his [the attorney's] part. Respondent [attorney] conceded he authorized [his office manager] to negotiate settlements, and that he did not get involved in the non-litigation cases, reasoning it was "routine" and that non-lawyers deal with insurance adjusters better than lawyers. As convincing evidence of his adequate supervision of his employees, respondent [attorney] referred to the existence of his "employee office manual," which according to respondent had the appropriate checklists and guidelines for his employees to process his cases. . . . Respondent conceded that he supervised [his office manager's] performance exclusively based on graphs evidencing how many cases she settled and the gross income generated from the cases.

Id. at 682-683.

Needless to say, the Supreme Court of Louisiana did not find this to be either the adequate supervision of the attorney's staff or the appropriate delegation of the practice of law. The attorney's characterization of settlement negotiations as "routine" or "cookie-cutter" was "clearly at odds" with the philosophy of the court that every client deserves the benefit of the lawyer's legal training and skill to resolve the particular issue before him. *Id.* at 686. It should be no surprise that Mr. Sledge was disbarred for this conduct.

A paralegal's claim that he was doing "nothing more than relaying information" will not shield him from prosecution for the unauthorized practice of law. *The Florida Bar v. Neiman*, 816 So. 2d 587, 589 (Fla. 2002). The claims regarding the UPL committed by Neiman, a paralegal, were numerous. Although interviewing clients is perfectly acceptable paralegal practice, this paralegal took it a step farther by commenting that it sounded like a "good case." *Id.* Legal research normally performed by a paralegal turned into UPL when Neiman reported the results directly back to the client. *Id.* It is good office protocol to return phone calls from other attorneys; however, again, Neiman took his role of paralegal one step too far, by not only speaking to opposing counsel but also arguing about issues of liability, evidence, and settlement. *Id.* at 590. Neiman, a paralegal, was very successful in "running the show" at the law office where he was employed. *Id.* at 594. However, this is unacceptable under the laws concerning UPL. The recommendation to the Supreme Court of Florida was very specific as to what actions taken by this paralegal were to be enjoined, and it provides a comprehensive list of prohibited actions. Paralegals who have been found guilty of UPL should be prevented from:

    a. having direct contact with any client, opposing counsel or third party, unless it involves the [paralegal]'s own personal legal matters;

    b. without limiting the above, discussing, construing or interpreting the applicability of any case law, statutory law or any other law with any opposing counsel or other third party;

    c. speaking on behalf of third parties at settlement conferences, meetings, negotiations or mediations, even with an attorney present;

    d. appearing on behalf of third parties at settlement meetings, negotiations or mediations without the attorney present for whom [the paralegal] is employed;

    e. without limiting the above, providing third parties advice on the strengths and weaknesses of any legal matter, or making decisions on behalf of others that require legal skill and a knowledge of the law greater than the average citizen;

    f. without limiting the above, advising third parties as to various legal remedies available to them and possible courses of action;

    g. preparing pleadings, motions or any other legal documents for others, and, without limiting the above, explaining to third parties the legal significance of any document;

    h. without limiting the above, having direct contact in the nature of consultation, explanation, recommendation, advice or assistance in the selection of any legal remedy or course of action;

    i. suggesting, directing or participating in the accumulation of evidence supporting any legal claim;

    j. holding [himself] out to third parties in such a manner that a third party places some reliance on [him] to handle legal matters;

    k. impliedly holding himself out as an attorney;

    l. without limiting the above, serving as a conduit or intermediary for the obtaining or relaying of any information for the preparation, consideration or evaluation of any legal matter from others who have never consulted with [the paralegal's] supervising attorney;

    m. soliciting or accepting attorney's fees;

    n. without limiting the above, corresponding with parties or attorneys of parties as the representative of any client relating to legal matters;

    o. signing any letter, pleading or other document on behalf of any attorney or under any attorney's signature, even with such attorney's consent. . . .

Id. at 595-596.

RESEARCH THIS

Find a case or ethics opinion in your jurisdiction that defines the "practice of law." What considerations did the court find important in describing what is or is not the practice of law (which is, therefore, confined to be practiced by attorneys)? Write your own definition for the "practice of law." After performing this task, write a paralegal job description detailing the duties and responsibilities of the position. Create a narrative of what the paralegals, both employees and freelancers, can and cannot do in order to stay within the UPL statutes of your jurisdiction.

The reviewing court was careful to point out that this did not unnecessarily restrict a paralegal's practice. Many other tasks are necessary for a law office to run properly, and these are properly delegated to the paralegal. Further, note that these prohibitions were very strictly construed against Neiman because of his flagrant abuse of his position at the firm. The most important factor to be considered is real supervision of a responsible attorney, something that was clearly lacking in the above case. Paralegals whose roles and duties are clearly delineated and known to clients do not run the risk of failing the test espoused by the *Neiman* court. "In common parlance, Neiman's activities fail the 'duck' test. That is, in common parlance, one would expect that if it looks like a duck, and walks, talks, and acts like a duck, one can usually safely assume it is a duck. Unfortunately, while Neiman at all times acted like an educated and licensed lawyer, he was not." *Id.* at 599.

HOW PARALEGALS CAN AVOID THE UNAUTHORIZED PRACTICE OF LAW

The burden of preventing the unauthorized practice of law does not fall solely on the shoulders of the supervising attorneys. Indeed, every member of the legal team should strive for compliance. This is particularly true for paralegals, as they have significant client contact. Further, clients cannot appreciate the subtle differences between giving them general information regarding their case and its progress and rendering legal advice. To complicate matters even further, paralegals often know the correct legal answer or have prepared the legal analysis regarding the issue, but are not permitted to communicate that to the client.

The paralegal's rapport (avoiding the use of the term "relationship," since that is a term of art saved for use with the attorney here) with the client is essential in the delivery of legal services. Often the paralegal is present at or in charge of the intake interview, or perhaps she is fielding the first phone call from the prospective client. Even these preliminary tasks present an opportunity to cross that line into the unauthorized practice of law. From the outset, the client should be informed of the paralegal's status and role as a member of the legal team. This is to avoid confusion on the part of the client as to whom he can look to for certain types of information. Legal advice, of course, cannot be given by the paralegal, and this constraint should be explained to the client in order to "head it off at the pass." Clients will call to check on the status of their cases, and if the attorney is unavailable, will also look to the paralegal for legal guidance. Once the boundaries of the duties of the paralegal have been established, the client will have been advised of this prohibition. Again, it is not that the paralegal does not know the answer, but that the protections of the ethical codes do not allow her to convey them directly to the client.

Paralegals may be most at risk for crossing the line in the situations that need them the most. Legal aid services provide free legal services to low-income residents in the jurisdiction. Often paralegals are used for intake screening, to determine the nature of the matter in order to refer the issue to the appropriate attorney, to ensure that the party is eligible for the legal services requested, and to screen for potential conflicts. The conversations between the paralegal and the potential client may or may not contain sensitive information, and the client may feel that a confidential legal relationship has been formed. This is a fact-sensitive issue that can be avoided by clear communication to the potential client during screening of the purpose and limitations of the role of the intake paralegal. In these situations, paralegals may find it difficult to refrain from answering an anxious client's legal questions. The desire to help, which probably drove the paralegal into employment at the Legal Aid Society in the first place, must be overcome by the paralegal's ethical obligations to refrain from the unauthorized practice of law.

The same holds true for paralegals engaged in other areas of law where anxiety runs particularly high. In bankruptcy, family law, wills/estates/trusts, landlord/tenant, and other document-based practices, it is very often the paralegal who actually prepares the first drafts of these papers. The worried client may be aware of this fact and the paralegal, having the information at hand, may be tempted to provide information regarding the matter. What type of communication is permissible, and when does it cross the line? The court has typically held that decisions regarding the choice of document to be prepared, the ramifications of that choice, and the actions to be taken by the client in furtherance of that choice are impermissible as the unauthorized practice of law. Conversely, paralegals have not stepped over the line when they have taken some of the above actions but have sought the final review and approval of a supervising attorney.

Other preliminary tasks also present potential hazards. Paper is everywhere in a law office, and much of it is in the form of letters. Constant correspondence is sent out to many different companies and individuals other than the client. These entities are not familiar with the role of the paralegal in the matter. As first impressions are everything, law firms often list their attorneys on their letterhead, indicating their bar admissions and certified specialties. Firms may also choose to list the names of their paralegals, and this is perfectly acceptable, as long as the paralegals are clearly identified as such. Indeed, it may give some clients a degree of comfort to know that qualified paralegals, whom the firm is proud to list, are employed on their cases. This may be particularly true where the paralegal has earned certifications from any of the national paralegal associations. Firms may also choose to supply their paralegals with business cards. Again, this is beneficial, in that the various parties who need information regarding a matter upon which a paralegal is working will be able to have the direct link to her. Signing correspondence, whether on letterhead indicating the paralegal's status or not, should also note under the signature the title of "paralegal," "legal assistant," or whatever other title is appropriate in the particular firm. Refer back to Figure 2.3 for the paralegal codes regarding this issue.

These issues related to correspondence have been addressed by various courts and ethics boards. The New Jersey Supreme Court Advisory Committee on Professional Ethics put it very clearly:

> It is not and should not be our intention to hamstring the effectiveness of the non-lawyer assistant by placing artificial barriers in the way of the performance of his or her duties. Thus, for example, the non-lawyer assistant may, we believe, properly sign firm letterhead in connection with routine tasks in many fields of law such as the gathering of factual information and documents. . . .

N.J. Eth. Op. 611, 1988 WL 356368 1.

The Committee's opinion went on to explain that other kinds of correspondence should not be signed by non-attorneys. Communications that include substantive legal issues or are sent to the court and opposing attorneys must be signed by the responsible attorney. The key to this issue is the substance of the correspondence. If the paralegal could not say or do what is accomplished in the letter without committing UPL, then the paralegal should not sign it.

> Such a rule has several beneficial effects including the following: It avoids the opportunity or temptation for the non-lawyer assistant to step over the line by rendering legal advice. . . . Second, it enables the responsible attorney to keep abreast of the matter by controlling important correspondence and so performing his essential function as the responsible attorney including his obligation of close supervision.

Id.

A paralegal's participation in pursuing a matter and its ultimate termination must comport with the aforementioned standards. *Any* action taken by a paralegal on behalf of the client impacting the client's legal rights and liabilities without an attorney's supervision will likely be found to be the unauthorized practice of law. Even if the conduct would have been permissible had it been overseen by an attorney who was ultimately responsible for the work product, it is an ethical violation in the absence of that oversight. The South Carolina Supreme Court rendered an opinion regarding the quality and type of oversight of a paralegal's conduct resulting in the unauthorized practice of law. The Court opined: "Meaningful attorney supervision must be present throughout

FIGURE 2.5 ▶
SIGNING
CORRESPONDENCE

NALA Guideline 5

[A] paralegal may perform any function delegated by an attorney, including, but not limited to the following: . . .

■ Author and sign letters providing the paralegal's status is clearly indicated and the correspondence does not contain independent legal opinions or legal advice.

NFPA EC 1.7(b)

A paralegal's title shall be included if the paralegal's name appears on business cards, letterhead, brochures, directories, and advertisements.

NFPA EC 1.7(c)

A paralegal shall not use letterhead, business cards or other promotional materials to create a fraudulent impression of his/her status or ability to practice in the jurisdiction in which the paralegal practices.

the process [of solicitation and representation]. The line between what is and what is not permissible conduct by a non-attorney is oftentimes 'unclear' and is a potential trap for the unsuspecting client." *Doe v. Condon*, 532 S.E.2d 879, 881 (S.C. 2000), citing *State v. Buyers Service Co., Inc.*, 357 S.E.2d 15, 17 (S.C. 1987). In *Doe*, the court found several different activities that constituted the unauthorized practice of law. The matter came before the court as the petitioner sought a declaratory opinion as to what proposed activities would be "out of bounds." Among other things, the paralegal intended to conduct educational seminars for the public on the topic of estate planning. Even answering "general" questions of the audience would involve the exercise of legal judgment, and therefore be prohibited.

ATTORNEYS AND THE UNAUTHORIZED PRACTICE OF LAW

Until now, the discussion has centered on the practice of law by non-attorneys; attorneys also can violate this rule, in two ways. First, the attorney can commit UPL herself in violation of ABA Model Rule 5.5 which prohibits an attorney from practicing in a jurisdiction in which he has not been formally admitted. Second, the attorney could violate the rule by assisting a non-attorney in committing UPL.

Multijurisdictional Practice

In today's trend toward globalization, many individuals and companies find themselves doing business across state lines and across national borders. The way that attorneys have traditionally practiced law does not accommodate this business model. As noted earlier in this chapter, attorneys must pass the bar for each state in which they practice. Traditionally, clients' interests were contained within the state in which they retained their attorneys. This simply is no longer the case. Engaging in the practice of law in a state where the attorney is not admitted is the unauthorized practice of law in that jurisdiction.

The problem is serious enough that in 2000, the ABA created a task force, the Commission on **Multijurisdictional Practice**, to study and report on this issue. The former version of the Multijurisdictional Practice Rule contained essentially only one sentence: "a lawyer shall not: (a) practice law in a jurisdiction where doing so violates the regulation of the legal profession in that jurisdiction; or (b) assist a person who is not a member of the bar in the performance of activity that constitutes the unauthorized practice of law." The goal of the ABA Commission was to find a balance between the interests of clients operating on national and international scales and of the states in protecting their citizens and maintaining the integrity of their own judicial systems. Clients have the right to retain the attorney of their own choosing; it places an undue burden upon them to have to retain an attorney for each state in which they operate.

multijurisdictional practice
The practice of law by an attorney outside the state in which that attorney was originally licensed, because the clients' interests are interstate or national in scale.

While every state has accommodations for a "one-time-only" admission where the client requires out-of-state assistance, the reality is that clients need their lawyers to operate in other jurisdictions on a more frequent basis. The "one-time-only" special dispensation for practice in the jurisdiction in which the lawyer is not admitted is called "pro hac vice"—literally, "for this turn." The attorney is required to submit an application to the court in front of which she desires to appear. Usually, a state also requires that an attorney admitted to practice in that state agrees to "sponsor" the petitioning attorney. The petitioned court may request any other reasonable information from the applicant that it deems necessary to make a determination as to whether leave to appear before the court is granted. This may include a substantial amount of detail regarding the applicant's current practice and reasons why the applicant should be permitted to practice in the jurisdiction. If there aren't any benefits to the client in having the out-of-jurisdiction attorney appear for the party, then the court is likely to refuse the application and deem it in the best interest of the client to have an in-state attorney appear on the client's behalf. This may also be seen as a protective measure for the in-state attorneys against infiltration of "border attorneys" (those practicing near the state line) who are not admitted to the practice in that state. Crossing borders has significant impact on these practitioners, much like the multijurisdictional practice issues discussed regarding lawyers. The Ohio Supreme Court has addressed this very issue in *Trumbull County Bar Ass'n v. Legal Aid State Services, Inc.*, 846 N.E.2d 35 (Ohio 2006). The legal service provider ran an online business based in Las Vegas, Nevada that purported to have expertise in preparing legal forms to be consistent with individual state standards. The incident that brought the service firm before the Ohio court was an adoption petition filed in Trumbull County, Ohio. The court found that the business was engaged in the unauthorized practice of law in Ohio, regardless of its place of operation, when it prepared legal papers to be filed in an Ohio court on behalf of its clients.

The new ABA Model Rule 5.5 adds much clarity, explanation, and guidance for practitioners who find themselves involved in multijurisdictional issues. The number of lawyers, and therefore the number of paralegals, who are going to find themselves in this situation will continue to rise. The multijurisdictional practice rules make more practical sense for attorneys and paralegals who practicing law today. Attorneys and paralegals have been given a means to serve their clients' interests without violating the ethics rules. Each state remains territorial and the particular rules regarding out-of-state legal representation must be investigated, but at least such representation is now possible.

Assisting Others in Committing the Unauthorized Practice of Law

A significant change made by the ABA commission to Rule 5.5 was the expansion of the concept that a lawyer should not assist *anyone* in the unauthorized practice of law. The previous definition suggested that lawyers should not assist only those who were not members of the bar, giving lawyers from another jurisdiction (members of the bar) a potential loophole, depending on how closely one read the rule. This modification makes it quite clear that any person who is not admitted to practice in the relevant jurisdiction should not be assisted in the practice of law. How does this play out in the law office? Attorneys, like many others, move from state to state for various reasons. If they are to be employed in a law firm, they must be admitted to practice in their new state. In *Bluestein v. State Bar*, 13 Cal. 3d 162, 118 Cal. Rptr. 175 (1974), a purported foreign attorney who was not licensed in California was listed on the California attorney's letterhead as "of Counsel," thus giving the appearance that he was an admitted, duly licensed attorney in that jurisdiction. The California attorney permitted the unlicensed person to consult with his clients regarding a matter arising in Spain. The California attorney was then held to have violated the ethical rules against aiding another in the unauthorized practice of law:

> Whether a person gives advice as to local law, Federal law, the law of a sister State, or the law of a foreign country, he is giving legal advice. . . . To hold otherwise would be to state that a member of the State Bar only practices law when he deals with local law, a manifestly anomalous statement. Giving legal advice regarding the law of a foreign country thus constitutes the practice of law, and the next question is whether such practice is unauthorized. Business and Professions Code section 6125 provides, "No person shall practice law in this State unless he is an active member of the State Bar."

Id. at 174.

It appears that the courts have interpreted the practice of law as the practice of any law, regardless of the source of that law. The conduct of an attorney who holds himself out as being able to practice law in a jurisdiction where he is not admitted also reflects upon his fitness to practice and violates his duty of candor towards the tribunals of that jurisdiction and their clients. In *In re Jackman*, the New Jersey Supreme Court found that a large New Jersey law firm had aided in an associate attorney's unauthorized practice of law where the managing partner knew about the associate's lack of admission to the New Jersey Bar. After about seven years at the New Jersey firm, the associate sat for the New Jersey Bar Exam. During this time, the associate was admitted to practice only in Massachusetts and had actually been put on inactive status in that jurisdiction. Further, the court supported the significant delay in the associate's certification to admission to the New Jersey Bar after having taken the bar exam to "underscore to this candidate the seriousness with which we view his earlier improper practice and his failure to be responsible in discerning his personal obligation to satisfy our admission and practice requirements." 761 A.2d 1103, 1110 (N.J. 2000).

However, most relevant to paralegal students is how the rules affecting attorneys pertain to them, persons who are clearly not members of the bar in any jurisdiction. Paralegals offer very valuable services to attorneys, services that are legal in nature. It is up to the trained professional determination of the attorney to determine how best to use the paralegal without overstepping the boundaries of the practice. Recall that paralegals are essential in some areas of practice in order to be able to deliver cost-effective legal services to members of the public who are most in need but sometimes least able to afford these services. This belief was highlighted in an Ethics Opinion of the Philadelphia Bar. An attorney had requested an advisory opinion regarding his acceptance of referrals and interpretation services provided by a bilingual paralegal. The Opinion could not address the attorney's concern over whether the independent paralegal was engaged in the unauthorized practice of law, because that is a fact-sensitive matter and would have to be determined by a court of law. However, the ethics committee did comment on the attorney's conduct with respect to these services provided by the paralegal. It found that as long as the attorney did nothing that could be construed as aiding and abetting in the unauthorized practice of law by that paralegal. The attorney, by necessity, had to rely on the assurances of the paralegal that he was not giving any legal advice during those translation services. *See* 1988 WL 236395 (Phila. Bar. Assn. Prof. Guid. Comm.).

While it seems intuitive from the above Rule that attorneys may not accept assistance from others in the practice of law, that is indeed what they are doing from the moment they employ a paralegal. If paralegals could not practice law, they would be of very little use in the office. Recall that that paralegals perform the authorized practice of law. For this reason, the ABA has created Model Rule 5.3. This Rule requires that all responsible lawyers in the firm must ensure that there are ways of monitoring their assistants' conduct and make certain that it is compatible with the professional obligations of the lawyers in the firm. This obligation underscores the importance of a paralegal's understanding of the Rules of Professional Responsibility that govern the attorneys in the relevant jurisdiction. See Figure 2.6.

FIGURE 2.6 ▶
PARALEGALS'
KNOWLEDGE OF THE
ATTORNEYS' RULES OF
PROFESSIONAL CONDUCT

NALA Guideline 1

Paralegals should:

- Understand the attorney's Rules of Professional Responsibility and these Guidelines in order to avoid any action which would involve the attorney in a violation of the Rules, or give the appearance of professional impropriety.

NFPA EC 1.3(e)

A paralegal shall not knowingly assist any individual with the commission of an act that is in direct violation of the Model Code/Model Rules and/or the rules and/or laws governing the jurisdiction in which the paralegal practices.

The main thrust of ABA Model Rule 5.3 is to permit attorneys to effectively use their paralegals, while reinforcing the necessity of supervision and the attorney's ultimate responsibility for not only the work product, but also the ethical performance of that work. This is precisely why paralegals need to study the applicable rules of ethics for their jurisdiction. A paralegal's conduct must comport with the standards of the supervising attorney. Without this mandate, the paralegal can become the "weakest link" in the chain of the provision of legal services to a client. Knowledge of the ethical standards serves to protect not only the paralegal and the attorneys in the office, but also the client's interests. To the extent that a paralegal is properly supervised and held accountable to the standards of ethics, she can practice law without overstepping the line into the unauthorized practice of law.

The duty of supervision is taken very seriously by the bar and the courts. An attorney's office must have all the proper procedures in place to ensure that a paralegal's actions are compatible with the attorney's ethical obligations. An attorney must ensure both that the paralegal is performing tasks in the same manner that the attorney is required to, and that the performance of those tasks enable the attorney to fulfill her own duties required under the ethical codes.

REEL TO REAL

Take a look, or a second look if you've already seen it, at *Erin Brockovich*; Julia Roberts portrayed this spunky legal assistant in the 2000 movie. The general plot follows the true story of Ms. Brockovich, who has lost a personal injury lawsuit and subsequently is employed by her attorney. During some routine filing, she finds some interesting connections between medical records and toxic leakage from the Gas and Electric Company that threatens the entire community's health. Examine the tasks assigned to and the actions taken by Ms. Brockovich, and evaluate whether any of them could be considered the unauthorized practice of law.

While proper procedures were in place in the attorney's office in *People v. Smith*, 74 P.3d 566 (Colo. 2003), his paralegal failed to follow through in ensuring that all client communications were transmitted to the attorney. The delegation of substantial work to a paralegal is perfectly acceptable; however, the attorney must properly supervise that work to make certain that the paralegal is taking the requisite actions. Failure to do so can, and in the *Smith* case did, result in the paralegal's commission of the unauthorized practice of law. The *Smith* court had little sympathy for the attorney, who claimed that the case neglect would not have occurred had the paralegal brought certain matters to his attention. The court found that it was the attorney's affirmative responsibility to take positive steps in supervision of the paralegal. Inaction or neglect by the paralegal did not excuse the attorney of responsibility and the finding that he was in violation of his ethical duties. For that reason, the attorney was suspended from practice for a period of nine months. Needless to say, it behooves the professional paralegal to maintain his personal integrity and responsibility for his own work product and work ethic in order to protect himself and his supervising attorneys.

Much in the same vein, ABA Model Rule 5.7 addresses this issue with regard to other law-related services provided by an attorney. If an attorney is involved in other businesses that are separate from but related to the law practice, the attorney must still comport with the applicable rules of professional conduct. The significance of this Rule relates to the idea that an attorney is always associated with "legal authority," wherever she might be. A business, although separate from the actual legal practice, will take on this authority and responsibility if there is an attorney involved in its management. Clients may not be able to make this complete separation between practice and business. Therefore, the ethical standards will follow the attorney into the business and impose standards upon the attorney where there normally would not be if the business were managed by a nonlawyer. It is in this setting as well that the attorney must control the output of his employees, so as not to give the impression that the business is rendering legal services. If that were the case, the attorney would be assisting in the unauthorized practice of law.

What are these other businesses that may cause this type of problem? Fields that are tangential to the provision of legal services, such as insurance, title searching, financial and estate planning, accountancy, medical consultations, political lobbying, and tax preparation, just to name a few, are susceptible to the ethical protections for clients. The list goes on, depending upon the specialty of the attorney. It is important for the staff of these tangential services to understand the nature of the proscriptions of the ethical rules in order to avoid the unauthorized practice of law.

Other groups of "practitioners" have the potential to be affected by UPL issues. Mediators and arbitrators are growing in number as the citizenry turns to alternate dispute resolution. In an effort to address this critical issue, the ABA Section of Dispute Resolution adopted a Resolution on Mediation and the Unauthorized Practice of Law in 2002. The Resolution had four main points.

First, it was determined that mediation is not the practice of law. Mediators do not represent the parties but rather function as an impartial negotiator to assist the parties in reaching a voluntary settlement. Second, while legal issues are addressed, these discussions do not constitute legal advice and there is no fiduciary relationship created. This is true even where the mediator is an attorney. Third, drafting the settlement agreement for the parties is not the practice of law as the mediator is acting merely as a scrivener. If the mediator inserts terms not agreed upon by the parties, he may be liable for UPL. The mediator must be clear that the suggestions made are merely for informational purposes and are not legal advice. Lastly, just like paralegals, mediators must make their role clear to the parties. If any party needs legal advice, that party will need to seek independent legal counsel before proceeding. Through this Resolution, the ABA was able to underscore the importance of alternative dispute resolution in the rendering of legal services to the public: It performs a cost- and time-saving function in addressing societal needs similar to those that gave rise to the paralegal profession. The burden on the court system can be alleviated by offering an efficient and effective means of handling legal disputes.

The ABA Resolution espouses the following principles:

Mediation is not the practice of law. Mediation is a process in which an impartial individual assists the parties in reaching a voluntary settlement. Such assistance does not constitute the practice of law. The parties to the mediation are not represented by the mediator.

Mediators. Discussion of legal issues. In disputes where the parties. legal rights or obligations are at issue, the mediator's discussions with the parties may involve legal issues. Such discussions do not create an attorney-client relationship, and do not constitute legal advice, whether or not the mediator is an attorney.

Drafting settlement agreements. When an agreement is reached in mediation, the parties often request assistance from the mediator in memorializing their agreement. The preparation of a memorandum of understanding or settlement agreement by a mediator, incorporating the terms of settlement specified by the parties, does not constitute the practice of law. If the mediator drafts an agreement that goes beyond the terms specified by the parties, he or she may be engaged in the practice of law. However, in such a case, a mediator shall not be engaged in the practice of law if (a) all parties are represented by counsel and (b) the mediator discloses that any proposal that he or she makes with respect to the terms of settlement is informational as opposed to the practice of law, and that the parties should not view or rely upon such proposals as advice of counsel, but merely consider them in consultation with their own attorneys.

Mediators' responsibilities. Mediators have a responsibility to inform the parties in a mediation about the nature of the mediator's role in the process and the limits of that role. Mediators should inform the parties: (a) that the mediator's role is not to provide them with legal representation, but rather to assist them in reaching a voluntary agreement; (b) that a settlement agreement may affect the parties. legal rights; and (c) that each of the parties has the right to seek the advice of independent legal counsel throughout the mediation process and should seek such counsel before signing a settlement agreement.

Through this Resolution, the ABA was able to underscore the importance of alternative dispute resolution in the rendering of legal services to the public.

It is important for the paralegal to bear in mind the role she plays in the legal system as a whole, not just the law office where she is employed. The unauthorized practice of law can take place in a law office, where the paralegal is either unsupervised or improperly supervised, or outside of the firm or corporate setting, where paralegals or others perform legal services that are exclusive to the attorney's practice of law. While many paralegals may have the experience to answer the legal questions posed by their practice and clients, it is imperative that they understand the boundaries of their own profession and not cross the line into the unauthorized practice of law.

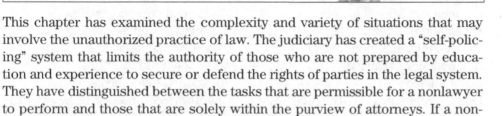

Summary

This chapter has examined the complexity and variety of situations that may involve the unauthorized practice of law. The judiciary has created a "self-policing" system that limits the authority of those who are not prepared by education and experience to secure or defend the rights of parties in the legal system. They have distinguished between the tasks that are permissible for a nonlawyer to perform and those that are solely within the purview of attorneys. If a non-attorney performs any of those tasks ascribed solely to attorneys, she has committed the unauthorized practice of law (UPL). The traditional tasks ascribed to attorneys alone include:

1. Acquiring clients and establishing the attorney-client relationship

2. Giving legal advice

3. Preparing legal documents

4. Managing a law practice

5. Representing clients in a court of law

6. Negotiating and settling legal claims

While the performance of these tasks by nonlawyers is clearly UPL, attorneys themselves can commit UPL in two situations: (1) practicing in a jurisdiction where they are not licensed, and (2) assisting others in committing UPL.

Understanding the rules relating to the unauthorized practice of law is essential for a paralegal in order to properly practice her profession within the boundaries of ethical conduct. Paralegals should be particularly vigilant in these areas:

1. Communicating with the client

2. Identifying themselves as paralegals

3. Writing and signing correspondence

4. Ensuring proper supervision by their employers

Independent paralegals (also known as "legal document preparers") face unique issues relating to UPL as they deliver legal services directly to the public. These professionals may be regulated by state statute, and must be mindful of the civil and criminal penalties that may be imposed for either UPL or professional negligence.

Key Terms and Concepts

Acquisition of clients	Legal documents
Attorney-client relationship	Management of law practice
Fiduciary relationship	Multijurisdictional practice
Freelance paralegal	Negotiation and settlement
Gatekeeping function	Paralegal manager
Independent paralegal	Representation in court
Legal advice	Substantive legal tasks
Legal Document Preparer (LDP)	Unauthorized practice of law (UPL)

Review Questions

MULTIPLE CHOICE

Choose the best answer(s) and please explain why you chose the answer(s).

1. "Legal advice" can best be defined as:
   a. The opinions of a lawyer
   b. Explanations of rights and liabilities of a citizen under the law
   c. Informing a client about any legal proceeding
   d. Describing the process of the judicial system
   e. All of the above
   f. None of the above

2. The judicial system prohibits nonlawyers from representing persons in court because:
   a. Nonlawyers have not paid the necessary dues to practice law

   b. Nonlawyers cannot know the intricate workings of the legal system

   c. The court cannot guarantee that the nonlawyers know the proper law and procedure

   d. Everyone has the right to represent themselves in court

3. Attorneys may be admitted "pro hac vice":
   a. When they want to practice in another jurisdiction
   b. When an established client has a legal issue in a jurisdiction where the attorney is not admitted
   c. Into multiple jurisdictions to ensure that they can represent corporate clients
   d. Before they are admitted to practice in the jurisdiction where they live

4. Which of the following is NOT traditionally accepted as a "lawyers only" task in the "practice of law?"
   a. Managing a law practice
   b. Acquiring clients
   c. Settling claims relating to a lawsuit
   d. Performing legal research

EXPLAIN YOURSELF

All answers should be written in complete sentences. A simple yes or no is insufficient.

1. In your own words, describe the difference between an attorney's practice of law and a paralegal's practice of law.

2. Why can't a paralegal negotiate and settle a matter for a client where the client has consented to that kind of representation?

3. Describe the problems associated with "multijurisdictional practice." Is there a good solution to the globalization problem faced by corporate counsel?

4. What is the biggest problem, in your opinion, faced by "independent paralegals"?

5. Explain an attorney's duty of supervision. Why is it so critical to the proper functioning of the legal system?

FAULTY PHRASES

All of the following statements are *false*. State why they are false and then rewrite each one as a true statement. Do not simply make the statement negative by adding the word "not."

1. All legal actions taken by nonlawyers constitute the unauthorized practice of law.

2. Paralegals may not prepare legal documents without committing UPL.

3. Once a retainer letter has been signed by the client, the attorney-client relationship has been formed.

4. All law office managers must be attorneys.

5. Attorneys cannot practice in multiple jurisdictions.

6. Paralegals should avoid signing correspondence to clients in order to avoid UPL.

PORTFOLIO ASSIGNMENTS

Write Away

1. In an effort to clarify the role of the paralegals in the firm, the managing partner asks you to write a paralegal job description detailing the duties and responsibilities of the position. The manager wants a narrative of what the paralegals, both employees and freelancers, can and cannot do in order to stay compliant with the UPL statutes of your jurisdiction.

2. Prepare a legal memorandum advising the managing partner of the firm's potential liability for the following actions taken by paralegals employed by the firm:

   a. Allen answered the law office's telephone and recognized the client's voice. He told the client that she had nothing to worry about in her matter because the attorney was on the other line right then with the opposing counsel and settling the case for her.

   b. Betty was out to lunch with the other paralegals in the firm and they began discussing the legal strategy of the biggest cases of product liability that the firm was handling.

   c. Carl met with new clients, Mr. and Mrs. Smith, to obtain some basic information from them. They have come to the firm to have their wills made. Carl took the liberty of suggesting that they see a financial advisor about their assets in order to protect them from estate taxes.

   d. Debbie drafted a will for her parents at their request. She told them they would have to see an attorney at her firm in order to have it finalized.

   e. Ernie spoke to opposing counsel regarding the discovery deadlines for a case he was working on. The other attorney became angry that Ernie was insisting that the firm receive the answers within the time required by the court rules and insisted that he be given an extension. Ernie said he would file a motion to compel seeking attorney fees if opposing counsel did not answer per the court rules.

Cases in Point

State v. Atchley, 108 Hawai'i 77, 116 P.3d 719, 2005 WL 1793458 (Haw. App.)

CONSTITUTIONALITY OF UPL STATUTES

(Under Rule 35(c) of the Hawai'i Rules of Appellate Procedure, a memorandum opinion or unpublished dispositional order shall not be cited in any other action or proceeding except when the opinion or unpublished dispositional order establishes the law of the pending case, res judicata or collateral estoppel, or in a criminal action or proceeding involving the same respondent.)

Intermediate Court of Appeals of Hawai'i.
STATE of Hawai'i, Plaintiff-Appellee,
v.
Kitty L. ATCHLEY, also known as Kitty L. Ah Loy, Defendant-Appellant.
No. 25322.
July 28, 2005.

Appeal from the Circuit Court of the Second Circuit (Cr. No. 02-1-0197(3)).

Burns, C.J., Foley and Nakamura, JJ.

SUMMARY DISPOSITION ORDER

Defendant-Appellant Kitty L. Atchley (Atchley) appeals from the Judgment filed on August 13, 2002, in the Circuit Court of the Second Circuit (circuit court). [FN omitted.] Atchley was a paralegal who operated a sole proprietorship known as Valley Isle Paralegal. She was not a licensed attorney and did not work under the supervision of an attorney. Between August and October of 2000, Atchley assisted Ellen and Richard Kamaka (the Kamakas) in obtaining an uncontested divorce, charging them approximately $300 for her services.

After a jury trial, Atchley was found guilty of practicing law without a license, in violation of Hawaii Revised Statutes (HRS) § 605–14 (1993).[2] Because Atchley had previously violated HRS § 605-14, she was subject to punishment for a misdemeanor. HRS

[2] Hawaii Revised Statutes (HRS) 605-14 (1993) provides, in relevant part:

> It shall be unlawful for any person . . . to do or attempt to do or offer to do any act constituting the practice of law, except and to the extent that the person . . . is licensed or authorized so to do by an appropriate court, agency, or office or by a statute of the State or of the United States. . . . Nothing in sections 605-14 to 605-17 contained shall be construed to prohibit the preparation or use by any party to a transaction of any legal or business form or document used in the transaction.

§ 605-17 (1993).[3] Atchley was sentenced to a one-year term of probation subject to conditions which included that she pay restitution to the Kamakas in the amount of $462.48[4] and perform 200 hours of community service.[5]

On appeal, Atchley argues that 1) HRS § 605-14 is unconstitutionally vague because it does not define what is meant by the "practice of law" and 2) the prosecutor engaged in misconduct in eliciting and the circuit court committed plain error in allowing testimony regarding Ellen Kamaka's conversation with a lawyer. After a careful review of the record and the briefs submitted by the parties, we conclude that Atchley's arguments have no merit.

I.

Atchley did not challenge the constitutionality of HRS § 605-14 on vagueness grounds in the court below. We agree with the State of Hawai'i (the State) that Atchley waived her right to raise this claim on appeal. *State v. Ildefonso,* 72 Haw. 573, 584-85, 827 P.2d 648, 655 (1992). But even if we consider her claim on the merits, Atchley is not entitled to relief.

In *Fought & Co., Inc. v. Steel Engineering and Erection, Inc.,* 87 Hawai'i 37, 46, 951 P.2d 487, 496 (1988), the Hawai'i Supreme Court indicated that

the phrase "practice of law," as used in HRS § 605-14, entails far more than appearing in court proceedings. The court cited the legislative history of HRS § 605-14 which reflected the legislature's recognition that the practice of law is not limited to appearing before the courts. It consists, among other things of the giving of advice, the preparation of any document or the rendition of any service to a third party *affecting the legal rights . . . of such party,* where such advice, drafting or rendition of services requires the use of any degree of legal knowledge, skill or advocacy.

Id. at 45, 951 P.2d at 495 (quoting Sen. Stand. Comm. Rep. No. 700, in 1955 Senate Journal, at 661) (emphasis in original).

In determining whether a statute is impermissibly vague, we consider judicial decisions clarifying or narrowing the statute. *Wainwright v. Stone,* 414 U.S. 21, 22–23 (1973); *State v. Wees,* 58 P.3d 103, 107 (Idaho 2002). A defendant raising a vagueness claim is assumed to have knowledge of court decisions interpreting the statute. *Winters v. New York,* 333 U.S. 507, 514-15 (1948). Atchley is therefore chargeable with knowledge of the *Fought* decision.

To prevail on her vagueness claim, Atchley must show that HRS § 605-14, as applied to her conduct, was unconstitutionally vague. *State v. Marley,* 54 Haw. 450, 457-58, 509 P.2d 1095, 1101-02 (1973); *State v. Kuhia,* 105 Hawai'i 261, 272, 96 P.3d 590, 601 (2004). In Atchley's case, the evidence showed that in return for a fee, Atchley assisted the Kamakas in preparing and filing form pleadings in the Kamakas' uncontested divorce action. In the course of preparing the forms, Atchley answered the Kamakas' questions and provided explanations on a variety of topics, including: 1) how granting Ellen Kamaka (Ellen) sole as opposed to joint custody of the Kamakas' two children would affect the rights of Richard Kamaka (Richard) to see his children; 2) whether child support payments would be made by Richard through the Child Support Enforcement Agency or directly to Ellen; 3) whether Ellen was eligible for alimony and whether alimony payments would be taxable; 4) how the divorce would affect Ellen's medical coverage under Richard's insurance plan; 5) whether Richard or Ellen would be named as the plaintiff; and 6) the procedures the Kamakas needed to follow to secure a divorce

[3] At the time Defendant-Appellant Kitty L. Atchley (Atchley) allegedly committed the offense in this case, HRS § 605-17 (1993) provided that the first violation of HRS § 605-14 was a violation, but that subsequent violations would constitute a misdemeanor. HRS § 605-17 was amended in 2001 and now provides that any violation of HRS § 605-14 is a misdemeanor. Atchley's prior violation of HRS § 605-14, for which she was fined $1,000, was reflected in a Judgment filed on August 10, 1999.

[4] Ellen Kamaka testified at trial that the Kamakas paid Atchley approximately $350. However, documents the Kamakas submitted at sentencing in support of their restitution claim showed that they paid Atchley approximately $300 for her services plus $160 for the cost of filing their divorce pleadings.

[5] Atchley's term of probation also initially included a condition that she serve 90 days in jail, which was stayed pending a compliance hearing. According to Atchley's brief, after a probation compliance hearing on May 1, 2003, the jail-term condition was removed.

decree. Without the Kamakas' knowledge or consent, Atchley completed certain forms and submitted a letter to the court falsely asserting that Ellen refused to submit financial statements. The Kamakas did not carefully review the documents Atchley filed, but accepted Atchley's assurances that "she knew what she was doing" and would "take care of everything."

In light of Atchley's extensive involvement in preparing the Kamakas' divorce pleadings and her providing the Kamakas' with legal advice, we conclude that HRS § 605-14, as applied to her conduct, was not unconstitutionally vague. In particular, the statute's prohibition against the unlicensed "practice of law" and court decisions interpreting that phrase gave Atchley fair warning that her conduct was illegal. *State v. Richie,* 88 Hawai'i 19, 31-32, 960 P.2d 1227, 1239-40 (1998). Our conclusion is supported by decisions in other jurisdictions which, under analogous circumstances, have rejected claims that statutes prohibiting the unlicensed practice of law were unconstitutionally vague. *E.g., Monroe v. Horwitch,* 820 F. Supp. 682, 686 (1993) ("The preparation of documents in simple divorce actions unequivocally constitutes the practice of law."); *Wees,* 58 P.3d at 108.

II.

In addition to seeking a divorce, the Kamakas were experiencing financial difficulties when they went to see Atchley. Ellen testified that in the context of discussing something related to bankruptcy, Atchley indicated that the Kamakas could call an attorney named Scott Holmes (Holmes). Ellen further testified that she later called Holmes. The State sought to establish that Holmes did not give the Kamakas any advice about their divorce. The State elicited testimony from Holmes that he had a short phone conversation with Ellen about a bankruptcy and that he would not have given the Kamakas advice about their divorce. Atchley did not object to the evidence regarding Ellen's conversation with Holmes.

We reject Atchley's claim that the prosecutor engaged in misconduct in eliciting and the court committed plain error in allowing testimony regarding Ellen's conversation with Holmes. Any attorney-client privilege relating to Ellen's conversation with Holmes was for Ellen, and not Atchley, to assert. Hawaii Rules of Evidence (HRE) Rule 503. Because Atchley did not object, there is no record of whether Ellen had previously waived or would have waived any privilege she had. Moreover, other than indicating that Ellen called Holmes with regard to a bankruptcy, neither Ellen nor Holmes revealed the details of their conversation. The key aspect of Holmes' testimony was that he would not have given the Kamakas any legal advice about their divorce. This portion of Holmes' testimony was not privileged. Under these circumstances, Atchley is not entitled to any relief under the plain error standard of review.

III.

IT IS HEREBY ORDERED that the August 13, 2002, Judgment filed in the Circuit Court of the Second Circuit is affirmed.

Source: Reprinted from Westlaw with permission from Thomson Reuters.

NJ Unauth. Prac. Op. 24, 126 N.J. L.J. 1306, 1990 WL 441613 (N.J. Comm. Unauth. Prac.)

New Jersey Supreme Court Committee on Unauthorized Practice
INDEPENDENT LEGAL ASSISTANTS
Opinion Number 24
November 15, 1990

Independent paralegals in New Jersey were understandably concerned over the ramifications of Opinion No. 24 of the Committee on the Unauthorized Practice of Law. In essence, it held that paralegals could not render services without being directly employed by an attorney. The Committee felt that the supervision would be per se inadequate and therefore, there could be no "independent" paralegals in New Jersey that were not simultaneously committing UPL just by the nature of their practice. These independent paralegals filed an appeal to the Supreme Court of New Jersey. The Court decided on the issue only of "independent contractor" paralegals employed by an attorney on a temporary or project-based term; the Court did not address those paralegals that rendered legal services directly to the public.

[. . .]

I

The Committee received inquiries from various sources regarding whether independent paralegals were engaged in the unauthorized practice of law. Pursuant to its advisory-opinion powers under *Rule* 1:22-2, the Committee solicited written comments and information from interested persons and organizations.

In response, the Committee received thirty-seven letters from a wide variety of sources. Additionally, the State Bar Association's Subcommittee on Legal Assistants ("Legal Assistant Subcommittee"), the National Association of Legal Assistants ("NALA"), and the National Federation of Paralegal Associates ("NFPA") provided the Committee with information on regulation, education, certification, and the ethical responsibilities of paralegals.

The Committee characterized the information that it received in two ways: first, the material expressed positive views on the value of the work performed by paralegals; second, all of the materials expressly or implicitly recognized that the work of paralegals must be performed under attorney supervision. None distinguished between paralegals employed by law firms and those functioning as independent contractors offering services to attorneys. Several recurring themes played throughout the submissions:

1. One need not be a full- or part-time employee of a single attorney to be under the direct supervision of an attorney and independent paralegals in particular work under the direct supervision of attorneys.
2. Independent paralegals provide necessary services for sole practitioners and small law firms who cannot afford to employ paralegals on a full-time basis.
3. Independent paralegals confer an invaluable benefit on the public in the form of reduced legal fees.
4. Independent paralegals maintain high standards of competence and professionalism.
5. Rather than exacting a *per se* prohibition, the Committee should consider regulations or standards or other alternative forms of guidance, such as licensure and certification.
6. A blanket prohibition on independent paralegals would work a disservice to the paralegals and the general public.

[. . .]

Two attorneys appeared before the Committee. One testified that as long as attorneys supervise independent paralegals, that those paralegals do not work full-time for one attorney or firm does not matter. The second attorney, a sole practitioner, testified that independent paralegals provide many benefits to both small firms and the general public alike. The Committee, he suggested, should focus on others, known as "legal technicians" or "forms practitioners," who offer their services directly to the public, rather than on independent paralegals who do not offer their services directly to the public but who are retained by attorneys.

II

After the hearing, the Committee issued Advisory Opinion No. 24, 26 *N.J. L.J.* 1306 (1990), in which it compared the amount of supervision attorneys exercise over employed paralegals and retained paralegals. It concluded that attorneys do not adequately supervise retained paralegals. *Id.* at 1338. The Committee linked the absence of adequate attorney supervision to several different factors.

[. . .]

It is the view of the Committee, moreover, that the paralegal practicing in an independent paralegal organization, removed from the attorney both by distance and relationship, presents far too little opportunity for the direct supervision necessary to justify handling those legal issues that might be delegated. Without supervision, the work of the paralegal clearly constitutes the unauthorized practice of law. We found, from the testimony and materials presented to our Committee, that the opportunity for supervision of the independent paralegal diminishes to the point where much of the work of the independent paralegal, is, in fact, unsupervised. That being the case, the independent practice by the paralegal must involve the unauthorized practice of law. The fact that some of the work might actually be directly supervised cannot justify the allowance of a system which permits the independent paralegal to work free of attorney supervision and control for such a large part of the time and for such a large part of the work. [*Ibid.*]

Based on those findings, the Committee concluded that attorneys are currently unable to supervise adequately the performance of independent paralegals, and that by performing legal services without such adequate supervision those paralegals are engaging in the unauthorized practice of law. *Ibid.*

We granted petitioners' request for review, ___ *N.J.* ___ (1991), and the Chairperson of the Committee granted their motion to stay the enforcement of Opinion No. 24.

III

No satisfactory, all-inclusive definition of what constitutes the practice of law has ever been devised. None will be attempted here. That has been left, and wisely so, to the courts when parties present them with concrete factual situations. See Milton Lasher, *The Unauthorized Practice of Law*, 72 *N.J. L.J.* 341 (1949) ("What is now considered the practice of law is something which may be described more readily than defined.").

[1] Essentially, the Court decides what constitutes the practice of law on a case-by-case basis. [Citations omitted]

The difficulties presented by our undefined conception of the legal practice are reflected in this Court's review of decisions of the Committee on the Unauthorized Practice of Law. For example, in *In re Application of the New Jersey Society of Certified Public Accountants*, 102 *N.J.* 231, 507 *A.*2d 711 (1986), (hereinafter *Application of CPAs*), the Court stated:

The practice of law is not subject to precise definition. It is not confined to litigation but often encompasses "legal activities in many non-litigious fields which entail specialized knowledge and ability." Therefore, the line between permissible business and professional activities and the unauthorized practice of law is often blurred. [*Id.* at 236, 507 *A.*2d 711 (citations omitted).]

The Court in *Application of CPAs* reviewed the Committee's Opinion No. 10, 95 *N.J. L.J.* 1209 (1972),

which held that a non-lawyer's preparation of an inheritance-tax return for another person constituted the unauthorized practice of law. The Court disagreed, and emphasized that "in cases involving an overlap of professional discipline we must try to avoid arbitrary classifications and instead focus on the public's realistic need for protection and regulation." *Application of CPAs, supra*, 102 *N.J.* at 237, 507 *A.*2d 711. Applying that standard, the Court modified Opinion No. 10 to permit CPAs to prepare inheritance-tax returns subject to the condition that the accountant notify the client that an attorney's review of the return would be helpful because of the legal issues surrounding its preparation. *Id.* at 241-42, 507 *A.*2d 711.

There is no question that paralegals' work constitutes the practice of law. *N.J.S.A.* 2A:170-78 and 79 deem unauthorized the practice of law by a non-lawyer and make such practice a disorderly-persons offense. However, *N.J.S.A.* 2A:170-81(f) excepts paralegals from being penalized for engaging in tasks that constitute legal practice if their supervising attorney assumes direct responsibility for the work that the paralegals perform. *N.J.S.A.* 2A:170-81(f) states:

Any person or corporation furnishing to any person lawfully engaged in the practice of law such information or such clerical assistance in and about his professional work as, except for the provisions of this article, may be lawful, but the lawyer receiving such information or service shall at all times maintain full professional and direct responsibility to his client for the information and service so rendered.

Consequently, paralegals who are supervised by attorneys do not engage in the unauthorized practice of law.

IV

Availability of legal services to the public at an affordable cost is a goal to which the Court is committed. The use of paralegals represents a means of achieving that goal while maintaining the quality of legal services. Paralegals enable attorneys to render legal services more economically and efficiently. During the last twenty years the employment of paralegals has greatly expanded, and within the last ten years the number of independent paralegals has increased.

Independent paralegals work either at a "paralegal firm" or freelance. Most are employed by sole practitioners or smaller firms who cannot afford the services of a full-time paralegal. Like large law firms, small firms find that using paralegals helps them provide effective and economical services to their clients. Requiring paralegals to be full-time employees of law firms would thus deny attorneys not associated with large law firms the very valuable services of paralegals.

[. . .]

New Jersey's Advisory Committee on Professional Ethics also has recognized the value of paralegals to the legal profession:

It cannot be gainsaid that the utilization of paralegals has become, over the last 10 years, accepted, acceptable, important and indeed, necessary to the efficient practice of law. Lawyers, law firms and, more importantly, clients benefit greatly by their work. Those people who perform Para professionally are educated to do so. They are trained and truly professional. They are diligent and carry on their functions in a dignified, proper, professional manner. [ACPE Op. 647, 126 *N.J. L.J.* 1525, 1526 (1990).]

The New Jersey State Bar Association also specifically recognizes the important role of the paralegal. On September 15, 1989, its Board of Trustees voted to allow associate membership for paralegals and legal assistants.

We also note that the American Bar Association ("ABA") has long given latitude to attorneys to employ non-lawyers for a variety of tasks. For example, Ethical Consideration 3-6 of the ABA *Model Code of Professional Responsibility* provides as follows:

A lawyer often delegates tasks to clerks, secretaries, and other lay persons. Such delegation is proper if the lawyer maintains a direct relationship with his/her client, supervises the delegated work, and has complete professional responsibility for the work product. This delegation enables a lawyer to render legal services more economically and efficiently.

V

No judicial, legislative, or other rule-making body excludes independent paralegals from its definition of a paralegal. For example, the ABA defines a paralegal as follows:

A person qualified through education, training or work experience; is employed or *retained* by a lawyer, law office, government agency, or other entity; works under the *ultimate* direction and supervision of an attorney; performs specifically delegated legal work, which, for the most part, requires a sufficient knowledge of legal concepts; and performs such duties that, absent such an assistant, the attorney would perform such tasks. (Emphasis added).

The ABA definition expands the role of a legal assistant to include independent paralegals, recognizing that attorneys can and do retain the services of legal assistants who work outside the law office.

New Jersey's ethics Rules also recognize independent paralegals. This Court has adopted the ABA's *Model Rules of Professional Conduct* to govern the conduct of New Jersey State Bar members. *R.* 1:14 (adopting the ABA *Model Rules* "as amended and supplemented by the Supreme Court"). The central provision governing the attorney's use of lay employees is *RPC* 5.3:

With respect to a non-lawyer employed *or retained by* or associated with a lawyer:

(a) Every lawyer or organization authorized by the Court rules to practice law in this jurisdiction shall adopt and maintain reasonable efforts to ensure that the conduct of non-lawyers *retained* or employed by the lawyer, law firm or organization is compatible with the professional obligations of the lawyer.

(b) A lawyer having direct supervisory authority over the non-lawyer shall make reasonable efforts to ensure that the person's conduct is compatible with the professional obligations of the lawyer; and

(c) A lawyer shall be responsible for conduct of such a person that would be a violation of the Rules of Professional Conduct if engaged in by a lawyer if:

(1) The lawyer orders or ratifies the conduct involved;

(2) The lawyer has direct supervisory authority over the person and knows of the conduct at a time when its consequences can be avoided or mitigated but fails to take reasonable remedial action; or

(3) The lawyer has failed to make reasonable investigation of circumstances that would disclose past instances of conduct by the non-lawyer incompatible with the professional obligations of a lawyer, which evidence a propensity for such conduct. (emphasis added).

The emphasized language indicates that *RPC* 5.3 applies to independent retained paralegals and not just to employed paralegals.

[. . .]

VI

Under both federal law and New Jersey law, and under both the ABA and New Jersey ethics Rules, attorneys may delegate legal tasks to paralegals if they maintain direct relationships with their clients, supervise the paralegal's work and remain responsible for the work product.

Neither case law nor statutes distinguish paralegals employed by an attorney or law firm from independent paralegals retained by an attorney or a law firm. Nor do we. Rather, the important inquiry is whether the paralegal, whether employed or retained, is working directly for the attorney, under that attorney's supervision. Safeguards against the unauthorized practice of law exist through that supervision.

Following the introduction of *RPC* 5.3, the Practicing Law Institute correctly noted:

[M]any firms will not be prepared to shoulder [the responsibility of supervising paralegals] within their existing procedures. Accordingly, effective measures will have to be undertaken to ensure compliance. These will include not only procedures and controls, but also communication, training and education of staff employees in the responsibilities inherent in relevant Model Rules.

Although we agree that those concerns must be addressed, we emphasize that they apply equally to employed paralegals and to independent paralegals.

[. . .]

Again, the problem is not with independent paralegals but with the absence of any binding regulations or guidelines.

Underlying many of the Committee's concerns is its belief that the attorney will not be able to comply with *RPC* 5.3 due to the lack of physical proximity to the retained paralegal. That "physical distance" led the Committee to conclude that for an attorney to maintain direct supervisory authority over an independent paralegal who often will not work in the same office as the attorney is too difficult.

We recognize that distance between the independent paralegal and the attorney may create less opportunity for efficient, significant, rigorous supervision. Nonetheless, the site at which the paralegal performs services should not be the determinative factor. In large law firms that have satellite offices, an employed paralegal frequently has less face-to-face contact with the supervising attorney than would a retained paralegal.

[. . .]

Moreover, nothing in the record before the Committee suggested that attorneys have found it difficult to supervise independent paralegals. Indeed, the paralegals testified that the use of word processing made an attorney's quick review of their work possible. Most of the independent contractors who testified worked under the supervision of attorneys with whom they had regular communication.

Although a paralegal's unsupervised work does constitute the unauthorized practice of law, that issue is not unique to independent paralegals. Rather, we emphasize again, it is the lack of educational and regulatory standards to govern their practice that is at the heart of the problem.

VII

Regulation and guidelines represent the proper course of action to address the problems that the work practices of all paralegals may create. Although the paralegal is directly accountable for engaging in the unauthorized practice of law and also has an obligation to avoid conduct that otherwise violates the Rules of Professional Conduct, the attorney is ultimately accountable. Therefore, with great care, the attorney should ensure that the legal assistant is informed of and abides by the provisions of the Rules of Professional Conduct.

Although an attorney must directly supervise a paralegal, no rational basis exists for the disparate way in which the Committee's opinion treats employed and independent paralegals. The testimony overwhelmingly indicates that the independent paralegals were subject to direct supervision by attorneys and were sensitive to potential conflicts of interest. We conclude that given the appropriate instructions and supervision, paralegals, whether as employees or independent contractors, are valuable and necessary members of an attorney's team in the effective and efficient practice of law.

We modify Opinion No. 24 in accordance with this opinion.

For modification—Chief Justice WILENTZ and Justices CLIFFORD, HANDLER, POLLOCK, GARIBALDI and STEIN-6.

Opposed—None.

Source: Reprinted from Westlaw with permission from Thomson Reuters.

Part Two

The Attorney-Client Relationship

Chapter 3

Maintaining Competency, Diligence, and Communications

Chapter Objectives

The student will be able to:

- Discuss the attorney's "competing" duties to both follow the directive of the client and to render independent legal judgment
- Define "competency" as it relates to the ability to practice law
- Identify the elements of competency as derived through the ABA standards
- Recognize the importance of diligence in the legal profession and the requirements of prompt communications with the client
- Evaluate a situation that could implicate an attorney and/or a paralegal in a professional malpractice action

This chapter examines the roles and responsibilities of all the parties involved in the attorney-client relationship. *How* can an attorney be sure he is able to render competent representation; *when* must the attorney respond to the client; *what* constitutes legal malpractice; and *who* is responsible for the failures and harm that may result from unskilled representation?

Just as the paralegal and the attorney have a working relationship wherein both parties need to respect the roles that each play, so the attorney has a working relationship with the client. The attorney's role is to provide guidance along a complex and sometimes treacherous path in achieving a favorable outcome. It is the client's role to decide what would be a favorable outcome. The client is truly the master of the case; ultimately, the decision making rests with the client. An attorney cannot take any actions that are not approved by the client. However, it is the attorney's ethical duty to try to persuade the client to take the best path to achieve the desired result. Sometimes that involves telling the client that her desired result is not possible.

An attorney must delicately address these two obligations to the client: (1) to follow the client's course and (2) to render independent judgment, sometimes in spite of the first obligation. The paralegal has a central role in this relationship. Often it is the paralegal that serves as liaison between them. In order to facilitate the relationship, the paralegal should be aware of its boundaries.

RENDERING INDEPENDENT LEGAL JUDGMENT

independent legal judgment
The attorney's determination of the best course to pursue to obtain the client's objectives, based upon the attorney's obligation to rely upon her own professional assessment of the legal situation, without undue influences from outside forces.

ABA Model Rule 2.1 states that the attorney's role is that of an advisor. This element, rendering independent legal judgment, is what defines the lawyer. All the years of schooling and practice are essentially to lead her to a true assessment of the situation presented by the client. One must always recall that an attorney's first obligation is to the court and the pursuit of justice. This is true even in a transactional matter that is not pursued in litigation. Fairness to all the parties involved is the goal. A client may be the impetus behind the case, but it is the lawyer that has the knowledge and skill to strategize and manage the case. It is the attorney's ethical duty to expose all the facts to the client, including the unpleasant ones, and make a fair, honest, and objective assessment of the matter to counsel the client properly.

Additionally, as the law itself is not isolated from the principles of morality, socioeconomics, or politics, an attorney's advice does not have to be isolated from them either. A strict answer couched in purely legal terms may not be of value to some clients, who may fail to understand the ramifications of a course of action. The relationship between a lawyer and his client is a fiduciary one. That means that the lawyer must look out for the best interests of the client, even if the client isn't sure what those interests are. It would be hard to imagine that the attorney in an adoption or surrogacy arrangement would not be counseling his client using morality and politics as guideposts for assessing the outcome of the court's decisions.

There is a difference in the "exercise of independent professional judgment" that sets the attorney apart from the paralegal. The very definitions of a paralegal and of the unauthorized practice of law make the paralegal unable to render her legal conclusions and legal opinions *independently* to the client. This does not mean that the paralegal does not or cannot, independent of the

◀ **FIGURE 3.1**
USE OF PARALEGALS'
PROFESSIONAL
JUDGMENT

NALA Guideline 3

Paralegals may perform services for an attorney in the representation of a client, provided:

- The services performed by the paralegal do not require the exercise of independent professional legal judgment

NFPA EC 1.6(a)

A paralegal shall act within the bounds of the law, solely for the benefit of the client, and shall be free of compromising influences and loyalties. Neither the paralegal's personal or business interest, nor those of other clients or third persons, should compromise the paralegal's professional judgment and loyalty to **the client.**

◀ **FIGURE 3.1**
USE OF PARALEGALS'
PROFESSIONAL
JUDGMENT

attorney and other influences, render a professional opinion regarding the matter. There may be many occasions in which the paralegal is called upon to analyze and plan the best course of action for a client and report the results *to the supervising attorney*. Both NALA and NFPA have identified the significance of maintaining professionalism in their ethical codes; however, they seem to be in conflict at first blush. Figure 3.1 sets forth their rules. It is important to note that NALA prohibits the paralegal from exercising independent professional judgment vis-à-vis the client—not the attorney.

The exercise of professional judgment by the paralegal is essential in order to assist the attorney. Forming theories, rendering opinions, and other applications of knowledge to the facts are perfectly acceptable where the final product is given to the supervising attorney. The line is drawn where the paralegal attempts to render this advice to the client without the supervision of an attorney. Recall from the previous chapter that rendering legal advice is the practice of law solely retained by attorneys. Why is this "guard" in place? It is the responsibility of the lawyer to create and maintain the relationship with the client, and the attorney is ultimately the person responsible for the outcome of her decisions. The paralegal may properly relay information from the attorney to the client that consists of the attorney's independent professional judgment, but the paralegal may not directly relay her own opinion to the client.

BALANCE OF AUTHORITY BETWEEN ATTORNEY AND CLIENT

balance of authority
The balance between the right of the client to choose the desired outcome of the case and the obligation of the attorney to determine the best legal course to obtain that result.

Rule 1.2 clearly delineates the **balance of authority between lawyer and client**. In summary, the Rule states that it is the client, not the attorney, that sets the "end goal" of the matter. While the attorney must explain the options that a client may pursue, she is not making the ultimate decisions. The client is the person who directs the course of action to be taken. It may be helpful to think of the relationship in ownership terms. The client owns the case or matter, and the attorney consults with the client to determine the best way to fix it. Just as people bring their cars to expert mechanics to be fixed, a client brings her troubles to the attorney. Most people do not know the best way to fix their cars, but have a certain idea of how far they are willing to go to solve a problem. The mechanic may not agree with the owner's decision to fix it up no matter what the cost, but as long as the mechanic has been honest in the assessment of the problem and in the cost to fix it, then he is obligated to follow the directive of the owner.

What happens when the client insists on the less desirable or potentially harmful or more costly course? That is where the attorney may find himself in a bind. Rule 1.2(b) specifically states that any actions taken at the direction of the client is not attributable to the attorney and "does not constitute an endorsement of the client's political, economic, social, or moral views or activities." With regard to the terms of the agreement for representation, generally speaking, parties may come to any contractual agreement they wish. When a client decides to take a certain course of action that the attorney disagrees with, it is the duty of the attorney to counsel against it, but if the client insists on that course, the attorney must follow those wishes. Specifically, the rule states that the client has full authority over the decision to settle a matter. For example, an attorney was advised by the Pennsylvania Ethics Committee that he would not be prohibited by the ethics rules in allowing a client to enter into a settlement agreement whereby she would give up child support in exchange for her ex-husband's giving up a claim of custody. The committee found that the attorney under Rule 1.2 had to follow the wishes of the client insofar as they were reasonable, were made without coercion, and did not prejudice the children's interests. The attorney was not under any obligation to agree with his client's choice. *See* 2000 WL 1616247 (Pa. Bar. Assn. Comm. Leg. Eth. Prof. Resp.). In criminal cases, the client has final say on the plea to be entered, whether to waive a trial by jury, and whether or not the client will testify.

An attorney may also find herself torn between the law and her client's conduct. When should a client's course of conduct be reported to the appropriate agency? Almost everyone feels a little reluctance when writing out the annual tax check to the government; some clients take this a step further and fail to pay taxes at all. When this fact is discovered, what are a lawyer and a paralegal to do? Neither of them may knowingly assist or counsel a client in furtherance of this plan of tax evasion. For instance, attorneys and paralegals cannot effect a transaction that would result in tax evasion or other fraud to escape tax liability. However, once a past transgression has been discovered in confidence, they are not under an obligation to report it. The attorney should counsel her client to pay these taxes otherwise the client is clearly in violation of the law. The tricky situation arises when the attorney finds himself as a counselor during the questionable conduct. *See* Lawyer's Duty During Client's Fraudulent Conduct, 2001 WL 34004974 (Conn. Bar. Assn.). An attorney must insist that his client cease the unlawful conduct and attempt to rectify the situation without compromising the client's position and the attorney's obligation of confidentiality. The affirmative duty to report criminal or fraudulent conduct to the proper authorities only applies prospectively. Attorneys and paralegals must report only on future conduct of their clients which they know will be unlawful. A full discussion of this obligation will be undertaken in Chapter 4.

The test, as demonstrated in the above opinions, is whether or not the attorney believes that the client is making a decision that is relatively reasonable under the circumstances, is not made as the result of force or threat, is not made in furtherance of fraud, and/or does not pose a threat to third-party interests that are not protected. The attorney's agreement with the client's decision is not relevant. Her participation may be limited by law or by her own moral compass so that she declines representation or counsels against such conduct, but she is not responsible for the client's ultimate poor decision making. It should go without saying that, on the flip side, an attorney will be found guilty of malpractice where he pursues a course of action that is both inconsistent with his client's wishes and is deleterious to the outcome of the case. *See Attorney Grievance Commission of Maryland v. Costanzo*, 68 A.3d 808, 820 (Md. 2009) (attorney failed to pursue a claim against the defendants that the client had indicated were responsible for the client's financial injury. Instead the attorney drafted a complaint against another entity. The attorney was disbarred; the court found that he had "abandoned a client by failing to pursue the client's interests." *Id.* at 822.).

COMPETENCY

An attorney is responsible for the establishment of the general parameters of representation and the explanation of the roles that he will play in the relationship with the client. Resting squarely on the shoulders of the attorney is the responsibility of determining whether he is competent to represent that particular client in the matter at hand. Competency is also reflected through the general office of the attorney. This means that the attorney must ensure the competency level of his paralegals, including verifying that the work performed by paralegals under his supervision is performed satisfactorily.

ABA Model Rule 1.1 is not particularly specific with regard to competence. It merely asserts that an attorney must possess the legal knowledge and skill to handle the matter, and must be thorough and prepared in the representation. The paralegal codes are no more elucidating; they are set forth in Figure 3.2.

Through cases, ethics opinions, and commentary, the rule becomes more clear. The most enlightening source, however, is the record of malpractice suits. Incompetency not only makes an attorney liable in ethics; it also gives rise to a professional malpractice suit if the plaintiff (former client) can prove the elements of that tort. Competency applies to both attorneys and paralegals and so will be discussed in both contexts. Indeed, an attorney can be held responsible for the incompetency of her paralegal, and a paralegal may be independently sued for negligence in the execution of his duties. For this reason, the ABA has also written the Guide for the Utilization of Paralegal Services.

competency
The ability to perform legal tasks with the requisite knowledge and skill to obtain a satisfactory result in the relevant field.

FIGURE 3.2 ▶
A "COMPETENT"
PARALEGAL

NALA Guideline 4

In the supervision of a paralegal, consideration should be given to

■ Designating work assignments that correspond to the paralegal's abilities, knowledge, training and experience

NFPA EC 1.1(a)

A paralegal shall achieve competency through education, training, and work experience.

**continuing legal
education (CLE)**
Continuing legal education
designed to enhance legal
services to the public and
ensure that the legal
professional maintains a
certain level of expertise
and competence.

What does it mean to be *competent*? Generally speaking, it means that the lawyer or paralegal has the right skills and appropriate knowledge to handle the matter presented. These skills and this knowledge are acquired through a number of ways. First, the person's basic legal education should prepare her for the general role of either attorney or paralegal. The educational requirements for both have already been discussed in Chapter 1. But formal education is not the only means of acquiring knowledge; indeed, in the law it is not even adequate. Actual practice on the job is necessary in order to understand the complexities of the legal system, manage the law office, and handle opposing counsel and clients. Furthermore, the law is always changing and evolving; new laws are created constantly to keep pace with societal influences. Even the ways in which lawyers practice law change to reflect new technologies. For this reason, most (40 out of 50) states require that attorneys acquire a certain number of continuing legal education (CLE) credits per year after they have been admitted to the bar of those states.

Keeping apace of developments in the law and its practice is so critical to the proper, competent rendering of legal services that in 1986, the ABA promulgated a Model Rule regarding mandatory or minimum continuing legal education as a requisite to practice. It is the ABA's desire that all the states will put these minimums into place so that there is a consistency and assurance of competency across the board. The Model Rule would require 15 hours of CLE each year. This could be satisfied by attending approved CLE courses, teaching, writing for CLE, receiving in-office training, and using other modes, as long as the educational efforts meet conditions set forth in later sections of the Model Rule for CLE. Further, the attorneys must report their CLE credits in order to assure compliance with the minimum requirements. In those states that do have CLE requirements, failure to meet the minimum standards will result in the denial of the right to practice in that jurisdiction where the attorney is delinquent. (*See Kentucky Bar Association CLE Commission v. McIntyre*, 937 S.W.2d 708 (Ky. 1997). In this matter, the attorney did not comply with the state's CLE requirements, despite having received several deficiency notices. "The failure to maintain licensing requirements constitutes a serious charge for which suspension is an appropriate remedy for non-compliant members.")

The newest and fastest changing aspect in maintaining competency is technology. In 2012, the ABA adopted this following **bold** addition to comment 8 to Rule 1.1 that specifically addresses this duty: "To maintain the requisite knowledge and skill, a lawyer should keep abreast of changes in the law and its practice, **including the benefits and risks associated with relevant technology**, engage in continuing study and education and comply with all continuing legal education requirements to which the lawyer is subject" [emphasis added]. As of this writing, almost half the states have adopted a formal ethical rule to this effect. California has issued Formal Opinion 2015-193, which requires attorneys to be technically competent as the situation requires. "While e-discovery may be relatively new to the legal profession, an attorney's core ethical duty of competence remains constant." *Id.* at 2. The California Bar opines that every litigation in this technological age potentially involves e-discovery and that all lawyers should be prepared for it.

> We start with the premise that "competent" handling of e-discovery has many dimensions, depending upon the complexity of e-discovery in a particular case. **The ethical duty of competence requires an attorney to assess at the outset of each case what electronic discovery issues might arise during the litigation, including the likelihood that e-discovery will or should be sought by either side.** If e-discovery will probably be sought, the duty of competence requires an attorney to assess his or her own e-discovery skills and resources as part of the attorney's duty to provide the client with competent representation. If an attorney lacks such skills and/or resources, the attorney must try to acquire sufficient learning and skill, or associate or consult with someone with expertise to assist. [Emphasis added.]

The full opinion can be found at: http://ethics.calbar.ca.gov/Portals/9/documents/Opinions/CAL%202015-193%20%5B11-0004%5D%20(06-30-15)%20-%20FINAL1.pdf.

In fulfilling the competency requirement, understanding technology goes beyond e-discovery. Technology has impacts in potentially all aspects of practice, even procedural and evidentiary matters. When a lawyer presents electronic evidence, there may be more "admitted" than what appears at first. The Court in *State v. Ratcliff*, 849 N.W.2d 183 (N.D. 2014), determined that the DVD recordation of the crime included both the video and audio. Although during the trial the jury only viewed silent surveillance video of the crime, during a review of the DVD in deliberations the jury also heard the audio component of the "evidence." "When another form of electronic information is introduced—say an electronic document—questions may arise whether they contain metadata. If so, is metadata being admitted along with the information on the face of the document? Knowing the answer will be important to lawyers, who must 'provide competent representation to a client.'" *Ratcliff* at 195 (Crothers, concurring). This issue of understanding what metadata is and whether or not to particularly request it has been the subject of numerous lawsuits. Federal Rules of Civil Procedure Rule 34, "Producing

Documents, Electronically Stored Information, and Tangible Things, or Entering Onto Land, for Inspection and Other Purposes," specifically permits metadata to be requested and states that the party must provide "any designated documents or electronically stored information—including writings, drawings, graphs, charts, photographs, sound recordings, images, and other data or data compilations—stored in any medium from which information can be obtained either directly or, if necessary, after translation by the responding party into a reasonably usable form." F.R.C.P. 34(a)(1)(A). However, the requesting attorney or paralegal must be savvy enough to "specify the form or forms in which electronically stored information is to be produced." F.R.C.P. 34(b)(1)(C).

Acquiring and maintaining new skills in both the relevant practice area(s) and technology is vital not only for attorneys. The national paralegal associations have also set forth minimum continuing legal education credits required each year for paralegals. As membership in these associations is voluntary, the requirements are not binding on paralegals in general. However, for those paralegals who hold one of the certification designations (CLA, CP, PACE, ALS, PLS, or PPC), the organizations do require CLE credits to be reported by the paralegals in order to maintain their status. There are countless offerings by these organizations that relate to new technologies in e-filing, e-discovery, litigation software, trial presentation, and data and case management. NALA requires evidence of completion of 50 hours of continuing legal education every 5 years, 5 hours of which must be on the subject of legal ethics. To maintain NFPA's PACE credential, a paralegal must complete 12 hours of continuing legal or specialty education every 2 years, with at least 1 hour in legal ethics. NALS requires 75 hours every 5 years with at least 5 hours devoted to legal ethics. The newest national certifying body, AAPI, which also requires higher education, mandates 18 hours of which 2 must be in ethics. The continuing legal education requirement time frames coincide with the organizations' certification renewal periods.

In its definition, the ABA identifies two general components of competency: (1) knowledge and skill, and (2) thoroughness and preparation.

What does each of these elements encompass, and how does one know if they have been satisfied since there are so many facets to the practice of law?

IN-CLASS DISCUSSION

What minimum requirements, if any, for continuing paralegal education (CPE) do you think should be required in your state? Do you think that CPE is necessary for practicing paralegals? Why? Does your state offer CLE seminars specifically for paralegals? What types of topics are offered; what topics would you like to see addressed?

Knowledge

It is impossible to assert that every attorney or paralegal knows everything about the law. Even specialists cannot know everything about their particular field. Increasingly, attorneys and the paralegals who work for them are becoming specialized in one field, because the law is becoming more complex. Many attorneys now cross-refer clients to these specialists when they cannot handle the matter competently. Relying on memory of the law is actually an ethical violation! It is imperative that an attorney be certain of the current state of the law, and the only way to do this is to perform the necessary research. Researching is one of the tasks commonly assigned to a paralegal. NALA's Guideline 5 specifically lists research as one of the tasks properly delegated to a paralegal and for which paralegals have competency. Failure to research has been found to be a sanctionable ethical offense by many courts and ethical boards. The requisite knowledge that an attorney or paralegal must have is the knowledge of how to apply the law once it has been found. Knowing how courts are likely to rule given the state of the law and applying it to the particulars of the matter at hand is the test of competency. Knowing *how* to find the answer, not already having the answer, is the essence of proper lawyering.

What this means in practical terms is that an attorney does not necessarily have to have experience in handling a matter in a particular area of law in order to handle a matter. Law schools expose their students to many areas of law in order to assure a certain level of familiarity with the issues involved in the diverse areas of law. General practitioners, those whose offices take on a variety of matters, may often face issues they have never dealt with before. Legal practice is much like a continuing education process anyway, as the law in an attorney's area of concentration may change. The practice of law does not require specialization, and therefore, these attorneys are fully competent to handle the matter as long as they acquire the requisite knowledge during the course of the client's matter. An assessment of the attorney's ability to do the research and analysis will determine whether the case can be undertaken. A more complex specialty or fact pattern of a particular matter may require that the attorney refer the case to anther with the relevant competency.

SPOT THE ISSUE

Natalie is a general practitioner with her own office. She has handled various kinds of cases over the ten years since she graduated law school, but has never drafted a will with a spendthrift trust provision. Natalie recalls how much she liked her estates professor in law school, so she consults her notebooks and casebook from that class to help her draft the will. The client seems pleased with the will, and it is properly executed in Natalie's office.

Has Natalie fulfilled her ethical requirements in taking on this new matter? Why or why not? What details would change your decision? What if Natalie had her paralegal thoroughly research the issue and draft the will instead of consulting her former coursework?

Skills

An attorney must be able to execute, or follow through with, the knowledge acquired in order to properly represent a client. Knowing how to do something is not quite the same as doing it well. This is where the skill of an attorney becomes relevant with regard to his competency level. Knowing how to perform research is merely the starting point. The skill is in finding the relevant law, identifying the legal issues involved, analyzing the legal ramifications of the legal authority, applying the law to the current fact pattern, composing a viable argument, and writing the necessary documents accurately and persuasively. Further, an attorney is skilled in making decisions as to how best to proceed in a legal matter. A skillful attorney strategizes on if, when, and how to negotiate and how to conduct the trial.

These are finely honed skills that are (or should be) continually improved upon as an attorney practices. They are nebulous, as each matter requires different handling and finesse. While paralegals develop and hone complimentary skills to those of attorneys, at its base, a paralegal's skill set is more easily definable. A paralegal should also be able to perform research, draft preliminary documents in legal style, accurately and concisely summarize information, identify material facts, and handle procedure both in the office and with the courts. Perhaps the trademark skills of a paralegal are (or should be) impeccable organization and the ability to manage multiple assignments

FIGURE 3.3 ▶
BASIC SKILLS OF A
COMPETENT PARALEGAL

NALA Guideline 5

Except as otherwise provided by statute, court rule or decision, administrative rule or regulation, or the attorney's rules of professional responsibility, and within the preceding parameters and proscriptions, a paralegal may perform any function delegated by an attorney, including, but not limited to the following:

- Conduct client interviews and maintain general contact with the client after the establishment of the attorney-client relationship, so long as the client is aware of the status and function of the paralegal, and the client contact is under the supervision of the attorney.
- Locate and interview witnesses, so long as the witnesses are aware of the status and function of the paralegal.
- Conduct investigations and statistical and documentary research for review by the attorney.
- Conduct legal research for review by the attorney.
- Draft legal documents for review by the attorney.
- Draft correspondence and pleadings for review by and signature of the attorney.
- Summarize depositions, interrogatories and testimony for review by the attorney.
- Attend executions of wills, real estate closings, depositions, court or administrative hearings and trials with the attorney.
- Author and sign letters providing the paralegal's status is clearly indicated and the correspondence does not contain independent legal opinions or legal advice.

REEL TO REAL

In *The Verdict* (1982), Paul Newman's character, Frank Galvin, is an alcoholic attorney on the brink of destroying his career. He struggles with his situation during his one last chance to prove his competency as an attorney in a medical malpractice defense matter. How does this attorney overcome his difficulties? Would it be ethical for him to take on this matter or for his firm to give him responsibility for it based upon his demonstrated competency level? Why or why not? If you were his paralegal, what would or should you do? Would it be ethical for you to assist him knowing about his condition? Why or why not?

effectively. As seen in NALA 3.3, NALA lists the basic skills of a paralegal in its ethical guidelines. NALA's emphasis on the supervision of an attorney under-scores the importance of the paralegal's knowledge of the ethical mandates for attorneys. The list is not all-inclusive. Both the attorney and paralegal are responsible for ascertaining the proper delegation of work. Not only must they each know their own limits of competency, they must understand each other's limitations. It is a cooperative effort.

Thoroughness

Not only must attorneys and paralegals acquire the requisite knowledge and skills; they also must perform thoroughly the tasks related to them. It is not enough to have *some* of the information; it is vital to have *all* of it. The practice of law is detail oriented. Cases turn on very specific facts; materiality is not necessarily dependent upon the amount of information available. In other words, size doesn't matter in determining the importance of a fact or an issue. It may be easy to overlook an element of the case without a thorough review of the file materials; it may be easy to miss the defining case without thorough research; it may be easy to miss an argument without a thorough examination of the issues; and it may be easy to miscalculate the probable or possible outcomes without a thorough analysis of the relevant law. Truly, "God is in the details" (Ludwig Mies van der Rohe, German-American architect, 1886–1969). The real challenge for legal professionals is to accomplish the level of thoroughness required in the most efficient manner possible. This is why competency in all skill sets is so important, as it relates to time management. A paralegal must learn to manage the amount of time spent on a task while still being thorough. It is a delicate balance between efficiency and thoroughness.

Preparation

After all the preliminary work is done and it's showtime for the attorney, she must be prepared. All information must be at her fingertips, accessible and comprehensible. It is usually a matter of teamwork, and the attorney relies on her team to have her prepared to face any situation or contingency. It is not enough to have competently, skillfully, and thoroughly prepared only the client's side of the issues. An attorney must be prepared for what the opposing side will counterargue. Courts have little patience or tolerance for ill-prepared attorneys. Indeed, a Vermont attorney was indefinitely suspended from the practice of law until he could prove that he was fit to practice; in other words, the court found him incompetent. In that case, a judge filed a complaint with the ethics board regarding the attorney's inadequate preparation of legal submissions to the court.

> All members of the Board agreed with the hearing panel's finding that between 1985 and 1992 respondent repeatedly submitted legal briefs to this Court that were generally incomprehensible, made arguments without explaining the claimed legal errors, presented no substantiated legal structure to the arguments, and devoted large portions of the narrative to irrelevant philosophical rhetoric. The briefs contained numerous citation errors that made identification of the cases difficult, cited cases for irrelevant or incomprehensible reasons, made legal arguments without citation to authority, and inaccurately represented the law contained in the cited cases. All members of the Board also agreed with the hearing panel's conclusions that respondent's briefs were not competently prepared and fell below the minimum standard for brief-writing expected of a practicing attorney. . . .
>
> *In re Shepperson*, 674 A.2d 1273, 1274 (Vt. 1996).

Clearly, the justice system does not usually tolerate those who "wing it" or have a "good enough" attitude; inadequate preparation is obvious and inexcusable. This applies not only to the substance of the preparation, but also to the adherence to technical requirements of a submission. To adequately prepare, the paralegal should consult all local rules of court with regard to the particulars of documents and appearances, and sufficient time should be allocated in order to comply with those requirements. Competent preparation takes time. Time and paralegal support is apparently what the lawyers in *Bradshaw v. Unity Marine Corp.*, 147 F. Supp. 2d 668 (S.D. Tex. 2001), did not have. Both lawyers apparently submitted their pleadings "entirely in crayon on the back sides of gravy-stained paper place mats." The full text of the case appears at the end of this chapter and is well worth the read simply for the humor of its author, Judge Kent.

DILIGENCE

diligence
Acting within the legally proscribed time or promptly responding to a client's or party's request.

Connected to the definition of competency is the exercise of **diligence** in pursuing a matter for the client. Having legal knowledge and skill is of no use unless the attorney takes prompt action upon it to preserve his client's interests in the matter. ABA Model Rule 1.3 simply states that an attorney needs to be reasonably diligent and prompt when representing a client, and as Figure 3.4

NFPA 1.1(c)

A paralegal shall perform all assignments promptly and efficiently.

illustrates, the paralegal's mandate is no clearer. This again underscores that the interpretation of reasonable actions and time frames must be determined in light of a particular matter. Each matter must be individually evaluated to determine the boundaries of ethical behavior for diligence.

With rare exception, all matters are subject to deadlines. Delay can cause anything from minor inconvenience, such as the rescheduling of a real estate closing, to annihilation of a claim, such as the lapse of the Statute of Limitations. Diligence relates not only to legally required time limits but also to the general progress of the matter as it develops in the attorney's office. Procrastination is unacceptable in the practice of law. There are many clients' needs that must be addressed and they often, if not always, overlap. Difficulties and delays will invariably arise; the fact of a delay does not automatically indicate that there has been a lapse in diligence. The most diligent and conscientious paralegals and attorneys find themselves behind schedule and affected by postponements; there are circumstances beyond their control. Diligence does not require that the delays be avoided entirely—only that the paralegal and attorney have put forth their best efforts to facilitate and expedite the matter.

In a "snowball effect" case, an attorney was found to have violated the ethics rules relating to diligence and promptness. *Attorney Grievance Commission of Maryland v. Ficker*, 706 A.2d 1045 (Md. Ct. App. 1998). The constant "putting off" of matters and dealing in a very high volume of cases resulted in an utter collapse of the entire practice. This is generally referred to as ***pervasive neglect***. The court discussed eight separate cases in which the attorney had failed to exercise diligence in pursuit of his clients' interests. Perhaps taken one by one, they would not have had the same impact as all of the transgressions viewed at once. The attorney was in the habit of interviewing clients and then assigning them to either himself or an associate. The problem with this habit was that the assignment came the day before trial. There was no way that either Ficker or his associates could prepare to appear and represent their clients. Failure to file proper motions on the theory that the request could be made in person on the court date was violative of the duty of diligence, in that it subjected the clients, the court, and other attorneys to unanticipated circumstances and further delay. The attorney was found lacking in diligence in almost every aspect of his practice, including following through with reasonable investigation of his clients' claims. A diligent attorney checks facts before cavalierly assuming that the matter is a simple one. *Id.* at 28.

> *Ficker essentially operated his practice like a taxicab company [. . .].*
> *What he apparently, and inexcusably, failed to realize is that, while*
> *perhaps any competent taxi driver can transport a passenger from one*
> *point to another on a moment's notice, legal services cannot routinely be*

pervasive neglect
Continued disregard for matters pending in the law office, deadlines, and other obligations that seriously impacts clients' interests and indicates an utter lack of diligence.

dispensed on that basis with an acceptable degree of competence. As the direct result of Ficker's practices, not only was the court inconvenienced but [the client] was faced with the unacceptable prospect of either falling on his sword or going to trial with a lawyer he never hired and who knew little or nothing about his case.

Id. at 32.

Additionally, the court noted that the entire office was lacking in any method of tracking cases and clients. Attorneys have a duty to remain diligent: to review cases periodically to ensure that no dates are missed and that the other parties are current in their obligations in the matter. The directives as far as timing of an attorney's actions can also come from the client. If a client instructs an attorney to take certain steps on her behalf or in connection with a matter, the attorney must do so in as prompt a manner as possible, as much as the attorney may not want to. Failure to abide by a client's directives in a prompt manner is also violative of the duty of diligence. *See In re Caldwell*, 715 N.E.2d 362 (Ind. 1999).

Diligence is perhaps where paralegals can help most in the law office. Having the procedural knowledge of court schedules and deadlines, the paralegal can "calendar" important dates. Factual knowledge of the firm's caseload will enable the paralegal to appropriately monitor their status and alert the responsible attorney. There is a great deal of information to keep track of in the law office. The Colorado Bar has created a checklist, set forth in Figure 3.5, for analyzing whether dates or information are falling through the cracks.

One of the most effective tools in use by paralegals and other professionals is the "Tickler File System." A tickler file is designed to tickle your memory so that tasks do not get forgotten in the onslaught of activity at work. It keeps track of assignments that need to get done on a certain day and lets you put reminders on a date. Tasks are grouped not only by project, but also by day and month. The system is flexible and lets you re-file tasks as deadlines or priorities change. Essentially, you need a folder or compartment for each day of the month and then a folder for each subsequent month. In the morning, the folder for that day is taken out and assignments and reminders are already in place so that they can be tackled without resorting to mere memory. At the end of the day, either all tasks are completed and the folder is empty or an uncompleted task can be placed in the front of the next day's folder. Color-coding by kind of project or matter and filing the supporting materials with the task can add

RESEARCH THIS

Find a case or ethical opinion in your jurisdiction that addresses the issue of "pervasive neglect" culminating in a sanctionable offense violating an attorney's duty of diligence.

◄ **FIGURE 3.5**
DOCKETING AND
CALENDARING

Missing a filing deadline or court appearance can be extremely damaging to a client as well as causing embarrassment and a potential malpractice claim for you. Each firm member should maintain an individual calendar in addition to a master calendar for the entire firm. Answer the following questions to determine how well you are doing in this area:

	Yes	No	N/A
Do we keep individual calendars, i.e. attorney and secretary/paralegal?			
Does your calendar include (as applicable):			
a) statutes of limitations?			
b) all court appearances?			
c) client and other appointments?			
d) real estate closing dates?			
e) all self-imposed, discretionary deadlines (i.e., promises made to others, promises made to you and work deadlines you have set for yourself?			
Do we maintain a master calendar?			
Do we have a good system for updating and maintaining each calendar in case of scheduling changes?			
Do we use reminder slips (tickler slips) to draw the attorney's attention to an upcoming deadline?			
If the calendar is maintained on the computer, do we frequently print out a copy to use in case of power failures or other computer problems?			

dimension to the file so that all the information is readily accessible. Of course, law offices are increasingly going paperless; many electronic calendaring systems will also let you create this kind of system with their various reminder and task functions.

COMMUNICATIONS WITH THE CLIENT

Lastly, in order to assert that one is competent, the legal professional has to keep the lines of **communication** open between himself and his client. Recall that the matter really "belongs" to the client. In order for a client to make decisions regarding the handling of the matter, he must be informed as to

communication
The obligation of an attorney to keep his client informed of the status of the matter, and to respond promptly to the client's requests for information in a candid manner.

the status of the matter and the legal ramifications of his decisions. Further, in order to satisfy the demands for diligence, an attorney must promptly answer the inquiries of his client. Attorneys, just like other professionals, are very busy, but unlike other professionals, they can be sanctioned for failing to respond to their clients. Additionally, in helping to steer the ship, attorneys must adequately explain the legal process and how the client's matter fits within it. The general public is not aware of the intricacies of the legal system and particulars of the laws in their jurisdiction; if they were, there would be little need for lawyers!

ABA Model Rule 1.4 sets forth the requirements for communicating with clients. It requires that the attorney consult with the client regarding the means to achieve the client's objectives and other pertinent matters, and to keep the client informed about the status of the matter. It clearly underscores the vital importance of communication with the client in all aspects of his representation. NALA has also recognized the critical supportive role of the paralegal in keeping the lines of communication open. See Figure 3.6.

These communications must also be made openly and forthrightly. Concealment and falsity are unacceptable as well. It is not good enough just to be talking; that exchange must be made in good faith and support the fiduciary nature of the relationship. While most people do not like to be the bearers of bad news, it is a requirement for attorneys to speak candidly about any issues that have arisen in the course of the matter. It may also be necessary for a paralegal to be that bearer of news as well.

It cannot be stressed enough that the client is in charge of the direction of the matter. It is the client's objectives, not necessarily the best or most reasonable or most achievable objectives in the estimation of the attorney, that must be met or at least attempted. The end and the means to the end are the prerogative of the client; the attorney counsels, advises, and in some cases warns, but does not take action without the authority of the client. In a strange manifestation of diligence, an attorney cannot make decisions unilaterally, of her own accord, even if the issue is urgent and time is urgent. She must communicate with the client and make her best efforts at securing the client's consent.

FIGURE 3.6 ▶
PARALEGALS'
DUTY TO COMMUNICATE

NALA Guideline 5

Except as otherwise provided by statute, court rule or decision, administrative rule or regulation, or the attorney's rules of professional responsibility, and within the preceding parameters and proscriptions, a paralegal may perform any function delegated by an attorney, including, but not limited to the following:

■ Conduct client interviews and maintain general contact with the client after the establishment of the attorney-client relationship, so long as the client is aware of the status and function of the paralegal, and the client contact is under the supervision of the attorney.

An absent or evasive client simply cannot be helped, even if it is in his best interest to take a specific action.

For example, *In re Samai*, 706 N.E.2d 146 (Ind. 1999), dealt with an attorney who was representing a client in an automobile personal injury matter. Having contacted the insurance company and set up a medical examination of his client, the attorney attempted to contact the client again and again. He was unable to locate her and had no further contact. However, being diligent and perhaps not wanting to prejudice his client and to keep the matter moving along, the attorney sent a demand letter for a $5,000 settlement of the claim. The insurance company counter-offered $2,000, which the attorney accepted on behalf of his client. This would have been bad enough, but the attorney aggravated the situation by then using the settlement proceeds to his own benefit. The failure to communicate coupled with the "selfish motive" warranted an 18-month suspension from the practice of law.

It is vital that these communications emanate from the responsible attorney. While it is true that paralegals play a vital role in keeping clients current in the progress of their matters, it is not their role to substitute for the required consultations with the attorney. Further, the attorney and paralegal should maintain communications so as not to mislead the client. In *People v. Milner*, 35 P.3d 670 (Colo. 2001), the attorney's paralegal took over communications with the client and made certain representations and misrepresentations regarding the progress of the case that did not come to fruition due to the lack of diligence of the attorney. The attorney was not affirmatively contacting the client and not affirmatively supervising the paralegal's contact with the client. There was a litany of charges in a variety of individual matters brought against this attorney and paralegal team. Essentially, it was determined that the attorney abandoned her clients, causing serious or potentially serious harm. This was aggravated by her failure to properly supervise the communications between her paralegal and her clients. It should come as no surprise that Milner was disbarred. The Colorado Bar's checklist for Client Relations, used to avoid such missed or faulty communications, is included as Figure 3.7.

As in any relationship, honest and candid communication is vital. An attorney cannot perform his tasks without input from the client; therefore, the client should be kept informed of all elements of the matter, and it is the task of the attorney to educate the client as to the status of the law and how it will impact the client in order for the client to make the choices necessary to keep the matter going forward. A competent attorney diligently communicates with his client, adverse parties, and the tribunal. While these ethical standards as they are applied are fact specific, there are certain acts or omissions that are clearly violative of the attorney's duties in the attorney-client relationship. Perhaps the best way to evaluate an attorney's conduct is to determine what another responsible attorney would do in the same situation. Reasonable actions are gauged by how most attorneys act in or react to the specific circumstances.

FIGURE 3.7 ▶
CLIENT RELATIONS
CHECKLIST

The relationship with the client is a critical consideration for law office management. Everything that happens in a law firm has a direct or indirect effect on the client. The way a law firm conducts its business will also influence its relationship with its clients.

Law firms are often set up so that the critical element of administrative support is service to the attorney. The attorney, in turn, serves the client. Today, a client-centered law firm involves all personnel directly serving the client. The attorney is a team member involved in providing overall service to the client.

Examine your client relation efforts by asking the following questions:

	Yes	No	N/A
Do we return clients' phone calls and email within 24-48 hours?			
Do we perform all the work we told the client we would?			
Do we send follow-up letters after a meeting or telephone conversation in which new decisions have been reached?			
Do we complete the work in a timely fashion?			
Do we follow up with clients at least every six weeks even when their cases are inactive?			
Do we acknowledge staff members for good client relations?			
Do we ask the client for feedback as the matter moves along?			

SPOT THE ISSUE

Albert Attorney has recently taken on many new cases. This increased workload has caused him to rely more heavily on his staff, consisting of both a paralegal and a secretary. He has told his paralegal to prepare seven new bankruptcy petitions, four wills, and five complaints, and to file them with the courts. He then instructs his secretary to call the clients to tell them that everything is taken care of. This pattern of behavior continues for the next several months, as Albert is simply swamped with his caseload.

The clients are, in general, receiving information from Albert's secretary regarding the filing of the necessary papers. One client has called several times to speak with Albert, but has been unable to get him in the office. The paralegal has offered to help answer this client's questions and has sent letters regarding the next court dates. However, this client is not happy that he has not been able to speak with Albert directly, although all his questions have been answered. Albert is pleased, as the office appears to be running relatively smoothly. Can you foresee any problems with this way of running the office and handling cases? While the paralegal appears to be competent, is the paralegal acting ethically in managing the entire office and communicating with the clients?

LEGAL MALPRACTICE

Lack of competency, diligence, or communication can also give rise to a civil lawsuit with separate and additional penalties: the malpractice claim brought by a client against the attorney. While some of the elements of these two claims are the same, there are different standards of proof required in order to recover for malpractice. In both an **ethical complaint** and a **legal malpractice** suit, the claimant needs to prove *that the relationship itself does exist*, and, therefore, the attorney owes the client a duty to protect his interests. Without the relationship, there can be no duty towards that person. The claimant is without a cause of action at that point. Secondly and also similarly, the client must show that the attorney acted unreasonably by failing to have (or acquire) the requisite knowledge, and failed to exercise the ordinary skill of a practicing attorney. There is a difference between malpractice and errors in professional judgment that end in an unsuccessful outcome.

> There can be no liability for acts and omissions by an attorney in the conduct of litigation which are based on an honest exercise of professional judgment. This is a sound rule. Otherwise every losing litigant would be able to sue his attorney if he could find another attorney who was willing to second guess the decisions of the first attorney with the advantage of hindsight. . . .
>
> *Clary v. Lite Machines Corporation,* 850 N.E.2d 423, 431 (Ind. 2006) (the court also determined that an attorney is liable for mistakes in legal research, a task that is often delegated to paralegals).

The difference between the ethical complaint and the malpractice suit is found in the last two elements of a civil cause of action: The attorney must be the proximate cause (the third element) of actual harm to the client (the fourth and last element). In order to show that he was harmed by the attorney, the client needs to show that he would have been successful in the underlying action. In other words, his loss in the matter must be attributable to the attorney. If the client would have lost no matter how incompetent the attorney, then there is no harm. While the defense of the malpractice suit can assert "no harm, no foul," the ethical boards are equally as concerned with the impact on the client as they are with the actual violation. The fact of the violation is enough to warrant a sanction. No harm to the client needs to be proven in order to bring the attorney before the ethical board; the harm is presumed to be against the profession itself.

ethical complaint
A report of suspected unethical activity on the part of an attorney to the ethical committee of the state bar association or another appropriate tribunal. The committee may investigate to determine if an ethics violation has, indeed, occurred.

legal malpractice
A civil cause of action wherein a client may sue his attorney for failures in the representation that caused the client actual harm. The client may be entitled to money damages and possibly punitive damages in excess of actual pecuniary loss if the attorney's conduct was egregious.

PARALEGAL MALPRACTICE

The way legal malpractice suits contrast with lawsuits against paralegals is still relatively uncharted territory. Paralegals *are* practicing law inside the law office, and while they should be held to the standard of care applicable in their jurisdiction, ultimately they do not have a direct, independent relationship with the client as the attorney does. This is the primary hurdle that generally cannot be overcome in order to hold paralegals liable for legal malpractice. The cause of action requires the fiduciary relationship, which is generally absent in the case of a paralegal. It is absent not because the paralegal does not have a relationship with the client, but because the primary responsibility for that relationship rests with the attorney. *See In re Estate of Divine*, 635 N.E.2d 581, 588 (Ill. App. 1994) (the court "refuse[d] to find that [the paralegal] owed [the client] a fiduciary duty simply because she worked for [the] attorney, and we refuse to hold that paralegals are fiduciaries to their employers' clients as a matter of law").

Attorneys are held responsible for the actions or inactions of their paralegals that cause harm to the clients, under the doctrine of *respondeat superior* ("let the superior answer"). This means that the supervising attorney is held liable for the malpractice of the paralegal. Essentially, the attorney is in a position to review the paralegal's actions and direct the course of the conduct, and therefore is in a position to avoid the mistake.

> The label "paralegal" is not in itself a shield from liability. A factual investigation is necessary to distinguish a paralegal who is working under an attorney's supervision from one who is actually practicing law. A finding that a paralegal is practicing law will not be supported merely by evidence of infrequent contact with the supervising attorney. As long as the paralegal does in fact have a supervising attorney who is responsible for the case, any deficiency in the quality of the supervision or in the quality of the paralegal's work goes to the attorney's negligence, not the paralegal's.

> *Tegman v. Accident & Medical Investigations, Inc.*, 30 P.3d 8, 13 (Wash. App. 2001).

This vicarious responsibility for the actions of the paralegal is understood by the malpractice insurance carriers covering attorneys. The policies generally also cover the errors of employees, as long as the employee was acting within the scope of her employment. Problems arise where there is no supervising attorney to hold responsible. Paralegals who are directly working for and representing individuals can and should be held to a certain standard of care for which they can be held liable for breaches of their duty. *See Busch v. Flangas*, 837 P.2d 438 (Nev. 1992) (the court determined that if the paralegal held himself out as having the legal ability to competently prepare all the necessary documents and protect the client's legal interests, he should be subject to a legal malpractice claim for negligent provision of legal services). Other courts have decided that paralegals could not be held liable for legal malpractice because they are not attorneys and therefore cannot enter into the requisite attorney-client relationship that gives rise to the duty of care. *See Palmer v. Westmeyer*, 549 N.E.2d 1202, 1209 (Ohio App. 1988). However, a caveat to that generalization exists when the nonlawyer holds herself out as an attorney. In that case, courts have found that the nonlawyer, by misrepresenting herself, opened herself up to a viable legal malpractice claim. This uses the same line of reasoning as *Busch*. *See Pytka v. Hannah*, 15 Mass. L. Rptr. 451, 2002 WL

31862712 (Mass. Super. 2002) (not reported in N.E.2d). The court found that all of the facts necessary to uphold a cause of action for legal malpractice were satisfied as against the nonlawyer except for the fact that he was not a member of the bar subject to that particular charge. However, "the allegations still f[e]ll well within charges of negligence, deceit, misrepresentation and breach of contract." *Id.* at 8. The non-attorney defendant was found liable for the client's losses and punitive damages were further assessed. In total, almost one million dollars in damages were assessed against him, and the plaintiff was further granted interest, fees, and costs to be added to that judgment. The unauthorized practice of law can be very costly for those disrespecting the rules. Paralegals, according to the definition of their role in the law office, cannot establish an attorney-client relationship. However, where liability may not attach for legal malpractice, it certainly may lie in an action for the unauthorized practice of law. Any paralegal holding himself out as capable of providing direct services, and therefore being outside the scope of an attorney's vicarious liability under malpractice, can be sued for the damages incurred as a result of the unauthorized practice of law.

The newest issue to arise in the context of legal malpractice relates to those LLLTs (Limited License Legal Technicians) who *do* create an independent relationship with their own clients. Those practicing in this format will need to protect their license just like attorneys do. In addition to the continuing education requirements, LLLTs will be expected to set up IOLTA accounts to manage their clients' funds and maintain professional malpractice insurance. For example, under the Washington State Admission and Practice Rules (APR), Regulation 12A requires an LLLT to "show proof of ability to respond in damages resulting from his or her acts or omissions in the performance of services permitted under APR 28 by submitting an individual professional liability insurance policy in the amount of at least $100,000 per claim and a $300,000 annual aggregate limit." As much of the criticism against LLLTs has focused on the potential for harm to the consumer of legal services, this extra protection should provide some measure of comfort; not only does the LLLT have a license to pursue their livelihood on the line, there is also a financial safety net should they harm a client.

Summary

An attorney must maintain a working relationship between herself and her clients. There are two competing obligations in performing this duty: following her own independent legal judgment and following the desired course of the client. This requires that the authority and control over the matter must be shared between the attorney and the client.

Both attorneys and paralegals must be competent to handle each type of case presented to them. This means that they have the requisite knowledge and skill and have approached the matter with thoroughness and preparation. These efforts must also be made with diligence; the matter must be pursued promptly in order to preserve the client's interests in the case. In order for the client to make decisions regarding the case, the attorney needs to maintain communications with the client in a timely manner.

An attorney lacking in any of the above-mentioned attributes may find himself the subject of a legal malpractice action. The private action initiated by the client is separate and in addition to any ethical sanctions and penalties to be imposed by the relevant ethical board. Paralegals, although they are not subject to their own ethical boards with sanction powers, can be sued individually for their lapse in the standard of care attributable to the paralegal profession.

Key Terms

Balance of authority

Communication

Competence

Continuing legal education (CLE)

Diligence

Ethical complaint

Independent legal judgment

Legal malpractice

Limited License Legal Technician (LLLT)

Pervasive neglect

Review Questions

MULTIPLE CHOICE

Choose the best answer(s) and please explain *why* you chose the answer(s).

1. A "competent" attorney has which of the following attributes?
   a. Legal research skills
   b. Knowledge of her ethical obligations
   c. Specialized training in a particular area of law
   d. Excellent oral advocacy skills
   e. A and B
   f. B and C
   g. All of the above

2. Diligence requires that an attorney:
   a. Return all phone calls from the client himself
   b. Keep the client informed of the particulars of the case
   c. Write letters to the client once a week
   d. File motions on the due date

3. "Pervasive neglect" means that the attorney:
   a. Does nothing on a case
   b. Has a habit of putting things off until the last minute

c. Has repeatedly failed to maintain diligence in a number of cases

d. Assigns all the work on a matter to her paralegal

EXPLAIN YOURSELF

All answers should be written in complete sentences. A simple yes or no is insufficient.

1. Explain the meaning of "competency." How does a paralegal know whether he is competent to handle a matter?

2. Describe the elements of proper communication with the client (it is more than just returning phone calls!).

3. What does it mean to be thorough and prepared with respect to a legal matter?

4. Do you think paralegals should be held responsible for their supervising attorney's ethical infractions? Why or why not? Could this cut down on malpractice lawsuits overall? Would that be a benefit to paralegals? How?

5. What are the most important skills of a paralegal?

FAULTY PHRASES

All of the following statements are *false*. State why they are false and then rewrite each one as a true statement. Do not simply make the statement negative by adding the word "not."

1. In order for an attorney to take on a new kind of matter that she has not previously handled in practice, she must have studied that particular area of law in school.

2. An attorney must always follow the instructions of the client with regard to the handling of the case.

3. An attorney must personally answer all the requests for information from the client.

4. Diligence requires that the attorney or paralegal find all the cases in the jurisdiction that answer the question presented in the matter.

5. As long as the paralegal in the office is keeping the clients happy, the attorney is doing his job.

6. Paralegals cannot be sued for malpractice because their supervising attorneys are responsible for all their work.

7. Paralegals are held responsible for their supervising attorney's ethical violations under the theory of *respondeat superior*.

PORTFOLIO ASSIGNMENT

Write Away

Compare the following scenarios and write a letter to each client in response to each. Assume you are a paralegal at a general practice firm and have been given three files to review:

- Client A is getting a divorce and his wife is trying to obtain sole custody of the children.
- Client B wishes to write her will.
- Client C is involved in a complex litigation which is currently in the discovery phase.

After reading all the relevant facts of these cases:

- Client A asks how many times women get custody of the children in these kinds of matters and what his chances are in obtaining sole custody.
- Client B asks whether she can have her sister sign as a witness to the will and whether she should set up a trust for her children.
- Client C wants to know how much time is left for submitting answers to interrogatories served on him by the defendant and what his chances are at getting the counterclaim against him dismissed.

Cases in Point

Board of Professional Responsibility of the Supreme Court of Tennessee

Formal Ethics Opinion Number 81-F-24
December 31, 1981

An inquiry has been made concerning the propriety of an attorney who is not competent to handle criminal cases accepting representation in a criminal case.

There has been a long standing practice in the courts of a mid-state county to appoint all attorneys in the county to represent indigents accused of criminal offenses by rotation without regard to their practice, intention to practice or interest in becoming or remaining proficient in the area of criminal law.

Canon 2 of the Code of Professional Responsibility states the axiom that a lawyer should assist the legal profession in fulfilling its duty to make legal counsel available. Certain Ethical Considerations under Canon 2 state the aspirational objectives toward which attorneys should strive in making legal counsel available. They state principles upon which the attorney can rely for guidance. The relevant portions of the Ethical Considerations under Canon 2 are:

EC 2-16
. . . persons unable to pay a reasonable fee should be able to obtain necessary legal services, and

lawyers should support and participate in ethical activities designed to achieve that objective.

EC 2-25

Historically, the need for legal services of those unable to pay reasonable fees has been met in part by lawyers who donated their services or accepted court appointments on behalf of such individuals. The basic responsibility for providing legal services for those unable to pay ultimately rests upon the individual lawyer, and personal involvement in the problems of the disadvantaged can be one of the most rewarding experiences in the life of a lawyer. Every lawyer, regardless of professional prominence or professional workload, should find time to participate in serving the disadvantaged. The rendition of free legal services to those unable to pay reasonable fees continues to be an obligation of each lawyer, but the efforts of individual lawyers are often not enough to meet the need. Thus it has been necessary for the profession to institute additional programs to provide legal services. Accordingly, legal aid offices, lawyer referral services and other related programs have been developed, and others will be developed, by the profession. Every lawyer should support all proper efforts to meet this need for legal services.

EC 2-26

. . . in furtherance of the objective of the bar to make legal services fully available, a lawyer should not lightly decline proffered employment. The fulfillment of this objective requires acceptance by a lawyer of his share of tendered employment which may be unattractive both to him and the bar generally.

EC 2-29

When a lawyer is appointed by a court or requested by a bar association to undertake representation of a person unable to obtain counsel, whether for financial or other reasons, he should not seek to be excused from undertaking the representation except for compelling reasons. Compelling reasons do not include such factors as the repugnance of the subject matter of the proceeding, the identity or position of a person involved in the case, the belief of the lawyer that the defendant in a criminal proceeding is guilty, or the belief of the lawyer regarding the merits of the civil case.

EC 2-30

Employment should not be accepted by a lawyer when he is unable to render competent service . . . .

Disciplinary Rule 6-101(A)(1) states, in part:

A lawyer shall not handle a legal matter which he knows or should know that he is not competent to handle . . . .

The Disciplinary Rules, unlike the Ethical Considerations, are mandatory in character and state the minimum level of conduct below which no lawyer can fall without being subject to disciplinary action. Therefore, an attorney who is not competent to handle criminal cases should respectfully decline appointment by the court of such cases in accordance with the authorities cited herein.

Approved and adopted by the Board.
Ethics Committee:

A. B. Goddard
Jack C. Raulston
John T. Henniss DISSENTS

Source: Reprinted from Westlaw with permission from Thomson Reuters.

493 B.R. 158
United States Bankruptcy Court,
D. Nevada.
In re Wayne A. SEARE, a/k/a Wayne Andrew Seare; and Marinette Tedoco,
a/k/a Marinette Morales Tedoco, Marinette Fitzpatrick, Debtors.
Dignity Health, f/k/a Catholic Healthcare West, d/b/a St. Rose Dominican
Health Foundation, Plaintiff,
v.
Wayne A. Seare, Defendant.
Bankruptcy No. BK–S–12–12173–BAM.
Adversary No. 12–01108–BAM.
April 9, 2013.
As Corrected April 10, 2013.

BRUCE A. MARKELL, Bankruptcy Judge.

I. INTRODUCTION

When a consumer consults a lawyer, there is a reasonable expectation that the lawyer's advice will address the consumer's concerns. Here, that didn't happen. Although the consumers here—debtors Wayne Seare and Marinette Tedoco—gave their attorney what any attorney would need to identify their problem, the attorney gave bad advice. When the bad advice was discovered, the attorney, Anthony J. DeLuca, doubled down. He refused to assist Seare and Tedoco further, whether or not they had the money to pay him for it, which, as Chapter 7 debtors, they did not. DeLuca justified his inaction by pointing to provisions in his standard form retainer agreement that Seare and Tedoco had signed. For the reasons given in this opinion, that conduct was wrong.

II. DETAILED FACTS

A. The St. Rose Litigation

Seare's legal odyssey began in December 2010 when he filed a complaint in the United States District Court for the District of Nevada alleging employment discrimination against his former employer, St. Rose Dominican Health Foundation ("St. Rose"), the plaintiff in this adversary proceeding. In the district court proceeding, Seare submitted evidence in the form of e-mails that he had "embellished" to boost his claims. (Evid. Hr'g Tr. 10:16–17.) Ultimately, the district court ordered sanctions against Seare,

dismissed his lawsuit with prejudice, and ordered him to pay St. Rose's attorney's fees. (Dist. Dkt. No. 36.)

In awarding these attorney's fees, the district court found that Seare knowingly provided false information to the court, allowed his attorney to file an amended complaint based upon the false information, and instituted and conducted litigation in bad faith—amounting to "fraud upon the court." (Id. at 3.) The district court then entered judgment on October 25, 2011 in the amount of the attorney's fees, or $67,430.58 (the "Judgment"). (Dist. Dkt. No. 37.)

B. The Garnishment

By January 2012, St. Rose had obtained a writ of execution and served the related writ of garnishment on Seare's current employer. (Dist. Dkt. Nos. 41, 43.) Seare's desire to have the garnishment permanently stopped drove Marinette Tedoco (his wife) and him (collectively, the "Debtors") to DeLuca to seek legal counsel about whether to file for bankruptcy. (Evid. Hr'g Tr. 3–4.)

C. The Initial Consultation

On February 13, 2012, Seare and Tedoco consulted with DeLuca at his law office. [. . .] They met personally with DeLuca, which, as it turned out, was the only direct contact they had with him during the entire case. (Id. at 3–4.) Among other documents, they gave DeLuca copies of both the Order for Wage Garnishment and Wage Sanctions. (Id. at 2.) According to the Debtors, DeLuca flipped through the court papers and stated that hospital bills are dischargeable. (*Id.*)

After the short meeting with DeLuca, the Debtors were placed in a small room to sign and initial the 19-page retainer agreement (the "Retainer Agreement") under which they hired DeLuca. (*Id.* at 5.) DeLuca's staff periodically checked to see if they had completed the forms, but no one sat with them to explain any part of the Retainer Agreement. (*Id.*)

The Debtors proceeded to execute the Retainer Agreement and retain DeLuca with a $200 down payment. In addition, DeLuca provided them with a 19-page "Frequently Asked Questions" document (the "FAQ"). (Ex. N.) The Debtors signed every relevant page and initialed every relevant paragraph of the Retainer Agreement. (Ex. G.) At the bottom of every page (right above the Debtors' signatures) is the statement: "I have read, understand, and agree to this page and its contents." (*Id.*) On the last page (right above the Debtors' signatures) is the statement: "I have read and received the foregoing NINETEEN (19) pages and I understand and agree to its terms and conditions." (*Id.* at 19.)

Notably, DeLuca did not sign or initial the Retainer Agreement. (*Id.*) The first page, a welcome page of sorts that thanks prospective clients for their business and instructs them to sign and initial the following pages, is a form letter with DeLuca's printed signature. (*Id.* at 1.) It states that the Retainer Agreement is only valid if the Debtors sign and initial at every location indicated. (*Id.* at 1, 19.) The Retainer Agreement is evidently the same for all clients, with only a few differences in fees depending on whether the case is filed under Chapter 7 or Chapter 13. For the Debtors' Chapter 7 case, DeLuca's flat fee was $1,999.99. (*Id.* at 3.)

The Retainer Agreement separates basic services from those services that require additional fees:

> BASIC SERVICES: Services to be performed by DeLuca & Associates include:
>
> a. Analysis of debtor's financial situation and assistance in determining whether to file a petition under the United States Bankruptcy code whether in Chapter 7 or chapter 13. . . .
> b. Review, preparation and filing of the petition, schedules, statement of affairs, and other documents required by the bankruptcy court;
> c. Representation at the meeting of creditors.

> d. Reasonable in person and telephonic consultation with the client. . . .

> ADDITIONAL FEES: There are circumstances which may require additional fees. Additional attorney fees will be charged for additional services including but not limited to: Addressing allegations of fraud or nondischargeability; . . . Adversary Proceedings. . . . (*Id.* at 5, 7.)

The Retainer Agreement does not explain the relationship between items and The Retainer Agreement includes a fraud disclaimer: "DEBTS THAT DO NOT GO AWAY: Non-dischargeable debts (debts you must re-pay), or debts not affected by client's bankruptcy, include but are not limited to the following: . . . debts incurred through fraud. . . ." (*Id.* at 11.) It also includes a request for copies of "ALL LAWSUITS you have been involved in within the last (2) years. . . ." (*Id.* at 12.) The FAQ also explains that debts incurred through fraud are nondischargeable. (Ex. N at 18.)

D. The Bankruptcy Case is Filed

[. . .]

E. The Adversary Proceeding is Filed

[. . .]

F. DeLuca's Refusal to Defend

Within several days, on June 4, 2012, DeLuca sent the Debtors an e-mail informing them of their discharge and that, as of the discharge date, their case was completed. (Ex. H at 2–3.) The e-mail appears to be a form message. It does not mention the particulars of the Debtors' bankruptcy or the then-recently filed adversary proceeding. (*See id.*) It states, "we are very happy to inform you that you can now move forward with a fresh start on life, free from the stress of excessive debt. Now you can place your financial situation back on the right track." (*Id.* at 3.)Also on June 4, the Debtors responded via e-mail to DeLuca's communication. (Ex. H at 2.) They thanked DeLuca for his e-mail and for "all the help in completing our [b]ankruptcy." (*Id.*) They asked whether the St. Rose Debt was discharged, since they understood that St. Rose was going to pursue the adversary proceeding against them. (*Id.*) They closed the e-mail by asking DeLuca to "[p]lease let us know what we need to do." (*Id.*)

On June 5, 2012, DeLuca's office responded. (*Id.* at 1–2.) They reminded the Debtors that St. Rose had expressed its intention to pursue the Judgment against the Debtors at the Section 341 meeting of creditors. (*Id.* at 1.) The e-mail also stated that on April 16, 2012 DeLuca had received a "fax cover letter . . . with an attached Stipulation and Order regarding the discharge-ability [*sic*] of subject debt in question as to Mr. Sear [*sic*] only." (*Id.*) It then informed the debtors that DeLuca had responded to the fax by advising St. Rose's counsel that he "would not sign off on any [s]tipulation regarding the discharge-ability [*sic*] of any debt listed in the schedules." (*Id.*) Put more bluntly, DeLuca rejected the proposed stipulation and order without consulting with Seare. It is unclear whether DeLuca informed St. Rose that he was not representing Seare in the adversary proceeding. The e-mail then explained that DeLuca had performed all the duties for which he was contracted and that DeLuca would not represent Seare in the adversary proceeding. (*Id.* at 1–2.) It recommended that Seare retain another attorney, Mr. Terry Leavitt, to handle the adversary proceeding. (*Id.* at 2.)

On June 6, 2012, the Debtors replied to the e-mail. (*Id.* at 1.) They admitted to understanding that DeLuca was hired only to "do our bankruptcy," but were very upset and frustrated that the fax containing the proposed stipulation and order was never sent to them. (*Id.*) They asserted that they were never even aware that DeLuca had received those documents from St. Rose; "[n]ot informing your clients of very important documents and failing to return phone calls are unacceptable and unprofessional customer service." (*Id.*) They requested copies of the proposed stipulation and order and the adversary complaint. (*Id.*) Also on June 6, DeLuca sent a letter to the Debtors informing them that he would not represent Seare in the adversary proceeding. (Ex. I.) The substance of the letter is essentially the same as the earlier e-mail. (*See* Exs. H, I.)

[. . .]

On August 2, 2012, the court held a scheduling conference for the adversary proceeding. DeLuca did not appear on behalf of Seare, who explained that DeLuca told him that DeLuca does not represent clients in adversary proceedings. (Dkt. No. 14 at 2.) St. Rose's counsel stated that she had informed DeLuca shortly after the Debtors filed their petition of St. Rose's intent to file a nondischargeability action. (*Id.*)

G. The Order to Show Cause

On August 3, 2012, the court issued its "Order to Show Cause Why This Court Should Not Sanction Anthony J. DeLuca for Failing to Represent Debtor in the . . . Adversary Proceeding" (Dkt. No. 14.) The court was concerned that DeLuca had not complied with specific provisions of Nevada's Rules of Professional Conduct, made applicable to this proceeding by Local Rule IA 10–7(a). The court ordered DeLuca to explain why nonrepresentation in the adversary proceeding was reasonable and to establish the Debtors' informed consent for the limitation. It set a hearing on the Order to Show Cause ("OSC") for September 13, 2012. Meanwhile, the adversary proceeding continued. On August 10, 2012, the court ordered a scheduling conference for September 13, which was later continued to October 19. On August 17, St. Rose filed its discovery plan. (Dkt. Nos. 17, 18, 21, 24.)

On August 22, 2012, DeLuca filed his brief in response to the Order to Show Cause (the "Reply Brief"). (Bankr. Dkt. No. 24.) The Reply Brief suffered from several procedural and substantive defects. DeLuca incorrectly filed the brief on the docket in the main bankruptcy case rather than the adversary proceeding. In addition, he did not file a certificate of service until October 24, 2012, one day after the evidentiary hearing at which the court ordered him to provide copies of his filings to Seare. (Dkt. No. 30.) DeLuca also failed to submit the retainer agreement that the Debtors had signed; instead, he submitted a blank, boilerplate document. (Bankr. Dkt. No. 24, Ex. B.) Substantively, DeLuca did not address the specific provisions of the Nevada Rules of Professional Conduct that the court had raised in the Order to Show Cause. (*See* Bankr. Dkt. No. 24.)

[. . .] On October 19, 2012, Seare filed his "Hearing Brief" regarding the Evidentiary Hearing. (Dkt. No. 29.) The same day, DeLuca filed his supplemental brief in anticipation of the Evidentiary Hearing (the "Supplemental Brief"). (Bankr. Dkt. No. 27.) Again, he incorrectly filed it on the docket for the main bankruptcy case rather than the adversary proceeding. He also failed to file a certificate of service until one day after the Evidentiary

Hearing. (Dkt. No. 31.) In addition to the brief, he filed a witness list, exhibit list, and various exhibits. (Bankr. Dkt. Nos. 28, 29.)

H. The Evidentiary Hearing

[. . .]

I. St. Rose and Seare Settle the Adversary Claim

[. . .]

III. THE PARTIES AND THEIR POSITIONS

These facts present the legal issue of when consumer bankruptcy attorneys such as DeLuca may limit the scope of their representation, a practice colloquially referred to as "unbundling." While unbundling is permissible, it must be done consistent with the rules of ethics and professional responsibility binding on all attorneys. Those rules allow a lawyer to limit his or her representation only when it is reasonable under the circumstances to do so, and only when the client gives informed consent to the limitation. In this case, DeLuca met neither of these requirements. As a defense, DeLuca asserts that his retainer overrides such mandatory rules. As will be seen, his position is incorrect; to the extent his retainer is inconsistent with the applicable rules of professional responsibility, his retainer is unenforceable, and his abandonment of his clients violated norms applicable to lawyers generally.

A. DeLuca's Arguments

DeLuca's primary argument is that the Debtors had the burden to inform him that the Judgment was based on Seare's fraud, and that they failed to meet this burden. [. . .] From this dubious premise regarding the Debtors' duties, he argues that the decision to unbundle all adversary proceedings, regardless of their relation to the relief requested or needed by a debtor was reasonable, and that the reasonable assumption of any attorney would be that a debt owed to a hospital is for medical care rather than a fraud judgment. (OSC Hr'g Tr. 4:8–18.) Had he known of the nature of the Judgment, so he argues, he would have declined to represent the Debtors in the first place. (Bankr. Dkt. No. 24 at 2.) He claims that he undertook representation based on

"incomplete, inaccurate, or intentionally omitted information regarding the fraudulent nature of a significant portion of the Debtors' debt." (*Id.* at 3.) He further argues, using the benefit of hindsight, that it is reasonable to limit services when the client is a known liar. (Bankr. Dkt. No. 27 at 14.)

DeLuca's next argument is that the Debtors gave informed consent to the exclusion of adversary proceedings. He asserts that the Retainer Agreement "specifically excludes adversary proceedings as part of the services provided . . . for the basic fee." (Bankr. Dkt. No. 24 at 2.) [. . .] In short, his argument is that the Debtors executed the Retainer Agreement with the knowledge that (1) such debts are nondischargeable; (2) St. Rose would likely bring an adversary proceeding; (3) adversary proceedings were excluded from the flat fee; and (4) his representation ended when the clients obtained their discharge.

[. . .] DeLuca next asserts that the right to contract includes the right *not* to contract. (Bankr. Dkt. No. 27 at 9.) "It is certainly within the discretion of DeLuca & Associates to limit its representation of Debtor(s) that have a proven track record of defrauding their own lawyer, opposing counsel, and the Court." (*Id.;* see Evid. Hr'g Tr. 39:7–18.) After he learned of the fraud, he decided that "representation of Mr. Seare represented a liability" to his firm and himself personally because, he contends, under the Bankruptcy Abuse Prevention and Consumer Protection Act ("BAPCPA"), attorneys may be held liable for the frauds of their clients. 11 U.S.C. §§ 526–528, 707(b)(4) (2012). The court interprets this argument as a justification for DeLuca's affirmative refusal to represent DeLuca in the adversary proceeding, communicated in the letter on June 6, 2012, rather than the reasonableness of the unbundling in the first place, because DeLuca only learned of the fraud after representation had commenced. In spite of the "danger," DeLuca chose to represent Seare in settlement negotiations with St. Rose, after the OSC Hearing, because it seemed like the best way to extricate himself from the matter. (Evid. Hr'g Tr. 45:15–46:7.)

Finally, DeLuca tops off his defense with an argument under the United States Constitution. He claims that the "basic services bargained for between the parties did not include litigation or adversary proceedings." (Bankr. Dkt. No. 27 at 8.) To impose additional terms that were not bargained for would violate the

Thirteenth Amendment, so he argues, because he would be obligated to perform work against his will and without compensation. (*Id.*) DeLuca asserts the "right to be free from involuntary servitude" and "enforced compulsory service of one to another." (*Id.* (citations omitted).)

B. Seare's Contentions

[. . .] The Debtors claim that during their meeting with DeLuca, they "specifically and clearly" stated the nature of the Judgment to him and provided court documents for his review. (Dkt. No. 47 at 5.) Tedoco claims that they told DeLuca that the Judgment was from a sexual harassment case lost by Seare in which he had "embellished" e-mails. (*Id.*) Seare and Tedoco have both asserted that DeLuca affirmatively told them, even after hearing this information, that the St. Rose Debt was dischargeable. (*Id.* at 2, 5, 6; Evid. Hr'g Tr. 13:3–7.) She states that the only reason they hired DeLuca was because he assured them of the dischargeability of the St. Rose Debt. (Dkt. No. 47 at 5.) Seare testified that, although he understood the contract language concerning the nondischargeability of debts incurred through fraud, he relied upon DeLuca's alleged assurances of nondischargeability over the language in the Retainer Agreement. (Evid. Hr'g Tr. 15:13–16:13.) Moreover, Seare did not read the FAQ because DeLuca had already answered their questions. (*Id.* at 17:22–24.)

[. . .] The Debtors also claim that DeLuca did not properly communicate with them or keep them informed of the progress in their case. Throughout the representation, Tedoco claims, DeLuca's office was nonresponsive. (Dkt. No. 47 at 3–4.) The Debtors only spoke to DeLuca himself during the initial consultation; after that, even if they left messages for him, one of his staff returned the call. (*Id.*) Sometimes, the calls were only returned after leaving multiple messages. (*Id.* at 4.) The Debtors are also upset that the proposed stipulation and order that DeLuca received from St. Rose, approximately one month before St. Rose filed the Complaint, were not promptly forwarded to them. (Ex. H.) DeLuca did not even consult with the Debtors before informing St. Rose that he would not sign off on the proposed documents. (*See id.*)

C. Seare's Credibility

There is a factual question about whether DeLuca affirmatively told the Debtors that the St. Rose Debt was dischargeable. [. . .] Seare also stated that DeLuca did not tell the Debtors that the debt was *not* dischargeable or that there might be an adversarial proceeding. (*Id.*) Of these assertions, the court finds two facts: (1) the issue of Seare's fraud at the district court was not overtly discussed during the initial consultation; and (2) DeLuca did not affirmatively represent that the St. Rose Debt was dischargeable.

Although DeLuca does not remember meeting the Debtors, reading any district court documents, or what specifically was said during the consultation, the court does not believe Seare's testimony that DeLuca told the Debtors that the St. Rose Debt was dischargeable. The court finds it much more likely that he simply "thumbed through" the district court documents without paying them much heed, and that he did not affirmatively represent either way whether the debt was dischargeable. Similarly, his cursory review of the district court documents would not have led him to conclude that an adversary proceeding was likely.

The court finds that DeLuca failed to inquire about the nature of the Judgment during the consultation. If the Debtors did mention any of the facts underlying the Judgment, either the facts as presented did not clearly amount to fraud or DeLuca was not sufficiently attentive to reach that conclusion on his own. If he did know it was for fraud, then he surely would have told the Debtors that St. Rose would likely seek to have the debt found nondischargeable in an adversary proceeding.

The court believes Seare's testimony that DeLuca did not explain anything about adversary proceedings during the consultation—what they are, whether one was likely in this case, or what the potential consequences could be. [. . .]

In sum, the court finds that DeLuca did not affirmatively represent that the St. Rose Debt was dischargeable. Nor did he explain anything about adversary proceedings, either in general or in relation to the Debtors' particular circumstances. He moved quickly and did not pay sufficient attention to the Debtors' individual goals and needs. His boilerplate forms and standardized approach belie a manner of legal practice that is all too common in consumer bankruptcy—an approach which may suffice for a lot of people, a lot of the time, but is prone to failing clients with circumstances that do not fit the mold of the prototypical consumer debtor. While the court applies several ethical rules and sections of the Bankruptcy Code to DeLuca's conduct, each of which addresses related yet unidentical concerns, the root problem is a view of legal practice as a mass consumer good rather than a relationship founded on trust and individualized attention. The practice of law is a professional service, not a prepackaged, one-size-fits-all product.

IV. LEGAL ANALYSIS

Resolution of this matter involves the intersection of contract law and the regulation of lawyers generally. DeLuca strenuously contends that he should be able to limit his representation of clients by contract. If he cannot, he asserts, he cannot run his practice prudently. Seare, on the other hand, wants DeLuca to follow the requirements binding on all lawyers. The contentions of both parties thus require a brief review of the nature of the legal profession.

A. The Nature of the Legal Profession

Lawyers are not plumbers. They cannot indiscriminately dismiss clients at their whim, or even if their clients don't pay on time. Lawyers are professionals that owe fiduciary duties to their individual clients, and must continue to represent them even if initially rosy predictions turn sour. Am. Bar Ass'n, Section Of Litig., Handbook on Ltd. Scope Legal Assistance 91 (2003) ("ABA Handbook"); see Restatement (Third) of Law Governing Lawyers § 16 (2000).

[. . .] The duties that a lawyer owes her client also flow from this understanding of what it means to a be a "professional"—that a lawyer's superior knowledge and training place clients in a position of trust and dependence such that the lawyer has obligations to individual clients beyond that of two equal parties to a transaction or contract. Instead, a lawyer is a fiduciary that owes the duties of candor, good faith, trust, and care to a client. ABA Handbook 91.

[. . .]

B. The Applicable Law and its Application to the Facts

1. Interplay Between State and Federal Law

[. . .]

2. Unbundling

Before assessing the specific rules and statutes at issue, a thorough discussion of unbundling is necessary. Unbundling is the practice of limiting the scope of services that an attorney will provide—"dividing comprehensive legal representation into a series of discrete tasks, only some of which the client contracts with the lawyer to perform." Amber Hollister, *Limiting the Scope of Representation: Unbundling Legal Servs.*, 71 Or. St. B. Bull. 9, 9 (2011). It is growing ever more common in general, and in family law and bankruptcy law in particular. [. . .]

The practice of unbundling also recognizes that the attorney-client relationship need not fit an identical mold for each client; parties have the right to contract for the services they deem appropriate to the situation. [. . .] Unbundling raises concerns, however. The push to limit representation may come from the attorney, who often benefits from and has superior knowledge of the possible ramifications of excluding certain services. [. . .]

If limited representation is selected, "the lawyer must also alert the client to reasonably related problems and remedies that are beyond the scope of the limited-service agreement." [. . .] In light of the above, the court agrees that adversary proceedings can be unbundled, so long as the limitation complies with the applicable rules and statutes, and that a lawyer may charge additional fees for adversary proceedings. The analysis now turns to the applicable rules and statutes.

3. Nev. Rule of Prof'l Conduct 1.1—Duty of Competence

a. Legal Standard

Under Nevada Rule 1.1, which is identical to ABA Model Rule 1.1, "[a] lawyer shall provide competent representation to a client . . . the legal knowledge, skill, thoroughness and preparation reasonably necessary for the representation." Nev. Rule of

PROF'L CONDUCT 1.1 (2011). [. . .] Whether a lawyer fulfilled the duty of competence depends on the client's objectives. [Citations omitted.] The lawyer's duty is to competently attain the client's goals of representation. In the absence of a valid limitation on services, a lawyer must provide the bundle of services that are reasonably necessary to achieve the client's reasonably anticipated result, unless and until grounds exist for the lawyer's withdrawal. [Citation omitted.]

In other words, the duty of competence both informs and survives any and all limitations on the scope of services. [. . .] To determine the client's objectives, a lawyer must properly communicate with the client to understand the client's expectations, learn about the client's particular legal and financial situation, and independently investigate any "red flag" areas. See CAL. ETHICS PRIMER 1–2. A bankruptcy lawyer cannot assume that a client knows what a bankruptcy will or will not do for her. She may understand that bankruptcy eliminates some debts but is unlikely to know anything else about bankruptcy or even whether she wants or needs to file. [. . .]

The client's objectives may, and likely will, change through the course of a proper initial consultation. Because potential clients do not understand bankruptcy law, their pre-consultation expectations may be unreasonable or unachievable. The lawyer must "inquir[e] into and analy[ze] . . . the factual and legal elements of the problem" ABA MODEL RULE 1.1 cmt. 5. [. . .] Put another way, the law of mutual mistake has no place in the retention of an attorney. The attorney bears the burden of failing to ascertain the client's objectives and/or failing to shape their objectives to conform to the remedies available under bankruptcy law. Once again, the lawyer is the expert, not the client.

b. Application

DeLuca's first failure—the root cause of his other failings—was to not define the goals of the representation, which resulted from a lack of communication with the Debtors at the initial consultation. He apparently treats all debtors the same, as if the discharge of all dischargeable debts is always the primary goal. [. . .]

DeLuca argues that the Debtors had the burden to inform him that the debt was incurred through fraud, as the Retainer Agreement states that debts incurred through fraud "do not go away" and requests copies of all lawsuits within the last two years. Because the Debtors knew that the Judgment was based on fraud, so DeLuca argues, the burden was on them to communicate that fact to him. DeLuca's argument fails, however, because he improperly placed the burden on the Debtors to make the legal conclusion that fraud, as defined in the Bankruptcy Code, includes the fraudulent act that Seare committed in the district court. [. . .] DeLuca is the bankruptcy expert, not the Debtors. [. . .] He did not apply the knowledge and skill he has acquired through many years of consumer bankruptcy practice to the Debtors' needs. [. . .]

4. NEV. RULE OF PROF'L CONDUCT 1.2(c)—Scope of Services

Unbundling is permissible only if "the limitation is reasonable under the circumstances and the client gives informed consent." NEV. RULE OF PROF'L CONDUCT 1.2(c).

a. Reasonable Under the Circumstances

(1) Legal Standard

"'Reasonable' . . . denotes the conduct of a reasonably prudent and competent lawyer." NEV. RULE OF PROF'L CONDUCT 1.0(h) (2011). Like the term "profession," precisely defining "reasonable" is elusive. A leading treatise states that a limitation is reasonable if it is "not harmful to the client." HAZARD & HODES, *supra*, at § 5.10. [. . .]

(2) Application

Turning to DeLuca's decision to unbundle adversary proceedings, the first issue is timing—when the decision to exclude adversary proceedings was made. There are only three options; the decision was either made before DeLuca met with the Debtors, during the initial consultation, or sometime during the representation of the Debtors in the main bankruptcy case. DeLuca's use of boilerplate contracts that exclude adversary proceedings from the flat fee indicates that the decision to unbundle was made before DeLuca ever met the Debtors. The court does not find fault with the practice of using pre-prepared forms that limit the scope of services included in a flat fee, but the decision to unbundle must be reasonable under the circumstances. Boilerplate forms with limited services may be used only if the unbundled services are not reasonably necessary to achieve a particular client's objectives. As aptly demonstrated by the Debtors in this case, not all clients are the same. By treating them all the same, the decision to unbundle was effectively made before DeLuca ever met the Debtors. This is unreasonable and violates Nevada Rule 1.2(c).

[. . .] Unlike during the initial consultation, by June the Complaint had already been filed. To say the least, representing Seare in the adversary proceeding was reasonably necessary to achieve his objective of discharging the St. Rose Debt. In fact, prevailing in the adversary proceeding was the only way that Seare could discharge the St. Rose Debt. Unbundling this service after the Complaint was already filed was patently unreasonable and violated Nevada Rule 1.2(c).

b. Informed Consent

(1) Legal Standard

The second element of Nevada Rule 1.2(c)—informed consent—is "the agreement by a person to a proposed course of conduct after the lawyer has communicated adequate information and explanation about the material risks of and reasonably available alternatives to the proposed course of conduct." NEV. RULE OF PROF'L CONDUCT 1.0(e) (2011). The analysis involves two questions: (1) whether the information disclosure was sufficient; and (2) whether the consent was valid. *Struffolino,* at 225. [. . .]

Not only must the risks of proceeding pro se in a particular situation be explained, but more broadly, the attorney must advise the client of the risks *inherent* in unbundling legal services. HAZARD & HODES § 1.2:401. "The chief risk is that purchasing a cheap solution may result in a poor solution that will have to be undone later at a greater cost." (citation omitted) [. . .] Because the required information that a lawyer must provide is situation-specific, boilerplate disclosures in contracts of adhesion are highly suspect. *Cf. In re Cuddy, 322 B.R. at 18* (finding ethical problems with contracts of adhesion that unbundle legal services). [. . .]

(2) Application

DeLuca failed both aspects of informed consent. First, he did not adequately communicate the material risks of unbundling adversary proceedings—either in general or in the Debtors' situation—or the available alternatives to such unbundling. Without adequate information upon which to base a decision, valid consent was impossible. Second, the means of the consent—initialing and signing DeLuca's contract of adhesion—did not sufficiently demonstrate that the Debtors understood the import of proceeding without representation in adversary proceedings.

5. NEV. RULE OF PROF'L CONDUCT 1.5—Attorneys' Fees

[. . .]

6. NEV. RULE OF PROF'L CONDUCT 1.4—Communication with Clients

a. Legal Standard

Even if a limitation is reasonable and the client gives informed consent, the lawyer is not discharged of all duties surrounding the unbundled matter. The lawyer still has the duty to communicate under Nevada Rule 1.4, which is identical in pertinent part to ABA Model Rule 1.4. NEV. RULE OF PROF'L CONDUCT 1.4 (2011); ABA MODEL RULE 1.4 (2002). The lawyer shall "[r]easonably consult with the client about the means by which the client's objectives are to be accomplished; . . . [k]eep the client reasonably informed about the status of the matter; [and] . . . [p]romptly comply with reasonable requests for information. . . ." NEV. RULE OF PROF'L CONDUCT 1.4(a) (2011). [. . .]

b. Application

DeLuca first violated Nevada Rule 1.4 by failing to reasonably consult with the Debtors about the means to achieve their objectives. NEV. RULE OF PROF'L CONDUCT 1.4(a)(2) (2011). Because he did not understand that their primary goal was to permanently stop the garnishment, to the near exclusion of discharging other debts, a meaningful consultation about which means best served the Debtors' goals was rendered impossible. [. . .]

DeLuca also violated Nevada Rule 1.4 by failing to timely respond to requests for information by the Debtors. NEV. RULE OF PROF'L CONDUCT 1.4(a)(4) (2011). Tedoco argues that throughout the representation, DeLuca's office was nonresponsive and failed to keep the Debtors informed of the progress in their case. [. . .] DeLuca could not simply ignore the requests for direct communication. The Debtors paid for DeLuca's ongoing professional legal counsel, not just for a one-time meeting. [. . .] For these reasons, DeLuca violated Nevada Rule 1.4.

7. The Bankruptcy Code

[. . .]

V. SANCTIONS

A. The Purpose of Sanctions

A lawyer's primary obligations are to her client, but she also owes duties to the public, the legal system, and her profession. The ABA has recognized this in articulating that "the purpose of lawyer discipline proceedings is to protect the public and the administration of justice from lawyers who have not discharged, will not discharge, or are unlikely properly to discharge their professional duties to clients, the public, the legal system, and the legal profession." AM. BAR. ASS'N, JOINT COMM. ON PROF'L SANCTIONS, STANDARDS FOR IMPOSING LAWYER SANCTIONS 13 (2005) (the "ABA STANDARDS"). [. . .]

B. The Range of Sanctions

[. . .] The *ABA Standards* includes a non-exhaustive list of potential sanctions, which the court may impose individually or collectively: (1) disbarment; (2) suspension; (3) interim suspension; (4) reprimand, a declaration that the lawyer's conduct was improper without limiting the lawyer's right to practice; (5) admonition, a non-public reprimand; (6) probation, which allows the lawyer to practice under specified conditions; (7) reciprocal discipline; and (8) various other sanctions and remedies, such as restitution, assessment of costs, limitation upon practice, appointment of a receiver, requiring that the lawyer take the bar examination or professional responsibility examination, or requiring that the lawyer attend continuing education courses. ABA STANDARDS 14–16. [. . .]

C. The *ABA Standards*

[. . .] The *ABA Standards* dictates consideration of four criteria: (1) the duties violated, whether owed to a client, the public, the legal system, or the profession; (2) the lawyer's mental state, whether she acted intentionally, knowingly, or negligently; (3) the seriousness of the actual or potential injury caused by the lawyer's misconduct; and (4) the existence of aggravating or mitigating circumstances. ABA STANDARDS 9; *In re Nguyen,* 447 B.R. at 277.

1. The Duties Violated

The most important duties are those owed to the client—loyalty, diligence, competence, and candor. ABA STANDARDS 9–10. In descending order of importance are the duties owed to the general public, the legal system, and the legal profession. *Id.* at 10. The public is entitled to be able to trust lawyers to protect their property, liberty, and lives. *Id.* Accordingly, lawyers should behave with honesty and integrity. *Id.* Being able to trust lawyers to protect one's property is especially important for consumer bankruptcy debtors, who typically seek representation in dire circumstances and face a complex legal process. The system is harmed where lawyers create or use false evidence or intend to deceive the court, and where the lawyer's behavior puts an unreasonable burden on the court. *Id.* The profession is harmed where an attorney's practices reflect poorly on the profession or contribute to a decline in the overall quality of services provided by attorneys in a practice area or region. *See id.*

DeLuca violated his duties to the Debtors, the public, the legal system, and the legal profession. The court considers his violations of the duties of competence and diligence to be of the utmost concern. He failed to perform the most essential of functions—ascertaining the client's objectives. This failure was the first domino. He could not competently unbundle adversary representation without knowing how crucial such representation could be in the Debtors' situation. Nor could he obtain informed consent. He did not diligently represent the Debtors; he failed to keep them properly informed. Whether framed under the duty of competence or diligence, he failed his duty to provide the debtors with transparent information about the scope of services and his fee structure under the Retainer Agreement. The Debtors were not in a position to understand the benefits and risks of filing for bankruptcy, the likely costs to them, in terms of time and money, and the other options available. He failed the core attorney duty of treating each client as an individual. He unbundled based on his needs, not those of the Debtors. *See* ABA HANDBOOK 7.

DeLuca violated his duty to the public by practicing in a manner that erodes the public's trust in attorneys. He treats all clients the same, creating the impression that attorneys are more interested in fees than solving individual client's problems. He does not explain that his fee structure, which unbundles various services, may not be standard practice or that it creates certain risks. *See* RESTATEMENT (THIRD) OF LAW GOVERNING LAWYERS § 19 (2000). This fosters the same impression of profits over clients. The public may grow more distrustful of lawyers if they feel channeled into limited forms of representation that do not respond to individual needs. Because laypeople are unlikely to understand the advantages and risks of unbundled legal services, the general public is harmed to the extent that DeLuca's practice is becoming the norm for consumer bankruptcy attorneys. *See id.*

DeLuca's conduct also harmed the legal system. While his behavior did not rise to deceit, his abandonment left the court system to deal with a pro se litigant in a complicated adversary proceeding. The court faces considerable administrative challenges with pro se litigants, and if the court takes any action to assist the pro se litigant, however innocent, the court may face allegations of impartiality. *See In re Cuddy, 322 B.R. at 17.* DeLuca's Rule 2016(b) disclosure states that adversary proceedings are excluded from the $2,000 flat fee, rather than that adversary proceedings are excluded from DeLuca's scope of services entirely. The court does not find that DeLuca violated his obligations under Rule 2016(b). The court merely points out that it had no way to know that DeLuca would not represent Seare in the adversary proceeding.

2. DeLuca's Mental State

The *ABA Standards* defines three mental states—intent, knowledge, and negligence—in descending order of culpability. ABA STANDARDS 10. "Intent" is when the lawyer acts "with conscious objective or purpose to accomplish a particular result." *Id.* "Knowledge" is when the lawyer acts "with conscious awareness of the nature or attendant circumstances of his or her conduct both without the

conscious objective or purpose to accomplish a particular result. *Id.* "Negligence" is when a lawyer "fails to be aware of a substantial risk that circumstances exist or that a result will follow, which failure is a deviation from the standard of care that a reasonable lawyer would exercise in the situation." *Id.*

DeLuca's failure to investigate the Debtors' circumstances—the wage garnishment and the Judgment—was negligent. The reasonable lawyer in that initial consultation would have performed an independent investigation. DeLuca failed to be aware of the substantial risk of an adversary proceeding that the Debtors were nearly certain to face, and consequently could not advise them about the risks associated with such a proceeding. Not all of his conduct, however, was merely negligent.

He knowingly created a system that fails to explain the risks of particular cases to clients. His system intends to do generally, by use of standard form contracts, that which can only be done specifically. He knowingly chose to unbundle certain legal services for all clients, regardless of their circumstance. The Retainer Agreement and the FAQ are the only information provided to clients, and they do not explain the risks of unbundled services, either general or specific to one's case. These documents are insufficient to form the basis of informed consent. He repeatedly failed to call the Debtors back when they specifically requested that he, not his staff, return the calls. The repeated nature of this failing contributes to the conclusion that he treats all clients the same and does not provide individualized service.

He knowingly took steps during the course of representation to make sure that he would not represent Seare in the adversary proceeding. He knowingly structured the Retainer Agreement to require extra fees for adversary representation, yet he did not quote a price to Seare for representation in this adversary proceeding. Instead, he sent Seare the nonrepresentation letter. He also knowingly failed to forward the proposed stipulation and order that St. Rose sent to him one month prior to filing the Complaint. Further, he knowingly failed to sign the Retainer Agreement.

3. Seriousness of the Injury

"The extent of the injury is defined by the type of duty violated and the extent of actual or potential harm." ABA STANDARDS 11.

The court first examines the actual injuries to the Debtors. The Debtors spent considerable time pursuing the bankruptcy case and $2,000 in legal fees. If they had known that the St. Rose Debt was nearly certain to face a nondischargeability allegation, they may not even have filed in the first place. [. . .]

The potential injuries to the Debtors, and to Seare in particular, are also significant. If Seare and St. Rose had not settled, they would still be embroiled in litigation and preparing for trial. Seare would either be facing a complex proceeding pro se or paying alternative counsel. The cost of that counsel would likely be greater than what DeLuca would have charged because another lawyer would have had to become familiar with the case. The emotional toll for Seare and Tedoco would also likely be great if the proceedings were ongoing.

[. . .] The court finds DeLuca's arguments unavailing. The Debtors, and Seare in particular, suffered substantial actual and potential injury from DeLuca's unethical behavior.

The injury to the public, the legal system, and the profession, must also be considered. DeLuca's conduct has eroded the public trust by serving as an example of one more lawyer that values efficiency and what is best for him over the client's needs. Regrettably, the court has had to expend considerable time and resources to pursue this sanctions matter. The profession suffers, albeit intangibly, where the overall level of consumer bankruptcy practice is dragged down by unethical behavior. These harms are impossible to quantify, but they are nonetheless real.

4. Aggravating or Mitigating Factors

The court may consider aggravating and mitigating circumstances in deciding what sanction to impose. ABA STANDARDS 25. Aggravating factors justify an increase in the degree of discipline imposed. *Id.; In re Nguyen, 447 B.R. at 277.* They include (1) dishonest or selfish motive; (2) a pattern of misconduct; (3) multiple offenses; (4) refusal to acknowledge wrongful nature of conduct; and (5) substantial experience in the practice of law. ABA STANDARDS 26–27. To lesser or greater extent, all of these factors are present for DeLuca. He knowingly created a system that maximizes efficiency, and therefore profit, in exchange for less client interaction and less attention to clients' particular needs and goals. This can only be characterized as selfish, and a violation of the fiduciary duty to

place clients' needs first. That he uses a standard form contract that fails to properly explain the risks of unbundling demonstrates a pattern of misconduct. Just in his dealings with the Debtors he committed multiple ethical offenses, although they really stem from the same set of mistakes. He has refused to admit his mistakes; he has repeatedly blamed the Debtors for failing to provide the correct information. Lastly, he is a highly experienced consumer bankruptcy practitioner. He is obligated to be aware of his duties under the ethical rules and under the Bankruptcy Code.
[. . .]

D. The Sanctions Imposed

DeLuca violated the most important duties of a lawyer—those to his clients—as well as duties to the public, the legal system, and the legal profession. Many of his actions were done knowingly, while in some instances they were merely negligent. As a consequence of these violations, the Debtors suffered substantial actual and potential injury. The public, the legal system, and the legal profession were also victims. While he made several attempts to rectify the Debtors' injuries, the aggravating factors overwhelm the mitigating factors.

[. . .] Based on the *ABA Standards* and the court's authority under Sections 105(a), 329(b) and 526(c), the court hereby imposes the following sanctions on DeLuca:

1. Disgorgement of Fees

The court orders the disgorgement of all attorney's fees that the Debtors paid to DeLuca, including but not limited to the $1,995.00 paid under the Retainer Agreement. [. . .]

2. Publication of this Decision

The court orders that this opinion be submitted for publication in West's *Bankruptcy Reporter*. Publication is a form of reprimand, which the *ABA Standards* expressly endorses for negligent violations. The seriousness of the harms caused by DeLuca supports a public reprimand. "Only in cases of minor misconduct, when there is little or no injury to a client, the public, the legal system, or the profession, and when there is little likelihood of repetition by the lawyer, should private discipline be imposed." ABA STANDARDS 13. While DeLuca himself may not engage in the same conduct in the future, the purposes of sanctions are to deter such conduct by all attorneys.

[. . .]

3. Continuing Education

The court orders DeLuca to complete five hours of continuing education regarding collection and enforcement of judgments, and ten hours regarding ethical responsibilities to clients. He must complete the courses within one year of the date of entry of this opinion. [. . .]

4. Provision of this Decision to Future Clients

Finally, the court orders DeLuca to provide a copy of this opinion to every client in the next two years (commencing on May 1, 2013) who is sued in an adversary proceeding, but only if DeLuca declines to represent them in that adversary proceeding for any reason. If DeLuca properly declines to represent a client in an adversary proceeding—where such limitation is reasonable under the circumstances and the client gives informed consent—then this opinion will merely serve to confirm that DeLuca's limitation on services is proper. If not, then the opinion will serve to put clients on notice that DeLuca has unethically unbundled services in the past and that unbundling contains certain risks.

[. . .] This sanction also informs the bar that being caught for unethical conduct has repercussions beyond just paying a fine and moving on. Whether to behave ethically should not just be a business calculation that weighs the cost of being caught against the potentially higher profits of streamlining representation to the point at which each client is treated like the next. DeLuca's sanctionable conduct occurred in a case in which an adversary proceeding was filed—a rare occurrence. [. . .]

Noncompliance with any of the above may result in the imposition of additional sanctions or a finding of contempt of court.

VI. CONCLUSION

DeLuca's business model automatically divorces representation in a consumer's main Chapter 7 case from representation in any adversary proceeding that arises after filing—a practice known generally as "unbundling." While unbundling is not necessarily

evil, it must be done intelligently and in accordance with the applicable rules of professional responsibility. One of the aspects of a regulated profession such as law is that the ethical and other rules governing lawyers restrict a lawyer's freedom of contract with his or her clients. These rules require that limitations in representation such as unbundling have to be consistent with the goals of the legal representation, and that the client must give informed consent to the limitations. This should not be exceptional. These rules and the practices of most attorneys are consistent with unbundling of adversary proceedings in most bankruptcy cases.

Here, however, they failed. They failed because DeLuca failed to ascertain the Debtors' goals, and failed to properly inform himself of the circumstances surrounding Seare's wage garnishment. Underlying these failures was DeLuca's system which generically treats all clients the same, with little or no individualized differentiation. But the practice of law is not a one-size-fits-all consumer good; it is a profession that demands individual attention to each client. Lawyers have fiduciary duties to clients, and by definition a fiduciary duty means lawyers must place clients' interests above their own. DeLuca has done the opposite, by knowingly designing a system that prioritizes efficiency and uniformity above the particularized needs of each client.

DeLuca violated multiple state ethical rules and sections of the Bankruptcy Code as set forth above. Yet all these violations stem from a single source— his "mill" system of processing cases. By blindly adhering to his system in this case, DeLuca violated Nevada Rules 1.1, 1.2, 1.4, and 1.5, and Bankruptcy Code sections 526, 528, and 707(b)(4)(C). The court believes that the sanctions imposed should sufficiently incentivize DeLuca to practice consumer bankruptcy in a manner that pays appropriate attention to the details of each client's case, and should sufficiently deter other attorneys from unethically unbundling legal services.

Based on the foregoing, the court ORDERS Anthony J. DeLuca SANCTIONED as set forth above.

This opinion constitutes the court's findings of fact and conclusions of law under Rule 7052, made applicable here by Rule 9014(c).

Source: Reprinted from Westlaw with permission from Thomson Reuters.

Chapter 4

Confidentiality

This chapter will examine the duty of confidentiality that pertains to all attorneys in all matters handled on behalf of their clients. *Who* holds the privilege, *why* does the duty exist, *what* is covered by the duty of confidentiality, and *when* can it be waived by the client or avoided by the attorney? Most important, the text discusses *how* the duty affects the responsibilities of paralegals.

At the very core of the attorney-client relationship is the trust the client has in his attorney to look out for his best interests and to protect him in the matter at hand. The only way to assure a client that the attorney can be trusted is to protect the communications between them. An attorney must gather very private details from a client, details the client would rather personally retain, in order to properly assess the situation and strategize for the plan of action. Without this assurance of confidentiality, the client has no incentive to disclose all the facts to his attorney. The "[a]ttorney-client privilege serves the cause of justice by promoting candor between counsel and client, which candor is encouraged by the promise that the lawyer will not later reveal the client's confidences or use them to advance the cause of another client." *Daniels v. State*, 17 P.3d 75, 84 (Alaska App. 2001). The attorney's obligation to keep these **confidences** is absolute. Therein lies the key; the ethical rule applies to communications made to an attorney in her capacity as counselor-at-law regarding the representation of the client. The client can feel secure knowing that the information received by the attorney, through any means, from any source, will not be disclosed by the attorney.

confidences
Any communication from the client to the attorney which the client intends to be kept private from everyone else.

DUTY VERSUS PRIVILEGE

The absolute nature of the duty of confidentiality is tempered by the scope of the application of the **attorney-client privilege**. This is an important distinction. The duty belongs to the attorney and requires that she not reveal *any* information relating to the client; the privilege belongs to the client and permits the client to keep *certain* information from being revealed and used against him. Not everything transmitted (i.e., papers, emails, telephone conversations, etc.) between the attorney and client is covered by the privilege, but it is all covered by the duty. The duty arises from the moment that a client consults the attorney, whether or not that attorney is ultimately retained, and continues indefinitely. The client does not have to affirmatively request that the information be kept private; this automatically is covered under the duty. However, the privilege is an evidentiary rule. It applies only to communications made in confidence between an attorney and client that are of a sensitive nature relating specifically to the representation and known only to the client and attorney.

attorney-client privilege
The legal relationship established between attorney and client allowing for the free exchange of information without fear of disclosure.

The burden of demonstrating the applicability of the attorney-client privilege rests on the party asserting the privilege. *See Matter of Bevill, Bresler & Schulman Asset Mgmt. Corp.*, 805 F.2d 120, 126 (3d Cir. 1986). The party asserting this privilege must show each of the following:

(1) [T]he asserted holder of the privilege is or sought to become a client;
(2) the person to whom the communication was made (a) is a member of the bar of a court, or his subordinate and (b) in connection with this communication is acting as a lawyer;

(3) the communication relates to a fact of which the attorney was informed (a) by his client (b) without the presence of strangers (c) for the purpose of securing primarily either (i) an opinion on law or (ii) legal services or (iii) assistance in some legal proceeding, and not (d) for the purpose of committing a crime or tort; and

(4) the privilege has been (a) claimed and (b) not waived by the client.

Idenix Pharmaceuticals, Inc. v. Gilead Sciences, Inc., 2016 WL 4060098 (D. Del. 2016) citing *In re Grand Jury Investigation*, 599 F.2d 1224, 1233 (3d Cir. 1979) (internal quotation marks omitted). (The *Idenix* court held that the portion of an e-mail sent by defendant company's founder and director of the board to an employee chemist stating that lawyer had been hired and that chemist should meet him was not privileged.) *See Avgoustis v. Shinseki*, 639 F.3d 1340, 1344 (Fed. Cir. 2011) ("Courts have consistently held that the general subject matters of clients' representations are not privileged.").

This differs from the **duty of confidentiality** in that the duty does not require that the information come from the client with the intent that it be kept a secret; even if the attorney learns of public information about the client, she is still bound not to repeat it. This may not at first seem necessary; however, statements of an attorney made about a client are cloaked with a certain amount of authority. While the public may know the information, it is substantiated when it is repeated by an attorney, someone who has a fiduciary relationship with the person. These privileged communications are, with few strict exceptions, never revealed to any third parties. The purpose of the rules of confidentiality is to preserve the nature of the attorney-client relationship. Paralegals are bound by the same code of silence as explained in Figure 4.1.

ABA Model Rule 1.6 pertains to the ethical constraints regarding the dissemination of information about the client. The foremost principle regarding confidentiality is, in most circumstances, to remain silent about any and all information about the client and the representation.

duty of confidentiality
An absolute prohibition against the attorney's disclosure of any information gained about his client, regardless of the source of that information. It is much broader than the matter covered under the attorney-client privilege.

NALA Guideline 1

Paralegals should:

- Preserve the confidences and secrets of all clients.

NFPA EC 1.5

A PARALEGAL SHALL PRESERVE ALL CONFIDENTIAL INFORMATION PROVIDED BY THE CLIENT OR ACQUIRED FROM OTHER SOURCES BEFORE, DURING, AND AFTER THE COURSE OF THE PROFESSIONAL RELATIONSHIP.

EC 1.5(a) A paralegal shall be aware of and abide by all legal authority governing confidential information in the jurisdiction in which the paralegal practices.

◀ **FIGURE 4.1**
PARALEGAL'S DUTY OF CONFIDENTIALITY

WAIVER

waiver of confidentiality
Authorization by the client, through his words or actions, of the disclosure of otherwise protected information obtained by his attorney.

It is important to understand that the client "owns" the information. Any and all information relating to the client is the client's "property." The client creates the duty of confidentiality on the part of the attorney and paralegal by disclosing information to them, and the client can destroy the duty as well. The client may choose to *waive* the protection afforded to him by the rules of confidentiality. A **waiver of confidentiality** may be either implicit or explicit. A client may explicitly authorize his attorney to reveal the otherwise confidential information; this should be done only as a consequence of informed consent. In a situation where a client wishes to disclose certain information, the attorney should explain the legal ramifications of that disclosure. Once information is no longer protected, it can be used against the client. Implicit waiver exists where the disclosure is necessary under court rules or orders, as it is assumed that a client would and will consent to comply with the law. A client may also waive the confidential nature of a communication made to his attorney if he makes it knowingly in a non-confidential setting. This may include speaking in front of third parties, speaking in public places without regard for who may overhear, or performing other actions that express the client's disregard for confidentiality and intent to waive the privacy of the information. The deciding factor in making the determination of whether the communication is made in confidence or whether that confidence has been waived is the intent of the client. The mere presence of third parties or the place or manner of communication is not determinative. It is reasonable to expect that the presence of a close family member or friend with whom the client already has a confidential relationship would not violate the confidentiality of the communication. It is also reasonable that the time when a person needs to seek the advice of counsel is the very time when he also needs the support of another person with whom he has a close relationship. In *Newman v. State*, 384 Md. 285, 291, 863 A.2d 321 (2004), the attorney requested that the defendant's close friend be present in the meetings for a "cool head in the room." In another situation where the confidentiality of the client was preserved, a young man's father was permitted to attend the consultations and meetings with his attorney regarding his DUI charge. *Kevlik v. Goldstein*, 724 F.2d 844 (1st Cir. 1984). The key is whether the client considered the communications in front of the third person to be confidential. Where this expectation is unreasonable or the client is careless, the confidentiality is broken. In *People v. Harris*, 57 N.Y.2d 335, 343, 442 N.E.2d 1205, 1208 (Ct. App. 1982), the substance of the accused's telephone conversation with her attorney was admissible. The accused spoke knowing that the police officer was still in the room. The court found that the privilege never attached, as the accused did not intend the statement to be confidential in that situation. The officer "did nothing to purposely overhear the conversation or conceal his presence from defendant. Generally, communications made in the presence of third parties, whose presence is known to the defendant, are not privileged from disclosure." An interesting twist on this scenario occurred in *People v. Shurka*, 596 N.Y.S. 2d 428, 91

A.D.2d 724 (1993), wherein the court refused to suppress statements between co-defendants which were in Hebrew and overheard by an officer present in the room who also happened to speak Hebrew. "There is no dispute that the defendant had invoked his right to counsel prior to the time the inculpatory statements were overheard. However, that the prosecution did nothing to elicit these statements [internal citations omitted]. [T]he mere presence of an officer who, unbeknownst to the defendant, understood his non-privileged communications, is not equivalent of the police-orchestrated telephone call" designed to elicit such statements, which would be essentially an "extension of police questioning." The court in *Shurka* determined that the Hebraic speakers were careless and therefore waived the protection of confidentiality.

It is important to note that a client may freely communicate with his attorney in the presence of the attorney's staff, including her paralegals, without destroying the confidential nature of the communications. These personnel are considered agents of the attorney and therefore are considered extensions of the attorney and bound by these rules. The extension of the "cone of silence" extends to those professionals engaged for the purposes of preparing the matter for litigation. Paralegals often meet with clients without the attorney present. This is part of the vital time-saving role that paralegals play in the law office. Clients should feel comfortable in disclosing confidential information to paralegals, knowing that the information is protected under the ethical rules as it is transmitted to the attorney. Further, paralegals have a duty to keep their supervisors informed of the confidential information obtained by them from the client. *See* NFPA's rule in Figure 4.2. In this way, all the legal service providers in the office can render their best efforts, because they have all the information available and can better understand of the facts of the matter.

The protection of confidentiality extends not only to paralegals, but also to other agents retained by the attorney or paralegal to assist them in preparing the client's matter. For example, in *Commonwealth v. Noll*, 662 A.2d 1123, 1126 (Pa. Super. 1995), *appeal denied*, 543 Pa. 726, 673 A.2d 333 (1996), statements made to an accident reconstructionist hired by the attorney were confidential because they were made in order to determine whether the client had a viable lawsuit. Similarly, in *Cottillion v. United Refining Company*, 279 F.R.D. 290, 305 (W.D. Pa. 2011), the emails between the attorney and the actuarial consultants wherein the attorney requested an interpretation of the financial data that was the subject of the lawsuit maintained the privilege of confidentiality. "If the third party consultant is involved in the giving of legal advice, the privilege obtains." *Id.*, citing *In re CV Therapeutics, Inc. Securities Litigation*, 2006 WL 1699536, 6 (N.D. Cal. 2015).

NFPA EC 1.5

(e) A paralegal shall keep those individuals responsible for the legal representation of a client fully informed of any confidential information the paralegal may have pertaining to that client.

◀ **FIGURE 4.2**
TRANSMITTING CONFIDENTIAL INFORMATION TO SUPERVISORS

SPOT THE ISSUE

Daniel has gotten himself into some hot water; he has been charged with driving under the influence (DUI) and is in need of some legal help. Bob the Bartender at Daniel's local pub suggests that Daniel call Larry, a lawyer who specializes in DUI defense. As it happens, not long after Bob and Daniel have spoken, Larry walks into the bar and, coincidentally, sits down next to Daniel. Larry and Daniel strike up a friendly conversation, and Daniel reveals that he is in need of an attorney for his DUI defense. Larry, happy to have found another client, volunteers to listen to all the details of Daniel's run-in with the law.

What are the ethical implications of this situation? What details would you add to argue either that no attorney-client confidentiality exists or that it does exist? What is Larry's duty to Daniel? Is this information privileged? Why or why not? On what facts does your answer depend? What if Larry were a paralegal (not an attorney) who worked for a DUI defense firm? Would your answer change? Why or why not?

For guidance, see Cal. St. Bar Comm. Prof. Resp. Formal Op. 161 (2003).

SPOT THE ISSUE

Attorney Smith represents the National Dressmakers Association (NDA) by and through its Board of Directors. The Board has consulted Attorney Smith with regard to some of the contracts its members are entering into with suppliers. Attorney Smith has asked his paralegal to prepare a memorandum regarding the legality of some of the proposed terms. The Board is planning a meeting and has invited the National Tailors Association (NTA) as its guest to discuss these matters. The attorney's memo was attached to the meeting agenda and was discussed. One month later, the NDA files a lawsuit against various suppliers based upon these contracts. The suppliers demand that the NDA produce the legal memorandum discussed at the board meeting with the NTA, claiming that the NDA's disclosure at the meeting waived the confidentiality of the document. The NDA refuses to do so, stating that the NTA's participation in the meeting did not break the confidential nature of the document.

Review the following:

Under the common interest rule, individuals may share information without waiving the attorney-client privilege if: (1) the disclosure is made due to actual or anticipated litigation; (2) for the purpose of furthering a common interest; and (3) the disclosure is made in a manner not inconsistent with maintaining confidentiality against adverse parties. Whether the parties shared a "common interest" in the anticipated litigation must be evaluated as of the time that the confidential information is disclosed.

Holland v. Island Creek Corp., 885 F. Supp. 4, 6 (D.D.C. 1995).

Do you think the legal memorandum is confidential, or has the NTA waived that protection?

REQUIRED DISCLOSURE

Prevention of Death or Serious Bodily Harm

The second section of ABA Model Rule 1.6 sets the parameters for those instances in which the client does not consent to disclose, but the attorney *may*, in her professional discretion, reveal the information to the appropriate authority. NFPA has a parallel ethical consideration. See Figure 4.3.

The first category of **permitted disclosure** relates to the attorney's or paralegal's reasonable belief that the client will likely lead contribute to the death or substantial bodily harm of another person. The attorney or paralegal must have a reasonable belief that her client will go through with the threat of harm to another before the duty of confidentiality can be violated. The communication regarding a future criminal act is not protected. Of course, the attorney should try to dissuade the client from going through with the malicious act and advise him as to the serious legal ramifications of his potential actions. If the paralegal is the one in possession of this information, the previously discussed ethical consideration imposes a duty upon the paralegal to report the potentially harmful act to the responsible supervising attorney, who can then take the appropriate legal actions.

permitted disclosure
The right of an attorney to reveal certain information learned from his client, even without the client's consent, in certain circumstances.

> We believe that conscientious lawyers, faced with the decision of whether or not to exercise their discretionary power to make the limited disclosure "necessary to prevent" a threatened crime, should consider a number of factors. The basic considerations would be the seriousness of the potential injury (especially when the threatened crime involves death or grave bodily injury), its likelihood and imminence, and the apparent absence of any other feasible way in which such prospective harm can be prevented. The lawyer may also appropriately give weight to other factors of potential relevance, including the extent to which the client may have attempted to involve the lawyer in the prospective crime, the circumstances under which the lawyer acquired the information of the client's intent, and any possibly aggravating or extenuating factors. As already noted, however, disclosure under this exception should be limited to what the lawyer believes necessary to prevent the crime.

N.Y. Eth. Op. 562, 1984 WL 50017 4 (N.Y. St. Bar. Assn. Comm. Prof. Eth.).

The determination is not an easy one to make; it is extremely fact-sensitive, and can potentially be second-guessed by a reviewing court. There are two

---

NFPA EC 1.5

(d) A paralegal may reveal confidential information only after full disclosure and with the client's written consent; or when required by law or court order; or when necessary to prevent the client from committing an act that could result in death or serious bodily harm.

◄ **FIGURE 4.3**
DISCLOSURE TO
PREVENT HARM

competing interests at stake in making this determination; the attorney or the paralegal must choose between protecting her client's trust and confidence and ensuring the personal safety, even the very life, of a third party.

The pivotal issue is whether the legal professional has information prior to the commission of the future act that she reasonably believes will occur. Indeed, an attorney may be compelled to disclose confidential information where it may prevent death or substantial bodily injury to a third party. The information does not have to withstand an inquiry as to the probability of its veracity. It is enough that there exists a possibility of saving a life or intercepting the commission of another crime or fraud. This was exactly the case in *Henderson v. State*, 962 S.W.2d 544 (Tex. Crim. App. 1997), wherein the attorney for the accused was compelled to produce maps made by the accused that law enforcement believed might lead them to the missing child. The public policy in protecting the well-being of the child outweighed the accused's right in privileged communications to her attorney. "Even if authorities believed that the chance of the maps leading to a live baby was remote, they were entitled to pursue that remote possibility. If the child had been abandoned, or secreted with an accomplice of appellant's, his life or health might have been in jeopardy. Hence, authorities could obtain the maps in an attempt to terminate a kidnapping." *Id.* at 557.

Crime-Fraud Exception

The second possibility of disclosure relates to the "crime or fraud" exception to the attorney-client privilege and the obligation of the legal professionals in the office to keep all the confidences of the client. If the information exchanged between the attorney and the client was used by the client to directly further the client's misconduct, then the attorney may reveal that secret information to the proper authorities. Essentially, the client has waived the privileged nature of the communication by using it toward an end not tolerable by justice system. To misuse an attorney's advice and abuse her trust is to forfeit the privilege. *U.S. v. Gorski*, 807 F.3d 451 (1st Cir. 2015). The attorney may be totally in the dark with regard to his client's purpose for seeking the advice; if it turns out that the client has misused the information, it is no longer subject to the privilege. The inquiry hinges upon the client's intent to use the information to further his illegal purpose. *Id.* at 462, citing *In re Jury Proceedings (Violette)*, 183 F.3d 71, 75 (1st Cir. 1999). Because the privilege is so well-established and vital to the performance of an attorney's duty, it is not lightly disregarded. "It does not suffice that the communications may be related to a crime" (*United States v. White*, 281 U.S. App. D.C. Cir. 39, 43, 887 F.2d 267, 271 (1989); nor is it enough to show that the client communicated to his attorney right before his commission of a crime or fraud (*In re Sealed Case*, 107 F.3d 46, 50, 323 U.S. App. D.C. Cir. 233, 237 (1997).) "[T]he court must determine that the communication was itself in furtherance of the crime or fraud, not merely that it has the potential of being relevant evidence of criminal or fraudulent activity."

1 JOHN W. STRONG, MCCORMICK ON EVIDENCE 382 (5th ed. 1999). Just like the first exception to the privilege for preventing death or substantial bodily harm to another, the "crime-fraud" exception applies prospectively. The privilege is not broken when the client discusses his past criminal or fraudulent activity—that may very well be why he is consulting an attorney in the first place! These rules are prophylactic in nature. They are designed to prevent future or ongoing harm. It is the attorney's duty to try to assist his client to navigate his way through the justice system, not to cover up, assist, counsel, or otherwise provide information to thwart the process. *In re Federal Grand Jury Proceedings 89-10*, 938 F.2d 1578, 1581 (11th Cir. 1991):

> A determination of whether the crime-fraud exception applies involves application of a two part test:
>
> First, there must be a prima facie showing that the client was engaged in criminal or fraudulent conduct when he sought the advice of counsel, that he was planning such conduct when he sought the advice of counsel, or that he committed a crime or fraud subsequent to receiving the benefit of counsel's advice.
>
> Second, there must be a showing that the attorney's assistance was obtained in furtherance of the criminal or fraudulent activity or was closely related to it.

There must be strong evidence of a nexus between information that the legal professional has in her possession and the planned crime or fraud perpetrated by the client. A **"fishing expedition"**—a request for disclosure to see what information the attorney may have—is not permitted, as it fails to meet this standard. *See In re Marriage of Decker*, 153 Ill. 2d 298, 606 N.E.2d 1094 (1992). In that case, a woman filed an emergency motion and subpoena for any information relating to the whereabouts of her ex-husband, who may have abducted their child by failing to return the child after visitation. The court first wrestled with the decision of whether the initial burden was met: whether the woman had enough information to lead a reasonable person to believe that the ex-husband's attorney had relevant information regarding his plan to kidnap the child. The second issue revolved around whether an *in camera* **inspection** of the materials that potentially contained this information was appropriate, to determine whether the "crime-fraud" exception applied and the privileged information should be made known in order to apprehend the ex-husband. The determination that indeed a crime had been committed was not enough to prove that there was any communication between the attorney and client that was related to that plan to carry out the crime. The court opined that a very specific question posed would clarify the determination.

> "Did your client ask your advice on how to commit this [specific illegal] act, knowing it to be unlawful?" The answer to this question would subject the information to minimal disclosure, and an affirmative answer would remove the privilege for that information.

Id. at 325.

"fishing expedition"
A request by an opposing party for potentially damaging information from the attorney, on the premise that the opposing party needs it to prevent harm, but without specific evidence of an actual threat of harm.

***in camera* inspection**
A proceeding in the judge's chambers during which the judge can examine the proffered evidence outside of the jury's presence to determine the necessity of disclosure of the confidential information.

SPOT THE ISSUE

Sam is a criminal defendant indicted for embezzlement and represented by Eddie, Esq. During their meetings, Sam reveals that he has recently purchased several vacation condos in Florida and California. He seems very pleased that he has no mortgages, as he has paid in cash for the full purchase price. He sees this as a sound investment strategy. Eddie seems surprised at his ability to come up with that kind of money right on hand as Sam had difficulty making bail. Eddie recalls reading a recent ethics opinion that he found his paralegal filing in the office library.

> [W]e do not believe that the Code intends to encourage attorneys to be unduly naive or disregard the obvious. There are some circumstances in which an attorney may be aware of facts which fall short of actual knowledge but which still impose on him an obligation to make inquiry to determine whether his client is engaged in unlawful conduct. A lawyer may not purposely close his eyes to what he perceives to be circumstances indicative of illegal or fraudulent conduct by a client. Such selective blindness may be a disservice to the client and, in some cases, has led to disciplinary proceedings against the attorney.
>
>   Likewise, an attorney need not turn a blind eye to circumstances that would lead a reasonable person to believe that a client intends to commit a crime even though the lawyer does not "know" that this is the client's intent. If a lawyer reasonably concludes after due inquiry that the client has the intention to commit a future crime, then the lawyer is permitted, but not required, to make disclosure to the appropriate authorities to prevent the crime. Once the threshold of reasonable belief of the client's intention to commit a crime is surmounted, in determining whether to make permissive disclosure, the lawyer should consider a number of factors, including "the seriousness of the potential injury to others if the prospective crime is committed, the likelihood that it will be committed and its imminence, the apparent absence of any other feasible way in which the potential injury can be prevented, the extent to which the client may have attempted to involve the lawyer in the prospective crime [and] the circumstances under which the lawyer acquired the information of the client's intent."
>
> N.Y.C. Eth. Op. 2202-1, 2002 WL 1040180 (N.Y.C. Assn. B. Comm. Prof. Jud. Auth.).

What do you think Eddie should do, given this opinion?

Anticipating Perjury

perjury
A witness's knowingly false and willful assertion as to a matter of fact, opinion, belief, or knowledge material to an inquiry, made under oath in a judicial proceeding as part of his or her evidence.

Perhaps the most abhorrent fraud is that perpetrated against the justice system's search for the truth: perjury. While there is no prohibition against presenting all defenses for the accused, the ethical rules that require an attorney from refraining from perpetrating a fraud or crime also prevent an attorney from permitting the client from lying under oath. If an attorney has a reasonable belief that his client will not tell the truth in presenting testimony, he is prohibited from affirmatively offering that evidence into court. If the client insists on presenting oral testimony in court, there are several options open to the attorney. The primary preference is to convince the client either not to take the stand or to refrain from lying. It is the attorney's duty to also explain the ramifications of that course of action. Permitting the client to commit perjury is, in itself, an ethical violation, as it is the **subornation of perjury**, which is a criminal offense. Once a client has committed perjury, it is the attorney's duty to report it to the court. Indeed, not only is the disclosure permitted as an exception from the attorney-client privilege; it is required by the ethics rules. The client needs to be made well aware that the attorney will disclose the perjury to the court. This is perhaps the most powerful weapon the attorney has to prevent the commission of perjury. *Nix v. White-side*, 475 U.S. 157, 106 S. Ct. 988, 89 L. Ed. 123 (1986).

With enough advance notice of the proposed perjurous testimony, the attorney can choose to apply to withdraw as counsel. This move has potentially positive outcomes for the attorney, but negative repercussions for the client and potentially for the court. While the attorney removes herself from the perils of an ethical violation, she may place another attorney in the same predicament. Additionally, this successive attorney may not be aware of the falsity of the proposed testimony and the intention of the client to commit perjury. To permit withdrawal is to facilitate the commission of perjury; the attorney who is aware of the potential fraud is no longer in the position to prevent it. Further, the court may not permit the withdrawal on the basis that it will prejudice the client's interests. Withdrawal is unlikely if the trial date is very close, as it would not permit the substituted counsel to adequately prepare. The court may also deny the motion to withdraw as counsel if the facts supporting withdrawal are not sufficient to convince the judge that there is the possibility of perjury. In making the motion, the attorney must disclose enough information to illustrate the possibility of perjury without making it clear exactly what parts of the proposed testimony is false—a difficult showing at best.

The "middle ground" between full disclosure and full preservation of confidentiality by withdrawing as counsel is the disassociation from or "nonsponsorship" of the testimony. If the client cannot be dissuaded from potentially committing perjury and insists on giving testimony on his own behalf, the client may give that testimony in a narrative form without the assistance of the attorney's direct examination. While the savvy juror would understand that this testimony is suspect because the attorney is not participating in offering the testimony into evidence, it is better than the alternative. Some courts have suggested that the attorney may conduct direct examination of his client as to the "nonsuspect" portions of the testimony, and then permit a narrative of that portion of the client's testimony which the attorney cannot support, as it is potentially perjury. This would also permit the attorney to include the direct-exam portion of the testimony in his closing argument as properly admitted evidence. This "bifurcation method" of dealing with the client's testimony has been criticized by other courts and the ABA:

> [T]his is the worst approach of all. . . . This [approach] would be far worse for the client than saying nothing, not to mention it would be virtually impossible to control once the client takes the stand. And what about

subornation of perjury
Assistance by an attorney in carrying out a witness's offer of false testimony.

cross? How can you possibly prepare your clients for that? Tell them not to answer any questions that they do not like?

ABA Criminal Justice Section, Ethical Problems Facing the Criminal Defense Lawyer at 162 (1995).

"[This] suggestion is impractical, as it may call attention to testimony of the defendant that is not argued by trial counsel, and would likely lead to counsel's making an incoherent final argument." *Commonwealth v. Mitchell*, 438 Mass. 535, 550, 781 N.E.2d 1237, 1249 (2003).

With so much at stake, how does an attorney determine whether the client's testimony is perjury that should be reported? Clients may not always be wholly truthful with their attorneys or fully disclose all the facts known to them. The standard upheld by most courts is that an attorney must have a "firm factual basis" and proof beyond a reasonable doubt that the proffered testimony rises to the level of lying under oath.

Prevention of Further Harm

The third exception to the rule of confidentiality is related to the one just above. However, this third rule contemplates that the legal professional has

---

IN-CLASS DISCUSSION

Lou has been indicted for "loan sharking" (lending money to people and charging very, very high interest on those loans). Lou is a rather large man and has been known to intimidate those with whom he deals. He tells his attorney's paralegal, Claude, that he can get plenty of witnesses to testify on his behalf. In fact, Lou's friend is a police officer, and Lou is *sure* he can *persuade* him to give positive testimony.

The police officer agrees to help Lou out and will in fact lie under oath for him without Lou's attorney knowing about the falsity of the testimony. Should Lou's attorney or paralegal be responsible for subornation of perjury in this case?

See Ex parte Castellano, 863 S.W.2d 476 (Tex. Crim. App. 1993).

RESEARCH THIS

Find a case in your jurisdiction that addresses the situation where an attorney or a paralegal is faced with a client who is contemplating committing perjury. How does your state court decide what is the attorney's or paralegal's most appropriate response and means to handle the issue? Remember to look not only at case law, but also at the ethics opinions from the appropriate body.

no knowledge of the planned criminal or fraudulent conduct, but learns of it after the fact. In this instance, if the attorney or paralegal can prevent further damage caused by her client's illegal conduct, she must do so. The New Jersey court stated:

> The Rule reads, "and if his client refuses or is unable to do so, he shall reveal the fraud to the affected person or tribunal." No prior case has stated precisely that the word "shall" in the above Rule is intended to be mandatory. "Shall" is defined in Webster's New Collegiate Dictionary as "ought to, must, will have to, used to express a command or exhortation, used in laws, regulations or directives to express what is mandatory". The clear meaning of "shall" in the Rule must be deemed "mandatory"; otherwise, the purpose of the Rule would be frustrated.
>
> *N.J. Eth. Op. 520, 112 N.J. L.J. 369, 1983 WL 106230 4 (N.J. Adv. Comm. Prof. Eth.); see also* Utah Ethics Advisory Op. 00-06, 2000 WL 1523292 (Utah St. Bar).

The Utah Ethics Board decided that silence in the face of a fraud or crime is equivalent to aiding in it. The attorney must first attempt to convince the client to rectify the situation; if the client is unwilling, then the attorney must reveal the truth to correct the result of the fraud or crime. The attorney has a duty also to the victim, to prevent the nondisclosure of the crime or fraud from getting worse. For example, having discovered his client's embezzlement of corporate funds, the attorney should take some measure to prevent the coming financial disaster as his client siphons the money.

Prevention of or Self-Defense Against Professional Malpractice

The fourth exception to the general close-mouthed position of the attorney essentially permits the attorney to look for legal advice in order to himself comply with the applicable rules. This manifests itself in the numerous and

REEL TO REAL

Witness for the Prosecution (1957) stars two cinematic powerhouses, Tyrone Power and Marlene Dietrich, locked in a courtroom battle over witness testimony. Dietrich's character is the wife of the accused murderer of a rich middle-aged widow. The defense's only alibi witness is his wife; however, she has agreed to take the stand on behalf of the prosecution. Evaluate her credibility, her motives for possible perjury, and the prosecution's decision to put her on the stand.

Contemporary powerhouses also clash in *A Few Good Men* (1992). The movie stars the sparring Jack Nicholson and Tom Cruise, giving rise to one of the most-quoted movie lines: "You want answers, I want the truth. You can't handle the truth."

varied ethics opinions rendered by courts and ethical boards. An attorney may find himself in a situation where his ethical duties are unclear. In an effort to do the right thing, the attorney writes to the supervising ethical body posing a hypothetical situation in which matches the one he has found himself. This disclosure of confidential client information is necessary in order for the attorney to comply with his duty to the profession and to properly counsel his client. The paralegal student will notice, upon finding an opinion rendered by a supervising ethical board or committee, that neither the name of the inquiring attorney nor that of his client is ever revealed in a published opinion. They are set forth as anonymous hypothetical situations in order to preserve the confidentiality of the client and ensure that no one can deduce from the facts set forth who the client may be. It is unclear whether paralegals have access to this kind of advice when they are in possession of such information.

Finally, an attorney or paralegal may reveal information necessary to defend himself against allegations of ethical violations or professional misconduct with regard to the representation of that particular client. To deny a legal professional the opportunity to disclose the content of conversations with his client would be to strip him of the ability to counter the contentions leveled against him. This exception to the privilege applies to accusations brought by both the former client and by third parties who allege that the legal professional was a participant in the former client's wrongdoing. This most often manifests itself as a defense to a malpractice claim. Not only attorneys are covered under malpractice claims and the related insurance; paralegals are as well. If a client challenges the attorney's or the paralegal's competence through either a civil claim or an ethical charge, the attorney may testify as to the relationship and produce documents that would otherwise be privileged. The ability to defend oneself and one's professional integrity is important enough that the courts have determined that the disclosure may be made even prior to an indictment. *See In re Friend*, 411 F. Supp. 776, 777 (S.D.N.Y. 1975). In this matter, the attorney applied for court permission to turn over certain client documents to a United States Grand Jury that was investing his former client and which would help to establish that the attorney acted properly in trying to assure his client's compliance with the law. "Although, as yet, no formal accusation has been made against Mr. Friend, it would be senseless to require the stigma of an indictment to attach prior to allowing Mr. Friend to invoke the exception [to the privilege] in his own defense." The disclosure may be made even in a case where the attorney is made subject to public criticism by "bad-mouthing" from the former client where the accusations leveled against the attorney suggest a breach of contract, fiduciary duty, malpractice, or violation of ethics.

> A lawyer may reveal protected information in self-defense against an accusation of alleged wrongdoing, regardless of whether there is a formal suit, criminal indictment or disciplinary charge. . . . It requires that the allegation be public and specific such that a person would reasonably conclude that the lawyer is subject to a claim or charge for such misconduct *and*

that the claim or charge is looming and will be brought before a body empowered to rule on such claim or charge.

NYCLA Eth. Op. 722, 1997 WL 232485 (N.Y. Cty. Law. Assn. Comm. on Prof'l Ethics) (emphasis added).

Ethics requires that confidences be broken only where the context of the disparaging comments would lead the listener to believe that the client is about to or could bring an action against the attorney and that the action is imminent. Mere gossip or general complaining is not enough to dissolve the duty of confidentiality; the duty of confidentiality is nearly sacrosanct.

UNINTENTIONAL DISCLOSURE

Whereas the preceding discussion focused on the purposeful ability of the legal professional to disclose confidential information, this section addresses those situations where the information is disclosed by accident. How does this **unintentional disclosure** occur? The most common scenario plays out in the failure of general office procedures. Failure to properly manage client files, mailing lists, faxes, and emails can all result in an inadvertent disclosure of sensitive documents. Mindful performance of these tasks by every member of the office is essential to maintaining confidential information. Monitoring these processes may be a key role played by paralegals. The discovery process offers the greatest access to confidential information, as the opposing party often has access to the set of client documents held by the attorney. If a close pre-discovery screening of the files for sensitive information has not been performed by either the attorney or, more likely, the paralegal, these documents will be exposed to opposing counsel. It is imperative to identify and remove all the confidential information from the client's files. Careful use of mailing lists, fax and e-mail is also necessary to keep documents and correspondence from reaching the wrong persons. It is often the legal secretary's or paralegal's job to maintain distribution lists of the parties involved in the suit and their corresponding counsel. Lack of clarity or ease of use of these lists makes it possible to transmit confidential information unintentionally. *See People v. Terry*, 1 Misc. 3d 475, 764 N.Y.S.2d 592 (N.Y. Co. Ct. 2003), wherein the defendant intended to send a letter to his attorney and put the correct name on the envelope; however, the address was mixed up with the District Attorney's office in charge of the prosecution of the case. The letter was then opened and read by the District Attorney. The court determined that the fault truly lay with the District Attorney and his personnel, because it was clearly sent in error and they should not have opened or read the material. The court determined that the inadvertent disclosure did not constitute a waiver by the client who sent the letter and the information contained in it could not be used against the defendant.

unintentional disclosure
The accidental release of sensitive client information to a third party.

What are the ramifications of this accidental disclosure? There are essentially three conclusions:

1. The privilege is lost, as it is considered waived, and the information can be used by the receiving party.
2. The privilege cannot be waived by accidental disclosure by the attorney, because waiver requires intent to disclose by the holder of the privilege, who in this case is the client. Only a knowing disclosure by the client can operate as a waiver of confidentiality.
3. The disclosure may constitute a waiver, depending on the circumstances surrounding it.

This third approach is a "middle ground" between the first two extremes, both of which operate unfairly on one party or another, or compromise the duties of either the sending or receiving attorneys. The circumstances that the court must examine to determine whether the accidental disclosure should act as a waiver of confidentiality or not are these:

1. The degree of care taken by the disclosing party—or, whether the precautions and the office procedures are reasonably and functionally able to prevent accidental disclosures
2. "The presence of extenuating circumstances, the most obvious being the press of massive discovery going forward under the pressure of deadlines, where even caution in producing documents is likely to generate occasional mistakes" (*Elkton Care Center Associates Ltd. Partnership v. Quality Care*, 145 Md. App. 532, 545 805 A.2d 1177, 1184 (2002), citing Christopher B. Mueller & Laird C. Kirkpatrick, *Evidence* § 5.29 at 450-52 (4th ed. 1995))
3. The number and significance of the accidental disclosures
4. The extent of the disclosure
5. The time between the disclosure and the attempts to rectify the situation
6. The overriding interests of justice that may be served by relieving a party of its error

See Sampson Fire Sales v. Oaks, 201 F.R.D. 351, 360 (M.D. Pa. 2001).

There is a duty upon the receiving party to maintain the overarching ethical principle of client confidentiality, maintain the highest standards of the profession, and ensure fairness in the legal process. An attorney or paralegal receiving this kind of sensitive confidential information should do three things:

1. Refrain from viewing the material as soon as she realizes that it is privileged information
2. Notify the sender about the disclosure
3. Follow the instructions regarding the return or destruction of documents or seek a resolution in court

Only the second task *must* be promptly undertaken as a requirement of the Model Rules of Professional Responsibility. *See Nova Southeastern University, Inc. v. Jacobson*, 25 So. 3d 82 (Fla. DCA 2009). The first and third are moral and ethical considerations that the legal professional may and should consider in making his decision, but he is not bound by the formal rules to follow them. *See* ABA Formal Opinion 06-440 (2006); this Opinion formally withdrew the previous opinion, 94-382, which did require all three steps to be taken. However, this retraction does not leave the door open for unscrupulous or questionable activity in obtaining and using privileged or confidential information. Where confidential information is obtained through tortious or criminal conduct, the attorney retaining and using the information may be sanctioned for such an offence. *See Maldonado v. New Jersey*, 225 F.R.D. 120 (D.N.J. 2004). The prosecuting attorney in that case clearly took advantage of the mysterious appearance in the plaintiff's mailbox of a confidential letter written by the defendants and addressed to their attorney. The most egregious conduct of an attorney taking advantage of unintended disclosure will likely result in a dismissal of the entire matter. In *Perna v. Electronic Data Systems Corporation*, 916 F. Supp. 388 (D.N.J. 1995), the plaintiff obtained access to the opposing counsel's briefcases, which they had left in the plaintiff's office instead of toting them to lunch as they were conducting discovery. Plaintiff found "work product" documents inside and then delivered them to his attorney. The court found that the plaintiff's "act of browsing through and photocopying the documents, knowing that the documents were his adversaries, is an unthinkable and extraordinary act. Further, he had his partner serve as a 'lookout' as he engaged in this clandestine behavior. Thus, the inappropriateness of his knowing and willful act is extreme in and of itself." *Id.* at 399. "The sanction of dismissal is generally reserved for those extreme circumstances where deception is willful and the act was inconsistent with the orderly administration of justice." *Id.* at 400.

Even the most innocent situations may pose a threat to a client's confidential information. Friends and family often ask about a paralegal's day: "Hi, honey, I'm home; how was your day?" It is a social norm to talk about things going on at work as you gather for lunch or dinner. A paralegal must be especially careful not to talk about matters in any specific or identifiable way, because many people do not understand the full scope of a legal professional's duty of confidentiality. It may be particularly hard not to discuss a high-profile matter in which the paralegal is involved. Recall that even if the information is publicly known, it is unacceptable for the legal professional to reveal it, as it might color the facts with a certain authority.

The reality of maintaining these confidences is not so cut and dried. For instance, can you recall how many paralegals were talking with just a little too much detail about their cases at the last paralegal association luncheon/dinner you attended? Or, how about that novice paralegal seeking guidance from you on how to accomplish a paralegal task, but who gave enough information about the client that the person at the next table in the restaurant could identify the client?

Suppose that person who overheard your conversation was from the adversary's lawyer's office and the information revealed client confidences to that person? And finally, imagine attending an interview for a paralegal job and being asked by the interviewing attorney to discuss the kinds of cases in which you have been involved. Wanting the job, wanting to impress the attorney sufficiently to secure the job, yet trying to be careful, you slip—hook, line and sinker—you've divulged a client confidence and lost any chance at ever getting a job with that firm or company.

Susan D. Daugherty, Loose Lips Sink Ships . . . or Paralegals, THE NATIONAL PARA-LEGAL REPORTER ONLINE 1998.

Clearly, paralegals must always be vigilant about their conversations about their work. As a legal professional, it is not always possible to leave work at the office and shed your duties as you "clock out." The ethical obligations remain in force 24 hours a day, seven days a week, no matter whom the paralegal is with or where the paralegal is.

UNPROTECTED COMMUNICATIONS

unprotected communications
Information that must be disclosed to the opposing party if requested during the discovery phase of litigation.

While clients would like to believe, or mistakenly do believe, that any and all documents in the possession of their attorneys and all communications between themselves and their attorneys are protected by the duty of confidentiality, the truth is that only those that relate to the representation of the client are protectable (not necessarily protected). Documents by the box-load may be brought to the attorney's office in preparation for litigation; however, the change in their location does not change their status from discoverable and unprotected to privileged. All documents that existed prior to the preparation for litigation are "fair game"; merely bringing or sending documents to your attorney does not make them confidential. Communications between the attorney and client that deal solely with a matter of fact are not ordinarily privileged, unless the communication of those facts were shown to be "inextricably linked" to the giving of legal advice. *See State v. Carpenter*, 2001 WL 1561058 (Conn. Super. 2001) (unpublished opinion), wherein the defendant sent letters attached to various documents, including newspaper clippings regarding the crime and possible suspects, to her attorney. The defendant claimed that these documents were privileged because although they dealt with public facts, when viewed in conjunction with the confidential letters, they revealed an ongoing legal strategy and were inextricably linked to the confidential legal advice rendered by her attorney. Letters (or emails) sent by clients to counsel as "courtesy copies" (a.k.a. cc's) to make sure the attorney has the information contained in them are not protected by confidentiality rules. These letters are "not sent or received for purpose of giving or receiving legal advice" but are sent merely for informational purposes. *See Isom v. Bank of America, N.A.*, 628 S.E.2d 458, 462 (N.C. App. 2006). "[A] document, which is not privileged in the hands of the client, will not be imbued with the privilege merely because the document is handed over to the attorney." *Id.*, citing *Mason C. Day Excavating, Inc., v. Lumbermens Mut. Cas. Co.*, 143 F.R.D. 601, 607 (M.D.N.C. 1992) (internal citations omitted).

Information that may have been intended by its creator to be confidential may not be actually protected by attorney-client confidentiality rules. The court must strike a balance between the sanctity of confidentiality and judicial search for the truth. The court will generally uphold the confidentiality of information, but only if it satisfies the prerequisites for this protection. (See the four conditions set forth in *State v. von Bulow* at the beginning of this chapter.) Information that is not communicated between attorney and client for the purpose of legal representation or seeking legal advice is not covered, despite the intention of the party. *See Cangelosi v. Capasso*, 851 N.E. 2d 954 (Ill. App. 2d. Dist. 2006), wherein a nurse took notes regarding her patient for her own use. She intended that they would be confidential and kept them secret for two years at which time she gave them to an attorney representing that former patient, who was bringing a medical malpractice action. Those notes contained the nurse's factual observations of what she saw and heard during treatment. The notes, although intended to be confidential by their creator, the nurse, were not protected by attorney-client privilege, because the nurse had no relationship with an attorney at the time of their creation and was not preparing the documents for a pending lawsuit, although she suspected that an action could be brought against the doctor.

Physical evidence of a crime is not protected by the privilege. It is impermissible for an officer of the court to fail to turn over relevant physical evidence of a crime.

The attorney should not be a depository for criminal evidence (such as a knife, other weapons, stolen property, etc.), which in itself has little, if any, material value for the purposes of aiding counsel in the preparation of the defense of his client's case. Such evidence given to the attorney during legal consultation for information purposes and used by the attorney in preparing the defense of his client's case, whether or not the case ever goes to trial, could clearly be withheld for a reasonable period of time. It follows that the attorney, after a reasonable period, should, as an officer of the court, on his own motion turn the same over to the prosecution.

> We think the attorney-client privilege should and can be preserved even though the attorney surrenders the evidence he has in his possession. The prosecution, upon receipt of such evidence from an attorney, where charge against the attorney's client is contemplated (presently or in the future), should be well aware of the existence of the attorney-client privilege. Therefore, the state, when attempting to introduce such evidence at the trial, should take extreme precautions to make certain that the source of the evidence is not disclosed in the presence of the jury and prejudicial error is not committed. By thus allowing the prosecution to recover such evidence, the public interest is served, and by refusing the prosecution an opportunity to disclose the source of the evidence, the client's privilege is preserved and a balance is reached between these conflicting interests. The burden of introducing such evidence at a trial would continue to be upon the prosecution.

Sowers v. Olwell, 394 P.2d 681, 684-685 (Wash. 1964).

Again, the court performs a balancing act between the rights of the defendant and the needs of the justice system. After all, the real goal of the law is to ensure fairness not only to the parties involved but also to society as a whole. These are generalized rules and precepts which require judicious application to specific facts in order to arrive at a fair outcome.

WORK PRODUCT RULE

In fairness, it is only right that a person gets to control that which she has worked on herself and is her own original product. She should not be required to share the fruits of her own labor. This is the guiding principle behind the **work product** rule. Materials prepared by attorneys and paralegals in connection with their client's representation in anticipation of litigation are protected as "work product," and this type of material is protected against disclosure. This is not "privileged information," because privilege refers to the client's ownership and the legal professional's fiduciary duty towards him; work product, rather, is independently immune from discovery, and that immunity is very rarely pierced. There are two types of "work product":

work product
An attorney's written notes, impressions, charts, diagrams, and other material used by him or her to prepare strategy and tactics for trial.

1. Mental impressions: These are the attorney's thoughts on how to conduct the litigation, including, but not limited to, trial strategies, theories of the case, and structured legal arguments.
2. Informational material: The underlying factual research material, witness interviews, internal legal memoranda, and similar means of compiling data (even the way a non-protected document was summarized or indexed) are protected, as they are the result of the way in which an attorney or paralegal thinks and approaches the case. The underlying facts are not protected, but the way they are organized and analyzed in these documents is protected.

Either type of work is the result of the attorney's brainpower, a compilation of information that has been sifted through the attorney's (or paralegal's) mind. The landmark case on this issue is *Hickman v. Taylor*, 329 U.S. 495, 67 S. Ct. 385, 91 L. Ed. 451 (1947). The United States Supreme Court acknowledged that an attorney's work product was not covered under the attorney-client privilege, yet it was equally protectable.

> Historically, a lawyer is an officer of the court and is bound to work for the advancement of justice while faithfully protecting the rightful interests of his clients. In performing his various duties, however, it is essential that a lawyer work with a certain degree of privacy, free from unnecessary intrusion by opposing parties and their counsel. Proper preparation of a client's case demands that he assemble information, sift what he considers to be the relevant from the irrelevant facts, prepare his legal theories and plan his strategy without undue and needless interference. That is the historical and the necessary way in which lawyers act within the framework of our system of jurisprudence to promote justice and to protect their clients'

interests. This work is reflected, of course, in interviews, statement, memoranda, correspondence, briefs, mental impressions, personal beliefs, and countless other tangible and intangible ways—aptly though roughly termed by the circuit court of appeals in this case as the "work product of the lawyer." Were such materials open to opposing counsel on mere demand, much of what is now put in writing would remain unwritten. An attorney's thoughts, heretofore inviolate, would not be his own.

Id. at 510-511.

The court in *Surf Drugs, Inc. v. Vermette*, 236 So. 2d 108, 112 (Fla. 1970), acknowledged that the concept of attorney work product is "incapable of precise definition" but that it included, generally, all those things that the attorney does not intend to offer into evidence, but rather creates for her own use in preparation for litigation. The *Surf* court listed other products of the attorney which could not be compelled to be disclosed:

> [the] personal views of the attorney as to how and when to present evidence, his evaluation of its relative importance, his knowledge of which witnesses will give certain testimony, personal notes and records as to witnesses, jurors, legal citations, proposed arguments, jury instructions, diagrams and charts he may refer to at trial for his convenience but not to be used as evidence.

Work product can be anything; its defining characteristics are that it is the result of the attorney's own thought process and that it will not be introduced as evidence to support his client's case.

PARALEGALS' DUTY TO MAINTAIN CONFIDENTIALITY

ABA Model Guideline 6 for the Utilization of Paralegal Services states that "[a] lawyer is responsible for taking reasonable measures to ensure that all client confidences are preserved by a paralegal." It is unquestionably necessary that a paralegal and every other employee of the attorney maintain the client's information as a secret. Recall the breadth of the duty of confidentiality: Nothing communicated between the attorney and the client may be revealed by the attorney without the permission of the client. It does not matter if the information is available from other sources. With regard to confidentiality, it matters only that the client has spoken to his legal representative in his capacity as such. This holds true for all the employees of the attorney, but has particular applicability to paralegals, as they are the employees most often exposed to client information. A paralegal's role on the legal team makes it essential that she know all the details of the matter; to perform her duties as a paralegal would be impossible without this level of exposure to potentially sensitive information. This may not be the case for other employees of the legal office, who are responsible for the business maintenance of the office, rather than the practice of law. Reflecting the importance of the preservation of client confidences, both NALA and NFPA have incorporated mandates of confidentiality into their standards of professional conduct for paralegals. See the Appendices for the complete text and commentary of these Codes.

How does a paralegal put these ideals into practice? A law firm should have well-established policies and procedures for dealing with such information. There are many ways of handling sensitive information: These may include, but are not limited to, keeping files in a secure location; marking or separating privileged information from the general files; proper storage and eventual destruction of closed files; use of security-enabled computers and systems; use of databases that are carefully constructed so that discoverable information is kept separate from confidential information using private areas for phone calls; and requiring confidentiality agreements with outside vendors. Paralegals are also prohibited from using "inside information" to their own gain. This may occur most frequently in mergers and acquisitions and stock information exchanges to which the paralegal is privy. The Colorado Bar Association produced a very helpful checklist so that legal professionals could perform a "self-test" evaluating the care taken in their office to protect client confidentiality. See Figure 4.4.

FIGURE 4.4 ▶
CONFIDENTIALITY
CHECKLIST

Clients depend on their lawyer to safeguard the information they provide. The Rules of Professional Conduct provide for only limited situations where this trust may be broken. Since trust is very difficult to reestablish once it has been broken, it is important that you take steps to ensure that every member of the firm does all they can to safeguard client information.

	Yes	No	N/A
Do all new employees sign a confidentiality form acknowledging they have discussed confidentiality with you, read the relevant Rules of Professional Conduct, and will not breach the confidentiality of any client during and after their association with the firm?			
Do we make sure no client files or other confidential materials are ever left in the reception area or other public access areas?			
While conferring in person with clients, do we avoid taking calls or otherwise talking with other clients so as to protect client identities and confidentialities?			
Are the fax machines and copiers located away from where non-firm persons may be able to see confidential materials?			
If we are in an office-sharing arrangement, have we discussed confidentiality with the landlord, other tenants and any employees who may be privy to confidential information (e.g., receptionist, word processor, etc.)?			

SPECIAL ISSUES WITH TECHNOLOGY

Technology can be both a boon to efficiency and the bane of the law office's existence. Electronic records and communications are at once transient and permanent. As society has become more familiar with technology, its use has skyrocketed; however, with comfort come complacency and carelessness. It is quite easy to hit a button on the computer keyboard and thereby create a confidentiality breach.

What are the specific threats to confidentiality posed by technology? The primary offenders are these:

1. **Cell phones and other wireless devices.** Conversations are easily intercepted as this technology relies on radio broadcast signals rather than land lines. Many people use them so frequently that they forget that they are in public, not in their private office.

2. **Email.** This mode of communication should generally not be used for sensitive information. If communication via email is necessary, after the client's consent to use this kind of communication is obtained the user should be sure it is encrypted. PDF files can be password protected; just be sure that the password is not transmitted in the same email as the document!

3. **"Metadata."** This is the invisible information contained in an electronic document that does not necessarily appear when the document is viewed or printed. It keeps information about the history and management of a document, how, by whom and when it was created, collected, accessed, and modified. This includes the file's name, location in a directory, file format, type, size, and permission or security information (who can read, run or write the data). Some of this may be particularly useful and incriminating, but it can be misleading, too, in that some documents may list the form's creator but not the author of a particular modification to it. This is important in tracing the authenticity and context of an electronic document. Sometimes the metadata can be inaccurate, as when a form document reflects the author as the person who created the template but who did not draft the document.

4. **Access from the "outside."** Passwords and "firewalls" are necessary with regard to computer access. Databases should be maintained in a way to prevent secure information from being "lifted."

5. **Teleconferences.** Skype, GoToMeeting, and other video communication platforms should be used only where the transmission is certain to reach the client, and no one else should have access to these accounts or passwords in order to log in. Further, these technologies permit the recording of the communication, and this feature should be disabled.

6. **Fax machines.** While fax machines have been relegated to "last resort" use as a means for transmission, there are still offices that may use this technology. Fax numbers that are dialed incorrectly and speed dial errors can result in the threat that the dialer may accidentally transfer confidential information to a third party. *See Beverly v. Reinert*, 239 Ill. App. 3d 91, 606 N.E.2d 621 (1992). Another interesting point with regard to fax

machines emerges in office-sharing situations. In a shared office, who is the recipient of the fax? *See* the ABA article "How to Protect Client Confidences in a Shared Office Suite" by Wells Anderson and Joseph M. Hartley of the Practice Management Section (Volume 19, Number 6, September 2002).

As technology increases, so will both the attorney's and the paralegal's vigilance in maintaining procedures to maintain client confidences. Convenience and ease of use makes electronic means more tempting to use than other, more traditional means of communication. However, traditional and, unfortunately, slower exchanges can be thought out and better controlled. It is perhaps the paralegal's most valuable contribution to the law office to manage the most efficient and protective way to handle these technological issues. Again, the Colorado Bar provides a helpful checklist for dealing with these special issues relating to confidentiality. See Figure 4.5.

FIGURE 4.5 ▶
TECHNOLOGY AND
CONFIDENTIALITY
CHECKLIST

Office technology is nothing more than the tools to best serve your clients. The challenge is to have the knowledge to use these tools fully. Indeed, it may soon be that a lawyer's professional competence will include the use of technology to benefit clients.

	Yes	No	N/A
Do all our lawyers and staff use computers?			
Do we use a networked (if applicable) calendar program?			
Is everyone trained to usefully use our software?			
Is the office locked every night to discourage theft?			
Do we use case management software?			
Do we use email with client permission?			
Is our e-mail marked "Confidential Privileged Communication"?			
Do we back up our data at least weekly?			
Do we attempt periodic "restores" of data (to check if it works)?			
Do we train new employees about our computer system?			
Do we use computer virus filters and a firewall?			
Does our voicemail tell callers to limit their message?			
Do we need a password to access data?			
Do we have confidentiality agreements for cleaning services, contract staff and computer maintenance vendors who have access to our computer systems?			

SURF'S UP

Find several (four or five) lawyer websites (any jurisdiction) wherein the visitor can pose a question to the lawyer or firm. What kind of information does the site seek to obtain? Are there any disclaimers regarding confidentiality or the attorney-client relationship? Compare the websites. Does one do a better job of protecting confidentiality of the submitted information than the others? How?

This issue was dealt with in the California State Bar Standing Committee on Professional Responsibility and Conduct in 2005. See the Case in Point at the end of the chapter to explore the issue further.

It is an onerous but important responsibility to maintain the confidences of the client in almost any and every situation. It is not just for the individual client that the rules of confidentiality exist; it is for the preservation of the integrity of the legal profession (either attorney or paralegal) itself. When the duty is excused, it must be for an imperative reason. It is vital that a paralegal understand the parameters of the duty in order to comply with the ethical obligations that are faced every day at work.

Summary

Attorneys have an absolute duty to maintain their clients' confidence and not reveal any information relating to the representation of the client. Further, "work product," the the mental impressions of the attorney or information gathered and formatted by the attorney or paralegal is also protected from disclosure. The attorney-client privilege is narrower in scope, in that it prevents disclosure only of information that is communicated between the attorney and client relating to the representation.

A client may waive the confidential or privileged nature of the information. An attorney may reveal confidential or privileged information without the client's consent only in limited circumstances:

1. To prevent death or substantial bodily harm to another

2. To prevent the client from committing a crime or fraud, including perjury

3. To prevent future substantial financial harm to another

4. To secure legal advice regarding compliance with the ethical rules

5. To defend against a malpractice claim

6. To comply with any other court order or law

An attorney may unintentionally disclose sensitive client information through a variety of ways and, depending on the means taken to rectify the exposure, there may be a waiver of the privilege. The means to correct the disclosure can include any of the following:

1. The degree of care taken by the disclosing party to avoid the disclosure

2. Extenuating circumstances

3. The number and significance of the accidental disclosures

4. The extent of the disclosure

5. The time between the disclosure and the attempts to rectify the situation

6. The overriding interests of justice that may be served by relieving a party of its error

The party on the receiving end of the inadvertent disclosure should, in the broader interest of fairness and justice:

1. Refrain from viewing the material as soon as he realizes that it is privileged information

2. Notify the sender about the disclosure

3. Follow the instructions regarding the return or destruction of documents or seek a resolution in court

There are some communications and documents that are not protected from disclosure to opposing parties. Documents that were in existence prior to the preparation for litigation are discoverable, as are communications solely of fact between attorney and client, unless they are inexorably linked to the giving of legal advice.

As a logical complement to the attorney's ethical duty of confidentiality and the client's right of privilege in those communications, the paralegal is held to the same standard of secrecy. As it is often the paralegal's role to deal with the technology that drives the law office, it is important that the paralegal understand the issues involved with its utilization and the preservation of confidential information.

Key Terms

Attorney-client privilege	Permitted disclosure
Confidences	Subornation of perjury
Duty of confidentiality	Unintentional disclosure
"Fishing expedition"	Unprotected communications
In camera inspection	Waiver of confidentiality
Perjury	Work product

Review Questions

MULTIPLE CHOICE

Choose the best answer(s) and please explain *why* you chose the answer(s).

1. The attorney-client privilege:
   a. Requires the attorney to keep all his client's secrets
   b. Attaches to all private work prepared by the attorney in preparation for litigation
   c. Restricts the attorney from speaking to anyone about his client's matters
   d. Is the same as the attorney's duty of confidentiality

2. If a client insists on taking the stand and the attorney thinks the client will commit perjury:
   a. The attorney can permit narrative testimony
   b. The attorney must withdraw from the case
   c. The client doesn't have to take an oath
   d. The attorney can use that testimony in her closing statement

3. In defense of a professional malpractice claim:
   a. An attorney can hand over all his files to the judge for an *in camera* inspection
   b. The attorney may not testify
   c. The attorney may disclose confidential information about the client
   d. The attorney may disclose confidential information that relates to the relationship and actions taken in the matter
   e. All of the above

EXPLAIN YOURSELF

All answers should be written in complete sentences. A simple yes or no is insufficient.

1. Describe the difference between the attorney's duty of confidentiality and the attorney-client privilege.

2. Explain the exceptions to the attorney's duty of confidentiality. When may an attorney divulge his client's secrets?

3. Explain the "crime-fraud" exception to the duty of confidentiality.

4. What should a paralegal do after receiving unintentionally disclosed confidential information from opposing counsel? What is the attorney ethically bound to do?

5. What is the work product rule? Does it apply to paralegals as well as to attorneys?

"FAULTY PHRASES"

All of the following statements are *false*. State why they are false and then rewrite each one as a true statement. Do not simply make the statement negative by adding the word "not."

1. The attorney-client privilege requires that the attorney not reveal any information about her client relating to her representation.

2. A person who overhears the attorney and client's conversations ruins the privilege, and that eavesdropper can testify as to the private conversation.

3. An attorney must be absolutely sure his client will commit a crime before he can reveal that information.

4. Opposing counsel can seek to obtain privileged documents, and the court must allow them to see the information if they have performed an *in camera* inspection of the materials.

5. Once confidential information is inadvertently disclosed, opposing counsel may use it in their case.

6. All communications between an attorney and a client are protected by the attorney-client privilege.

7. Electronic communications are not protected by either the rules of confidentiality or attorney-client privilege.

PORTFOLIO ASSIGNMENT

Write Away

Prepare an interoffice memorandum regarding the proper procedures for handling client communications. Be sure to address the various types of communications (both traditionally written and electronic) and what special considerations should be taken into account when dealing with them. As this memorandum will be circulated to all office personnel, be sure to explain why the method of handling the communications is so important under the ethical considerations.

Cases in Point

Issue: does a lawyer who provides electronic means on his web site for visitors to submit legal questions owe a duty of confidentiality to visitors who accept that offer but whom the lawyer elects not to accept as clients, if the attorney disclaims formation of an attorney-client relationship and a "confidential relationship"?
Formal Opinion Number 2005-168
2005

STATEMENT OF FACTS

Searching the Internet for law firms that specialize in divorce, Wife finds Law Firm's web site. The W site describes Law Firm's family law practice, lists the firm's California address, and notes that all of the firm's attorneys are licensed to practice exclusively in California and are available to represent any person who wishes to pursue or defend a divorce action in a California court. [FN omitted.] The web site contains a link entitled "What are my rights?" Wife clicks on that link and is taken to a new page, which contains an electronic form. At the top of the form appears the legend: "Wondering about a legal problem you have?" The form asks for the inquirer's name and her contact information, for a statement of facts related to the reader's legal problem, and for any questions the inquirer wishes to pose to Law Firm.

After typing in her contact information, Wife explained that she was interested in obtaining a divorce. She related that her Husband, a Vice-President at Ace Incorporated in Los Angeles, was cohabiting with a co-worker. She also stated that her 13-year-old son was living with her and asked if she could obtain sole custody of him. She noted that Husband was providing some support but that she had to take part-time work as a typist, and was thinking about being re-certified as a teacher. She revealed that she feared Husband would contest her right to sole custody of her son and that, many years ago, she had engaged in an extra-marital affair herself, about which Husband remained unaware. Wife stated that she wanted a lawyer who was a good negotiator, because she wanted to obtain a reasonable property settlement without jeopardizing her goal of obtaining sole custody of the child and keeping her own affair a secret. She concluded by noting she had some money saved from when she was a teacher, and stating, "I like your website and would like you to represent me."

Immediately below the text box in which Wife described her case was a list of "Terms," which stated:

Terms

- I understand and agree that I may receive a response to my inquiry from an attorney at Law Firm.
- I agree that by submitting this inquiry, I will not be charged for the initial response.
- I agree that I am not forming an attorney-client relationship by submitting this question. I also understand that I am not forming a confidential relationship.
- I further agree that I may only retain Law Firm or any of its attorneys as my attorney by entering into a written fee agreement, and that I am not hereby entering into a fee agreement. I understand that I will not be charged for the response to this inquiry.

Below the foregoing list of "Terms" are two buttons, one which reads "SUBMIT" and the other which reads "CANCEL," with the following statement:
By clicking the appropriate button below, I agree to:
SUBMIT my inquiry pursuant to the foregoing terms.
CANCEL my inquiry.

Wife clicked on the "SUBMIT" button; had she clicked "CANCEL," Law Firm's computer would have refused to accept her information.

Upon receiving Wife's inquiry, the law firm discovered that Husband had already retained Law Firm to explore the possibility of a divorce from Wife. The next day, an attorney in Law Firm sent Wife an e-mail, which stated:

We regret we will be unable to accept you as a client because there is a conflict with one of our present clients. Good luck with your case.

We address whether Law Firm may be precluded from representing Husband as a result of the firm's contact with Wife on the ground that Law Firm has obtained material confidential information.

DISCUSSION

A. Introduction

In California State Bar Formal Opn. No. 2003-161, we set forth an analytical framework for determining when a lawyer might be deemed to have entered into an attorney-client relationship, or otherwise have taken on a duty of confidentiality, when people ask a lawyer about a legal problem in a setting other than the lawyer's office. [. . .]

B. Must Law Firm Keep Confidential the Information Wife Transmitted?

As we noted in California State Bar Formal Opn. No. 2003-161, the attorney-client relationship, with all of the duties attendant upon that relationship—including confidentiality—"is created by contract, either express or implicd." [Citations omitted.] Law Firm never expressly agreed to enter into a client-lawyer relationship with Wife and, for the purposes of this opinion, we also assume that Law Firm did not form an implied-in-fact attorney-client relationship with Wife either. [Citations omitted.]

[. . .] Here, by providing the link that states, "What are my rights?" in combination with directions to submit facts that related to a legal problem she was "[w]ondering about," Law Firm has invited the consultation with Wife, and has done so for the purpose of considering whether to enter into an attorney-client relationship with the inquirer. [FN omitted.]

Law Firm has attempted to avoid taking on a duty of confidentiality by requiring each inquirer to agree that (1) by submitting a question, the inquirer is not forming an attorney-client relationship or a "confidential relationship"; and (2) whatever response Law Firm provides will not constitute legal advice but, rather, "general information." To assess whether Wife's agreement to these terms prevented Law Firm from taking on a duty of confidentiality, we apply the "reasonable belief" test we set forth in California State Bar Formal Opn. No. 2003-161: "If the attorney's conduct, in light of the surrounding circumstances, implies a willingness to be consulted, then the speaker may be found to have a reasonable belief that he is consulting the attorney in the attorney's professional capacity." We do not believe that a prospective client's agreement to Law Firm's terms prevented a duty of confidentiality from arising on the facts before us, because Law Firm's disclosures to Wife were not adequate to defeat her reasonable belief that she was consulting Law Firm for the purpose of retaining Law Firm.

[. . .] As we explained earlier, and elaborated fully in California State Bar Formal Opn. No. 2003-161, a lawyer can owe a duty of confidentiality to a prospective client who consults the lawyer in confidence for the purpose of retaining the lawyer. Thus, that an attorney-client relationship did not arise from Wife's consultation with Law Firm did not prevent Law Firm from taking on a duty of confidentiality to Wife. [FN omitted.]

Second, Wife's agreement that she would not be forming a "confidential relationship" does not, in our view, mean that Wife could not still have a reasonable belief that Law Firm would keep her information confidential. [. . .] Without ruling out other possibilities, we note that had Wife agreed to the following, she would have had, in our opinion, no reasonable expectation of confidentiality with Law Firm: "I understand and agree that Law Firm will have no duty to keep confidential the information I am now transmitting to Law Firm." [FN omitted.]

Another way in which Law Firm could have proceeded that would have avoided the confidentiality issue entirely would have been to request from web site visitors only that information that would allow the firm to perform a conflicts check. For example, under the facts presented, Law Firm would first want to ensure that it does not represent the other spouse. Law Firm could explain that it is seeking the information to determine whether representing the visitor might create a conflict with one of its present clients, preventing it from representing the visitor. Law Firm could request that the inquirer provide relevant information such as the names of the parties, children, former spouses, etc., and, given the subject area, any relevant maiden names. [. . .]

In the situation presented, however, Law Firm chose neither to make a plain-language reference to the non-confidential nature of communications submitted to its web site, nor to first screen visitors for potential conflicts with its existing clients. Having taken the course it did, Law Firm may be disqualified from representing Husband should the court conclude that the information Wife submitted was material to the resolution of the dissolution action. [FN omitted.]

CONCLUSION

A lawyer may avoid incurring a duty of confidentiality to persons who seek legal services by visiting the lawyer's web site and disclose confidential information only if the lawyer's web site contains a statement in sufficiently plain language that any information submitted at the web site will not be confidential.

This opinion is issued by the Standing Committee on Professional Responsibility and Conduct of the State Bar of California. It is advisory only. It is not binding upon the courts, the State Bar of California, its Board of Governors, any persons or tribunals charged with regulatory responsibility or any member of the State Bar.

Source: Reprinted from Westlaw with permission from Thomson Reuters.

UNPUBLISHED OPINION. CHECK COURT RULES BEFORE CITING.

Court of Appeals of Michigan.
CHRYSLER CORPORATION, Plaintiff-Appellant,
v.
Paul V. SHERIDAN, Defendant-Appellee.
No. 227511.
July 10, 2001.

Before: WHITE, P.J., and WILDER and ZAHRA, JJ.
PER CURIAM.

Plaintiff appeals by leave granted the circuit court's order denying plaintiff's motion for return of a privileged document. We reverse.

FACTS

Plaintiff filed this suit on December 27, 1994, claiming defendant wrongfully disclosed its trade secrets. A preliminary injunction was entered in 1996, prohibiting defendant from disclosing plaintiff's confidential, proprietary information. On February 23, 2000, the trial court dissolved that injunction. Soon thereafter, plaintiff learned of an affidavit defendant submitted in connection with a separate suit filed in Texas. Plaintiff

claimed the substance of that affidavit referred to confidential information that plaintiff had not previously disclosed. On March 8, 2000, plaintiff filed a motion and brief for reconsideration of the court's decision to dissolve the injunction. Plaintiff specifically identified and attached to the brief three exhibits: Exhibit A was a copy of the trial court's February 23, 2000 opinion and order dissolving the preliminary injunction; Exhibit B was a copy of defendant's twenty-one-page affidavit filed in the Texas case; and Exhibit C was a copy of the trial court's March 27, 1996 opinion granting a preliminary injunction. Defendant's affidavit was attached to plaintiff's brief as Exhibit D, and behind defendant's affidavit was a copy of a two-page e-mail written by plaintiff's lead national trial counsel, David Tyrrell. The e-mail was not identified as a separate exhibit and was not referenced in defendant's affidavit, plaintiff's motion for reconsideration or the brief supporting plaintiff's motion for reconsideration.

On March 23, 2000, plaintiff filed an emergency motion for return of the document and for a temporary restraining order, alleging that the e-mail was subject to the attorney-client privilege and that it had been inadvertently attached to the affidavit. Plaintiff requested that the court enter an order stating that no privilege had been waived and that defendant be ordered to return all copies of the document and to refrain from further dissemination and disclosure of the document. After a hearing on the issue, the trial court ruled the e-mail is not privileged and denied plaintiff's motion for its return. In a short opinion and order denying plaintiff's motion for return of any copies of the e-mail, the court stated, in pertinent part:

Here, the document is not marked confidential or privileged. The unrelated attorney who first forwarded the document did not mark it confidential. The in-house counsel of the client forwarded the document without marking it confidential. When received by the court and defense counsel, the document was not marked confidential. Rather, it appears related to the arguments in the motion to which it was attached. When received by Defendant's counsel, the document was further distributed around the country. Assuming the document was subject to privilege and its attachment to the exhibit was an inadvertent error, there was little to notify the recipients that the document may be subject to a privilege. As such, this court finds that the document is not now subject to a privilege and Plaintiff's motion for return of privileged document and restraining order is denied.

The instant appeal followed.

ANALYSIS

A. Standard of Review

The sole issue before us is whether the trial court erred in determining the e-mail document is not subject to the attorney-client privilege. Whether the lower court properly construed the privilege is a legal question we review de novo. *Reed Dairy*

Farm v. Consumers Power Company, 227 Mich. App. 614, 618; 576 N.W.2d 709 (1998). If the lower court properly construed the privilege, application of the privilege to the facts of the case is reviewed for an abuse of discretion. *Franzel v. Kerr Mfg.,* 234 Mich. App. 600, 614; 600 N.W.2d 66 (1999). An abuse of discretion may be found if we conclude that an unprejudiced person reviewing the facts and law would find no justification or excuse for the trial court's ruling. *Id.* at 617.

B. Common Law Privilege and Waiver

The common law attorney-client privilege attaches to direct communications between a client and his attorney and communications made through their respective agents. *Reed Dairy Farm, supra.* Where the client is an organization, the privilege extends to communications between attorneys and agents or employees of the organization authorized to speak on its behalf in regard to the subject matter of the communication. *Id.* at 619.

Although a communication is subject to the attorney-client privilege, that privilege may be waived. *Franzel, supra* at 616; *Sterling v. Keidan,* 162 Mich. App. 88, 91-92; 412 N.W.2d 255 (1987). In *Franzel,* this Court clarified the following with respect to waiver of the attorney-client privilege:

(1) The attorney-client privilege has a dual nature, i.e., it includes both the security against publication and the right to control the introduction into evidence of such information or knowledge communicated to or possessed by the attorney; (2) This dual nature of the privilege applies where there has been inadvertent disclosure of privileged material; (3) An implied waiver of the privilege must be judged by standards as stringent as for a "true waiver," before the right to control the introduction of privileged matter into evidence will be destroyed, even though the inadvertent disclosure has eliminated any security against publication; (4) A "true waiver" requires "'an intentional, voluntary act and cannot arise by implication,'" or "'the voluntary relinquishment of a known right'"; and (5) Error of judgment where the person knows that privileged information is being released but concludes that the privilege will nevertheless survive will destroy

any privilege. [*Franzel, supra* at 613-614, citing *Sterling, supra* (internal citations omitted).]

Thus, regardless whether a party is charged with an intentional or implied waiver of the attorney-client privilege, there can be no waiver without an intentional, voluntary act. Inadvertent disclosure of a privileged communication does not constitute a waiver. *Id.*

C. The E-Mail was Privileged and Production of it did not Constitute a Waiver of the Privilege

Proper analysis of this issue requires us first to examine whether the e-mail is protected under the attorney-client privilege. If that question is answered in the affirmative, we must then consider whether the privilege was waived when the copy of the e-mail was attached to plaintiff's motion and brief for reconsideration. It is undisputed the e-mail was drafted by a member of plaintiff's national legal counsel. While neither the e-mail itself nor its copies were expressly marked "confidential" or "privileged," the undisputed facts establish it was distributed to members of plaintiff's legal counsel in confidence. Defendant does not claim Tyrrell sent the e-mail to anyone other than plaintiff's agents or counsel. Nor is there evidence that plaintiff's in-house counsel sent the document to any party other than plaintiff's trial counsel in the present case. The e-mail was specifically addressed to plaintiff's in-house counsel and contains Tyrrell's candid impressions of defendant's suspected knowledge of various issues. It also contains Tyrrell's opinions, conclusions and recommendations in regard to defendant's affidavit and defendant's qualifications as a witness against plaintiff. Under these circumstances, we conclude the e-mail was intended as a confidential communication between plaintiff's agents and counsel pertaining to on-going and future litigation, and is subject to the attorney-client privilege. *Reed Dairy Farm, supra* at 618-619.

We conclude as a matter of law that the production of the e-mail was inadvertent and neither plaintiff nor its counsel waived the privilege by this inadvertent production. Plaintiff's trial counsel in the present case submitted a detailed affidavit below, asserting the e-mail was inadvertently attached to the motion.

The attorney who signed the motion for reconsideration appeared in court on the hearing date prepared to testify that the e-mail was inadvertently attached to the motion for reconsideration, and to submit to cross-examination by defendant and examination by the court. Defendant did not examine the attorney and did not present any evidence to dispute these assertions. Instead, defendant argued that the privilege does not apply or was waived because the e-mail related to the motion for reconsideration. The trial court appears to have accepted defendant's argument, at least in part, as it concluded that the e-mail related to the contents of plaintiff's motion for reconsideration. The trial court abused its discretion in reaching this conclusion.

The content of the e-mail reflects the opinions and factual assertions of plaintiff's counsel in the Texas litigation. The e-mail is not presented in the form of an affidavit. This document, as attached to the motion for reconsideration, is of no evidentiary value to a court. It is not documentary evidence of any kind. Had plaintiff intended to present the opinions or factual assertions of Texas counsel as evidence to support its motion for reconsideration, such information would have been offered by way of an affidavit. Moreover, each of the marked exhibits offered in support of the motion for reconsideration is specifically referenced in the brief supporting the motion. Significantly, the e-mail, which was not marked as an exhibit to the motion, is not referenced anywhere in the motion, the brief or the exhibits supporting the motion. In sum, we conclude that an unbiased person viewing all of the facts presented would not be justified in concluding that the e-mail was intentionally attached to support the motion for reconsideration. The facts and circumstances presented below do not support the conclusion that plaintiff or its counsel no longer intended to maintain the document's confidentiality. *Sterling, supra* at 96. Plaintiff's counsel's inadvertent disclosure of the e-mail did not constitute a waiver of the attorney-client privilege that attached to the document. *Franzel, supra; Sterling, supra.*

We also are not persuaded that the absence of a statement in the e-mail notifying recipients of its confidential or privileged nature defeats the privilege or constitutes a waiver. No authority requires that a document be expressly marked confidential or privileged in order for it to be subject to the attorney-client privilege. As discussed *supra,* the e-mail was a confidential communication between plaintiff's counsel and agents involving legal issues and was subject to the attorney-client privilege. Plaintiff's counsel's inadvertent disclosure of the document did not constitute a waiver of the privilege.

CONCLUSION

Accordingly, we hold that the trial court abused its discretion in denying plaintiff's request for an order declaring that the privilege was not waived.

Reversed.

Source: Reprinted from Westlaw with permission from Thomson Reuters.

**United States District Court,
D. Kansas.
David BURTON, Plaintiff,
v.
R.J. REYNOLDS TOBACCO CO. and The American Tobacco Co., Defendants.
No. 94-2202-JWL.
May 1, 1996.
*MEMORANDUM AND ORDER***

LUNGSTRUM, District Judge.

I. INTRODUCTION

[. . .]

II. FACTS

The Tobacco Industry Research Committee ("TIRC") was formed in 1954 by members of the tobacco industry, including the defendants, to provide funding for research on the effects of tobacco use. In 1958, the TIRC changed its name to the CTR. The CTR's Scientific Advisory Board ("SAB"), which is composed of scientists, reviews grant proposals and provides funding to research projects they deem worthy. Between 1965 and 1990, the CTR began conducting its own scientific projects separate from the SAB's grant program under the name special projects.

On September 9, 1995, the plaintiff served the defendants with its Third Request for Documents. Request No. 1 sought all documents relating to the CTR special projects division or program. In their response dated October 11, 1995, the defendants objected to this request because it sought privileged or protected documents and because it sought documents relating to subjects other than those matters

at issue here, peripheral vascular disease and the alleged addictive nature of cigarettes. Subject to their objections, both defendants produced what they believe are non-privileged CTR Documents in their possession relating to the conditions they believe are at issue in this case. Defendant American did not withhold any documents because it believes that it does not possess any relevant, privileged CTR documents. Defendant Reynolds provided the plaintiff with a log indicating that it believes 24 CTR Documents were privileged and that nine CTR Documents were partially privileged. Defendant Reynolds provided the plaintiff with redacted copies of the nine allegedly partially privileged Documents. [. . .] Defendant Reynolds represents that these Documents are privileged because they consist of communications between Reynolds and its counsel, communications between its counsel and counsel for other tobacco companies, and internal company communications reflecting privileged information. On March 1, 1996, the plaintiff filed a motion to compel the defendants to produce the CTR Documents relevant to his claims. The plaintiff asserts that the impetus for its motion to compel arose from admissions made by another tobacco company's lawyer during a hearing in a separate case. [. . .]

III. DISCUSSION

A. Motion to Compel

1. Timeliness of Plaintiff's Motion

Defendant Reynolds opposes the plaintiff's motion on procedural as well as substantive grounds. In this case's Scheduling Order dated September 26, 1994, the court stated that

"Motions to compel discovery with accompanying memoranda and in compliance with D. Kan. Rule 206 and 219 shall be filed and served within 30 days of the default or service of response, answer, or objection which is the subject of the motions, unless the time for the filing of such motions is extended for good cause shown, or the objection to the default, response, answer, or objection shall be waived."

Without question, the plaintiff's motion to compel is out of time under that order, and Defendant Reynolds asks that it be denied on that basis.

The district court has wide discretion in its regulation of pretrial matters. [citations omitted] Although the plaintiff's motion to compel is clearly beyond the 30 day limit prescribed in the Scheduling Order, the court concludes that it should exercise its discretion in this instance, in the interests of justice, to permit the plaintiff to bring this motion. The litigation here involves a still evolving area of the law and the plaintiff raises serious substantive legal issues which the court is extremely reluctant to truncate based solely on its own procedural requirement designed primarily to expedite the orderly progress of garden variety lawsuits. Moreover, the court has been provided no showing that the defendants would be prejudiced by the plaintiff's delay and, in the event the plaintiff's allegations of fraud concerning the CTR Documents should have merit, the likelihood that the discovery would lead to relevant evidence is high. Thus, the plaintiff's motion to compel shall not be deemed to be time barred.

[. . .]

2. Relevance

The next hurdle for the plaintiff to clear is a showing that the material he seeks is relevant. The plaintiff's claims are based on his assertions that the defendants knew and had a duty to disclose to the public that the nicotine in their cigarettes was addictive, that the defendants knew and had a duty to disclose to the public that their cigarettes are a vasoconstrictor, and that the defendants knew and had a duty to disclose to the public that their cigarettes contributed to the development of peripheral vascular diseases including atherosclerotic peripheral arterial occlusive. Thus, the relevance analysis must focus on whether the information sought bears on whether the defendants knew during the relevant time period what the plaintiff alleges they knew.

The court believes that the 33 CTR Documents withheld by Defendant Reynolds would be relevant to this case to the extent the plaintiff could link the documents to a showing that the Defendant Reynolds knew during the relevant time period that nicotine is addictive, that its cigarettes are a vasoconstrictor, or that its cigarettes caused peripheral vascular diseases. [Citation omitted.] By contrast, Defendant American has not withheld any documents as privileged because it claims that it does not possess any CTR Documents which are relevant to the plaintiff's claim. Because the plaintiff has failed to show that Defendant American does possess CTR Documents relevant to his claims, the court denies the plaintiff's motion to compel with respect to Defendant American. [. . .]

The defendants argue that even if they had disclosed the information the plaintiff alleges they had in their possession, the plaintiff would have continued to smoke cigarettes because by 1952 the plaintiff was, in his mind, addicted to the nicotine contained in the defendants' cigarettes and, therefore, could not stop regardless of what information the defendants disclosed. The court disagrees. It may be one thing to recognize retrospectively, as the plaintiff claims, that he was addicted and thus was powerless to quit smoking based on warnings that tobacco use could be harmful to his health. It is quite something different to have been denied, as plaintiff also claims, the information that nicotine truly is addictive, thus depriving him of the impetus to seek professional assistance to overcome his dilemma. Had the defendants disclosed the information the plaintiff alleges the defendants had in their possession, the court believes that a reasonable jury could credit the proposition that the plaintiff, upon realizing that nicotine was addictive and that he had a high likelihood of contracting peripheral vascular disease from smoking, would, more likely than not, have sought medical attention to help him break his nicotine addiction.

Thus, the plaintiff's motion to compel does not fail on relevance grounds.

3. Privileges

a. Choice of Law

[. . .]

b. Attachment of Privilege

Under Kansas law, the attorney client privilege protects communications found by the judge to have been between a lawyer and his or her client in the course of that relationship and in professional confidence. K.S.A. § 60-426(a). The defendants contend that the CTR Documents are protected by the attorney client privilege because they involve communications between themselves and their lawyers in the course of their legal relationship and in professional confidence.

In order to be protected by work product immunity, the party asserting the privilege must show (1) that the material is a document or tangible thing, (2) that the material was prepared in anticipation of litigation, and (3) that the material was prepared by or for a party or by or for the party's representative. *Jones v. Boeing Co.,* 163 F.R.D. 15, 17 (D. Kan. 1995). The defendants contend that the CTR Documents are protected by the work product doctrine because they were prepared in anticipation of litigation.

Under Kansas law, the disclosure of privileged information by an attorney to counsel of actual or potential co-defendants does not constitute a waiver of the attorney client privilege based on the joint defense exception to the general rule that no privilege attaches to communications made in the presence of third parties. *State v. Maxwell,* 10 Kan. App. 2d 62, 66, 691 P.2d 1316 (1984). The joint defense privilege encompasses shared communications to the extent that they concern common issues and are intended to facilitate representation in possible subsequent proceedings. *Id.* It is also essential that the co-defendants have exchanged the information in confidence, "not . . . for the purpose of allowing unlimited publication and use, but rather . . . for the limited purpose of assisting in their common cause." *Id.* The defendants contend that the CTR Documents are protected by the joint defense privilege.

The plaintiff argues that none of these theories shield the communications from disclosure because the involvement with the CTR Documents by counsel was not in a legal capacity. However, the court finds no support in the plaintiff's submissions for that conclusion. Moreover, based upon the evidence available at this time, the court rejects the plaintiff's sweeping conclusory argument that lawyers and science simply do not mix. As a result, the court concludes that the defendants have made the necessary showing to assert the attorney client privilege, work product immunity, and the joint defense privilege concerning the CTR Documents. *Jones,* 163 F.R.D. at 16-17; K.S.A. § 60-426(a); *Maxwell,* 10 Kan. App. 2d at 66.

[. . .]

c. Waiver

Intentional disclosure to third parties of privileged information is a waiver of any privilege. *See Monarch Cement Co. v. Lone Star Indus., Inc.,* 132 F.R.D. 558 (D. Kan. 1990). The plaintiff contends that the defendants waived any privileges or immunities from disclosure which might have attached to the CTR Documents when they intentionally and knowingly chose to funnel them through the CTR, a third party committed to public disclosure. The defendants argue that the plaintiff has produced no evidence indicating that the CTR Documents were disclosed to CTR employees and have argued that the alleged funneling through the CTR does not constitute a waiver of any asserted privileges because disclosing the CTR Documents to the CTR employees did not make it substantially more likely that the CTR Documents would be disclosed to an adversary. [. . .] The court agrees with the defendants that, based upon the submissions of the parties, the plaintiff has not met his burden of showing that the defendants waived any privileges.

4. Crime-Fraud Exception—in Camera Review

a. Standard

During the court's telephone hearing on the plaintiff's motion to compel, plaintiff's counsel took the position that his strongest argument to obtain discovery of the CTR Documents is the so-called crime-fraud exception to the doctrines which otherwise would protect the confidentiality of certain legal communications. The crime-fraud exception's purpose is to assure that the seal of secrecy between lawyer and client does not extend to communications made for the purpose of getting advice for the commission of a fraud or crime. *United States v. Zolin,* 491 U.S. 554, 563, 109 S. Ct. 2619, 2626, 105 L. Ed. 2d 469 (1989). Under Kansas law, the attorney client privilege does not extend to communications regarding legal services "sought or obtained in order to enable or aid the commission or planning of a crime or tort." K.S.A. § 60-426(b)(1); *Aguinaga v. John Morrell & Co.,* 112 F.R.D. 671, 682 (D. Kan. 1986). Tenth Circuit law concerning work product is to the same effect. *See In re Vargas,* 723 F.2d 1461 (10th Cir. 1983). While the plaintiff must only make a prima facie showing that a crime or fraud has been perpetrated, the plaintiff may not use as evidence of the crime or fraud the very documents which are sought in discovery. *Aguinaga,* 112 F.R.D. at 682 (citing *In Re A.H. Robins Co., Inc.,* 107 F.R.D. 2, 9 (D. Kan. 1985)). [. . .]

The Kansas Supreme Court has recently addressed this issue in *Wallace Saunders Austin Brown & Enochs, Chartered, v. Louisburg Grain Co.,* 250 Kan. 54, 824 P.2d 933 (1992). That case involved a law firm suing its former client for payment of its legal fees. After the former client confessed judgment, the law firm attempted to execute its judgment on the former client's real estate located in Miami County, Kansas. After receiving a notice of sale from the law firm, the former client's judgment creditors filed a motion to set aside the law firm's writ of execution and deny the law firm's order for sale. Based on the judgment creditors' argument that the law firm's action constituted a collusive and improper attempt to defraud the former client's judgment creditors, the trial court set aside the law firm's writ of execution and set the matter for trial. *Id.* at 57, 824 P.2d 933. After the law firm refused to produce certain documents involving communications between the law firm and the former client based on the attorney client privilege, the judgment creditors filed a motion to compel the production of those documents based on their allegation that the law firm's suit for attorney fees was fraudulent and, therefore, the crime-fraud exception to the attorney client privilege applied. The Kansas Supreme Court stated that the crime-fraud exception requires that the moving party present a prima facie case to overcome the attorney client privilege. *Id.* at 61, 824 P.2d 933. A prima facie case requires "evidence which, if left unexplained or uncontradicted, would be sufficient to carry the case to the jury and sustain a verdict in favor of the plaintiff on the issue it supports." *Id.*

Although Kansas courts have enunciated the requisite burden for the party seeking the application of the crime-fraud exception, no Kansas court has addressed whether the requisite burden for a party seeking an in camera review based on the crime-fraud exception of allegedly privileged documents is any different. In 1989, the United States Supreme Court held, under federal law, that a district court may conduct an in camera review to determine the applicability of the crime-fraud exception if the party requesting such a review makes a showing of a factual basis adequate to support a good faith belief by a reasonable person that in camera review of the documents may reveal evidence to establish that the crime-fraud exception applies. *United States v. Zolin,* 491 U.S. 554, 572, 575-76, 109 S. Ct. 2619, 2632, 2632, 105 L. Ed. 2d 469 (1989); *see also Motley v. Marathon Oil Co.,* 71 F.3d 1547, 1551 (10th Cir. 1995). This evidentiary standard requires less than what is required ultimately to overcome the privilege. *Id.* at 572, 109 S. Ct. at 2632. [. . .]

There is a substantial conflict between the *Wallace Saunders* decision and the *Zolin* decision which must be confronted in attempting to determine whether Kansas would adopt the *Zolin*-like relaxed standard for in camera review. The *Wallace Saunders* decision does not permit the moving party to use the documents sought pursuant to the crime-fraud exception to help make the necessary prima facie case. By contrast, *Zolin* permits the moving party to use the documents sought pursuant to the crime-fraud exception to prove the crime-fraud exception after the moving party has made the necessary threshold showing and after the court has conducted an in camera review of the allegedly privilege documents and determined on its own that the documents evidence a basis for application of the crime-fraud exception. The *Wallace Saunders* limitation is grounded in the very words of the statutory privilege: . . . "Such privileges shall not extend (1) to a communication if the judge finds that sufficient evidence, *aside from the communication,* has been introduced to warrant a finding that the legal service was sought or obtained in order to enable or aid the commission or planning of a crime or a tort. . . .'' K.S.A. § 60-426(b)(1) (emphasis added). *Zolin,* by contrast, is rooted in federal common law and is not restricted by a comparable legislative pronouncement. Thus, there is no basis to conclude that the Kansas Supreme Court would adopt a more relaxed standard, like *Zolin.* If the disputed communications cannot be considered in determining whether the exception to the privilege applies and the decision rests on the application of the *Wallace Saunders* prima facie case test to the other existing evidence, then the purpose of an in camera review is not to help satisfy the burden of establishing the exception but, rather, to help determine whether the documents meet the substance of what the party seeking them has averred and whether they are, thus, subject to production as a result. Therefore, the court has applied the *Wallace Saunders* standard, not the relaxed *Zolin* standard, to determine whether the prima facie test has been met and to determine whether or not an in camera review should be ordered. [. . .]

b. Evidence

The plaintiff argues that lawyers for tobacco companies, including the defendants, were used to facilitate the perpetration of a continuing fraud. Specifically, the plaintiff contends that the lawyers for the tobacco companies used the CTR to deceive the public about the health risks associated with smoking. The plaintiff requests that the court review the CTR Documents in camera to determine whether they evidence this deception. In support of its in camera review argument, the plaintiff points to the following evidence: excerpts from the U.S. Food and Drug Administration ("FDA") Special Supplement titled "Nicotine in Cigarettes and Smokeless Tobacco Products is a Drug and These Products are Nicotine Delivery Devices under the Federal Food, Drug, and Cosmetic Act"; two articles published in the Journal of the American Medical Association ("JAMA") entitled "Lawyer Control of the Tobacco Industry's External Research Program," and "Lawyer Control of Internal Scientific Research to Protect Against Products Liability Lawsuits"; a statement from the TIRC entitled "A Frank Statement to the Public by the Makers of Cigarettes"; three letters/memos from Mr. Earnest Pepples, the former vice president and general counsel of the Brown & Williamson Tobacco Company; and the notes from a meeting of the tobacco companies' general counsels. [. . .]

The defendants object to these documents based on hearsay, authenticity, and relevance grounds, among others.

The court rejects the hearsay and authenticity arguments because under Federal Rule of Evidence 104(a), it is not bound by the rules of evidence on those subjects in determining the existence of a privilege and because it is sufficiently satisfied with the reliability of the proffered FDA, JAMA, and TIRC evidence to conclude that those items of evidence should be considered for this purpose. Those documents are also relevant to the plaintiff's claims.

The defendants also contend that any evidence not lawfully obtained cannot be used by the plaintiff to make his threshold showing for an in camera review. *Zolin,* 491 U.S. at 574, 109 S. Ct. at 2632. The defendants argue that the court should not consider the documents stolen from the Brown & Williamson Tobacco Company, which consist of three letters/memos from Mr. Earnest Pepples and the notes from a meeting of the tobacco companies' general counsels. Although *Zolin* is less than clear concerning the scope of the restriction which it articulates, and although there is no allegation that anyone associated with this plaintiff stole the documents, the court has determined not to consider them here because there is ample evidence to support the plaintiff's position without reference to the purloined documents.

[. . .]

The TIRC's Frank Statement essentially states that the members of the TIRC, which includes the defendants, do not believe that their tobacco products are injurious to the public health and that the TIRC will aid and assist in the research effort concerning all areas of tobacco use and health. The excerpts from the FDA Special Supplement discuss tobacco industry documents which the FDA contends reveal that nicotine is a drug, that consumers of tobacco products smoke cigarettes for the pharmacological effects of nicotine, that nicotine creates physical dependency, that nicotine has addictive properties and that tobacco company researchers and top officials are aware of and understand these facts.

The court believes that the plaintiff has carried his burden to make out a prima facie case of fraud based on the Frank Statement and the excerpts from the FDA's Special Supplement. The Frank Statement clearly indicates that the TIRC/CTR was created to research and disclose to the public the effects of tobacco use on people's health. The excerpts from the FDA's Special Supplement give rise to the inference that the members of the CTR knew during relevant time periods that nicotine was addictive and did not disclose that information to the public, which is in direct conflict with the Frank Statement. Moreover, the members of the CTR's silence on the issue of nicotine being addictive raises the inference, based on the Frank Statement, that the tobacco companies believed that nicotine was not addictive. In other words, this is evidence which, left unexplained or uncontradicted, would be sufficient to support the conclusion that the members of the CTR chose not to disclose information about nicotine being addictive to deliberately mislead the public about the effects of tobacco use. *Wallace Saunders Austin Brown &*

Enochs, Chartered v. Louisburg Grain Co., 250 Kan. 54, 824 P.2d 933 (1992). As a result, the court deems it necessary to conduct an in camera review of Defendant Reynolds' 33 allegedly privileged CTR Documents to determine whether any of them indicate that the defendants knew during the relevant time period that nicotine was addictive and failed to disclose that information despite the CTR's public representation that it would make such disclosures to the public. The motion to compel (Doc. # 214) is retained under advisement to that extent and is referred to United States Magistrate Judge Ronald C. Newman to conduct the review and rule on whether any of the documents are to be produced.

[. . .]

Source: Reprinted from Westlaw with permission from Thomson Reuters.

Chapter 5

Conflicts of Interest

Chapter Objectives

The student will be able to:

- Discuss the reasons for conflict rules in attorney-client relationships
- Analyze whether a conflict exists between clients, either current or former
- Explain the prohibited transactions between attorneys and clients in which the conflict is automatically assumed
- Acknowledge an "appearance of impropriety" in an attorney-client relationship even where an "official" conflict is lacking
- Discern between those conflict situations where waiver is proper and permissible and those where it is not
- Discuss "imputed conflicts" and how and when these apply
- Determine whether an "ethical wall" can overcome a potential conflict and describe how one is constructed

This chapter will examine the maze of conflict rules in order to sort out *who* may or may not be taken on as a client and *what* constitutes a conflict of interest between both former and present clients and between attorneys and clients. If a potential conflict exists, the rules also explain *how* to avoid or deal with the situation.

conflict of interest
A clash between private and professional interests or competing professional interests that makes impartiality difficult and creates an unfair advantage.

The same principles that require legal professionals to keep all client confidences also require them to avoid all situations that may compromise these client secrets and to maintain trustworthiness and integrity in client representation. The conflict of interest rules are really an extension of the confidentiality rules. Because of the knowledge that attorneys and paralegals have about their past and present clients, they are prohibited from either representing another party whose interests are adverse to either the attorney's present or former clients or entering into certain personal, financial, or business relationships and transactions with those clients. The practical consequence of these rules is the attorney's obligation to refuse employment from potential clients whose representation would violate the rules of professional conduct. In some situations, the analysis of the rules' application to the potential representation is clear-cut; in others, the potential representation does not pose an immediate or obvious conflict, and the attorney must analyze the future possible impact of taking on the representation. Even when the actual circumstances do not lead to any negative consequence to either attorney or client, the mere appearance of impropriety may result in a violation of the rules' overarching concern about the preservation of the integrity of the legal profession. Clients must be able to trust that an attorney will look out for their individual best interests and have unwavering loyalty to them. Again, this rests directly on the cornerstone of the duty of confidentiality. The ABA Model Rules (and those state codes based upon them) are broken down by (1) type of client and (2) type of relationship involved:

- Rule 1.7 deals with conflicts between current and/or potential clients.
- Rule 1.8 deals with particular conflicts between the current client and a transaction with the attorney.
- Rule 1.9 deals with conflicts involving former clients and potential new clients.
- Rule 1.10 deals with an entire firm's inability to take on a client due to the "infection" from an attorney's individual conflict based upon one of the three preceding rules.
- Rule 1.11 deals with a particular circumstance: when a former government/public attorney reenters the private practice. Due to the scope of public practice, returning to the private sector would be all but impossible if not for the exceptions in this Rule.

NALA's Model Standards do not separately address conflicts of interest. Rather, in the Comment to Guideline 1, the avoidance of conflicts is the responsibility of the supervising attorney. It is imperative that the paralegal "take any and all steps necessary to prevent conflicts of interest and fully disclose such conflicts to the supervising attorney."

NFPA does directly address a paralegal's duty to avoid conflicts of interest and essentially parallels the ABA Model Rules in this regard. (See Figure 5.1.)

◄ **FIGURE 5.1**
AVOIDANCE OF
CONFLICTS OF
INTEREST

NFPA 1.6

A paralegal shall avoid conflicts of interest and shall disclose any possible conflict to the employer or client, as well as to the prospective employers or clients.

CURRENT CLIENTS

The most obvious conflict situation arises where there is a direct conflict between the current representation of a client and another potential client's interests. It is simply an acknowledgement that "you cannot serve two masters" with equality and fairness. (See Figure 5.2.)

Legal professionals are bound to represent their clients in an attempt to obtain the best possible outcomes for the clients. This is not possible when one client's interest is adverse to another's. The best the attorney could do would be to meet in the middle at a reasonable compromise. An attorney's role is to be a zealous advocate, not a mediator. Taking actions inconsistent with this role as the "client's champion" is violative of the attorney's duties of confidentiality and competence. How? The attorney or paralegal cannot cordon off the part of his brain that knows secrets about one client and keep it separate from another that knows about adverse client interests. Even the most disciplined professional will be torn as to how to keep this information from affecting the representation of the other client. Additionally, the clients will most likely be unable to accept this arrangement and its potential for disloyalty. How do these conflicts affect competence? It is the attorney's and the paralegal's duty to act as other reasonable professionals in a similar situation; most reasonable attorneys and paralegals do not put themselves in a conflict position.

The ABA Model Rules contemplate that there are situations where a conflict or apparent conflict may exist, yet the attorney and client can still enter into this "conflictual" relationship. Neither of the paralegal codes address this issue as it pertains to the establishment of the attorney-client relationship. This decision as to whether or not a conflict does exist and whether it can be overcome is ultimately a legal judgment and solely within the purview of the practice of the attorney. Where the ethical rules may perceive a conflict, a client may not. It is acceptable to represent potentially adverse clients

◄ **FIGURE 5.2**
LOYALTY TO CLIENT

NFPA EC 1.6(a)

A paralegal shall act within the bounds of the law, solely for the benefit of the client, and shall be free of compromising influences and loyalties. Neither the paralegal's personal or business interest, nor those of other clients or third persons, should compromise the paralegal's professional judgment and loyalty to the client.

adverse
Characteristic of a position or interest that is inconsistent or opposite with another, so that they cannot be reconciled without compromising an important element of one or both positions or interests.

where they both consent to this representation. At this juncture, it is important to discuss what the ethical rules perceive as **adverse**. The term does not merely mean a directly contrary position between opposing parties in the same matter. "Adversity" lies in the inability of the attorney to render full and impartial representation of an individual client's best interest. While superficially it may appear that the multiple clients have concomitant interests in the transaction or litigation, the processes, strategies, theories of liability, and/or ultimate outcomes may diverge during the representation. The ethical rules seek to avoid this situation as well. The rules address possibilities as well as the apparent probabilities. The mere threat of this type of harm is enough to implicate a conflict of interest. *Ferrara v. Jordache Enterprises, Inc.*, 12 Misc. 3d 769, 771, 819 N.Y.S.2d 421, 423 (Kings Cty. 2006). (The driver and passenger were represented by the same counsel in an automobile accident case. In such a case, while their claims against the defendant are the same, there lies the possibility that the plaintiff-passenger may bring a counterclaim against the plaintiff-driver. Indeed, joining the driver as a defendant is necessary in order to preserve an opportunity for recovery if the defendant in the other vehicle is exonerated.) The preservation of independent professional judgment is paramount. Without these potential conflict prohibitions, the attorney would have the ability to take on potentially (although not actually) disharmonious clients and then have to try to disengage from the representation after work had been started.

> Indeed, the dual representation mandates the disqualification of counsel in regard to his continuing representation of either of these plaintiffs since such continued representation would necessary result in a violation of the firm's fiduciary obligations to preserve client confidentiality and vigorously represent the clients' interests.

> *Id.* at 770.

informed consent
Permission that is voluntarily given after having received and understood all relevant information relating to the situation's risks and alternatives.

In some circumstances, the parties may consent to the adverse multiple representation. This consent must be obtained after the attorney has fully explained the possible ramifications of the multiple representation; this is the concept of **informed consent**. It is not enough that the clients are informed of the existence of the potential conflict; it requires that "each affected client be aware of the relevant circumstances and of the material and reasonably foreseeable ways that the conflict could have adverse effects on the interests of that client." *North Carolina State Bar v. Merrell*, 777 S.E.2d 103, 114 (N.C. Ct. App. 2015) citing comment 18 to Rule 1.7. In other situations, despite the attorney's full disclosure of the implications of multiple representation and the clients' informed consent, the multiple representation is prohibited. *See Baldasarre v. Butler*, 132 N.J. 278, 295-296 (1993) ("The disastrous consequences of Butler's dual representation convinces us that a new bright-line rule prohibiting dual representation is necessary in commercial real estate transactions where large sums of money are at stake, where contracts contain complex contingencies, or where options are numerous. The potential for conflict in that type of complex real estate transaction is too great to permit even consensual dual representation of buyer and seller. Therefore, we hold that an attorney may not represent both the buyer and the seller in a complex commercial real estate transaction even if both give their informed consent."). The courts are generally in agreement that where two or more parties can assert claims against each other in the same litigation, these clients are unable to give informed consent. The attorney, by definition, cannot reasonably, responsibly, and diligently represent these clients without some compromise in loyalty, either actual or perceived. Even where the attorney feels he can act with clinical neutrality, the appearance of impropriety will taint the representation. Further, in truth, clinical neutrality is not the role of the attorney in representing a client. The attorney has an ethical duty of zealous representation which includes a certain conviction or passion for the interests of the individual client. "Because dual representation is fraught with the potential for irreconcilable conflict, it will rarely be sanctioned even after full disclosure has been made and the consent of the clients obtained." *LaRusso v. Katz*, 30 A.D.3d 240, 244, 818 N.Y.S.2d 17, 20 (2006). The court has the ultimate responsibility for the fairness of the justice system, and the "existence of conflict undermines the integrity of the court." *State v. Davis*, 840 A.2d 279, 284 (N.J. App. Div. 2004).

The current conflict may even exist between the attorney and the client. An attorney must not have a financial or other personal interest in the outcome of the case in which he is representing a client. This is clearly demonstrated where the attorney represents a client in a bankruptcy matter and that client owes the attorney money for unpaid legal fees. The representation is subject to **material limitation** by the attorney's interest and those duties owed to the other creditors of the client. *In the Matter of Disciplinary Proceedings against Krueger*, 709 N.W.2d 857, 861 (Wis. 2006) (These proceedings were further exacerbated by the fact that the attorney failed to disclose his status as a creditor of the client on the court papers and collected the fees after they were discharged in bankruptcy in violation of the code. The attorney was suspended from practice for 60 days and was required to pay the costs of the disciplinary proceeding in the amount of $20,489.37).

material limitation
The inability to render neutral and unbiased services or advice.

SPOT THE ISSUE

Two independent businessmen, Bert and Ernie have regularly used Attorney Elmo to draft their commercial leases on their respective properties. Last week, during a meeting, Bert and Ernie decided to create a joint-venture agreement to buy and lease commercial real estate together. They now approach Attorney Elmo to draft this agreement. Can he do so? Why or why not? What are the potential problems in this dual representation? What facts, if different, would change the outcome?

IN CLASS DISCUSSION

Mary, a newly hired paralegal at the highly regarded Smith and Thompson Law Firm, has just been assigned to participate in the defense of some local teenagers who attempted to carry out a Columbine-like shooting spree at their high school. Luckily, no one was killed, but several students were seriously wounded. Mary is devoutly religious and is adamantly supportive of gun control. She feels deep sympathy for the children and parents affected at the school and is convinced that stricter gun control laws could have prevented the tragedy. What is Mary's best response to this situation at work?

In determining whether a conflict of interest exists, an attorney must take all these factors into consideration:

- Actual or apparent adversity
- The ability to give informed consent
- The degree of limitation presented by the lawyer's own interests and ethical duties to his clients

disinterested lawyer
The standard to which potentially affected attorneys must measure their actions. An attorney must detach himself from any personal interest in the matter and act accordingly.

Then, the attorney must determine whether a **disinterested lawyer**, one who is unrelated and unaffected by the situation, "would believe that the lawyer can competently represent the interest of each." *Ferrara v. Jordache Enterprises, Inc.*, 12 Misc. 3d 769, 771, 819, N.Y.S.2d 421, 423 (2006). In order to avoid a possible conflict of interest that might be violative of the ethical rules, an attorney must examine the situation from three perspectives:

1. **The perspective of the client**—in order to determine whether an individual client would feel betrayed by another's representation. This encompasses the element of *direct adversity*.
2. **The perspective of the attorney's own conscience**——in order to determine whether the representation presents some underlying bias that would place the attorney's interests over those of her client, thereby *materially limiting* her ability to function as the client's advocate.
3. **The perspective of the justice system and public at large**—in order to determine whether other, outside attorneys would consider the representation a conflictual one (the *disinterested lawyer standard)* and whether the integrity of the court would be compromised in the eyes of the public if the representation were permitted (in other words, if it would *appear improper*).

There are particular circumstances that present themselves with sufficient predictability and are serious enough to warrant specific treatment, and that are encapsulated in ABA Model Rule 1.8. Most of these situations relate to the intimate knowledge of the client's financial situation and the possibility that the

SURF'S UP

Attorneys are increasingly using the internet to obtain new clients. Many of these websites contain forms on which to submit legal questions. What happens when two opposing parties submit the same question simultaneously to the attorney? Can the attorney disclaim the existence of an attorney-client relationship even after she has received confidential communications from both potential clients?

Read the following excerpt from The State Bar of California's Standing Committee on Professional Responsibility and Conduct, Formal Opinion No. 2005-168:

> After typing in her contact information, Wife explained that she was interested in obtaining a divorce. She related that her Husband, a Vice-President at Ace Incorporated in Los Angeles, was cohabiting with a co-worker. She also stated that her 13-year-old son was living with her and asked if she could obtain sole custody of him. She noted that Husband was providing some support but that she had to take part-time work as a typist, and was thinking about being re-certified as a teacher. She revealed that she feared Husband would contest her right to sole custody of her son and that, many years ago, she had engaged in an extra-marital affair herself, about which Husband remained unaware. Wife stated that she wanted a lawyer who was a good negotiator, because she wanted to obtain a reasonable property settlement without jeopardizing her goal of obtaining sole custody of the child and keeping her own affair a secret. She concluded by noting she had some money saved from when she was a teacher, and stating, "I like your web site and would like you to represent me."
>
> [. . .]
>
> Upon receiving Wife's inquiry, the law firm discovered that Husband had already retained Law Firm to explore the possibility of a divorce from Wife. The next day, an attorney in Law Firm sent Wife an e-mail, which stated:
>
> "We regret we will be unable to accept you as a client because there is a conflict with one of our present clients. Good luck with your case."

> We address whether Law Firm may be precluded from representing Husband as a result of the firm's contact with Wife on the ground that Law Firm has obtained material confidential information.
>
> [. . .]
>
> [W]e discussed situations in which there was some question about whether the attorney had agreed to be consulted, noting that the attorney must "evidence, by words or conduct, a willingness to engage in a confidential consultation with any of the individuals." Here, by providing the link that states, "What are my rights?" in combination with directions to submit facts that related to a legal problem she was "[w]ondering about," Law Firm has invited the consultation with Wife, and has done so for the purpose of considering whether to enter into an attorney-client relationship with the inquirer.
>
> Law Firm has attempted to avoid taking on a duty of confidentiality by requiring each inquirer to agree that (1) by submitting a question, the inquirer is not forming an attorney-client relationship or a "confidential relationship"; and (2) whatever response Law Firm provides will not constitute legal advice but, rather, "general information." To assess whether Wife's agreement to these terms prevented Law Firm from taking on a duty of confidentiality, we apply the "reasonable belief" test we set forth in California State Bar Formal Opn. No. 2003-161: "If the attorney's conduct, in light of the surrounding circumstances, implies a willingness to be consulted, then the speaker may be found to have a reasonable belief that he is consulting the attorney in the attorney's professional capacity." We do not believe that a prospective client's agreement to Law Firm's terms prevented a duty of confidentiality from arising on the facts before us, because Law Firm's disclosures to Wife were not adequate to defeat her reasonable belief that she was consulting Law Firm for the purpose of retaining Law Firm.
>
> First, our assumption that Law Firm did not form an attorney-client relationship with Wife is not conclusive concerning Law Firm's confidentiality obligations to Wife. An attorney-client

relationship is not a prerequisite to a lawyer assuming a duty of confidentiality in such a situation. As we explained earlier, and elaborated fully in California State Bar Formal Opn. No. 2003-161, a lawyer can owe a duty of confidentiality to a prospective client who consults the lawyer in confidence for the purpose of retaining the lawyer. Thus, that an attorney-client relationship did not arise from Wife's consultation with Law Firm did not prevent Law Firm from taking on a duty of confidentiality to Wife.

Second, Wife's agreement that she would not be forming a "confidential relationship" does not, in our view, mean that Wife could not still have a reasonable belief that Law Firm would keep her information confidential. We believe that this statement is potentially confusing to a lay person such as Wife, who might reasonably view it as a variant of her agreement that she has not yet entered into an attorney-client relationship with Law Firm. Cf. Virginia State Bar Ethics Opn. 1794 (June 30, 2004) (Lawyer's use of a disclaimer in non-Internet setting that stated "I understand that my initial interview with this attorney does not create an attorney/client relationship and that no such relationship is formed unless (sic) actually retain this attorney" is not effective in preventing the lawyer from incurring duty of confidentiality to prospective client). Had Law Firm written its agreement with Wife with a plain-language reference that her submission would lack confidentiality, then that would have defeated a reasonable expectation of confidentiality. Accord, Barton v. District Court (9th Cir. 2005) 410 F.3d 1104, 1110 (Law firm should have spoken clearly to the laymen to whom its website was addressed about what commitments it did and did not make by a plain English explanation on the website).

Without ruling out other possibilities, we note that had Wife agreed to the following, she would have had, in our opinion, no reasonable expectation of confidentiality with Law Firm: "I understand and agree that Law Firm will have no duty to keep confidential the information I am now transmitting to Law Firm."

Another way in which Law Firm could have proceeded that would have avoided the confidentiality issue entirely would have been to request from web site visitors only that information that would allow the firm to perform a conflicts check. For example, under the facts presented, Law Firm would first want to ensure that it does not represent the other spouse. Law Firm could explain that it is seeking the information to determine whether representing the visitor might create a conflict with one of its present clients, preventing it from representing the visitor. Law Firm could request that the inquirer provide relevant information such as the names of the parties, children, former spouses, etc., and, given the subject area, any relevant maiden names. Regardless of the precise language used, it is important that lawyers who invite the public to submit questions on their web sites, and do not want to assume a duty of confidentiality to the inquirers, plainly state the legal effect of a waiver of confidentiality. (See also D.C. Ethics Opn. 302 (providing tentative "best practices" guidance on attorney communications over the Internet to avoid formation of attorney-client relationships, including the use of prominent "click through" disclaimers).) We note that by suggesting a means for lawyers to avoid inadvertently taking on a duty of confidentiality to web site visitors, we do not mean to suggest that this methodology is the only means for doing so.

In the situation presented, however, Law Firm chose neither to make a plain-language reference to the non-confidential nature of communications submitted to its web site, nor to first screen visitors for potential conflicts with its existing clients. Having taken the course it did, Law Firm may be disqualified from representing Husband should the court conclude that the information Wife submitted was material to the resolution of the dissolution action.

attorney may take advantage of that knowledge in a transaction with the client. Other rules deal with the basic intimate relationship between the attorney and the client.

Business Dealings with the Client

The ABA Model Rules present a general prohibition against both entering into a business transaction with a client and being involved in a business interest that is in conflict with that of the client. This reflects the concern that while the client would be relying upon the expertise of his attorney, the attorney would be looking out for his own best interest in the deal, not that of his client. The conflict lies in the dual role the attorney is attempting to play in the transaction, he is both counsel and party and cannot serve these two masters with equal fairness; his loyalty is divided.

> [The rule] specifically limits business transactions between lawyers and clients when the lawyer and client have "differing interests" in the transaction and when "the client expects the lawyer to exercise professional judgment [in the transaction] for the protection of the client. . . ." When these circumstances are present, a lawyer must refrain from entering into the transaction unless the client has consented after full disclosure by the lawyer. Business ventures between lawyers and their clients are normally discouraged.
>
> *Iowa Supreme Court Bd. of Professional Ethics and Conduct v. Fay*, 619 N.W.2d 321, 325 (Iowa 2000), citing *Committee on Prof'l Ethics & Conduct v. Carty*, 515 N.W.2d 32, 35 (Iowa 1994).

Courts have further noted that business dealings with a client are inherently dangerous because attorneys possess superior knowledge and education in legal dealings. "It is an area wrought with pitfalls and traps and the Court is without choice other than to hold the attorney to the highest of standards under such circumstances." *In the Matter of Lowther*, 611 S.W.2d 1, 2 (Mo. 1981); *see also In the Matter of Disciplinary Action Against Giese*, 662 N.W.2d 250, 257 (N.D. 2003); *In the Matter of Smyzer*, 108 N.J. 47, 56 (1987) (The attorney invested his client's money in stocks; however, the attorney failed to disclose his interests in those companies. "As the record makes painfully clear, [the attorney] chose not to make full disclosure to his clients, all of whom were financially unsophisticated individuals relying heavily on [their attorney] for investment advice." This also resulted in the comingling of his clients' funds and his own. The attorney was disbarred for this failure of his fiduciary duties.).

The situations in which an attorney or paralegal may have an adverse interest in another transaction involving his client come up rather often, as the practice of law is closely related to other business services. Attorneys and paralegals may have business relationships with insurance providers, medical professionals, realtors, brokers, accountants, and others to whom they customarily refer their clients. These referrals may ordinarily not pose a problem. However, if the attorney or paralegal has an interest in the business to which his client was referred, a potential conflict exists. Legal professionals in their fiduciary capacity may have made the referrals to a proper professional; however, where the attorney or paralegal has a financial stake in the company to which the client was referred, the referral is improper. The attorney or the paralegal has an incentive to refer clients to his monetary gain, rather than to the most competent or appropriate service provider for the client. *See Falanga v. State Bar of Georgia*, 1996 WL 33370668, 10 (N.D. Ga. 1996) ("Part of [the attorney's] 'marketing plan' consisted of networking with the chiropractors. [He] would meet with the doctors to tell them about his firm, occasionally taking them to lunch, and ask them to recommend his firm to their patients. The Bar asserts that the conflict of interest arises because, in those instances where a chiropractor's bill is to be paid out of settlement proceeds, an attorney who has benefited from the doctor's referral may be less inclined to scrutinize the doctor's bill for fear of alienating him and losing his referrals. An attorney dependent on the chiropractor's referrals for a substantial portion of his business is likely to have a conflict between his client's best interests and the continued relationship with the doctor."). This prohibition also pertains to referrals for which the attorney hopes to gain future benefit. While an attorney may send clients to a particular professional in the hopes of obtaining that professional as a client or to gain reciprocal referrals, this may not be a condition of the referral. The test is whether a disinterested attorney would look at the situation and determine that the involved attorney was looking out for his client's best interest.

This prohibition extends even so far as to exclude an attorney or paralegal from representing a family member in a business transaction with one of his clients. The same kind of conflict exists, as the attorney or the paralegal is torn between loyalties, despite having no direct benefit derived for himself out of the transaction. In *In the Matter of Hurd*, 354 A.2d 78 (N.J. 1976), an attorney took on dual representation of his own sister and a long-time family friend in a real estate transaction. The record became unclear whether the parties intended a sale, some other sort of transfer, or loan/mortgage, but what was clear was the fact that the attorney had divided interest. He could not remove himself from his loyalty to his sister, and accepted her version of the arrangement to the detriment of the other client.

A strict prohibition would be a burden both for enterprising attorneys and hard-working paralegals and for those residents of smaller communities where the businesses are naturally interdependent. Therefore, the ethics rules do allow for these transactions, provided that several conditions are met. First, the terms of the transaction and the deal as a whole must be fair and

FIGURE 5.3 ▶
RELATIONSHIPS THAT
CAUSE CONFLICT

NFPA EC 1.6(c)

A paralegal shall avoid conflicts of interest that may arise from family relationships and from personal and business interests.

REEL TO REAL

Both family relations and personal convictions are involved in the conflict between a young lawyer and his client in the 1996 movie *The Chamber*, based on John Grisham's novel. It stars Chris O'Donnell as the young lawyer and Gene Hackman as the racist murderer on death row. The twist lies in the fact that the murderer is the lawyer's own grandfather. While the lawyer despises racism, he defends his grandfather. Is this representation ethically responsible? Why or why not? How could the grandson/lawyer justify his representation?

reasonable. The standards of "fairness" and "reasonableness" are measured by an objective standard, as if those terms were arrived at by two parties dealing at arm's length with each other, and having the advice of independent counsel. Further, these fair and reasonable terms must be fully disclosed in writing to the client and the client must be able to understand them. This may require the attorney to write the agreement in plainer language than he normally uses when dealing with other legal professionals. There is an additional writing requirement: The client must be advised of the benefit of obtaining a neutral third-party lawyer to render advice regarding the transaction. The requirement that the attorney put this request in writing underscores its importance. Securing advice from another attorney who has no previous relationship to either the involved attorney or the client ensures that at least one attorney is looking out for the client's best interests; this puts the interested attorney and his client on a level playing field. It is a protection against potential over-reaching or advantage-taking. To memorialize these precautions and to ensure that they are indeed undertaken, there is also the requirement that the client give this informed consent in a writing signed by the client. Much of this emphasis on the writing requirement relates to problems of proof. The rules of professional ethics are strictly enforced, and attorneys must comply with all of their seemingly rigorous protocol. A violation of any part of a rule renders the attorney culpable; further, the attorney bears the heavy burden of proof to show that the dealings were fair and reasonable to the client. *See Brigham v. Brigham,* 11 So. 3d 374 (Fla. Dist. Ct. App. 2009). Generally, these transactions between an attorney or paralegal and a client are discouraged; no harm needs to be proven in order to void the agreement for failure to comply with these requirements. If, however, the client has been harmed and the attorney or paralegal has appeared to have benefited in the transaction, it is presumed that the agreement is invalid.

Maintaining Confidentiality in a Conflict Situation

Attorneys and paralegals are privy to sensitive information regarding their clients. It is imperative not only to avoid disclosure of this confidential information, but also, in the absence of disclosure, to avoid using it to one's own advantage. For example, an attorney representing a mother in a child support action obtained information regarding the father's whereabouts and financial status. During his investigation of the mother's file, the attorney also discovered that both the parents were indebted to the local welfare agency for some of the costs associated with the birth of their child. The welfare agency was a client of the attorney in question; therefore, the attorney had to withdraw from the representation of the mother. All would have been well and good had the attorney stopped there. However, the attorney violated the ethics rules when he contacted the welfare agency and gave them information obtained from the mother's file about the father so that the agency could seek collection from him. Of course, the mother was later added as a defendant to that suit as well. The attorney was not ethically permitted to reveal the information obtained from the file to the disadvantage of his client, the mother, without her consent. *See Matter of Anonymous*, 654 N.E.2d 1128 (Ind. 1995). Also implicated is the duty to preserve the confidences of former clients, discussed under ABA Model Rule 1.9. Many of these situations involve several ethical rules. The ethics rules seem relatively duplicative, but this underscores the importance of their essence and inviolability. Overlapping coverage can help to ensure their applicability to almost any questionable situation.

Financial Incentives Prohibited

The ethical rules also prohibit an attorney from obtaining any personal financial interest in the outcome of the client's matter that may affect how the attorney handles the case. This is exclusive of fee arrangements that may be contingent upon a positive resolution of the matter and recovery for the client. The concern is that the attorney will not be able to render neutral, independent professional advice where the attorney has a stake in the outcome. While it may be true that the attorney's advice would benefit both himself and the client, it may just as well be true that there are two or more outcomes possible, some of which would be better for the client and some of which would be better for the attorney at the expense of the client's best interest. It is only human nature to desire the best possible outcome for oneself.

Substantial gifts given by clients to either the attorney or the paralegal are also prohibited "financial incentives." The key to understanding this section is to define a **substantial gift**. Small tokens of appreciation or presents given on holidays or birthdays usually are permitted; after all, legal professionals are people too. It is the elaborate or expensive gift that is prohibited. Why? Those who lavish gifts upon someone usually expect something in return. In some circumstances, these gifts may also be seen as rewards or bribes. Attorneys may not be compensated over and above their initial fee arrangements with their clients. Paralegals may not be compensated for their performance over and above their salaries and regular bonuses. A successful outcome is not grounds for extra compensation; gifts cannot serve as incentive for the attorney or the paralegal to put forth extra efforts to win. An attorney

substantial gift
A gift from client to attorney large enough to have a significant impact on the attorney's ability to perform services in a neutral and detached manner.

must render zealous representation and the paralegal must render her best efforts to their clients under the ethical rules. There should be no such thing as the ability to work harder to gain a better outcome for a client. A legal professional should always work at the outermost limit of effort and professionalism—the best cannot, by definition, get any better.

The real issue posed by this rule is the meaning of the word "substantial." Courts have not defined this standard in any clear terms and have acknowledged that every case is so fact sensitive that to attempt to define "substantiality" across the board would be ineffectual.

> The issue as to allowance of anything more than a token gift or gift of nominal value is whether or not the proposed gift "represents general standards of fairness." The reason for that conclusion lies in the fact that nowhere in the Rules is there a definition of "substantial." Moreover, there would appear to be no case law nor any published opinion indicating what constitutes a "substantial gift." And, even if there were cases indicating what is considered "substantial," it would not be likely that results reached in one case would help in deciding another.
>
> *PA Eth. Op. 95-177, 1996 WL 928114 (Pa. Bar Assn. Comm. Leg. Eth. Prof'l Resp.).*
>
> Other factors may also be taken into consideration in determining the nature of the gift. [I]ts value should be assessed at the time the [gift or bequest] is [given or] prepared, and both the size of the [donor's] estate and the financial status of the lawyer should be considered when deciding if the gift is substantial. This analysis could be helpful in that, at least, it tells one that the determination of substantiality takes place at the time of the document preparation."
>
> *PA Eth. Op. 90-146, 1990 WL 709667 (Pa. Bar Assn. Comm. Leg. Eth. Prof'l Resp.)*

SPOT THE ISSUE

Walter, a very wealthy and generous friend of Peter, an attorney, requested that Peter draft his last will and testament. The will bequeathed his sizable estate to his four married sons, but should all four predecease him and leave no surviving children, Peter would receive 25 percent of the estate, and the remainder would go to his alma mater, the School of Hard Knocks. Upon Walter's death last year, all four sons received their share of the estate as they had all survived their father. Therefore, Peter received nothing. Indeed, Peter had never expected to receive anything under the will, as the contingency (that all four sons predecease their father) was so improbable. Therefore, Peter did not believe that the 25 percent bequest would constitute a substantial gift from his friend and client, Walter. Is Peter correct? Why? For a hint, see *In re Disciplinary Action against Boulger,* 637 N.W.2d 710 (N.D. 2001).

This rule against securing a financial interest in the outcome of the client's matter or accepting a gift is bent in cases where the legal professional's family is involved. The ethical rules allow people to take advantage of having a lawyer or paralegal in the family and permit lawyers and paralegals to take care of their families. This includes writing wills or other property transfers for family members, even where the family member/lawyer takes as a beneficiary from the relative/client. In the case of estates or property transfers, the subject matter is of a "substantial" nature; it is more than a mere token of affection or gratitude, but is permitted. Other than this familial exception, attorneys and paralegals are not generally permitted to be beneficiaries under their clients' wills. The reason for this is clear: Legal professionals, in their fiduciary, confidential, and trusted roles, have substantial influence over their clients. Courts and ethical tribunals have recognized this potential for abuse and have determined that the "receiving" attorney or paralegal must show that he did not unduly influence or take advantage of his client in any way that resulted in the bequest. The courts will presume fraudulent conduct; it is the attorney's burden to show otherwise.

> [I]f a lawyer accepts a gift from his client he is peculiarly susceptible to the charge that he unduly influenced or overreached the client and that, other than in exceptional circumstances, a lawyer should insist that an instrument in which his client desires to name him beneficially be prepared by another lawyer selected by the client. Indeed, public policy necessitates such a shift in the burden of proof. In its absence, an attorney may freely misappropriate testator's property or make himself a beneficiary in a will knowing full and well that at the death or incapacity of the client all evidence against the lawyer would die with the client. A disciplinary proceeding is not intended for the purpose of punishment, but rather to determine the fitness of an officer of the court to continue in that capacity and to protect the courts and public from unfit persons.

Matter of Smith, 572 N.E.2d 1280, 1286 (Ind. 1991).

This prohibition against taking substantial gifts from non-relative clients extends to those that are contingent or merely possible beneficiaries. *See In re Boulger,* 637 N.W.2d 710, 712 (N.D. 2001), wherein the court rejected the attorney's argument that the contingencies drafted into the will that would trigger the testamentary gift to him were so unlikely to happen that the conditional bequests were not actually substantial gifts under the ethical rule's prohibition.

Taking advantage of a client's situation also applies when Hollywood calls. Popular media such as books, television shows, and movies are constantly being created with legal issues and lawyers as the central themes and characters. Indeed, not only is it hard to watch an evening of prime time on any of the networks without encountering a legal drama, but also an entire network, CourtTV, has arisen in response to the demand. The temptation to cash in on the demand for stories has been expressly prohibited by the ABA Model Rules.

Violation of this ethical provision can be dealt with in the most severe manner permissible under the ABA Standards for Imposing Lawyer Sanctions, Section 7.1. Where an attorney knowingly violates his professional duties to his client with the intent to obtain a benefit for himself at the expense of his client or the justice system, disbarment is generally appropriate. This prohibition extends even to the selling of the attorney's own story as it relates to the representation of her clients.

> In signing the option contract for "The Garnett Harrison Story," Harrison [the attorney] violated Rule 1.8(d) of the Rules of Professional Conduct. Such transaction, for which Harrison was paid $10,000, is prohibited as creating a conflict of interest between a lawyer and client. Her clients—at that point, the estate of Dorrie Singley, and Bernice Singley as administratrix—may not have been injured by Harrison's signing of the option contract. However, *the potential serious injury to the legal profession is manifest. Realization of personal profit from representation of a client creates an appearance of impropriety which the profession can ill afford.* Therefore, disbarment is proper under this Rule.

> *Harrison v. Mississippi Bar*, 637 So. 2d 204, 227 (Miss. 1994) (emphasis added).

The key to this prohibition is its effect or potential effect upon the legal system, its integrity, and the public's confidence in its truth-finding and justice-rendering role. A legal professional who has a financial interest in the profitability of the client's story as a book or movie also has an incentive to make that story as marketable and appealing as possible. This may be at odds with the outcome that is best or most just for the client. Even if this were not so, there would always be doubts surrounding the motivation for the actions taken by the attorney or paralegal. This **"appearance of impropriety"** standard applies in many circumstances, under many ethical rules. The legal profession regards the preservation of the dignity of the law as so important that the mere possibility of harm and actual harm can be met with equally stringent discipline.

appearance of impropriety
A standard used to evaluate whether actions which are not strictly prohibited are still deemed unethical, because an ordinary citizen would suspect them as inappropriate behavior for a legal professional.

Recall that the client is the "master of the claim" and therefore is ultimately in charge of the direction and settlement of the matter. The attorney's role is to properly steer the course in the legal system to achieve the client's desired result. Any incentives an attorney has to direct the end result towards her own gain are prohibited, even if those incentives are never realized or intended. Again, the attorney must avoid the mere possibility and public perception of them. Another way to acquire a financial interest in the outcome of the client's matter is to loan money to him. The attorney then has her own agenda in settling the matter for the maximum amount possible, which may not be the best outcome for the client, particularly if that client wishes to end the matter quickly.

Another prohibition relates to financial aid to clients. Essentially, it is impermissible to provide assistance to the client in connection with pending or contemplated litigation. There are two exceptions to the "no-loan" rule, and they are strictly enforced. Any money advanced by the attorney's office that does not qualify as court costs or expenses of litigation is prohibited. The attorney's intent in making any other sort of loan, the loan terms, and/or the client's needs are irrelevant to the determination that the ethical rule has been violated. There are many situations where attorneys may be sympathetic to the plight of their clients; however, in all cases the courts will find an ethical violation. This is based upon the desire to prevent "(1) clients selecting a lawyer based on improper factors, and (2) conflicts of interest, including compromising a lawyer's independent judgment in the case and creating the potentially conflicting roles of the lawyer as both lawyer and creditor with divergent interests." *State ex rel. Oklahoma Bar Ass'n v. Smolen*, 17 P.3d 456, 462 (Okla. 2000). The attorney was not permitted to advance living expenses to his worker's compensation client until the final disposition of the case. Dramatically, in *Matter of K.A.H.*, 967 P.2d 91 (Alaska 1998), the attorney was not permitted to advance money to the widow and children of a seaman killed on an Alaskan crab boat so that they could pay rent and move out of their car! Along the same lines, in *Toledo Bar Assn. v. Crossmock*, 111 Ohio St. 3d 278, 855 N.E.2d 1215 (2006), the attorney was not permitted to advance funds for medical treatment for his personal injury client. It is not that courts have turned a deaf ear to the financial troubles of clients; they simply have sent a clear message that the integrity of the justice system must be preserved by prohibiting these loans between legal professionals and clients.

Financial influences can come from outside sources—those that are not related to the actual action but have an interest in the outcome. Since the beginning of law practice in America, the "American Rule" with regard to fees has been in place. The American Rule provides that parties pay for their own legal services and costs. The victor in the litigation battle does not also win the costs of retaining the attorney in the recovery. This practice is reflected in the ethics rules, which essentially require that the client pay for his own representation.

As always, there are exceptions to the general prohibition. There are situations where a third party/non-client can agree to pay for the client's legal costs. The first should be familiar: Most, not all, actions to be undertaken by an attorney relative to representation can be validated by informed client consent. The client must understand the risks involved in permitting the attorney to accept payment from another source. One of the characteristics of the practice of law is the exercise of independent professional judgment. In potential conflict with this duty is the desire of this third party, who is paying the bills for the client, to have some say in how the matter is pursued—how the money is spent, so to speak. This is impermissible, and therefore any monetary influence a third party may have over the attorney-client relationship is prohibited. Further, the principle of client confidentiality must be maintained. The third party paying for the legal services has not paid for access to the private communications between the attorney and client. Recall NFPA's EC 1.6(a): "Neither the paralegal's personal or business interest, nor those of other clients or *third persons*, should compromise the paralegal's professional judgment and loyalty to the client" (emphasis added).

This danger of interference with the attorney-client relationship by payment rendered by an outside party surfaces most often in insurance coverage matters. The client is the insured person, while the payer is the insurance company. The insurance company has a vested interest in keeping the cost of handling the insured's matter at a minimum, and the client has the opposite incentive: to get as much work as possible out of the attorney, to obtain the best possible outcome for the matter.

The tension between insurer control of defense and settlement of claims and the exercise of an attorney's independent judgment on behalf of an insured exists in part because of the unsettled nature of the insured, insurer, defense counsel relationship. The insured purchases insurance from an insurance company. The insurance company promises to defend claims against the insured and to indemnify the insured for judgments and settlements. The insurance company hires an attorney to defend claims against insureds. The insured agrees to cooperate.

The relationship has been described as a "tripartite relationship." The precise nature of the relationship among an insured, an insurer, and defense counsel is enigmatic.

There are different views as to whether the insured and insurer are both clients, or whether the insured is a single client and the insurer is a third party payer, or whether the relationship is characterized otherwise. . . . Within this patchwork of views regarding the nature of the relationship among the insured, insurer and defense counsel, questions emerge regarding what is ethical conduct for insurance defense attorneys. The unsettled nature of the relationship stimulates the search for ethical guidance.

Whether an insurance defense attorney may abide by an insurer's "litigation management guidelines" without violating ethical duties of the legal profession has been the subject of advisory opinions in this state and other states. The majority view is that certain carrier imposed limitations give rise to ethical problems . . . . In conclusion, it is this Board's view that it is improper under [the ethical rules] for an insurance defense attorney to abide by an insurance company's litigation management guidelines in the representation of an insured when the guidelines interfere with the professional judgment of the attorney. Attorneys must not yield professional control of their legal work to an insurer.

OH Adv. Op. 2000-3, 2000 WL 1005223, 2-3 (Ohio Bd. Com. Griev. Disp.) (citations omitted). *See also Petition of Youngblood,* 895 S.W.2d 322, 328 (Tenn. 1995) ("The employer cannot control the details of the attorney's performance, dictate the strategy or tactics employed, or limit the attorney's professional discretion with regard to the representation. Any policy, arrangement or device which effectively limits, by design or operation, the attorney's professional judgment on behalf of or loyalty to the client is prohibited by the Code, and, undoubtedly, would not be consistent with public policy.").

In what ways can third-party payers influence the professional judgment of the legal professionals?

Guidelines that restrict or require prior approval before performing computerized or other legal research are an interference with the professional judgment of an attorney. Legal research improves the competence of an attorney and increases the quality of legal services. Attorneys must be able to research legal issues when they deem necessary without interference by non-attorneys.

Guidelines that dictate how work is to be allocated among defense team members by designating what tasks are to be performed by a paralegal, associate, or senior attorney are an interference with an attorney's professional judgment. Under the facts and circumstances of a particular case, an attorney may deem it necessary or more expedient to perform a research task or other task, rather than designate the task to a paralegal. This is not a decision for others to make. The attorney is professionally responsible for the legal services. Attorneys must be able to exercise professional judgment and discretion.

Guidelines that require approval before conducting discovery, taking a deposition, or consulting with an expert witness are an interference with an attorney's professional judgment. These are professional decisions that competent attorneys make on a daily basis.

Guidelines that require an insurer's approval before filing a motion or other pleading are an interference with an attorney's professional judgment. Motion by motion evaluation by an insurer of an attorney's legal work is an inappropriate interference with professional judgment and is demeaning to the legal profession. If an insurer is unsatisfied with the overall legal services performed, the insurer has the opportunity in the future to retain different counsel.

OH Adv Op. 2000-3 at 6-7.

This long list of prohibited interferences underscores the importance of the exercise of independent professional judgment and the maintenance of the sanctity of the confidentiality and inviolability of the attorney-client relationship—one that is free from "outsider" influence driven by financial interests. A paralegal working with an attorney must be cognizant of these situations. Paralegals are highly involved in insurance cases and must take care to avoid influence from third-party insurance carriers. Where the third party is trying to assert such influence, the paralegal clearly must adhere to the ethical standards to maintain her professional integrity and independence. (See Figure 5.4.)

Multiple Representation

Independence as a theme for the manner in which the attorney must operate also pertains to the situation where the attorney has permissibly represented

FIGURE 5.4 ▶
WORK PROHIBITED
WHERE THERE IS A
CONFLICT

NFPA EC 1.6(f)

A paralegal shall not participate in or conduct work on any matter where a conflict of interest has been identified.

two or more clients in the same matter. After clearing the initial conflict of interest hurdle and determining that a present conflict does not exist, an attorney still must maintain separation between or among the clients. Each client retains his own cause of action, and the attorney must treat the clients as if they were independent of each other. This means that the end result must also be separable; there are no "two-for-one" deals in making settlements simply because the attorney is handling more than one client in the matter.

Of course, the most common requirement, informed consent in writing, is also present if the attorney and clients wish to enter into a multiple representation agreement. It is very important for clients to be fully aware of the potential pitfalls associated with multiple representation and to know their rights with respect to each other. In essence, the client must not fare any worse than he would have if he had obtained independent counsel. The clients must all come to an agreement about the goals and amount of settlement that will be acceptable. Further, once the aggregate settlement has been made, the proceeds need to be divided according to that written agreement reflecting the understanding of the represented clients, and all of those clients must be consulted at the various stages of the settlement procedure. Particularly susceptible to an aggregate settlement without full consultation is the probate of estates. The estate is made up of several persons with an interest in the disposition of the entire estate. For example, in *In re Hoffman*, 883 So. 2d 425, 433-434 (La. 2004), the attorney settled the matter after consulting with one of the three siblings, albeit the one who was given most of the control over the matter. The court found that the attorney had to give the other siblings an "opportunity to exercise their absolute right to control the settlement decision . . . it is of no moment whether the Walker siblings had actually agreed to divide the settlement funds equally. Prior to accepting the settlement offer, respondent should have resolved with all of his clients the issue of the allocation of the settlement proceeds." It is important to note that the the estate itself is not the client in these matters; the clients are the living persons who are retaining the attorney to assist them with a problem in the probate and distribution of the estate, and the attorney must consult with them. "Rejecting the lawyer's argument that he was required to consult only with the personal representative of the decedent's estate, whom the lawyer asserted was the 'true client,' the court pointed out that the lawyer 'had three clients in the action and owed to each the right of disclosure and consent in accepting and distributing the award.'" *Id.*, citing *State ex rel. Oklahoma Bar Ass'n v. Watson*, 897 P.2d 246 (Okla. 1994).

Waiver of Claims Against the Legal Professional

While fee agreements will be handled in a later chapter, it is helpful to note here that an auxiliary agreement, one that addresses the attorney's quality of performance, is prohibited under ABA Model Rule 1.8. Attorneys cannot attempt to contractually limit their own or their paralegal's liability for malpractice claims or to settle a malpractice claim unless the client is represented by a disinterested third-party attorney in making the arrangement. In essence, the lawyer cannot escape a claim for malpractice by having his client waive that claim in a pre-representative contract. While these types of agreements, limitation of liability and limitation of damages, are common in ordinary business transactions, they are disfavored in the lawyer-client relationship. For that reason, any proposal that the attorney or paralegal will not be held accountable for acts of malpractice requires that the client knowingly waive these rights with consultation and advice from an independent attorney. The same holds true for any settlement regarding a potential claim for malpractice. The client cannot settle her rights with respect to her claim against the attorney or paralegal absent consultation from an outside disinterested attorney. The courts consider an attorney's accountability so important that it is not necessary for the client to prove that any malpractice occurred; the mere waiver of the right to sue for malpractice is grounds enough for the finding of an ethical violation. *In re Disciplinary Proceeding against Greenlee*, 143 P.3d 807 (Wash. 2006), illustrates this point. The client requested written confirmation from the attorney that no further fees were owed, just $1,595 in costs. The attorney agreed to this only if the client agreed to sign a mutual release which included the release of any claims she might have against the attorney. No claim was filed against the attorney; however, the court, deciding the matter as a case of first impression, stated that none need exist because

> [o]ne of the primary purposes of attorney discipline is the protection of the public from attorney misconduct, and disciplinary rules should be interpreted to advance that purpose. As a general matter, the rule seeks to protect unrepresented clients when a lawyer seeks release of liability in situations where the lawyer's interests either directly conflict or have the potential to directly conflict with the client's interests.

> *Id.* at 813 (citations omitted).

It is clear that agreements to release the attorney from potential liability at the outset of representation remove the attorney's incentive to do his very best and align himself with his client's best interests. Settling a potential claim after representation without permitting the client to consult outside counsel permits the attorney to take advantage of his established relationship with his client, and is essentially also a violation of the rules forbidding communications with unrepresented persons. The client is essentially unrepresented in the settlement, because the attorney is looking out for his own interest at the cost of the client.

Stake in the Outcome of the Case

Legal professionals should be looking out for their client's best interests. The best interest of the client may be (1) a protracted litigation, (2) extensive aggressive settlement negotiations rewarded with a large judgment, or (3) a quick settlement. Which course is actually most desirous? The client may prefer a swift resolution to a large judgment. The attorney, understandably, wants to take the course that will render the most money in fees. Therefore, at times, the attorney's interest in the outcome of the case may diverge from that of the client. The attorney is bound to take the route that the client most desires. The ethics rules prohibit an attorney or a paralegal from acquiring a stake in the outcome of the case or in the subject matter in contention. This removes another level of temptation to increase the duration, the settlement, or the judgment in order to secure a higher fee.

There are two exceptions to this rule that are necessary in order to protect an attorney's ability to collect the monies duly owed. The first permits an attorney to use client property (including the client's files at the attorney's office) as collateral or security in order to ensure that the fees and expenses will get paid. *See Skarecky & Horenstein, P.A. v. 3605 North 36th Street Co.*, 825 P.2d 949 (Ariz. App. 1991) (the law firm's acceptance of a client's assignment of the beneficial interest of a deed of trust, intended to secure payment of attorney's fees in a lawsuit concerning the promissory note secured by that deed of trust, did not violate the ethical rules prohibiting the acquisition of a **proprietary interest** in the cause of action). These fees and liens are not tied to the cause of action, but rather exist because the lawyer performed work. The second exception permits an attorney to accept matters on a contingent fee basis. This is a common arrangement in personal injury, class action, and other types of damage cases. It is absolutely prohibited in most family law matters and criminal cases. While the fees in a contingency arrangement are usually much higher than those billed hourly, the situation is attractive to clients, as they have no bill for services to pay unless there is a recovery. The only restraint in other kinds of civil cases is the requirement that the contingency fee be reasonable. This usually translates into 33 percent of the recovery; however, there are many other kinds of contingencies that are permissible as long as they are reasonable. The reasonableness is determined on a case-by-case basis. One instance where the fee is unreasonable deals with basing the contingency on the demanded amount in a complaint or, in the case of a defendant, on the reduction in amount from that claimed in the complaint to actual judgment. Plaintiffs often overstate the amount of damages sought; there is no penalty for doing so. Therefore, the contingency based upon these figures is completely unrelated to the actual settlement of the matter and, therefore, commonly found unreasonable.

> A plaintiff may sue defendant for $1,000,000, but the fact that sum is named in the complaint does not necessarily mean that plaintiff's claim can fairly be said to be for that amount. Plaintiff's counsel often overstate the amount to which their client is entitled, and indeed have little incentive for restraint. Thus, the amount demanded cannot automatically be the number from which the savings resulting from a judgment or settlement can reasonably be calculated.
>
> *ABA Comm. on Ethics and Prof'l Responsibility, Formal Op. 93-373 at 1001: 181-182 (1993).*

proprietary interest
A definite financial stake in the outcome of a case or matter which may influence the attorney to take a path that is not in the best interest of his client but rather will result in a greater monetary recovery for the attorney.

The reasonableness of the contingent recovery is the same as that in any fee arrangement. (Fee arrangements are discussed at length in the next chapter.) Among other factors, the contingent fee must bear some relationship to "[t]he time and labor required, the novelty and difficulty of the questions involved, and the skill requisite to perform the legal service properly." *Clark v. General Motors, LLC*, 161 F. Supp. 3d 752, 765 (W.D. Mo. 2015) (The Court found that the 40 percent contingency fee arrangement with a widow who lost her husband in a fatal car crash due to the defective ignition switch was "unreasonable at its inception." In reviewing the attorney's work, the Court determined that "the law firms invested 450 total hours in this case, [so] collecting a $1,527,728.00 fee [was] equivalent to charging a blended rate of $3,395 an hour," which was over six times their standard rate. *Id.* at 764). *See also Brown & Sturm v. Frederick Road Ltd. Partnership*, 137 Md. App. 150, 768 A.2d 62 (2001) (the proposed compensation, which would have been based upon sales, leases, or development of the farm, bore little relation to the actual work being done, and appellants [lawyers] could conceivably have received substantial sums of money for rendering few or no legal services).

Sexual Relationships Prohibited

The last prohibition relating to the relationship with the client that naturally causes a conflict of interest is extremely personal. Legal professionals must not commence a sexual relationship with a client. It is never a good idea to become romantically involved with anyone you must work with on a professional basis. This rule states the obvious. However, the Pennsylvania Bar Association Committee on Legal Ethics and Professional Responsibility felt it necessary to examine the issue of attorney-client sexual relations in 17 pages of analysis, ultimately concluding that this type of relationship should not be permitted.

> Several problems arise when an attorney engages in sexual contact with a client. The lawyer-client relationship is grounded on mutual trust. A sexual relationship that exploits that trust compromises the lawyer-client relationship. Also, an attorney is in a fiduciary relationship with a client. Many authorities support the proposition that when an attorney has sexual involvement with a client, the fiduciary relationship the attorney owes to a client is breached.
>
> *1997 WL 671579, 3.*

The only exception is where the relationship came first. This relates back to the benefit of having an attorney in the family. Of course, a person may look to her significant other who is a lawyer for legal assistance. "[A] woman may choose her lover as her lawyer, but not her lawyer as her lover." Linda Fitts Mischler, *Reconciling Rapture, Representation, and Responsibility: An Argument Against Per Se Bans on Attorney-Client Sex*, 10 Georgetown J. Legal Ethics 209, 237 (Winter 1996).

All of these prohibitions, with the exception of the last (romantic) one, relate to all attorneys and paralegals in the firm. Any act that is prohibited to one of them is prohibited to all of them. ABA Model Rule 1.8 sets forth very specific prohibitions in the relationship between an attorney and a current client, so that clarity can prevent potentially disastrous results due to the inherent conflict in these situations. The Rule sets forth ten prohibited activities, although most have exceptions to them if certain requirements are met. In simple sum, the following behaviors are prohibited:

1. Entering into business transactions with a client, unless a transaction is fair, written in easy-to-understand language, and able to be reviewed by a disinterested attorney, which equates to informed consent
2. Using information obtained from a client against the interests of that client, unless the client gives informed consent
3. Accepting a substantial gift from a client, unless the client is a family member
4. Securing media or literary rights in the client's action
5. Giving financial assistance to a client, except to advance litigation costs and filing fees
6. Accepting payment from a third party, unless the attorney notifies the client and the third party neither makes decisions nor obtains client confidences
7. Making an aggregate settlement on behalf of two or more clients in the same matter without first obtaining informed consent
8. Limiting liability for malpractice claims
9. Obtaining a proprietary interest in the cause of action, except to secure a valid attorney lien or create a contingency fee arrangement
10. Starting a romantic relationship with a client

All of these rules are designed to ensure that the legal professionals act in their clients' best interests and not for any personal gain that may interfere with the proper management of the case.

FORMER CLIENTS

Current clients are not the only ones to whom legal professionals owe certain duties of loyalty. Former clients are also protected. Without the professionals' preserving of certain aspects of the relationship "to the grave," clients would have little confidence in the relationship. If an attorney or a paralegal were able to use personal and potentially harmful confidential information about a client after the matter was closed, then the client would be reluctant to enter into the relationship at all. Therefore, the ethical rules address how an attorney or a paralegal must conduct herself with regard to the client after the representation has ended. (See Figure 5.5.)

This rule is of importance to paralegals who assist in intake of clients and perform "**conflict checks**." (See Figure 5.6 for a sample intake form.) Many case management systems can perform this electronically through the firm's database; however, this functions only as well as the method of input does. The

conflict check
A procedure used to verify potential adverse interests before accepting a new client.

FIGURE 5.5 ▶
CONFLICTS ARISING
FROM PRIOR
EMPLOYMENT

NFPA EC 1.6(b)

A paralegal shall avoid conflicts of interest that may arise from previous assignments, whether for a present or past employer or client.

"ghost" of the former client remains in the office of the attorney. If a new client comes in looking for representation, the attorney (or, most likely, the paralegal) will need to check to see if any former clients were involved with this potential client. If there is a conflict between a former client and the new potential client, further inquiry needs to be made. The prohibitions against taking this potential client are not as strict as if the existing client were currently being represented. For the prohibition to stand, the potential client must be looking for representation that relates to the same or substantially similar subject matter as the previous representation of the former client. The rule is based on the premise that a client's confidences remain forever inviolate. For legal professionals to have intimate knowledge of a former client's matters and then be able to turn around and use it to that former client's disadvantage totally eviscerates the principles of confidentiality. If the new client is looking for representation regarding a different matter, the attorney will be permitted to take the case. This is where the rule of current clients (ABA Rule 1.7) differs from that of former clients (ABA Rule 1.9). There is some latitude in taking a new client that has some sort of conflict with a former client, whereas there is a ban on taking a new client that has some sort of conflict with a current client.

For example, Attorney Able represents Larry Lumberman in his lawsuit against Donald Developer regarding an outstanding balance owed for lumber and supplies to one of Donald's many construction projects. Obviously, during the representation of Larry, Able could not represent Donald in any matter according to Rule 1.7 (assuming that Larry did not consent to the concurrent representation). However, after Larry's matter is over and Able has concluded all representation of Larry, Able would be able to take Donald on as a new client in a matter involving the sale of any of the development projects or other matters not related to the collection matter in which he represented Larry.

How do courts determine whether a conflict exists when a former client brings a motion to disqualify his former firm from representing a new client with a potential conflict? The key to understanding this disqualification based upon the subject matter is to determine what "substantially similar" means in this context.

> The key to making a determination about the former client disqualification is to understand what a "substantially similar" matter is. Thus, an attorney should be disqualified if he has accepted employment adverse to the interests of a former client on a matter substantially related to the prior representation. This test has been honed in its practical application to grant disqualification only upon a showing that the relationship between the

All information is protected by the ethical duty of attorney-client confidentiality.

New Client: ☐   Prior Client: ☐

File Number:_____   Date Form Completed:

Client Information

Name:_____   S.S.#:_____

Address:_____

Home Telephone:_____   Work Telephone:_____

Employer Name:_____

Employer Address:_____

Emergency Contact(s): (Name) (Relationship) (Telephone)

_____

Marital Status: Single ☐   Married ☐   Divorced ☐   Separated ☐

Spouse Information

Name:_____   S.S.#:_____

Address:_____

Home Telephone:_____   Work Telephone:_____

Employer Name:_____

Employer Address:_____

Children (names, ages):_____

How did you learn of this firm/attorney?

_____

Referred By: Client ☐   Attorney ☐   Other ☐_____

SUBJECT MATTER: _____

STATUTE OF LIMITATIONS DEADLINE: _____

Previous legal consultations? With whom? _____

Previous medical consultations? With whom? _____

BRIEF STATEMENT OF FACTS: _____

_____

NAMES OF POTENTIAL WITNESSES: _____

_____

CONFLICT CHECKING:

✓ All business / employment relationships:

✓ Family names / relationships:

✓ Persons or entities involved in this matter:

✓ Persons or entities with whom you have been legally involved, including prior
    lawsuits:

What final result is client looking for?_____

Case Name/Number:_____   Practice Area:_____

Originating Attorney:_____

Assigned Attorney(s):_____

issues in the prior and present cases is "*patently clear*" or when the issues are "*identical*" or "*essentially the same.*"

Bergeron v. Mackler, 623 A.2d 489, 493-494 (Conn. 1993) (citations omitted; emphasis added).

Why do courts seem to narrow the definition so that in many situations the attorney will be able to take on a new client even where that client's interests are directly adverse to those of the former client? This is because the legal system balances protecting the confidentiality of the former client with the new client's right to freely engage the counsel of his choice. Too many restrictions with regard to former clients would result in too many attorneys being "conflicted out" and unable to render the services the new client desires. Imagine the impact a more stringent rule would have on small-town practices. With only four or five attorneys to choose from, once a client has consulted with all of them on various matters, no one else in the town could engage those attorneys as counsel in a matter against the first client. They all would have some degree of confidences relating to that first client. This is why the ethical rules put the "substantially similar" requirement in place: to allow subsequent clients the most choice in selecting counsel.

The same standard applies to paralegals. In order to determine whether the law office can take on a matter, the paralegals must determine whether they have had any former dealings with the potential new client. In this determination, it is important for paralegals to appreciate the responsibility of confidentiality fully. Only as much of the prior client's information as is necessary can be revealed in order to make the conflict determination. (See Figure 5.7.)

Once a potential conflict has been identified, further analysis is required; it involves looking at the question of whether subsequent representation would be "materially adverse" to the former client.

The court must make a case-specific inquiry to determine the degree to which the current representation may actually be harmful to the former client. This fact-intensive analysis focuses on whether the current representation may cause legal, financial, or other identifiable detriment to the former client. Additionally, we must determine "whether the attorney's exercise of individual loyalty to one client might harm the other client or whether his zealous representation will induce him to use confidential information that could adversely affect the former client.

Simpson Performance Products, Inc. v. Robert W. Horn, P.C., 92 P.3d 283, 288 (Wyo. 2004) (citations omitted).

FIGURE 5.7 ▶
IDENTIFYING A CONFLICT

NFPA EC 1.6(e)

A paralegal shall reveal sufficient non-confidential information about a client or former client to reasonably ascertain if an actual or potential conflict of interest exists.

Rule 1.9(b) essentially reiterates the prohibitions set forth in subsection (a) of that Rule. What subsection (b) does is expand the disqualification to an entire firm when that attorney moves employment. It is clear that the rule regarding former clients follows the attorney to his new firm and will also follow paralegals.

The issue to be determined here is whether the "transplanted" legal professional had significant contact with the former client's matter. In making this determination, three factors are generally considered: "(1) factual similarities between the two representations, (2) similarities in legal issues, and (3) the nature and extent of the attorney's involvement with the case and whether he was in a position to learn of the client's policy or strategy." *Ochoa v. Fordel, Inc.*, 146 Cal. App. 4th 898, 908, 53 Cal. Rptr. 3d 277, 285, citing *Adams v. Aerojet-General Corp.*, 86 Cal. App. 4th 1324, 1332, 104 Cal. Rptr. 2d 116 (2001). If the attorney or paralegal has obtained no confidences either through contact with the client or through other legal professionals in the firm, then there is no need for the protections afforded by this rule. The attorney and/or paralegal will generally carry the burden of proof showing that he did not have the opportunity to obtain sensitive client information during his prior association with his former firm.

Not only is an attorney prohibited from taking on a new client where the rules apply, but the attorney is also prohibited from using any information obtained from the former representation to the former client's detriment in any way or disclosing the information under any circumstances not permitted by these rules. The last section of Rule 1.9 underscores the importance of the everlasting duty of confidentiality.

Lastly, ABA Model Rule 1.10 functions to subsume all the above prohibitions and apply them to all the attorneys and paralegals associated in a firm. This rule makes it clear that the conflict follows the attorney or paralegal when she changes firms, thereby "infecting" the new firm and clearing the old firm of its previous conflict. The theory behind attributing the "taint" of conflict to every other attorney in the firm rests on the fact that attorneys talk to one another, both socially in the coffee room and professionally for advice. Therefore, the law assumes that what one attorney in the firm knows, they all know. Such **imputed conflict** does not apply in the case where the conflict is personal to the individual attorney. Conflicts resulting from personal bias or revulsion or a sexual relationship are not transferred to all the attorneys in the firm.

imputed conflict
Applies when one attorney or paralegal in a law office has an individual conflict with a client whom the law office wishes to represent. The conflict is attributed to the whole firm.

Generally, the taint of conflict is removed when the conflicted attorney or paralegal leaves the firm; however, if there are others who may have shared in some way in the former representation, the taint may remain. The purpose of the entire set of ethical rules is reinforced: Where there is a possibility that an attorney or paralegal could use information gained from the confidential relationship with a client to the client's detriment, the attorney is prohibited from taking on that representation.

The last two subsections of ABA Model Rule 1.10 are administrative in essence. Subsection (c) permits the effected client(s) to waive the conflict with informed consent under the same circumstances that are required under Rule 1.7. Subsection (d) provides that governmental attorneys moving from

RESEARCH THIS

Find a case in your jurisdiction that discusses the disqualification and conflicts rules as they pertain to a former government employee who has entered into private practice. Explain the "substantial responsibility" standard applied to determine whether the former government attorney incurs a conflict of interest.

public to private practice are not governed by these rules of conflict. It would be very hard for a former governmental attorney or other legal professional to avoid conflicts, as they deal with so many cases from so many different firms. For this reason, there is a separate ethical rule to deal with this special situation. Rule 1.11 is not covered here as it is particular to this one circumstance.

In order to comply with all of these ethical requirements, meticulous record-keeping is essential. Even the most conscientious legal professional will be unable to keep track of all clients and the substance of their representation. (See Figure 5.8.)

From the first day on the job, a paralegal must have a system of keeping track of all clients and matters assigned to her. Ethical compliance is an immediate obligation. Followed to a strict end, this may mean that the more experience a paralegal has, the less able she is to change firms without conflicting herself out. The more clients a paralegal comes in contact with, the more potential conflicts exist. In essence, a paralegal could work herself into a situation where she had little option for changing firms! In order to permit paralegals to advance their careers at other offices, there must be some way of screening out the "taint." This screen is usually referred to as either an "ethical wall" or a "Chinese wall" (meaning that it is purportedly as solid and defendable as the Great Wall of China). (See Figure 5.9.)

A paralegal who creates a conflict situation in the firm may be "walled off" from participating in the matter that creates the conflict. This isolation from the matter is similar to the tenets of confidentiality, with its "cone of silence." There are many steps in creating this wall, and every firm must have a method for putting it into place if necessary. Additionally, if an adversary seeks to disqualify the firm based upon a paralegal's taint, the firm must have documented its steps to show that it has done its very best to keep the paralegal and the other members of the firm who are participating in the matter separate from the

FIGURE 5.8 ▶
CONFLICT RECORDS

NFPA EC-1.6 (d)

In order to be able to determine whether an actual or potential conflict of interest exists a paralegal shall create and maintain an effective recordkeeping system that identifies clients, matters, and parties with which the paralegal has worked.

NFPA EC 1.6(g)

In matters where a conflict of interest has been identified and the client consents to continued representation, a paralegal shall comply fully with the implementation and maintenance of an Ethical Wall.

◀ **FIGURE 5.9**
ETHICAL WALL

persons actively working on it. The following steps should be taken to attempt to prevent the transmission of confidential information:

ethical wall
A set of internal office procedures by which a law firm can isolate or screen attorneys and paralegals who present a conflict with matters in the office and can prevent the disclosure of clients' confidential information.

1. The office should have a written statement regarding the importance of confidential information, along with ongoing ethical educational programs to enforce compliance.
2. The "infected" employee may be required to sign a confidentiality agreement wherein he agrees not to disclose any information relating to the conflict situation.
3. An office meeting may be required to inform other employees that they are not to discuss the matter with the "tainted" employee. They may also be required to sign an agreement not to discuss the matter.
4. Files must be kept in a secure location to restrict access. Files that create a conflict situation should be marked as such and kept away from general circulation. The files must be marked so they can be easily identified.
5. Client consent should be obtained where conflict or potential conflict situations arise.

This list is not all-inclusive or exhaustive. The measures taken will depend upon the structure and administration of the particular law office. The main point is to keep the tainted employee away from those who are working on the matter in a way that makes it as if the tainted employee were not present to create the conflict. The sensitive and fiduciary nature of the relationship between the legal professional and the client is held sacrosanct, and any impingement on that is strongly disfavored. Clients must feel that their interests are being advanced with no reservations on the part of the legal professionals who work for them. Conflicts chip away at this trust and must be avoided or mitigated to the furthest extent that they can be.

Summary

The ethics rules regarding conflicts of interest are broad in scope and applicable to every attorney-client relationship, and last indefinitely. Where there is a doubt as to whether the attorney may take on a new client or should withdraw as counsel, the preferred choice (where there is not a prejudicial effect upon the client) is to defer to the conflicts rules and disengage from the relationship.

There are very specific requirements that must be fulfilled in order to enter into or maintain an attorney-client relationship or generally prohibited transaction. The requirement that is found in almost every rule is the concept of "informed consent." Because attorneys have superior knowledge of the law and legal relationships, they cannot use this to the detriment of their clients who look to them for advice. Clients generally assume that their attorney is looking out for their best interests, and this is generally a good assumption, because the ethics rules impose this burden upon them. However, in this chapter, we have seen that there are certain circumstances in which this premise may not be true. In these instances the client must be informed of the terms and consequences of the proposed arrangement in clear, easy-to-understand terms and must have the ability to consult with outside counsel for advice on those terms.

Simply stated, every attorney and every paralegal owes an uncompromised duty of loyalty to each current and former client. Further, most of these conflicts are imputed to the entire firm for which the legal professional works. Essentially, the firm must demonstrate loyalty to the individual client as well. All of these conflicts rules work in concert with the confidentiality rules to ensure that a client feels protected and the fiduciary relationship remains intact and unmarred by any outside interests.

Key Terms

Adverse
Appearance of impropriety
Conflict check
Conflict of interest
Disinterested lawyer
Ethical wall

Imputed conflict
Informed consent
Material limitation
Proprietary interest
Substantial gift

Review Questions

MULTIPLE CHOICE

Choose the best answer(s) and please explain *why* you chose the answer(s).

1. "Informed consent":
   a. Requires the attorney to tell the prospective client about every current client the attorney represents
   b. Means the client has waived the conflict of interest
   c. Restricts the attorney from speaking to anyone about his client's matters
   d. Is a client's voluntary, written permission, after full disclosure of the risks, for the attorney to take on potentially conflicting clients

2. The "appearance of impropriety" standard:
   a. Disqualifies attorneys who lack moral character
   b. Requires an attorney to refuse or withdraw from representation where the representation would make a person question the attorney's motives

   c. Requires an attorney to submit her potentially disqualifying representation to the ethics board for an opinion as to its validity

   d. Disqualifies an attorney who has committed an ethics violation in open court

3. An attorney cannot enter into a business transaction with a client unless:
   a. The transaction is fair and reasonable on its terms
   b. The terms are in writing
   c. The client has an opportunity to seek independent counsel
   d. The client gives informed consent
   e. All of the above
   f. None of the above; an attorney should never go into business with his client

EXPLAIN YOURSELF

All answers should be written in complete sentences. A simple yes or no is insufficient.

1. When can an attorney concurrently represent two or more clients that may have a potential conflict?

2. Explain the concept of "adversity" as it pertains to a conflict of interest.

3. What is the "disinterested lawyer standard" and when does it apply?

4. Are attorneys always prohibited from accepting gifts from clients?

5. What is an "imputed conflict"? Does it apply to paralegals as well as to attorneys?

FAULTY PHRASES

All of the following statements are *false*. State why they are false and then rewrite each one as a true statement. Do not simply make the statement negative by adding the word "not."

1. An attorney may never represent a present client who has a conflict with a former client.

2. A client can always waive a conflict of interest.

3. Gifts are considered substantial if they exceed $10,000 and, consequently, legal professionals are always prohibited from accepting them.

4. Clients must always pay for their own representation.

5. Attorneys can limit the amount of money that a client can recover from a malpractice suit in the retainer agreement.

6. Because courts favor settlement over trial, an attorney is permitted to take on quarreling clients in order to encourage a speedy resolution to the matter.

7. An attorney is ethically prohibited from having any romantic or sexual relationship with her client.

PORTFOLIO ASSIGNMENT

Write Away

The law firm where you are employed has just hired a new attorney. However, Connie, the new attorney, has worked at another law firm wherein she represented an opposing party in one of the matters you are currently working on. Your supervising attorney has asked you to prepare an interoffice memorandum explaining the steps that the law office should take to screen Connie and why these steps are necessary. Make sure you are detailed enough that all members of the entire staff know what they should do in this situation.

Case in Point

Court of Appeals of Arizona, Division 1, Department E.
SMART INDUSTRIES CORP., MFG., and Lutes Enterprises, Inc., Petitioners,
v.
SUPERIOR COURT of the State of Arizona, In and For the COUNTY OF YUMA, The Honorable H. Stewart Bradshaw, a judge thereof, Respondent Judge,
Darryl and Marilyn ST. GERMAINE, Real Parties in Interest.
No. 1 CA-SA 93-0320.
April 7, 1994.
Review Denied July 28, 1994.

OPINION

JACOBSON, Presiding Judge.

Petitioner Smart Industries, a defendant in the underlying personal injury suit, seeks review of the trial court's denial of its motion to disqualify plaintiffs' lawyer after defendant's counsel's former legal assistant was hired by plaintiffs' lawyer. [FN omitted] This special action requires us to decide whether the same rules of imputed disqualification that apply to lawyers also apply to nonlawyer personnel who change employment between law firms.

Factual Background

In December 1990, real parties in interest Darryl and Marilyn St. Germaine (collectively, "the St. Germaines" or "plaintiffs"), through their former lawyer Richard D. Engler, filed a personal injury suit alleging products liability and premises liability against Smart and other defendants. The St. Germaines subsequently retained their present counsel, Don B. Engler, the brother of Richard D. Engler, to represent them in this action. Don Engler is a sole practitioner in Yuma.

Smart retained the law firm of Mower, Koeller, Nebeker, Carlson & Haluck ("Mower, Koeller") to defend it in that litigation. The Yuma office of Mower, Koeller consists of two lawyers and three support staff. Co-counsel Constance Miller and William A. Nebeker of that firm worked on the case. Ms. Miller also worked with her secretary, Janet Gregston, who has been employed "in a secretarial/

paralegal capacity" at Mower, Koeller since September 1991. According to Ms. Miller's affidavit, Ms. Gregston's paralegal duties involved extensive work on the St. Germaine/Smart litigation:

[Ms. Gregston] worked extensively [on this case] in numerous confidential settings. . . . [She] was privy to exhaustive client confidences, correspondences between counsel and clients, strategic planning, litigation preparation and documentation, pretrial conferences with clients, lay and expert witnesses. She participated in the preparation of trial exhibits and is shown in one test video which may be presented at trial.

According to counsel for Lutes, Ms. Gregston participated in numerous discussions with co-defendants, clients, and experts, involving strategic planning for a cooperative defense.

On October 8, 1993, approximately 60 days prior to the firm trial date, Ms. Gregston suddenly terminated her employment at Mower, Koeller. [FN omitted.] On October 18, 1993, she began new employment as a legal secretary for plaintiffs' lawyer Don Engler. According to Mr. Engler's avowal to the court:

[C]ontrary to Mrs. Gregston's duties while in Ms. Miller's employ . . . her duties [in Engler's employ] do not include a broad spectrum of "paralegal" tasks. To the contrary, Mrs. Gregston was employed to perform the specific professional duties of a legal secretary.

This means that Mrs. Gregston is responsible only to prepare those pleadings, motions and correspondence which [Engler] dictates, in conformance with [his] directions. Mrs. Gregston's contact with clients generally, and in this case in particular, is limited to receipt of telephone messages and placing of telephone calls for the undersigned.

Mr. Engler also avowed that he had given "specific and segregated authority" to a separate paralegal with her own secretary for "[a]ll matters relating to discovery, client conferences, preparation of discovery motions for final review . . . , trial exhibits, and pretrial statements . . ." and that "Mrs. Gregston has no responsibility in regards to these matters whatsoever." Similarly, Ms. Gregston's affidavit states that, prior to her employment with Mr. Engler, she was informed that she would not be asked to reveal any confidences she had learned in her prior employment,

and to report to Mr. Engler if she were ever questioned by anyone in the office regarding her knowledge gained from her employment at Mower, Koeller. However, Ms. Gregston's initials and signature appear on several pleadings in this case, both in the underlying litigation and in special action papers filed in this court. Thus, it is apparent she is presently performing secretarial work on this case.

On November 15, 1993, Smart filed a motion to disqualify Engler as plaintiffs' counsel, based on imputed disqualification of Engler's firm under ER 1.10, Rule 42, Rules of the Arizona Supreme Court, [FN omitted] because of Ms. Gregston's employment by Engler. [FN omitted.] The motion relied heavily on the California case of *In re Complex Asbestos Litigation,* 232 Cal. App. 3d 572, 283 Cal. Rptr. 732 (Dist. 1 1991).

In response, Mr. Engler argued that ER 1.10 had no application in a nonlawyer context, and that California case law was distinguishable. Furthermore, he contended, he had met the requirements of the applicable ethical rule, ER 5.3, [FN omitted] by instructing Ms. Gregston not to divulge confidences. Thus, he concluded, disqualification was not required.

At a hearing on the motion, the trial court questioned its authority to order disqualification based on the conduct of a nonlawyer. The court subsequently ruled as follows:

The issue covered by this order is whether the plaintiffs' attorney must be disqualified to continue to act by reason of the fact that he has hired a secretary/legal assistant who formerly worked for counsel for a defendant and who, it is contended, did a great deal of work on this case and has considerable "inside information" about the case.

. . . .

Plaintiffs' counsel has contended that he has studiously insulated himself from any possible knowledge his employee might have, and the court accepts this as true.

Were this an attorney there would be absolutely no doubt in the court's mind that disqualification would be proper. This is not an attorney.

Not being an attorney, two thoughts are raised.

The first is that the court really has no method of protecting the privilege of confidentiality which Ms. Miller's client is entitled to enjoy.

The second is that there is no code of conduct in place which would guide a lawyer. The code of conduct is that of the employer.

The upshot of all of this is that the continued representation of the plaintiff by her attorney and a defendant attorney's former employee looks bad. It cannot be but perceived by the public that something fishy is going on. Thus, it smells bad, too.

However bad it may appear, mere appearance of evil is not a sufficient basis for the court to disqualify an attorney. While it may be that he should, ethically, withdraw, the court is not in a position to force the issue.

ORDERED that the motion to disqualify plaintiffs' counsel is overruled.

Smart petitioned for special action from this order.

DISCUSSION

A. Standard of Review

Rulings on disqualification motions are within the discretion of the trial court, limited only by the applicable legal principles. See, e.g., In re Complex Asbestos Litigation, 283 Cal. Rptr. at 739. Our review is thus limited to a determination whether the trial court abused its discretion. Id.

B. Application of Ethical Rules to Disqualification Motions

The trial court apparently questioned its authority to disqualify a lawyer based on the conduct of a nonlawyer, when that conduct falls outside the scope of the disciplinary system. Smart argues that the court's ruling therefore may have constituted a failure to exercise discretion, as much as an abuse of discretion. As a preliminary matter, then, we determine the basis for the trial court's authority to disqualify a lawyer based upon employment of nonlawyer personnel.

. . . A trial court's authority to apply an ethical rule to govern a disqualification motion in a litigation setting derives from the inherent power of the court to control judicial officers in any proceeding before it. See In re Complex Asbestos Litigation, 283 Cal. Rptr. at 739. As one court has defined this inherent authority:

> Attorney disqualification of counsel is a part of a court's duty to safeguard the sacrosanct privacy of the attorney-client relationship which is necessary to maintain public confidence in the legal profession and to protect the integrity of the judicial process.
>
> Panduit Corp. v. All States Plastic Mfg. Co., 744 F.2d 1564, 1576 (Fed. Cir. 1984).

The trial court's quandary in this case, however, was that the disqualification motion was based on the conduct of a nonlawyer, over whom the Model Rules have no effect in a disciplinary setting. However, as both Smart and the St. Germaines point out, the operation of ER 1.10(b) may be extended to the conduct of nonlawyers through ER 5.3. This duty imposes on a lawyer the duty to supervise a nonlawyer employee, which includes "reasonable efforts to ensure that the person's conduct is compatible with the professional obligations of the lawyer. . . ." ER 5.3(b). The duty of supervision also includes lawyer responsibility for any nonlawyer conduct "that would be a violation of the rules of professional conduct if engaged in by a lawyer," if the lawyer orders, has knowledge of, or ratifies such conduct. ER 5.3(c).

The lawyer's duty of supervision over, and responsibility for, the conduct of a nonlawyer assistant under ER 5.3 clearly encompasses the protection of client confidences communicated to a nonlawyer assistant, such as a paralegal or secretary. See id. at 433 n.8, 844 P.2d at 600 n.8 (obligations over nonlawyer include insuring client confidentiality). Under these combined principles, we conclude that a trial court has authority, in a litigation setting, to disqualify counsel on the basis of a nonlawyer assistant's conduct that would violate an ethical rule protecting a client's confidential communications to a lawyer. Therefore, to the extent that the trial court's ruling in this case may have been based on the erroneous assumption that it lacked authority to disqualify a lawyer based on the conduct of a nonlawyer, that ruling constitutes a failure to exercise discretion necessary "to safeguard the sacrosanct privacy of the attorney-client relationship which is necessary to maintain public confidence in the legal profession and to protect the integrity of the judicial process." See Panduit, 744 F.2d at 1576; see also Rule 3(a), Arizona Rules of Special Actions (special actions may address failure of judicial officer "to exercise discretion which he has a duty to exercise").

C. Application of Imputed Disqualification Rules to a Nonlawyer Assistant

Having concluded that a trial court has the authority, in a litigation context, to disqualify counsel based on the conduct of a nonlawyer assistant that is incompatible with the lawyer's ethical obligations, we turn next to the standard to be applied in determining whether disqualification is mandated under the facts of this case.

This is a case of first impression in Arizona. Indeed, we note that very few jurisdictions have considered the issue, either in the context of litigation case law or in ethical opinions. Those that have addressed the issue tend to apply the same standards to nonlawyers as are applied to lawyers under the jurisdiction's applicable disciplinary rules regarding imputed disqualification.

Thus, if, under the jurisdiction's applicable ethical rules, a lawyer can be saved from imputing disqualification to his or her new firm by appropriate screening mechanisms, then a paralegal's or secretary's potential conflict in the new firm can be avoided by the same mechanisms, sometimes described as "Chinese Walls," or "cones of silence." *See, e.g., Kapco; In re Complex Asbestos Litigation.* However, if the jurisdiction does not recognize such a "screening" option as adequate protection against a lawyer's potential conflict in the new firm, then it usually does not recognize such an exception to the imputed disqualification rule for a nonlawyer assistant. *See, e.g., Glover Bottled Gas Corp.;* Kansas Bar Ass'n Ethical Op. No. 90-555.

Arizona law does not recognize screening devices to avoid imputed disqualification of the new law firm to which a lawyer moves when that lawyer possesses client confidences and the new firm has interests adverse to that client. *Towne,* 173 Ariz. at 369, 842 P.2d at 1382. In *Towne,* we interpreted ER 1.10(b) and the comments thereto, as adopted by our supreme court, to require that, when a lawyer in possession of client confidences moves from one firm to another, that movement imputes absolute disqualification to the new firm in any matter materially adverse to the client. *Id.* at 365, 842 P.2d at 1378. We adopted the trial court's conclusion that the firm and the lawyer had "scrupulously maintained" an ironclad wall to screen him from any adverse representation of the client undertaken by the new firm. [FN omitted.] *Id.* at 368, 842 P.2d at 1381. However, we concluded:

Unfortunately, these efforts do not suffice.

. . . .

The language of ER 1.10 is absolute. When, as in this case, the moving lawyer has acquired

protected information, the rule admits waiver or consent as the only exception to imputed disqualification of the receiving firm. This mandatory bright line was drawn in deliberate contradistinction to ER 1.11, which permits a screening solution when lawyers move from government practice to private firms. . . .

. . .

ER 1.10, as adopted in Arizona, rejects walling off a tainted attorney as an alternative to imputed disqualification of the firm.

Id. at 368-69, 842 P.2d at 1381-82 (citations and footnotes omitted) [FN omitted].

We are also reluctant, however, to adopt the reasoning of those jurisdictions that have declined to adopt the "cone of silence" screening defense for lawyers, but then have blindly applied this rule to the analogous nonlawyer situation without first examining whether any distinction exists between the two situations.

In ABA Informal Opinion, the Committee was asked whether, under the Model Rules, a law firm that hires a paralegal who was formerly employed by another lawyer must withdraw from representation in a matter adverse to a client of the former firm about whom the paralegal had obtained substantial information relating to the suit. The employing firm proposed to "screen the paralegal from receiving information about or working on the lawsuit and will direct the paralegal not to reveal any information relating to the representation of the sole practitioner's client gained by the paralegal during the former employment." *Id.* at 318. Although acknowledging that ER 1.10(b) does "not recognize screening the *lawyer* from sharing the information in the employing firm as a mechanism to avoid disqualification of the entire firm" (emphasis added), the Committee nonetheless found screening the *nonlawyer* to be an acceptable alternative to disqualification of the new firm, for the following reasons:

In the case of nonlawyers changing firms, however, additional considerations are present which persuade the Committee that the functional analysis [of the Seventh Circuit] in *Kapco* is more appropriate than would be a rule requiring automatic disqualification once the nonlawyer is shown to have acquired information in the former employment relating to the representation of the opponent.

It is important that nonlawyer employees have as much mobility in employment opportunity as possible consistent with the protection of clients' interest. To so limit employment opportunities that some nonlawyers trained to work with law firms might be required to leave the careers for which they are trained would disserve clients as well as the legal profession. Accordingly, any restrictions on the nonlawyer's employment should be held to the minimum necessary to protect confidentiality of client information.

Id. at 320.

We note that a similar "issue of fairness" was recognized by the Kansas Bar Association even though it ultimately rejected screening of nonlawyers as an alternative to disqualification:

A rigid rule of "if the employee possess[es] information which if possessed by an attorney is a conflict, the hiring firm is disqualified" raises important questions, not the least of which is the anomalous proposition that the more skilled a legal assistant or other employee becomes to the employer and the more information he or she acquires on cases in the firm, such assistant becomes *less* valuable to other firms with significant caseloads with the current employer. . . . [A] literal reading [of this rigid rule] would stymie a legal assistant's career, or at the very least make them "Typhoid Marys," unemployable by firms practicing in specialized areas of the law where the employees are most skilled and experienced.

KBA Ethics Op. No. 90-005 at 6-7.

Noting this concern for the ability of nonlawyers to change employment, the California court in *Complex Asbestos Litigation* added its concern for the rights of clients to obtain counsel of their own choosing; balanced against those concerns, however, are "the need to maintain ethical standards of professional responsibility," and "the paramount concern" for "the preservation of public trust in the scrupulous administration of justice and the integrity of the bar." 283 Cal. Rptr. at 740. We too agree that all these concerns are relevant and important in determining a disqualification issue; however, we are wary of allowing a literal reading of a rule appropriate for lawyers to become a means of injustice to the parties when applied to nonlawyers if there are valid reasons to draw distinctions between them.

. . .

We believe that this reason for treating government lawyers differently in the context of imputed disqualification cases applies equally to nonlawyer assistants, who, unlike lawyers in private practice, generally have neither a financial interest in the outcome of a particular litigation, nor the choice of which clients they serve. Moreover, in our opinion, the public perception of what is expected of lawyers as compared to nonlawyers is different, probably based on the "independent contractor" status enjoyed by lawyers as compared to the "master/servant" role of nonlawyer assistants. Our analysis, thus, is directed to determining the scope and extent of a supervising lawyer's ethical duty under ER 5.3, to insure that a nonlawyer's conduct in this "master/servant" setting is compatible with other ethical obligations.

In ABA Informal Opinion, the Committee construed the lawyer's duty under Model Rule 5.3, to assure that a nonlawyer's conduct is "compatible" with the lawyer's ethical obligations. "Compatible" requirements to preserve confidentiality under Model Rule 5.3 in the supervision of the nonlawyer, but not "identical" to those imposed on lawyers under Model Rule 1.10(b), included the following:

(a) appropriate instruction and supervision concerning the ethical aspects of their employment, particularly regarding the obligation not to disclose information relating to representation of the client;

(b) admonitions to be alert to all legal matters, including lawsuits, in which any client of the former employer had an interest. The nonlawyer should be cautioned:

   (1) not to disclose any information relating to the representation of a client of the former employer; *and*

   (2) *that the employee should not work on any matter on which the employee worked for the prior employer or respecting which the employee has information relating to the representation of the client of the former employer.*

Id. at 320-21 (emphasis and blocked format added).

We conclude that the screening requirements articulated above are sufficient to satisfy a lawyer's duty under ER 5.3 to supervise a nonlawyer employee in a manner that will assure conduct "compatible" with the lawyer's ethical obligations. Thus, satisfaction of these requirements will prevent disqualification of the firm based on a nonlawyer's potential conflict even though a stricter standard is imposed on lawyers by operation of ER 1.10(b). *See Towne.* [FN omitted.]

Applying these concepts to this case, however, we conclude that Smart is entitled to disqualification of plaintiffs' counsel under the undisputed facts before us. First, there is no question that Ms. Gregston obtained client confidences in her former employment; the St. Germaines do not contend that her involvement in the case was any less than lawyer Miller has alleged. Second, there is no question that these client confidences are substantially related to the representation by her current employer; indeed, she is now on the other side of the same lawsuit, which is pending trial. It is also clear on this record that Smart did not consent to her employment by opposing counsel, nor did Smart waive its objection to her new employment. [FN omitted.]

We understand that plaintiffs' counsel instructed Ms. Gregston not to divulge any client confidences gained in her former employment, and, as previously mentioned, we accept as true counsel's avowals, in both this court and the trial court, that he has insulated himself from any possible disclosure. However, this instruction and insulation do not necessarily satisfy the minimum requirements necessary under ER 5.3 to prevent disqualification. In this case, counsel does not dispute that Ms. Gregston has not been screened from participation in the actual litigation with which she was intimately involved in her former employment; rather, she has initialed and signed pleadings and correspondence in this record. She has also submitted personal affidavits as evidence, in both the trial court and in this court. Counsel's avowal that Ms. Gregston's duties are limited to typing and taking phone messages is not sufficient to remove her from involvement in the case in a manner that would significantly decrease the likelihood of a prohibited disclosure, even inadvertently. *See, e.g.,* Maryland State Bar Ethics Op. 90-17 (secretary whose duties are "limited to typing" must be screened from information about or participation in matters involving clients of her former employer); *see also LaSalle Nat'l Bank v. County of Lake,* 703 F.2d 252 (7th Cir. 1983) (promise not to discuss case was inadequate screening). Furthermore, we observe that counsel's refusal, after a strong suggestion by the trial court to withdraw, to even offer to screen this employee from working on the very matter which gave rise to the problem shows an apparent insensitivity by counsel to the valid concerns of the adverse client that confidences may be disclosed by the nonlawyer who had such a significant involvement on the other side of the case for over two years. [FN omitted.] Such conduct by counsel is insufficient to protect the "reputation of the bar as a whole." *Id.* at 259.

Under the facts of this case, we conclude that the trial court should have granted the motion to disqualify plaintiffs' counsel, and abused its discretion in failing to do so. No screening mechanism was utilized to assure Smart that its confidences were preserved, and, at this stage of the litigation, given Ms. Gregston's participation on behalf of the St. Germaines, we cannot fashion any remedial action that counsel could employ to mitigate Smart's perception that its confidences could be compromised, or to satisfy the duties imposed by ER 5.3.

CONCLUSION

For the foregoing reasons, we hold that the trial court abused its discretion in denying Smart's motion to disqualify. We remand this matter to the trial court for entry of an order consistent with this opinion. [FN omitted.]

Source: Reprinted from Westlaw with permission from Thomson Reuters.

Chapter 6

Fees and Client Property

Chapter Objectives

The student will be able to:

- Evaluate the reasonableness of attorney's fees using the appropriate factors
- Determine whether paralegal fees could be part of an award of fees
- Recognize improper fee-sharing or fee-splitting arrangements and how they apply to employed paralegals
- Discuss the attorney's (and paralegal's) duty to ensure that a client's property is kept securely

This chapter will examine particular issues that affect the attorney-client relationship at its core. *How much* can an attorney reasonable charge for her services? *When* can she charge the client for legal services performed by the paralegal? *What* should the law firm do with clients' money and property when it is under the firm's control?

There are few issues that affect the very essence of attorney-client relationships more than money. As parties consider entering into the agreement, they need to understand not only their individual roles as either the attorney or the client, but also the details relating to the duties and disclosures required from the attorney to assist the client in obtaining the larger goal of representation. These can be discussed in a chronological manner. First, the attorney must set a reasonable fee for her services in order for the client to determine whether or not to enter into the relationship, by weighing the cost with the expected benefit in going forward. Second, the attorney must determine whether the paralegal's tasks will be billable and/or recoverable. Third, there must be strict control over what an attorney does with the fees, monies, and property of the client. Along with the duty of confidentiality (keeping a client's secrets safe), an attorney must also be able to safely keep a client's property. This means that she must have places and procedures already set up before taking on the matter that will require them.

ESTABLISHING FEES

Perhaps one of the most notorious issues surrounding attorneys is the cost of legal services. Indeed, the development of the paralegal profession was a direct response to this issue. While ABA Model Rule 1.5 speaks at length regarding fees, there is no restriction on the amount of fee, as long as it is "reasonable." The issue of fees is not new.

> Justice should be administered economically, efficiently, and expeditiously. The attorney's fee is, therefore, a very important factor in the administration of justice, and if it is not determined with proper relation to that fact it results in a species of social malpractice that undermines the confidence of the public in the bench and bar. It does more than that; it brings the court into disrepute and destroys its power to perform adequately the function of its creation.

> *Baruch v. Giblin*, 122 Fla. 59, 164 So. 831 (1936).

The retainer agreement that creates the service contract between the attorney and client varies widely. At its core, it establishes the work to be performed and the fees to be paid. A sample is provided in Figure 6.1. However, there is great diversity in forms; this is illustrated well in the Table of Contents of *Legal Representation and Fee Agreements for the Maryland Lawyer: Forms and Comments*, 2d ed. by Christopher L. Beard, Esq., C. Michael Bradshaw, and The Honorable Richard C. Goodwin (available through the Maryland Institute for Continuing Professional Education for Lawyers, Inc., which can be accessed at: http://msba.inreachce.com/. (See Figure 6.2. Yes, it's long; that's the point. There are so many nuances that affect the final agreement.)

Chapter 10. Civil Rights

VII. Attorney's Fees

B. Procedural Forms

§ 10:385. Retainer agreement—Between client and attorney

Form of Retainer Agreement

1. [Name of client] hereby agrees to retain [name of attorney] as [his/her] attorney to represent [him/her] with respect to all claims against [name of defendant] or any other person (including a corporation or governmental body) arising out of incidents occurring on or about [list of dates of incidents], in which [name of client] was subjected to discriminatory treatment in [specification of nature of discrimination] because of [his/her] [race/color/creed/sex/marital status/national origin].

2. Client hereby authorizes the attorney to retain, associate, join, or dismiss additional attorneys on client's behalf as the attorney deems necessary. Client further authorizes the attorney or other attorney(s) designated by the attorney to conduct any negotiations on client's behalf, and, as the attorney deems necessary, to commence any litigation or other proceedings, including actions in any appropriate forum.

3. It is further understood and agreed that the attorney may employ any qualified person(s) to assist in the preparation of the case to the extent permitted by the law.

4. It is expressly agreed between the attorney and client that the client shall have the obligation to pay a fee from all amounts and other consideration recovered in cash, as well as in kind or otherwise, as a result of a settlement compromise, or judgment, including punitive damages unless an equal or greater attorney fee is awarded by court order or judgment, or by a provision in any settlement agreement reached with any other party expressly providing a sum certain for a reasonable attorney fee.

5. The attorney reserves the right to seek a court award of attorney fees to be paid by the defendant or defendant's attorney and the client agrees to pay the attorney the amount of any such fee actually recovered from the defendant, whether or not this amount exceeds the fee established by reference to paragraph 6, below.

6. The fee shall be determined by applying the following agreed schedule of compensation to any recovery:

   a. [percentage of amount recovered]% on the first $1,000 recovered to the attorney;

   b. [percentage of amount recovered]% on the next $19,000 recovered to the attorney;

   c. [percentage of amount recovered]% on the next $30,000 recovered to the attorney;

   d. [percentage of amount recovered]% on any amount recovered over $50,000 to the attorney.

   This fee schedule shall apply to any consideration received from the defendant, whether in kind or as a cash recovery or settlement, but shall not preclude the attorney from a greater recovery, if so provided by paragraph 5.

continued

◀ **FIGURE 6.1**

SAMPLE RETAINER AGREEMENT
Source:
5 FEDERAL PROCEDURAL FORMS § 10:385. Chapter 10. Civil Rights. VII. Attorney's Fees. Reprinted with permission from Thomson Reuters.

FIGURE 6.1 ▶
SAMPLE RETAINER
AGREEMENT
(CONTINUED)

7. It is understood and agreed that the attorney may advance any and all disbursements incurred by the attorney in connection with this representation, including, but not limited to filing and service fees, costs of discovery and investigations, expert witness and subpoena fees, photocopying, printing, and other incidental expenses, etc. The client authorizes the attorney to withhold from any award recovered in connection with this representation, an amount equal to any unreimbursed disbursements or costs, prior to calculating the permissible fee.

8. The permissible fee provided for in the above schedule shall be computed on the net sum recovered after disbursements advanced by the attorney in connection with the institution and prosecution of the claim have first been reimbursed to the attorney by the client.

9. The foregoing fee agreement shall not apply to legal services rendered on any appeal, review proceeding or retrial, and this agreement shall not be deemed to require the attorney to take an appeal.

Billing

timesheet
An accurate, daily record of time spent on each task performed by an attorney or paralegal for each client.

An unavoidable element to the practice of law is the **timesheet**. (See Figure 6.3: Daily Time Record.) Attorneys and paralegals watch the clock all day, recording how much time it takes to complete each and every task of the day and to what client it is attributable. Very often there are "work codes" or abbreviations used for tasks that are performed frequently. Examples are "TC" for telephone call, "DR" for draft, "RR" for receipt and review of correspondence, "LR" for legal research, and so on. Whether that amount of time is actually billed to the client is another matter; this is referred to as the **billable hour**. Supervising attorneys have the discretion to reduce the bill to compensate for inexperience or other factors. For example, imagine the new associate is assigned a relatively complex complaint to draft, not having had much drafting experience. Hoping to impress the partner, the associate spends ten hours on the complaint. At $100 an hour, the actual timesheet reflects $1000 due for that work; however, the supervising attorney knows that this is not a reasonable amount of time for an average associate to spend on the matter. She, therefore, reduces the amount to five hours on the client's bill, reflecting the real value of the service rendered to the client. The new associate is not in any trouble for this "loss" in billables, as the other five hours are considered part of the learning curve, a known and anticipated "expense" of training a new lawyer or paralegal. The importance of accurate time records cannot be overemphasized. An attorney may lose money that may have been properly earned but is reduced through a court's intervention as "unreasonable" due to improper documentation. Essentially, the court is not finding that the time spent or hourly fee is necessarily unreasonable, but that not having accurate time records is unreasonable and punishable by that reduction. *See In re Trust of McDonald*, 858 S.W.2d 271, 279 (Mo. App. 1993) (The attorney billed $30,000 in fees representing "over 400 hours"; however, he did not keep very good time records. The court found the fee was excessive in the absence of adequate evidence of having spent that time). Further, summarization of work performed without

billable hour
Time (totaling one hour) spent on a client's matter for which the client is responsible to pay, as the attorney's effort relates to and benefits the client's matter.

MARYLAND ATTORNEY FEE AGREEMENTS
FORMS AND COMMENTS
TABLE OF CONTENTS

continued

FIGURE 6.2 ▶

TYPES OF MARYLAND
ATTORNEY
FEE AGREEMENTS
(CONTINUED)

continued

FIGURE 6.2 ▶
TYPES OF MARYLAND
ATTORNEY
FEE AGREEMENTS
(CONTINUED)

FIGURE 6.3 ▶
DAILY TIME RECORD

TIME CONVERSIONS:

6 minutes = .1 hour
12 minutes = .2 hour
18 minutes = .3 hour
24 minutes = .4 hour
30 minutes = .5 hour
36 minutes = .6 hour
42 minutes = .7 hour
48 minutes = .8 hour
54 minutes = .9 hour

DATE:

Client	File No.	Task Performed	Supervising Attorney	Time Spent

specifics can result in a reduction of permissible fees. The Court in *Colorado Hospitality Services Inc. v. Owners Ins. Co.*, 154 F. Supp. 3d 1173, 1179 (D. Colo. 2015), opined that weekly summaries of work performed, particularly with vague notations such as "trial preparation," were unacceptable.

double-billing
Charging two or more clients for the same services and/or same time period.

While sloppy or absent time records may result in a reduction of the attorney's fee, inaccurate timesheets result in severe disciplinary action. Padding timesheets and **"double-billing"** are absolutely unacceptable in the legal profession. Both these practices involve fraud and dishonesty, which are prohibited under the ethical rules and impinge on the integrity of the profession itself. Padding time refers to adding extra minutes or hours that were not spent onto those that were spent. As with any ethical violation, the claim that no actual harm occurred is not a valid defense. Even if the supervising attorney reduces the amount of time billed to accurately reflect the actual time spent, or the time doesn't get billed to the client at all as in a contingent fee case, the act of padding is its own violation. Junior associates may feel the pressure to bill as many hours as humanly possible and may even fear for their jobs; however, this does not excuse the padding, even when done with the permission of the supervising attorney. One associate testified that he

> [decided] to "pad" my bills in the plaintiff's personal injury contingency fee cases on which I was working by logging time that I did not actually work.

I felt this was the most acceptable solution to my dilemma, because (a) bills in plaintiff's personal injury contingency fee cases are not paid by the client, so there was no real damage done to anyone by a "padded bill," and (b) when my total hours were checked by the partners of the firm, the amount would be high enough to keep my job. While this was not a perfect solution to a tough dilemma, it was the best, in my view, under the circumstances.

In re Lawrence, 884 So. 2d 561, 563 (La. 2004) (attorney was suspended for three months).

Double-billing is the practice of charging two clients for the same time period; like being in two places at once, it is humanly impossible to work for two parties at once. In some circumstances this practice can result in charging for more hours than there are in a day! For example, an attorney flying out to a witness deposition may choose to bill Client A, for whom the witness is relevant, for his travel time, *or* he may choose to work on another matter entirely, for Client B. Those five hours spent in the plane will be billed to either one of the clients, but not *both*. His timesheets should not show six hours' worth of billing (three to Client A for the travel, and three to Client B for the work). Consider what would happen if after his three-hour deposition, he chose to spend six hours doing research that was relevant to two separate but very similar matters, and billed each client for those six hours. This would result in 25 hours of work in one day! ($5 \times 2 + 3 + 6 \times 2$). This may very well be a hard-working attorney (after all, the real time spent equals 14 hours of billable time), but no one can work 25 hours in a 24-hour day. Some courts have characterized double-billing not only as dishonesty, but also as misappropriation: essentially, stealing from clients. *See Disciplinary Counsel v. Holland*, 835 N.E.2d 361 (Ohio 2005) (although the attorney was not ultimately convicted of the charge of grand larceny, he was suspended for one year and was forced to repay the amount he had overcharged).

SURF'S UP

Technology has increased attorneys' productive capacity and has made it possible to "short-cut" some tasks and to perform others from a distance, where previously this was impossible. Cloud-based storage and File Transfer Protocol (FTP) sites allow attorneys to send electronic documents via the internet; database and knowledge-sharing sites make it possible to access information at the speed of sound instead of spending hours in the library; networked office computers gain access to the entire firm's work product. How has all this affected fees and billing practices? While the streamlined nature of technology has decreased the billable hours spent on a task, the value of obtaining and maintaining the technology has increased the per-hour earnings of attorneys.

Reasonable Fees

Setting of a reasonable fee is "measured" by balancing the following factors. Performing this analysis will not render a mathematically certain rate; it can only really determine whether a fee is truly exorbitant and, therefore, unreasonable. There are many factors to be taken into account when trying to determine whether a fee is reasonable. The first is straightforward: the amount of time and labor required to perform the tasks necessary to representation. Simple tasks cost less than more complicated, time-consuming ones. Aside from being simple or complex, a matter may pose new or unique challenges for the attorney and paralegal that may merit a higher fee. Highly skilled legal professionals can also garner higher fees because the client is paying for that talent. Of course, legal professionals with extensive experience in a particular field or those held in high regard by their peers are paid for their reputations as much as they are for their skill. These are factors that are characteristic of the individual legal professional. There are other factors under the control of the client that may affect the reasonableness of the fee. If the client is highly demanding of exclusive time with the attorney or paralegal and this prevents that professional from working on other matters, the fee may be higher. Additionally, if the client imposes significant time constraints on the attorney, then the fee can be increased. Rush orders always carry a premium. Objective factors are also taken into account when setting a reasonable fee. Attorneys are selling a commodity, and the local market will often determine the range of fees. Most firms or individual attorneys will charge about the same fee for similar legal services. It only makes ordinary business sense to do so. Further, the greater the amount of money at stake, the higher the fee may be to secure it. A multimillion-dollar real estate transaction can be billed out at a higher rate than a modest residential home purchase. Risk is allocated not only to the clients' outcomes but also to how the attorney plans on collecting the fee. Fixed fees based on hourly billing or other reliable and objectively determinable factors carry little risk of loss (aside from client nonpayment). Contingent fees, however, carry the risk that the attorney may not get paid any fees at all if the case is lost. Generally, contingent fees end up being higher than fixed fees due to this risk taking on the part of the attorney.

    A **reasonable fee** is determined by the above factors, and the courts have added several others in reviewing whether an attorney charged a fee that should be fairly recoverable. All of these fee review matters are evaluated on a case-by-case basis, as there is no standardization of attorneys' or paralegals' fees, either nationally or by state. Generally, when speaking of fees, people often simply ask for the hourly rate charged and then multiply it by the anticipated time it will take to complete the tasks at hand. But the base calculation only addresses the first two factors considered above. This is the **"lodestar calculation"** approach, which only can approximate the amount of fee.

    This lodestar calculation is just a starting point which can guide the rest of the inquiry into whether the fee is reasonable. The elements of novelty and difficulty must also enter into the equation. In this way, an attorney can estimate the amount

reasonable fee
A charge for legal services that accurately reflects the time, effort, and expertise spent on a client matter.

lodestar calculation
A mere guidepost for determining the amount of fees to be charged, by multiplying the time to be spent on the task by the attorney's hourly rate.

of time needed to competently prepare for the matter. If time expended were the only measure of reasonableness, attorneys and paralegals would have little incentive to work at their most efficient speed and, ironically, the most experienced legal professionals might receive less compensation for their efforts, because it would take them less time than their novice counterparts.

> The general agreement in all jurisdictions is that the time and labor spent by the attorney in performing services for which compensation is sought is an important factor to be considered in setting a reasonable fee. However, it is also commonly agreed that the time element must be considered in connection with other factors. Fees cannot fairly be awarded on the basis of time alone. The use of time as the sole criterion is of dubious value because economy of time could cease to be a virtue; and inexperience, inefficiency, and incompetence may be rewarded to the detriment of expeditious disposition of litigation.

Oliver's Sports Center, Inc. v. National Standard Ins. Co., 615 P.2d 291, 294 (Okla. 1980).

Factors to Consider

Courts have long-held that the following twelve factors all need to be considered in determining the reasonableness of attorney's fees:

1. Time and labor required.
2. The novelty and difficulty of the questions.
3. The skill requisite to perform the legal service properly.
4. The preclusion of other employment by the attorney due to acceptance of the case.
5. The customary fee.
6. Whether the fee is fixed or contingent.
7. Time limitations imposed by the client or the circumstances.
8. The amount involved and the results obtained.
9. The experience, reputation and ability of the attorneys.
10. The "undesirability" of the case.
11. The nature and length of the professional relationship with the client.
12. Awards in similar cases.

Evans v. Sheraton Park Hotel, 503 F.2d 177, 187-188 (D.C. Cir. 1974) (internal citations omitted).

Some of the above factors are relatively straightforward, while others require a more nuanced examination. Taking on an entirely new issue of law, one that has never been tested in the courts in the relevant jurisdiction before, or challenging the validity of an existing law takes time as well as courage. Novelty is also rewarded by an increase in attorney's fees. This will often be tied to the expenditure of a substantial amount of time. *See Rackow v. Illinois Human Rights Comm'n*, 504 N.E.2d 1344, 1351 (Ill. App. Ct. 1987):

> Additionally, while [. . .] counsel did not request it, the administrative law judge applied a multiplier of 1.5 to insure that reasonable attorney fees

were awarded, as this was a case of first impression before the Human Rights Commission. He noted that the amount of attorney fees may be large as compared with the relatively small amount of monetary damages, but justified his decision because this was a case of first impression and because the uniqueness of Illinois law under these circumstances required extensive research and analysis.

Further, spending time on one client's matter may prevent the legal professional from working on a matter for another. Despite the current emphasis on multitasking, attorneys and paralegals (as well as most other professionals) can and should do only one thing at a time. To reemphasize, working on more than one matter at a time is impermissible "double-billing" under the ethics rules. However, taking one case may not preclude taking another of a similar nature or one of a type with which the attorney has a good deal of experience, as these can be dealt with efficiently. Preclusion of other employment depends primarily upon the factors of complexity of the matter and experience of the attorney. On the other hand, some matters may be time intensive and therefore genuinely preclude work on other matters. *See Kittler and Hedelson v. Sheehan Properties, Inc.*, 203 N.W.2d 835 (Minn. 1973). In this case, the attorney was required to be absent from his office on extended and frequent international travel in order to properly handle the matter. Also, time limitations imposed by the client or by the circumstances would warrant a higher fee. The shorter the time period in which the legal professional has to operate, the more she must concentrate solely on that matter; the pressure adds an "urgency surcharge."

Attorneys are not immune from the economic principle of supply and demand. The "market" will reach some sort of average range in an area; consumers of the service will not (or should not) bear costs greatly in excess of this range. To determine whether a fee is reasonable, looking at the fee customarily charged in the locality for similar legal services is a good indicator. It is, of course, like all the other factors, not determinative, but merely one point of reference. This factor must be broken down into its elements:

customary fee
A rate generally charged in a given locality by lawyers of the same level of expertise and area of practice.

1. How does one arrive at the **customary fee**?
2. What is the relevant locality?
3. What is the degree of similarity between the services?

First, a court's evaluation of the "customary fee" begins with testimony from attorneys regarding the fees charged by them and their colleagues. Of course, as in any dispute, opinions will be offered on both the high and low sides of the issue. The court can then make some average calculation based upon this testimony. However, the average fees will depend largely on the second factor, the locality. In *Eve's Garden, Inc. v. Upshaw & Upshaw, Inc.*, 801 So. 2d 976 (Fla. App. 2001), the attorneys testifying as to the customary fee in the locality used the judicial circuit as the defining jurisdiction. The appellate court did not agree with the trial judge, who noted that the circuit included metropolitan areas in which attorneys often charged higher rates similar to the amount requested by the plaintiffs. The locality in this instance was a rural community and attorneys charged significantly less than attorneys in the metropolitan areas of the circuit. The locality must be sufficiently similar in nature and proximity to the place in which the action is brought. If there are no attorneys in that locality that practice a particular kind of law due to its uniqueness or complexity, then a court may look outward to the prevailing rates where that special attorney normally practices. *See Standard Theatres, Inc. v. State Dept. of Transp., Div. of Highways*, 349 N.W.2d 661 (Wis. 1984) (The attorney chosen by the condemnee in this condemnation case did not have an office in the county where the proceedings took place, but had practiced in this specialty area for decades. The Court found the "reasonable and necessary attorney fees [did] not mean that a condemnee must retain counsel from the locality where the condemned property is located in order to receive full compensation of attorney fees.") The next factor really refers to comparing "apples to apples": Not only the locality, but also the nature of the matter must be sufficiently similar. This analysis may include the number of parties, amount in controversy, difficulty of obtaining evidence, witness preparation, amount of documentation needed (either reviewed or prepared), and a host of other factors, in addition to the relevant area of law.

The amount of money at stake or the value placed on the results by the client also plays a part in determining whether the fee is reasonable. Fee agreements can reflect the understanding that the higher the stakes are, the higher the fee is. In some cases, an attorney can be awarded over and above the contingency fee agreement by using a "multiplier" to compensate the attorney for the results obtained for his client. A trial court may determine whether a multiplier is necessary by considering the following factors:

> (1) whether the relevant market requires a contingency fee multiplier to obtain competent counsel; (2) whether the attorney was able to mitigate the risk of nonpayment in any way; and (3) whether any of the factors set forth in Rowe are applicable, especially, the amount involved, the results obtained, and the type of fee arrangement between the attorney and his client. Evidence of these factors must be presented to justify the utilization of a multiplier.

> *Alvarado v. Cassarino*, 706 So.2d 380, 381 (Fla. App. 1998).

These factors are weighed with the likelihood of success as seen from the outset of the matter. The riskier the venture, the more apt the court is to employ a multiplier anywhere from 1.5 to 2.5. In the *Alvarado* case, the trial court applied a contingency risk multiplier of 1.5 to the attorney's fee of $57,570, which resulted in a total recovery by the attorney of $86,355 for his work.

Contrary to this multiplication of the fee for hard, risky work is the court's ability to reduce the recoverable contingent fee because it is not reasonable in the circumstances. In *People v. Egbune*, 58 P.3d 1168, 1173–1174 (Colo. 1999), the attorney and client entered into a 35 percent contingent fee agreement. The matter settled quickly for $17,500 and the attorney collected a fee of $6,122.

While this seems mathematically reasonable, the surrounding circumstances rendered it unreasonable. The attorney worked for only three weeks and "did no more than make a few phone calls to the insurance adjuster, meet with his client, examine some medical treatment records and do some research at the law library to determine the reasonable range of settlement for [these types of] claims." The attorney's work did very little to enhance the client's claim and therefore he was not entitled to such a large share of it.

Attorneys are essentially skilled craftsmen; you pay not only for the time spent on a project but also for the talent of the particular "artist." Delicate or complicated matters may take more finesse rather than more time and the attorney should be compensated for this effort. This is where the "lodestar" approach fails. Adeptness should be ultimately rewarded. One court eloquently stated it this way:

> The evidence before me bearing upon an attorney's fee is as follows. This is a private anti-trust suit which was not preceded by a public or even another private suit in the same industry. Plaintiff's chief counsel, James D. Saint Clair, Esq., in his thoroughness of preparation, economy of effort, choice of emphasis, quality of examination and cross-examination, presentation of argument, analysis of the law, courtesy to parties, witnesses, opposing counsel, and the Court, and that indefinable distinction with breathes excellence, can stand comparison with any lawyer who has appeared before me in the last dozen years. The success that he achieved, while founded on the merit of plaintiff's case, was by no means inevitable. In hands less gifted and with a lawyer less persuasive to a jury, plaintiff's cause might well have gone a-gley. Here as in earlier cases, plaintiff's counsel has shown that despite his relative youth and his short career at the bar, he is quite capable of holding his own against the most experienced advocates of our profession. With becoming deference to his seniors, but with unflinching courage in examining witnesses, in meeting opposing arguments, and in resisting what he regarded as unsound rulings from the bench, plaintiff's counsel set a model not likely to be surpassed. [...] Sometimes the figure may seem high. But so far as price is determined by unique excellence and by social usefulness, the advocate is especially worthy of large recompense. [...] Unless excellence in the trial lawyer is properly recompensed, the best men will not spend their time in court, and thus there will dry up the most essential sources of an independent bar.

Cape Cod Food Products v. National Cranberry Ass'n, 119 F. Supp. 242, 242-243 (D.C. Mass. 1954).

certified specialist
An attorney who has been acknowledged to have specialized and demonstrated knowledge in a particular area of law by a bar-recognized legal association.

Experience and reputation also garner significant premiums. Usually an attorney with both of these can efficiently handle a certain matter better than another without them. Specialists and boutique firms fall into this category. A "**certified specialist**," an attorney that has proven her ability to the bar association, may certainly reasonably demand a higher fee.

Last in our discussion is the nature and length of the professional relationship with the client, which factors into the "reasonableness" equation.

IN-CLASS DISCUSSION

The real-life drama surrounding Anna Nicole Smith did not get laid to rest at her funeral in February of 2007. The paternity suit filed (and won) by Larry Birkhead resulted in exorbitant legal fees nearing one million dollars. His attorney, Debra Opri, filed a lawsuit for unpaid legal bills and Mr. Birkhead countersued, claiming Attorney Opri had agreed to represent Mr. Birkhead for free because the publicity would benefit her career. Mr. Birkhead's lawsuit accused Attorney Opri of charging Mr. Birkhead not only for costs directly associated with his representation but also for her travel expenses, dinners with friends, and entertainment expenses. While Mr. Birkhead was capable of making the payments demanded by Attorney Opri, he maintained that the fee agreement stated that he would not be charged for her services. Who do you think is at fault in this situation? What could have been done to avoid the fee disagreement? Is the purported fee arrangement fair? Should this type of arrangement be allowed in celebrity or high-profile cases? Why or why not?

Under appropriate circumstances, an attorney who is the attorney for a client who has frequent and continuing legal problems may make appropriate adjustment of the amount of the fee charged. What would be a reasonable fee to such a client may not be the same as for a client who sees the lawyer for the first time.

Peebles v. Miley, 439 So. 2d 137, 143 (Ala. 1983).

It may be that the attorney is rewarding client loyalty and/or that the attorney is better able to use efficiencies of scale when dealing with the same client over and over. The background information remains the same, the risk of nonpayment is probably not present (attorneys are not apt to agree to represent a client in a new matter when there are significant outstanding bills), and the possibility exists of reusing work product and general familiarity with the issues; all of these factors weigh in favor of a previous client "discount." On the other hand, an attorney may know what is in store for him if he does take on another matter for this client and therefore, being warned of the difficulties that might be encountered yet again, may choose to adjust the fee upward to compensate for the reasonably anticipated hardships in taking on another matter for this client.

PARALEGAL FEES

The range of reasonableness is extraordinarily large in determining an attorney's fee. Practically speaking, a better measure is to establish that the fee is not unconscionable and then justify its sum by balancing the above factors. The same approach is taken in determining a paralegal's fee to be awarded in a case. This is not to say that paralegals are directly compensated or earn individual fees payable to them, but rather that, if an attorney is awarded fees by a court, the attorney may properly include billable hours performed by a paralegal in the total submission for compensation. For an example of this type of submission, see Figure 6.4.

The bill for the paralegal services should be at the prevailing market rate for paralegals in that jurisdiction, not at the cost of the services to the attorney. In other words, even if the paralegal is paid $25 per hour, the attorney can bill at the prevailing rate, which can be significantly higher, as in Figure 6.4. *See also* NALA's National Utilization and Compensation Survey, which is conducted approximately every two years (available on their website under "Research and Survey Findings"). Paralegals' work is part of the "attorney work product" for which the office collects its fee. The United States Supreme Court validated this approach in *Missouri v. Jenkins*, 491 U.S. 274, 109 S. Ct. 2463, 105 L. Ed. 2d 22 (1989). The plaintiff, Jenkins, brought a suit against the State of Missouri under a civil rights statute that also permitted the award of attorney's fees. The State argued that the paralegal fees should be calculated at their actual cost to the attorney to prevent a "windfall" to the firm. The Court rejected this argument. "By encouraging the use of lower cost paralegals rather than attorneys wherever possible, permitting market-rate billing of paralegal hours encourages cost-effective delivery of legal services and, by reducing the spiraling cost of civil rights litigation, furthers the policies underlying civil rights statutes." *Id.* at 288.

> The award of paralegal fees is not limited to civil rights proceedings. In any case where a statute or other legal authority permits the prevailing party to recover attorney's fees and costs against the opposition, paralegal fees may be included. This award of fees is contrary to the traditional "American Rule," where each party is responsible for his own attorney's fees. The requirement for submitting expenses to the court for an award is reasonableness, proper justification, and detail in calculating that fee. The Supreme Court of Rhode Island stated it simply: Our legal community, like the majority of jurisdictions in the United States, separately lists the paralegal services that are compensable. Therefore, the trial justice may use his discretion in determining whether the proffered fees are reasonable and whether the paralegal work performed was *a necessary element in the proceeding*."

Schroff, Inc. v. Taylor-Peterson, 732 A.2d 719, 721 (R.I. 1999) (emphasis added).

FIGURE 6.4 ▶
SAMPLE CALCULATION
FOR SERVICES

Employee	Billable Hours	Rate	Total
Senior Attorney	1,000	$350	$ 350,000
Associate	1,200	$250	$ 300,000
Paralegal	1,500	$115	$ 172,500
Total Compensation			$ 822,500

RESEARCH THIS

Find the local prevailing rates for paralegal time in your locality. You can look online for paralegal salary surveys or career information sites, contact recruiters, or do it the old-fashioned way and interview employers.

It is important to note that the purpose of the billed paralegal work must be sufficiently specified so that the court can make a determination that the paralegal work was a necessary element in preparing the matter. If the type of work is not described adequately, the court can deny reimbursement for those paralegal fees. This, of course, brings the paralegal back to her duty to accurately record her time and work in the daily timesheet.

Applauding paralegals' skills at keeping these necessary records, the court in *Role Models America, Inc. v. Brownlee*, 353 F.3d 962, 974 (Ct. App. D.C. 2004), found that the only properly kept time records were those kept by the paralegals and therefore all of their fees were recoverable.

Here, by contrast, the legal assistants' time records, unlike the attorneys' and the law clerk's, provide adequate detail and show that these employees performed suitable tasks. We will therefore award reimbursement for the full number of hours requested for the legal assistants' time, with the exception of the two hours that a legal assistant spent visiting this court to pick up a brief and the time that a legal assistant spent on three separate occasions filing a brief.

FEE ARRANGEMENTS

While all of these factors have weight in determining what a reasonable fee is and that may be a subject of much debate, there is very little debate over the requirement of clear communication to the client. The ideal is to memorialize the agreement in writing so that all possible future questions will have a baseline to refer to. This fee agreement is the first manifestation of the fiduciary relationship between the parties. The attorney is bound not to procure the agreement by misrepresentation or to "overreach" for the highest fee possible in the matter. The writing protects both parties. Courts will not generally disturb the fee arrangement as agreed to by the parties. However, in cases where there is evidence of undue influence or overreaching by counsel, "the courts as a matter of public policy give particular scrutiny to fee arrangements... casting the burden on attorneys who have drafted the retainer agreements to show that the contracts are fair, reasonable, and fully known and understood by their clients." *Shaw v. Manufacturer's Trust, Co.*, 499 N.E.2d 864, 866 (N.Y. 1986) (internal citations omitted).

In order to prove such good faith and fairness, an attorney seeking to enforce a contract for attorney's fees must show:

(1) the client fully understood the contract's meaning and effect,
(2) the attorney and client shared the same understanding of the contract, and
(3) the terms of the contract are just and reasonable.

Alexander v. Inman, 974 S.W.2d 689, 694 (Tenn. 1998) (internal citations omitted).

It is important to note that it is not just the attorney's fees that must be spelled out in detail. If a paralegal will be working on the matter, that fee must be agreed upon as well. Any costs that will be passed on to the client, such as copying, phone charges, mailing, travel expenses, and other necessary payments made on the client's behalf, must be included in the fee agreement. Simply stated, the client should not be surprised at the charges included on the bill: He may be upset about the amount, but he shouldn't be taken by total surprise.

Contingency Fee Arrangements

contingency fee
The attorney's fee calculated as a percentage of the final award in a civil case.

The ABA Model Rules address in a separate section the validity of **contingency fees**. Because these fees may result in enormous sums of money, far more than the attorney would recover under the "normal" hourly billing method, the rules specifically state that they must be in writing. This writing must be as specific as possible in setting forth how the fee shall be calculated and whether costs are included or excluded in that amount. Additionally, many cases terminate before they are fully tried in court. Therefore, the attorney must stipulate how a fee will be calculated if the matter settles without a trial. The rules of ethics put great emphasis in contingent fee cases on the specificity of the required writings and accountings.

SPOT THE ISSUE

Carrie has worked as a paralegal for a construction law boutique firm for a while and, with her help, the firm was recently successful in challenging a state's public bidding process for a local construction project. It was a long and arduous task. The relevant statute pertaining to these kinds of suits permits the challenging/prevailing party to recover costs associated with the suit. The lead attorney has requested $100,000. The trial court denied this amount and significantly reduced the fees to $12,000. The court also denied the fees billed by the paralegal on this matter, as it considered those costs to be part of "overhead" in running the practice. Apparently, the trial court decided that the attorney should have spent only 120 hours on the matter and should be billing $100 per hour for his services. Is the court correct? Why or why not? What factors should the court have taken into consideration? Make an argument using the factors discussed above to receive the full amount requested: $100,000.

Contingent fees essentially give the attorney a stake in the outcome of the case. The larger the settlement or judgment amount, the larger the fee collected. This incentive to strive for a bigger settlement is ethically prohibited in cases involving certain domestic relations matters or in any criminal matter. A contingent fee in a domestic relations matter is not per se invalid whereas any contingency fee in any criminal matter is prohibited. A contingency based upon obtaining the divorce itself or upon the amount of the settlement is prohibited. For example, it is impermissible to charge a contingency fee based upon the amount of alimony received in the divorce or based upon the amount received in the division of property. Contingency fees in other kinds of domestic relations matters are subject to strict scrutiny to evaluate whether they are proper in the circumstances.

> As a general rule, contingent fee agreements are begrudgingly permitted in domestic relations cases. Because public policy favors marriage and discourages attorneys from promoting bitter divorce battles for financial gain, contingent fees are subjected to enhanced scrutiny and rarely are found to be justified. As a matter of fact, so unsavory are contingent fees in domestic relations cases that a higher quantum of proof is necessary to enforce a contingent fee.
>
> *Alexander* at 693.

Generally speaking for domestic relations matters and definitively speaking for defending criminal cases, contingent fees are to be avoided.

Alternative Fee Arrangements

The legal industry has undergone a paradigm shift in the area of fee structuring. The increasingly savvy, cost-conscious client has forced law firms to take a second look at the traditional method of hourly billing. "Alternative fee arrangements" (AFAs) are essentially all those billing practices that are not hourly fees. Or, stated in the positive, AFAs are based upon the value of the services rendered such as fixed or capped fees that allocate more risk to the firm. The lawyers and firm have more incentive to engage in the most effective *and* time-saving efforts on behalf of the client. For example, if an attorney agrees to fix her fee at $2,500 for the matter, she has every incentive not to go over that cost or else she and her firm will not be paid for that "extra work." An AFA can address the issue that clients perceive in the rates that lawyers charge for their services; many complain that the amount of the fee is disproportionally large compared with the legal services rendered. It is simply a matter of getting value for their money. AFAs can lower the risk for clients because they can estimate how much the total bill will be to pursue their matter, rather than be at the mercy of the inflatable billable hour. The risk of protracted litigation or negotiation is shared with the lawyer because the attorney is also incentivized to conclude the matter before the fee cap is reached. Of course, the ethical rules require all fee arrangements to be not only in writing but also clearly communicated to and consented to by the client.

alternative fee arrangements
Billing practices that are not tied to time spent on a matter but rather based on the value of the services rendered, such as fixed or capped fees that allocate more risk to the firm.

While the billable hour is not at risk of becoming extinct, there has clearly been a shift to this new billing method for some firms and attorneys at least some of the time. How can attorneys, firms, or even independent paralegals decide whether to bill under an AFA? The ABA's Law Practice Management Section can provide this guidance.

There are five key elements to consider when making the shift to AFAs:

1. Focus on historical time investments. Lawyers [and paralegals] should be recording time using task-based billing codes. This will enable law firms to determine how much time is required to complete specific tasks and will assist the firm in developing sound AFAs.
2. Improving time management. Law firms that use AFAs must pay serious attention to their lawyer/other timekeeper capacity and utilization. This is an area where project management skills will become essential. Firms will need to get serious about the proper leveraging of lawyers/other timekeepers to maximize client value, provide more predictability and minimize firm costs.
3. Adhering to budgets and time-tracking procedures. Lawyers will need to be trained to review and live by case or matter budgets. Again, this becomes a project management issue. Despite the many perceived imperfections of recording time, tracking time is a logical means of measuring the firm's effectiveness in efficiency and managing productivity.
4. Evolution of AFA systems. As law firms learn more about their costs and better understand client concerns, they will refine their pricing strategies. Pricing systems might include blends of hourly rates, fee caps, menu, project and portfolio pricing. The key is to keep the AFA as simple as possible. Many law firms develop pricing systems that are often too complex and clients become frustrated and lose interest.
5. Profitability. Understanding how much it costs the firm to produce a billable hour per task and per lawyer [or paralegal] is essential to AFA success. Successful firms are heavily focused on efficiency and value, and have been successful in changing the paradigm not only in terms of timekeeping and economic monitoring, but in changing internal behaviors.

See Frederick J. Esposito, Jr., *The New Normal—Alternative Fee Arrangements and Project Management for Lawyers*, 37 ABA Law Practice Magazine, Nov./Dec. 2011.

The second ethical concern (after clarity in communication) involves the intersection between fee arrangements controlled by ABA Model Rule 1.5 (discussed in this chapter) and Model Rule 1.8 (discussed in Chapter 5) that prohibit the attorney from entering into a business relationship with the client. As AFAs, albeit indirectly, determine the fee earned with the outcome of the case, there will be additional scrutiny applied to the AFA in question to determine whether it goes beyond the "reasonable fee" permitted by Rule 1.5 and the disclosure and consent standards required by Rule 1.8.

FEE SPLITTING/SHARING

On some level all lawyers in a law office share their fees with all the other employees; they are the sole source of office income. There is nothing wrong with this. The fees from individual clients are pooled into the general operating account and from there they lose their individuality. Salaries and other expenses are disbursed from this general account. The prohibition on fee splitting and fee sharing arises where particular, identifiable client proceeds are disbursed to another individual in payment for work performed on that matter. This can come in the form of splitting the particular client's fee with lawyers outside the firm or sharing the fee with non-attorneys inside or outside the firm. This is not to say that paralegal time spent on a matter cannot be billed out and collected in a particular matter. Paralegal fees are considered part of recoverable attorney's fees, which simply means these fees must not be directly paid to the paralegal out of the individual recovery.

Attorneys can and sometimes should consult with professional colleagues who are not members of their own firm. Perhaps an attorney has come across an issue that cannot be readily and effectively handled within her own firm. Her best option is to consult an attorney who specializes or has expertise in the area she is struggling with. However, the attorney may not seek this assistance without the consent of her client. To do so would be to essentially delegate some work and responsibility without the client knowing that the matter was being handled in some way by an attorney she did not contract. If the client does consent to the services and the proportion of work to be performed by the other attorney, the other requirements are that:

1. The proportion of work and the proportion of fee be relatively equal. An attorney doing 30 percent of the work should receive roughly 30 percent of the total fee.
2. The attorneys assume joint responsibility for the representation. An attorney cannot contribute to the total "product" without also bearing some blame if it all goes wrong. The contributing attorney becomes a fiduciary of the client as well. It is as if the attorneys have formed a partnership for the purposes of this client.
3. The fee-sharing agreement must be in writing.
4. The total fee is reasonable.

Of course, the attorney who is consulted must still be in good standing. An attorney who hired a suspended attorney to work as a paralegal in the office was himself suspended for three months (reduced from the original recommendation of an 18-month suspension) for sharing legal fees with the suspended attorney who had worked on particular matters. *Attorney Grievance Comm'n of Maryland v. Brennan*, 714 A.2d 157 (Md. 1998); *see also In Matter of Martin*, 105 A.3d 967, 976 (Del. 2014) (The "supervising" attorney was suspended for one year for permitting his suspended attorney colleague to continue to work in the office as a paralegal. The court found it determinative that the "supervising" attorney "did not compensate [the suspended attorney] as a paralegal on an hourly basis for any of that work. Instead, the two men continued to operate under the same, pre-suspension fee-sharing agreement that they had entered into when they were both duly licensed lawyers. There is clear and convincing evidence that [supervising attorney's] payment to [the suspended attorney] of his full share of the settlement without an 'appropriate division' for pre- and post-suspension work was a violation of Rule 5.4(a).")

This fee-sharing arrangement is entirely prohibited in the circumstance where a paralegal has worked for the attorney. Paralegals, no matter how much work or how well they perform in a case, cannot be allocated a percentage of the recovery based upon the percentage of work done, even where the client consents. This prohibition extends to paralegal contract agencies as well. The court in *In re Watley*, 802 So. 2d 593 (La. 2001), determined that the paralegal agency, "We the People," could not collect a percentage of the attorney's fees earned on personal injury cases on which the contract paralegals worked. The payments made into this "paralegal pool" were impermissible under the relevant ethics rules; the agency was still a nonlawyer. The attorney's actions were not shown to have caused direct harm to the represented clients; there were no underlying malpractice actions. The court found that the fee-sharing arrangement had the potential to harm clients. The harm came from the paralegals' and agency's financial interest in the attorney's fees. This financial stake in the outcome of the case could cause the agency or the paralegals to interfere with the attorney's independent legal judgment. *Id.* at 597. Further, attempts to disguise a fee-sharing arrangement as an hourly wage will be closely examined, as they were in *State Bar of Texas v. Faubion*, 821 S.W.2d 203. The independent paralegal/investigator was paid a percentage of the fee recovered in the case based on his "involvement" in the matter. The wage was not actually based upon the number of hours worked, but was calculated as a percentage of the recovery. The paralegal was paid in the form of a salary out of the firm's operating account on regular paydays. This was where the acceptability ended. The amount of his paycheck was in the range of 20 to 33 percent of the fee received in a particular case, depending on the paralegal's time and involvement in the case. Essentially, once payment to the paralegal is tied to a particular case, it crosses the line into unethical fee sharing. *See also Reich & Binstock, LLP v. Scates*, 455 S.W.3d 178, 180 (Tex. App. 2014) (The prohibition against fee-splitting applies to any nonlawyer, including experts. The lawyers and the expert "agreed that the expert would be paid an additional $30 per hour for that same [kind of] work upon 'settlement' of the case. The attorney stated that the expert's additional fee was a 'bonus,' which would only be paid if the law firm made a profit after expenses and client distribution." As the bonus payment was contingent upon the outcome of the case, the court determined that it amounted to an impermissible fee-sharing arrangement.)

REEL TO REAL

Both *Regarding Henry* (1991, starring Harrison Ford) and *The Firm* (1993, starring Tom Cruise) deal with attorney's fees indirectly, as both films expose the perils of becoming a slave to wealth. How do these attorneys deal with the pressure to bill for their services? Do you think this accurately reflects the practice of law? In what way? Can you think of a way to cut down on this kind of pressure? How would you have reacted in these situations?

SAFEKEEPING OF PROPERTY

Clients should feel safe in trusting their attorneys to keep not only their interests but also their property (including money) safe. Perhaps the mantra of all attorneys is, or should be, this: Do not mix clients' property with your own. This is the ethical mandate that, when broken, garners the most severe penalties. Maintaining separation is most easily done with personal or real property that is not money. If a client needs the attorney to hold onto some pieces of an estate she is administering, safe deposit boxes at the local bank can be easily secured for the client's benefit, and that is the most reasonable place to safely keep such items. Where attorneys find themselves getting into trouble is in the handling of money. The best practice is absolutely scrupulous accounting and meticulous separation of client funds from attorney funds. Mixing of these two kinds of accounts is impermissible; the mere **commingling** of the funds, even if the funds are completely accounted for or if the amount of commingling is small, is an ethical violation.

Often, attorneys are in possession of client funds that are intended to cover future legal fees incurred on the matter. Retainer fees may be either characterized as a nonrefundable payment to engage the attorney or as a prepayment sum to be drawn upon as fees are earned. In the first case, the money goes straight to the attorney's working account. The client relinquishes any interest in that money, which is nonrefundable; by accepting the client, the attorney has earned it. On the other hand, a prepayment sum that is intended to be drawn on as the attorney bills for services remains the client's money until it is earned; the attorney must not put any unearned portion in her working account.

Money must be identified as to its source, where it is going, and why; it must be placed in the appropriate account and be used only for its intended purpose. Promptness and accurate record keeping are essential. In the real world in personal accounts, people juggle money from account to account to cover withdrawals and payments, eventually coming out even in the end. It is a rare person who hasn't taken a little out of savings to cover a bill or two in a tight month, or failed to balance the checkbook to the penny every month. However, this is unacceptable practice in a law firm, even without improper motive. Mere sloppiness and the resulting inaccuracies, failure to keep records, and other poor accounting practices can result in severe

commingling
The mixing of a client's funds with the attorney's personal funds without permission; an ethical violation.

sanctions. This may be true even when the attorney had the interests of his clients in mind when he made certain improper disbursements, for example by postdating a check or giving more money in settlement than originally agreed on. The absence of dishonest intent is only a mitigating factor in the decision to sanction the attorney for these accounting failures. The fact remains that the violations of the ethical rule to the safekeeping of property were committed. *See Attorney Grievance Com'n of Maryland v. MBA-Jonas*, 919 A.2d 669 (Md. 2007) (The attorney was suspended indefinitely with the right to apply for readmission after 90 days. While all offenses were unintentional, the court found that they attorney "engaged in conduct prejudicial to the administration of justice, [. . .] in addition to certain discrete violations related to his escrow account, including overdrawing his trust account on several occasions, the respondent managed his escrow account 'carelessly' failing to reconcile it monthly, 'maintained inaccurate settlement sheets and kept very few records.") To keep track of the office procedures involving these issues, see Figure 6.5.

misappropriation
The unlawful and unethical taking of a client's property for the lawyer's own use, regardless of intent or duration of time the property is kept.

On the opposite side of the spectrum is the knowing **misappropriation** of client funds. Anytime an attorney takes money that should properly be left in a client trust account and uses it for her own purposes, she is guilty of misappropriation.

An attorney not only must leave money in the client trust account until it is properly earned and disbursed, but is under an ethical duty to notify the client that the office has received those funds for the client. Further, the disbursement to the client of the monies or property received must be promptly made and an accounting, if requested, must be supplied. A significant delay in delivery of the client's money or property constitutes misappropriation as well.

It does not matter for what reason the attorney improperly kept or took the funds: to cover payroll or other office expenses, to pay a court fee on another matter, to take a vacation. All of these reasons are improper, because misappropriation is not related to what the money was intended for; the attorney doesn't have to have a devious plan. Further, it doesn't matter whether the attorney intended only to "borrow" the money and meant to pay the money back, or even that he indeed did paid it back; the money was used for a purpose for which it was not intended.

> Misappropriation of client funds undermines the relationship between attorney and client and damages the legal profession as a whole. Indeed, this court and others have not minced words when addressing it, describing it as "always indefensible," something "we cannot tolerate," a form of "ethical dereliction," "the gravest form of professional misconduct," and an act that "reflects poorly on the entire legal profession and erodes the public's confidence in lawyers." As we explained in *Babilis*, a seminal Utah case in this area, intentional misappropriation of client funds "strikes at the very foundation of the trust and honesty that are indispensable to the functioning of the attorney-client relationship and, indeed, to the functioning of the legal profession itself.
>
> *In the Matter of the Discipline of Lundgren*, 355 P.3d 984, 987-988 (Utah 2015) (internal citations omitted), citing *In re Discipline of Babilis*, 951 P.2d 207, 217 (Utah 1997).

	Yes	No
All expenses of representation are posted to the clients' files on a regular basis (filing fees, travel, other outsourcing).		
Outsourced services and vendors' prices and invoices are reviewed for accuracy and posted to the proper account.		
All internal costs are posted to the clients' files on a regular basis (postage, long distance calls, other office overhead attributable to one particular client).		
All entries are reviewed for completeness and accuracy.		
All bills to clients are reviewed and approved by the supervising attorney prior to posting.		
All bills are sent to clients at the same time each month or other regular schedule.		
All payments are recorded regularly to the clients' files.		
All accounts receivable are updated and followed up on a regular basis.		
All client trust funds are kept in a proper Attorney Trust Account separate from operating funds and accounts.		
All client trust accounts are reviewed for accuracy and updated regularly.		

◄ **FIGURE 6.5**
BILLING AND EXPENSE
CHECKLIST

It is very clear that the courts take attorneys' fiduciary obligations to their clients with the utmost seriousness.

> Respondent's restitution of the funds prior to notification of the random audit of his records indicates that he did intend only to "borrow" funds in the sense that he planned to use the funds for his own purposes only temporarily before restoring them. Nevertheless, restitution does not alter the character of knowing misappropriation and misuse of clients' funds. Intent to deprive permanently a client of [his or her] funds . . . is not an element of knowing misappropriation. Nor is the intent to repay funds or otherwise make restitution a defense to the charge of knowing misappropriation. A lawyer who uses funds, knowing that the funds belong to a client and that the client has not given permission to invade them, is guilty of knowing misappropriation. . . . It makes no difference whether the money is used for a good purpose or a bad purpose, for the benefit of the lawyer or for the benefit of others, or whether the lawyer intended to return the money when he took it, or whether in fact he ultimately did reimburse the client; nor does it matter that the pressures on the lawyer to take the money were great or minimal. The essence of Wilson is that the relative moral quality of the act, measured by these many circumstances that may surround both it and the attorney's state of mind, is irrelevant: it is the mere act of taking your client's money knowing that you have no authority to do so that requires disbarment.

Matter of Blumenstyk, 704 A.2d 1, 3-4 (N.J. 1997).

In every relationship, including that between attorney and client, parties will fight over money. Where there is a dispute over who has the right to certain property, it is the attorney's job to keep that property (including controverted fees) in the client trust account until the court (or other resolution) decides how the property is to be dispersed.

When the controversy is over fees, the attorney can dispense only those funds that are not in dispute. For example, if the client's matter settled for $100,000 and the fee arrangement provides for a 25 percent contingent fee, it may appear at first blush to the client that the attorney should send a check for $75,000 from his client trust account and transfer $25,000 to her own business account. However, the attorney claims that the fee arrangement provides that the costs associated with the prosecution of the claim come off the top first, and then the disbursements are made according to the contingent fee arrangement. If the costs totaled $10,000, then the client would be entitled to $67,500 and the attorney to $22,500. Under the ethics rules, the unquestioned amounts should be disbursed and the disputed amount ($10,000) should remain in the client's trust account until the matter is settled.

The safekeeping of property rules are really very simple to understand; however, they tend to get attorneys in the most trouble. There is a clear-cut, bright-line mandate: Never, never move a client's property unless and until the party is clearly entitled to it without dispute. Further, all property must be accounted for to the last penny and identifiable as to where it came from, for what purpose it was handed into the attorney's hands, which party is entitled to it, and why that party is entitled to it.

Summary

The provisions discussed in this Chapter have one thing in common: They all underscore the importance of trust and respect in the way attorneys handle their clients. Attorneys must not gouge their clients with exorbitant fees, and must handle client property with scrupulous care.

Key Terms

Alternative fee arrangements
Billable hour
Certified specialist
Commingling
Contingency fee
Customary fee

Double-billing
Lodestar calculation
Misappropriation
Reasonable fee
Timesheet

Review Questions

MULTIPLE CHOICE

Choose the best answer(s) and please explain *why* you chose the answer(s).

1. Timesheets must be filled out:
   a. On a daily basis
   b. As soon as possible after the assignment or meeting is completed
   c. To include both billable and non-billable time
   d. All of the above

2. Double-billing:
   a. Is the practice of sending two collection statements to a client per month
   b. Means that the firm will collect twice as much in fees as it originally expected
   c. Is always unethical
   d. Is permitted if the attorney can reuse some work previously completed for another client in the same kind of matter

3. Paralegal fees may be recoverable when:
   a. A paralegal has worked over ten hours on a file
   b. A paralegal has been assigned legal work in a matter
   c. The total amount of fees requested by the attorney is not excessive
   d. The requested amount is a reflection of reasonable time and legal effort spent on the matter

4. Paralegals may be paid:
   a. In an amount equal to the percentage of effort they put forth in an individual matter
   b. Bonuses for a good year of work and effort put in on all the cases
   c. Out of the client trust account
   d. By the client directly

5. When fees owed are in dispute, a paralegal:
   a. Cannot get paid
   b. Must create a separate client trust account for that disputed amount
   c. Still draws her salary because her money is not tied to an individual case
   d. Must report attorney misappropriation to the ethics board

EXPLAIN YOURSELF

All answers should be written in complete sentences. A simple yes or no is insufficient.

1. Describe an attorney's duty of safekeeping of property. To what kind of property does it attach?

2. What is comingling of funds? Are there any circumstances when it is permitted?

3. When can an attorney split his fee with another professional?

4. What are the factors to be considered in determining whether a paralegal's fee may be recoverable in court?

FAULTY PHRASES

All of the following statements are *false*. State why they are false and then rewrite each one as a true statement. Do not simply make the statement negative by adding the word "not."

1. A customary fee is usually determined by what other local law firms charge.

2. All legal matters can use the method of contingency fee billing.

3. A reasonable fee is one that multiplies the number of hours spent on a legal matter by the attorney's hourly wage.

4. An attorney can split a fee with his paralegal for her work performed on the matter.

5. A paralegal sets his own fees in each matter he handles in the law office.

6. All paralegals in the same law office must be billed out at the same rate to every client.

PORTFOLIO ASSIGNMENT

Write Away

Create a table or spreadsheet that will serve as your own time-sheet for the next three days. Keep track of every task you perform and how long that takes. The "client" may be yourself, your family, your professors, your boss, etc. The point of this writing assignment is to take a critical look at how you spend your time and decide whether this use is efficient. Once the time-sheet has been filled in, review it to determine which tasks should be "billable" and which should not. For example, doing your homework for class is billable work. Your knowledge and skill is being utilized to create "work product." Taking a long shower or watching a movie is not billable time.

Case in Point

2004 WL 253453 (E.D. La.)
Only the Westlaw citation is currently available.

United States District Court, E.D. Louisiana.
Edith L. STAGNER
v.
WESTERN KENTUCKY NAVIGATION, INC.
No. Civ. A. 02-1418.
Feb. 10, 2004.

[. . .]

[T]he Court ordered counsel for the defendant to provide the Court with (1) an affidavit attesting to their education, background, skills and experience and (2) sufficient evidence of rates charged in similar cases by other local attorneys with similar experience, skill and reputation no later than January 9, 2004. Defendant's counsel complied and the Court is now ready to rule on the amount of attorney's fees that should be awarded.

[. . .]

II. ANALYSIS

[. . .]

The defendant seeks to recover attorney's fees in the amount of $627.50. The defendant contends that Kathy Bilich, paralegal, expended a total of 1 hour on matters regarding the motion to compel at an hourly rate of $60.00. The defendant further contends that Zachary Stump, attorney, expended a total of 2.9 hours drafting and revising the motion to compel at an hourly rate of $110.00, and attorney Danica Benbow spent 1.1 hours in connection with the motion at an hourly rate of $135.00.

[. . .]

B. Standard

The determination of a reasonable attorney's fee award involves a two-step process. See Rutherford v. Harris County, 197 F.3d 173, 192 (5th Cir. 1999). The court must first determine the "lodestar" by multiplying the reasonable number of hours expended and the reasonable hourly rate for each participating attorney. See *Hensley*, 461 U.S. at 433. This "lodestar" method serves as the initial estimate of a reasonable attorney's fee. Blum v. Stenson, 465 U.S. 886, 888, 104 S. Ct. 1541, 79 L. Ed.2d 891 (1984).

The second step involves the application of twelve factors the Fifth Circuit applies in determining what amount is warranted. Johnson v. Georgia Highway Express, Inc., 488 F.2d 714, 717-719 (5th Cir. 1974). These factors are: (1) the time and labor required; (2) the novelty and difficulty of the questions presented; (3) the skill required to perform the legal service properly; (4) the preclusion of other employment by the attorney due to acceptance of the case; (5) the customary fee; (6) whether the fee is fixed or contingent; (7) time limitations imposed by the client or the circumstances; (8) the amount of money involved and the results obtained; (9) the experience, reputation, and ability of the attorneys; (10) the undesirability of the case; (11) the nature and length of the professional relationship with the client; and (12) awards in similar cases.

Once the lodestar is computed by multiplying the reasonable number of hours by a reasonable hourly rate, the court may adjust the lodestar upward or downward depending on its analysis of the twelve factors espoused in Johnson. See Dodge v. Hunt Petroleum Corp., 174 F. Supp. 2d 505, 508 (N.D. Tex. 2001). Thus, in light of the Johnson factors, the Court may reduce the award resulting from the lodestar calculation if the documentation of hours worked is inadequate or if the calculation includes hours that were not "reasonably expended." See Hensley, 461 U.S. at 433-434.

C. The Lodestar

1. Reasonable Fee

The party seeking attorney's fees has the burden of establishing the reasonableness of the fees by "submitting evidence supporting the hours worked and the rates claimed." Rode v. Dellarciprete, 892 F.2d 1177, 1183 (3rd Cir. 1990) (citing Hensley, 461 U.S. at 433). Thus, counsel for the defendant "must produce satisfactory evidence-in addition to [their] own affidavits-that the requested rates are in line with those prevailing in the community for similar services by lawyers of reasonably comparable skill, experience and reputation." Blum v. Stenson, 465 U.S. 886, 896 n.11, 104 S.Ct. 1541, 79 L. Ed. 2d 891 (1984); Watkins v. Fordice, 7 F.3d 453, 457 (5th Cir. 1993).

The Court must determine the reasonable number of hours expended in the litigation and the reasonable hourly rate for the participating attorneys. See Louisiana Power & Light Co. v. Kellstrom, 50 F.3d 319, 324 (5th Cir. 1995). The lodestar is then computed by multiplying the number of hours by the reasonable hourly rate. Id.

2. Reasonable Hourly Rate

Attorneys' fees are to be calculated at the prevailing market rates in the relevant community for similar services by attorneys of reasonably comparable skills, experience, and reputation. Blum v. Stenson, 465 U.S. 886, 895, 104 S. Ct. 1541, 79 L. Ed. 2d 891 (1984). In the instant case, it is uncontested that the relevant community here is the New Orleans, Louisiana legal market.

[. . .]

Evidence of rates may be adduced through direct or opinion evidence as to what local attorneys charge under similar circumstances. The weight to be given to the opinion evidence is affected by the detail contained in the testimony on matters such as similarity of skill, reputation, experience, similarity of case and client, and breath of the sample of which the expert has knowledge. Norman, 836 F.2d at 1299.

a. Zachary Stump
[. . .]

b. Danica Benbow
[. . .]

c. Kathy Bilich

Kathy Bilich ("Bilich"), a paralegal with Frilot, Partridge, Kohnke & Clements, L.C., submits that for all of the work she performs on behalf of clients, the firm charges an hourly rate of $60.00. As proof of the reasonableness of the rate, the defendant has only provided the affidavit of Kathy Bilich, the paralegal performing the work.

Bilich states that she graduated high school in 1975, attended Tulane Paralegal School, completing courses for Legal Research and Writing, and she also has a certificate from the University of Colorado for Paralegal Studies. Bilich further states that she has twenty-five years of legal experience.

The defendant has not offered evidence, other than the affidavits, that the rates charged for the services are in line with the prevailing rates charged by attorneys or paralegals of similar experience or education in the community. However, Stagner does not oppose the hourly rates requested by the defendant, the itemization of costs submitted by the defendant, or the hours expended on bringing the motion. Further, as discussed below and based on the Court's own knowledge:

i. Attorney rates
[. . .]

ii. Paralegal rate

It is well established that prevailing parties can recover for fees expended by paralegals working on the file.[10] Kathy Bilich, in her affidavit stated that she was billed at her customary rate of $60.00 per hour. Further, this rate has not been contested by Stagner.

In, Baza v. Chevron Oil Service Co., the Court allowed the paralegals to bill at their customary rates of $50.00 and $60.00 per hour, finding the rates reasonable, within the prevailing market range in New Orleans, and uncontested by opposing counsel. 1996 WL 711506 at *2 (E.D. La. Dec. 10, 1996); see also Jimenez v. Paw-Paw's Camper City, Inc., 2002 WL 257691 at *20 (E.D. La. Feb. 22, 2002) (finding that $60.00 per hour was a reasonable rate for paralegal services). Considering Bilich's education in paralegal studies and her twenty-five years of legal experience, her customary rate of $60.00 per hour is reasonable.

However, in order to recover for paralegal fees, the services rendered by the paralegal must be legal in nature, or work traditionally performed by an attorney. See Jones v. Armstrong Cork Co., 630 F.2d 324, 325 n.1 (5th Cir.1980). Work that is legal in nature includes, for example, "factual investigation, locating and interviewing witnesses, assistance with depositions, interrogatories and document production, compilation of statistical and financial data, checking legal citations and drafting correspondence." Missouri v. Jenkins, 491 U.S. 274, 288, 109 S. Ct. 2463, 105 L. Ed. 2d 229 (1989).

The legal activities undertaken by paralegals must be distinguished from other activities that are purely clerical in nature, such as typing, copying, or delivering pleadings. See Lalla v. City of New Orleans, 161 F. Supp. 2d 686, 710 (E.D. La. 2001). Pure clerical or secretarial work may not be billed at a paralegal rate. Jenkins, Id.

Counsel for the defendant is seeking to recover for one hour of paralegal services for the following: 1.) 0.2 hours for a telephone conference with Dr. Parnell regarding IME; 2.) 0.4 hours for review of the file regarding Stagner's IME and supporting information prepared for motion to compel; 3.) 0.2 hours for telephone conference with Tim Young regarding IME and motion to compel; and 4.) 0.2 hours for telephone conference with Dr. Parnell regarding fees. These time entries reflect work that is legal in nature as opposed to pure secretarial tasks, and counsel for the defendant should be allowed to recover for the services performed by Bilich.

3. Reasonable Number of Hours Expended

The party seeking attorneys' fees must present adequately documented time records to the court. Watkins v. Fordice, 7 F.3d 453, 457 (5th Cir. 1993). As a general proposition, all time that is excessive, duplicative or inadequately documented should be excluded from any award of attorney's fees. Raspanti v. United States Dept. of the Army, 2001 WL 1081375 at *6. Attorneys must exercise "billing judgment" by "writing off unproductive, excessive, or redundant hours" when seeking fee awards. Id. (citing Walker v. United States Dep't of Housing & Urban Dev., 99 F.3d 761, 769 (5th Cir. 1996)). The fee seeker's attorneys are "charged with the burden of showing the reasonableness of the hours they bill and, accordingly, are charged with proving that they exercised billing judgment." Walker, 99 F.3d at 770. When billing judgment is lacking, the court must exclude from the lodestar calculation the hours that

---

[10] The cost of paralegal services are to be included in the assessment and award of attorney's fees if the following criteria are met:

1. the services performed must be legal in nature;
2. the performance of such services by the paralegal must be supervised by an attorney;
3. the qualifications of the paralegal performing the services must be specified in the application or motion requesting an award of fees in order to demonstrate that the paralegal is qualified by virtue of education, training, or work experience to perform substantive work;
4. the nature of the services performed by the paralegal must be specified in the application/ motion requesting an award of fees in order to permit a determination that the services performed were legal rather than clerical in nature;
5. the amount of time expended by the paralegal in performing the services must be reasonable and must be set out in the motion; and
6. the amount charged for the time spent by the paralegal must reflect reasonable community standards of remuneration.

See Jones v. Armstrong Cork Co., 630 F.2d 324, 325 n.1 (5th Cir. 1980). See also Fees for Paralegal Services: Are They Recoverable, 461 PLI/Lit. 185 (1993); Associated Builders, 919 F.2d at 380.

were not reasonably expended. *Hensley*, 461 U.S. at 434.

In reviewing the time sheets submitted by the defendant, seeking to recover fees for a total of five hours expended on the motion to compel, the Court finds that the hours are not excessive, duplicative, or unreasonable.

4. Fees/Costs

Lastly, the defendant seeks to recover attorney fees and costs in the amount of $200.00. This amount is reflective of the cancellation fee charged by Dr. Melvin Parnell for Stagner's failure to appear for the medical exam. [. . .]

The invoice submitted by the defendant indicates that Dr. Parnell charged defendant's counsel $200.00 for Stagner's "no-show office consult," on October 21, 2003. However, these costs cannot be said to have been incurred in bringing the motion to compel. Therefore, the request for reimbursement for the "no-show office consult" is denied.

5. The Johnson Factors

"The lodestar . . . is presumptively reasonable," and should be enhanced or reduced only in exceptional cases. Watkins v. Fordice, 7 F.3d 453, 459 (5th Cir. 1993) (citing City of Burlington v. Dague, 505 U.S. 557, 567, 112 S. Ct. 2638, 120 L. Ed. 2d 449 (1992)). After carefully reviewing the record, the Court finds that the Lodestar amount is reasonable and finds that no further reduction or enhancement is required. In making this recommendation, the Court has considered and applied the factors articulated in Johnson as required by the Fifth Circuit.

Accordingly,

IT IS ORDERED that the defendant's application for attorney's fees in connection with the previous Motion to Compel Independent Medical Examination (doc. # 29) is GRANTED IN PART and DENIED IN PART as follows:

1.) GRANTED to the extent that the defendant seeks to recover fees for attorney and paralegal time expended in bring the motion to compel. The defendant is entitled to recover for 1 hour at an hourly rate of $60.00 for paralegal work, 2.9 hours at an hourly rate of $110.00 for work performed by Zachary Stump, and 1.1 hours at an hourly rate of $135.00 for work performed by Danica Benbow, or an amount of $427.50.

2.) DENIED to the extent that the defendant seeks to recover $200 .00 for the cancellation fee charged by Dr. Parnell for Stagner's failure to attend the scheduled examination on October 21, 2003.

Source: Reprinted from Westlaw with permission from Thomson Reuters.

Chapter 7

Special Clients and Situations

Chapter Objectives

The student will be able to:

- Acknowledge that each client must be individually evaluated for special needs or circumstances
- Differentiate between the organization and the "control group" as a client and recognize the significance of the difference
- Discuss the special considerations involved in dealing with clients with diminished capacity
- Explain the circumstances where an attorney should either decline or terminate representation of the client

This chapter will examine particular issues that affect the attorney-client relationship at its core. *Who* is the client when the client is not a real person, but a legal entity such as a corporation? *Why* are some clients in need of special care, and *what* is the attorney's heightened duty toward them? *When* should an attorney decline or terminate representation of a client?

There are a few special issues that affect the very essence of attorney-client relationships. As both parties consider entering into the agreement, they need to understand not only their individual roles as either the attorney or the client, but also the details relating to the duties and disclosures required from the attorney to assist the client in obtaining the larger goal of representation. Legal professionals must evaluate the client to determine if there are any special considerations relating to that kind of representation. Where the client is actually a business entity, the people who make up that organization must be treated in a manner slightly different from the way the attorney treats a client who is an individual. Similarly, persons who have special needs due to some infirmity should be treated with particular care not necessarily due to other individual clients. Finally, if the attorney feels that taking on the representation is not in either party's best interest or within the attorney's competency, the attorney cannot simply show the client the door. Even absent a formal attorney-client relationship, the attorney still owes certain duties to the declined or terminated client. All of these requirements stem from the same underlying core as the rest of the ethics rules: preservation of the integrity of the legal profession and society's confidence in it.

AN ORGANIZATION AS A CLIENT

A client is traditionally thought of as the person who sits across the desk from the attorney and explains the recent problem plaguing him. However, in many cases, the client is actually not the individual sitting in the chair, but what he represents: an organization. These entities are recognized as autonomous legal beings that have collective separate interests from the human beings that run them. ABA Model Rule 1.13 addresses this situation in great detail; neither NALA nor NFPA does so, because both groups defer to the rules of attorney ethics in this matter. The client is the organization, and therefore, the attorney's fiduciary duty is to that organization, not necessarily to its board of directors, president, or shareholders. Of course, the only way for the organization to make its legal needs known to the attorney is through its authorized representatives, those individuals who control the organization and its direction. This group of people is commonly referred to as the "control group."

It is important to remember exactly who the client is and what interests must be protected. The rule of confidentiality attaches to those communications made by the agents of the organization who seek the advice of the attorney and who are acting within their capacity in the organization. Confidentiality is not limited to any one class of persons, like the control group, but rather to the kind of communication made. The United States Supreme Court made this position clear in *Upjohn Co. v. United States*, 449 U.S. 383, 101 S. Ct. 677, 66 L. Ed. 2d 584 (1981): that the attorney-client privilege applies to communications made by corporate employees concerning matters pertinent to their job tasks, regardless of the employee's status or position in the corporation, as long as that communication was made to the corporation's attorney in order for him to formulate and render legal advice to the corporation. In other words, the significance lies not in *who* said it, but rather in *what* was said and *why*.

Tied to confidentiality is the duty of loyalty; the identity of the client is vital in determining a conflict of interest. Corporate America is not set up as insular units of business. An organization is made up of different people playing different roles. Whether an organization is comprised of one shareholder or one thousand, the client remains the one focus of the attorney. This focus must be clearly conveyed to all others with whom the attorney must deal, particularly to those who may be confused as to the role the attorney is playing and the party to whom her loyalty is pledged.

Conflicts of Interest within the Organization

Conflicts are evaluated under the same analysis for organizations as individual personal clients. Multiple representation may be permissible if no actual conflict exists and the clients consent. This means that the organization's directors, officers, members, shareholders, employees, and various other affiliated persons can be represented by that attorney and paralegal. The legal professional must bear in mind the ethical constraints of the relevant conflicts rules. For paralegals, reference should be made to NFPA EC 1.7 and NALA Guideline 1, both of which have been discussed in previous chapters.

Further, many large corporations have subsidiaries that exist as independent business entities. Representing a large conglomerate can impose substantial conflict for attorneys not exclusively employed by that corporation—also known as "outside counsel." How does an attorney determine if a conflict exists when a subsidiary is involved? Is the subsidiary the same as or different from the parent company? The California State Bar opined:

> Though the question of whether a parent and its subsidiaries must be treated as the same or different entities for conflict purposes is one of the most frequently arising questions in corporate practice, there are surprisingly few judicial or ethics authorities on the issue presented. Nevertheless, we do not believe that majority or even sole ownership of a subsidiary corporation should be controlling in determining who is the client for conflict purposes unless the subsidiary is merely an alter ego of the parent corporation. Notwithstanding the ownership interest which a person or entity has in a corporation, the ethical rules make clear that the client is the corporation which is represented by the attorney. When the subsidiary involved is a wholly-owned subsidiary, instances will be infrequent, though not impossible, where parent and subsidiary can have interests adverse to each other. Regardless of the ownership of his or her client, the duty of the lawyer to keep paramount the interests of the entity which he or she actually represents is still the same. The fact of total ownership does not change the parent corporation's status as a constituent of the subsidiary. The duties which an attorney owes to a constituent are defined in and go no further than those set out in [the ethics rules]. . . . On the facts presented here, the parent is not a party to the suit against the subsidiary,

and there is no prospect that it will be made a party. The representation against the subsidiary can therefore have no direct consequences on the parent; the only adversity can be that indirect adversity which might result from the diminution in the value of the parent's stock in the subsidiary if the attorney's suit against the subsidiary is ultimately successful. *This possible indirect impact is insufficient to give rise to a breach of the duty of loyalty owed to the parent. The attorney's duty of loyalty does not encompass the obligation to refrain from actions which may have only indirect adverse effects on existing clients in matters unrelated to those which the attorney is handling for such clients.*

CA Eth. Op. 1989-113, 1989 WL 253261 (emphasis added).

The attorney must continuously look out for the best interests of the organizational client. The personal interests of the agents must be separated from the proper goals of the organization; this is again an exercise in focusing on the issue of who the client really is: the organization, not any of its constituents. There are occasions where a person associated with the organization may take actions that are detrimental to the organization's interest, may subject the organization to legal process, or may do other substantial injury. If this is the case, then the attorney must first inform a higher authority or the highest in the organization, depending upon the severity of the potential harm and status of the wrongdoer. This is the first step an attorney should take when he has come into knowledge that a member of the organization is committing or omitting some act that will harm the organization's best interests, or intends to do so. It is an internal "whistle-blower" protection for the attorney, and permits the disclosure of information without violation of confidentiality or privilege. While this provision may look as though there is little to keep an attorney quiet after communicating with a member of the organization, the rule has a rather high standard for a protected disclosure.

This is similar to the standard that applies to individual clients: The attorney must know or suspect with reasonable certainty that the member is going to cause harm to the organization. Additionally, the harm threatened must be so substantial as to rise to the level of imperiling the organization by violating a legal obligation or the law. Poor business judgment or imprudence cannot be avoided by counsel's intervention using this rule. The principle of disclosing the least amount of confidential information possible to avoid the potentially disastrous consequences applies here as well. The first line of defense is to ask the "offender" in the organization to reconsider his position on the matter. Should that approach fail, then the attorney must go to a higher-ranking member and request that remedial measures be taken.

Permitted Disclosures

So far, the damage control has occurred "in house." However, where the questionable conduct emanates from the highest officer(s) able to act, or where these officers have been notified but refuse to act in the best interest of the organization, the attorney can disclose the relevant information to the appropriate outside authority. The act or omission involving the highest authority in the organization must be a clear violation of law before the attorney can act to disclose confidential information to others, to prevent the reasonably certain and substantial harm to the organization.

Once litigation or other proceedings have been instituted against the organizational client, of course the normal attorney-client confidentiality and privileges apply. The attorney is not required to disclose information that relates to the defense of the organization against charges of wrongdoing. The reporting requirement applies to actions or inactions taken by the organization during the normal course of business.

There are certain sectors that are more heavily regulated, for good reason, than others. The Securities and Exchange Commission (SEC) tolerates very little in the way of questionable business practices. The Commission places additional reporting requirements on the attorneys and paralegals for businesses governed by its regulations. Section 307 of the Sarbanes-Oxley Act of 2002 (SOX) required the Securities and Exchange Commission (the Commission) to issue rules setting forth minimum standards of professional conduct for attorneys appearing and practicing before the SEC. This section functions as another avenue to guide attorneys practicing in this area.

SOX underscores and reemphasizes the ABA Model Rule regarding the Organization as Client. The first part of SOX § 307 equates to ABA Model Rule 1.13 (b); it requires the "attorney to report evidence of a material violation of securities law or breach of fiduciary duty or similar violation by the company or any agent thereof, to the chief legal counsel or the chief executive officer of the company (or the equivalent thereof)." The second part equates to Rule 1.13 (b) which requires lawyers to act in the best interest of the organization and, if necessary "the lawyer *shall* refer the matter to higher authority in the organization, including, if warranted by the circumstances to the highest authority that can act on behalf of the organization as determined by applicable law" (emphasis added). The second section of § 307 states that

> if the counsel or officer does not appropriately respond to the evidence (adopting, as necessary, appropriate remedial measures or sanctions with respect to the violation),[it requires] the attorney to report the evidence to the audit committee of the board of directors of the issuer or to another committee of the board of directors comprised solely of directors not employed directly or indirectly by the issuer, or to the board of directors.

This mirrors the obligation of the attorney under the ABA Model Rule 1.13(c) to reveal as much information as is necessary to avoid substantial injury to the organization.

These ethical rules and regulations, in part a response to scandals like Enron, have caused attorneys for businesses to question whether they are acting as trusted counselors or governmental informants. The SEC requires the attorney to report mere evidence of the violation, whereas the Model Rules require knowledge on the part of the attorney that a violation has occurred or will occur.

Legal Professionals' Protections after Disclosure

If an attorney does "blow the whistle" on her employer, the ethics rules provide protection for the attorney. If an attorney believes that she has been fired or forced to withdraw for making a justified disclosure to protect the organization from harm, then she can take whatever steps she feels are professionally necessary to protect herself. This protective rule applies also to paralegals who feel it necessary to report misconduct.

retaliatory discharge
A client's firing of the attorney for the attorney's failure to pursue the client's unethical or imprudent course in handling its legal affairs.

constructive discharge
An attorney's cessation of the performance of legal work due to the client's insistence on pursuing unethical or imprudent means to achieve its desired result in the legal matter.

The ABA Model Rules afford an attorney a means to defend herself against **retaliatory discharge**: Her employer cannot fire her because she made the requisite disclosures to the appropriate authorities. In addition, the attorney may properly withdraw from representing the organization. In the instance where the company is the sole client of the attorney, the unemployment is deemed to be a **constructive discharge** rather than a resignation. This would equate to a wrongful termination claim against the client. Under normal circumstances, this is unacceptable in the attorney-client relationship. The fiduciary duties owed to the client prohibit this potentiality; it is incongruous to expect almost absolute trust from the client and to uphold the attorney's duty of loyalty with the ominous threat of suit at the hands of the fiduciary. However, as an employee of an organization, the attorney is entitled to the same economic protection that other contractually bound employees enjoy. This includes employment protection. Losing this client could mean losing an attorney's entire livelihood.

The attorney-plaintiff in *O'Brien v. Stolt-Nielsen Transportation Group, Ltd.*, 48 Conn. Supp. 200, 209, 838 A.2d 1076, 1083 (2003), claimed that he was constructively discharged from employment at the company because he was "ethically and legally barred from rendering legal services to, and remaining in, the management of Stolt-Nielsen while the company's alleged illegal activities continued." The attorney followed the requisite course of reporting the questionable actions to the highest authorities in the company, but the company failed to stop the activity. The attorney-plaintiff sought not only money damages but also a declaratory judgment that would allow him to reveal confidential client information to the court and law enforcement authorities.

This step, requesting the court's permission to reveal the information, is necessary in such an instance of revealing past acts of the client. The Court in *Heckman v. Zurich Holding Company of America*, 242 F.R.D. 606, 607 (D. Kan. 2007), upheld the attorney's right to sue the organizational client under a claim for retaliatory discharge for whistle-blowing (the attorney reported that the organization had engaged in illegal conduct). Of course, this would involve a breach of confidentiality between the discharged in-house attorney and the former employer. The solution? While the attorney was permitted to "reveal confidential information under Rule 1.6(b)(3) to the extent necessary to establish such claim . . . the Court f[ound] that a protective order which limits the unnecessary disclosure of such information [was] appropriate." *Id.* at 612. However, if the attorney had knowledge of an ongoing crime or fraud, that information could be revealed under the "prevention of a crime-fraud" exception of the ethical rules. This serves as a reminder that while in-house counsel and other attorneys dealing with organizations as a client have a special rule that applies to them, it works in concert with the other rules covering all attorneys.

CLIENTS WITH DIMINISHED CAPACITY

In a perfect world, clients not only present the attorney with all the relevant information, but also are capable of understanding the legal situation and agree with the attorney's well-reasoned advice. The fact that this very seldom happens can pose problems for attorneys working with "average" clients. The problems and efforts increase when an attorney finds himself working with a client with **diminished capacity**. This can mean that the client is a minor, is physically or mentally ill or impaired, or has some other disability that affects her capacity to appreciate the situation, comprehend the attorney's advice, and/or make a reasoned decision. The attorney must try to overcome these challenges to maintain as normal a relationship as possible with this type of client and, of course, act in the best interest of the client. ABA Model Rule 1.14 addresses the issues in dealing with this type of client. The most difficult task in this respect may be that the client takes a position that is not in his best interest and the attorney must "disobey" the directives of the client.

Acting in the best interests of the client may not be possible without the assistance of other professionals, or at least of family members. The least drastic and invasive actions should be attempted first; an example would be a consultation with the family to suggest creating a power of attorney to take charge of the affected client's interests. Should that prove unsuccessful or ineffective, evaluation and counseling from a professional may be necessary. Lastly, **guardianship/conservatorship** should be sought. It is a delicate situation and introduces another person's opinion as to what is best for the client. The goal is to permit the client to retain as much independence and dignity as possible in the handling of his legal affairs.

Indeed, even making the decision to seek protection for the client is not easy:

> The most difficult task is determining whether under Rule 1.14(b) you must take protective action with respect to your client. You must believe that your client cannot act in her own best interests, but this should not be based upon what you believe are ill-considered judgments alone. If you feel that you have doubts about your client's ability to act in her own best interests, it may be appropriate to seek guidance from an appropriate diagnostician. [. . .]
>
> Before you attempt any protective action, you must determine that other, less drastic, solutions are not available. Examples of less drastic solutions in the ABA Formal Opinion are: "involvement of other family members who are concerned about the client's well-being, use of a durable power of attorney or a revocable trust where a client of impaired capacity

diminished capacity
A client's incapacity to understand legal ramifications of his decisions, as a result of immaturity or of some mental or physical infirmity.

guardianship/ conservatorship
The appointment of a third party who has the legal authority and fiduciary duty to care for a diminished person and/or his property. The individuals are known as either a guardian or a conservator.

has the capacity to execute such a document, and referral to support groups or social services that could enhance the client's capacities or ameliorate the feared harm." These types of avenues should be examined and explored prior to taking protective action.

After a thorough review of the situation, your professional judgment may lead you to believe that protective action is necessary. This could mean applying for the appointment of a conservator (voluntary or involuntary) or guardian ad litem.

While Rule 1.14 does allow a lawyer to take protective action on behalf of a client, it is not a mandate a lawyer must follow. Obviously, many lawyers would feel uncomfortable filing for protective action for their client. Termination of representation is permissible, but must be performed "without material adverse effect on the interests of the client."

Conn. Ethics Op. 97-19, 1997 WL 700686 (Conn. Bar Assn.).

Lastly, in dealing with a client of diminished capacity, all the rules of confidentiality take on an added dimension, as the attorney needs to consult with outside parties in order to effectuate proper representation. In this regard, the attorney may reveal only client confidences that are directly related and absolutely necessary for the third party to know in order to assist the attorney in making the best decisions for the client. Failure to properly consult the guardian of the client can also result in sanctions. It is not enough for the attorney to assume the guardian's consent to actions that may have been the client's plan prior to incompetency.

To be sure, an adjudication of incompetency . . . does not obviate the need for a guardian or judge to consult a ward's feelings or opinions on a matter concerning his care. It does not make the ward any less worthy of dignity or respect in the eyes of the law than a competent person. It does not deprive the ward of fundamental liberty interests. But the rights and interests of one adjudicated to be incompetent must of necessity and for the benefit or advantage of the ward, often be vindicated in a manner different from that of the mentally competent.

In re Guardianship of Hocker, 791 N.E. 2d 302, 307 (Mass. 2003) (internal citations omitted).

Therefore, it is clear that the attorney is also obligated to communicate with the guardian against his client's wishes.

SPECIAL CIRCUMSTANCES

Declining Representation

Attorneys do not have to take on prospective clients who may pose difficulties, for whatever reason; they may decline to represent a person. While the underlying reasons for declination are not subject to any rules, the way in which the person is treated is. Primarily, any person who approaches an attorney in any setting and seeks legal advice about any situation, whether or not the attorney is competent in that area, is considered a **prospective client**, and shall be treated according to the ethical rules. The governing ABA Model Rule is 1.18. The key to understanding when the ethical rules kick in is determining whether the person knows he is speaking to an attorney and intends to communicate with him about a legal issue. It is a very broad interpretation and is designed to safeguard the integrity of the profession. It is well known and well established that attorneys must keep communications secret. Extending this protection to any person who seeks advice, a "prospective client," ensures that people will feel comfortable seeking legal assistance.

The Rules specifically state that any communications made in this initial consultation are held confidential, as if they were made by an actual client. This duty of confidentiality does not depend on whether the attorney takes on the person as an actual client or whether any fees were paid. The moment the prospective client opens his mouth, the ethical "cone of silence" applies. The duties to this "prospective client" are the same as those that apply to former clients, as discussed in Chapter 5.

Further, declination of representation is *mandated* where taking on the prospective client would create a conflict of interest with a current client. The conflict would arise where the prospective client's interests are materially adverse to those of the current or former client in the same or a substantially related matter. Once an attorney has obtained enough information from the initial communications from the prospective client to determine that a conflict exists, he must prevent the prospective client from further revealing information and decline the representation. No other member of that firm may take on that prospective client, according to the imputed disqualification rule of conflicts.

As in the previously discussed conflicts rules, an attorney would be able to overcome the conflict and take on the representation only if the parties affected knowingly waived the conflict in writing or the affected attorney were properly screened from the matter if the firm decided to take on the representation. Of course, notice of these precautions must be given to a prospective client. This provision allows the prospective client to be represented by the firm of his choice.

Mandated Termination of Representation

On the other hand, if the attorney has already taken on a matter that has gone sour, the attorney may properly withdraw from that representation only as long as the ethical requirements are met. There are two categories of withdrawal or declination of representation: when it is *mandatory* for the attorney to withdraw and when it is *permissible* to withdraw. **Mandatory withdrawal** occurs if an attorney finds herself in a situation where:

1. The rules of professional ethics will be violated if the attorney continues to represent the client, or

---

prospective client
A person who knowingly seeks the advice of an attorney relating to legal matters.

mandatory withdrawal
Withdrawal of an attorney from representation where that representation will result in a violation of ethical rules, or the attorney is materially impaired, or the attorney is discharged.

2. The attorney is impaired by a physical or mental condition that materially interferes with her ability to represent the client, or

3. The attorney is fired by her client.

In a mandatory withdrawal, the attorney has no discretion as to whether the relationship needs to end; it must end. The attorney can no longer represent that particular client. There may not be a provision in the attorney-client agreement specifying the amount due under circumstances requiring withdrawal prior to the natural termination of the matter. This may be particularly true in cases where the attorney is working on a contingency fee basis. The attorney may be able to recover fees in *quantum meruit* for the work that he did perform if:

1. Counsel's withdrawal was mandatory, not merely permissive, under statute or State Bar rules;

2. The overwhelming and primary motivation for counsel's withdrawal was the obligation to adhere to these ethical imperatives under statute or State Bar rules; counsel commenced the action in good faith;

3. Subsequent to counsel's withdrawal, the client obtained recovery; and

4. Counsel has demonstrated that his [or her] work contributed in some measurable degree towards the client's ultimate recovery.

Duchrow v. Forrest, 156 Cal. Rptr. 3d 194, 213 (Cal. Ct. App. 4th 2013).

The first enumerated provision underscores the importance of understanding the ethical rules and their application in any situation. It is impermissible to violate the ethical rules; therefore, if the representation will result in an ethical violation, the representation is prohibited. The second provision addresses the condition of the attorney. Practicing the law is not easy; the stress and fast pace can put a strain on an attorney's general well-being. Add to this any personal, physical, and mental problems the attorney may be experiencing, and this strain can result in a diminished fitness to practice. The disability suffered by the attorney must be influencing the legal tasks required in his practice. In other words, the performance of the attorney must be directly caused by and compromised by the disability. Without this causal connection, the attorney may continue without threat of a violation of his ethical duties. The simple fact that an attorney is under stress, overworked, or dealing with a myriad of problems, either mental or physical, does not mean that he has diminished capacity to practice law. The disability must impact the lawyer's fitness to practice law.

There is a tension here: How is a compromised attorney to recognize when she needs to decline work, withdraw, or seek help? Unfortunately, an attorney may not realize that she is unable to perform at the appropriate competency level, and an ethical violation may result. However, the fact that the attorney did not purposefully neglect or falter in his practice, but rather suffered under a disability, will mitigate the sanction imposed. The ABA has set forth in Rule 9.32 of the Standards for Imposing Lawyer Sanctions the circumstances

quantum meruit
"As much as is deserved." The reasonable value of services rendered to cover labor and costs where no other specific amount is the subject of an enforceable contract.

under which a mental disability, including a chemical dependency, will be considered. The affected attorney must be able to show:

1. Medical evidence that she is impaired by a chemical or mental disability, and that
2. The misconduct was caused by the chemical dependency or mental disability, and that
3. She has sustained a meaningful and successful period of rehabilitation from the chemical dependency or mental disability, and that
4. This recovery has stopped the misconduct, and that
5. The recurrence of the misconduct is unlikely.

It is not enough that an attorney suffers from a disability that causes her to falter in her legal and ethical duties to her clients. She also must show that she is willing and able to recover from the disability, that the recovery is substantial in both time and effect, and that the recovery will affect positively how the attorney resumes her practice. Indeed, after the period of rehabilitation, the attorney must apply to the Bar to show the extent of recovery in order for the Bar to assess whether the attorney should, indeed, be reinstated.

The compassionate nature of the disciplinary board was aptly demonstrated in *Lawyer Disciplinary Bd. v. Dues*, 218 W. Va. 104, 624 S.E.2d 125 (2005). In the time frame of just two years, Attorney Dues suffered a heart attack, underwent triple bypass surgery, was admitted to the hospital on three occasions for various physical ailments, and had a prostate operation. All of these physical problems led to severe depression, and Attorney Dues began psychiatric treatment. It was only after these problems occurred that Attorney Dues was found to have committed 39 violations of his professional duties. He presented "unchallenged medical evidence that his legal deficiencies were directly connected to the serious depression that flowed from his physical problems." *Id.* at 113. The court empathized and opined: "the unique facts of this case convincingly demonstrate that, in addition to his clients, Mr. Dues was also a tragic victim in this matter. He was the victim of a mental disease that 'the legal community has been slow to recognize . . . as a legitimate disease that merits attention.'" *Id.* citing, Todd Goren & Bethany Smith, "*Depression as a Mitigating Factor in Lawyer Discipline*," 14 G. J. Legal Ethics 1081, 1082 (2001). *See also Lawyer Disciplinary Board v. Blyler*, 787 S.E.2d 596, 613 (W. Va. 2016) (The evidence established that the attorney's mitigating circumstances warranted a lesser discipline. The "significant personal, emotional, and financial toll placed on Mr. Blyler while caring for his wife as she suffered through early onset Alzheimer's disease, which required Mr. Blyler's continual care and assistance in every activity of life as she progressively declined both physically and cognitively. It is plain that Mr. Blyler was devoted to the needs of his dying wife while continuing to serve a community with his small, general, rural law practice.")

On the other hand, where an attorney uses the fact of having a disability to escape responsibility, the disciplinary board is not sympathetic. An attorney

RESEARCH THIS

Find the Lawyer's Assistance program in your jurisdiction. Make note of its mission statement and contact information. What services do they offer?

REEL TO REAL

For a refreshing comedic break, watch *All of Me* (1984), starring Steve Martin and Lily Tomlin. Tomlin's character is a wealthy heiress who, in preparing for her death, arranges to have her soul transferred into a younger woman's body. However, her soul ends up in the body of her lawyer, played by Martin. Would this unconventional problem be considered grounds for an attorney to withdraw from representation of clients under the theory of mental impairment?

SURF'S UP

Stress can be a killer, not only of productivity, but of sanity. Surf the internet to find ways to handle the pressures associated with an overload of work. Technology and the internet can be a "virtual" lifesaver. It is important to test drive many different ways of handling your own to-do list. Find the appropriate program to do just that. It may already be on your computer, like Outlook® or other calendaring programs. Almost every mobile device has some task or calendar manager and there is a myriad of apps for this purpose! Don't let technology burden your paralegal career—use it to enhance your productivity and lower your mental stress levels so that you can perform at your best.

diagnosed with bipolar II disorder was suspended from practice for three years for his 22 ethical violations. The attorney's conduct involved dishonesty in lying to clients and judges and falsifying documents in order to cover up his mistakes in practice. His treating psychiatrist testified that dishonesty is not a symptom of bipolar II disorder. The violations could not be connected to the underlying mental disease, and, therefore, the disability could not have caused the attorney's improper actions. Consequently, the disability was not a mitigating factor in deciding how to sanction the attorney. *Lawyer Disciplinary Bd. v. Scott*, 213 W. Va. 209, 215, 579 S.E.2d 550, 556 (2003).

IN-CLASS DISCUSSION

Evaluate the "disabilities" suffered by two attorneys in capital murder cases. If you were on the Appellate Panels, would you have ruled the same way? Should these attorneys have withdrawn? Should they be ethically sanctioned for their failure to withdraw in these situations? Note that in both trials, the defendants had co-counsel (each was represented by another attorney who assisted the counsel in question).

In the first case, the Applicant's first claim is that he was actually or constructively denied counsel because of his retained attorney's persistent habit of napping during the trial.

> He argues that when Mr. Benn slept through significant portions of his trial, applicant was totally deprived of that counsel's assistance. Applicant notes that in United States v. Cronic, the Supreme Court held that a defendant's Sixth Amendment rights are violated "if the accused is denied counsel at a critical stage." Under Cronic and its progeny, a defendant is denied counsel not only when his attorney is physically absent from the proceeding, but when he is mentally absent as well, i.e., counsel is asleep, unconscious, or otherwise actually non compos mentis. This prong of Cronic is epitomized by the "inert" or "potted plant" lawyer who, although physically and mentally present in the courtroom, fails to provide (or is prevented from providing) any meaningful assistance. In this situation, courts presume prejudice based upon the actual or constructive denial of counsel "when such absence threatens the overall fairness of a trial."
>
> See Ex parte McFarland, 163 S.W.3d 743, 752 (Tex. Crim. App. 2005) (citations omitted).

In the second, the attorney (Mr. Portwood), not only admitted to a problem with alcohol abuse (drinking 12 shots of rum per night during the trial, contrary to the findings of the court below), he was later pulled off another death penalty case and sent to a detoxification facility. The attorney later died of a liver-related illness. The defendant's appeal to the Supreme Court of the United States was denied, and Mr. Frye was executed in August of 2001.

> Frye also contends, in connection with his ineffective assistance claim, that Portwood's asserted alcohol dependency rendered him incapable of providing constitutionally effective assistance up to and during the sentencing phase of the trial. We are indeed troubled by Portwood's acknowledgment of a decades-long routine of drinking approximately twelve ounces of rum each evening. However, the district court found that Portwood "never consumed alcohol during the work day and never performed any work on the case when he had consumed alcohol." We agree with our sister circuits that, in order for an attorney's alcohol addiction to make his assistance constitutionally ineffective, there must be specific instances of deficient performance attributable to alcohol. In this case, there is no evidence of specific instances of defective performance caused by Portwood's alcohol abuse. Furthermore, it is significant that Frye was not represented by Portwood alone—he had the benefit of two court-appointed lawyers assisting in his defense.
>
> Frye v. Lee, 235 F.3d 897, 907 (4th Cir. 2000) (citations omitted).

Lastly, an attorney must withdraw if his client terminates the relationship. The attorney is essentially employed by the client at the client's will. If the client wishes to "fire" his attorney, that is his prerogative. "Public policy strongly favors a client's freedom to employ a lawyer of his choosing and, except in some instances where counsel is appointed, to discharge the lawyer during the representation for any reason or no reason at all." *Hoover Slovacek LLP v. Walton*, 206 S.W.3d 557, 562 (Tex. 2006). However, the attorney will be able to recover the value of his services rendered to the client prior to the termination by the client. Attorneys are entitled to collect the proper fees for their time and effort, even if the fee arrangement was originally contingent. The firing of the attorney does not allow the client to obtain free counsel. If the attorney must resort to the court for collection of his fee, a reasonable fee will be determined and awarded to the attorney in a contingent fee case. It is not based upon the actual settlement or judgment obtained by the former client. Fees can also be collected by securing an attorney lien on the proceeds of the matter. The right to place such a lien is dependent upon the circumstances surrounding the client's termination of the attorney. If the attorney was discharged for cause (the attorney violated some duty owed to the client), then the attorney has no right to place a lien on the matter; on the other hand, if the client terminated the relationship without cause, the attorney does have the right to place the lien. *See Friedman v. Park Cake, Inc.*, 825 N.Y.S.2d 11 (N.Y. App. Div. 2006).

Permissive Termination of Representation

The attorney has the option of withdrawing in many other situations that arise in practice. The operative language in ABA Model Rule 1.16 is that the attorney *may* withdraw, but does not have to, in the following situations:

1. There is no material, adverse effect on the client's interests if the attorney chooses to withdraw;
2. The lawyer reasonably believes the client will use, continue to use, or has used the attorney's services to perpetrate a crime or fraud;
3. The attorney is repulsed by or has a fundamental disagreement with the client's actions or decisions in the matter;
4. The attorney has previously notified the client of the client's failures to fulfill his obligations under the retainer agreement and the client has continuously and substantially failed to satisfy those obligations. The attorney may withdraw after such warning has been given;
5. The attorney will suffer unreasonable financial burden by continuing to represent the client;
6. Actions or inactions by the client have rendered the representation unreasonably difficult; or
7. Other good cause exists which justifies withdrawal.

permissive withdrawal
The attorney's chosen termination of representation of the client in certain circumstances that comply with the attorney's ethical obligations to the client.

Many of these factors are present in any one case. Most, if not all of the time, finances play some part in the **permissive withdrawal** of the attorney. Either the client refuses to pay bills as they come due or the representation itself has become too expensive to go forward (factors 4 and 5 above). Generally, withdrawal will require the attorney to make a motion to the court to obtain permission to terminate the relationship. At that time, the court will first examine whether the client will be adversely affected by the withdrawal. There is a presumption that the longer an attorney has represented the client and the closer it is to the time of trial, the more likely it is that a client will be adversely affected. Withdrawals on the eve of trial, without exceptional excuse, are not granted. If the request to withdraw is not granted, the attorney must continue to represent his client to the best of his ability.

In making the application to withdraw, the attorney must only disclose as much information as is necessary to effectuate the withdrawal; the attorney must keep as much client information secret as possible pursuant to his ethical duty of confidentiality. "In this case the motion was filed early on in the appeal, and withdrawal will not unduly disrupt the proceedings. We see no need for this counsel to explain why he wishes to withdraw in more detail, as such an explanation could be detrimental to the client or protected by the attorney-client privilege." *Horan v. O'Connor*, 832 So. 2d 193, 194 (Fla. App. 2002). In that matter, the attorney withdrew from representation due to "irreconcilable differences" that arose between the attorney and the client, "rendering the [attorney] unable to ethically and fairly represent [client] in this matter." *Id.*

Similarly, where an attorney determines that a case lacks merit, the economic incentives to pursue the matter dissipate, adding insult to injury. This is particularly true in a contingency fee case. See *Elton v. Dougherty*, 931 So. 2d 201 (Fla. App. 2006), wherein the attorney decided that the case lacked merit and he was no longer willing to advance costs necessary to proceed. The client could not afford to pay the costs, and, therefore, the court found "that the attorney's and client's interests were in insurmountable conflict."

No matter what the reason, economic or otherwise, the attorney must preserve the client's rights and advise him of any issues that they need to be aware of before full termination of the relationship. Former clients are still protected by attorneys' ethical obligations. An attorney must do all he can to make sure that the client is not harmed by the withdrawal, and facilitate the transfer of the matter to another attorney if necessary. The disengaging attorney must surrender client files and property and return unearned legal fees. These protections are of utmost importance when timing is critical, as when the Statute of Limitations is running. There is no "bright line rule" as to how close to trial or to the end of the filing period for the cause of action is too close, making it impermissible for counsel to withdraw.

SPOT THE ISSUE

Ronald, a relatively new client, has just learned that Leonard, the lawyer handling his matter, has delegated many substantial legal tasks to Connie, his very competent paralegal. Ronald voiced his unsubstantiated and uneducated opinions about the way that Leonard was handling the matter. He thought that Leonard should do all the work, since Leonard was the one who signed the retainer agreement. Ronald disparaged Connie's abilities to perform the tasks assigned to her. Ronald stubbornly refused to go to another lawyer; he wanted only Leonard to work on the matter. What options does Leonard have in dealing with Ronald?

Every case is determined on its own facts and parties involved. Where a few weeks may be enough time for a simple legal issue, it may not be for a complex matter. Or, with regard to the parties, the time required for a savvy businessperson familiar with legal affairs to obtain new counsel may not be enough for another individual.

> The letter of termination, moreover, while it referred to the two-year statute of limitations and "suggest[ed]" plaintiff contact another lawyer immediately, did not specify the critical date. Finally, a fact-finder could also conclude that the period of time left to plaintiff before the statute of limitations had run was unreasonably short, particularly in view of the preceding six-month period following [the attorney]'s receipt of Dr. Stein's favorable report. In this regard, we note that medical malpractice cases are ordinarily difficult representations and are not lightly or casually undertaken by serious and responsible lawyers. It is by no means clear that plaintiff could have obtained a new lawyer who, in three weeks, would have been able to review her file, make the necessary evaluations, and agree to file a complaint, particularly after knowing that her previous lawyer, who had represented her for twenty-one months, had suddenly declined to continue.

Gilles v. Wiley, Malehorn & Sirota, 345 N.J. Super. 119, 127, 783 A.2d 756, 761 (App. Div. 2001).

The attorney must take the individual client's capacity to deal with the situation at hand into consideration when withdrawing from the representation. Recalling the discussion of clients with special needs due to diminished capacity, the protection of the client's interests during and after withdrawal becomes paramount. The key to handling this potentially delicate situation is to understand the capacity of the disabled client to comprehend the ramifications of the withdrawal. While letters of disengagement may work for clients of normal functioning, a client with special needs may need more explanation. The attorney's benevolent intent is immaterial if the communication is ineffective. In *Cuyahoga Cty. Bar Assn. v. Newman*, 102 Ohio St. 3d 186, 808 N.E.2d 375 (2004), the attorney represented a gentleman who had been injured in an accident, leaving him physically and mentally disabled. He helped this client for years and free of charge, as he considered him a friend. Of course, the attorney asserted that he did not mean to financially harm his disabled client. The attorney sent his client a letter in which he stated that he would not be acting as his attorney for a certain matter involving a commercial lease. The court found that the brief letter of withdrawal was insufficient to give the client proper notice given the capabilities of his client, and that the attorney knew or should have known that the client would not be able to understand the significance of the letter. Not only was the withdrawal improper because it was ineffectual under the ethical rules; the attorney, in fact, had violated his ethical obligations by "abandon[ing] his client's interests during the course of a professional relationship and caus[ing], at least in part, the client's personal liability for defaulting on the lease." *Id.* at 190. This brings us to the lesson learned in this section:

Write a carefully crafted letter of disengagement, specifically noting all deadlines and ramifications of withdrawal, and have the client confirm his understanding of it.

Returning to the reasons why an attorney may choose to withdraw, the crime or fraud factor most often relates to false statements made in legal documents or to client perjury. In those cases the attorney has the option of withdrawing if the client persists in this course of conduct despite admonitions from the attorney. Pursuit of unmeritorious claims is not only punishable by ethical sanctions, but also penalized under the civil rules' "frivolous claims" prohibition; in that instance, the attorney should be permitted to withdraw. For example, in *Pritt v. Suzuki Motor Co., Ltd.*, 513 S.E.2d 161 (W. Va. 1998), the attorney learned that his client was faking the extent of his injuries and that the activities in which the client was engaging were completely inconsistent with the plaintiff's theory of the case. The attorney was permitted to withdraw due to the client's use of the attorney's services to perpetrate fraud on the court. In *Staples v. McKnight*, 763 S.W.2d 914 (Tex. App. 1988), the attorney would be permitted to withdraw if she believed and could show reasonable basis for her belief that her client intended to commit perjury.

Whether a client's actions or suggestions for conducting the case are repugnant or not is highly fact sensitive. What is clear is that inconsiderate or distasteful conduct towards other parties or counsel is ground for withdrawal. The North Carolina Court opined that while an attorney should zealously represent the interests of her clients, taking unfair advantage of a colleague who is suffering from an ailment or disability is inconsiderate or repugnant. The attorney can avoid the client's propositions to use offensive tactics and is, on the contrary, ethically obligated to "treat[] with courtesy and consideration all persons involved in the legal process. . . . If the client is insistent and the client-lawyer relationship is no longer functional because of the disagreement about tactics, the lawyer may withdraw from the representation pursuant to Rule 1.16(b)(4)." 2003 N.C. Eth. Op. 2, 2003 WL 24306941.

While the ethical rules speak to ideals, they are not confined to them. The practice of law involves the practical issues of running a business as well. For that reason, factors 4 and 5 above speak to the financial and operational issues that occur in representation. Clearly, the client has an obligation to pay certain costs and fees associated with the matter; additionally, the client has an obligation to stay in communication with the attorney. Non-responsiveness to efforts by the attorney to consult with the client is a "breach" of the client's "duty" to help move the case forward. *Benefield v. City of New York*, 824 N.Y.S.2d 889 (2006). If these obligations are not met, the attorney has the right to withdraw as counsel. Similarly, if the attorney's practice, indeed, his very livelihood, is placed in jeopardy due to the financial stresses of handling the matter, the attorney may be able to withdraw. In a case of first impression, the Appellate Division of New Jersey weighed the public policy considerations involved in permitting a firm to withdraw as counsel under a contingent fee arrangement in a large, costly, and prolonged tobacco litigation. Weighing against such a withdrawal, the trial court opined and the appellate court agreed:

> The fact that no competent counsel appears willing to invest the time and energy on such basis clearly reflects that withdrawal will have "material adverse effect on the interests" of plaintiffs. The question before us therefore is whether the representation of plaintiffs in this case will cause such an unreasonable financial burden as to permit withdrawal of counsel under [Rule] 1.16(b)(5). . . . This argument [of unreasonable financial burden] is not compelling in the context of a contingency fee relationship which, by its nature, involves uncertainty and risk and requires the parties to make predictions as to (1) the likelihood of recovery, (2) the length of time until recovery and (3) the probable size of recovery. Given their litigation experience, lawyers are in a better position than clients to make these predictions.

Smith v. R.J. Reynolds Tobacco Co., 267 N.J. Super. 62, 75-77, 630 A.2d 820 (App. Div. 1993).

The court recognized that the firm took on this risk, and determined that to permit withdrawal on the ground that maintaining the litigation had become too costly would "stigmatize" such risky yet socially important claims. "As for plaintiffs, the disappointment at having been abandoned mid-stream is likely to undermine faith in the legal system and to reinforce the notion that access to the courthouse is a function of wealth." *Id.* at 78. However, on the other hand:

> Denial of the present motion would serve only to discourage lawyers confronted with requests by clients to pursue ground-breaking claims on their behalf. While the risk of bearing litigation costs and the costs of lawyer and paralegal time without compensation will always exist in such cases if, as here, the lawyer's compensation is contingent, denying permission to withdraw here would threaten otherwise courageous counsel with the need to contemplate that no matter how bleak and desperate the financial costs of carrying litigation costs had become, the firm would be required to stagger on and complete the course. For a court to require such heroic undertakings would also add to the threat of imposed litigation costs that defendants can often dictate in a case through cost-generating and delay-producing moves in the course of the litigation. If anything, such a decision would only add to the incentives of defendants to engage in such practices.

Id. at 81.

This extensive examination of the financial burdens and risks on the part of both attorneys and clients underscores the case-sensitive nature of such requests to withdraw as counsel. The legal system balances all the factors as described in ABA Model Rule 1.16, to determine the most just result for the parties involved and for the maintenance of confidence in the system as a whole. Clients should not feel as though attorneys can desert them midstream without a means to reach their goals.

Summary

The provisions discussed in this chapter have one thing in common: They all underscore the importance of trust and respect in the way in which attorneys handle their clients. They must identify their client and act only in the client's best interest despite outside influences either from those who would take advantage of a disabled client or the directors of an organizational client. Where an organization is the client, the duty of loyalty is owed to the organization as a whole, not to an individual member. All clients, prospective, current or past, must be respected and their information kept confidential to the extent required under the rules. Respect for the client's best interest may manifest itself in declining representation or withdrawing from representation if representation would result in an ethical violation. There are certain situations that require an attorney to withdraw:

1. The rules of professional ethics will be violated if the attorney continues to represent the client, or

2. The attorney is impaired by a physical or mental condition that materially interferes with her ability to represent the client, or

3. The attorney is fired by her client.

There are certain situations in which the attorney may choose to withdraw or to continue representation. These exist where:

1. There is no material, adverse effect on the client's interests if the attorney chooses to withdraw;

2. The lawyer reasonably believes the client will use, continue to use, or has used the attorney's services to perpetrate a crime or fraud;

3. The attorney is repulsed by or has a fundamental disagreement with the client's actions or decisions in the matter;

4. The attorney has previously notified the client of the client's failures to fulfill his obligations under the retainer agreement and the client has continuously and substantially failed to satisfy those obligations. The attorney may withdraw after such warning has been given;

5. The attorney will suffer unreasonable financial burden by continuing to represent the client;

6. Actions or inactions by the client have rendered the representation unreasonably difficult; or

7. Other good cause exists which justifies withdrawal.

Whether the issue involves special clients or special circumstances, paralegals and attorneys must act in the best interests of each client and do their best to deal with the situation at hand with all the ethical mandates in mind. All of the matters dealt with in this chapter pose challenges for legal professionals. It is the purpose of the ethical rules to provide parameters in which to deal with them.

Key Terms

Constructive discharge
Diminished capacity
Guardianship/Conservatorship
Mandatory withdrawal

Permissive withdrawal
Prospective client
Quantum meruit
Retaliatory discharge

Review Questions

MULTIPLE CHOICE

Choose the best answer(s) and please explain *why* you chose the answer(s).

1. Where the attorney represents an organizational client:
   a. He also represents all the shareholders of that corporation
   b. He may represent other members of the organization if there is no conflict of interest
   c. He can share confidential corporate information only with the board of directors
   d. All subsidiary companies of the organization are also clients of the attorney for the parent company
   e. All of the above

2. An attorney must maintain an organization's confidential information unless:
   a. She chooses to represent the organization's employees instead
   b. The SEC requests all the records of the company
   c. The organization chooses to pursue a criminal or fraudulent activity
   d. She has been retaliatorily discharged as counsel

3. An attorney may permissively withdraw from representation:
   a. Only with the court's approval at a hearing or at trial
   b. If he is fired by the client
   c. If the client continues to pursue an ill-advised course of action
   d. When the attorney is found guilty of ethical misconduct

4. An attorney who has agreed to represent a client with diminished capacity must obtain a guardian when:
   a. The client is unable to make her own decisions in her representation
   b. The family of the disabled client asks the attorney to obtain one
   c. The client has made poor decisions regarding her representation
   d. The client is completely unable to understand the ramifications of her decisions regarding her representation

EXPLAIN YOURSELF

All answers should be written in complete sentences. A simple yes or no is insufficient.

1. Who is the client when the attorney handles matters for a corporation?

2. What are the duties owed to a client with diminished capacity?

3. When *must* an attorney withdraw or decline representation of a client?

4. Describe a situation in which an attorney should withdraw for mental impairment or disability. What can you as a paralegal do in this circumstance?

FAULTY PHRASES

All of the following statements are *false*; state why they are false and then rewrite each one as a true statement. Do not simply make the statement negative by adding the word "not."

1. All employees of a corporation who have relevant information about the legal matter at issue are protected under attorney-client privilege.

2. A client with diminished capacity does not have the same rights of attorney-client privilege as other clients.

3. An attorney must take on all clients who come to his office who present him with a problem in the area of law in which he specializes.

4. An attorney must decline to represent a potential client who suffers from diminished capacity because the potential client cannot act for herself.

5. An attorney who drinks alcohol or uses drugs should withdraw from the representation of clients.

6. An attorney can appeal her client's decision to terminate the representation if the attorney is fired right before trial.

7. An attorney may cease to work on a client's matter until he is paid for his work.

PORTFOLIO ASSIGNMENT

Write Away

Draft a letter of disengagement to your client, Sly Stone. Explain why the law firm can no longer represent him. Use any of the reasons explained in this chapter and be sure to include enough details to justify the termination of the relationship. Also make note of any important steps that Mr. Stone should take after receiving the letter. Provide for return of any client property, if necessary.

Case in Point
Corporate Clients

44 Pa. D. & C. 3d 513, 1987 WL 46863 (Pa. Com. Pl.) Court of Common Pleas of Pennsylvania, Allegheny County.

Monah

v.

Western Pennsylvania Hospital

No. G.D. 86-8881.

February 23, 1987

WETTICK, A.J.

This is a medical malpractice action in which plaintiffs' negligence claims include the negligent monitoring of the patient following surgery in the recovery room of defendant, Western Pennsylvania Hospital. Plaintiffs have filed a motion to compel Western Pennsylvania Hospital to produce a written statement of the head nurse in the recovery room. The nurse is an eyewitness to the events in the recovery room at the time that plaintiff suffered a cardiac and respiratory arrest.

The nurse is an employee of Western Pennsylvania Hospital. Her statement was prepared prior to the commencement of the lawsuit at the request of in-house counsel for the hospital. For purposes of this motion to compel, we assume that this statement was prepared to assist counsel in evaluating the hospital's potential liability and that counsel did not reveal the contents of this statement to any third persons. Western Pennsylvania Hospital contends that this statement is protected by the attorney-client privilege because this was a statement by an employee of the corporation to corporate counsel while both were acting in the course of their employment. Plaintiffs, on the other hand contend that the attorney-client privilege does not extend to factual statements of an employee who is only a witness to an incident.

The law is settled that the attorney-client privilege extends to corporations. *Upjohn Co. v. United States,*

449 U.S. 383, 101 S. Ct. 677 (1981). Because a corporation is capable of communicating with its attorneys only through its agents, it is necessary to determine which communications between corporate counsel and employees or other agents of the corporation come within the scope of the attorney-client privilege.

All communications between corporate employees and corporate counsel should not be protected. For example, a corporation should not be able to assert the attorney-client privilege to protect a statement of an employee injured in the course of his employment made to corporate counsel at counsel's request in a FELA action by this employee against the corporation arising out of the incident described in the statement; or to protect statements by fellow laborers, sympathetic to the injured employee, made to corporate counsel; or to protect statements that an employee made to corporate counsel as part of a corporate investigation to determine whether the employee had been embezzling corporate funds. In these situations, the employees making the statements have none of the attributes of a client making a statement to his or her counsel and counsel has none of the responsibilities to these employees that an attorney owes to a client.

There is no Pennsylvania appellate court case law that has considered the issue of what statements made by employees to corporate counsel are protected by the attorney-client privilege. Furthermore, the issue has not arisen frequently in other jurisdictions because most jurisdictions protect attorney work product from discovery and this protection encompasses most statements that corporate employees make to corporate counsel. However, this issue has been thoughtfully addressed by a sufficient number of appellate courts so that the different approaches available to a court have been carefully examined. The opinions in *Consolidation Coal Co. v. Bucyrus-Erie Co.*, 432 N.E. 2d 250 (Illinois Supreme Court, 1982), *Leer v. Chicago, Milwaukee, St. Paul and Pacific Railway Co.*, 308 N.W.2d 305 (Minnesota Supreme Court, 1981), cert. denied, 455 U.S. 939 (1982), and *Marriott Corp. v. American Academy of Psychotherapists Inc.*, 277 S.E.2d 785 (Georgia Court of Appeals, 1981), thoroughly review the development of the case law.

Prior to 1981, most jurisdictions followed one of two tests. The first test—the control group test—was initially adopted in *City of Philadelphia v. Westinghouse Electric Corp.*, 210 F. Supp. 483 (E.D. Pa., 1962). This test extends the attorney-client privilege only to corporate employees who will be directly involved in making any decision that may be based on the advice of counsel. The rationale for the test is that the employee, by virtue of his or her position with the corporation, will be acting as the corporation when he or she is consulting with counsel. This test focuses on the status of the employee within the corporate hierarchy.

"[I]f the employee making the communication, of whatever rank he may be, is in a position to control or even to take a substantial part in a decision about any action which the corporation may take upon the advice of the attorney, or if he is an authorized member of a body or group which has that authority, then, in effect, he is (or personifies) the corporation when he makes his disclosure to the lawyer and the privilege would apply. In all other cases the employee would be merely giving information to the lawyer to enable the latter to advise those in the corporation having the authority to act or refrain from acting on the advice." *Id.* at 485.

This test has been criticized because it fails to protect confidential communications that are essential in order for corporate counsel to provide legal advice. Top level executives frequently do not have the information necessary for counsel to render legal advice to the corporation. They will be reluctant to authorize

counsel to obtain such information from lower level employees who have direct knowledge of the corporate operations if this information is not protected. This, in turn, will prevent corporations from utilizing counsel to learn how to obey the law according to the critics of the control group test. *Marriott Corp. v. American Academy of Psychotherapists Inc., supra.; Upjohn Co. v. United States, supra.*

The second test—the subject-matter test—was initially formulated in *Harper and Row Publishers Inc. v. Decker*, 423 F.2d 487 (7th Cir., 1970); affirmed by an equally divided court, 400 U.S. 348 (1971). Under this test, the communication of an employee who is not a member of the control group with corporate counsel is privileged if the employee made the communication at the direction of a supervisor and if the subject matter upon which the lawyer's advice was sought by the corporation and dealt with in the communication was within the performance of the employee's duties. This test has been criticized because it protects almost all communications between a corporate employee and corporate counsel. In response to this criticizm, the Court of Appeals for the Eighth Circuit in *Diversified Industries Inc. v. Meredith*, 572 F.2d 596 (1978) (en banc), adopted a third test—the Weinstein test—which is a refined subject matter test initially proposed by Judge/Professor Weinstein. Under the Weinstein test, the attorney-client privilege will be available to a corporation if the following requirements are met:

"(1) [T]he communication was made for the purpose of securing legal advice, (2) the employee making the communication did so at the direction of his corporate superior, (3) the superior made the request so that the corporation could secure legal advice, (4) the subject matter of the communication is within the scope of the employee's corporate duties, and (5) the communication is not disseminated beyond those persons who, because of the corporate structure, need to know its contents." *Id.* at 609.

In 1981, in the case of *Upjohn Co. v. United States, supra*, the United States Supreme Court rejected the use of a narrow control group test because this test fails to protect confidential communications of employees who are not members of the control group made to counsel in order for counsel to acquire the information necessary to give informed advice. In this case, outside counsel was retained by the board of directors of the corporation to learn whether corporate funds had been paid to foreign governments to secure governmental business for the corporation. The ultimate purpose of counsel's investigation was to give legal advice to the board of directors. At counsel's request, the control group instructed management employees outside of the control group to provide information to counsel.

The Internal Revenue Service issued a summons for the production of this information which these corporate employees had furnished counsel. The corporation raised, inter alia, the attorney-client privilege as a basis for its refusal to provide any information furnished to corporate counsel. The court of appeals rejected the corporation's contention, holding that any information supplied by an officer or agent not responsible for directing the corporation's activities in response to legal advice which counsel furnished was outside the scope of this privilege. The United States Supreme Court reversed, stating that the narrow control group test sanctioned by the court of appeals cannot control the development of this area of the law. The court concluded that the information was protected because of the need by corporate counsel, if he or she is to adequately advise the client, to obtain relevant information from middle and lower level employees. The court did not propose a substitute test but, instead, stated that the scope of the privilege will be determined on a case-by-case basis.

While the *Upjohn* case is not binding on state courts, the case will be carefully considered by any state court that is addressing the issue of the applicability of the attorney-client privilege to communications by corporate employees to corporate counsel. The result in *Upjohn* appears to be consistent with the goals and purposes of the attorney-client privilege. The *Upjohn* case dealt with information which counsel obtained from management employees as to corporate practices that they may have pursued on behalf of the corporation. Counsel's inquiries did not involve incidents which a corporate employee may have witnessed but, instead, dealt with policies made or followed by employees on behalf of the corporation.

This court's conclusion that the result in *Upjohn* is consistent with the attorney-client privilege as recognized by the Pennsylvania courts does not mean that the control group test should be completely abandoned. In fact, it would appear that the *Upjohn* court's

dissatisfaction with the Sixth Circuit's ruling stemmed from its use of a rigid control group test that did not bring within the scope of the attorney-client privilege employees who are apparently acting as the corporation (although possibly outside the scope of any specific direction from upper management).

An important rationale for the *Upjohn* holding was that the application of the attorney-client privilege to the communications that were involved "puts the adversary in no worse position than if the communications had never taken place." 101 S. Ct. at 685. In the present case, the application of the attorney-client privilege to the communication by the head nurse to corporate counsel would place plaintiffs in a worse position that if the communication had never taken place.

This nurse is a potential witness for plaintiffs. If she would testify on behalf of plaintiffs, Western Pennsylvania Hospital would be in a position to impeach her testimony through the use of a statement that was never made available to plaintiffs. Thus, if this court were to protect this statement, we would be creating a situation in which Western Pennsylvania Hospital could use this witness without any fear that her statement could be used to impeach her testimony while plaintiffs, if they called this nurse as a witness, would run the risk of impeachment based upon a statement that they have never seen.

The attorney-client privilege was initially developed to protect people, not corporations. If the nurse was the client of the attorney who obtained her statement, the attorney-client privilege would bar the attorney from using this statement to impeach the nurse. Thus, if this court were to protect this statement, we would be placing the corporation in a better position than if it were an individual.

While there may be situations in which the attorney-client privilege should be applied in a manner that places the corporation in a better position than an individual client, this result must be supported by strong policy considerations. These policy considerations do not exist where the communication from the employee to corporate counsel involves only the factual description of a witness to an incident that resulted in injury or death. There is no need to protect this information in order for a corporation to conduct its business affairs because the communication does not involve matters concerning confidential corporate practices. If the purpose for the communication is to assess the corporation's liability, the communication need not be protected because the same information may be obtained by plaintiff through discovery. If the purpose for the communication is to obtain evidence that will be unavailable to the plaintiff, the communication should not be protected.

The choice of the test to be applied to communications of corporate employees to corporate counsel depends on the manner in which the court balances the competing interests of the corporation in protecting employee communications with counsel and of the litigant in obtaining full discovery of the relevant facts in order that the law's protections are extended to those persons whom the law seeks to protect. In the case of *Consolidated Coal Co. v. Bucyrus-Erie Co., supra* (which was decided after and gave consideration to *Upjohn*), the court concluded that a broad control group test strikes the proper balance between the state's broad discovery policies which are essential to a fair disposition of the lawsuit and the needs of the corporation to obtain legal advice. Thus, the court held that a factual report of an engineer who had examined the pieces of the machine in question was not protected by the attorney-client privilege.

A similar approach was followed by the Minnesota Supreme Court in *Leer v. Chicago, Milwaukee, St. Paul and Pacific Railway Co., supra* (which also was decided after and gave consideration to the *Upjohn* opinion). In that case, the corporate railroad was seeking to protect statements of other members of a switching crew who had observed the accident in which plaintiff, a switchman, was injured. The court concluded that the attorney-client privilege should not extend to suppress statements of witnesses to the incident because of the state policy favoring a liberal construction of the discovery rules. The court ruled that "when an employee is merely a witness to an accident and not a party to a subsequent action, communications made with him in a general investigation do not create an attorney-client relationship." 308 N.W.2d at 309.

This court recognizes that other jurisdictions have more broadly construed the attorney-client privilege to protect the statements of employees who witnessed

an accident made to corporate counsel in connection with pending or threatened litigation. *See State of Missouri ex ref. Missouri, Highways and Transportation Commission v. Legere, 706 S.W.2d 560 (Missouri Court of Appeals, 1986)*; *Macey v. Rollins Environmental Services*, 432 A.2d 960 (Superior Court of New Jersey, 1981). This court declines to follow these cases because these communications do not need to be protected in order for corporate counsel to properly prepare a defense or to give legal advice to the corporation. Furthermore, an extension of the attorney-client privilege to such communications is inconsistent with the broad discovery provisions of the Pennsylvania Rules of Civil Procedure governing discovery of trial preparation material, such as Pa. R.C.P. 4003.3 which protects from discovery only the mental impressions, conclusions, or opinions respecting the value or merit of a claim or defense or respecting strategy or tactics with respect to a representative of a party other than the party's attorney, and rule 4003.5 which does not protect the facts known or opinions held by a regular employee of a party who may have collected the facts or rendered the opinions under the direction of counsel for a party. In jurisdictions, such as Pennsylvania, which do not protect factual information obtained in anticipation of litigation, a broad construction of the attorney-client privilege as to communications to corporate counsel from corporate employees who are witnesses to the incident would create an unfair result. The rules of discovery would permit the corporation to obtain each statement that counsel for an adverse party obtained from a corporate employee who witnessed the incident while the attorney-client privilege would protect from discovery each statement that corporate counsel obtained from the same employee.

For these reasons, the court enters the following ORDER

On this February 23, 1987, it is hereby ordered that plaintiffs' motion to compel is granted and that the statement of the recovery room nurse shall be produced within 20 days.

Source: Reprinted from Westlaw with permission from Thomson Reuters.

Part Three

The Legal Professionals' Roles in the Justice System

Chapter 8

Advocacy and Litigation Issues

Chapter Objectives

The student will be able to:

- Differentiate between meritorious claims and defenses and potentially frivolous ones and provide an explanation of the choice
- Acknowledge the importance of expediting litigation despite the temptation to use dilatory practices
- Discuss the obligation of honesty in presenting information to a tribunal and identify when certain disclosures must be made in order to effectuate justice
- Identify the rules pertaining to communications with opposing and third parties
- Evaluate an attorney or paralegal's actions during the litigation process in light of their obligations of fairness

This chapter will examine the legal professional's role as an advocate and/or litigator. *How* are the participants in the litigation process obligated to act towards one another and towards the justice system? To *whom* may a lawyer or paralegal speak in either a transactional or a litigious matter? *What* can the legal professional communicate to others? Most importantly, this section of the ABA Model Rules emphasizes the foundations of justice and fairness as the reason *why* attorneys and paralegals are required to act in a certain way in presenting claims and defenses in the adversarial process.

In the previous five chapters (Chapters 3 through 7), the duties of the attorney to her client have been explored. In the following four chapters (Chapters 8 through 11), the responsibilities of the attorney to the justice system will be explained. It is important to bear in mind that both transactional matters and litigation are components of the justice system; however, most frequently the adversarial nature of legal representation presents itself in litigation. There may be times when the client, the justice system, and/or the employment situation of the attorney may cause a problem or conflict for the attorney. The purpose of the ethics rules in this area is to guide the attorney through the problem's resolution, which will undoubtedly favor the maintenance of the integrity of the profession and the administration of justice. The question posed in this part of the text is this: How can the attorney balance her responsibilities in order to ensure that her actions comport with all of the applicable ethical rules?

For the same reason discussed previously, the paralegal must be able to understand why a firm or an attorney is acting in a certain manner in order to do his part to ensure compliance. A paralegal cannot do that which an attorney cannot do under the ethics rules. Often, the paralegal is involved in preparing the submissions to the tribunal, and, therefore, takes an active role in ensuring that the attorney fulfills her duties of honesty and fairness to everyone and every entity with whom she comes in contact.

advocacy
To engage in the profession of taking on clients to actively support their cause.

adversarial model
The American system of retaining separate independent and oppositional counsel to engage in zealous representation of individual clients.

There are particular issues that arise in the context of **advocacy**. The "in-your-face" **adversarial model** under which the American system operates, and indeed, has been honed to a sharp edge, tempts both the attorney and the client to take any advantage. However, justice is not served by "pot-shots" taken at an adversary; justice is served by exposing truths in their proper light. Already the paralegal student can see the conflict within the trial attorney's psyche: how to protect his client's vulnerability without misleading the tribunal and without overly assisting his adversary.

The ABA Model Rules are presented relatively chronologically and will be discussed in that order. The attorney and paralegal must:

1. Present plausible causes of action and defenses to those claims in the pleading or other initial papers to the tribunal (ABA Model Rule 3.1)
2. Keep the litigation moving through the system by not purposefully causing delay in the preparation for trial (ABA Model Rule 3.2)
3. Be honest with the court in all matters, even when that honesty may compromise the client's interest (ABA Model Rule 3.3)
4. Deal fairly with all parties involved in the litigation (ABA Model Rule 3.4)
5. Remain neutral and respectful to the justice system and its processes (ABA Model Rule 3.5)
6. Refrain from revealing to the media certain information covering the litigation which may have an adverse impact on the proceedings (ABA Model Rule 3.6)
7. Treat all "non-clients" with respect, keeping an eye on the justice system's overriding interest in fairness (ABA Model Rules 4.1–4.4)

MERITORIOUS CLAIMS AND DEFENSES

After the attorney has decided to pursue litigation as the means to achieve her client's goals, she must file a complaint with the court or other proper tribunal competent to hear the matter. Recall that the client may determine the ultimate end to be achieved, but it is the attorney who must direct the course to that end. Therefore, she is responsible for the content of all presentations to the court—after all, the client retained her for just that reason. The attorney knows (or should know) the proper course of conduct and submission to the tribunal. To impress the importance of proper submissions upon practicing attorneys, they are held to be responsible for the content of the documents that they have prepared or have been prepared under their supervision. Pleadings, motions, and other papers sent to the court for its consideration must be signed by an attorney who will vouch for their credibility. This is not to say that the allegations contained therein are absolutely true, but rather that the attorney has made a reasonable inquiry into the plausibility of the facts and legal arguments set forth. The signature requirement for court submissions makes someone, usually the attorney, accountable, and without the signature, the paper will be stricken. The court must be assured that it is not wasting its time on a matter that an attorney will not stand behind.

Paralegals are involved in these processes of collecting information from the client and witnesses and drafting the initial documents submitted to the court. Indeed, NALA's Guideline 5 sets forth these duties as some of those properly delegated to a paralegal. (See Figure 8.1.)

As the paralegal's work will form the foundation of the attorney's work product submitted to the opposing party and the tribunal, it is imperative that the paralegal scrupulously adhere to the ethical requirements that underpin the adversarial system.

How does an attorney make the determination as to whether or not the cause of action has merit and is properly submitted to a tribunal for adjudication? In this situation, an attorney has two sources of guidance: ABA Model Rule 3.1 and the Federal Rules of Civil Procedure Rule 11. It is very important to note that most cases are *not* handled in federal court. The Federal Rules are discussed in this text as an example only. Paralegals and students must always check the rules in their relevant jurisdictions. ABA Model Rule 3.1 prohibits an attorney from bringing any issue before the court for which he cannot make a good faith argument in law and that he cannot support with some factual basis. Essentially, it prohibits nonsense or baseless claims. The true key to understanding this rule is to understand the **good faith** requirement imposed upon the attorney. This is where Federal Rule 11 is helpful. Most states have enacted similar rules pertaining to frivolous claims. Subsection (b) of Federal Rule 11, "Representations to Court," presents the situations in which the attorney would not be acting in good faith in presenting the issue to the tribunal. The attorney can be said to be acting in good faith only if, after a reasonable inquiry into the matter, he asserts that:

1. It is not being presented for any improper purpose, such as to harass or to cause unnecessary delay or needless increase in the cost of litigation;

good faith
An attorney must reasonably believe in the validity of the claim(s) asserted and present them for a proper purpose for adjudication by the tribunal.

FIGURE 8.1 ▶
DUTIES PROPERLY
DELEGATED TO
PARALEGALS

NALA Model Standards and Guidelines for the Utilization of Paralegals: Guideline 5

Except as otherwise provided by statute, court rule or decision, administrative rule or regulation, or the attorney's rules of professional responsibility, and within the preceding parameters and proscriptions, a paralegal may perform any function delegated by an attorney, including, but not limited to the following:

- Conduct client interviews and maintain general contact with the client after the establishment of the attorney-client relationship, so long as the client is aware of the status and function of the paralegal, and the client contact is under the supervision of the attorney.
- Locate and interview witnesses, so long as the witnesses are aware of the status and function of the paralegal.
- Conduct investigations and statistical and documentary research for review by the attorney.
- Conduct legal research for review by the attorney.
- Draft legal documents for review by the attorney.
- Draft correspondence and pleadings for review by and signature of the attorney.
- Summarize depositions, interrogatories and testimony for review by the attorney.
- Attend executions of wills, real estate closings, depositions, court or administrative hearings and trials with the attorney.
- Author and sign letters providing the paralegal's status is clearly indicated and the correspondence does not contain independent legal opinions or legal advice.

2. The claims, defenses, and other legal contentions therein are warranted by existing law or by a non-frivolous argument for the extension, modification, or reversal of existing law or the establishment of new law;

3. The allegations and other factual contentions have evidentiary support or, if specifically so identified, are likely to have evidentiary support after a reasonable opportunity for further investigation or discovery; and

4. The denials of factual contentions are warranted on the evidence or, if specifically so identified, are reasonably based on a lack of information or belief.

It is helpful to take each of these instances of good faith in turn. First, the attorney must promise that he is not bringing the matter to court just to bully another party. Mere unsubstantiated threat to sue is a violation of the attorney's duty to use the justice system only for proper purposes; actual misuse of the justice system is a more serious sanctionable offense violating both relevant rules of conduct. Further, even if the matter is properly brought before the court, it is impermissible to use any procedure in the court rules to achieve an improper purpose. For example, an attorney may not bring motion after motion that essentially seek the same result just so the other party is forced to take time out of case preparation in order to answer them, and as a consequence the matter is delayed. More specifically, an attorney would be hard pressed to justify this sequence of motions as a good faith tactic: first, a motion for a more definite statement on the pleadings; second, another motion for the same; then, a motion to dismiss for failure to state a cause of action; then, a motion to dismiss on the pleadings; then, a summary judgment motion; and so on. All of these in rapid succession would not advance the proper purpose of these motions, but rather cause delay and frustration for the opposing counsel. This may also play out in the discovery phase of litigation, where an attorney drowns the opposition in superfluous and repetitive requests for production of information. A paralegal should be on alert for a supervising attorney's aggressive tactics in this regard. The court may also find that only part of the claim brought before the court is without merit, and dismiss that element of the matter. See, for example, *Hudson v. Moore Business Forms, Inc.*, 836 F.2d 1156 (9th Cir. 1987), wherein the plaintiff filed suit against her former employer alleging wrongful discharge and sex discrimination. Her employer counterclaimed, alleging that she had breached her employment duties of loyalty and good faith in performing her work. While the employer's claim of $200,000 in compensatory damages may have been a reasonable request for extension of the law of tort damages in an employment context, the $4 million sought in punitive damages was found to be wholly frivolous. The request for $4.2 million in total damages was determined to have no plausible factual or legal basis and was made for the improper purpose of harassing the plaintiff and discouraging others from bringing similar suits against the employer.

Second, legal professionals must know not only the law, but also the boundaries of the law and when and if those borders should be crossed. Attorneys and paralegals have an obligation to the legal system to uphold those laws that are just and to advocate for change where the law or interpretation of the law is not just or equitable. To confine legal professionals by maintaining that any challenge to existing law is **frivolous** is to abrogate the very nature of our legal system. "[T]he Rule does not seek to stifle the exuberant spirit of skilled advocacy or to require that a claim be proven before a complaint can be filed. The Rule attempts to discourage the needless filing of groundless lawsuits. And we have recognized that creative claims, coupled even with ambiguous or inconsequential facts, may merit dismissal, but not punishment." *Newsome v. Gallacher*, 2014 WL 4199616 at 5, (N.D. Okla. 2014) citing, *Hunter v. Earthgrains Co. Bakery*, 281 F.3d 144, 153 (4th Cir. 2002) (internal citations omitted). Laws change and develop over time in order to address the contemporary needs of society. Without challenges to the existing laws, past legal horrors like segregation and discrimination would still be in place. However, merely a desire to avoid the proper application of a just law to the present situation because it adversely impacts the client is not a good faith argument to have it changed. This truly good faith argument for change may be unconventional given the relevant precedent, however, "Rule 11 must not be construed so as to conflict with the primary duty of an attorney to represent his or her client zealously. Forceful representation often requires that an attorney attempt to read a case or an agreement in an innovative though sensible way. Our law is constantly evolving, and effective representation sometimes compels attorneys to take the lead in that evolution. Rule 11 must not be turned into a bar to

frivolous
Having neither factual merit nor legal purpose.

legal progress." *Operating Engineers Pension Trust v. A-C Co.*, 859 F.2d 1336, 1344 (9th Cir. 1988).

Third, conjecture and hypothesis based upon legal theory are not the sole basis for a claim; there must also be supporting facts that can be applied to the legal standards set forth in the law. The fact-finder, usually the jury, must be able to hear evidence that could convince them that the party has a **viable claim**; without evidence there can be no claim. This does not mean that the attorney must have her hands on all the supporting documentation at the time the pleadings are filed, but rather that she is satisfied that there exist such facts and evidence to support the claim. The standard applied in this situation is whether another attorney similarly situated would feel that the matter has enough factual support to bring the matter before the court. The attorney must make a reasonable inquiry as to the merits of the case before proceeding.

In deciding whether an attorney signing a pleading made a reasonable inquiry into the facts and law of a case, the court uses an objective standard, asking what a reasonable attorney should have done under the circumstances that existed at the time of the challenged filing. Applying this objective standard, a court should consider these factors in determining whether an attorney made a reasonable inquiry to the facts:

> whether the signer of the documents had sufficient time for investigation; the extent to which the attorney had to rely on his or her client for the factual foundation underlying the pleading, motion, or other paper; whether the case was accepted from another attorney; the complexity of the facts and the attorney's ability to do a sufficient pre-filing investigation; and whether discovery would have been beneficial to the development of the underlying facts.
>
> An attorney may rely upon his or her client for the factual basis for a claim when the client's statements are objectively reasonable, but this does not mean that an attorney always acts reasonably in accepting a client's statements. Whether it is reasonable to rely on one's client depends in part upon whether there is another means to verify what the client says without discovery. A party and attorney may not rely on formal discovery after the filing of a suit to establish the factual basis for the cause of action when the required factual basis could be established without formal discovery. In addition, in deciding whether to rely on one's client for the factual foundation of a claim, an attorney must carefully question the client and determine if the client's knowledge is direct or hearsay and is plausible; the attorney may not accept the client's version of the facts on faith alone. Allegations by a client of serious misconduct of another may require a more serious investigation. While the investigation need not be to the point of certainty to be reasonable and need not involve steps that are not cost-justified or are unlikely to produce results, the signer must explore readily available avenues of factual inquiry rather than simply taking a client's word.

Wisconsin Chiropractic Ass'n v. State of Wisconsin Chiropractic Examining Board, 676 N.W.2d 580, 589-590 (WI App 2004) (citations omitted).

---

viable claim
A claim for which the fact-finder can supply a redress in law by applying the relevant legal standard to the presentable and substantiated facts.

The Wisconsin court's point regarding client statements cannot be overemphasized, particularly for paralegals. Clients will, understandably, slant their recounting of the underlying facts to best support their claims, and it is often the paralegal's responsibility to perform client intake interviews, or at least attend them in order to take notes. Understanding the motivation for the client's accounting of the situation and evaluating his reliability and truthfulness is critically important at this early stage.

The last subsection of Rule 11 deals with properly defending against allegations. Just as a plaintiff may not wantonly hurl accusations at a defendant, so a defendant cannot recklessly deny them. While the burden of proving the essential elements of the cause of action lies with the plaintiff (generally speaking), the defendant cannot deny those factual elements that either are indeed known to her to be true or for which she has no knowledge as to the truth of the matter asserted.

IN-CLASS DISCUSSION

While many people thought the case brought against McDonald's alleging damages because Big Macs made the plaintiff fat was absolutely ridiculous, it was not frivolous under either ABA Model Rule 3.1 or Federal Rule 11 standards. The plaintiff was claiming that although he knew that Big Macs were not healthful, the marketing of the product caused him to consume too many and therefore caused him harm. This may appear to be a case of "assumption of the risk"; if the plaintiff is aware of the danger and proceeds anyway, there should be no recovery against the other party who presented the risk of harm. Why, then, did the attorney for the plaintiff file suit when everyone knows that fast food is not good for you and will make you fat if you eat too much of it? It looks like a loser from the start, doesn't it? Or does it? Didn't hundreds of plaintiffs win millions of dollars alleging the very same thing with respect to cigarettes?

SURF'S UP

Late hours and work overload may cause some attorneys to lash out in papers that, of course, will never be filed – very similar to those letters that we write to purge ourselves of tension and stress and then promptly shred or burn. But unforgiving technology doesn't let you retract that scathing e-mail that got sent because you inadvertently pushed the "enter" or "send" button. Similarly, a Colorado attorney, blowing off some steam onto yet another dreaded motion, probably did not intend to send the motion in Figure 8.2 by electronic filing.

FIGURE 8.2 ▶
MOTION FOR EXTENSION
Source: www.abovethelaw.
com

EFILED Document

DISTRICT COURT, WATER DIVISION 7, COLORADO 1060 2nd Ave. Durango, CO 81301	Co La Plata County District Court 6th JD Filing Date: Mar 4 2007 11:28 AM MST Filing ID: 14001012 Review Clerk: Paula Petersen
IN THE MATTER OF THE APPLICATION FOR WATER RIGHTS OFTHE SOUTHWESTERN WATER CONSERVATION DISTRICT, Applicant.	▲ COURT USE ONLY ▲
ATTORNEY FOR OPPOSER: REDACTED Denver, CO 80222 REDACTED	Case No.: 01 CW 54
MOTION FOR RULE 6(b)(2) EXTENSION TO RESPOND TO BILLS OF COSTS	

Certificate of Compliance with Conferral Requirement

The undersigned certifies that opposing counsel do not consent to the extension.

Opposer Citizens Progressive Alliance ("CPA"), through its attorney undersigned and pursuant to Rule 6(b)(2), C.R.C.P., respectfully requests another one-day extension, to Monday, March 5, 2007, to respond to the Applicant's (and other opposers') bills of costs. As grounds therefor, the undersigned states that she had almost completed this response on the due date, which was Friday, March 2, but suspended her work in order to take a friend out to dinner for his birthday. When she came back, she was unable to finish it, due to the wine. :-) The response is filed herewith.

WHEREFORE, inebriation constituting excusable neglect, and no prejudice inuring to the other parties, the court should grant the present extension, as it is in the interest of justice.

EXPEDITING LITIGATION

Misusing the system to gain an unfair advantage may begin as described above; by contrast, later in the process, after a valid claim has been asserted, the abuse may take the form of overt disregard for and explicit impediments to the procedural deadlines imposed by the court rules. ABA Model Rule 3.2 requires that attorneys, and therefore their paralegals, make reasonable efforts to keep the litigation moving at a pace consistent with their obligations to the client and the legal system. Not only must legal professionals keep track of the timeline for litigation in a passive manner; they must also actively try to advance the resolution of the matter.

> That rule imposes an affirmative duty on lawyers to make reasonable efforts to expedite litigation. The caveat—consistent with the interests of the client—insures that a lawyer's efforts to expedite litigation do not conflict with the client's legitimate interests. The comments [to the ethics rule], however, make it clear that "delaying tactics" are discouraged.
>
> *Matter of Shannon*, 876 P.2d 548, 563 (Ariz. 1994).

There may be times when delay would actually benefit the client, giving the client more time to make submissions or raise funds for the continuation of the matter. This presents a false conflict between the lawyer's duty to expedite litigation and to zealously represent and preserve the client's interest. The judges in *Iowa Supreme Court Attorney Disciplinary Board v. Weiland*, 862 N.W.2d 627 (Iowa 2015), found that the rules of procedure and professional responsibility required the attorney to "disclaim such motivation [preservation of the claim by delay] as a legitimate interest of a client." *Id.* at 637. These disciplinary matters highlight the balancing act that attorneys must play in managing the progress of their cases. Hastiness, like excessive delay, is rarely congruous with good lawyering. Somewhere between these two extremes, the proper approach can be found. Paralegals play a vital role in finding and maintaining that balance through essential calendaring and case management systems. It is sometimes proper to request extensions of time in order to be thorough or due to extenuating circumstances not under the attorney's control or influence. However, prolonging the matter in order to gain strategic or financial advantage or simply to wear down the opposition's patience is unacceptable. The "reasonable lawyer" standard is used in determining whether the delay is tolerable. The essential question is whether another attorney or paralegal acting in good faith in carrying out her duties and obligations would take a similar course of action. The reasoning behind the request for an extension must have some purpose other than delay or advantage-taking. As in many areas of life, judging the conduct by the standard of the "Golden Rule"—treat others as you want to be treated—provides the best guidance.

CANDOR TOWARDS THE TRIBUNAL

The underlying foundation of the entire justice system is honesty: "[c]andor and truthfulness are two of the most important moral character traits of a lawyer." *Attorney Grievance Comm'n of Maryland v. Myers*, 333 Md. 440, 635 A.2d 1315 (1994). The attorney previously had been suspended for three years for an intentional misrepresentation to the court. At this hearing, the court stressed the importance of truthfulness and disbarred the attorney for this second offense involving misrepresentation to the court. Although history and the notorious media have not always borne that ideal out, attorneys, aware of the severe sanctions possible, generally comply. To ensure that attorneys understand the sanctity of this principle, ABA Model Rule 3.3 is very specific as to the attorney's duties and makes it clear that in all situations where there is a conflict, candor toward the tribunal outweighs the attorney's duty to keep his clients' confidences. Figure 8.3 lists the various obligations of a legal professional to maintain honesty in the administration of justice.

knowing
Believing with a reasonable and substantial probability (it is not necessary to be absolutely certain).

The key to understanding these obligations and their applicability is the definition of **knowing.** Where is the line to be drawn between knowledge and ignorance? There is a gray area of uncertainty between these two states of mind; how should the determination be made that an attorney or a paralegal "knew" a fact or statement of law was false? Since the purpose of the ethical rules is to protect the public and maintain the respectability of the profession, the courts have decided to err in favor of the public and the integrity of the legal system and hold that a negligent submission to a tribunal is a knowing misstatement subject to sanction. Attorneys are trained to make reasonable investigations into facts and law; they are required to make inquiry into the veracity of the underlying basis of their submissions to the tribunal. When they do not do so, they are making not an intentional misrepresentation, but rather a negligent declaration that they know is unsupported and therefore could be false. This knowledge of potential falsity and the potential to mislead or deceive is enough to achieve the "knowing" standard of the ethics rules. "By making no inquiry into the truth or falsity of her statement regarding the [. . .] incident, [the attorney] 'knowingly' misrepresented the facts." *In re Dodge,* 108 P.3d 362, 366 (Idaho 2005). Once the attorney formulates the intent to deceive by making a false statement to the tribunal, ABA Model Rule 8.4 comes into force. Professional misconduct is defined as engaging in conduct involving dishonesty, fraud, deceit, or misrepresentation. Similarly, NFPA prohibits such conduct in EC 1.3(b). (See Figure 8.4.) Violations such as fraud and

FIGURE 8.3 ▶
ENSURING HONESTY
AND TRUTHFULNESS
BEFORE A TRIBUNAL

Attorneys and paralegals are obligated to:

1. Refrain from making any statement of fact or law that the legal professional knows is false
2. Correct any previously made false statement of material fact
3. Disclose controlling legal authority (statutes, cases, rules, etc.) that is known by the legal professional and is directly adverse to the position of the client and which has not been disclosed to the tribunal by opposing counsel
4. Refrain from offering evidence that the legal professional knows to be false. An attorney may refuse to offer evidence that the attorney reasonably believes to be false, although the attorney cannot prohibit a criminal defendant from testifying in his own behalf if he chooses to exercise that right.
5. Correct any false evidence submitted once the attorney becomes aware of its falsity
6. Prevent or remediate criminal or fraudulent conduct of his client where those activities are related to the proceedings

NFPA EC 1.3

A paralegal shall avoid impropriety and the appearance of impropriety and shall not engage in any conduct that would adversely affect his/her fitness to practice. Such conduct may include, but is not limited to: violence, *dishonesty*, interference with the administration of justice, and/or abuse of a professional position or public office (emphasis added).

◀ **FIGURE 8.4**
THE IMPROPRIETY OF DISHONESTY

misrepresentation by their legal definitions require the intent to deceive another regarding a material fact. Dishonesty may not require a specific intent to make a false statement regarding a material fact only. Any false statement impinges upon the trustworthiness and honesty of the legal professional. Every statement by an attorney to the court should be deliberately made, and this deliberateness should not depend upon the importance of that fact. It also does not matter if the court actually relied upon that false statement in making its decision, or whether any harm may have resulted from it. The mere fact of making a false statement to the court that the attorney knew was not necessarily true or verified is enough to form the basis of a sanction.

> If an attorney does not know if an assertion is true or cannot point to a reasonably diligent inquiry to ascertain the truth of the statement, the attorney can remain silent, profess no knowledge, or couch the assertion in equivocal terms so the court can assess the assertion's probative value. The standard of affirming facts to the court cannot be the negligence standard, which is the argument presented to the Court by [the attorney]. . . . It is not unrealistic to expect an attorney making a representation to the court purporting to come from personal knowledge to take reasonable steps to assure she is speaking truthfully.

Id. at 367-369.

Materiality does impact the legal professional's obligation when it comes to correcting a previously made statement. If, at the time that the legal professional made the submission to the court, it was true or the legal professional reasonably believed it to be true, but later, the legal professional discovers that it was incorrect, the attorney must make a supplemental disclosure to the court correcting the statement that is now known to be false. All litigants are entitled to a fair hearing and to judgments based upon a complete and truthful record. The obligation to supply the tribunal with correct information may last even beyond the final judgment, although the usual limit is the termination of the matter, by either settlement or final judgment, or the end of the time period for review on appeal. In *Washington v. Lee Tractor Co., Inc.*, 526 So. 2d 447 (La. App. 1988), the plaintiff sued the tractor company for personal injuries he sustained after falling off the tractor sold to the plaintiff's employer and used by the plaintiff in his course of work. The defendant tractor company obtained summary judgment in its favor based upon an affidavit from the tractor company's president that asserted that the tractor was not sold by

materiality
Having a reasonable and recognizable importance in the process of evaluating a situation, such that its omission might affect the determination of fact or law.

his company and therefore the company was not liable for the plaintiff's personal injuries. The tractor company believed this information to be true at the time the affidavit was made. One month later, the tractor company found the invoice indicating the sale of the tractor. The lawyers for both sides agreed to reinstate the lawsuit; however, plaintiff's counsel informed the defendant that the suit would not be pursued. Approximately nine months later, plaintiff hired new counsel who contacted defense counsel to go forward with the reinstatement. Defense counsel at this time refused to honor the former agreement to reopen the matter. On application to the court, plaintiff was able to reopen the case and the summary judgment was annulled. The court found defense counsel's actions unacceptable and unethical because the summary judgment was obtained by knowingly false evidence and counsel is bound "to correct a false statement of material fact" (RPC 3.3), and the Rules

> place a distinct burden on an attorney who discovers the existence of false evidence to take 'reasonable remedial measures' , and that such duty is unlimited in time, and do not abate at the end of the proceeding. . . .
>
> In essence, failure to correct false evidence, even if originally offered in good faith, is violative of this rule. . . . The failure to rescind the falsely obtained summary judgment has deprived Mr. Washington of his action against Lee. Defendant would not otherwise have been entitled to the summary judgment on the grounds for which it was prayed, without the supporting affidavit. By failing, and then refusing to have the summary judgment rescinded, and thus correct the record, the judgment has been allowed to stand. The result is unconscionable as the plaintiff is left without a remedy through no fault of his own. Therefore, we hold that these events constitute a [violation of the ethical rules].

Washington at 448-449.

There could be no more important fact than that which forms the basis for judgment, like the affidavit in the *Washington* case. The obligation applies to material facts only. What, then, does "material" mean? A fact is considered "material" if

> (a) a reasonable man would attach importance to its existence or nonexistence in determining his choice of action in the transaction in question; or
> (b) the maker of the representation knows or has reason to know that its recipient regards or is likely to regard the matter as important in determining his choice of action, although a reasonable man would not so regard it.

Watts v. Krebs, 962 P.2d 387, 391 (Idaho 1998) (quoting *Edmark Motors, Inc. v. Twin Cities Toyota*, 727 P.2d 1274, 1276 (Idaho Ct. App. 1986) (citing Restatement (Second) of Torts § 538(2) (1977))).

Essentially, if the submitted fact would have impacted the decision in any way and the attorney making the representation knew that the average "reasonable" person would regard that fact as an important factor—*or* if perhaps a "reasonable" person would not perceive the submitted fact as important, but the *legal professional* knows or suspects that the person will place importance on the fact and base some of her decision upon that fact (whether logically or not)—the *legal professional* has a duty to correct or update that decision-maker by informing her of any changes in the original submission.

The third listed obligation seems almost counterintuitive to the adversarial system; however, attorneys and paralegals are ethically bound to reveal to the court the legal authority in the **controlling jurisdiction** in the matter, whether or not the authority is adverse to the attorney's position. It would be nearly impossible, relatively redundant, and ineffectual to mandate that all law that may impact the matter before the court be revealed and discussed. Indeed, a legal professional's skill set includes the ability to analyze and artfully choose not only the relevant legal authority to present to the court, but also the most persuasive authority, because it is most factually similar to the matter at hand. Clearly, the law that is most persuasive is that which comes from the controlling jurisdiction, where a decision has been made by a higher court within the jurisdictional hierarchy. Of course, the attorney or paralegal will willingly reveal the authority that bolsters her cause. If authority exists that is not favorable to the attorney's case, she must not ignore it. The duty of the attorney in that case is, in zealous advocacy for her client, to argue that the adverse authority is distinguishable from the matter at hand or was based upon an improper application of the law and therefore should not be applied. "The concept underlying this requirement of disclosure is that legal argument is a discussion seeking to determine the legal premises properly applicable to the case." *In re Thonert*, 733 N.E.2d 932, 934 (Ind. 2000). Indeed, this "open discourse" is appreciated by the courts and was remarkably noted in *Seidman v. American Express Company*, 523 F. Supp. 1107, 1110 (E.D. Pa. 1981): The trial court "commended" the defense attorney for calling attention to a case that was handed down after the defense's oral argument that severely undercut the position that the defendant had taken at oral argument.

The courts are apt to take a more expansive view of what legal authority should be disclosed, rather than a narrow view—again, in an effort to make a determination on the merits of the case and to properly ascertain a just and fair result. Courts and other legal bodies use their words very carefully: "directly adverse" is not the same as "controlling" when dealing with precedent.

> The meaning of "directly adverse" is explained in Formal Opinion No. 280 issued by the American Bar Association's Committee on Professional Ethics and Grievances. The Committee had been asked to clarify the "duty of a lawyer . . . to advise the court of decisions adverse to his client's contentions that are known to him and unknown to his adversary." The Committee wrote:
>
> We would not confine the [lawyer's duty] to "controlling authorities"—i.e., those decisive of the pending case—but, in accordance with the tests hereafter suggested, would apply it to a decision directly adverse to any proposition of law on which the lawyer expressly relies, which would reasonably be considered important by the judge sitting on the case.

controlling jurisdiction
The legal system in which the tribunal sits whose higher courts' opinions are binding authority upon the lower courts.

The Committee then defined the duty of disclosure:

The test in every case should be: Is the decision which opposing counsel has overlooked one which the court should clearly consider in deciding the case? Would a reasonable judge properly feel that a lawyer who advanced, as the law, a proposition adverse to the undisclosed decision, was lacking in candor and fairness to him? Might the judge consider himself misled by an implied representation that the lawyer knew of no adverse authority?

Tyler v. State, 47 P.3d 1095, 1104-1105 (Alaska App. 2001).

The implication for attorneys and paralegals is clear: perform complete and thorough research and deal with it all, the good and the bad, in an honest, albeit persuasive, manner. This may mean that the paralegal will have to present her supervising attorney with cases that he doesn't necessarily want to hear about, but must be able to face and deal with. What if the other side has not been so diligent? What if opposing counsel has failed to find the law that is supportive of its side? The first attorney is required to essentially do the opposition's work for it. Yes, the ideal is to have adversaries that are vigorously defending their positions with their own arguments and legal support; however, "the old idea that litigation is a game between the lawyers has been supplanted by the more modern view that the lawyer is a minister of justice." *In re Greenberg*, 104 A.2d 46, 49 (N.J. 1954). Counsel cannot take advantage of the sloppy lawyering of opposing counsel. Adverse authority in the controlling jurisdiction must be presented to the court.

Even more egregious than failing to disclose, which is essentially a sin of omission, is actively and knowingly offering false evidence, a sin of commission. The rules and violations thereof are much clearer; either the evidence is substantiated and verifiable or it is not. The *Greenberg* case, *supra*, stated clearly that while attorneys should be able to argue perceptions of the facts and what they might indicate and submit those to the jury for its consideration, an attorney must not "present his inferences from the facts as if they were the very facts themselves. When he is indulging, as he has every right to do, in inferences or reasoning from the facts, he must say so [. . .] and to be effective he should state the facts in the record from which he is making inferences." *Greenberg* at 47-48. A simple example of the difference between fact and inference is as follows: Upon awakening, a person notices that her driveway is wet; she may infer that it rained during the night, but she has no factual basis without consulting the weather authority that it did in fact rain during the night. This prohibition applies not only to matters in an attorney's professional trial files, but also to those in her personal affairs that may end up in court. An attorney who sued in small claims court based on a simple breach of an equipment purchase submitted a letter he had written regarding the matter to settle the dispute. He was caught in a fabrication of evidence; he claimed to have sent this letter to the company that was suing him with a courtesy copy to the attorney representing the company. As it turns out, on the date that the letter was dated, the current attorney for the company was still in law school! The attorney, in an attempt to extricate himself from the knowing submission of false evidence, argued that it was merely a "petty business dispute" arising out of his poor temper in a personal matter which did satisfactorily settle out of court and therefore was not material to any disciplinary action. The court opined that "[t]his interpretation of the events grossly understate[d] their seriousness." *In the Matter of Barratt*, 663 N.E.2d 536, 539 (Ind. 1996). The attorney was suspended from practice for an entire year; this demonstrated the court's acknowledgment of the seriousness of the violation, as it reflected deleteriously upon the integrity of the profession and adversely upon the attorney's fitness to practice law. The lesson here for all legal professionals is to be scrupulous in all dealings with others.

The attorney must not only maintain his own honesty, but actively prevent others under his control from submitting false evidence. If the attorney is or becomes aware of a false submission from either his client or his witness, he must take action to correct it. The corrective action may go as far as withdrawing as counsel and disclosing the falsehood to the tribunal. The drafters of the Model Rules were not insensitive to the harshness of such a result. In comment 11 to Rule 3.3, they acknowledged that the client would naturally and understandably feel betrayed by the attorney's or paralegal's disclosure of the client's false testimony. However, the more evil of the two alternatives is the legal professional's assistance in the deception of the court. The truth-finding mission of the justice system can be served only by imposing this absolute obligation upon those who serve the system. Above all, the attorney must remain true to his highest role as an officer of the court, and the paralegal must steadfastly support that function.

Nowhere is this tension between loyalty to the client and duty to the court more strongly felt than in the criminal context. Criminal defendants have been given certain constitutional protections in judicial proceedings not afforded to civil matters due to the severity of punishment that can be imposed upon those found guilty of a crime. Where life and liberty, both constitutional protections, are threatened, the court has the highest duty to ensure fairness and just adjudication based upon the merits, and to afford the opportunity for the defendant to avail herself of all proper defenses. **Due process** may require that the defendant be given an opportunity to testify on her own behalf, and the United States Supreme Court has considered it a corollary to the Fifth Amendment right not to present evidence against oneself: i.e., if a defendant has the right not to speak, she should have the right to speak if she so chooses. In the landmark case *Nix v. Whiteside*, 475 U.S. 157, 106 S. Ct. 988, 89 L. Ed. 2d 123 (1986), the United States Supreme Court was presented with a case wherein the criminal defendant claimed a violation of his Sixth Amendment right to assistance of counsel when his attorney told him not to state in his own defense testimony that he saw "something metallic" (alluding to the fact that the defendant believed his murder victim to have had a gun but did not in fact see one); the attorney also told the defendant that if he insisted in presenting that testimony, the attorney would have to disclose the perjured testimony to the court. The Supreme Court found that the Sixth Amendment

due process
The ensuring of appropriateness and adequacy of government action in circumstances infringing on fundamental individual rights.

does not and cannot extend to subornation of perjury. "The Model Rules do not merely *authorize* disclosure by counsel of client perjury; they *require* such disclosure." *Id.* at 168 (emphasis in the original). The only deprivation in this case was the defendant's loss of his proposed submission of perjury; this, in the Court's view, is not only a good thing, but reasonable and proper under the Professional Rules of Conduct, and did not, therefore, deny or impair the defendant's Sixth Amendment right to effective assistance of counsel. "The right to counsel includes no right to have a lawyer who will cooperate with planned perjury. A lawyer who would so cooperate would be at risk of prosecution for suborning perjury, and disciplinary proceedings, including suspension or disbarment." *Id.* at 173.

The recurrent theme throughout these ethical obligations is the overarching duty of fairness in the justice system. To take advantage of the lack of actual knowledge of the court, jury, or adversary by submitting false legal authority, facts, or other evidence is to undermine the purpose of the system itself: to render justice based upon the truth. One court characterized this behavior as an attempt at "victory of unbridled egotism and arrogance over the judicial process and the rule of law." *Candolfi v. New York City Transit Authority*, 156 Misc. 2d 964, 969, 595 N.Y.S.2d 656 (N.Y. City Civ. Ct. 1992).

This theme of candor and justice is extended to opposing parties and counsel as well. The thrust of ABA Model Rule 3.4 is the openness of the exchange of evidence or other relevant material between attorneys and the honest communication of information. In short, it is really about fighting fair. Fairness can be achieved only through full access to the truth. Attorneys and paralegals are prohibited from obstructing access to evidence and from destroying, altering, or falsifying evidence or any other material or document that may have evidentiary value. Evidence can also come in the form of testimony. Legal professionals must not advise or assist a witness to offer false testimony.

In a situation where one party has control of the evidence or information necessary to properly prepare for the resolution of the matter, opposing counsel must be given an opportunity to examine that evidence. Clearly, parties may wish that certain documentation indicating weakness, or worse, acknowledging fault, remained hidden; however, this cannot be the case where the legal system insists upon determining matters upon their merits. The infamous shredding, destruction, or modification of materials before responding to discovery requests is unacceptable and almost invariably, the parties get caught. Particularly horrendous is manipulation of the evidence by the attorney himself, not just at his "suggestion." For example, in the case of *Bank of Hawaii v. Kunimoto*, 984 P.2d 1198 (Haw. 1999), counsel for the defendant in a bankruptcy judgment went into receivership; creditors were looking for payment on the $1.6 million judgment. The receiver requested, properly, financial information and an accounting of all assets either currently or previously owned. In an attempt to protect their client, the attorneys withheld certain stock issuance information that they alleged was not relevant because it had been transferred to the defendant's father years before. However, counsel knew that the receiver was entitled to the information and the court had ordered the defendant's father and sister to testify in court as to the stock. Despite this, counsel accepted the transfer of title of the stock in question to their firm in purported payment for legal fees and then, still aware that the court and receiver were interested in this stock, the firm sold it to liquidate the asset and kept the proceeds. The Court found that counsel "recklessly or knowingly deceived the Court, withheld material, responsive information and documents regarding the CPB stock, and recklessly or knowingly disregarded, if not the letter, then certainly the spirit of Court orders and Court proceedings regarding the CPB stock." *Id.* at 386. The court ordered the disgorgement of the $90,000 from the sale to the receiver. In addition, counsel, who were acting under a limited admission to the Hawai'i bar (*pro hac vice*), were ordered to disclose the fact that their status was terminated in this matter and to give the reasons for their termination should they ever apply to any court in Hawai'i again.

An attorney or a paralegal who engages in this type of dishonest conduct, offering false or falsified evidence, is not fit to practice. An attorney and a paralegal must remain loyal first to the proper functioning of the justice system, and secondly, to their client. In an attempt to "get the heat off his client," an attorney had false bills of sale witnessed by another one of his clients after he noticed that the witness line was left blank for stolen equipment. He then submitted them to the court as proof that his client was not acting as a "fence" in the subsequent sale of the goods. Digging himself deeper, the attorney testified at his grievance hearing that he was unaware, at the time he prepared the receipts, that the equipment was stolen. An unlikely story, given that he previously had defended this client on larceny charges. The attorney's violation by altering and/or creating false evidence in violation of the subsequent subsection is regarded as the most serious kind of misconduct.

> Fundamental honesty is the base line and mandatory requirement to serve in the legal profession. The whole structure of ethical standards is derived from the paramount need for lawyers to be trustworthy. The court system and the public we serve are damaged when our officers play fast and loose with the truth. The damage occurs without regard to whether misleading conduct is motivated by the client's interest or the lawyer's own.

> *Iowa Supreme Court Board of Professional Ethics and Conduct v. Romeo*, 554 N.W.2d 552, 554 (Iowa 1996).

Even mere hinting to a witness to alter his testimony is prohibited. Where an attorney knew that testimony might be damaging to his client, he told the grand jury witness: "Look, do me a favor. Just don't hurt the old guy, will you?" *Matter of Verdiramo*, 475 A.2d 45, 46 (N.J. 1984). The attorney was merely trying to protect his client, whom he characterized as "a genuinely nice human being who screwed up what checks went into what account." *Id.* The motive behind the attorney's misconduct is irrelevant.

> Attempted subornation of perjury is an inexcusable and reprehensible transgression. It is an obstruction of the administration of justice.

Respondent's actions project a public image of corruption of the judicial process. . . . Professional misconduct that takes deadly aim at the public-at-large is as grave as the misconduct that victimizes a lawyer's individual clients. Because such a transgression directly subverts and corrupts the administration of justice, it must be ranked among the most egregious of ethical violations.

Id. at 185-186.

Whether the attorney actively engaged in the fraud upon the court, as in the Romeo disciplinary matter, or merely suggested that he would rather not see his client hurt by a full account of the truth in a witness's testimony, the attorney violated his obligation of honesty just the same. Any contravention of the rules subjects the attorney to severe discipline.

The openness and forthrightness required also pertains to dealings with third persons (non-clients and non-attorneys). To instruct witnesses or others holding relevant materials not to disclose that information is to obstruct access to potential evidence and is impermissible for the same reasons discussed above. The only two exceptions here apply to those persons in a close and potentially confidential relationship with the client and that kind of information that, if withheld, would pose no harm to the party seeking it. The first exception is easily understood: Information from a client's spouse or another person who stands in an intimate relationship with the client and to whom the initial disclosures from the client would have been presumed to be secret or protected due to the relationship should be held safe. This protects the expectations of the client when the information was shared with the third party. There are certain parties to whom it is expected that private disclosures will or must be made in order to facilitate the purpose of the relationship. Second, if the person from whom information is sought will not be adversely affected by the refusal to disclose the information, then that person may properly refuse to divulge the information. This will come up in the context where an informal request is made to a person not a party to the litigation and the information sought could be obtained through other means. If, however, a subpoena (formal request) has been issued, the attorney may not counsel the third party to fail to respond, because that would subject the third party to court sanctions (an adverse effect resulting from the refusal to render up the requested information). An attorney can advise another to refrain from voluntarily giving out the information only where there will be no adverse consequence. As officers of the court, attorneys and paralegals are expected to obey the orders and rules of procedure and other obligations to the letter. If an attorney decides that he has a valid and ethical basis upon which to rest his refusal to comply with an order or rule, he must present his excuse for refusal to comply openly to the court. In this way, the court can make the final determination of whether the attorney is properly maintaining his duties to both client and court. An attorney is not permitted to merely self-diagnose the problem and, once it is concealed from the court, take action upon it. An attorney is not the final arbiter of the conflict of duty; he has an obligation to expose the issue to the tribunal.

The rules of civil procedure for discovery underscore the theory that full, open, and honest disclosure of information is vital to just adjudication. They set forth mandates that opposing counsel exchange documents, answer interrogatories, conduct depositions, and the like within a certain time period. In this way, the matter can move forward at a predictable pace and the parties are fully aware of all supporting documentation for their claims and defenses. Again, in this area, paralegals are indispensable. Case management and calendaring are of the utmost importance. All discovery requests must be reasonably made and answered. Very often this duty falls upon the paralegal to accomplish in accordance with the rules of court procedure and ethical obligations of diligence and candor.

In a series of egregious failures to comply with the rules of discovery, including failure to supply opposing counsel with requested information, failing to make any requests for discovery until after the court-appointed time, and making motions for extensions of discovery time just in case he decided to make formal discovery requests, an attorney subjected himself to serious ethical sanctions. In his practice, the attorney felt that he was better able to serve his clients by keeping costs down and doing only as much informal discovery as necessary. He would interview witnesses on his own and not rely on information gathered through opposing counsel. In the same vein, he failed to make appropriate disclosures to opposing counsel. The court appointed another independent attorney to supervise the violator; this monitoring attorney would have access to all the violator's paperwork regarding the management of his practice. Specifically, and probably humiliatingly, the monitoring attorney would meet with the violator twice a month and the violator would have to report "whether he has failed to timely respond to requests for discovery, to motions to compel, or to orders to show cause." He also had to "maintain a comprehensive calendar of court appearances, discovery deadlines, and other pleading deadlines." *In re Boone*, 7 P.3d 270, 284 (Kan. 2000). The courts have the ability to fashion appropriate remedies to ensure that attorneys do not flout their obligations under both the rules of procedure and the rules of ethics.

Particularly damaging is dishonesty or deceitful tactics in open court. Juries can be unduly influenced by the dramatics of the courtroom, and the matter of admissibility of evidence is enough to confuse an experienced attorney, let alone a layperson. Further, it is simply human nature to draw conclusions, whether substantiated or not, and nearly impossible to disregard a statement once heard; one court characterized the damage of an attorney's misconduct in front of the jury as "like trying to un-ring a bell." *Love v. Wolf*, 226 Cal. App. 2d 378, 392, 38 Cal. Rptr. 183 (1964). In order to provide the factfinder with a clear stream of evidence to consider, all matters not relevant or unsupported by admissible evidence should not be brought up in open court. The record should be "clean" for the jury to consider the evidence fairly.

It is fair to say that the average jury, in a greater or less degree, has confidence that these obligations [of candor], which so plainly rest upon the prosecuting attorney, will be faithfully observed. Consequently, improper suggestions, insinuations, and, especially, assertions of personal knowledge are apt to carry much weight against the accused when they should properly carry none.

Berger v. U.S., 295 U.S. 78, 88, 55 S. Ct. 629 (1935).

The ABA Model Rules require attorneys to refrain from making any remarks that are not supported by the information properly before the court.

While trial advocacy is an art, there are some boundaries that must not be crossed. Attorneys are granted considerable latitude when crafting their opening and closing arguments, as well as in how they phrase their questions on examination of witnesses.

> Aggressive advocacy is not only proper but desirable. Our jurisprudence is built upon a firm belief in the adversary system. Moreover, in a long trial, as this one was, vigorously prosecuted and defended, frayed tempers leading to intemperate outbursts are a to-be-expected byproduct. Skilled advocates are not always endowed with "high boiling points." Juries, characteristically composed of average men and women, may be assumed able to withstand substantial blandishments without surrendering their ability to reason soberly and fairly. Recognizing these factors, reviewing courts are not, and should not be, overly eager to reverse for conduct which is merely moderately captious.
>
> But there is a limit. The misconduct here was intentional, blatant, and continuous from opening statement, throughout the trial, to closing argument. It was committed by a seasoned and experienced trial lawyer and the record leaves no doubt it was carefully contrived and calculated to produce a result.

Love, supra, at 393-394.

During trial, testimony procured from cross-examination must refer only to evidence that has been or will be admitted for consideration to the jury. An attorney may become a master at the **leading question** designed to elicit the desired answer from the opposing side's witnesses. However, cross-examination questions may not refer to supposed facts that are not supported by evidence received in court. Infamous tactics like these—"Isn't it true that . . ." and "Did you know that . . ."—may refer only to that which is substantiated by supporting evidence. The attorney cannot use the question to suggest that certain facts exist when indeed they do not. "These 'did you know that' questions designed not to obtain information or test adverse testimony but to afford cross-examining counsel a device by which his own unsworn statements can reach the ears of the jury and be accepted by them as proof have been repeatedly condemned," *supra*, at 391 (citations omitted).

Similarly, the closing arguments of counsel must refer only to the facts presented during the trial that were properly admitted before the court. This would exclude unsubstantiated allusions of counsel during testimonial evidence, as discussed above.

> [I]t is first necessary to reiterate certain well established principles of law concerning closing arguments. The purpose of a closing argument is to

leading question
The phrasing of an interrogatory so as to suggest the desired answer.

assist the jury in arriving at a verdict, with all facts presented fairly. Considerable latitude of expression on anything that is in evidence must be allowed counsel. The closing arguments of counsel must be confined to those matters that are in evidence or admitted and uncontroverted. When counsel oversteps the boundaries of proper argument, the trial judge need not wait for opposing counsel to object but under appropriate circumstances the court can halt the improper argument. [. . .] It is the duty of the court to control counsel within reasonable bounds and to restrict the argument to the evidence in the case.

Foerster v. Illinois Bell Tel. Co., 315 N.E.2d 63, 67 (Ill. App. Ct. 1974) (citations omitted).

Clearly, if an attorney is prohibited from alluding to inadmissible evidence, she is just as clearly prohibited from expressing her personal opinions on the credibility of a witness (insinuating or declaring outright that the witness is a liar) or on the justness of the cause (characterizing the claim or defense as ridiculous) or on the guilt or innocence of the litigant (usurping the very job of the jury). Where "the assistant prosecutor referred to defense evidence as "lies," "garbage," "garbage lies," "[a] smoke screen," and "a well conceived and well rehearsed lie" there was a clear violation of the rule. *State v. Smith*, 470 N.E.2d 883, 885 (Ohio Ct. App. 1984). Paralegals attending trial and sitting at counsel table assisting their supervising attorneys must take care not to use body language to send negative signals to the jury. Commentary upon the evidence and to suggest what a jury may infer for itself from the properly admitted evidence is proper; reaching beyond this is unethical. Argument is not the same as assertion. Essentially, if attorneys were able to present their own opinions on the matters considered by the court, they would be acting as unsworn witnesses themselves. An attorney is not permitted, as a general rule, to act as a witness in a case where he is also acting as an advocate. See ABA Model Rule 3.7 (Lawyer as Witness).

Closely allied to the requirement of honesty in a tribunal is the idea that the third persons (non-parties) involved in the litigation should remain unbiased and be able to openly evaluate the merits of the case properly presented to them. Attorneys and paralegals are prohibited from seeking to influence anyone involved with the justice system. This includes judges, jurors, prospective jurors, bailiffs, clerks, and other court personnel. The tasks of judges and jurors in the justice system require that they maintain a respectful distance and neutrality in all matters before them. Attorneys frequently appear before the same judges in the various cases they handle. It is important for both parties to retain a respectful distance and decorum despite the familiarity that may develop between them. These players in the system have a mutual obligation to ensure that they do not take advantage of their respective roles and circles of influence. In a rather startling matter, a judge met with an attorney who was frequently before him in court and asked why the attorney didn't "turn [his] two hundred and fifty thousand dollar case into a million?" and, of course, give the judge his share of the increased collected fee. *Committee on Legal Ethics of the*

West Virginia State Bar v. Hobbs, 439 S.E.2d 629, 630 (W. Va. 1993). But the judge was not the only one sanctioned in this matter. The duty to remain neutral and abide by all the relevant ethical rules is mutual. Even though the attorney voluntarily came forward after the judge was indicted on other matters, the hearing court found that the attorney had expected to gain an advantage in this or other matters.

> In this case, the ethics violations are serious. Secret payments of money to a presiding judge are a direct attack on one of the most vital areas of our legal system. To paraphrase *In re Barron*, 155 W. Va. 98, 102, 181 S.E.2d 273, 275 (1971) (disbarment for bribing a juror), we find it difficult to consider an offense which is more destructive or corruptive of the legal system of West Virginia than secret payments, however categorized, to a presiding judge. Protection of the public against members of the Bar who are unworthy of the trust and confidence essential to the attorney/client relationship is a primary purpose of professional discipline.

Hobbs at 611.

This attempt to influence any official, not just a judge, in the litigation will most likely result in disbarment, due to the grave implications it has on the effective administration of justice. *See Matter of Kassner*, 93 A.D.2d 87, 461 N.Y.S.2d 11, (N.Y.A.D.1983), *app. denied*, 59 N.Y.2d 604, 464 N.Y.S.2d 1025, 451 N.E.2d 504 (1983), wherein the attorney was disbarred after attempting to bribe the judge's secretary in an attempt to gain a favorable verdict. This rule against improper influence is intuitive and, fortunately, crops up infrequently in practice, although it makes for wonderful plot complications in television dramas and movies. Remember, any action that is prohibited for an attorney cannot be performed by a paralegal; the ethical obligations are the same.

The interaction with the judge, juror, or other official need not be so drastic as bribery or other extreme conduct. In order to preserve the inviolability of the process, any **ex parte** communications with these types of persons are prohibited. NFPA EC 1.2 (a) specifically prohibits paralegals from making such communications. (See Figure 8.5.) Ex parte communications are those that are made by an attorney to the tribunal without opposing counsel present that relate to the substance of the matter. General inquiries about court dates or other procedural questions are not generally considered prohibited communications. The types of communication that are prohibited, with exceptions for emergencies, are those that attempt to gain an unfair advantage. Secret communications do not correspond with candor toward the tribunal. All exchanges of information must be made openly and with the participation of both sides. Both sides should at all times be able to present and respond at the same time. This ensures that no unfair advantage can be taken. It does not matter whether the attorney actually gained any unfair advantage or not due to the ex parte communication. The simple fact that the exchange took place and could have had some effect on the legal rights of the parties in the matter before the court is enough. The violation does not depend upon how the

ex parte
A legal professional's communications regarding the substance of the matter to the tribunal without opposing counsel present.

NFPA EC 1.2(a)

A paralegal shall not engage in any ex parte communications involving the courts or any other adjudicatory body in an attempt to exert undue influence or to obtain advantage or the benefit of only one party.

◀ **FIGURE 8.5**
EX PARTE
COMMUNICATION

judge reacts to the improper communication; the attorney's actions are determinative of the issue. *See In re Complaint of Thompson,* 940 P.2d 512, 515 (Or. 1997). In this way, there is a "bright-line" rule prohibiting the ex parte communication, and therefore, an attorney can clearly determine his obligation under the rule and conduct himself accordingly. The rule against ex parte communication applies even when the attorney does not talk about the facts of the matter before the court:

> Even though petitioner did not discuss the merits of his case with the juror, the record amply supports the trial judge's conclusion that petitioner attempted indirectly to influence her. By initiating a friendly conversation, buying drinks, and discussing his personal history and religious beliefs, petitioner attempted to arouse sympathy on his behalf. "The harm inherent in deliberate contact or communication can take the form of subtly creating juror empathy with the party. . . . Petitioner's conduct may in itself have been criminal. At the very least, it was grossly unethical. As an attorney, petitioner must have been aware that any outside influences on the jury's deliberative processes are inimical to our system of justice."In a criminal case, any private communication, contact, or tampering, directly or indirectly, with a juror during a trial about the matter pending before the jury is, for obvious reasons, deemed presumptively prejudicial, if not made in pursuance of known rules of the court and the instructions and directions of the court made during the trial, with full knowledge of the parties." Thus, it is unethical for an attorney to communicate with a juror outside the courtroom during the course of a trial. Petitioner's blatant violation of this rule plainly demonstrates an unfitness to practice law.
>
> *In re Possino,* 37 Cal. 3d 163, 170, 207 Cal. Rptr. 543 (1984) (internal citations omitted).

REEL TO REAL

Runaway Jury (2003), starring John Cusack, Gene Hackman, Dustin Hoffman, and Rachel Weisz, illustrates how vulnerable juries can be. With a huge jury verdict in the works and major public policies on the line, the defendant (a gun manufacturer) hire jury consultants who turn out to be much more influential than is proper. View *Runaway Jury* and look for the jury tampering from both outside the courtroom and inside the jury.

The prohibition of ex parte communications is not limited to attorneys or paralegals who are directly involved in either prosecution or defense of matter. In *People v. Honeycutt*, 20 Cal. 3d 150, 141 Cal. Rptr. 698 (1977), a juror contacted his own attorney for advice during deliberations in a criminal case. Not only is the juror guilty of misconduct, but, under the ethics rules, so is the outside attorney who is communicating with the juror. Paralegals are also prohibited from consulting with anyone involved in a proceeding. Friends and family may ask for advice, commentary, or explanation when they are involved as jurors in the legal system. This is understandable. However, it is imperative that paralegals refrain from offering any information. These ex parte communications, whether they come from a participating attorney, outside attorney, judge, or other official, have the potential to compromise the proceedings. The juror would be receiving information not properly admitted into evidence; this would constitute an obstruction of justice and a knowing violation on the part of the attorney of the ethical mandate to refrain from interfering with the judicial process.

This obligation of noninterference does not end with the termination of the litigation in all circumstances. As discussed above, attorneys may find themselves before the same judge in another case, so they must remain at a professional distance at all times. This is not the case with jurors. Once the matter is over, the attorney is unlikely to see them in the legal context again. However, the ethical rules still prohibit talking to jurors even *after* the case has concluded under some circumstances. An attorney or a paralegal must not communicate in any way with a juror after discharge of the jury where such communications are

1. Prohibited by court order or other law or rule
2. Unwanted by the juror, where the juror has told that to the legal professional
3. In furtherance of misrepresentation, coercion, duress, or harassment

The second and third subsections are self-explanatory with regard to their impropriety. Under what circumstances would a communication be prohibited by law or court order? There are two major reasons for seeking to communicate with jurors post-trial: (1) to determine whether there has been any improper conduct during the jury deliberations to form a ground to challenge the verdict based upon jury misconduct, and (2) to determine on what basis the verdict was reached.

In the first instance, the attorney must apply for leave of court to contact the jurors to evaluate the potential for a challenge to the jury's conduct, and the attorney must demonstrate in a sworn affidavit some specific evidence of misconduct. "Federal courts have generally disfavored post-verdict interviewing of jurors. We have repeatedly refused to 'denigrate jury trials by afterwards ransacking the jurors in search of some new ground, not previously supported by evidence, for a new trial.'" *Haeberle v. Texas Intern. Airlines*, 739 F.2d 1019, 1021 (5th Cir. 1984), citing *United States v. Riley*, 544 F.2d 237, 242 (5th Cir. 1976), *cert. denied*, 430 U.S. 932, 97 S. Ct. 1554, 51 L. Ed. 2d 777 (1977).

The second reason may have arguable implications in First Amendment rights (freedom to speak and associate with other members of the public); however, the privacy interests of the jurors to be free of harassment and the respectability of the jury system outweigh the "curiosity" of attorneys and litigants. *Haeberle* at 1022.

Impartiality and Decorum

As is the custom with ethics rules, there is a final "catch-all" provision that applies in all these situations in both the ABA Model Rules and the NFPA Rules. Attorneys and paralegals are prohibited from disrupting or disrespecting the decorum of the tribunal. (See Figure 8.6.) This appears to be where the issues involving the use of social media content and contacts arise. There have been many cases of jurors using social media inappropriately during jury deliberations that have given rise to claims and appeals for juror misconduct and violations of the defendant's right to a fair and impartial jury. Attorneys and paralegals have access to a vast amount of information about jurors through their social media accounts. It is reasonable and expected that legal professionals will conduct research on potential jurors and, of course, the *voir dire* process' goal is to impanel a "fair" jury. However, the New York City Bar rendered "Formal Opinion 2012-2—Jury Research and Social Media" (May 30, 2012) which sets boundaries on the use of social media and what constitutes unethical ex parte communication.

> We conclude that if a juror were to (i) receive a "friend" request (or similar invitation to share information on a social network site) as a result of an attorney's research, or (ii) otherwise to learn of the attorney's viewing or attempted viewing of the juror's pages, posts, or comments, that *would* constitute a prohibited communication if the attorney was aware that her actions would cause the juror to receive such message or notification. We further conclude that the same attempts to research the juror *might* constitute a prohibited communication even if inadvertent or unintended. In addition, the attorney must not use deception—such as pretending to be someone else—to gain access to information about a juror that would otherwise be unavailable. Third parties working for the benefit of or on behalf of an attorney must comport with these same restrictions (as it is always unethical pursuant to Rule 8.4 for an attorney to attempt to avoid the Rule by having a non-lawyer do what she cannot). Finally, if a lawyer learns of juror misconduct through a juror's social media activities, the lawyer must promptly reveal the improper conduct to the court.

NFPA EC 1.3(a)

A paralegal shall refrain from engaging in any conduct that offends the dignity and decorum of proceedings before a court or other adjudicatory body and shall be respectful of all rules and procedures.

◄ **FIGURE 8.6**
DECORUM IN
PROCEEDINGS

Where no specific rule applies, but the attorney or paralegal has clearly engaged in some improper conduct that has negative consequences on the trial, the disciplinary board can rest its findings in the "catch-all" provision. For example, in *Disciplinary Counsel v. LoDico*, 833 N.E.2d 1235, 1237 (Ohio 2005), two judges found the attorney in contempt for his "pervasive and continuing pattern of misconduct in their courtrooms." His behavior was egregious and the antics hard to comprehend outside of a TV courtroom drama series.

> [The attorney]'s misconduct began even before the jury was impaneled, with inappropriate, loud, and rude statements that wrongly impugned the integrity of a prospective juror during voir dire. Respondent was cautioned about his conduct in the courtroom early in the trial proceedings. [. . .] Rather than curtailing his misconduct, however, respondent continued his behavior, at one point throwing money and credit cards on the bench in anticipation of a sanction and telling the Judge, '[G]o ahead and fine me.'" [. . .] Disregarding [the] Judge's orders, he spoke loudly at sidebars in an apparent effort to ensure that the jury heard his statements, including his suggestions that witnesses were lying. [. . .] [Attorney]'s pattern of misconduct in [the] courtroom appears to have been an effort to create "an atmosphere of utter confusion and chaos, quoting the trial court's contempt charge." Rather than advancing the pursuit of justice, [the attorney] advanced obstruction, obfuscation, and opprobrium.

> *Id.* at 233-234, citing *Mayberry v. Pennsylvania* (1971), 400 U.S. 455, 462, 91 S. Ct. 499, 27 L. Ed. 2d 532.

Trial Publicity

Some rules address the conduct within the confines of the individual tribunal in order to maintain the dignity of the justice system, and others focus on the perception of the matter as portrayed to the public at large. The relationship between attorneys and the media is mutually impactful, but not necessarily mutually beneficial, in high-profile cases. A legal professional is not prohibited from making statements outside the courtroom (extrajudicial statements); however, she must be careful in what she does say, as public sentiment is a powerful weapon inside the jury deliberations. The ABA Model Rules do permit basic facts to be disseminated because the public also has a right to know what is going on.

> The judicial system, and in particular our criminal justice courts, play a vital part in a democratic state, and the public has a legitimate interest in their operations. *See, e.g., Landmark Communications, Inc. v. Virginia*, 435 U.S. 829, 838-839, 98 S. Ct. 1535, 1541-1542, 56 L. Ed. 2d 1 (1978). "[I]t would be difficult to single out any aspect of government of higher concern and importance to the people than the manner in which criminal trials are conducted." *Richmond Newspapers, Inc. v. Virginia*, 448 U.S. 555, 575, 100 S. Ct. 2814, 2826, 65 L. Ed. 2d 973 (1980). Public vigilance serves us

well, for "[t]he knowledge that every criminal trial is subject to contempo-
raneous review in the forum of public opinion is an effective restraint on
possible abuse of judicial power. . . . Without publicity, all other checks
are insufficient: in comparison of publicity, all other checks are of small
account." *In re Oliver*, 333 U.S. 257, 270-271, 68 S. Ct. 499, 506-507, 92 L.
Ed. 682 (1948).

Gentile v. State Bar of Nevada, 501 U.S. 1030, 1035, 111 S. Ct. 2720, 2724, 115 L. Ed.
2d 888 (1991).

Indeed, the Sixth Amendment of the United States Constitution requires a
public trial in criminal cases, as the Framers understood the need to ensure
fairness to the accused and to ensure the community's confidence in the judicial system. The Framers did not set a priority between the First and Sixth
Amendments probably because the factors in each case must be delicately balanced to secure justice in that particular circumstance. There are certainly
more factors to consider when celebrities are involved or during a particularly
notorious crime.

ABA Model Rule 3.6 sets forth the kinds of information that can be disseminated. The real danger lies not in the factual content of the statement, but
rather the connotations, implications, and inferences that can be drawn by
the public because the information is coming from an attorney. The information
may be imbued with authority because of its source. It matters who the mes-
senger is in this circumstance. Therefore, statements other than the most basic
information are prohibited. Attorneys are confined to:

1. Stating the type of claim asserted and/or any defenses available
2. Identifying their client (unless there is a legal prohibition or exception, as
   in the case of minors)
3. Stating information available from public records
4. Stating that there is an investigation in progress
5. Advising of the progress or stage of litigation and any court scheduling
6. Requesting assistance in obtaining information regarding the matter
7. Warning the public about any danger posed by the person or people
   involved in the matter
8. Advising of the status of the criminal arrest, investigation, and officers
   involved (if applicable)

All of these types of information should seem relatively familiar, as they are
regularly reported on news broadcasts. If you pay attention to interviews with
attorneys, you will notice which information they readily make public and
which is not commented on at all. Naturally, social media has compounded
the problem exponentially. The Court in *State v. Polk*, 415 S.W.3d 692 (Miss.
Ct. App. 2013), was particularly disconcerted by the use of Twitter by the Circuit Attorney, who consistently tweeted on the case during the length of trial.

[E]xtraneous statements on Twitter or other forms of social media, particularly during the time frame of the trial, can taint the jury and result in
reversal of the verdict. We doubt that using social media to highlight the

evidence against the accused and publicly dramatize the plight of the victim serves any legitimate law enforcement purpose or is necessary to inform the public of the nature and extent of the prosecutor's actions. Likewise, we are concerned that broadcasting that the accused is a "child rapist" is likely to arouse heightened public condemnation. We are especially troubled by the timing of Joyce's Twitter posts, because broadcasting such statements immediately before and during trial greatly magnifies the risk that a jury will be tainted by undue extrajudicial influences.

Id. at 696.

The United States Supreme Court rendered an opinion regarding the potential impact of these restrictions not just on an attorney's ethical obligations, but also on the attorney's First Amendment right to free speech. The

---

IN-CLASS DISCUSSION

Evaluate whether the commentary to the press was appropriate under the ethical rules regarding trial publicity—whether it may have been prejudicial or was consistent with Constitutional protections.

> In July of 1993, Rothman was retained by Mr. C. and his son, a minor, to seek redress against the popular singer, Michael Jackson, for alleged torts against the boy. Rothman contacted Jackson and began to negotiate on behalf of the C. family, but did not immediately file a lawsuit, as the family wished the matter kept confidential.
>
> While negotiations were proceeding, a psychological evaluation of the boy, which had been filed with the Los Angeles County Department of Children's Services, as required by California's child abuse reporting laws was "leaked" by a person or persons unknown. However, no claim has been made that Rothman or his clients were responsible for the leak. In any event, whoever caused the leak, its result was what Rothman characterizes as a "firestorm" of publicity, for Jackson is a celebrity among celebrities, and the charges contained in the psychological evaluation were sensational.
>
> The defendants responded to this negative public exposure by calling a press conference on August 29, 1993, and by making other statements to the media thereafter, in which the defendants not only denied the charges against Jackson, but made countercharges that Rothman and his clients had knowingly and intentionally made false accusations against Jackson in order to extort money from him. Extortion is, of course, a crime and the charge was inevitably damaging to Rothman's professional reputation. Moreover, as an additional consequence of the extortion charges, Rothman felt compelled to withdraw from his representation of the C. family, causing him significant economic damage, as the C.'s eventually retained other counsel who negotiated a settlement with Jackson that was never disclosed to the public, but was reputed to be over $25 million.
>
> *See Rothman v. Jackson*, 49 Cal. App. 4th 1134, 1138-1139 (1996).

RESEARCH THIS

Social media outlets like Facebook and Twitter, tabloids, pop culture magazines, TV broadcasts—they are all littered with celebrity goings-on, and the juiciest morsels often relate to legal battles. Find the truth behind the sensational headlines. Pick a current high-profile legal battle that is garnering a lot of media attention and perform your own unbiased legal research on the matter. Evaluate the ethical implications of the public commentary on the matter.

ethical obligations prohibit an attorney from statements to the press that he knows or reasonably should know will have a substantial likelihood of materially prejudicing the trial. Essentially, information that goes beyond the basic can be considered to be prejudicial to the litigant's right to a fair trial.

> The "substantial likelihood of material prejudice" standard is a constitutionally permissible balance between the First Amendment rights of attorneys in pending cases and the State's interest in fair trials. Lawyers in such cases are key participants in the criminal justice system, and the State may demand some adherence to that system's precepts in regulating their speech and conduct. Their extrajudicial statements pose a threat to a pending proceeding's fairness, since they have special access to information through discovery and client communication, and since their statements are likely to be received as especially authoritative. The standard is designed to protect the integrity and fairness of a State's judicial system and imposes only narrow and necessary limitations on lawyers' speech.
>
> *Gentile* at 1031.

Even if the press could report the occurrences as public information gained from open access to the court proceedings, the attorney and his staff may be prohibited from discussing the same information. The key to understanding this principle is to understand the perception of the public. The source of the information is just as critical as the information itself. It is the difference between getting your news from the Wall Street Journal, the publication of record with an impeccable reputation for accuracy and integrity, and getting it from one of the tabloid magazines that thrive on scandal and creatively captioning paparazzi snapshots of the rich and famous. Attorneys are presumed, whether correctly or not, to have insider information, and what they say is given authority and taken to be true. They are not neutrals to the matter, as they are allied with either the prosecution or the defense and are ethically bound to zealously advocate for their respective positions. This may either cause what they say to be slanted in itself or cause their speech to be unduly influential. Understandably and consistently with the other rules, all attorneys associated in a firm are bound to conform their actions to the obligations of each individual attorney. This also holds true for the paralegals and other support staff in the firm. What an attorney is prohibited from doing, so are all employees and agents of the attorney.

An exception exists where an attorney is put in a defensive position due to another person's statement regarding the matter. By making a potentially harmful comment, that party has "opened the door" for the attorney to respond as appropriate in order to protect her client's interests in receiving a fair trial. The response must be purely remedial in nature and cannot divulge information beyond that which has been released publicly by the other party or the press.

Truthfulness in Statements to Others

Of course, it is not only inside the courtroom that an attorney represents the honor of the justice system; in all his dealings, including those with non-clients and those not participating in the litigation, he must act with the same candor and respect. The various parts of ABA Model Rules 4.1 through 4.4 ("Transactions with Persons Other than Clients") essentially reiterate and underscore this duty to uphold the reputation and respect of the justice system with everyone.

SPOT THE ISSUE

Prosecutors owe a dual loyalty: to the public as their champion against those who threaten their security and peace, and to the criminal justice system. They are often called upon to comment on criminal investigations and recent apprehensions.

Paul the prosecutor recently attended a press conference and made several statements to the media regarding the anticipated prosecution in two separate murders that had the town up in arms.

He described Suspect #1's confession and the circumstances surrounding his custodial statements to police:

The police were able to obtain a confession completely consistent with the suspect's constitutional rights; he confessed within just a few hours with incredible details that only the murderer would have known. He was then provided the opportunity to rest and he commented that it was one of the best nights of sleep he had gotten in a long time.

In the morning at dawn, he was taken up to the crime scene, was videotaped by police, and went over in detail by detail every step of what he did to the victim. Suspect #1 provided a full and detailed account of the assault and murder.

As for Suspect #2, the prosecutor stated this:

The County Police were able to determine definitively that indeed it was Suspect #2 who had committed the second notorious murder. They were able to do so by following him. They conducted surveillance for over 24 hours. And then when they actually found him, he was wearing a unique shoe, a very unique boot, and the print of that boot matched the print that was found at the scene of the crime, and then further questioning revealed, in fact, he was the person that had done it. We have a confession from the perpetrator as well as scientific and forensic evidence to corroborate that confession. We have found the person who committed the crime at this point and the case against Suspect #2 will be a strong case.

For guidance, see Attorney Grievance Commission of Maryland v. Gansler, 377 Md. 656, 835 A.2d 548 (2002).

Relying on everything that was discussed regarding trial publicity, it is merely an extrapolation of the principle that statements made by legal professionals have a certain added authority, and, therefore, they are obligated to be careful in making statements to others. Misstatements of law or fact are not permissible in any context. Delegation or blame placed on another person involved in the misrepresentation does not absolve the attorney of her responsibility to ensure that communications to third persons are not misleading or false. Encouraging or instructing a client to make a false statement to a third party is still violative of the ethics rules, as if the attorney had made the statement himself, because it is clothed in his authority when made in the context of a legal matter. *See In re Mitchell*, 822 A.2d 1106 (D.C. Ct. App. 2003), wherein the attorney apparently instructed the client to inform the third party creditor to the client that the personal injury suit was "on appeal" and therefore the attempt at collecting the debt from the lawsuit proceeds was not yet ripe. This was a false statement in an attempt to avoid payment. It doesn't matter that the falsification was through his client, nor would it matter if the misrepresentation were through another third party. The attorney may be held responsible if he knew that the false statement was made. There is also the continuing obligation to correct any prior statements that either were unknowingly incorrect at the time they were made or were true at the time but have become incorrect.

> Making a false statement includes the failure to make a statement in circumstances in which nondisclosure is equivalent to making such a statement. Thus, where a lawyer has made a statement that the lawyer believed to be true when made but later discovers that the statement was not true, in some circumstances *failure to correct the statement is equivalent to making a statement that is false*.

Carpenito's Case, 651 A.2d 1, 4 (N.H. 1994) (emphasis added).

Persons Represented by Counsel

Respect for third persons extends to acknowledging the fact of their representation by another attorney or the fact that they should be represented by another attorney in the matter for which the attorney seeks to speak to them. There are specific rules addressing the propriety of communicating with persons represented by counsel and rules for when they are not. If a person is represented by counsel, legal professionals are not permitted to communicate with her. All communications must be made through the represented person's attorney. There are two exceptions to this general prohibition: The attorney may have permission from the other attorney to contact his client directly, or there may be a court order or rule that permits this direct communication.

It is very important to note that paralegals, support staff, and other persons working with the attorney (whether or not an agency relationship exists) must respect these rules as well. (See NFPA EC 1.2(b) in Figure 8.7.) This was the case in *In re Conduct of Burrows*, 629 P.2d 820 (Or. 1981). A rape and robbery suspect was approached by the prosecuting attorney to turn into an informant regarding the local drug scene in exchange for a reduction or dismissal of the other pending charges. The suspect met with the prosecutor and police officers in the prosecutor's office and they told him they would not discuss the rape matter because he was represented by an attorney. After the meeting and in the presence of the prosecutor, the police told the suspect not to mention the undercover work to his attorney in the rape case; the prosecutor said nothing. The police worked with the suspect for months without ever contacting the suspect's attorney. The court found that the prosecutor was guilty of communicating with a represented person about the subject matter of the case. In his defense, the prosecutor first claimed that the role of drug informant was not the "subject of the representation"; however, the court found this to be too limited an interpretation. The suspect's activities in cooperation with the police had a direct impact on the charges levied against him. The suspect received a more favorable plea agreement on the charges for which he was represented as a consequence of his cooperation with the police.

> It is entirely possible, if not probable, that an accused needs competent legal counsel representation during the evolution of an agreement for leniency in exchange for cooperation with law enforcement agencies. . . . In short, we think that where it was clear that [suspect]'s undercover drug activities were likely to, or at least were expected to, impact the pending criminal charges, the subject matter of the communications necessarily involved the pending criminal charges.

> *Id.* at 143.

Having determined that there indeed was communication regarding the "subject of representation," the prosecutor then argued that it was not himself that was communicating with the represented suspect.

> Further, we are not aware of any rule of law or principle which enables an attorney to excuse his failure to obtain an opposing attorney's consent by delegating the task to non-lawyers who, albeit deceptively, failed to follow through with their instructions. It would be difficult to hypothecate a set of circumstances which better illustrate the folly and danger of a principle of ethics which would permit a lawyer to excuse his misfeasance or nonfeasance by delegating to, and then later blaming, a non-lawyer. The overzealous and at times deceptive conduct of one or more of the police officers involved in this episode aptly illustrate the point.
>
> In any event, by the time the police officers were instructed to inform [the suspect's attorney], two proscribed meetings had been held and the die was practically cast. [The suspect's attorney] merely would have been presented with a fait accompli.
>
> In our opinion, both attorneys violated [the rule] by communicating, or causing others to communicate, with [the suspect] without obtaining [the suspect's attorney]'s consent.
>
> [. . .] We also find that [the prosecutor] acted to conceal the communications by his failure to countermand the police officers' suggestion to [the suspect] that he not tell [the suspect's attorney].

> *Id.* at 143-144.

◀ **FIGURE 8.7**
COMMUNICATION
WITH REPRESENTED
PERSONS

NFPA EC 1.2(b)

A paralegal shall not communicate, or cause another to communicate, with a party the paralegal knows to be represented by a lawyer in a pending matter without the prior consent of the lawyer representing such other party.

Any communications that could not be made by the attorney could also not be made by any person with whom she is working. To allow an attorney to delegate or assign away her ethical responsibility is impermissible, as it would give the attorney a loophole to avoid compliance with the ethical rules.

Persons Not Represented by Counsel

Particularly susceptible are those persons who are not represented by an attorney and who are then contacted by an outside legal professional. Why? Because the roles of attorneys are not always clear to those not accustomed to legal affairs. A legal professional cannot state or imply that he is unbiased in the matter. He is not a neutral mediator in his role as advocate for an individual client. Recall that legal professionals are ethically bound to represent their clients to the best of their ability. This is incongruous with an assertion of neutrality. Both attorneys and paralegals have an affirmative duty to either avoid or correct misunderstandings regarding their role in a matter. (See Figure 8.8.)

Essentially, the "best practice" of this rule boils down to only speaking to an unrepresented person only in order to advise her to seek her own counsel. However, the rule does not act as a "gag order." If the unrepresented person consents to speak to the attorney after being advised of both the interests represented by the attorney and the advisability of obtaining independent counsel, then the attorney may communicate with that person without fearing a violation of the rule. The only proscription is against giving legal advice to an unrepresented person who may have interests adverse to those of the attorney's client. Rendering legal advice may indeed threaten to irreparably compromise the unrepresented person's legal position. What are the dangers? Any statements made by the unrepresented person may be admitted against them later if those comments are deemed "statements against interest"—or, in a worst-case scenario, a settlement could be made concerning a legal matter contrary to the actual rights and liabilities in the matter.

◀ **FIGURE 8.8**
DISCLOSURE OF
PARALEGAL'S STATUS

NFPA EC 1.7(a)

A paralegal's title shall clearly indicate the individual's status and shall be disclosed in all business and professional communications to avoid misunderstandings and misconceptions about the paralegal's role and responsibilities.

Recall that the line between client and third party becomes blurred in the instance where the attorney represents an organization. The legal entity of the business is the party to which the attorney owes his loyalty, despite the fact that the communications are made solely through real persons. Information may be gathered through either current or former employees by the organization in order to properly represent the entity. There are a myriad of dangers here for those unrepresented persons, as they may feel that their interests are aligned with those of their employer where the matter does not involve a direct suit between them, but rather, the employee is acting as a third-party witness to the underlying facts. Recognizing that a balance needs to be struck between the need to protect those persons not represented by counsel and the need to obtain information for the organizational client, the court in *In re Environmental Ins. Declaratory Judgment Actions*, 600 A.2d 165 (N.J. Super. Law Div. 1991), set forth strict requirements for the attorneys making contact with the company's employees. The attorneys were required to first send a letter "to that employee explaining who they were and who they represented, what their purpose was and what their rights were with respect to agreeing to being interviewed." Then, once the contact was made to conduct the interview, the court mandated the following:

> No interview of any former employee shall be conducted unless the following script is used by the investigator or attorney conducting the interview:
>
> 1. I am a (private investigator/attorney) working on behalf of _____ . I want you to understand that _____ and several other companies have sued their insurance carriers. That said action is pending in the Union County Superior Court. The purpose of the lawsuit is to determine whether _____ insurance companies will be required to reimburse _____ for any amounts of money _____ must pay as a result of environmental property damage and personal injury caused by _____. I have been engaged by _____ to investigate the issues involved in that lawsuit between _____ and _____, its insurance company.
> 2. Are you represented by an attorney in this litigation between _____ and _____?
> If answer is "YES," end questioning.
> If answer is "NO," ask:
> 3. May I interview you at this time about the issues in this litigation?
> If answer is "NO," end questioning.
> If answer is "YES," substance of interview may commence.

Id. at 173.

It may seem incredibly controlling of the court to require such formal actions by the attorneys before interviewing third parties, but that is how seriously the court takes its responsibilities to monitor conduct and ensure fairness to all members of the public, regardless of their manner of involvement in a legal matter. It is significant to note that the court recognized that it may not be the attorney herself making the contact with the unrepresented person, but an investigator. The court intended that any person acting on behalf of and/or at the direction of the attorney be bound by the same rigorous requirements of disclosure. Of course, paralegals play a significant role in the fact-gathering stage of litigation and are therefore also bound by such mandates of fairness in disclosure. The "best practice" note for paralegals is to immediately identify oneself as the paralegal for the attorney in the matter and state which party that supervising attorney represents.

Respect for Others

The last rule is another "catch-all" provision. Attorneys are required to treat all persons with respect to maintain the integrity of and confidence in the justice system. Attorneys and their agents, like paralegals, cannot forget that they are representing the legal system to the general public. Tactics designed solely to embarrass, delay, or burden a third party violate the legal professional's ethical responsibility to both individuals and tribunals.

Misuse of the position of attorney or paralegal by using tactics that are intended to harass a non-client in order to gain advantage over that non-client is prohibited. Any person who is not a client, including another attorney, is covered under this catch-all. Attorneys send confrontational letters to each other in order to obtain their desired results; however, stepping over the line by making that confrontation public is not permitted, as there is no other purpose but to embarrass the other attorney. *See In the Matter of Comfort*, 159 P.3d 1011 (Kan. 2007). The attorney not only sent a "sharp-worded," if not "vitriolic," letter to the opposing counsel advising him of a potential conflict of interest on the opposing counsel's part (and also insinuating other ethical violations), but he also "published" it to nine city officials. The court found the attorney in violation of his ethical obligations because opposing counsel was a non-client and therefore covered under the prohibition against misuse of his position. The Court did not accept the First Amendment defense of the sharp-tongued attorney opining that:

> A lawyer, as a citizen, has a right to criticize a judge or other adjudicatory officer publicly. To exercise this right, the lawyer must be certain of the merit of the complaint, use appropriate language, and avoid petty criticisms. Unrestrained and intemperate statements against a judge or adjudicatory officer lessen public confidence in our legal system. Criticisms motivated by reasons other than a desire to improve the legal system are not justified.

Id. at 1025, citing *In re Johnson*, 729 P.2d 1175, 1178 (Kan. 1986).

In the *Comfort* matter, there was no other reason for sending copies of the letter to the various city officials than to embarrass opposing counsel.

The spirit of this rule is abstention from taking unfair advantage of anyone other than a client. This is not to say that attorneys may take advantage of their clients; those actions are even more egregious and are covered under other rules in a much more formal and detailed manner. Until now, the discussion regarding communications with others has focused on actions or failures to act where there is a duty. But what happens when information is simply sent to an attorney's office without any request by the attorney or the paralegal? The attorney or paralegal is merely the passive recipient of the communication and has done nothing in contravention of the ethical requirements. Reinforcing the idea that legal professionals should "do the right thing" with respect to third persons, any information that (1) is mistakenly sent to the attorney's office and (2) may be used to the attorney's advantage and (3) is known to be sensitive and confidential must be reported to the sender. The attorney or receiving paralegal must let the sender know that the "cat may be out of the bag" with regard to certain information. Additionally, the attorney cannot then use that information to her advantage. By giving notice to the sender, the legal professional can alert the sender to this possibility, and therefore the sender can react appropriately. Of course, the initial recipient of this inadvertent communication may be the paralegal, who is often the manager of information in the firm. In order to ensure that the attorney complies with the ethical obligations to treat all third parties with respect, the paralegal will need to bring the inadvertent disclosure to the attorney's attention. The motto of this ethical requirement is to "fight fair" with all potential players, not just those directly involved in the litigation. This rule closes the loophole where the information received is not already covered by attorney-client privilege. Clearly, where opposing counsel mistakenly sends confidential information to the other attorney, the privilege rules attach to cover that situation. Where third parties, like witnesses, send information, this rule is required to cover the situation and guarantee the respect for the third party's interests.

The overall principle here was best summed up over two hundred years ago by Thomas Jefferson in a letter to George Hammond: "It is reasonable that everyone who asks justice should do justice" (1792). From the commencement of litigation, an attorney should work within the standards set forth by the courts to ensure a just and fair result, not merely the one that the client desires. The initial papers filed with the court should accurately, truthfully, and in good faith represent the facts and law applicable to the client's position. Once litigation has commenced, the attorney has the duty to assist in moving it forward to a proper and legally satisfactory resolution even where the client's interests may be subordinated to those of truth-seeking. The attorney must always be mindful of his chief allegiance to the justice system and its processes.

Summary

Respect for the legal profession manifests itself in respect for the other legal professionals, all parties involved in the matter, and those persons not directly affected by the outcome. Each individual matter should be handled in a manner that reflects positively on the adversarial and adjudicatory process. There are seven means to achieve this result specifically discussed in the ABA Model Rules and also reflected in NFPA's Ethical Code. They require:

1. Presentment of meritorious claims and defenses. The legal professional must have a good faith belief that the pleading contains plausible causes of action and defenses to those claims.

2. Keeping the litigation moving through the system by not purposefully causing delay in the preparation for trial.

3. Being honest with the court in all matters, even when that honesty may compromise the client's interest. This may require disclosure of confidential information or adverse legal authority.

4. Dealing fairly with all parties involved in the litigation.

5. Remaining neutral and respectful to the justice system and its processes, particularly in dealing with court personnel and jurors.

6. Refraining from revealing certain information to the media covering the litigation that may have an adverse impact on the proceedings.

7. Treating all "non-clients" with respect, keeping an eye on the justice system's overriding interest in fairness in communicating with other persons.

Key Terms

Adversarial model	Good faith
Advocacy	Knowing
Controlling jurisdiction	Leading question
Due process	Materiality
Ex parte	Viable claim
Frivolous	

Review Questions

MULTIPLE CHOICE

Choose the best answer(s) and please explain *why* you chose the answer(s).

1. A frivolous claim:
   a. Extends or modifies existing law
   b. Is always permissible as a defense in a criminal case
   c. Is sanctionable unless supported by a belief that it is necessary
   d. Unduly burdens the process of litigation

2. An attorney's ongoing duty of candor to the tribunal requires:
   a. The attorney to submit all the case law found during his research process
   b. The paralegal to call and update the court before trial if any facts change
   c. The attorney to present only information which he reasonably believes to be true
   d. All of the above

3. If an attorney wants to speak to a third-party witness, she must:
   a. Call him and identify herself as an attorney for the opposition
   b. Determine whether or not he is represented by counsel
   c. Subpoena the witness to testify
   d. Submit written interrogatories to opposing counsel

EXPLAIN YOURSELF

All answers should be written in complete sentences. A simple yes or no is insufficient.

1. Explain an attorney's duty to reveal contrary legal authority to the court.

2. Why is it impermissible for an attorney to speak about a matter he is handling in public?

3. Describe the kind of courtroom behavior that would result in an ethical complaint against the attorney.

4. A frivolous claim is best described as . . .

FAULTY PHRASES

All of the following statements are *false*. State why they are false and then rewrite each one as a true statement. Do not simply make the statement negative by adding the word "not."

1. An attorney must always perform an independent factual investigation to support all her client's claims prior to filing suit.

2. An attorney cannot ask for extensions of time, because he has an ethical duty to expedite litigation.

3. An attorney is obligated to reveal all her sources of law under her duty of candor to the tribunal.

4. A lawyer's inviolate duty of confidentiality outweighs his duty of candor to the tribunal.

5. Attorneys can express their opinions on the value of the evidence presented at trial in their closing arguments.

6. After trial an attorney is permitted to ask the jurors how they deliberated and rendered the verdict.

7. An attorney can simply ignore her client's perjured testimony; she is not in violation of the rules unless she directed the false testimony.

8. Ex parte communications are permitted where the attorney is familiar with the judge.

PORTFOLIO ASSIGNMENT

Write Away

Draft a memorandum for all paralegals in your office that explains their ethical obligations regarding their code of conduct in a courtroom or other tribunal when they accompany the supervising attorney. Make sure you include enough details and cover all possible situations that may arise in contentious litigation.

Cases in Point

■ Compare the outcome of these two cases both involving the Facebook "friending" of a judge.

Youkers v. State, 400 S.W.3d 200 (Tex. App. 2013)
Court of Appeals of Texas,
Dallas.
William Scott YOUKERS, Appellant
v.
The STATE of Texas, Appellee.
No. 05–11–01407–CR.
May 15, 2013. Discretionary Review Refused Aug. 21, 2013.

SYNOPSIS

Background: State filed motion to revoke defendant's community supervision. Defendant entered open plea of true to State's allegations and requested reinstatement of his supervision. The 219th Judicial District Court, Collin County, Scott Becker, J., sentenced defendant to eight years' imprisonment and thereafter denied his motion for new trial. Defendant appealed.

Holdings: The Court of Appeals, MURPHY, J., held that:

1. as a matter of apparent first impression, designation of trial judge as "friend" of victim's father on social media website was insufficient to show bias, as basis for recusal;

2. trial judge's statement when imposing sentence did not reflect bias, partiality, or failure to consider full range of punishment;

3. government's mail delay did not render assistance of defendant's attorney ineffective;

4. denial of defendant's motion for new trial was not based on defendant's alleged refusal to waive attorney-client privilege; and

5. trial judge improperly assessed court-appointed attorney fees against defendant.

Affirmed as modified.

OPINION

Opinion by Justice MURPHY.

William Scott Youkers appeals the revocation of his community supervision and eight-year prison sentence for his conviction of assaulting his girlfriend. He contends (1) the trial judge lacked impartiality or neutrality based on ex parte communications, including a Facebook friendship with the girlfriend's father; (2) his trial counsel's assistance was rendered ineffective due to the Collin County Detention Center's delay in delivering a letter from his attorney; (3) the judge erred by denying his motion for new trial based on Youkers's refusal to waive his attorney-client privilege regarding the contents of the letter; and (4) the judge improperly assessed court-appointed attorney's fees. We modify the judgment to delete the award of attorney's fees and affirm the judgment as modified.

BACKGROUND

Youkers was on parole for a previous felony conviction of tampering with evidence when he was indicted for assaulting his girlfriend, who was pregnant with his child. *See* Tex. Penal Code Ann. § 22.01(b)(2)(B) (West 2011). Youkers pleaded guilty to the assault allegations. Pursuant to a plea agreement, the judge assessed a ten-year prison sentence, suspended for five years, and a $500 fine. Approximately three months later, the State filed a motion to revoke Youkers's supervision, contending he violated the terms and conditions of his supervision by testing positive for methamphetamines, failing to submit to a urinalysis, failing to report as scheduled to his supervision officer, and failing to pay court-ordered fees and costs.

Youkers entered an open plea of true to the allegations in the motion and requested reinstatement of his community supervision. Youkers explained that he previously "didn't have a stable place to live," but he was now living with his mother, had started attending school, and hoped to continue studying. The judge sentenced Youkers to eight years' imprisonment and thereafter denied his motion for new trial. Youkers appealed.

DISCUSSION

Youkers raises three issues on appeal. In his first two issues, which have subparts, Youkers contends the trial judge abused his discretion in denying Youkers's motion for new trial. We review a trial court's ruling on a motion for new trial under an abuse of discretion standard. *Smith v. State*, 286 S.W.3d 333, 339 (Tex. Crim. App. 2009). In conducting our review, we do not substitute our judgment for that of the trial court. *Webb v. State*, 232 S.W.3d 109, 112 (Tex. Crim. App. 2007). We give great deference to the trial court's ruling and will overrule that decision only if it is arbitrary or unreasonable. *Lewis v. State*, 911 S.W.2d 1, 7 (Tex. Crim. App. 1995). A trial court abuses its discretion in denying a motion for new trial only when no reasonable view of the record could support the trial court's ruling. *Holden v. State*, 201 S.W.3d 761, 763 (Tex. Crim. App. 2006).

Judicial Bias

Youkers's first ground for reversing the trial judge's denial of his motion for new trial is his challenge to the judge's neutrality. Youkers describes two sources evidencing bias—(1) the judge's Facebook friendship with the father of Youkers's girlfriend, which continued during the pendency of the revocation hearing, and (2) emails to the judge from Youkers's community supervision officer.

Facebook Friendship

After the judge sentenced Youkers to an eight-year prison term, Youkers filed a motion for new trial complaining "[t]here was an undisclosed friendship" between the judge and the father of Youkers's girlfriend, improper communications between the two, and influence over the judge by the father. He asserted the communications and relationship created both actual and apparent bias. Youkers relied on a private message the judge received on the judge's Facebook page approximately one week before Youkers's original plea and the ongoing status of the judge and the father as Facebook "friends."

The judge testified at the hearing on Youkers's motion for new trial that he knew the father because they both ran for office in the same election cycle. He testified they were designated as "friends" on Facebook and were "running at the same time," but that was "the extent of [their] relationship." The two were not related, and, other than the private Facebook messages, they had had no other contacts through Facebook. At the time of the hearing, they were still Facebook "friends."

The Facebook communications began with a message from the father to the judge seeking leniency for Youkers. That message was posted just prior to Youkers's original plea. The judge responded online formally advising the father the communication was in violation of rules precluding ex parte communications, stating the judge ceased reading the message once he realized the message was improper, and cautioning that any further communications from the father about the case or any other pending legal matter would result in the father being removed as one of the judge's Facebook "friends." The judge's online response also advised that the judge was placing a copy of the communications in the court's file, disclosing the incident to the lawyers, and contacting the judicial conduct commission to determine if further steps were required. The father replied with a message apologizing for breaking any "rules or laws" and promising not to ask questions or make comments "relating to criminal cases" in the future.

At the hearing on Youkers's motion for new trial, the judge confirmed that he followed through based on his Facebook message—he placed a copy of the Facebook communications in the court file, he contacted both Youkers's attorney and the State's attorney to inform them of the communications, and he contacted the judicial conduct commission regarding the communications. He said these were the only Facebook communications he had with the father and he had not read any of the father's Facebook posts.

Youkers's complaint is that the judge's Facebook relationship with the father created actual and apparent absence of impartiality. Although Youkers's motion for new trial addressed both the communications and the online status of the father and the judge as Facebook "friends," his complaint on appeal focuses only on the online status.

No Texas court appears to have addressed the propriety of a judge's use of social media websites such as Facebook. Nor is there a rule, canon of ethics, or judicial ethics opinion in Texas proscribing such use. The general premise that judges are not prohibited from using social media is consistent with the current standards suggested by the American Bar Association, as well as recent articles addressing the topic. *See, e.g.,* ABA Standing Comm. on Ethics & Prof 1 Responsibility, Formal Op. 462 (2013) (concluding judge may participate in electronic social networking); Judge Susan Criss, *The Use of Social Media by Judges,* 60 THE ADVOC. (TEX.) 18 (2012); Judge Gena Slaughter & John G. Browning, *Social Networking Dos and Don'ts for Lawyers and Judges,* 73 TEX. B.J. 192 (2010).

Allowing judges to use Facebook and other social media is also consistent with the premise that judges

do not "forfeit [their] right to associate with [their] friends and acquaintances nor [are they] condemned to live the life of a hermit. In fact, such a regime would . . . lessen the effectiveness of the judicial officer." Comm. on Jud. Ethics, State Bar of Tex., Op. 39 (1978). Social websites are one way judges can remain active in the community. For example, the ABA has stated, "[s]ocial interactions of all kinds, including [the use of social media websites], can . . . prevent [judges] from being thought of as isolated or out of touch." ABA Op. 462. Texas also differs from many states because judges in Texas are elected officials, and the internet and social media websites have become campaign tools to raise funds and to provide information about candidates. *Id.; see also* Criss, *supra,* at 18 ("Few judicial campaigns can realistically afford to refrain from using social media to deliver their message to the voting public. Social media can be a very effective and inexpensive method to deliver campaign messages to the voting public").

While the use of social media websites such as Facebook "can benefit judges in both their personal and professional lives," the use presents concerns unique to the role of the judiciary in our justice system. ABA Op. 462. An independent and honorable judiciary is indispensable to justice in our society. *In re Thoma,* 873 S.W.2d 477, 496 (Tex. Rev. Trib. 1994, no appeal). Thus, judges must be mindful of their responsibilities under applicable judicial codes of conduct. *See* ABA Op. 462; TEX. CODE JUD. CONDUCT, *reprinted in* TEX. GOV'T CODE ANN., tit. 2, subtit. G, app. B (West 2005).

The preamble to the Texas Code of Judicial Conduct first reminds us of the role of the judiciary and provides that intrinsic to all sections of the code are the precepts that judges must respect and honor their judicial office as a public trust. TEX. CODE JUD. CONDUCT, Preamble. The individual canons are intended to state basic standards for judicial conduct and to provide guidance to judges. *Id.* Several of those canons are relevant to our analysis of Youkers's issue.

Canon two provides that judges "should act at all times in a manner that promotes public confidence in the integrity and impartiality of the judiciary" and "shall not allow any relationship to influence judicial conduct or judgment." *Id.* Canon 2(A), (B). It follows that the judge may not "convey or permit others to convey the impression that they are in a special position to influence the judge." *Id.* Canon 2(B). Similarly, canon four cautions a judge to conduct all extra-judicial activities to avoid casting reasonable doubt on the judge's capacity to act impartially as a judge. *Id.* Canon 4(A).

Canon three also addresses the judge's duty of impartiality and prohibits, with limited exceptions, any direct or indirect ex parte communications concerning the merits of a pending or impending judicial proceeding. *Id.* Canon 3(B)(8). An ex parte communication is one that involves fewer than all parties who are legally entitled to be present during the discussion of any matter with the judge. *Erskine v. Baker,* 22 S.W.3d 537, 539 (Tex. App.-El Paso 2000, pet. denied). Ex parte communications are prohibited because they are inconsistent with the right of every litigant to be heard and with the principle of maintaining an impartial judiciary. *Abdygapparova v. State,* 243 S.W.3d 191, 208 (Tex. App.-San Antonio 2007, pet. ref'd). This proscription applies regardless of whether the communication occurs through a social media website, in the judge's chambers, or elsewhere. That is, while the internet and social media websites create new venues for communications, our analysis should not change because an ex parte communication occurs online or offline.

A judge must recuse in any proceeding in which "the judge's impartiality might reasonably be questioned" or "the judge has a personal bias or prejudice concerning the subject matter or a party." Tᴇx. R. Cɪᴠ. P. 18b; *see also Gaal v. State,* 332 S.W.3d 448, 452 (Tex. Crim. App. 2011). Recusal based on bias is not required simply because of a business relationship or acquaintance with a party. *See Woodruff v. Wright,* 51 S.W.3d 727, 737–38 (Tex. App.-Texarkana 2001, pet. denied) (noting appearance of impropriety determined by reasonable person with all facts; mere business relationship, that included judge's performance of wedding ceremony for defendant and defendant's surgery on family member of judge, insufficient for reasonable person to find bias).

Merely designating someone as a "friend" on Facebook "does not show the degree or intensity of a judge's relationship with a person." ABA Op. 462. One cannot say, based on this designation alone, whether the judge and the "friend" have met; are acquaintances that have met only once; are former business acquaintances; or have some deeper, more meaningful relationship. Thus, the designation,

standing alone, provides no insight into the nature of the relationship. *See Lueg v. Lueg,* 976 S.W.2d 308, 311 (Tex. App.-Corpus Christi 1998, pet. denied) (concluding recusal not required where one party's attorney was judge's past campaign manager; that designation alone provided no insight into the nature of the relationship). Further context is required. *See id.;* ABA Op. 462.

The judge testified at the hearing on Youkers's motion for new trial regarding the nature of the relationship with the father. He stated they were running for office at the same time—that was "the extent of [their] relationship." That evidence, with no other context, provides no insight into any relationship that would influence the judge and lead to bias or partiality. *See Lueg,* 976 S.W.2d at 311. The record also does not show the father had a role in Youkers's revocation hearing or was called as a witness.

The record regarding the earlier Facebook communications also provides no additional context that would support Youkers's suggestion of bias. We first observe the communication was not adverse to Youkers; the father sought leniency. Additionally, the judge stated that he ceased reading the father's message once he realized it was an ex parte communication; he emphasized, "I have not considered any of the information in your e-mail as it would be improper for me to do so." The judge also acted in full compliance with the Texas Committee on Judicial Ethics' recommended procedure for treatment of ex parte communications. *See* Comm. on Jud. Ethics, State Bar of Tex., Op. 154 (1993) (providing that judge receiving ex parte communication from litigant may comply with canon 3B(8) by placing the communication in clerk's file; providing the communication to all parties; determining if the communication is proper; and, if it is not, advising the communicant that all ex parte communications must cease).

Youkers asserts that even if actual bias is absent, the evidence shows an appearance of bias. Specifically, he relies on an affidavit from Youkers's mother filed in support of the motion for new trial. In that affidavit, the mother states that "[the father] said that he had influence with [the judge] and would help [Youkers] with his case." The appearance of impropriety must be determined by a "reasonable person" who is in possession of all of the facts. *Woodruff,* 51 S.W.3d at 738. A reasonable person in possession of all of the facts in this case likely would conclude the contact between the judge and the father did not cause the judge to abandon his judicial role of impartiality; besides the evidence that the judge and the father's acquaintance was limited, any appearance of bias created by the Facebook communications was dismissed quickly by the judge's handling of the situation.

We acknowledge the judge had an obligation not to let the father convey the impression that he was in a special position to influence the judge. Tex. Code Jud. Conduct, Canon 2(B). Assuming the father made the improper statement to Youkers's mother suggesting he had influence with the judge, the record contains no evidence the judge was aware of the statement. Importantly, the judge quickly disposed of any suggestion by his full disclosure of the Facebook communications, and his judgment in no way supports any implication of influence. Based on the facts in this record, we conclude the trial judge did not abuse his discretion in denying Youkers's motion for new trial based on his Facebook-based claims of bias.

Community Supervision Officer

Youkers also complains that ex parte emails sent by his community supervision officer created judicial bias. Youkers was placed on five years community supervision on June 2, 2011. Approximately two months later, on August 18, the officer emailed the judge letting the judge know she was sending a notice of violation regarding Youkers's case. She stated that, "I just wanted to give you advanced notice so that you would keep an eye out for it. I am very concerned about this case." The officer then emailed a notice of violation to the State. On September 20, the officer sent another email to the judge. Attached to this email was a memorandum from the officer advising the judge that "[i]t is believed that Mr. Youkers is a major threat to both himself and others." The State filed its motion to revoke Youkers's community supervision that same day, and a capias was issued based on Youkers's probation violation.

Youkers argues this record shows the judge predetermined Youkers's sentence based on his community supervision officer's emails informing the judge of Youkers's "poor character" before the probation hearing; he claims this information was not introduced as evidence at any hearing in the case "yet it clearly prejudiced [the judge's] impartiality such that he was unable to consider the full range of punishment and mitigating evidence."

The State contends Youkers waived this complaint because he failed to raise the issue in the motion for new trial or at the hearing. Youkers asserts he could not raise this complaint in the motion for new trial because the emails were not part of the "public" file and he was unaware of them until the Clerk's Record was filed in this appeal.

The Clerk's Record filed in this appeal is the record that was available to the public. That record shows the community supervision officer's August 18 email was stamped with the Collin County District Clerk's file mark on August 19, 2011 and was filed prior to the September 20 motion to revoke. Similarly, the September 20 email and memorandum (the same date the motion to revoke was filed) are part of the same record; they are placed in the file directly after the motion to revoke and just before the file-marked capias showing the sheriff's return of service. Accordingly, Youkers's statements that the communications were not disclosed and not discoverable are incorrect. Youkers thus has failed to preserve any objection to the communications by failing to present his complaint to the trial judge. See Tex. R. App. P. 33.1(a). The record also contains no evidence the judge predetermined Youkers's sentence or failed to consider the evidence presented.

Due process requires a neutral and detached hearing body or officer. *Brumit v. State,* 206 S.W.3d 639, 645 (Tex. Crim. App. 2006). Absent a clear showing of bias, a trial court's actions will be presumed to have been correct. *Id.* A judge's remarks during trial that are critical, disapproving, or hostile to a party "usually will not support a bias or partiality challenge, although they *may* do so if they reveal an opinion based on extrajudicial information." *Gaal,* 332 S.W.3d at 454.

As evidence of the judge's bias, Youkers identifies statements made at the revocation hearing, which he asserts show a predetermined sentence based in part on the officer's emails. Specifically, the judge stated that the reason he was "leaning towards greater force rather than less force" was because "when a smart person is left unmonitored or lightly monitored, they are the ones who are more able to quickly figure out how to get around . . . and not necessarily follow the rules." He further explained to Youkers that he was giving him two years less than the maximum sentence "in the hopes that you use your intelligence to realize that you've got to fix these things and not keep trying to fix them to the minimum to where people stop watching you. Because the moment you are unwatched, you are untrustworthy."

These statements are supported by the evidence. Youkers's mother testified about Youkers's "high IQ" shortly before the trial judge commented regarding Youkers's intelligence. She described Youkers as having "been through a lot in his life," detailing some of the abuse he had suffered from his father. When the judge questioned Youkers's mother regarding "the least amount of force" needed to "get [Youkers] to stop screwing up," his mother explained that "now" he had a child he loved very much and he had a passion to go to school. She then admitted "[n]obody was stopping him from doing that" earlier and she could not "make excuses." She agreed she would probably "try to train him until he's 43" because she is "his mom" and loves him. The judge also asked the mother "[w]hat's different today than any of the other times that he's come before the Courts and asked for mercy?" Continuing to admit she could not make excuses for her son, she described terrible abuse he had endured as a child and asked that her son be given a chance.

Youkers also testified. He said his mother had "rules" she expected him to abide by when he lived with her; yet when he stayed with others, he "used." He stated he needed help, including "a stable place to stay." Additionally, Youkers's record showed numerous violations. His prior probation for the tampering with evidence conviction was revoked because he did not "show up." He admitted he used drugs while on probation for that conviction and he assaulted his pregnant girlfriend by choking her. He then received probation for the assault family violence conviction, and he again used methamphetamine and quit attending counseling at Hope's Door because he was not living close enough to ride his bike.

It was only after hearing all of the evidence that the judge stated, "[b]ased on the totality of the information presented to the Court at [the] hearing and [his] review of the file," he was sentencing Youkers to eight years in prison. The judge added the statement (about which Youkers complains) that he believed he was "making a mistake and it should be a bigger number"; he was giving Youkers two years less

than the maximum sentence "in the hopes that [Youkers] use [his] intelligence to realize that [he's] got to fix these things and not keep trying to fix them to the minimum to where people stop watching [him]. Because the moment [he is] unwatched, [he] is untrustworthy."

The evidence supports the judge's comments, which do not reflect bias, partiality, or the judge's failure to consider the full range of punishment. See *Brumit*, 206 S.W.3d at 645. We conclude the trial judge did not abuse his discretion in overruling Youkers's motion for new trial based on complaints regarding tribunal partiality.

Ineffective Assistance of Counsel

Youkers also asserts that a mail delay at the Collin County Detention Center rendered his trial attorney's assistance ineffective. Specifically, he blames the center for the mail delay, which resulted in his failure to receive a letter from his attorney advising of a plea offer. Youkers claims that immediately after the revocation hearing in which the judge sentenced him to an eight-year prison term, he returned to his cell to find a letter from his attorney. The letter had been sent approximately six days earlier. Youkers testified by affidavit that "[w]hen I read the letter I was devastated, had I received it earlier it would have caused me to change my plans and accept the plea offer which had been offered me by the State."

Youkers does not argue he was unaware of the offer at the revocation hearing. Conversely, he testified he spoke with his attorney before the hearing. That attorney is the same attorney who drafted the letter Youkers claims he did not receive. The attorney advised Youkers prior to the revocation hearing of the State's two-year offer as well as a second offer she was able to negotiate. Specifically, Youkers's attorney testified she had the opportunity to speak with Youkers before the revocation hearing. She said she had spoken with the prosecuting attorney before the hearing, and the State was willing to "continue [Youkers] on probation and let him go into [Substance Abuse Felony Punishment]." She testified she conveyed both offers to Youkers, but he "decided not to take [the SAFP] offer or the two TDC. . . ." Thus, Youkers was aware of two plea offers and refused both.

Despite Youkers's and his attorney's testimony at the revocation hearing, Youkers claims he would have taken the offer had he read the letter. The wording of the letter was not before the judge. Nor is the letter before this Court. Youkers stated in his affidavit that the letter contained "some critical advice and the result of an investigation [his trial attorney] had conducted." In her testimony at the hearing on Youkers's motion for new trial, his attorney verified the letter contained the terms of the offer made by the State, "what the rights on a revocation are, the ramifications, the range of punishment, etcetera." When the State tried to question the attorney about the letter's specific contents, however, Youkers's appellate attorney (who represented him during the hearing on the motion for new trial) objected on the basis of the attorney-client privilege. The judge sustained the objection.

To prevail on an ineffective assistance of counsel claim, an appellant typically must show by a preponderance of the evidence both deficient performance and prejudice. *Strickland v. Washington,* 466 U.S. 668, 687, 104 S. Ct. 2052, 80 L. Ed. 2d 674 (1984); *Williams v. State,* 301 S.W.3d 675, 687 (Tex. Crim. App. 2009). He must demonstrate under the first prong that his attorney's performance fell below an objective standard of reasonableness under prevailing professional norms. *Strickland,* 466 U.S. at 687-88, 104 S. Ct. 2052; *Ex parte Lane,* 303 S.W.3d 702, 707 (Tex. Crim. App. 2009). To meet the second prong, the appellant must show the existence of a reasonable probability, sufficient to undermine confidence in the outcome, that but for his attorney's deficient performance, the result of the proceeding would have been different. *Strickland,* 466 U.S. at 694, 104 S. Ct. 2052; *Ex parte Lane,* 303 S.W.3d at 707. Prejudice may be presumed in a few situations. *Ex parte McFarland,* 163 S.W.3d 743, 752 (Tex. Crim. App. 2005). One of those is "state interference" with counsel's assistance. *Id.; see also Strickland,* 466 U.S. at 692, 104 S. Ct. 2052.

Both the United States Supreme Court and the Texas Court of Criminal Appeals have recognized the Sixth Amendment's right to counsel can be violated when the government adversely affects an attorney's ability to perform the attorney's duties. *See Geders v. United States,* 425 U.S. 80, 91, 96 S. Ct. 1330, 47 L. Ed. 2d 592 (1976); *Batiste v. State,* 888 S.W.2d 9, 18–19 (Tex. Crim. App. 1994). Relying on *Geders,* Youkers argues that an ineffective assistance of counsel claim can be premised on government action that blocks the free flow of communication between attorney and client, and "it is clear that this right is violated where the government takes any actions—intentional or otherwise—that hinders this right."

In *Geders,* the Supreme Court concluded that a trial court's order banning attorney-client consultation during an overnight recess deprived the defendant of his Sixth Amendment right to trial counsel. *See Geders,* 425 U.S. at 91, 96 S. Ct. 1330. Similarly, the Texas Court of Criminal Appeals concluded a prisoner's right to counsel was violated by a sheriff's refusal to allow the defendant to speak to his attorney outside the sheriff's presence. *See Turner v. State,* 91 Tex. Crim. 627, 241 S.W. 162, 164 (1922). Neither factual scenario is present here.

Youkers was not deprived at any time of his right to consult with his attorney. Nor does he claim he was not allowed to confer with counsel in private. Instead, he argues it is well established that a failure to inform a defendant of a plea offer made by the State is an omission that falls below an objective standard of reasonableness.

To support this claim, Youkers also relies on *Ex parte Lemke,* 13 S.W.3d 791, 795 (Tex. Crim. App. 2000), *overruled on other grounds by Ex parte Argent,* 393 S.W.3d 781 (Tex. Crim. App. 2013). In that case, the defendant's attorney told him the State had not offered any plea bargains, when in fact the State had offered him two. *Ex parte Lemke,* 13 S.W.3d at 794. The defendant became aware of the plea offers several months after his sentencing when he testified against his trial counsel in an unrelated matter. *Id.* at 794-95. The court concluded the attorney's failure to relay the offer to his client fell below an objective standard of professional reasonableness and, as a remedy, required the government to reinstate the original offer. *Id.* at 796, 798.

Youkers's facts are distinguishable from *Ex parte Lemke.* The trial attorney in *Ex parte Lemke* failed to tell the defendant that there was any plea offer on the table; the defendant was left with the justified misunderstanding that the State had provided no offer. *Id.* at 794. In contrast, Youkers testified his trial attorney told him about the plea offer before the revocation hearing, the attorney confirmed the information provided, and Youkers rejected the offer. Youkers, unlike the defendant in *Ex parte Lemke,* did not miss the opportunity to accept a plea offer because he did not know about it. He missed the opportunity because he chose not to accept it.

The burden of proving ineffectiveness rests upon the defendant and requires proof by a preponderance of the evidence. *Rodriguez v. State*, 899 S.W.2d 658, 665 (Tex. Crim. App. 1995). Youkers has not met that burden, and the trial judge did not abuse his discretion in denying Youkers's motion for new trial.

Waiver of Attorney-Client Privilege

Youkers also contends the judge abused his discretion in denying his motion for new trial because the judge improperly based his denial on Youkers's refusal to waive his attorney-client privilege. Youkers testified in support of his motion for new trial he would have accepted the State's plea offer had he received his attorney's letter earlier. Yet he refused to testify to the contents of the letter based on the attorney-client privilege. In response to the judge's observation that Youkers's argument "he would have changed his actions based on what's in the letter . . . would make the contents of that letter quite relevant," Youkers's attorney insisted the contents of the letter were privileged. The judge asked, "Since he's talking about them, don't you think he's waived it?" His attorney maintained there was no waiver, and the judge sustained the objection.

During closing arguments on Youkers's motion for new trial, the judge interrupted Youkers's attorney and asked, "You want me to grant a Motion for New Trial based on the contents of a letter that I don't know if it says something of any significance or it says the moon is made of green cheese?" The attorney responded that the motion should be granted because Youkers was "prevented from receiving a communication from [his] attorney" and he "testified had he received it timely he would have altered his course in a criminal action." The judge questioned how—without knowing the contents of the letter—Youkers would "expect any fact finder to make a credible determination as to whether or not that belief is reasonable or unreasonable?" The attorney argued Youkers's testimony that the letter made a difference to him and it would have changed his course of conduct had he received it was sufficient to show "denial of significant aid from his attorney." The judge denied the motion.

Youkers claims error in the judge's denial of his motion, arguing to "deny a motion for new trial based upon the correct raising of a privilege . . . was to deny [Youkers] his Constitutional right to effective counsel due to his refusal to waive a well established privilege." The State responds that Youkers has produced no evidence the motion was denied because he refused to waive the privilege; while the judge did raise questions regarding whether he could grant the motion without knowing the contents of the letter, the judge did not state this was the basis of his denial. The State also argues Youkers waived his attorney-client privilege by raising the ineffective assistance of counsel claim. Youkers did not request findings of fact and conclusions of law to establish the basis of the judge's ruling.

The attorney-client privilege is not absolute; it may be waived. *Ballew v. State*, 640 S.W.2d 237, 240 (Tex. Crim. App. [Panel Op.] 1980). One way the privilege can be waived is by litigating a claim against an attorney for a breach of legal duty. *See Joseph v. State*, 3 S.W.3d 627, 637 (Tex. App.-Houston [14th Dist.] 1999, no pet.).

Youkers necessarily placed in issue privileged communications when he argued his attorney breached her legal duty to provide effective assistance of counsel. By doing so, he effectively waived his attorney-client privilege. *See id.*, at 638. When he refused to disclose the contents of the letter on which he relies as the basis for a new trial, he failed to provide sufficient evidence to meet his burden of proving his attorney was ineffective. *See Rodriguez*, 899 S.W.2d at 665 (noting defendant bears burden of proving by preponderance of evidence counsel's ineffective assistance). Simply stated, Youkers cannot hide behind the privilege. He was required to meet his burden of showing ineffective assistance of counsel, and the attorney-client privilege does not relieve Youkers of that burden. On this record, we cannot conclude the judge abused his discretion by denying Youkers's motion for new trial.

Assessment of Attorney's Fees Against Youkers

Youkers's final argument is that the trial judge erred in assessing court-appointed attorney's fees against him. Specifically, the judge found Youkers to be indigent and provided court-appointed counsel as requested by Youkers. Yet the judge assessed the court-appointed attorney's fees as costs and taxed the fees against Youkers as part of the judgment revoking his community supervision. The State agrees the assessment was in error.

Once a trial court finds a criminal defendant to be indigent, the defendant is presumed to remain indigent for the remainder of the proceedings unless a material change in the defendant's financial resources occurs. *See* Tex. Code Crim. Proc. Ann. art. 26.04(p) (West Supp. 2012). For the trial court to assess attorney's fees, it must determine the defendant has the financial resources that enable the court to offset those costs. *Id.* art. 26.05(g); *see also Mayer v. State*, 309 S.W.3d 552, 556 (Tex. Crim. App. 2010); *In re Daniel,* No. AP-76959, 2013 WL 1628937, at *2 (Tex. Crim. App. 2013) (orig. proceeding). The record also must show some factual basis to support the trial court's determination. *See Barrera v. State*, 291 S.W.3d 515, 518 (Tex. App.-Amarillo 2009, no pet.).

The record contains no evidence of a material change in Youkers's financial circumstances once the judge found him to be indigent. Accordingly, the evidence is insufficient to justify the trial judge's assessment of attorney's fees against Youkers. *See Mayer*, 309 S.W.3d at 556.

When the evidence does not support the assessment of attorney's fees as court costs, the proper remedy is to modify the judgment to delete the requirement. *Id.* at 557. We therefore modify the judgment revoking Youker's community supervision by deleting the assessment of attorney's fees.

CONCLUSION

Youkers has failed to show actual or apparent lack of tribunal neutrality. The judge's designation as a Facebook "friend," without context providing insight into the nature of the relationship, was insufficient to show bias. Youkers also failed to meet his burden of showing the government's mail delay rendered his attorney's assistance ineffective. The plea offer purportedly referenced in the letter was conveyed by his attorney prior to the revocation hearing and Youkers rejected the offer. The judge also did not abuse his discretion in denying Youkers's motion for new trial when Youkers refused to disclose the contents of the letter and the only information known to the judge—that the letter contained a plea offer—was conveyed to Youkers properly and timely. We therefore overrule issues one and two. Regarding issue three, that the trial judge improperly assessed court-appointed attorney's fees against Youkers, we sustain the issue and modify the judgment to delete the assessment. We affirm the judgment as modified.

Source: Reprinted from Westlaw with permission from Thomson Reuters.

Chace v. Loisel, 170 So. 3d 802 (Fla. Dist. Ct. App. 2014)

District Court of Appeal of Florida, Fifth District.
Sandra CHACE, Petitioner,
v.
Robert LOISEL, Jr., Respondent.
No. 5D13-4449.
Jan. 24, 2014.

SYNOPSIS

Background: Wife filed petition for writ of prohibition to quash the order of the trial court, Linda D. Schoonover, Respondent Judge, denying her motion to disqualify the trial judge presiding over her dissolution of marriage case.

Holding: The District Court of Appeal, Cohen, J., held that trial judge's ex parte communication with wife presented a legally sufficient claim for disqualification of judge, particularly since wife's failure to respond to judge's social media "friend" request created a reasonable fear of offending judge.

Petition granted.

OPINION

Cohen, J.

Petitioner, Sandra Chace, seeks a writ of prohibition to quash the trial court's order denying her motion to disqualify the trial judge presiding over her and Respondent Robert Loisel, Jr.'s dissolution of marriage case. Upon review, we conclude that the trial court erred in denying Petitioner's motion.

The following allegations formed the basis for Petitioner's motion to disqualify. Prior to entry of final judgment, the trial judge reached out to Petitioner, ex parte, in the form of a Facebook "friend" request. Upon advice of counsel, Petitioner decided not to respond to that invitation. Thereafter, the trial court entered a final judgment of dissolution, allegedly attributing most of the marital debt to Petitioner and providing Respondent with a disproportionately excessive alimony award. Following entry of the final judgment, Petitioner filed a formal complaint against the trial judge, alleging that the judge sent her a Facebook "friend" request and then retaliated against Petitioner after she did not accept the request. Respondent later filed a motion for clarification of certain provisions in the final judgment, which is currently pending below. In the meantime, Petitioner had learned of other cases involving similar ex parte social media communications by the judge that resulted in her disqualification. Subsequently, the subject motion to disqualify was filed, a hearing was held on that motion, and the motion was denied as legally insufficient. The instant petition was then filed in this Court.

If the grounds asserted in a motion for disqualification are legally sufficient to create a well-founded fear in the mind of a party that he or she will not receive a fair trial, it is incumbent upon a judge to disqualify herself. See *Fischer v. Knuck*, 497 So. 2d 240, 242 (Fla. 1986). To determine whether the motion is "legally sufficient," this Court must resolve whether the alleged facts, which, accepted as true, would prompt a reasonably prudent person to fear that she could not get a fair and impartial trial before that judge. An affiant's mere subjective fear is insufficient to form the basis for disqualification. *Id.*

It seems clear that a judge's ex parte communication with a party presents a legally sufficient claim for disqualification, particularly in the case where the party's failure to respond to a Facebook "friend" request creates a reasonable fear of offending the solicitor. The "friend" request placed the litigant between the proverbial rock and a hard place: either

engage in improper ex parte communications with the judge presiding over the case or risk offending the judge by not accepting the "friend" request.

In *Domville v. State,* 103 So. 3d 184 (Fla. 4th DCA 2012), *rev. denied, State v. Domville,* 110 So. 3d 441 (Fla. 2013), the Fourth District addressed a Facebook issue with regard to judges "friending" *attorneys* through social media. That court determined that a judge's social networking "friendship" with the prosecutor of the underlying criminal case was sufficient to create a well-founded fear of not receiving a fair and impartial trial in a reasonably prudent person. *Id.*

We have serious reservations about the court's rationale in *Domville.* The word "friend" on Facebook is a term of art. A number of words or phrases could more aptly describe the concept, including acquaintance and, sometimes, virtual stranger. A Facebook friendship does not necessarily signify the existence of a close relationship. Other than the public nature of the internet, there is no difference between a Facebook "friend" and any other friendship a judge might have. *Domville*'s logic would require disqualification in cases involving an acquaintance of a judge. Particularly in smaller counties, where everyone in the legal community knows each other, this requirement is unworkable and unnecessary. Requiring disqualification in such cases does not reflect the true nature of a Facebook friendship and casts a large net in an effort to catch a minnow.

That said, *Domville* was the only Florida case that discussed the impact of a judge's social network activity and, as such, was binding upon the trial judge in this case. See *Pardo v. State,* 596 So. 2d 665, 666 (Fla. 1992) (explaining that "in the absence of interdistrict conflict, district court decisions bind all Florida trial courts"). Although this case involves the "friending" of a party, rather than an attorney representing a party, for purpose of ruling on the motion to disqualify we find that the difference is inconsequential. In our view, the "friending" of a party in a pending case raises far more concern than a judge's Facebook friendship with a lawyer.

Beyond the fact that *Domville* required the trial court to grant the motion to disqualify, the motion to disqualify was sufficient on its face to warrant disqualification. The trial judge's efforts to initiate ex parte communications with a litigant is prohibited by the Code of Judicial Conduct and has the ability to undermine the confidence in a judge's neutrality. The appearance of partiality must be avoided. It is incumbent upon judges to place boundaries on their conduct in order to avoid situations such as the one presented in this case.

Because Petitioner has alleged facts that would create in a reasonably prudent person a well-founded fear of not receiving a fair and impartial trial, we quash the order denying the motion to disqualify and remand to the trial court for further proceedings consistent with this opinion. We trust that the issuance of a formal writ will be unnecessary.

PETITION GRANTED.

SAWAYA and PALMER, JJ., concur.

Source: Reprinted from Westlaw with permission from Thomson Reuters.

Chapter 9

Law Firms: Understanding the Structure and Management of the Practice

Chapter Objectives

The student will be able to:

- Differentiate between the ethical responsibilities of partners, supervising attorneys, and paralegals
- Acknowledge the importance of professional independence, free from monetary incentives or restrictions, in the practice of law
- Define and discuss the issues surrounding multijurisdictional practice of law
- Evaluate the paralegal's roles and responsibilities in maintaining ethical standards appropriate to the firm

This chapter will examine *how* law firms are structured; this hierarchical structure defines *who* is ultimately held responsible for the ethical breaches within a law firm. In order to ensure the professional independence of the attorney, the rules stipulate with *whom* fees may be shared and *what* restrictions may be placed upon an attorney's right to practice law. Although, clearly, paralegals cannot practice law outside of the work they perform in their own law firm, attorneys are also restricted as to *where* they may practice outside their jurisdiction of admission.

It is not enough that an attorney comply with his own individual ethical obligations as if he were "an island." Most lawyers do not practice in isolation; even solo practitioners usually have some sort of office assistance. Due to the sensitive nature of the work that attorneys perform, it is necessary for them to maintain controls over everyone that works on the attorneys' matters to ensure that there are no leaks of information or failures in performance of the requisite actions on the cases. It may seem that this is an exercise in micromanagement; however, with proper training and reporting procedures, all persons employed by the supervising attorney can feel satisfied that they are not the "weak link in the chain." The first rules discussed in this chapter address the responsibility of partners, managers, and other supervising attorneys toward the firm, clients, and other parties when another person acts on behalf of the firm. The second set of rules addresses the concern of placing certain ethical responsibilities upon an attorney where that individual lawyer is acting in a business relationship outside of her firm, but still in a legal context.

supervising attorney
A partner or manager having ultimate responsibility for the work product of other attorneys and paralegals in the firm.

SUPERVISORY RESPONSIBILITY FOR OTHER ATTORNEYS

As in any business, there is a certain organizational hierarchy that assigns responsibilities and ensures accountability. For a general representation of the structure of a large law office, see Figure 9.1. The personnel farther down the chart have less ethical responsibility for the acts of others. Of course, every member of the law office has full ethical responsibility for his own acts. Senior and managing partners, rewarded with large hourly fees and other perks of experience, are conversely burdened with the extra responsibility to oversee and ensure compliance with all members' ethical duties. Yes, they are their "brothers' keeper." It is not enough to know that they are maintaining their own cases and clients properly; it is their duty to ensure that the entire firm acts according to the ethical code. The ABA Model Rules specifically set out the responsibility of partners regarding each kind of employee of the firm: copartner, subordinate associate, or nonlawyer assistant.

A partner may be held accountable for actions or omissions of her equal. One might assume that after many years in practice and after gaining the status of partner, an attorney may enjoy autonomy—the right to handle her matters in the way she sees fit. This is true, but only to a certain extent. While partners are

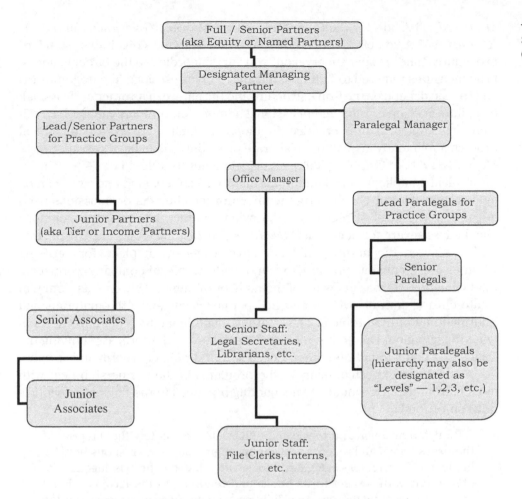

not in the habit of looking over each other's shoulders (they simply do not have time or energy for that), all partners in the law firm must make sure there are protocols in place that will effectuate ethical compliance, similar to quality control measures in other businesses. Rule 5.1 (c) holds a supervisory attorney responsible for another attorney's violation of the professional rules when:

1) The lawyer orders or, with knowledge of the specific conduct, ratifies the conduct involved; or

2) The lawyer is a partner or has comparable managerial authority in the law firm in which the other lawyer practices, or has direct supervisory authority over the other lawyer, and knows of the conduct at a time when its consequences can be avoided or mitigated but fails to take reasonable remedial action

"Whether an employee's ethical breaches are due to the employee's sub-standard performance or the deliberate circumvention of standard procedures, proper supervision must include mechanisms to determine whether the delegated tasks are being performed." *Attorney Grievance Comm'n of Maryland v.*

McDowell, 93 A.3d 711, 720 (Md. 2014), citing *Attorney Grievance Comm'n v. Kimmel*, 955 A.2d 269, 290 (Md. 2008). Of course, what constitutes "standard procedures" and "proper supervision" will vary according to the circumstances. "The measures required to fulfill the responsibility prescribed in paragraphs (a) and (b) can depend on the firm's structure and the nature of its practice. In a small firm, informal supervision and occasional admonition ordinarily might be sufficient. In a large firm, or in practice situations in which intensely difficult ethical problems frequently arise, more elaborate procedures may be necessary." *In re Myers*, 584 S.E.2d 357, 361 (2003), citing Comment to Rule 5.1.

negligent misconduct
Acts that are not done intentionally, but that do not comply with the standard of ordinary care and thought needed to fulfill the relevant ethical obligations.

Ethical compliance is so important that these supervising attorneys can be held responsible for even **negligent misconduct**; the acts or omissions need not rise to the level of reckless or knowing conduct, although the sanctions may be less severe for negligence. *See In re Froelich*, 838 A.2d 1117, 1118 (Del. 2003), wherein the attorney did not have a system in place for verifying whether the documents prepared by an outside paralegal company were accurately handled. He was unaware of the number of outstanding checks from real estate closing until his wife, a certified paralegal, reviewed the materials and informed him of the problem. The attorney made immediate attempts at rectifying the situation. Due to his voluntary disclosure and efforts at rectifying the issues, the court found him merely negligent and publicly reprimanded him.

As could be expected, many of the problems in the partnership deal with money, from the more mundane accounting practices to the flagrant misappropriation of funds.

> Although a managing partner cannot guarantee absolutely the integrity of the firm's books and records, it is the managing partner's responsibility to implement reasonable safeguards to ensure that the firm is meeting its obligations with respect to its books and records. As the Lawyers' Fund points out, meeting these responsibilities need not pose an onerous burden for the managing partner. It is, however, a serious responsibility.
>
> [. . .] Finally, even if we concluded there was no evidence that [the attorney] explicitly or implicitly directed the invasion of client trust funds, we still find clear and convincing evidence on this record that [the attorney] engaged in knowing misconduct. We agree with the Lawyers' Fund's assertion that the "sustained and systematic failure" of a managing partner to supervise a firm's employees to ensure compliance [. . .] may not be characterized as simple negligence. A lawyer who accepts responsibility for the administrative operations of a law firm stands in a position of trust vis-à-vis other lawyers and employees of the firm. The managing partner must discharge those responsibilities faithfully and diligently.

In re Bailey, 821 A.2d 851, 864-865 (Del. 2003).

All the ethical requirements regarding supervision of any employee have the same underlying theory. However, a supervising attorney is held more responsible for the acts and omissions of a subordinate lawyer and less responsible for those of his partners. Generally, partners are absolved of responsibility for their fellow partners' actions where there is no knowledge of the wrongdoing and where there are procedural safeguards in place. This is not necessarily the case where a subordinate attorney is involved. In *Kus v. Irving*, 736 A.2d 946 (Conn. Super. 1999), the court noted that the liability rules for partnerships were applicable and the ethical rules did not expand the liability as between law partners. As the other partners had no knowledge of the one partner's wrongdoing, they were protected from liability under the general business partnership rules. The court noted that a different conclusion would result if the other partners had supervisory authority over the miscreant attorney. The more experienced supervising attorney can be held liable for negligent acts of the subordinate lawyer because the ABA Model Rules impose not only a general safeguarding obligation as discussed above, but also require that the supervising attorney makes reasonable efforts to oversee that class of lawyers. It is not enough to let the procedural processes in place at the office function as all the supervision the subordinate lawyer is subject to; supervision requires a more active role. The additional supervision requirements work in tandem to ensure that the subordinate lawyer learns how to work within the ethics rules because these requirements place the burden on the supervising attorney to guarantee the supervision. Becoming a competent, ethical attorney requires this kind of "apprenticeship." The court found it "troubling" that there "was the lack of a review mechanism which allowed an associate's work to be reviewed and guided by a supervisory attorney." *In re Cohen*, 847 A.2d 1162, 1166 (D.C. 2004). The real issue was that the supervisory attorney, although she may not have had actual knowledge of ethical violations, should have exercised prudence and competence and therefore, "reasonably should have known" about the status of the matters handled by the subordinate lawyer. *Id.* at 1167 (emphasis added).

These rules do not necessarily impose vicarious liability, or what can be called "passive" responsibility, under a *respondeat superior* theory, but rather impose an active ethical duty upon the supervising attorney. The mere fact of the professional relationship does not create the responsibility. Part of a senior attorney's duty is to actively supervise lawyers that report to her. This responsibility can be broken down into three obligations, as shown in Figure 9.2. It is clear that liability will attach where the supervising attorney has actually ordered the offensive conduct. The subordinate lawyer is not absolved of responsibility if it is a clear ethical violation, but the supervising attorney does not absolve herself of responsibility because it was not she herself who violated the ethical rules. Accountability cannot be delegated; the supervising attorney will remain "on the hook." If, as a result of the supervision, the senior attorney learns of the violation and either condones it by doing nothing (**ratification**) or fails to act to prevent or lessen the consequences of the violation (avoidance, or **mitigation**), she is just as guilty of the **malfeasance** as the acting attorney. Essentially, the failure to act to remediate the violative actions of the subordinate attorney is an unethical omission with sanctionable consequences.

By placing some responsibility on the senior management of a firm, the rule prevents those attorneys who have the most influence over the

subordinate attorney
An attorney who must report to a supervising attorney, who then takes ultimate responsibility for the work product's compliance with the firm's ethical practices.

ratification
The adoption, as one's own, of the words or actions of another person.

mitigation
The lessening of the harmful effects of a course of action.

malfeasance
A wrongful, unethical, or tortious act.

FIGURE 9.2 ▶
HOLDING THE
SUPERVISING ATTORNEY
RESPONSIBLE

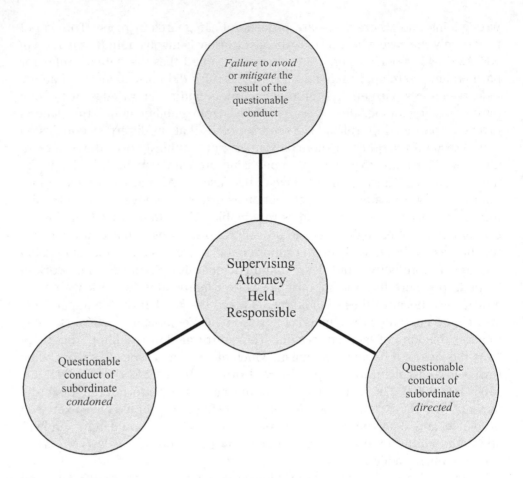

atmosphere of the firm from turning a blind eye to the behavior of the firm's attorneys. While partners are not required to guarantee that other attorneys in their firm will not violate the Rules of Professional Conduct, ignoring their supervisory responsibilities can lead to sanctions for those running the firm.

Undoubtably, the supervision of attorneys by other attorneys in their firm is one of the most effective methods of preventing attorney misconduct. However, that supervision must be reasonably competent or it is meaningless and that failure in itself can encourage unethical behavior. In situations where supervising attorneys fail to make reasonable efforts to ensure their subordinates follow the Rules of Professional Conduct, if the disciplinary proceedings only punished the individual attorney who committed the violation, the environment that fostered the attorney's unethical conduct would be allowed to continue.

In re Anonymous Member of South Carolina Bar, 552 S.E.2d 10, 14-15 (2001).

Clearly, this method of self-policing and the resulting accountability for all attorneys in a law firm maintains the integrity of the entire justice system and the confidence of the public in entrusting their most sensitive legal matters to it. Each ethical obligation builds upon another one, becoming more specific as to the duty to ensure that the law firm operates within the boundaries of ethics. Procedures must be implemented to ensure a means to monitor the activities of the attorneys in the firm; a supervisory attorney must take an active role in guiding the conduct of subordinate lawyers to ensure that they conform to the ethical rules; and finally, any attorney may be liable for the unethical acts of another lawyer in the firm if she has either ordered the violative conduct or knowingly ratified the conduct. A supervisory attorney will be liable for a subordinate attorney's unethical conduct if she knows of it and fails to act to either stop it or lessen the impact of it.

SUPERVISORY RESPONSIBILITY FOR NONLAWYERS

Just as attorneys are responsible for assuring that the other lawyers in the firm act in a manner that comports with the relevant ethical codes, so they must ensure that all nonlawyers employed by them follow the ethical rules that bind attorneys. Indeed, the ABA Model Rules explain the supervising attorney's responsibility for nonlawyers using the very same language they use regarding subordinate lawyers. To permit nonlawyer assistants to act in a way that is impermissible for the attorney is to completely undercut the ethical rules and render them useless, as the attorney could circumvent them by delegating a task to a nonlawyer in his employ. This rule applies to all persons retained by the attorney to assist them in his practice. It applies not only to the paralegals and legal secretaries, but also to the investigators and experts retained. "Ethical considerations are as applicable to representatives of lawyers as to lawyers themselves. Further, not to impose these rules when a lawyer's [representative] acts improperly would render the rules relatively meaningless." *In re Environmental Ins. Declaratory Judgment Actions*, 600 A.2d 165, 168 (N.J. Super. Ct. Law Div. 1991) (internal citations omitted).

There is a range of roles and skills that the support system of nonlawyers renders to the attorney. The extent of supervision needed depends upon the role and knowledge of the assistant. What is certain is that the attorney cannot delegate ultimate responsibility for the legal functions of these persons and must account for their ethical performance. Further, when attorneys delegate legal work to these **paraprofessionals**, clients must always understand their role in the rendering of the legal services. Without this comprehension, the client is not in a position to evaluate to whom she should be speaking and to what extent that paraprofessional can render assistance to the client. The client would be unable to alert the attorney to any issues that might pose an ethical issue during the course of the paraprofessional's work if this understanding were not accomplished. Without the client's input, the attorney could not comply with her obligations to supervise and to fix any problem that the nonlawyer assistant had created. *See Mays v. Neal*, 938 S.W.2d 830, 834 (Ark. 1997), wherein the court stated: "In sum, we must conclude, [. . .], that [the attorney] failed to properly delegate his legal work and responsibilities and failed to properly supervise work delegated to his assistants. If he had, he

paraprofessional
A person with the appropriate education, knowledge, and training to perform specialized work under the supervision of another professional who has the ultimate responsibility for the collaborative work.

IN-CLASS DISCUSSION

Arnold Jones usually handles family law and wills; however, on occasion he will handle some personal injury claims on behalf of his injured clients. As the majority of his practice does not consist of handling the money or property of his regular clients, he delegates the day-to-day management of both his trust and his operating bank account activities to his paralegal, Annie, whom he has employed for over 15 years. Arnold has given Annie authority to use his signature stamp to deposit money to both his trust and his operating accounts and to write checks from both accounts. Annie's office duties also include opening Arnold's mail, including his bank statements. Every year, Arnold uses an outside, professional accountant to reconcile transactions or activities involving his operating and trust bank accounts.

The office received two checks for a recent settlement in a personal injury matter: one from the insurance company and the other from the defendant directly for medical expenses. Annie endorsed the client's signature on the two checks, because Arnold usually obtains this kind of permission from his personal injury clients. This practice ensures that the settlement monies are available in a shorter time frame for disbursement. In conjunction with this, Annie used Arnold's signature stamp to make a deposit into the trust account.

This time, Annie knew that she would not be able to pay her rent. She decided to endorse the medical expense check over to herself because she didn't think anyone would miss that smaller check and she could repay the trust account before the accountant checked it. Arnold knew nothing of these transactions.

Should Arnold be held responsible for Annie's actions? Why or why not? Would you suggest different procedures in this office in order for it to comply with the ethical requirements?

This scenario is loosely based on *State ex rel. Oklahoma Bar Ass'n v. Mayes*, 977 P.2d 1073 (Okla. 1999).

would have been in the position at the least to have tried to resolve the questions that continued to resurface during his legal representation of [the client]."

Interestingly, ABA Model Rule 5.3 (Responsibilities Regarding Non-Lawyer Assistants) was used to defeat the attempt to regulate the paralegal profession independently. Recall from Chapter 2 the discussion surrounding *In re Opinion 24 of Committee on Unauthorized Practice of Law*, 607 A.2d 962 (N.J. 1992), as it relates to the unauthorized practice of law. ABA Model Rule 5.3 supplements the attorney's obligations to prevent the UPL by his support personnel by also requiring that there be procedures in place to ensure compliance with the rules. These may include ethics training in-house or sponsoring the nonlawyer's attendance at continuing legal education seminars. The paralegal, as the closest paraprofessional to the attorney, and one who is "extremely aware of the potential ethical dilemmas of the legal profession," is also responsible for his own conduct to a degree. *In re Opinion No. 24*, 607 A.2d at 971.

> Although fulfilling the ethical requirements of RPC 5.3 is primarily the attorney's obligation and responsibility, a paralegal is not relieved from an independent obligation to refrain from illegal conduct and to work directly under the supervision of the attorney. A paralegal who recognizes that the attorney is not directly supervising his or her work or that such supervision is illusory because the attorney knows nothing about the field in which the

paralegal is working must understand that he or she is engaged in the unauthorized practice of law. In such a situation an independent paralegal must withdraw from representation of the client. The key is supervision, and that supervision must occur regardless of whether the paralegal is employed by the attorney or retained by the attorney.

Id. at 127.

The court felt that the proper supervision of an attorney negated the need for a separate body to oversee, certify, or otherwise regulate the paralegal profession. The court stressed that the crux of the question regarding paralegals and the practice of law is the direct supervision of the attorney to ensure that all ethical requirements have been fulfilled. Essentially, the supervising attorney must make sure that the paraprofessional, whether employed or retained as an independent contractor, is performing all her duties as if she were an attorney. This is a clear instance of the interrelatedness of the ethics rules and underscores the importance of accountability.

This obligation of supervision is not relieved just because the supervising attorney has the utmost confidence in the abilities of her nonlawyer assistant. The rule regarding ethical supervision does not assume that the lawyer's assistant does not have the requisite knowledge or competence. It must assume that she does. Indeed, if the attorney were to delegate work to the assistant, she could do so only if the assistant were competent and capable of handling that aspect of the matter. Instead, this rule is designed to provide security and accountability on the part of the supervising attorney; an attorney never has the excuse that it was someone else's fault because that attorney did not do the actual work that was unacceptable even where that "someone else" had the requisite skill and knowledge to complete the task. This is the reason some states have amended their particular local ethics rules to forbid the hiring of a disbarred attorney as a legal assistant in almost any capacity (i.e., paralegal, office manager, etc.). It is only under the strictest of guidelines that a disbarred or suspended attorney may be employed in the law office. This requires that the disbarred or suspended attorney perform only preparatory work for the supervising attorney. This work must not involve client contact. "Any contact with a client is prohibited. Although not an inclusive list, the following restrictions apply: a suspended or disbarred lawyer may not be present during conferences with clients, talk to clients either directly or on the telephone, sign correspondence to them, or contact them either directly or indirectly." *In re Reinstatement of Parsons*, 890 So. 2d 40, 45 (Miss. 2003), citing *In re Wilkinson*, 834 P.2d 1356, 1362 (1992). *See also In re Chavez*, 1 P.3d 417, 424 (N.M. 2000) ("An unlicensed person may not use a licensed attorney simply as a facade to cover up the fact that he or she is engaging in the unauthorized practice of law.") There is a great temptation to let this disbarred attorney work without the same amount of supervision that another nonlawyer assistant would receive, because the supervising attorney knows that the disbarred attorney has the training and education to do the job assigned. This is an unacceptable practice.

These rules recognize that lawyers generally employ non-lawyers in their practice, including secretaries, investigators, clerks, and paralegals, and that such individuals assist the lawyer in the efficient rendition of the lawyer's professional services. However, a lawyer is completely responsible for the work product of his non-lawyer assistants and must give the assistants appropriate instruction and supervision concerning the ethical aspects of their employment. While appropriate delegation of tasks to non-lawyer assistants is allowed and encouraged, a lawyer may never permit non-lawyer assistants to engage in activities that constitute the practice of law or to hold themselves out as lawyers. The key to appropriate delegation is proper supervision by the lawyer, which includes adequate instruction when assigning projects, monitoring of the progress of the project, and review of the completed project. It is the lawyer's responsibility to see that his non-lawyer employees understand these limitations.

Applying these principles to the instant matter, there is little doubt that respondent failed to adequately supervise [the disbarred attorney]. The record demonstrates that respondent gave [the disbarred attorney] a free hand to meet with clients, handle legal fees, correspond with attorneys and insurance adjusters, render legal opinions, and negotiate settlements. Unquestionably, the evidence in the record in support of Counts I and II proves in a clear and convincing fashion that respondent violated Rules 5.3 and 5.5(b). Furthermore, respondent engaged in conduct prejudicial to the administration of justice when he permitted a legal pleading to be "notarized" with his "signature" by [the disbarred attorney], then filed into the public record.

In re Comish, 889 So. 2d 236, 244-245 (La. 2004) (citations omitted).

The court made it very clear that the supervising attorney had to actively oversee the disbarred attorney's work, not just be available for the disbarred attorney to consult with him where the disbarred attorney felt he needed assistance with handling a matter. The contact with clients is perhaps the most serious of the ethical violations because of the resulting harm that may occur. Another court severely sanctioned the supervising attorney because he had been warned of the potential harm. *See In re Gaff*, 524 S.E.2d 728 (Ga. 2000). In sum, any nonlawyer assistant must be supervised; the degree of review will vary depending upon the experience and track record of the person in question, but there must be that ultimate accountability on the part of the supervising attorney.

RESEARCH THIS

Find a case in your jurisdiction, either state or federal, that discusses an attorney's failure to properly supervise a non-attorney member of the staff (paralegal, secretary or other). What was the sanction imposed upon the attorney? Do you think it was fair in the situation? Why or why not?

PROFESSIONAL STATUS OF THE PARALEGAL

Many law offices consider paralegals to be indispensable professionals and integral to the structure and function of their organizations. Attorneys rely on paralegals' knowledge, skill, and training to accomplish complex legal tasks that otherwise would have to be performed by the attorneys. While attorneys are unquestionably considered professionals, there has been a considerable amount of debate as to the status of paralegals as "white-collar professionals" under the United States Department of Labor (DOL) regulations of the Fair Labor Standards Act. The distinction made between exempt and non-exempt employees serves to distinguish those employees who are covered by minimum wage and overtime regulations and those who are not. White-collar professionals are exempt. Employers are not required to pay a minimum wage or overtime pay to these professionals. The criteria for exempt status as a professional can be generally stated as follows:

1. The employee is salaried at a certain minimum. His wages are not subject to reductions or variations depending on the quality of the work or the amount of time worked in a week.
2. The employee is performing non-manual work that requires the exercise of discretion and independent judgment related to the management of the business of the employer.
3. The work requires advanced knowledge acquired through prolonged specialized intellectual instruction.

These three requirements for exempt status are the characteristics of a good paralegal. However, the DOL did not find that the paralegal profession as a whole qualified under all three conditions. The two most important factors discussed, which still form the basis for controversy, are "the exercise of discretion and independent judgment related to the management of the business" and "knowledge acquired by a prolonged course of specialized intellectual instruction."

The DOL asserted that paralegals do not exercise independent judgment because their work consists of using a set of skills and well-established techniques to formulate a course of action. These decisions are also confined to clearly defined parameters of action. The definition of discretion and independent judgment must relate to the management and business operations of the employer in order for an employee to qualify as exempt. The DOL relied on the ABA's rules against the unauthorized practice of law to support this position:

> [A] delegation of legal tasks to a lay person is proper only if the lawyer maintains a direct relationship with the client, supervises the delegated work, and has complete professional responsibility for the work produced. The implication of such strictures is that the paralegal employees you describe [in the request for a formal opinion from the DOL] would not have the amount of authority to exercise independent judgments with

regard to legal matters necessary to bring them within the administrative exception.

Additionally, an exempt employee must have acquired specialized academic training as a prerequisite for entrance into the profession. "The best prima facie evidence that an employee meets this requirement is possession of the appropriate academic degree." Herein lies the problem for paralegals. As discussed previously, paralegals are not required to have a particular undergraduate degree or graduate certificate in order to be employed as paralegals. Paralegals can have degrees in various fields of study; a great deal of their knowledge is acquired through hands-on working experience, as in an apprenticeship. "The learned professional exemption also does not apply to occupations in which most employees have acquired their skill by experience rather than by advanced specialized intellectual instruction." 29 C.F.R. § 541.301(d). The subsequent section, 29 C.F.R. § 541.301(e), clarifies the DOL's generally applicable position:

> **(7) Paralegals.** Paralegals and legal assistants generally do not qualify as exempt learned professionals because an advanced specialized academic degree is not a standard prerequisite for entry into the field. Although many paralegals possess general four-year advanced degrees, most specialized paralegal programs are two-year associate degree programs from a community college or equivalent institution. However, the learned professional exemption is available for paralegals who possess advanced specialized degrees in other professional fields and apply advanced knowledge in that field in the performance of their duties. For example, if a law firm hires an engineer as a paralegal to provide expert advice on product liability cases or to assist on patent matters, that engineer would qualify for exemption.

However, despite this broad determination, the DOL recognizes that every paralegal's employment situation and job responsibilities can differ in the amount of discretion and independent judgment exercised. Further, many paralegals do hold advanced specialized degrees, and the educational background of each paralegal can be analyzed to determine whether it comports with the exempt status requirements. The DOL's formal opinion in 2005 was based on an inquiry into six different paralegals. Their education ranged from little formal postsecondary education to a Masters in Business Administration (MBA) degree and national paralegal certifications. None of these paralegals met the requirements for exempt status. However, in *Austin v. CUNA Mut. Ins. Soc.*, 240 F.R.D. 420 (W.D. Wis. 2006), a "law specialist" sued her employer for failure to pay overtime. The employee argued that she and others in similar positions were non-exempt employees and therefore were entitled to overtime pay for hours worked in excess of 40 per week. To qualify for the position of "law specialist" within the Office of General Counsel, an applicant "needed a general college degree, a paralegal education or equivalent experience." *Id.* at 423. The plaintiff, Austin, had a Bachelor's degree in legal assistance and criminal justice and at the time of suit had worked as a paralegal for more than 25 years. At CUNA the paralegal plaintiff was responsible for managing cases where claims against the insurance had been filed. After a restructuring, her duties increased

> to include maintaining the litigation team's "Knowledge Management" database. To maintain the Knowledge Management database, plaintiff was required to read briefs from outside counsel and opinion letters from in-house lawyers, summarize the content of the brief or opinion letter, and index the summary by topic so it could be found again if similar issues arose in later cases.

> *Id.* at 427.

The court found that this type of work was included in the kind that requires the exercise of discretion and independent judgment directly related to management or general business operations. This kind of work includes, but is not limited to, the following:

> work in functional areas such as tax; finance; accounting; budgeting; auditing; insurance; quality control; purchasing; procurement; advertising; marketing; research; safety and health; personnel management; human resources; employee benefits; labor relations; public relations; government relations; computer network, internet and database administration; legal and regulatory compliance; and similar activities.

> *Id.* at 428-429, citing 29 C.F.R. § 541.201(b).

Employees who act as advisers or consultants to their employer's clients or customers perform work that is considered to be "directly related to management or general business operations." *Id.*, citing 29 C.F.R. § 541.201(c). Austin's work in assuring that her employer's insurance policies were properly administered and the contested claims were managed with outside counsel was considered "directly related to the [employer's] general business operations and crucial to its functioning." Therefore, under this element, performing work directly related to the management of the employer, the legal specialist was considered exempt.

The second element discussed, independence of the employee, also was decided in the employer's favor. The paralegal was found to be exempt from overtime. The court was careful to explain that

> [a]lthough the exercise of discretion and independent judgment implies that the employee has authority to make an independent choice, free from immediate direction or supervision, the term "discretion and independent judgment" does not require that the decisions made by an employee be free from review or that the employee have unlimited authority.

> *Id.* at 430, citing 29 C.F.R. § 541.202(c).

The number of times that the employee actually deviates from the standard practice of her employer is not determinative of her actual authority to do so. Austin had the discretion to reject outside counsel's recommendations on a particular matter if she disagreed with them. The fact that she rarely did so was not dispositive of that factor. The paralegal had the authority to act independently and to exercise discretion in handling cases worth up to $50,000. The fact that the paralegal could commit her employer to such a sum of money without supervisory approval was indicative of her independent authority. On this element as well, the paralegal was found to be exempt from overtime.

ATTORNEYS' INDEPENDENCE OF BUSINESS JUDGMENT

The ethical rules also prescribe the way in which lawyers may associate with other lawyers and nonlawyers in order to preserve the independence of the profession. Attorneys must always maintain their first loyalty to their clients; any interference that may result from a business association or fee payment arrangement is not permitted. While ABA Model Rule 5.4 has many subsections, its essence underscores the integrity of the individual attorney and the firm, which must remain free of outside influences. A point previously discussed must be underscored here: An attorney cannot share his fee with any nonlawyer; legal fees earned are a result of legal work that only an attorney can render. The reasoning behind all the restrictions on fee sharing is that no outside person without legal training should have any say in or any reward for legal services rendered. There are certain situations that may look like fee-sharing but are not; they are merely a function of the business of the office. A law firm may:

1. Pay money into the estate of a deceased attorney of the office over a reasonable period of time pursuant to an employment or benefit agreement.
2. Pay money to the estate or representative of a deceased, disabled, or disappeared attorney for the purchase of that attorney's practice.
3. Include nonlawyer employees in a firm retirement plan or other compensation plan, even where that plan is based on a profit-sharing arrangement. This practice encourages attorneys to take care of all their employees, regardless of their status as "attorney" or lack of it.
4. Share fees with a nonprofit organization that employed or otherwise recommended or retained the attorney in that matter for which the court awarded the fees. This exception encourages an attorney's predilection to charity.

RESTRICTIONS ON PARTNERSHIP

No attorney may include any nonlawyer in a partnership where the enterprise entails the practice of law. All partners must be attorneys, in order to preserve the integrity of the practice and to keep it free of any influences from the nonlawyer partners who may have different business goals and views from the attorney and who are not constrained by the professional rules of ethics as

SPOT THE ISSUE

Wanda is an attorney engaged in labor, wage, and hour practice with her paralegal William. They are trying to stir up more business and so send out this letter:

Dear Members of the Labor Union:
   We are so sure that we can champion your cause for fair labor practices in the courts of this state that we will gladly donate 20 percent of our portion of any recoveries made by your individual members back into the union.
   Signed, Wanda and William

   Wanda also had William contact the Employers' Association and make essentially the same offer.
   What, if any, ethical problems are involved with these letters?

REEL TO REAL

Watch *A Civil Action* (the 1998 film starring John Travolta, Robert Duvall, and William H. Macy) and keep your eye out for factors that may cloud an attorney's independent judgment and cause him to pursue a case to a bitter end. What do you think the triggers were to lead to this result? Do you think this happens in real life? Why or why not? What would you have done differently?

SURF'S UP

Technology and access to the internet have consolidated many services traditionally performed in the offices of lawyers. Real estate professionals, financial planners, tax preparers, and providers of probate and trust services all perform such services, and none of these are legal entities. Often these services are bundled into one service company, and many times their services are available online. The legal community must respond to this practice and can encourage service companies to take the step that foreign service companies have taken: mergers with law firms. This is referred to as "multidisciplinary practice."
   For more information on this subject, refer to the ABA's *Commission on Multidisciplinary Practice*.

attorneys are. This is not to say that attorneys cannot enter into business relationships with nonlawyers at all; what the ethical rule prohibits is a business wherein legal services are rendered. An attorney is free to form any other association with any other person for any other legitimate business purpose—just not a purpose that would involve the practice of law.

Finally, to further ensure that the attorney maintains her independent business judgment, without threat of compromise due to monetary incentive, the ethics rules disapprove of an attorney's accepting payment from any person other than her client. If that type of financial arrangement is made, the attorney cannot be influenced in any way by the desires of the third-party payor in making decisions about the case. This is true even where the attorney is in-house counsel for a company. This potential conflict arises quite often in the insurance context. The client is the insured policyholder; however, payment comes from the insurance company. There is tension, because the insured's claim may not be in the best financial interest of the insurance company. The attorney must do her best to follow the procedures set forth by the insurance company, but the company cannot in any way direct the course of the representation of the insured.

> Because a defense attorney is ethically obligated to maintain an independence of professional judgment in the defense of a client/insured, an insurance company possesses no right to control the methods or means chosen by the attorney to defend the insured. As one court stated, an insurance company cannot control the details of the attorney's performance, dictate the strategy or tactics employed, or limit the attorney's professional discretion with regard to the representation [of the insured].

Barefield v. DPIC Companies, Inc., 600 S.E.2d 256, 270 (2004).

The practice of law is considered exclusive territory for attorneys, and any potential threat to compromise their independent trained and skilled judgment is discouraged. It is ultimately the attorneys who have responsibility, and they are the only ones accountable under the ethics rules for breaches of the clients' trust.

MULTIJURISDICTIONAL PRACTICE

Attorneys

Clients can be located anywhere, particularly with the modern trend of globalization; almost every business is national on some scale. Corporate counsel has a particularly tough job trying to keep up with the interstate goings-on of their clients. As discussed in Chapter 1, each state must admit the attorney before its bar. Anyone not licensed in that particular state who practices there commits the unauthorized practice of law, even if that person is an attorney licensed in another state. Further, an attorney licensed in the state cannot assist another in practicing in that state where the other attorney is not licensed.

Recognizing the impossibility of counsel's ability to be admitted in every state where the client may be involved in legal issues, the ABA Model Rules provide two ways for the preferred and retained attorney to practice outside of the state in which he is licensed. The first admits the attorney to practice law in that jurisdiction *pro hac vice* (for this time only), in litigation or on another temporary basis. It is as if the attorney is a member of the bar of the other state for that matter alone.

There are certain attendant qualifications that must be satisfied in order for the out-of-state attorney to properly represent her client in the non-admitted jurisdiction. First and foremost, the attorney must be in good standing in her home state. This is a protective measure and easily understood: The non-admitted jurisdiction does not want a substandard attorney practicing and potentially harming its own citizens. If the attorney was not good enough to practice in her home state, she surely isn't good enough to practice outside of it. Secondly, the out-of-state attorney must associate with an attorney who is admitted in the jurisdiction in which the out-of-state attorney wishes to practice. This is an "insurance policy" of sorts for the outside jurisdiction; one of its own has vouched for the credentials of the out-of-state attorney and will remain actively involved in the representation in the matter. In this way the court can be assured that the out-of-state attorney can be made aware of the local rules of procedure, standards of conduct, and local laws.

Attorneys may, in good faith, perform preliminary work in preparation for the legal work in the outside jurisdiction without fear of committing the UPL. Courts have understood that in order to evaluate the need for admission into another state, there must be some investigation into the potential cause of action. Therefore, meetings, interviews, and document reviews are permitted without a temporary admission in that state. The object of the court is not to hamper the process and client representation, but rather to protect the integrity of the court system. The rules are designed to permit these activities—but only if they are related to a proceeding in which the out-of-state attorney is involved with the client in her home state. If the matter involves appearances before the court, then the attorney should seek formal admission by motion for *pro hac vice* status. Other tribunals do not have such a formal status. If the attorney regularly handles construction arbitrations in her home state for her client, she may be able to handle the same in another state for that client. The standard applied is whether those out-of-state activities "arise out of or are otherwise reasonably related to the lawyer's practice" where she is admitted to practice. RESTATEMENT (THIRD) OF LAW GOVERNING LAWYERS § 3 (2000). Comment e to this Section addresses this situation:

> Transactional and similar out-of-court representation of clients may raise similar issues, yet there is no equivalent of temporary admission pro hac vice for such representation, as there is in litigation. Even activities that bear close resemblance to in-court litigation, such as representation of clients in arbitration or in administrative hearings, may not include measures for pro hac vice appearance. Some activities are clearly permissible. Thus, a lawyer conducting activities in the lawyer's home state may advise a client about the law of another state, a proceeding in another state, or a transaction there, including conducting research in the law of the other state, advising the client about the application of that law, and drafting legal documents intended to have legal effect there. There is no per se

bar against such a lawyer giving a formal opinion based in whole or in part on the law of another jurisdiction, but a lawyer should do so only if the lawyer has adequate familiarity with the relevant law. It is also clearly permissible for a lawyer from a home-state office to direct communications to persons and organizations in other states (in which the lawyer is not separately admitted), by letter, telephone, telecopier, or other forms of electronic communication. On the other hand, as with litigation, it would be impermissible for a lawyer to set up an office for the general practice of nonlitigation law in a jurisdiction in which the lawyer is not admitted as described in § 2 [of the Restatement (third) of the Law Governing Lawyers].

There is, of course, another "catch-all" for legal services that do not fit in to either *pro hac vice* or other temporary admission categories. If the out-of-state attorney needs to perform legal services for his client and these services are reasonably related to the duties he performs in his home state, then he may reasonably expect that his activities out of state will be permissible. The goal of this rule is really to preserve efficiency. Requiring a client to retain outside counsel in another jurisdiction and then educating that counsel regarding the matter and the client's background may delay the proceedings and unduly burden the client.

Directly addressing the issues of national and global organizational clients, the ABA Model Rules provide that in-house counsel can operate in the non-admitted jurisdiction to provide the kind of services that are needed by the organization and that the attorney normally provides in the home jurisdiction. Recall that the client is only the organization and the attorney cannot represent the officers or employees individually in another jurisdiction, even if such representation would be related to the business entity that the attorney does represent. The ABA Model Rules on Multijurisdictional Practice really apply to in-house corporate lawyers, government lawyers, and others who are employed to render legal services to an organizational employer doing business in many different jurisdictions. The lawyer's ability to represent the employer outside the jurisdiction in which the lawyer is licensed generally serves the interests of the employer and does not create an unreasonable risk to the client and others, because the organizational client is in the best position to evaluate that individual lawyer's qualifications to perform the extrajurisdictional work. There may also be situations where the attorney is permitted to practice in that outside jurisdiction due to some other procedural rule or by federal law.

Paralegals

Because paralegals are not licensed as of yet in any state, they are not subject to the same restrictions as attorneys. They may freely move from state to state and practice their craft under the supervision of any admitted attorney. The paralegal's ethical obligations remain the same: to adhere to the local ethics rules and avoid the unauthorized practice of law in any jurisdiction. There may come a time when this issue becomes complicated, if some states license paralegals and some do not. This will potentially pose a practical obstacle to moving to another jurisdiction. As of now, however, this is not the case. Voluntary certifications do not affect a paralegal's right to practice across jurisdictions.

RESTRICTIONS ON THE RIGHT TO PRACTICE

Independence is the cornerstone of an attorney's practice. Outside influences are not permitted to sway the manner in which the attorney handles himself, his clients, or his advocacy. Clients are free to choose whichever attorney they feel most comfortable with and whom they trust with their matters. Acknowledging that business competition is a fact of life in the practice of law as well, ABA Model Rule 5.6 seeks to balance the clients' interest in selecting the attorney of choice, an individual attorney's interest in maintaining his livelihood, and the law firm's interest in its business.

Broadly speaking, no lawyer or firm can restrict another lawyer's right to practice law in any setting. This means that **covenants not to compete** are unenforceable against attorneys. When an attorney leaves a firm, he cannot be told if, where, when and with whom he may practice law. His professional autonomy is intact. The only agreement an attorney and the firm can make is one that restricts retirement benefits should the attorney seek to disengage from the firm. This is purely a business condition and does not relate to the practice of the individual lawyer, but rather restricts potential benefits that would accrue towards retirement based upon the profitability of the firm that the attorney is leaving. Any other financial disincentives to the departing attorney to restrict his practice, whether in client base, time, or geographic scope, are invalid.

covenant not to compete
An employment clause that prohibits an employee from leaving his job and going to work for a competitor for a specified period of time in a particular area doing substantially similar work.

> [W]hile the provision in question does not expressly or completely prohibit a withdrawing partner from engaging in the practice of law, the significant monetary penalty it exacts, if the withdrawing partner practices competitively with the former firm, constitutes an impermissible restriction on the practice of law. The forfeiture-for-competition provision would functionally and realistically discourage and foreclose a withdrawing partner from serving clients who might wish to continue to be represented by the withdrawing lawyer and would thus interfere with the client's choice of counsel.
>
> *Moskowitz v. Jacobson Holman, PLLC*, 2015 WL 6830266 at 4 (E.D. Va. 2015), citing *Cohen v. Lord, Day & Lord*, 75 N.Y.2d 95, 551 N.Y.S.2d 157, 550 N.E.2d 410, 411 (N.Y. 1993).

The "provision in question" that was struck down in the *Moskowitz* case stated in the firm's operating agreement that an equity partner who withdraws and takes clients with him will forfeit 50 percent of his payout. *See also Whiteside v. Griffis & Griffis, P.C.*, 902 S.W.2d 739, 744 (Tex. App. 1995) (The withdrawing attorney would be required to sell his stock back to the law firm at book value, "specifically defined to exclude good will unless [departing attorney] did not practice law or compete against corporation within 300 miles of designated city for period of five years." The court found this impermissible. "While an indirect financial disincentive against competition or a reasonable covenant not to compete may have vitality in a commercial setting, we believe the strong public-policy concerns surrounding client choice warrant prohibition of lawyer restrictions.").

Just as the firm cannot restrict an attorney's right to practice in order to protect its business activities, a client cannot hold that kind of power over an attorney's right to practice. The ethical rules do not allow a client to hold this kind of power over an attorney. This restriction may take the form of an agreement that the settlement will be entered into only as long as the attorney agrees not to represent other similarly situated clients against the restriction-requesting opposing party. In this situation, the opposing party has restricted the right of an attorney to take on other clients against her. This is what happened in *In re Conduct of Brandt*, 10 P.3d 906 (2000). The defendant offered to settle the matter with plaintiffs' counsel only if plaintiffs' counsel would agree to then leave those clients after the settlement was final and be retained by the defendant. Essentially, the defendant was trying to buy out the plaintiffs' attorneys and make it impossible for them to bring future claims against the defendant. The court found that the discussion during settlement negotiations of future employment that would disqualify the plaintiff's attorney in the future from representing that type of client by virtue of a conflict of interest once he was retained by the defendant was violative of Rule 5.6(b).

> First, permitting such agreements restricts the access of the public to lawyers who, by virtue of their background and experience, might be the very best available talent to represent these individuals. Second, the use of such agreements may provide clients with rewards that bear less relationship to the merits of their claims than they do to the desire of the defendant to 'buy off' plaintiffs' counsel. Third, the offering of such restrictive agreements places the plaintiff's lawyer in a situation where there is conflict between the interests of present clients and those of potential future clients.

> *Id.* at 918, citing ABA Comm. on Ethics and Prof'l Responsibility, Formal Op. 371 (1993).

This restriction on the attorney's right to choose which future clients he would take on is an unacceptable restriction on his right to practice law. Attorneys, as a whole, are fiercely independent, and their judgment cannot be permitted to be clouded with financial concerns and potential negative ramifications for their livelihood.

While the business of the practice of law is similar in many ways to other businesses, there are certain conditions that the attorneys in law firms must consider in order to remain faithful to their ethical obligations. There are added burdens on supervising attorneys to ensure not just the quality of the work being done in their firms, but also the ethical manner in which those legal tasks are performed. Due to the nature of their relationship with their clients, attorneys must be vigilant to ensure that there are no "cracks" in the system into which some work could fall; they would be held accountable for the mistake. The practice of law is relatively unforgiving of mistakes, as each one, even little ones, may have a substantial impact on the rights and liabilities of clients. That is also the reason attorneys must maintain their independence from outside influences. Those who are not attorneys do not understand the ethical implications of every element of the practice of law and are not held responsible for any transgression. Therefore, the attorney must depend upon his individual professional judgment alone in handling a matter for a client. Clients have every right to expect this duty of care from their attorneys and have a right to freely choose which attorney will represent their interests. This is the reason no outside influences, monetary incentives, or other restrictions on attorney access are permitted.

Summary

It is important for paralegals to understand the organizational structure of the law firm in order to implement best ethical practices. Supervising attorneys have the greatest responsibility for ensuring ethical compliance in the law office. Paralegal managers have the same sort of duty with regard to the supervised paralegals. The hierarchical structure of the branches within the office may seem duplicative with regard to ethical responsibility; however, that organization serves to ensure that the highest ethical standards of conduct are followed.

Office organization and ethical responsibility also affect the employment status of the personnel. Clearly, attorneys are white-collar employees exempt from wage and overtime mandates from the Department of Labor. Exempt employees:

1. Are salaried at a certain minimum. Their wages are not subject to reductions or variations depending on the quality of the work or the amount of time worked in a week.

2. Perform non-manual work that requires the exercise of discretion and independent judgment related to the management of the business of the employer.

3. Have advanced knowledge acquired through prolonged specialized intellectual instruction.

Paralegals have generally been considered "blue-collar," non-exempt employees. This has advantages and disadvantages, for the individual earning the overtime and for the profession as a whole and its public perception as a true "profession."

Ethics in a law office must be free from monetary incentives or other restrictions. It is imperative that attorneys maintain their independence in order to properly function as ethical professionals. This independence takes the form of rules regarding partnerships and prohibiting attorneys from forming business partnerships with nonlawyers or giving outside third parties control over the decision-making process of the attorney.

The globalization of business has also affected the practice of law. Attorneys are traditionally licensed in only one or two states, whereas businesses are often national in scale. This creates problems associated with multijurisdictional practice. Paralegals are not confined in a state-specific licensure scheme, so they are not restricted to any geographical area of practice.

Key Terms

Covenant not to compete   Paraprofessional
Malfeasance   Ratification
Mitigation   Subordinate attorney
Negligent misconduct   Supervising attorney

Review Questions

MULTIPLE CHOICE

Choose the best answer(s) and please explain *why* you chose the answer(s).

1. An attorney may share legal fees with a paralegal in the following circumstances:
   a. Pursuant to a written fee agreement with attorney's firm
   b. After a reasonable time after attorney's death
   c. Never
   d. As long as the paralegal agrees to accept whatever portion is deemed fair and appropriate by the attorney that reflects the value of the paralegal's services

2. A supervisory attorney is responsible for the conduct of:
   a. All subordinate employees
   b. Her partners
   c. All attorneys and support staff to whom she assigns/delegates work
   d. Only full-time attorneys, not any independent contractors like freelance paralegals

3. Multijurisdictional practice:
   a. Requires that an attorney pass the bar exam in every jurisdiction in which she intends to practice

b. Is never permitted by unadmitted attorneys

c. Requires that the attorney make a motion to be admitted *pro hac vice*

d. Is becoming more prevalent, and there are many ways to deal with the issues

EXPLAIN YOURSELF

All answers should be written in complete sentences. A simple yes or no is insufficient.

1. Describe the circumstances under which an attorney could apply for *pro hac vice* status in a matter.

2. When may an attorney share legal fees with a non-attorney?

3. Explain the difference between an attorney's responsibility for unethical conduct of one of his partners and the attorney's responsibility for one of the paralegals in the firm.

4. When is it permissible for an attorney to accept payment for legal services from a third-party non-client?

5. Should a law firm be able to require its paralegals to sign a covenant not to compete as part of their employment contracts?

FAULTY PHRASES

All of the following statements are *false*. State why they are false and then rewrite each one as a true statement. Do not simply make the statement negative by adding the word "not."

1. An attorney cannot be responsible for another lawyer's misconduct if the supervising attorney did not specifically direct that course of action.

2. A supervising attorney will not be ethically sanctioned for the actions of a subordinate if no harm was caused to the client.

3. An attorney may form a business with a non-attorney if only a small portion of that business involves the practice of law.

4. Covenants not to compete are enforceable against former attorney-employees as long as they are reasonable.

5. An attorney may practice in a jurisdiction in which she is not licensed as long as it is the kind of matter in which she customarily engages in her home jurisdiction.

6. A paralegal in another jurisdiction can assist an out-of-state attorney to prepare a legal matter for submission to the court.

7. A supervising attorney has no ethical obligation to correct the mistakes of his paralegal.

PORTFOLIO ASSIGNMENT

Write Away

Prepare a persuasive brief for submission to your local paralegal association explaining your position on the impact "non-exempt" (blue-collar) or "exempt" (white-collar) status has on the paralegal profession as a whole. There is no right or wrong answer, as good arguments can be made for the impact of either status on both the public's perception of the profession and an individual paralegal's opinion about her chosen career. Be sure to include enough detail in your argument to support your position.

Case in Point

■ As this case clearly demonstrates, office management requires that attorneys have the ability to *effectively* oversee the work performed by their paralegals. It is not enough to merely structure a firm to place paralegals under an attorney. The attorney must have a means of substantively reviewing the paralegal's work and ratifying the content to ensure that it complies with the attorney's professional ethical obligations.

State Bar of Michigan
Standing Committee on Professional and Judicial Ethics
Opinion Number R-1
December 16, 1988

SYLLABUS

A lawyer having direct supervisory authority over a nonlawyer shall make reasonable efforts to ensure that the person's conduct is compatible with the professional obligations of the lawyer.

A lawyer cannot adequately supervise the quality of legal services rendered by six civilian and eighteen prison paralegals to a prospective client population of 4,500 prisoners located in prisons throughout the State of Michigan, including the Upper Peninsula.

TEXT

The director of a legal services organization (LSO) is considering submitting a bid on a legal assistance program which the Michigan Department of Corrections may start pursuant to a recent federal court order. Under the program, LSO would provide assistance, not in-court representation, in post-conviction

and conditions of confinement cases to prisoners at six locations in four Michigan prisons. The staff would consist of one lawyer/director, six civilian paralegals and eighteen prisoner paralegals. The duties of the lawyer/director would include the hiring, training and supervision of the six civilian and eighteen prisoner paralegals at six separate locations throughout the state. While the duties would include other aspects of administering the program, it is the hiring, training and necessary supervision of the paralegals which generate concern. The civilian paralegals would be entrusted with a variety of responsibilities which would include visiting and assisting prisoners in segregation units, responding in writing to requests for legal assistance and supervising an average of three prisoner paralegals and an unknown number of prisoner law library clerks. The prisoner paralegals would be entrusted with duties which would include providing legal research and drafting assistance to civilian paralegals and conducting conferences with prisoner clients.

Estimates of new caseloads range to 1,718 persons per year. Additionally, there are currently 226 open cases. Case estimates are difficult because, first, the prisoner population at any prison constantly changes, thus even though capacity for a given facility may be 500 prisoners, several thousand persons could pass through the facility each year. Second, the percentage of persons requesting assistance fluctuates depending on the quality and speed of the responses. The more efficient and better staffed the LSO becomes, the greater the number of requests.

May the lawyer/director of LSO ethically accept the responsibility of supervising 24 or more nonlawyers or any number of nonlawyers in so many locations? May civilian paralegals under the lawyer/director's control provide on-site supervision over the work of prisoner paralegals?

Any issue addressed relative to the activities of paralegals operating under the supervision of licensed lawyers must be viewed with *MRPC 5.3* and *5.5* in mind. *MRPC 5.5* forbids a lawyer from assisting a person who is not a member of the bar in the performance of activity that constitutes the unauthorized practice of law. The comment following *MRPC 5.5* specifies that paragraph (b) does not prohibit a lawyer from employing the services of paraprofessionals and delegating functions to them, so long as the lawyer supervises and retains responsibility for the delegated work.

What constitutes the unauthorized practice of law in a particular jurisdiction is a matter for determination by the courts of that jurisdiction. Questions of law are beyond the scope of the Committee's jurisdiction. The inquirer is referred to the following resources: *State Bar v. Cramer, 399 Mich. 116 (1976)*; Vol. 59 No. 3 MBJ 173 (1980); Vol. 62 No. 8 MBJ 624 (1983); and Vol. 56 No. 8 MBJ 704 (1977).

MRPC 5.3 further defines and enhances the responsibility of the supervising lawyer by providing that not only does that lawyer have a responsibility not to aid in the unauthorized practice of law, but also must assure that the nonlawyer over whom he or she has direct supervisory authority does not engage in conduct incompatible with the professional obligations of the lawyer, or engage in conduct that would be a violation of the Michigan Rules of Professional Conduct if engaged in by a lawyer. The comment following MRPC 5.3 notes that the measures employed in supervising nonlawyers should take account of the fact that they do not have legal training and are not subject to professional discipline. It also says a lawyer should give nonlawyers personal assistance, appropriate instruction, and supervision concerning the ethical aspects of their employment, particularly regarding the obligation not to disclose information relating to representation of the client, and that the lawyer should be responsible for the work product of the nonlawyer.

Given the parameters set forth in *MRPC 5.3* and *5.5*, for the lawyer/director to assume the responsibilities as outlined would be to invite a violation of *MRPC 5.5* and could lead to a violation of *MRPC 5.3*. While it appears as though the legal assistants under the terms of the plan described would not be expected to engage in the practice of law by making court appearances or providing actual, technical representation, there is a distinct possibility and, in all likelihood, a probability that they will be engaged in advising clients of their legal rights. The proposed legal assistance program will utilize the Technical Assistance Manual on Offender Legal Service prepared by the American Bar Association's Commission on Correctional Facilities and Services as a guide in delivering services. The manual repeatedly stresses two things—the exigencies under which prisoners are operating in securing even the most basic legal services and the role of the lawyer in providing those services. It discusses in detail such prisoner problems as illiteracy, confusion, unsophistication and lack of access to the system. It also expressly contemplates the extreme reliance of such individuals upon the advice provided by the lawyer. Under the proposal submitted here for examination, it is clear that for all practical purposes, it would be the paralegals (civilian and prisoner) upon whom the bulk of the reliance for advice would be placed. This system does not provide the quality legal service to which the clients are entitled and the Michigan Rules of Professional Conduct require of lawyers.

The reasoning behind the adoption of the rules forbidding the unauthorized practice of law operates to substantiate the opinion that the activities proposed under the plan would present an unavoidable ethical dilemma. Initially, it must be remembered that paralegals are not subject to state licensure, nor are they subject to the requirements and regulations imposed upon the members of the legal profession. A nonlawyer who undertakes to handle legal matters is not governed as to integrity or legal competence by the same rules that govern the conduct of the lawyer. A lawyer is not only subject to license regulation, but also is committed to high standards of ethical conduct. The public is best served in legal matters by a highly trained and regulated profession committed to such standards. Only lawyers are subject to the special fiduciary duties in the lawyer-client relationship and to the regulations of an effectively policed profession.

Moreover, a layperson who seeks legal service often is not in a position to judge whether he or she will receive proper professional attention. The entrustment of a legal matter may well involve the confidences, the reputation, the property, the freedom or even the life of the client. Proper protection of members of the public demands that no person be permitted to act in the confidential and demanding role of a lawyer unless he or she is subject to high standards. In this instance, those who seek the legal services are particularly disadvantaged, and additional care must be taken to assure that the reliability of the assistance they receive is not impaired.

Given the fact that the lawyer/director would be expected to hire, train and supervise a minimum of six civilian and eighteen prisoner paralegals at six separate locations, it is difficult to perceive how the lawyer/director could provide the direct supervision required for each client and realistically assume full responsibility to each and every client for the actions or nonactions of the legal assistants. Moreover, given the number of paralegals and their locations as well as the potential caseload, it is our opinion that it would be physically impossible for the lawyer/director to provide the supervision required to avoid violating *MRPC* 5.5 or *MRPC* 5.3. Additionally, the direct supervision of the prisoner paralegals and an unknown number of prisoner law library clerks by civilian paralegals would be direct contravention of the requirement that they be directly supervised by a lawyer.

Finally, the ABA manual recommends a lawyer to prisoner ratio of one lawyer to four hundred prisoners per year, divided between a variety of "advice only" and more time consuming court action cases. In the plan being considered, the lawyer to client ratio would be one lawyer to 1,944 prisoners. That ratio is incompatible with the appropriate delivery of legal services and the stated purpose of the program to provide meaningful assistance to the prison population.

For the foregoing reasons, the inquirer's participation as supervising lawyer in the LSO as presently structured would violate *MRPC* 5.3 and 5.5.

Source: Reprinted from Westlaw with permission from Thomson Reuters.

Chapter 10

Advertising and the Solicitation of Clients

Chapter Objectives

The student will be able to:

- Understand the reasons for stricter restrictions on attorney advertising
- Discuss the kinds of advertising that are and are not acceptable under the rules and identify those advertisements that are "borderline"
- Distinguish between salesmanship and false and misleading legal advertising
- Identify situations where solicitations are prohibited
- Describe the proper use of the terms "specialization" and "certification"

This chapter will examine *what* an attorney or paralegal may say to a client in soliciting business, to *whom* the legal professional may speak in drumming up more business, *how* the advertisements and solicitations for new business must comply with certain ethical requirements, and *why* these requirements are different from those for normal commercial advertising.

Honesty and advertising—not two words one usually puts together in the same sentence. However, when it comes to attorneys' attempts at gaining clientele, they must go hand in hand. An attorney's commercial advertisement will never air during the Super Bowl, when the funniest and wittiest marketing powerhouses are out for the American consumer. However, in the short time that attorney advertising has been permitted, it has come a long way; whether for better or for worse is not yet evident.

OVERCOMING THE BAN ON ATTORNEY ADVERTISING

Historically, attorneys were not permitted to advertise their services *at all.* The first ABA Model Code of Ethics, written in 1908, prohibited any means of advertising other than printed business cards with the attorney's contact information. The legal profession, through many different associations, courts, and individuals, has sought to maintain the integrity and honor of this noble profession. The codes of conduct were slow to change: Until the late 1970s, only listings in the Yellow Pages that contained contact information, basic personal background information, and area of practice were permitted. The United States Supreme Court, in its landmark decision regarding attorney advertising, *Bates v. State Bar of Arizona*, 433 U.S. 350, 367, 97 S. Ct. 2691, 2700 (1977), acknowledged "that an advertising diet limited to such spartan fare would provide scant nourishment." The crux of the issue in *Bates* was the publication of a fee schedule in the attorneys' advertisements for legal services. The Court examined the origins of the "no advertising" rule and determined that it was no longer relevant and could not withstand a Constitutional First Amendment challenge for freedom of speech, albeit **commercial speech**.

commercial speech
A category of expression that has only limited protection under the United States Constitution because its purpose is not the dissemination of an idea, but rather the garnering of monetary rewards through commerce.

> It appears that the ban on advertising originated as a rule of etiquette and not as a rule of ethics. Early lawyers in Great Britain viewed the law as a form of public service, rather than as a means of earning a living, and they looked down on "trade" as unseemly. Eventually, the attitude toward advertising fostered by this view evolved into an aspect of the ethics of the profession. But habit and tradition are not in themselves an adequate answer to a constitutional challenge. In this day, we do not belittle the person who earns his living by the strength of his arm or the force of his mind. Since the belief that lawyers are somehow "above" trade has become an anachronism, the historical foundation for the advertising restraint has crumbled.

> *Id.* at 371-372.

Word of mouth, reputation in the community, and other referral systems had worked when the geographic practice areas of attorneys were relatively limited. But just as every segment of the economy has grown and become specialized, attorneys must reach out to find those with whom they can do business. The Supreme Court in *Bates* found the opposition without merit in their main arguments against attorney advertising and the publishing of legal rates. While attorneys do charge different rates for different clients and matters depending on many variables unique to each case, the general advertisement will not necessarily be misleading because of "the inherent lack of standardization in legal services." *Id.* at 373. The advertisement will not be able to completely address the particular concerns of each client and will not be able to give full background regarding the competency of the attorney, but that is not an excuse to ban that kind of speech altogether. The very nature of advertisement has those problems inherent in it for any service. "A rule allowing restrained advertising would be in accord with the bar's obligation to facilitate the process of intelligent selection of lawyers, and to assist in making legal services fully available." *Id.* at 377. The Supreme Court took a very balanced approach in protecting lawyers' interest in obtaining clients by the right exercise of free speech and the need to regulate these advertisements so as to protect the public from those who might take this opportunity to mislead the public for increased profits.

Indeed, globalization and the trend towards the **"unbundling" of legal services** can lead to significant advertising implications. Those attorneys who are engaged across international boundaries are potentially also subject to a different set of ethical rules of practice and advertisement. The unbundling of legal services wherein the lawyer agrees to provide only limited representation in a client's matter based (usually) upon discrete tasks, may also make the fee structure for these separate legal services more susceptible to ethical concerns. "When describing unbundled services, the lawyer should be clear and accurate about what fees and costs may be charged and should avoid using terms that are likely to be misleading if they cannot be substantiated. Characterizations of a lawyer's fees such as 'cut-rate,' 'lowest,' and 'cheap' are likely to be misleading if those statements cannot be factually substantiated." Colorado Bar Ass'n Ethics Comm. 101, "Unbundling/Limited Scope Representation" (2016), at 14, citing Colo. RPC 7.1, cmt. [5]. ABA Model Rule 1.2(c), as modified in 2002, does permit the unbundling of legal services upon the condition that "the limitation [of the scope of legal services] is reasonable under the circumstances and the client gives informed consent." The ABA's website has an "Unbundling Resource Center" for more information about this type of client representation.

unbundling of legal services
The component parts of a client's legal matter are broken down and the attorney provides representation to only an agreed-upon segment of the client's needs; also known as "limited scope representation."

REEL TO REAL

John Grisham's 1997 film *The Rainmaker* (starring Matt Damon and Danny DeVito, and directed by Francis Ford Coppola) portrays a young, freshly admitted attorney's struggle to start his career and obtain clients. Pay attention to the ethical interplay between Damon's character and DeVito's as they take on clients.

MODERN RESTRICTIONS ON ATTORNEY ADVERTISEMENT AND SOLICITATION

solicitation
An attorney's attempt to gain business, usually directed at a specific individual or group and involving an invitation to consult with the attorney regarding legal matters.

The current ABA Model Rules permit advertising and certain types of **solicitation** (invitations to consult with the attorney on a matter). Each jurisdiction has a set of rules based upon these general principles, but the ways in which the individual state courts have interpreted them can vary widely. At the core, an attorney is prohibited from making a false or misleading statement with regard to the lawyer or his services. Advertisements and solicitations must not misstate a fact or law or omit a fact such that the statement is rendered misleading.

"Materially Misleading" Communication

materially misleading
Characterized by false information upon which a member of the intended audience would rely in making a decision.

The rules of advertisement and solicitation apply to any and every kind of communication: oral, written, or electronic. The key to their application is the understanding of what constitutes a "materially misleading" communication. As in other contexts, a statement is material if it is one upon which a person would base some or all of his decision. If it doesn't make a difference to that person, then it isn't material. Different audiences, the targets of the advertising and solicitation, may consider different factors to be material, so it is important to examine the circumstances surrounding the communication as well. "[B]ecause the public lacks sophistication concerning legal services, misstatements that might be overlooked or deemed unimportant in other advertising may be found quite inappropriate in legal advertising." *Bates*, at 383. Unlike the typical commercials for consumer products that the public is used to seeing and hearing, legal advertisements must remain relatively conservative. They cannot use such normal marketing language as "best" or "premier"; nor can they make any comparative or statistical claims based upon their track record or client information. What attorneys cannot do in marketing their services is an exhaustive list of "shall-nots." If the advertisement presents self-praise, creates unjustified expectations in a potential client based upon past success stories, offers an opinion as to the quality of the attorney's services, implies that the attorney's services are better than those of others, omits the name of the firm or the attorney, or contains unverifiable information, it is misleading under the multitude of court cases dealing with this issue.

NFPA addresses specific misrepresentations that may tempt a paralegal to bolster her résumé or credentials. NFPA EC 1.7 (d) and (e). NALA's Guideline 1, although not specifically tailored to this particular issue, provides that legal assistants should disclose their status as legal assistants. (See Figure 10.1.)

Advertisements can be found to be misleading for a number of reasons. One advertisement that was found to be misleading came from the Florida law firm of Pape and Chandler. It featured an image of a pit bull. The court forced them to change their logo because the image of the pit bull was

NFPA EC 1.7

(d) A paralegal shall not practice under color of any record, diploma, or certificate that has been illegally or fraudulently obtained or issued or which is misrepresentative in any way.

(e) A paralegal shall not participate in the creation, issuance, or dissemination of fraudulent records, diplomas, or certificates.

"inherently deceptive because there is no way to measure whether the attorneys in fact conduct themselves like pit bulls so as to ascertain whether this logo and phone number convey accurate information. [. . .] In addition, the image of a pit bull and the on-screen display of the words "PIT-BULL" as part of the firm's phone number are not objectively relevant to the selection of an attorney. The referee found that the qualities of a pit bull as depicted by the logo are loyalty, persistence, tenacity, and aggressiveness. We consider this a charitable set of associations that ignores the darker side of the qualities often also associated with pit bulls: malevolence, viciousness, and unpredictability." *The Florida Bar v. Pape*, 918 So. 2d 240, 244-245 (2005). The Florida court "would not condone an advertisement that stated that a lawyer will get results through combative and vicious tactics that will maim, scar, or harm the opposing party, conduct that would violate our Rules of Professional Conduct. [. . .] Yet this is precisely the type of unethical and unprofessional conduct that is conveyed by the image of a pit bull and the display of the 1-800-PIT-BULL phone number." *Id.* at 246. Essentially, all the glitz and tools of the marketing industry are to be kept out of legal advertisement. To keep tabs on all of these new requirements and secure enforcement, attorneys must keep copies of all their advertisements on file for three years.

Another common method of misleading a potential client in advertisement is to refer to past, positive results in handling client matters. Particularly concerning are those advertisements that contain statements regarding high-dollar amount recoveries. While all of this information may be true, and indeed, it would have to be under the strict ethical rules of attorney advertising, it may nevertheless remain misleading to the average consumer. "The inclusion of past results in advertising carries a particularly high risk of being misleading. Such advertising will require the inclusion of more information than most types of advertising in order to comply [with the Ethical Rules]." *Rubenstein v. Florida Bar*, 72 F. Supp. 3d 1298, 1305 (S.D. Fla. 2014) (This case dealt with attorney advertisements on billboards, television, and radio. The court made special note that these types of media contain very little room or time for detailed information to be conveyed to the consumer.) Particularly prone to deception are those advertisements that contain client testimonials. They tend to contain impermissible "self-laudatory" commentary and inaccurate statements regarding attorney fees and costs. "The commercials that contained information about

IN-CLASS DISCUSSION

Review these recent attorney advertisements from a divorce law firm. The first billboard placed by the law firm had larger-than-life photos of a female torso practically bursting out of a lace bra and black thong and an extremely toned and muscular male torso. The firm was required to replace the ads with a less provocative ad. The second is the "more tame" replacement. It features photos of a female in a see-through negligee and thigh-high stockings and a male unbuttoning his shirt, again to reveal very toned abs. In neither advertising campaign were the faces of the models shown. The firm's slogan remained unchanged and reads, "Life is Short. Get a Divorce." The law firm defends its advertisements and clearly plans to continue this line of advertising. See http://www.fgalawfirm.com/ for more information about the Fetman, Garland and Associates law firm. Also note that attorney Corri Fetman is the female figure in the ads and is a former *Playboy* model and writes a column for the online magazine. Are these advertising tactics ethical under the relevant rules? Why or why not?

the firm's past successes, while not inaccurate, were self-laudatory and inherently misleading. Despite the praises of the former clients, there is no way to objectively determine whether the results achieved by the firm were exceptional, adequate, or poor, or even whether the firm was instrumental in the outcome of the cases. Comments about past successes may create unjustified expectations of similar outcomes in the future without taking into account the peculiarities of the particular cases." *Disciplinary Counsel v. Shane*, 692 N.E.2d 571, 573 (Ohio 1998). In cases where a contingency fee arrangement is in place, statements that clients who do not prevail will not be responsible for attorney's fees are also deceptive as even losing clients are still responsible for costs. "While it may be true that respondents' practice is not to bill costs and expenses to clients who lose, paragraph three of the standard fee agreement that respondents entered into with their clients provided that itemized "case" expenses "shall be billed to the Client over and above any billings for Attorney's fees." Indeed, were the respondents to agree otherwise, they would violate [the Rule], which states that a lawyer may advance expenses of the case "provided the client remains ultimately liable for such expenses." *Id.* citing *Zauderer v. Office of Disciplinary Counsel*, 471 U.S. 626, 652, 105 S. Ct. 2265, 2282, 85 L. Ed. 2d 652, 673 (1985)

Technology

The ways in which attorneys market their services are changing with both industry and the technology. For example, the New York State Unified Court System has continuously adopted new advertising rules for the state's attorneys as new technologies arise and become commonplace. These changes attempt to address a host of issues related to common marketing tactics and modes of communication, particularly concerning the use of the internet. The new rules cover computer-accessed communication, which they define as

> any communication made by or on behalf of a lawyer or law firm that is disseminated through the use of a computer or related electronic device, including, but not limited to, web sites, weblogs, search engines, electronic mail, banner advertisements, pop-up and pop-under advertisements, chat rooms, list servers, instant messaging, or other internet presences, and any attachments or links related thereto.

See NYRPC 1.0(c)

Further, New York adopted Disciplinary Rule 2–101 (G) which prohibits the use of pop-ups unless they are contained solely on the firm's individual website (e.g., the ads cannot populate as a banner ad as you are browsing the internet). As to the "catchiness" of the attorney's advertisement, endorsements or testimonials from clients with pending matters are prohibited, as are portrayals of a judge or a fictitious law firm. No mottos, nicknames, trade names or other titles that are not directly related to the business of the law firm and/or mislead, are not to be used, nor are attorneys permitted to use celebrity voice-overs in their commercials. Full disclosure of the fact that an advertisement uses actors or dramatizations must be prominently made; it must clearly display the label "ATTORNEY ADVERTISEMENT."

Social media has made this area of legal advertising decidedly murkier. Certainly, a lawyer's blog and Facebook page about the practice and updates and reflections on developments in the law could attract clients. What is less clear is the rise of Twitter as a viable source of information. Could tweets be considered advertisements if they contained certain information about the tweeting lawyer's practice? Given its unique character (an account holder does not control her audience like the ability to "friend" on Facebook), its word limit (140 character limit), and its ubiquity, Twitter poses a real challenge for lawyers and ethicists. Fortunately, the State Bar of California Standing Committee on Professional Responsibility and Conduct issued a detailed Formal Opinion (No. 2012-186) on this topic. The Committee held generally that "The restrictions imposed by the professional responsibility rules and standards governing attorney advertising are not relaxed merely because such compliance might be more difficult or awkward in a social media setting." Their determinations of five representative tweets appeared to hinge upon whether the tweeted statement relates to the "availability for professional employment." In a single month the attorney tweeted the following:

1. "Case finally over. Unanimous verdict! Celebrating tonight."
2. "Another great victory in court today! My client is delighted. Who wants to be next?"
3. "Won a million dollar verdict. Tell your friends and check out my website."
4. "Won another personal injury case. Call me for a free consultation."
5. "Just published an article on wage and hour breaks. Let me know if you would like a copy."

The Committee determined that the first and last tweets were not attorney advertisements as they did not specifically reach out to prospective clients, but are rather statements of fact about the attorney's activities. However, the remaining three statements are clearly solicitations for prospective clients to get in touch with the attorney. The second tweet violates the advertising rules because it relates a client testimonial; "an attorney cannot advertise that he has performed his services so well that his clients consequently praise him" *Id.* at 4. That second tweet also contains language of positive results and "could be interpreted as asking who wants to be the next victorious client." *Id.* The third tweet clearly intends to advertise the attorney's services as it "ask[s] the reader to tell others to look at her website so that they may consider hiring her." The fourth also clearly solicits for new clients as "an offer of a free consultation is a step toward securing potential employment." *Id.* at 5.

The old adage "Let the buyer beware" is not applicable in the area of legal services. The courts and bar associations have unequivocally decided that the buyer in this case, the client, deserves extra protection from the potential overreaching of attorneys in their quest to increase their client bases. Many of the disciplinary boards of the states have contended with the issue of which communications will be permitted and which ones go too far and put the public at risk of misunderstanding the services provided by the advertising attorney. In discussing the content and method of delivery, the courts have come far since the days of an all-out ban. Indeed, as each new method of delivery has become available and widely used, the court has reevaluated the ethical rules pertaining to the content of legal advertising.

overreaching
Taking unfair commercial advantage of another by going beyond normal and reasonable means to obtain the desired result.

> The trial court found that the prohibition of "drawings, animations, dramatizations, music or lyrics" in attorney advertising did not pass constitutional muster under the United States Supreme Court's attorney advertising decisions. The factual finding underlying that conclusion was that such techniques, while they may be factually deceptive, are not inherently so. The trial court found what the record overwhelmingly supports, namely that the use of these techniques "are only inherently misleading in the sense . . . [of] inducing action more on the basis of emotion than rational thought." The trial court explicitly determined that, despite this emotional aspect of these techniques, their prohibition would "preclude the effective use of legal services advertising and constitute more extensive regulation than necessary to serve the governmental interests in precluding false, misleading, and undignified advertising." Prohibiting these techniques would result in "tombstone" ads that would not "accomplish the intended purposes of attention-getting, recall assistance (memory storage), and supplying substantive legal services information to the public." At the same time, the trial court stressed that its factual finding assumed not only that ads would be required to be truthful and not misleading, but also that the requirement that ads be presented in a dignified manner would be maintained. Clearly concerned with the irrational aspect of creative advertising, the trial court also noted that "careful monitoring and measurement of the effect on the public of the use of the techniques is obviously necessary and desirable."

Petition of Felmeister & Isaacs, 518 A.2d 188, 191-192 (1986).

IN-CLASS DISCUSSION

Discuss the following scripts from the television advertisements of law firms. Which do you think violate ABA Model Rule 7.1, prohibiting false or misleading communications? Why? Describe the elements of the commercial that are potentially misleading. What could you change about them to make them comply with the ethical constraints? (Ignore the fact that the name of the law firm has been omitted; assume there is one in the actual commercial.)

1. The advertisement, known as the "Strategy Session," depicts a conference room where actors portraying insurance adjusters are discussing a claim. An older man, the "senior adjuster," asks a younger man, the "junior adjuster," how the claim should be handled. The junior adjuster describes the claim as ". . . a large claim, serious auto accident" and suggests they try to deny and delay to see if the claimant will "crack." The senior adjuster then asks which lawyer represents the victim, whereupon the junior adjuster responds: "The XYZ Law Firm." A metallic sound effect follows and the senior adjuster, now looking concerned, states: "The XYZ Law Firm? Let's settle this one." At this point in the advertisement, a well-known actor appears on screen and advises viewers, "[T]he insurance companies know the name The XYZ Law Firm." He invites individuals who have been injured in an auto accident to tell the insurance companies they "mean business" by calling The XYZ Law Firm. The actor provides the firm's telephone number, which also appears at the bottom of the screen. *See In re Keller*, 792 N.E.2d 865 (Ind. 2003).

2. In four of the television commercials, former clients of the firm appear, talking about actual situations in which they have employed the law firm. In one of the presentations, a client says that the firm "fought the law all the way to the state Supreme Court and we won." A client in another presentation says, "They really fought for me. They were aggressive and settled things quickly. I never expected the large settlement they won for me." A third client says, "They made things happen. And they got results. If you have the right attorneys, you can fight City Hall." The fourth former client says, "They fought for me and got me a very good judgment. Take my word for it, they're the best." The attorney adds at the end of the commercial: "There's no charge unless we win your case. What could be fairer?" *See Disciplinary Counsel v. Shane*, 692 N.E.2d 571 (Ohio 1998).

3. The following two commercials are from the same law firm:

    a. The "Divorce Case" scene shows a couple discussing a division of their property. After they agree to split everything "right down the middle," the husband uses a power saw to cut through a table and a sofa while their dog looks on soulfully, possibly with some concern that he may suffer the same fate. The announcer then states:

    > When a marriage gets in trouble, everyone wants to be fair. But that's not always so easy. Our law offices can help you through those difficult times. Because we understand that people facing a divorce don't need any more problems than they already have.

    b. The "Bankruptcy Case" shows a man sitting in his living room in front of a television set with a bowl of popcorn. Two men come in and proceed to strip the room of all its furnishings, including the television set and finally the bowl of popcorn. The announcer then states:

    > When financial tragedy strikes you, you don't have to lose everything; there are laws to protect you. Bankruptcy laws. Our law offices can help you protect yourself, because the law is designed to serve ordinary people. So are our law offices.

    See Grievance Committee for Hartford-New Britain Judicial Dist. v. Trantolo, 470 A.2d 228 (Conn. 1984).

SURF'S UP

Browse the websites of some of your state's biggest law firms. Are they in complete compliance with your state's ethical rules regarding attorney advertising? Do you think they "push the envelope" in some respects? Describe how.

This type of review of attorney advertising has been extended to the more modern methods of marketing such as blogs *See Hunter v. Virginia State Bar ex. Rel. Third Dist. Committee*, 744 S.E.2d 611 (Va. 2013), and websites *See Bedoya v. Aventura Limousine & Transp. Service*, 861 F. Supp. 2d 1346 (S.D. Fla. 2012).

RECOMMENDATIONS AND REFERRALS

"Money changes everything" is an adage true in legal advertising as well as in other areas. Protecting the integrity of the profession from "buying" clients is ABA Model Rule 7.2. The ethical rules recognize that legal professionals will have to pay for commercial advertisements. This is against the normal prohibition forbidding attorneys to pay for referrals. The advertising medium is not referring or in any way endorsing the use of the attorney. All media, such as television, newspapers, websites, and other public means of dissemination, charge for the advertising time and space they provide. The rules, therefore, must allow the attorney to pay for such advertisements without violating the "no payment for referral" rule. Lawyers may not give anything of value to individuals for their assistance in getting the word out about the attorneys' services. This means they are not to give out cash, bonuses, awards, or presents or to barter their services for anyone who recommends their legal services.

The exception on the "bartering" for services is that an attorney may recommend that his clients seek the professional services of another lawyer or other professional. This professional referral is constrained; the attorney may have a mutual referral agreement ("you scratch my back, I'll scratch yours") with the other attorney or professional only if the agreement is not exclusive and the client is made aware of the agreement. This serves two purposes. First, the non-exclusivity rule assures that clients have a meaningful choice among professionals and that the referring attorney gives the best referral to the most appropriate professional, not the one to whom she is bound by agreement. Such agreements cannot interfere with the attorney's independent professional judgment. Second, the client's awareness of the reciprocal referral agreement is necessary so that the client is able to decide for himself whether to seek independent counsel or the service of another professional, knowing that the attorney may have some favorable bias toward the referred professional.

An attorney referral system can be a type of clearinghouse to funnel potential clients to the appropriate attorney in practice and geographical area. It makes all the difference whether the advertising system is for-profit or not-for-profit. The only acceptable referral system is a non-profit one, as the monetary compensation for referral is not permitted. There is a difference between a true referral system and a paid group advertisement, wherein a specific group of lawyers combine their resources to advertise their services. As long as the advertisement clearly indicates that the group commercial is not an attorney referral service and indicates the participating attorneys, the commercial is permissible. In *Alabama State Bar Ass'n v. R.W. Lynch Co., Inc.*, 655 So. 2d 982, 983 (Ala. 1995), the defendant advertising agency produced an "Injury Helpline" television marketing program. Several law firms or solo attorneys jointly purchased advertising to be included in the pool of attorneys listed on the "Injury Helpline" commercial. The 30-second commercial expressly states: "Advertising paid by sponsoring attorneys. Not a lawyer referral service." The attorneys' or firms' names and addresses appear on the commercial, and a 1-800 toll-free telephone number is provided for the viewer to call. The calls are received by an answering service and the caller needs to supply only her name, telephone number, and zip code. The court found this to be an acceptable form of group advertisement and that it was not a referral service. The distinction was important because the advertising agency was run for profit. This allows the potential clients to ascertain whether they will be assisted in making their choices based on need (as in a true referral service) or simply directed to an answering service that then transferred their calls to the lawyer who paid for the right to service clients in that geographic area. Where there may be any confusion on the part of the consumer, the attorney is to err on the side of caution and make sure that if it is a paid advertisement, that fact is explicitly and prominently indicated.

> When advertising is done through a vehicle which is not explicitly referenced as an advertisement, and is not readily known to consumers as a place of pure advertising (as, for example, the Yellow Pages would be), there is a possibility that the presentation and language could lead a reasonably informed consumer to believe that the listing has some sort of professional or authoritative imprimatur, as a kind of endorsement, such as an authorized lawyer referral service might give (e.g., a web page presented as "anti-trust lawyers.com," as a hypothetical). Such a presentation could, intentionally or inadvertently, thus mislead consumers into believing it was other or more than simply a paid advertisement, and carried greater weight.
>
> NJ Atty. Advert. Op. 36, 15 N.J.L. 48, 182 N.J.L.J. 1206 (2006) (The Committee on Attorney Advertising was presented with a question regarding website advertising.).

Whether an attorney seeks clients through advertising or referral, the real harm to the consumer is in the monetary incentive to generate further business. Further, a referral system could not advertise any of the participating attorneys' services in a manner that would violate any of the other rules regarding communications of legal services. Essentially, the advertisement or not-for-profit referral service may not deliver the information about the attorneys' services in a manner in which the legal professional himself would be prohibited from doing so.

An interesting case was brought before Maryland's Attorney Grievance Commission involving the work of a paralegal and her assistance in gaining clientele for her employer. The paralegal, who was very successful in the thriving personal injury firm that she wished to leave, contacted an attorney whose personal injury practice could use some bolstering. The paralegal assured the attorney that she could help because of her work experience and the fact that she had "lots of contacts and friends." Her new employment contract gave her an $80,000 a year salary and included a term that she would need to increase the firm's practice by acquiring one hundred personal injury files within a year. The paralegal's former firm brought charges against the paralegal and her new firm, alleging that she stole closed client file information and was unethically soliciting former clients for the new attorney. The trial court found that

> [The attorney] knowingly hired [the paralegal] not for her legal or secretarial skills but with the primary motive/purpose of obtaining the personal injury clients that could be delivered through [the paralegal]'s access to the white copy of the information forms from [her prior employer] and/or her own personal client contacts. Rule 7.2(c), the advertising rule, is the most appropriate one to apply to this violation. While this particular form of payment for referrals is a matter of first impression now before this Court, it is analogous to paying "runners" or "bird dogs" for referrals as discussed under 7.2(c). These are similar practices for which the Court has previously disciplined lawyers. [The paralegal] brought no specific qualifications that would justify such an exorbitant compensation package; thus, it is clear that she was being compensated for her services in bringing in clients.

> *Attorney Grievance Comm'n of Maryland v. Wills*, 705 A.2d 1121, 1124 (Md. Ct. App. 1998).

However, the Appellate Court of Maryland could not find that the sending of letters to the former clients associated with the paralegal's prior firm was in violation of the ethical rules pertaining to advertising or solicitation. While the salary was very high, it could be paid for both her paralegal skills and her advertising services. She merely prepared proper letters for distribution to potential clients. The letters themselves were not in violation of the rules for advertising and solicitation and, therefore, if the paralegal were performing a function that the attorney could ethically perform, even though those services were linked to paying her for her time in preparing advertisements, the paralegal was not in any violation either. The trial court's decision was reversed and the complaint dismissed. Compare this to an opinion from the Pennsylvania Legal Ethics committee, which found that giving a paralegal an extra paid

RESEARCH THIS

Find and compare two cases in your jurisdiction that deal with the propriety of attorney advertising: one which held that the advertising material was in compliance with your local rules and one holding that it was not. What were the defining factors that led to these opposite conclusions? What could you change about each one to get the opposite result? (i.e., what would have put the valid advertisement "over the line" and what would have kept the unethical one within the regulations?)

day off for referring a new client to the firm was impermissible. The relevant ethics rule prohibits lawyers from giving "anything of value" to nonlawyers as an "expression of thanks" for the referral. *See* PA Eth. Op. 2005-81 (Pa. Bar. Assn. Comm. Leg. Eth. Prof. Resp.), 2005 WL 2291089. Each jurisdiction may interpret this "value" question in its own way; the Arizona courts permit gifts valued at less than $100 and the D.C. courts have decided that attorneys may give nonlawyers "a cash payment or gift certificate in exchange for referrals, as long as the payment or gift is not contingent on the success of the case referred." *Id.*, citing DCB Legal Ethics Comm., Op. 286 (1998).

DIRECT CONTACT WITH PROSPECTIVE CLIENTS

Televised commercials, radio spots, and letters are all ways to reach out impersonally to potential clients. There is significantly more danger associated with in-person solicitation of clients. The directness, influence, pressure, immediacy, and surrounding circumstances may overpower the consumer into making a less than well-thought-out decision regarding the retention of the particular attorney. For this reason, legal professionals are prohibited from contacting potential clients "live." This is set forth in ABA Model Rule 7.3. The contact is considered "in person" or "live" if the communications can be made instantaneously between the attorney and client. This includes use of the telephone and electronic means of communication.

As in almost every other rule, there are exceptions to the general prohibition against contacting a prospective client in person. The first exception permits in-person or other "live" contact only if the other party is an attorney or if the contacting legal professional already has a relationship of some sort with the potential client. It guards the potential client's privacy first of all, but most of all it protects the potential client's ability to reflect upon the decision. The danger of pressure from one attorney to another is significantly less than that of pressure on a lay consumer who contacts a legal professional. Presumably, other attorneys are not influenced by the "silver-tongued" solicitor and understand their right to take the time to make an informed decision about retaining the contacting attorney. The second group excepted from this rule already knows the attorney and/or paralegal and therefore has reason to have and expect contact with her. An attorney or a paralegal has more to lose if certain strong-arm tactics are used with family, close friends, and former clients. Indeed, the attorney and/or the paralegal may be motivated to help these individuals not by monetary gain, but by a sense of duty and loyalty.

ambulance chaser
A derogatory term used to describe attorneys that make direct in-person or mailed solicitation to injured persons very shortly after an accident, so that they seem to be waiting at the ambulance door for them.

Most of the case law in this area of in-person solicitation involves the notorious **ambulance chasers**, those attorneys or their agents who contact victims shortly after their incidents in an effort to be retained. The danger here lies in the fact that the legal professional may engage in overreaching not only in selling his services immediately, but also in taking advantage of the potential client's vulnerability during this time. Attorneys and courts have taken this issue very seriously, as it potentially infringes not only on an attorney's right to pursue his livelihood, but also on the First Amendment right of freedom of speech (albeit commercial speech), which is entitled to less protection than other kinds of expression not fueled primarily for pecuniary gain. Two United States Supreme Court cases address this very issue of in-person solicitation. In the first, *Ohralik v. Ohio State Bar Association*, 436 U.S. 447, 98 S. Ct. 1912, 56 L. Ed. 2d 444 (1978), the attorney/acquaintance of the family of the injured visited her in the hospital and, over the course of a few days spent talking with her and her family, secured a contingent fee contract to represent her personal injury claim. The injured client fired the attorney a few days after signing the contract. The Court found that while the First Amendment does protect "restrained advertising" to address society's interest in obtaining information about the availability of legal services, each state has a countervailing interest in protecting its citizens against overreaching by attorneys in securing their services. *Id.* at 455. The Court found that "in-person solicitation of professional employment by a lawyer does not stand on a par with truthful advertising about the availability and terms of routine legal services." *Id.* Therefore, there is no comparison between the advertisements in *Bates, supra,* wherein a print advertisement set forth standard fees, and the in-person solicitation of business. While both advertise the availability of legal services, there are significant and material differences.

> Unlike a public advertisement, which simply provides information and leaves the recipient free to act upon it or not, in-person solicitation may exert pressure and often demands an immediate response, without providing an opportunity for comparison or reflection. The aim and effect of in-person solicitation may be to provide a one-sided presentation and to encourage speedy and perhaps uninformed decision-making; there is no opportunity for intervention or counter-education by agencies of the Bar, supervisory authorities, or persons close to the solicited individual.

> *Ohralik* at 457.

Whereas printed informational material, like *Bates*, offers potential clients the opportunity to make a reliable and informed decision, direct in-person or live solicitation does not. "Subsequent decisions, however, have made clear that the holding in *Ohralik* is narrow, and that "the constitutionality of a ban on personal solicitation will depend upon the identity of the parties and the precise circumstances of the solicitations." *Texans Against Censorship, Inc. v. State Bar of Texas*, 888 F. Supp. 1328, 1352 (E.D. Tex. 1995). For instance, some jurisdictions have held that telephone calls are not as invasive or persuasive as in-person solicitations and therefore may be a valid means of outreach to potential clients.

> In determining whether telephonic communications are a mode of expression "rife with possibilities for overreaching, invasion of privacy, the exercise of undue influence, and outright fraud," it is necessary to examine whether lawyers will be able to employ their arts of persuasion over the telephone to the same degree as in personal meetings with prospective clients. It appears likely that lawyers will be more limited in their ability to employ persuasive techniques over the telephone than in a face-to-face confrontation. In some face-to-face situations, such as the hospital room solicitation described in *Ohralik*, it may be particularly difficult for a consumer to end a conversation with a lawyer. With telephone solicitations, however, the consumer need only hang up the telephone receiver to end the matter. It is thus evident that the recipients of telephone solicitations have a much more effective means of ending unpleasant or harassing calls than those subjected to an in-person solicitation.

Id. at 1353 (internal citations omitted).

If the person with whom the attorney would like to make contact has made it known, either directly or through circumstance, that she does not wish to be contacted, the attorney must not solicit employment from that person. The rule is clear in its directive: "No means no." However, the rule also prohibits solicitation, either impersonal or face-to-face, that involves coercion, duress, or harassment. It is much harder to discern this situation. One circumstance is clear: Overzealousness in trying to be the first one to see the victim is in violation of that prohibition. In order to protect the public from these evils

SPOT THE ISSUE

Ernie, the insurance salesman, contacted Sally after Ernie saw her advertisement regarding Sally's insurance malpractice firm. Ernie asked Sally if she might consider hiring him to assist in finding plaintiffs for Sally's prospective class action suit against a large insurance company. Ernie said that other attorneys had utilized his services in the past. Sally hired Ernie as a paralegal in her firm and since he had such an extensive insurance background, simply gave him a client package that contained a client intake form, a set of questionnaires, and Sally's retainer agreement. Ernie contacted 100 potential clients and successfully signed 63 as clients using the supplied retainer agreement.

Discuss the possible ethical violations. For a hint, see *Mississippi Bar v. Turnage,* 919 So. 2d 36 (Miss. 2005).

proscribed by the rule, most, if not all, states ban attorneys from contacting victims in personal injury or wrongful death matters for 30 days. This gives the victim some "breathing room" to regain reason and objectivity regarding the incident. The courts, bar associations, and disciplinary boards are constantly trying to maintain or improve the public's perception of the legal profession. In an effort to adopt appropriate ethical rules to assist in this endeavor, the Florida Bar undertook a two-year study of the effects of lawyer advertising on public opinion. As a result of this study, the Florida Bar instituted a 30-day blackout period during which an attorney could not solicit the accident victims or their families. A lawyer referral service (Went For It, Inc.) challenged the constitutionality of the rule changes. The United States Supreme Court, once again, found that the public's interest in remaining free from overreaching or unduly influential communications from attorneys seeking employment outweighs the free speech concerns of the attorneys involved in purely commercial speech.

> While it is undoubtedly true that many people find the image of lawyers sifting through accident and police reports in pursuit of prospective clients unpalatable and invasive, this case targets a different kind of intrusion. The Bar has argued, and the record reflects, that a principal purpose of the ban is protecting the personal privacy and tranquility of [Florida's] citizens from crass commercial intrusion by attorneys upon their personal grief in times of trauma. The intrusion targeted by the Bar's regulation stems not from the fact that a lawyer has learned about an accident or disaster (as the Court of Appeals notes, in many instances a lawyer need only read the newspaper to glean this information), but from the lawyer's confrontation of victims or relatives with such information, while wounds are still open, in order to solicit their business. In this respect, an untargeted letter mailed to society at large is different in kind from a targeted solicitation; the untargeted letter involves no willful or knowing affront to or invasion of the tranquility of bereaved or injured individuals and simply does not cause the same kind of reputational harm to the profession unearthed by the Bar's study.

Florida Bar v. Went For It, Inc., 515 U.S. 618, 630, 115 S. Ct. 2371, 2379, 132 L. Ed. 2d 541 (1995).

disclaimer
A legal notice that serves to advise the recipient that the disseminator of the information will not be held responsible or liable for the content of the advertising.

There are technical requirements that apply to the above substantive provisions. The first attempts to protect the public by requiring a standard **disclaimer** on any and all attorney communications that seek to gain employment for the lawyer. The label "Advertising Material" must be prominently displayed, either printed or stated, as appropriate to the method of transmission. The second qualifies the substantive rules by providing an exclusion for prepaid or group legal plans. These potential clients may be solicited by the organization itself, as they are subscribers to the plan and on some level have consented to the direct solicitation for services. However, the participating attorney cannot herself contact these subscribers, and the attorney cannot be an owner or director of that organization. This underscores the dangers in direct attorney solicitation and the evils associated with paying for legal referrals.

FIELDS OF PRACTICE AND SPECIALIZATION

The last two ABA Model Rules on this subject are very specific in application and concern how the attorney represents himself or his firm to the public at large. Traditionally, most lawyers were involved in **general practice firms**, but there has been an increasing trend toward specialization in the profession. Attorneys and **boutique firms** are concentrating on one particular or a related group of legal matters. In order for any potential client to identify which attorney she should contact for assistance, it is necessary to permit these attorneys and firms to advertise their areas of legal practice.

This applies to the advertising rules in that an attorney may place an advertisement indicating that he is willing to take on a particular kind of case or class of plaintiffs without violating the rule against solicitation. In *Zauderer v. Office of Disciplinary Counsel of Supreme Court of Ohio*, 471 U.S. 626, 639-640, 105 S. Ct. 2265, 2276, 85 L. Ed. 2d 652 (1985), the United States Supreme Court held that where an advertisement was truthful and not misleading as to the facts of the type of litigation and that the attorney was handling such matters for other similarly situated plaintiffs, there was no ethical violation:

> The advertisement did not promise readers that lawsuits alleging injuries caused by the Dalkon Shield [an intrauterine birth control device] would be successful, nor did it suggest that [the attorney] had any special expertise in handling such lawsuits other than his employment in other such litigation. Rather, the advertisement reported the indisputable fact that the Dalkon Shield has spawned an impressive number of lawsuits and advised readers that [the attorney] was currently handling such lawsuits and was willing to represent other women asserting similar claims. The heart of the analysis as to the permissibility of advertising the area of concentration is the deceptive or misleading standard used in the other advertising rules.

It is extremely important to distinguish between an area of practice as a **specialization**, (an attorney who chooses to concentrate in a specific area) and a **certified specialist** in a particular area of law. A certified specialist must apply to her own state in order to be authorized to use such a title. Each state is in control of the areas in which it offers ABA-accredited certification programs, just as each state is in control of its own bar admission standards. There are a few national certification programs, such as the National Board of Trial Advocacy. These certifying boards all have some elements in common: They all have demanding standards for the applicants; require extensive experience in the area of specialization; and require continuing legal education, an exam, recommendations from judges, and other such credentials. (For detailed information on the areas in which an attorney can become certified, please consult the ABA Standing Committee on Specialization.) Thus, it is very different for an attorney to say she specializes in one area of the law rather than to claim to be a specialist in a type of practice. The attorney who

general practice firm
An attorney or firm that will handle almost any type of legal matter that is presented by clients.

boutique firm
An attorney or firm that handles only certain types of legal matters that are usually highly detailed and related to each other and that require specialized knowledge and experience.

specialization
An attorney who has chosen to practice in a certain area of the law and has developed a concentration in this kind of legal matter.

certified specialist
An attorney who has applied for and obtained state and bar acknowledgement of extensive knowledge and expertise in an area of law through demonstrable evidence of testing scores and experience.

concentrates in an area of law should make it very clear that she is not a specialist certified by any state or national body. To blur the line between the two is to invite an ethical infraction regarding the advertisement of the lawyer's services.

In 1990, the United States Supreme Court decided that an attorney had a First Amendment constitutional right to advertise his certification in a specialized area. The Court opined that while opinions as to the quality of an attorney's legal work are impermissible under the ethical rules, a designation from an accredited certifying body as to the background qualifications of an attorney are not, as they are verifiable statements that can indicate a certain level of quality that has been achieved. The state bar that opposed the attorney's right to list this credential on his letterhead contended that the statement may be misleading to potential clients.

> To the extent that potentially misleading statements of private certification or specialization could confuse consumers, a State might consider screening certifying organizations or requiring a disclaimer about the certifying organization or the standards of a specialty. A State may not, however, completely ban statements that are not actually or inherently misleading, such as certification as a specialist by bona fide organizations such as NBTA.

> *Peel v. Attorney Registration and Disciplinary Comm'n of Illinois*, 496 U.S. 91, 112, 110 S. Ct. 2281, 2292-2293, 110 L. Ed. 2d 83 (1990).

Similarly, paralegals who have earned a certified status through a paralegal association/organization as discussed in the first chapter have a right to use that designation. Relying on *Peel*, the New York State Bar Association determined that the "certified" status of a paralegal employed at the firm is subject to the same inquiry as the status of an attorney. As long as the association bestowing the credential is a bona fide organization, the standards for certification are objectively clear and the title is not misleading, the credential can be used.

A relatively new issue has developed in attorney "credentialing," the use of LinkedIn "endorsements." As discussed above, lawyers may not advertise that they are specialists in any area of law unless they have achieved that credential according to their state bar rules. However, LinkedIn allows other users to check boxes that indicate which skills the lawyer possesses. This is not an assertion by the lawyer, but it may become problematic if they are inaccurate. The public may not make such an exacting analysis of the difference between a member's endorsement of a lawyer's litigation skills and the lawyer's actual certification for "Trial Advocacy." There is a one sure-fire way to avoid this confusion: A lawyer may choose to opt out of endorsements altogether and/or manage the endorsements that appear on their profile page. Each individual legal professional will need to determine whether the endorsements are a valuable marketing tool for his career, as there does not appear to be a definitive statement from the ethics committees on this point.

FIRM NAMES AND LETTERHEAD

The most public and widespread "advertisements" for attorneys are their firm name and their letterhead; these two are "everywhere" and project a certain image (or at least the attorneys hope that they do). For a paralegal, the most important thing to remember is that the firm's reputation is carried on every piece of letterhead that leaves the office. No matter how trivial the correspondence, the paralegal should ensure that it is well written, free of errors, uses the appropriate tone, and is formatted correctly.

Traditionally, firm names are composed of the "list" of equity partners in order of seniority; however, this is not required under ABA Model Rule 7.5. **Trade names**, such as "Toxic Tort Tamers, Inc.," could be employed, as long as they passed muster under the other advertising rules regarding deceptive or misleading tactics. Most important, the trade name must not insinuate that the firm is in any way a governmental entity or associated with governmentally sponsored legal services or charitable organizations. It seems clear from the various cases handling violative trade names that the use of words like "legal services," "legal clinic," "claim service," and "consumer law center" are all potentially misleading, as they may suggest a relationship with those organizations that truly do provide free or no-cost legal aid services by and through governmental and charitable agencies. New Jersey went so far as to opine:

> A law firm name may include additional identifying language such as "& Associates" only when such language is accurate and descriptive of the firm. Any firm name including additional identifying language such as "Legal Services" or other similar phrases shall inform all prospective clients in the retainer agreement or other writing that the law firm is not affiliated or associated with a public, quasi-public or charitable organization. However, no firm shall use the phrase "legal aid" in its name or in any additional identifying language.

Matter of Vincenti, 704 A.2d 927, 937 (1998).

However, the Florida Bar has clarified the use of "legal clinic" and it is permissible under their Rule 4-7.9 only "if the lawyer's practice is devoted to providing routine legal services for fees that are lower than the prevailing rate in the community for those services." *In re Amendments to the Rules Regulating the Florida Bar—Advertising*, 971 So. 2d 763, 790-791 (Fla. 2007). Therefore, it behooves a legal professional to consult her jurisdiction's rules before going to the expense of having letterhead printed.

Most of the time, firm names are made up of the list of named partners in the firm. Without any other indication on the letterhead, the law firm is presumed to practice solely in the jurisdiction where the office is located. However, as clients' matters became more complicated and the effects of globalization were felt, attorneys became licensed in more than one jurisdiction to better serve their clients' interests, and the firms opened up offices in different states. Where it is the case that attorneys in the firm are able to practice in

trade name
The title of a company that it uses in commerce to identify and distinguish it from others in the field.

various office locations, the letterhead must indicate where each attorney is licensed. Failure to identify the jurisdictional limitations of the attorneys in the firm is an ethical violation.

> Even where there is one office located in a single jurisdiction, the attorneys are bound to indicate where they are licensed to practice if they are not so licensed in the state where the one office is located. A Virginian attorney found himself in violation of this rule because, while he worked out of the Maryland office with his partner, he did not take any of the Maryland related cases. The Virginian attorney did not list his jurisdictional limitation and the court felt that this would be misleading because clients would believe he was licensed where he maintained an office. It is as if he were holding himself out as a Maryland attorney, when in fact, he was not.

> *Attorney Grievance Comm'n of Maryland v. Johnson*, 363 Md. 598, 605, 770 A.2d 130, 135 (2001).

Requiring the specifics of jurisdictional admission is not limited to letterhead. The Court in *In re Winstead*, 69 A.3d 390, 398-399 (D.C. Ct. App. 2013), determined that the failure to specify the states in which the attorney was licensed to practice would extend to any correspondence relating to the matter at hand including the retainer agreement.

> While we recognize that certain transactional matters do not require a license to practice law, the language in the retainer agreements demonstrates that respondent was holding herself out as authorized to provide *legal* counsel. Respondent repeatedly used the title "Esquire" after her name, called herself "Counsel" throughout the retainer agreements, indicated that she could associate with other firms and seek attorney's fees, stated that she did not specialize in certain areas of law, and noted that she could provide litigation services for an additional fee. In context, respondent's statement that she could provide counsel for transactional matters would cause a reasonable recipient of the communications to be misled into believing that respondent was authorized to provide legal services. Accordingly, we conclude that the retainer agreements contained misleading communications that violated Rule 7.1(a).

Some states take the name of the firm very seriously and protect the public by requiring that all the attorneys whose names are used in a law firm's name be members of the bar of that state.

> The purpose of the rule is obvious. It is reasonable to expect that those listed in a law firm name are licensed to practice in this State. If those persons are not so licensed, the firm name is deceptive to consumers of legal services. To the extent law firm names with unlicensed lawyers defeat consumers' reasonable expectations, the disciplinary rule protects the public against deception.

> *On Petition for Review of Opinion 475 of Advisory Committee on Professional Ethics*, 89 N.J. 74, 77, 444 A.2d 1092, 1094 (1982).

The New Jersey Supreme Court would not permit the national firm "Jacoby & Meyers" to open a New Jersey office because neither Mr. Jacoby nor Mr. Meyers were admitted to the New Jersey Bar. Interestingly, there is no prohibition in continuing to use a long-dead partner's name in the firm name in which he participated; in actuality this provides a consistency of identification and an indicator of service. For example, the largest U.S. law firm, Baker & McKenzie, has long since lost both founding partners, but continues using that name with enormous success, employing over three thousand attorneys.

If a lawyer also happens to hold a public office, her name cannot be used in the firm's name. The prohibition prohibits an attorney or firm from appearing to hold any sway with a government official. Therefore, if one of the named partners is a government official, there is an inherent conflict.

Finally, the list of attorneys in the firm name is presumed to be the partners in a duly organized law firm. Partners owe each other certain duties of loyalty and are responsible for each other's actions, as discussed in the previous chapter. For attorneys to present their names as if they were associated in a partnership or other professional corporation when they are, in fact, not so related, is misleading and in violation of advertising Rule 7.5(d). Such a violation was found in *In re Weiss, Healy & Rea*, 109 N.J. 246, 536 A.2d 266 (1988), where eight in-house attorneys for an insurance company sought to "assemble" under the name of "Weiss, Healy & Rea." These attorneys worked together and shared information as to strategic decisions in the defense of the insurance company's insureds. However, they were all employees of the company and did not share in any profits, losses, or other expenses in the group; all of this was covered under the company.

> We believe that the message conveyed by the firm name "A, B & C" is that the three persons designated are engaged in the general practice of law in New Jersey as partners. Such partnership implies the full financial and professional responsibility of a law firm that has pooled its resources of intellect and capital to serve a general clientele. The partnership arrangement implies much more than office space shared by representatives of a single insurer. Put differently, the designation "A, B & C" does not imply that the associated attorneys are in fact employees, with whatever inferences a client might draw about their ultimate interest and advice. The public, we believe, infers that the collective professional, ethical, and financial responsibility of a partnership-in-fact bespeaks the "kind and caliber of legal services rendered.

Id. at 252.

New Jersey also dealt with an interesting question regarding the use of partners' names in more than one law firm. The facts were as follows:

> The Committee has received an inquiry from a law firm practicing under the name "A, B, C, D & E" which would like to merge and form a separate firm with a sole practitioner in another part of the State to be known as "A & X" or "A, B & X." Well-established in its geographical area, the inquiring firm does not wish to change its name. Nor does it wish to add the sole practitioner's name as it believes the firm name is already too long and would become unwieldy. However, because of his reputation, the firm believes it advisable that the sole practitioner's name be included in the name of the newly formed firm.

[. . .] The inquiring firm's formation of a second firm for the limited purpose of advancing the sole practitioner's name circumvents the rule. The newly formed firm would be owned in its entirety by the inquiring firm. It would in no way function as a separate, distinct, autonomous firm. Rather, it would be but an appendage or satellite office of the parent firm. Moreover, all of the members of the original firm would be members of the newly formed firm and listed as such on its letterhead. Therefore, these lawyers and the inquiring firm would be practicing under more than one name, which is prohibited by RPC 7.5(a).

It is clear that where attorneys seek to affiliate themselves for any other reason than the formation of a recognized business partnership under which they will practice as an independent group of attorneys, they will be in violation of the ethics rules. The firm name and letterhead must accurately reflect the true nature of the business relationship between the attorneys.

While it is clear that a paralegal's name will never appear in a firm name, paralegals may be listed on the letterhead with their appropriate designations as "paralegal" and any earned certifications after their names. The legal community has recognized the "growing presence of formally trained and/or experienced legal assistants and paralegals in the practice of law" and therefore acknowledged the desirability of including them on letterhead and allowing them to distribute business cards. Fla. Ethics Op. 86-4 (Fla. St. Bar Ass'n 1986). A New York Ethics Committee found that "[s]ince paralegals may have to deal with clients and members of the court system and the public while performing their duties, it will often be convenient for them to identify themselves and their affiliation by means of a business card." NYCLA Ethics Op. 673 (N.Y. Cty Law Ass'n Comm'n Prof'l Ethics 1989). NFPA has addressed this issue in its Ethical Consideration 1.7(c). (See Figure 10.2.)

There are so many titles that a paralegal can use—the designations vary from firm to firm and in different geographic regions. The vast majority of states hold that listing paralegals on letterhead and issuing them firm business cards is acceptable, even beneficial to the public. The prime consideration when including a paralegal on the firm letterhead or on business cards is to avoid misleading the recipient as to the paralegal's status. However, as the New York State Bar Association pointed out, the inquiry is whether "the various

FIGURE 10.2 ▶
A PARALEGAL'S TITLE
SHALL BE FULLY
DISCLOSED

NFPA EC 1.7

EC 1.7(a)   A paralegal's title shall clearly indicate the individual's status and shall be disclosed in all business and professional communications to avoid misunderstandings and misconceptions about the paralegal's role and responsibilities.

EC 1.7(b)   A paralegal's title shall be included if the paralegal's name appears on business cards, letterhead, brochures, directories, and advertisements.

EC 1.7(c)   A paralegal shall not use letterhead, business cards or other promotional materials to create a fraudulent impression of his/her status or ability to practice in the jurisdiction in which the paralegal practices.

titles clearly demonstrate that the paralegal is not an attorney." NY Ethics Op. 640 (N.Y. St. Bar Ass'n Comm'n Prof'l Ethics 1992). The committee determined that titles such as "paralegal" and "senior paralegal" are clearly permissible, as they unambiguously indicate that the person is not an attorney. However, the term "paralegal coordinator" is not permitted without further clarification, because it is not clear whether the person responsible for overseeing the paralegals is a paralegal himself or an attorney in charge of this task. The term "legal associate" is not permissible at all, because the title "associate" refers only to non-partner attorneys in the firm. These titles are merely examples, not an all-inclusive list. Other designations may be used, as long as they clearly define the status of the paralegal as a nonlawyer.

All public representations made by an attorney in any form—solicitation, advertisements, firm names, letterhead, and others—must be made in an honest and forthright manner. Any practice that could be deemed misleading or action that would constitute overreaching by the attorney can be sanctioned under the ethics rules. The purpose behind these strict rules is to ensure that the public retains its confidence in the legal profession. The old-fashioned notion of the noble profession in which attorneys should only "live to serve" without any need for efforts to attract clients has long passed, and the commercial aspects of the practice have been recognized. Attorneys are permitted to promote their services to potential clients. The time, place, and manner of those efforts can be regulated without the impingement of the attorneys' right to freedom of commercial speech. Advertising and solicitation of clients requires, as many of the other ethical constructs do, a balancing of the attorneys' needs and duties with those of clients and the public.

Summary

The practice of law is also a business that depends on attracting clients through general public advertisements and targeted solicitation to individuals or a class of persons. As in every other aspect of legal practice, there are ethical rules to delineate what legal professionals may say to the public in advertisements and solicitations. The statements may not be false or misleading. This prohibition also extends to advertisements that are overly aggressive or suggestive. Paralegals are prohibited specifically from enhancing their credentials under color of record or degree. Technology plays an important role in the delivery of legal advertisements, and there are restrictions placed upon television advertisements and website content to avoid overdramatization or overreaching by a legal professional. In-person solicitation is the most restricted form of attorney commercial contact, as it has the greatest risk for undue influence by the legal professional. Also potentially unduly influential is the use of certification and specialization designations. Paralegals must be particularly careful to clearly convey their status and title, both in using certifications and on the general firm letterhead and their own business cards. Always bear in mind that whatever an attorney cannot do in the advertising context, a paralegal cannot do either.

Key Terms

Ambulance chaser
Boutique firm
Certified specialist
Commercial speech
Disclaimer
General practice firm

Materially misleading
Overreaching
Solicitation
Specialization
Trade name
Unbundling of legal services

Review Questions

MULTIPLE CHOICE

Choose the best answer(s) and please explain *why* you chose the answer(s).

1. An attorney may use the title "certified trial attorney":
   a. Only on his letterhead and business cards, but not in his advertising
   b. Only after applying for and passing the requirements set forth by the appropriate association approved by the ABA
   c. If his practice is limited to litigation only
   d. All of the above
   e. None of the above

2. Advertising is materially misleading if:
   a. Recipients will believe the claims made by the attorney
   b. No reasonable person could believe the claims made by the attorney
   c. A recipient believes that the attorney can guarantee a winning result in her case
   d. The court determines that the facts contained in the advertisement are important to the public

3. An attorney may solicit clients:
   a. By bulk mail flyers indicating her areas of concentration of practice
   b. Through her paralegal
   c. Via the internet and website directories
   d. All of the above
   e. None of the above

EXPLAIN YOURSELF

All answers should be written in complete sentences. A simple yes or no is insufficient.

1. Why is attorney advertising more heavily controlled than other forms of commercial speech?

2. Describe in your own words what "materially misleading" advertising is.

3. How can an attorney become a certified specialist? Is that the only time she can advertise her area of concentration?

4. Explain the proper use of paralegals in obtaining new clients.

FAULTY PHRASES

All of the following statements are *false*; state why they are false and then rewrite each one as a true statement. Do not simply make the statement negative by adding the word "not."

1. A law firm's name must always be composed of the equity partners' surnames.

2. As long as the victim is a relative, an attorney may solicit legal business at the hospital.

3. Every attorney must become certified in his area of specialty.

4. As long as the advertisement has a disclaimer, the content of the ad cannot be considered materially misleading.

5. The Constitution protects the content of commercial speech as it pertains to all attorney advertisements.

6. Paralegals' names should not appear on the firm's letterhead.

7. All the members of a boutique firm are certified specialists in that area of law.

8. A satisfied client may not recommend her attorney to a friend without violating the attorney solicitation rules.

PORTFOLIO ASSIGNMENT

Write Away

Create the following for your law firm, which consists of 20 attorneys and 5 paralegals. Two of the named partners are certified by the American Board of Certification (see http://www.abcworld.org/abchome.html for details); the firm specializes in bankruptcy law; and you, one of the paralegals, hold a national paralegal certification.

1. A Yellow Pages advertisement
2. A bulk mailing to everyone in the town
3. A mailing directed at persons who are currently in foreclosure on their homes
4. A PowerPoint (or other visual) presentation outlining the concept for a television advertisement

Case in Point

Christie STEINER et al., Petitioners,

v.

The SUPERIOR COURT of Santa Barbara County, Respondent;
Volkswagen Group of America et al., Real Parties in Interest.
2d Civil No. B235347
Filed October 30, 2013
As Modified on Denial of Rehearing November 26, 2013

PERREN, J. [footnotes omitted]

An attorney's web site advertised her success in two cases raising issues similar to those she was about to try here. The trial court admonished the jury not to "Google" the attorneys or to read any articles about the case or anyone involved in it. Concerned that a juror might ignore these admonitions, the court ordered the attorney to remove for the duration of trial two pages from her web site discussing the similar cases. We conclude this was an unlawful prior restraint on the attorney's free speech rights under the First Amendment. Whether analyzed under the strict scrutiny standard or the lesser standard for commercial speech, the order was more extensive than necessary to advance the competing public interest in assuring a fair trial. Juror admonitions and instructions, such as those given here, were the presumptively adequate means of addressing the threat of jury contamination in this case.

Although the order was improper, it is no longer in effect and thus no relief can be granted. We deny the petition for writ of mandate.

FACTS AND PROCEDURAL BACKGROUND

Richard and Christie Steiner filed this personal injury action after Richard Steiner contracted lung cancer. They alleged his cancer was caused by exposure to asbestos in friction automobile parts manufactured and distributed by Volkswagen Group of America (Volkswagen), Ford Motor Company (Ford) and others. After the jury was impaneled, Volkswagen moved for an order requiring the Steiners' attorney, Simona A.

Farrise, to remove during trial two pages from her law firm Web site touting her recent successes against Ford in similar asbestos cases. The first page discussed a $1.6 million verdict against Ford and others, stating that "at least one jury managed to successfully navigate defendants' courtroom confusion and find these companies at fault." The second page described a $4,355,987 jury verdict against Ford. Volkswagen asserted that "human nature being what it is, [Volkswagen], in the interests of a fair trial, believes that plainly provocative and prejudicial information should not intentionally be prominently displayed on the internet, by the parties or their counsel in this case during trial. That will obviously prejudice the jury process during the trial and deliberations in this case, if it is encountered by a juror." Ford joined in the motion.

The Steiners argued that the request infringed upon counsel's constitutional right of free speech and that the more appropriate remedy was to admonish the jury not to search the Internet for information about the attorneys. The trial court, however, granted the motion at a hearing on August 22, 2011. After the parties expressed confusion over the scope of the order, the court clarified: "I had intended the decision here to be surgical. I was [not] directing [Ms. Farrise to] take down her whole website by any stretch of the imagination. It was the items that the Defense had pointed to that I was directing my thoughts to. [¶] Maybe I wasn't as clear as I should have been, but that's all. I wasn't asking you to do anything more than just take [down] the comments that the Defense pointed to in their motion, which was, I thought, very specific."

The trial court admonished the jurors not to Google the attorneys. It also gave the standard admonishments prior to opening statements. Those admonishments are not part of the record, but at the time they were given, CACI No. 100 stated: "During the trial, do not read, listen to, or watch any news reports about this case. . . . This prohibition extends to the use of the Internet in any way, including reading any blog about the case or about anyone involved with it or using Internet maps or mapping programs or any other program or device to search for or to view any place discussed in the testimony." (See CACI No. 100 (2011 ed.).)

The Steiners, Farrise and her law firm (collectively petitioners) sought a writ of mandate in this court seeking to reverse the trial court's order requiring Farrise "*to take down part of her firm's website during the pendency of the trial of this case* in order to assure that the jurors do not view it." (Original italics.) The petition stated the trial court initially ordered Farrise to take down the entire firm Web site, but subsequently "modified its order and limited application of the order to the discussion of two verdicts [Farrise] had obtained in other actions. . . ." We summarily denied the petition.

Thereafter, petitioners sought review of our denial in the California Supreme Court. In their petition for review, they changed the basis for their claim and represented to the Supreme Court that the trial court had ordered Farrise "*to take down her firm's entire website during the trial of this case* in order to assure that the jurors do not view it." (Original italics.) The petition for review stated that "[e]ven if the order were limited to the website's discussion of other cases, it would be an unreasonable and unnecessary prior restraint and would violate [counsel's] free speech rights. But the order is not so limited: It requires that [counsel] take down her *entire* website, even with respect to speech wholly unrelated to any other asbestos litigation." (Original italics.) This claim contradicts the claim made to this court and is unsupported by the record. Five days later, the Supreme Court granted review and transferred the matter to this court with instructions to issue an order to show cause. We complied. We also asked petitioners to explain the discrepancies in the petitions regarding the scope of the trial court's order.

In response, petitioners concede that the trial court did not order Farrise to take down the entire Web site and that only the two pages specified in the motion were removed. They nonetheless assert the trial court's written ruling, issued the day after the court made its clarifying comments on the record, created an "ambiguity" in the scope of the order. That ruling, which was part of a lengthy final pretrial conference order, stated: "Take it down for the time of the trial. The Court will make the same order with respect to any of the websites of the defendants upon request." Petitioners claim the word "it" arguably referred to the entire Web site rather than the two pages referenced in the motion and identified by the trial court. The record reflects, however, that the court drafted the ruling shortly after explaining it "had intended the decision here to be surgical," and was not "by any stretch of the imagination" directing removal of the entire Web site. It stated: "I'm going to print [the order], one copy—20 pages. . . . You're going to get it out there, Monday, and I'm going to say that th[e] motion is granted. And Miss Farrise has a copy of it if she feels that she'd like to writ it, then it's clearly part of my record. Now, that part's done and behind me. I think that's being [as] surgical as I can be."

On the day the petition for review was filed, the trial court issued a separate written order denying the Steiners' request to require defense counsel to take down portions of their Web sites. It explained "As I have said before, repeatedly, the Court is willing to surgically cut out any references in the websites of each side that could have a material effect on the outcome of this case; I do not find, in [the defense] websites any such offending material." Two days later, Volkswagen's counsel sent an e-mail to petitioners' counsel advising that "[y]our petition to the California Supreme Court improperly reflects that Judge Anderle ordered you to take down your entire website. This clearly is contrary to Judge Anderle's order that was issued on August 22, 2011." Citing counsel's ethical obligations, Volkswagen requested that petitioners "immediately advise the Supreme Court of [the] error." They chose not to do so.

Farrise restored the two pages to her firm Web site when the trial ended in October 2011. Volkswagen moved to discharge the order to show cause as moot. We deferred resolution of the motion until the show cause hearing.

DISCUSSION

A. Public Interest Exception for Mootness

Appellate courts generally will neither decide controversies that are moot nor render decisions on abstract propositions. (*Eye Dog Foundation v. State Board of Guide Dogs for the Blind* (1967) 67 Cal. 2d 536, 541, 63 Cal. Rptr. 21, 432 P.2d 717; see also *Mercury Interactive Corp. v. Klein* (2007) 158 Cal. App. 4th 60, 78, 70 Cal. Rptr. 3d 88.) "A case is moot when the decision of the reviewing court 'can have no practical impact or provide the parties effectual relief. [Citation.]' [Citation.] 'When no effective relief can be granted, an appeal is moot and will be dismissed.' [Citation.]" (*MHC Operating Limited Partnership v. City of San Jose* (2003) 106 Cal. App. 4th 204, 214, 130 Cal. Rptr. 2d 564 (*MHC*).)

Petitioners concede the writ petition is moot, but contend this matter falls within the public interest exception to the doctrine of mootness. (See *MHC, supra,* 106 Cal. App. 4th at pp. 214-215, 130 Cal. Rptr. 2d 564; *In re William M.* (1970) 3 Cal. 3d 16, 23, 89 Cal. Rptr. 33, 473 P.2d 737 ["[I]f a pending case poses an issue of broad public interest that is likely to recur, the court may exercise an inherent discretion to resolve that issue even though an event occurring during its pendency would normally render the matter moot"].) Petitioners assert that by granting review, the Supreme Court ordered us to decide "whether a court can or should order an attorney to remove *any* website postings that do not relate to the case pending before the court." This point is debatable given that the petition for review represented that the trial court ordered removal of Farrise's *entire* law firm Web site during trial. An order of that magnitude would have exceeded the scope of requested relief, among other things.

The actual order is much narrower, but it does raise questions as to a trial court's authority to issue an order restricting an attorney's free speech rights during trial to prevent potential jury contamination. Because any order restricting such speech during trial is likely to become moot before a writ petition can be heard, we agree it raises an issue of broad public interest that is likely to evade timely review. (See *Nebraska Press Assn. v. Stuart* (1976) 427 U.S. 539, 546-547, 96 S. Ct. 2791, 49 L. Ed. 2d 683 (*Nebraska Press*) [prior restraint on speech via

pretrial order evades review because of its inherently short duration].) We therefore deny Volkswagen's motion to discharge the order to show cause as moot and exercise our discretion to reach the petition's merits.

B. Unlawful Prior Restraint on Free Speech

Petitioners correctly assert the trial court's order placed a direct restraint on Farrise's right to freedom of speech under the United States and California Constitutions. (U.S. Const., 1st Amend.; Cal. Const., art. I, § 2, subd. (a).) "Orders which restrict or preclude a citizen from speaking in advance are known as 'prior restraints,' and are disfavored and presumptively invalid." (*Hurvitz v. Hoefflin* (2000) 84 Cal. App. 4th 1232, 1241, 101 Cal. Rptr. 2d 558, fn. omitted (*Hurvitz*); see *Nebraska Press, supra,* 427 U.S. at p. 559, 96 S. Ct. 2791 ["[P]rior restraints on speech and publication are the most serious and the least tolerable infringement on First Amendment rights."].) An order restricting the speech of trial participants, typically known as a "gag order," is a prior restraint. (*Hurvitz,* at pp. 1241–1242; 101 Cal. Rptr. 2d 558; *Saline v. Superior Court* (2002) 100 Cal. App. 4th 909, 915–916, 122 Cal. Rptr. 2d 813.) Although the right to a fair trial is also a protected constitutional right, a court seeking to insure a fair trial may not impose a prior restraint unless " 'the gravity of the "evil," discounted by its improbability, justifies such invasion of free speech as is necessary to avoid the danger.' " (*Nebraska Press,* at p. 562, 96 S. Ct. 2791.)

Relying upon *Gentile v. State Bar of Nevada* (1991) 501 U.S. 1030, 111 S. Ct. 2720, 115 L. Ed. 2d 888 (*Gentile*), Volkswagen contends that whenever an attorney's exercise of free speech potentially conflicts with a party's right to a fair trial, the trial court may reasonably impose a prior restraint on such speech. *Gentile* reviewed an order holding that a criminal defense attorney, who had made comments to the media concerning his client's innocence, had violated a Nevada disciplinary rule limiting an attorney's extrajudicial statements that have a " 'substantial likelihood of materially prejudicing' " the trial. (*Id.* at p. 1034, 111 S. Ct. 2720.) One of the issues was whether a stricter standard, such as the " 'clear and present danger' " test, should apply when addressing the speech of attorneys commenting on pending criminal proceedings. (*Id.* at pp. 1070-1071, 111 S. Ct. 2720.) The plurality opinion, authored by Chief Justice Rehnquist, concluded the lesser standard in the Nevada rule passed constitutional muster. (*Id.* at p. 1075, 111 S. Ct. 2720.) It explained that "[l]awyers representing clients in pending cases are key participants in the criminal justice system, and the State may demand some adherence to the precepts of that system in regulating their speech as well as their conduct." (*Id.* at p. 1074, 111 S. Ct. 2720.)

The matter before us does not involve the constitutionality of a state disciplinary rule regulating speech by attorneys in criminal proceedings. It involves the constitutionality of a single court order prohibiting an attorney in a civil proceeding from publishing speech about two other civil cases. *Gentile* did not discuss a trial court's authority to issue an order restricting an attorney's speech during a civil proceeding. (See *In re Morrissey* (E.D. Va. 1998) 996 F. Supp. 530, 539.) Given these distinctions, *Gentile* does not assist our review.

1. Standard of Judicial Scrutiny

As a general rule, gag orders on trial participants are subject to strict judicial scrutiny and may not be imposed "unless (1) the speech sought to be restrained poses a clear and present danger or serious and imminent threat to a protected competing interest; (2) the order is narrowly tailored to protect that interest; and (3) no less restrictive alternatives are available." (*Hurvitz, supra,* 84 Cal. App. 4th at p. 1241, 101 Cal. Rptr. 2d 558, fn. omitted; see *Maggi v. Superior Court* (2004) 119 Cal. App. 4th 1218, 1225, 15 Cal. Rptr. 3d 161 (*Maggi*).) The trial court did not apply this or any other standard because Volkswagen's motion did not address First Amendment concerns.

With the benefit of hindsight, Volkswagen contends the order is not subject to strict scrutiny, but rather to the less restrictive standard for commercial speech. Typically, "[l]awyer advertising is commercial speech and is accorded an intermediate measure of First Amendment protection." (*Revo v. Disciplinary Bd. of the Supreme Court* (10th Cir. 1997) 106 F.3d 929, 932; *Florida Bar v. Went For It, Inc.* (1995) 515 U.S. 618, 623, 115 S. Ct. 2371, 132 L. Ed. 2d 541 (*Florida Bar*).) Petitioners acknowledge Farrise's

Web site advertises her legal services and thus contains elements of commercial speech.

Central Hudson Gas v. Public Service Comm'n (1980) 447 U.S. 557, 100 S. Ct. 2343, 65 L. Ed. 2d 341 (*Central Hudson*), considered the constitutionality of a New York regulation banning promotional advertising by an electrical utility. Recognizing that commercial speech is accorded less protection, the court developed a four-prong intermediate scrutiny standard to examine whether state regulations on commercial speech are constitutionally valid: First, the court must determine whether the speech concerns lawful activity and is not misleading. If it satisfies that criteria, the court must decide whether the asserted governmental interest is substantial, whether the restraint directly advances that interest and whether it is "more extensive than is necessary to serve that interest." (*Id.* at p. 566, 100 S. Ct. 2343; see *Larson v. City and County of San Francisco* (2011) 192 Cal. App. 4th 1263, 1285 & fn. 7, 123 Cal. Rptr. 3d 40 (*Larson*); *People ex rel. Brown v. Puri-Tec* (2007) 153 Cal. App. 4th 1524, 1537, 64 Cal. Rptr. 3d 270 (*PuriTec*).) The court struck down the utility advertising ban under the fourth prong, concluding the public agency had failed to "show[ ] that more limited speech regulation would be ineffective." (*Central Hudson,* at p. 571, 100 S. Ct. 2343.)

Because *Central Hudson* addressed "whether a particular commercial speech regulation is constitutionally permissible" (*Thompson v. Western States Medical Center* (2002) 535 U.S. 357, 376, 122 S. Ct. 1497, 152 L. Ed. 2d 563), the cases applying it similarly involve the review of statutory or administrative regulations. Volkswagen cites no cases applying *Central Hudson* to judicial restraints on commercial speech. In fact, it cites no cases involving such restraints. Without conceding the issue, petitioners contend it is irrelevant which standard we apply because the trial court's order does not pass muster under even the less restrictive *Central Hudson* test. We agree, and consequently focus our discussion on that standard. In so doing, we do not decide whether *Central Hudson* extends to judicial restraints on commercial speech. We decide only that since the trial court's order "cannot satisfy this intermediate-scrutiny test, it necessarily fails under a strict scrutiny analysis." (*Baba v. Board of Supervisors* (2004) 124 Cal. App. 4th 504, 518, 21 Cal. Rptr. 3d 428.)

2. *Application of* Central Hudson

"The party seeking to uphold a restriction on commercial speech carries the burden of justifying it." (*Bolger v. Youngs Drug Products Corp.* (1983) 463 U.S. 60, 70-71, fn. 20, 103 S. Ct. 2875, 77 L. Ed. 2d 469.) Volkswagen asserts the restraint was proper under the first prong of the *Central Hudson* test because the challenged speech was misleading. (*Central Hudson, supra,* 447 U.S. at p. 566, 100 S. Ct. 2343; *Bates v. State Bar of Arizona* (1977) 433 U.S. 350, 383, 97 S. Ct. 2691, 53 L. Ed. 2d 810 ["[a]dvertising that is false, deceptive, or misleading of course is subject to restraint"].) It claims the two Web pages omitted pertinent information, such as that a settlement in one case resulted in the dismissal of all claims against Ford, and that another defendant secured a defense verdict. Volkswagen ignores, however, that it did not seek removal of the pages to prevent deceptive or misleading advertising. It sought removal to deny the jury access to the pages until the trial was over. Volkswagen presented no evidence or argument demonstrating the pages were subject to restraint as misleading advertising, and the trial court made no such finding. Thus, we have no basis to make that determination here.

Turning to the second prong, the parties agree that a substantial governmental interest exists in assuring the parties receive a fair trial. (See *Maggi, supra,* 119 Cal. App. 4th at p. 1225, 15 Cal. Rptr. 3d 161.) Their dispute centers on the third and fourth prongs. (*Central Hudson, supra,* 447 U.S. at p. 566, 100 S. Ct. 2343; *Keimer v. Buena Vista Books, Inc.* (1999) 75 Cal. App. 4th 1220, 1231, 89 Cal. Rptr. 2d 781.) Even if we assume the restraint directly advanced the stated governmental interest, it fails to withstand the fourth prong as it was more extensive than necessary to serve that interest. (*Larson, supra,* 192 Cal. App. 4th at pp. 1292–1293, 123 Cal. Rptr. 3d 40.) That prong requires ". . . a "fit" between the [government's] ends and the means chosen to accomplish those ends, . . . a fit that is not necessarily perfect, but reasonable; that represents not necessarily the single best disposition but one whose scope is "in proportion to the interest served," that employs not necessarily the least restrictive means but . . . a means narrowly tailored to achieve the desired objective." (*Florida Bar, supra,* 515 U.S. at p. 632, 115 S. Ct. 2371; see *Gerawan Farming,*

Inc. v. Kawamura (2004) 33 Cal. 4th 1, 23-24, 14 Cal. Rptr. 3d 14, 90 P.3d 1179 (*Gerawan*).) No such fit is to be found here.

Volkswagen maintains the restraint was necessary to reduce the chance of "an expensive and time-consuming new trial" if a juror inappropriately accessed Farrise's firm's Web site during trial. Volkswagen has not demonstrated, however, that "alternative, less-speech-restrictive [measures] would be less efficient or effective in accomplishing the government's objective." (*Gerawan, supra,* 33 Cal. 4th at pp. 23-24, 14 Cal. Rptr. 3d 14, 90 P.3d 1179; see *Thompson v. Western States Medical Center, supra,* 535 U.S. at p. 358, 122 S. Ct. 1497 ["If the Government can achieve its interests in a manner that does not restrict commercial speech, or that restricts less speech, the Government must do so"].) As emphasized in *Thompson,* "[i]f the First Amendment means anything, it means that regulating speech must be a last—not first—resort." (*Thompson,* at p. 373, 122 S. Ct. 1497.)

It is well established that "frequent and specific cautionary admonitions and jury instructions . . . constitute the accepted, presumptively adequate, and plainly less restrictive means of dealing with the threat of jury contamination." (*NBC Subsidiary (KNBC-TV), Inc. v. Superior Court* (1999) 20 Cal. 4th 1178, 1221, 86 Cal. Rptr. 2d 778, 980 P.2d 337 (*NBC Subsidiary*).) In *NBC Subsidiary,* our high court "stressed [its] adherence to the fundamental premise that, as a general matter, cautionary admonitions and instructions serve to correct and cure myriad improprieties, including the receipt by jurors of information that was kept from them. To paraphrase Justice Holmes, it must be assumed that a jury does its duty, abides by cautionary instructions, and finds facts only because those facts are proved." (*Id.* at pp. 1223-1224, 86 Cal. Rptr. 2d 778, 980 P.2d 337, citing *Aikens v. Wisconsin* (1904) 195 U.S. 194, 206, 25 S. Ct. 3, 49 L. Ed. 154.)

Although it applied strict scrutiny, *Freedom Communications, Inc. v. Superior Court* (2008) 167 Cal. App. 4th 150, 83 Cal. Rptr. 3d 861 (*Freedom Communications*) is instructive. To prevent witnesses from being influenced by the trial testimony of others, the trial court issued a gag order prohibiting the defendant newspaper from reporting on the witnesses' testimony. (*Id.* at pp. 152-153, 83 Cal. Rptr. 3d 861.) The Court of Appeal granted the newspaper's petition for writ of mandate, observing the "case law makes clear that the danger the trial court sought to avert by its prior restraint here—the risk that witnesses in a civil trial might be influenced by reading news reports of the testimony of other witnesses—cannot possibly justify the censorship imposed." (*Id.* at p. 153, 83 Cal. Rptr. 3d 861.)

The court emphasized that less restrictive alternatives were available to protect the plaintiffs' fair trial rights, including admonishing witnesses not to read press accounts of the trial. (*Freedom Communications, supra,* 167 Cal. App. 4th at p. 154, 83 Cal. Rptr. 3d 861.) It remarked that "such an admonishment would go farther in preventing the tainting of witness testimony because the gag order applies only to [the defendant newspaper] and not to other newspapers that cover the trial." (*Ibid.*) The same is true here. Although the trial court's order required Farrise to remove information from her Web site regarding prior verdicts involving Ford, it did not apply to any other Web sites discussing such verdicts. Thus, the trial court's admonitions not to research the parties or their attorneys did more to prevent potential jury misconduct than the removal of some of the available information on the Internet. (See *ibid.*)

Volkswagen cites no authority suggesting that a prior restraint of speech, whether commercial or otherwise, is the appropriate means of handling the threat of jury contamination. It maintains that while juror admonishments may have been sufficient to prevent juror misconduct in the past, they are no longer effective in today's world of 24-hour news, Google, Twitter and the Internet. It emphasizes that "jurors' ready access to information . . . has vastly increased the risk of prejudice from extrajudicial sources and has seriously weakened courts' ability to filter or control the flow of information." (See, e.g., *Russo v. Takata Corp.* (S.D. 2009) 774 N.W.2d 441, 452, 454 [juror's brief discussion with fellow jurors about his "Google search" results indicating "there were no other lawsuits against" the defendant seatbelt manufacturer was prejudicial and warranted vacation of defense verdict]; Amey, *Social Media and the Legal System: Analyzing Various Responses to Using Technology from the Jury Box* (2010) 35 J. Legal. Prof. 111, 130 ["'[I]t is unlikely that judges or lawyers will be able to eliminate juror misuse of the Internet,

and they should adjust to a world in which control of information to or from jurors is much less effective than it was before the advent of Google, Facebook and the next emerging technology.'"]; Artigliere, *Sequestration for the Twenty-First Century: Disconnecting Jurors from the Internet During Trial* (2011) 59 Drake L. Rev. 621 ["Judges and trial lawyers around the country are shocked by court systems' apparent inability to control the behavior of jurors"].)

Trial courts have grappled with this issue for several years. The parties cite dozens of law review and legal news articles addressing such topics as the "wired juror," "mistrial by twitter" and how to silence the "twittering juror." These articles discuss various ways courts are coping, including imposing courthouse technology bans, threats of contempt, extensive voir dire, stronger admonitions and pattern cautionary jury instructions reflecting the realities of the electronic age. (See, e.g., St. Eve & Zuckerman, *Ensuring an Impartial Jury in the Age of Social Media, supra,* 11 Duke L. & Tech. Rev. at pp. 18-20.) While recognizing the imperfections in these solutions, the authors stop short of suggesting that prior restraints of out-of-courtroom speech are the answer. The focus is on controlling jurors' behavior, not that of the trial participants.

The first line of defense against juror legal research is "to address the issue in jury instructions." (Morrison, *Can the Jury Trial Survive Google?* (Winter 2011) 25 Crim. Just. 4, 14.) As one state court observed, "given the simplicity, speed, and scope of Internet searches, allowing a juror to access with ease extraneous information about the law and the facts, trial judges are well advised to reference Internet searches specifically when they instruct jurors not to conduct their own research or investigations." (*Commonwealth v. Rodriguez* (2005) 63 Mass. Ct. App. 660, [828 N.E.2d 556, 568, fn. 11]; see Comment, *Silencing the 'Twittering Juror': The Need to Modernize Pattern Cautionary Jury Instructions to Reflect the Realities of the Electronic Age* (Fall 2010) 60 DePaul L. Rev. 181, 186 ["The traditional prohibition against external communication and outside research must be rewritten to meet the demands of the twenty-first century"].)

Consistent with this view, our Legislature enacted Statutes 2011, chapter 181, clarifying that jurors may not use social media and the Internet—such as texting, Twitter, Facebook and Internet searches—to research or disseminate information about cases, and can be held in criminal or civil contempt for violating these restrictions. The bill analysis highlighted that "[t]he use of [electronic and wireless] devices by jurors presents an ongoing challenge in preventing mistrials, overturned convictions and chaotic delays in court proceedings. In response, this common sense measure seeks to clarify and codify an informal practice among trial courts to authorize courts to appropriately admonish jurors against the use of electronic and wireless devices to communicate, research, or disseminate information about an ongoing case." (Assem. Com. on Judiciary, Analysis of Assem. Bill No. 141 (2011-2012 Reg. Sess.) Mar. 15, 2011, p. 1; see Chow, *Chapter 181: The End to Juror Electronic Communications* (2012) 43 McGeorge L. Rev. 581, 584-586.)

Among other things, the law amended Code of Civil Procedure section 611 to require the trial court to admonish the jury "that the prohibition on research, dissemination of information, and conversation applies to all forms of electronic and wireless communication." It also amended Penal Code section 166, subdivision (a)(6) to provide that a juror may be guilty of a misdemeanor for "[w]illful disobedience . . . of a court admonishment related to the prohibition on any form of communication or research about the case, including all forms of electronic or wireless communication or research."

The adoption of these amendments underscores that trial courts are appropriately focusing on tougher admonition rules and contempt consequences, rather than on trying to restrain speech on the Internet. This is particularly true where, as here, the speech does not directly concern the case before the court. It also is consistent with the tenet that admonitions are the presumptively reasonable alternative to restricting free speech rights. (*NBC Subsidiary, supra,* 20 Cal. 4th at p. 1221, 86 Cal. Rptr. 2d 778, 980 P.2d 337; *Freedom Communications, supra,* 167 Cal. App. 4th at p. 154, 83 Cal. Rptr. 3d 861.)

The trial court properly admonished the jurors not to Google the attorneys and also instructed them not to conduct independent research. We accept that jurors will obey such admonitions. (*NBC Subsidiary, supra,* 20 Cal. 4th at pp. 1223-1224, 86 Cal. Rptr. 2d 778, 980 P.2d 337.) It is a belief necessary to maintain some balance with the greater mandate that speech shall be free and unfettered. If a juror ignored these admonitions, the court had tools at its disposal to address the issue. It did not, however, have authority to impose, as a prophylactic measure, an order requiring Farrise to remove pages from her law firm Web site to ensure they would be inaccessible to a disobedient juror. Notwithstanding the good faith efforts of a concerned jurist, the order went too far.

DISPOSITION

The trial court's order constituted an unlawful prior restraint on Farrise's constitutional right to free speech. Because the order is no longer in effect, the trial court need not take any action. Having served its purpose, the order to show cause is discharged and the petition for writ of mandate is denied. The parties shall bear their own costs.

We concur:
GILBERT, P.J.
YEGAN, J.

Chapter 11

Maintaining the Integrity of the Profession

Chapter Objectives

The student will be able to

- Discuss the role that both attorneys and paralegals play in maintaining the distinguished character of the practice of law
- Define and discuss the "appearance of impropriety" standard as it applies to attorney and paralegal conduct
- Compare the obligation for truthfulness in all aspects of an attorney's life with those of other professionals
- Explain an attorney's and a paralegal's obligation to report professional misconduct to the proper authorities

This final chapter will explore and review the overarching ethical principles that mandate *how* legal professionals should act at all times, no matter *where* they are or *whom* they are with. Loyalty to the justice system takes precedence over all other professional obligations, and attorneys are required to report the misconduct of others in the profession in order to maintain the integrity of the profession and ensure that the public trust is truly earned and protected. Similarly, paralegals find themselves under reporting obligations pursuant to their own code of ethics.

The last set of rules deals with the general behavior of attorneys with respect to their various roles as counselors and as officers of the court. No matter what they do or in what capacity they act, all attorneys must behave in a manner that will honor the profession and the rule of law. Attorneys do not necessarily "clock out" when they leave the office; they remain representatives of the legal profession while they are in public, and those around them are conscious of their position. It is a demanding role to play, but this has been so since the origin of this "noble profession." Trust and confidence are not "on and off" characteristics; once instilled, they must be constantly nurtured and maintained by every attorney and judge at all times. This chapter will explore the overarching ethical requirements that attempt to ensure that attorneys act in compliance with all the specific rules previously discussed. It should be the aspiration of all paralegals also to adhere to these codes of conduct. While there is no uniform, enforceable ethical code for all paralegals, there are models and guidelines that should motivate the actions of all legal professionals.

DUTY OF HONESTY TO ADMISSIONS OR REVIEW BOARDS

The rules of ethics come full circle in ABA Model Rule 8.1. Where an attorney begins is a good indicator of where she will end. The boards of bar examiners in every jurisdiction take their jobs very seriously in setting standards and evaluating candidates for admission to practice law. Every bar candidate and every attorney sponsoring or recommending that candidate must be truthful in all the representations made in the application. There is an ongoing duty to correct or supplement any information that changes during the pendency of the application. This honesty and forthrightness is a continuing obligation throughout an attorney's career, during both normal practice and any disciplinary matters. The obligation of bar candidates and attorneys in both applications and disciplinary matters is trifold. First, and most obviously, no false statements of material fact can be made in connection with either proceeding. Second, silence can be misleading. The party before the board of bar examiners or disciplinary council cannot fail to speak where the candidate or attorney knows the board or council is mistaken about a material fact. "Letting it slide" may allow the party to avoid negative consequences, but it is not in compliance with the duty of candor to the tribunal. Third, the candidate or the attorney must comply with any proper demand for information pertaining to the bar admission or disciplinary action. This may pose a delicate situation where the information sought is the object of privilege and protected under the rules of confidentiality. Recall that confidentiality generally trumps all other rules requiring disclosure. The reason is the ultimate objective of the profession: to instill trust in the profession from the public and clients.

The confidentiality rule not only will protect disclosure of information requested by a disciplinary authority, but also is the only privilege an attorney can assert that will permit the attorney to refuse to disclose client information in a proceeding against the attorney. Even where a private citizen could assert a free speech protection, an attorney may not be granted that immunity. Political elections are fraught with mudslinging, and campaigns surrounding the election of judges to the bench are not immune from such attacks among the candidates. In a charge of making false statements in connection with a judicial election, the opposing attorney/candidate asserted a "journalistic" First Amendment right in that he was entitled both to speak publicly about his opponent, as he "had the intent to disseminate to the public the information obtained through [his] investigation" and to keep his journalistic sources confidential. *In re Charges of Unprofessional Conduct Involving File no. 17139*, 720 N.W.2d 807, 816 (Minn. 2006). The disciplinary board requested that the attorney reveal the source of his information that formed the basis of his defamatory statements about his judicial opponent. Despite the attorney's assertion that he had the right to keep his sources confidential (although not through attorney-client privilege), the court found that the attorney must disclose his sources in compliance with ABA Model Rule 8.1(b). The disciplinary board had shown that its "request [was] rationally related to the charges of professional misconduct or to a lawyer's defense to those charges and whether the request is unduly burdensome in light of the gravity and complexity of the charges. In this case, the identities of respondent's sources are extremely relevant—indeed, critical—to the ethical violation alleged." *Id.* at 814. Further, the protections generally afforded to all journalists claiming First Amendment privilege may be pierced where there is an inherent improbability of truth behind the statement, and the journalist may be compelled to disclose the sources so that they can be evaluated. Therefore, for two reasons, one based upon the obligation to disclose non-privileged information under the rules of confidentiality and the other constituting an exception to the journalistic privilege, the information had to be disclosed in the disciplinary matter.

RESPECT FOR THE LEGAL SYSTEM

The profession encompasses participants other than attorneys, and attorneys' conduct must also remain respectful of these persons. The deference that the attorneys must show to the system is manifested through their conduct towards judges and other legal officers of the judicial system. To improperly affront the working members of the judiciary or other court officials or their conduct in the public eye is to insult the system itself and undermine its integrity. A distinction again must be made here between proper exercise of the First Amendment free speech rights of lawyers and improper disparagement for purposes not related to acceptable criticism of the function of the individual or office. Attorneys are often disappointed in the outcome of their matters before judges or magistrates; however, airing their displeasure in a public forum is not acceptable where the attorney goes beyond the facts of the rendered decision.

In *In re Disciplinary Action Against Graham*, 453 N.W.2d 313 (Minn. 1990), the animosity between attorneys grew into one's conspiracy theory that the opposing attorney and the judge had fixed the outcome of a case. To support his allegations, the attorney accused the judge of substantial procedural irregularities that favored the opposing attorney's position. To expose the purported conspiracy to "decide the upcoming case [. . .] without regard to the law and facts," the complaining attorney wrote a letter to the U.S. Attorney alleging the judicial misconduct. *Id.* at 317-318. Had any of this been true or been made in proper political criticism based upon genuine or ascertainable facts, the attorney would not have been disciplined; indeed, he would have been in compliance with his ethical obligations to report actual, known misconduct. However, by his own testimony, he made these statements believing they were probably true but not having the certain knowledge he had claimed in his letter to the U.S. Attorney. Additionally, while he had accused the judge of improperly using political friendships and stated that these other persons had knowledge of the judge's improper intentions, the attorney could not identify any others purportedly involved in the matter. As a consequence, the disciplinary board found that his allegations were "false, frivolous, and made in reckless disregard of their truth or falsity." *Id.* at 319. The First Amendment protects the expression of even unpopular views and protects the speaker against liability for defamation when he criticizes public officials for their official conduct. An abuse of this privilege will not be tolerated in the legal profession.

> This court certifies attorneys for practice to protect the public and the administration of justice. That certification implies that the individual admitted to practice law exhibits a sound capacity for judgment. Where an attorney criticizes the bench and bar, the issue is not simply whether the criticized individual has been harmed, but rather whether the criticism impugning the integrity of judge or legal officer adversely affects the administration of justice and adversely reflects on the accuser's capacity for sound judgment. An attorney who makes critical statements regarding judges and legal officers with reckless disregard as to their truth or falsity and who brings frivolous actions against members of the bench and bar exhibits a lack of judgment that conflicts with his or her position as an officer of the legal system and a public citizen having special responsibility for the quality of justice.

Id. at 322.

The standard applied to attorneys in their exercise of free speech in criticizing judges and other elements of the legal system is higher than that of private citizens, because, in short, attorneys "know better." Attorneys have proven themselves worthy of public confidence by demonstrating legal competence and responsibility that others do not possess. The "reasonableness" standard applied in a review of an attorney's conduct will be that of another reasonable attorney, not just a reasonable person in general. This does not mean that an attorney is prohibited from making any derogatory statements at all regarding judges and their capacity to render accurate and just opinions. "Restrictions on attorney speech burden not only the attorney's right to criticize judges, but also hinder the public's access to the class of people in the best position to comment on the functioning of the judicial system." *In re Green*, 11 P.3d 1078, 1085 (Colo. 2000). An African-American attorney wrote three letters to the judge and opposing counsel accusing the judge of being a racist and a bigot in his treatment of the attorney. While these are strong words, the attorney had factual basis for making these allegations and they were substantiated personal opinion. As the comments were "opinion based upon fully disclosed and uncontested facts . . . [the court could] not, consistent with the First Amendment and the first prong of the New York Times test, discipline Green for his subjective opinions, irrespective of our disagreement with them." *Green* at 1086. It is important to note that these comments were made to a limited audience—only the judge and opposing counsel—although it is not clear whether the court would have been able to rule any differently had the comments been made available to the public at large. The attorney did not make them with any recklessness as to their truth or falsity and therefore the statements were not violative of the ethical rule. More recently and consistent with the above determination, the court in *Attorney Grievance Commission of Maryland v. Stanalonis*, 126 A.3d 6 (Md. 2015), decided that an attorney running for judicial office was permitted to exercise his right to free speech when commenting on the views of his opponent, a sitting judge at the time. The attorney produced a campaign flyer that slighted his opponent's qualifications and, as it turned out, erroneously misconstrued that judge's views on a critical legal issue. "Not all attorney statements that turn out to be untrue violate [RPC 8.4(c)]. 'While this Court has sometimes drawn fine distinctions among the four horsemen of the rule—dishonesty, fraud, deceit and misrepresentation—each pertains to a false statement by an attorney only if the attorney makes use of the false statement knowing that it is untrue.'" *Id.* at 16, citing *Attorney Grievance Comm'n v. Smith*, 109 A.3d 1184, 1196 (Md. 2015). The lower court determined that "the statement reflected negatively on the legal profession because the [attorney's] campaign made it without 'conducting a full and thorough investigation' into its accuracy." *Id.* at 17. However, the appeals court reversed this determination because the attorney had a "demonstrable basis" for believing the statement he published. The Appellate Court held that "[i]t is hard to imagine that making such a statement would negatively impact that public's perception of the legal profession, except insofar as any campaign material that of the opponent who, as in this case, is an attorney who holds public office. But such a standard would be incompatible with the State's current policy, incorporated in the State Constitution, of holding contested elections for circuit court judgeships and public legal officers such as the Attorney General and State's Attorneys. Accordingly, there was no violation of [RPC 8.4(d)]." *Id.* at 17-18.

DUTY TO REPORT MISCONDUCT

How does this code of personal conduct affect paralegals? The answer is stated eloquently in NFPA's Preamble to its Model Code of Conduct:

> Paralegals have recognized, and will continue to recognize, that the profession must continue to evolve to enhance their roles in the delivery of legal services. With increased levels of responsibility comes the need to define and enforce mandatory rules of professional conduct. Enforcement of codes of paralegal conduct is a logical and necessary step to enhance and ensure the confidence of the legal community and the public in the integrity and professional responsibility of paralegals.

> Paralegals play an essential role in the delivery of legal services to clients, and their conduct, just like that of attorneys, reflects upon their competency to hold the public trust. Honesty, integrity, and trustworthiness are personal characteristics that cannot be left at the door. A paralegal's work is influenced by her own personal ethical fiber, and the actions taken by a paralegal outside the office reflect upon the workings of the legal system as a whole. It may be a demanding profession; however, the importance of the work requires this level of personal character. Attorneys and paralegals are responsible for the public confidence in the legal system and hope in the attainment of justice.

> How do the ethical boards learn of these breaches of conduct by attorneys and paralegals? Clients, other attorneys, and court personnel can bring an ethical complaint against an attorney who has shown that he may not be fit to practice due to some action or statement. However, as the profession is **self-policing** (this means that it disciplines its own members), it must rely on its own members to report the misconduct. In order to be sure that lawyers do not have an incentive to shield each other from investigation into their activities, the ethical rules mandate that a lawyer with knowledge of another's misconduct must report it or be found to have violated the rules herself. It is unethical not to report a known violation of the rules by another attorney.

self-policing
The profession's practice of relying on its own members to report misconduct by others and to mete out punishment for infractions.

The same is true for paralegals holding a NFPA certification credential. NFPA affirmatively requires paralegals to report the misconduct of any other legal professional to the proper authorities, as stated in NFPA EC 1.3(d). (See Figure 11.1.) This is broad in scope and significant in practice. This canon requires a paralegal to report known misconduct not only of other paralegals, but also of attorneys. This could mean that the paralegal is reporting on her supervisory lawyer or partner! This is exactly what happened in the case of *Paralegal v. Lawyer*, 783 F. Supp. 230 (E.D. Pa. 1992) (As the case stemmed from a then-unresolved disciplinary matter, the "names have been changed to protect the presumptively innocent.") A paralegal brought a wrongful discharge case against her employer. She claimed that she was fired because she reported his misconduct (backdating a letter to avoid another disciplinary complaint). The court found that the paralegal had a viable cause of action for wrongful termination. She was protected after properly disclosing her supervising attorney's misconduct. The backdating of

NFPA EC 1.3(d)

A paralegal shall advise the proper authority of non-confidential knowledge of any action of another legal professional that clearly demonstrates fraud, deceit, dishonesty, or misrepresentation. The authority to whom the report is made shall depend on the nature and circumstances of the possible misconduct, (e.g., ethics committees of law firms, corporations and/or paralegal associations, local or state bar associations, local prosecutors, administrative agencies, etc.). Failure to report such knowledge is in itself misconduct and shall be treated as such under these rules.

◀ **FIGURE 11.1**
A PARALEGAL'S DUTY TO REPORT MISCONDUCT

documents to avoid discipline is clearly indicative of fraud, deceit, and an unfitness to practice law.

Knowledge

The imposition of a sanction against a non-reporting legal professional depends upon the establishment of **knowledge** and the subsequent failure to report what the attorney "knew." First, it should be noted that the information must be non-privileged. An attorney or paralegal cannot be required to report misconduct for which he is representing the accused colleague; that information is protected as a client confidence. Any other result would be illogical—it would mean that every professional legal malpractice attorney would have to report many of his clients if there were a reasonable basis for the claim against them! Where an attorney who does not stand in a relationship requiring confidentiality has "a firm opinion that the conduct in question more likely than not occurred" and that conduct is an ethical violation, the attorney has the duty to report the incident to the appropriate authority. *In re Riehlmann*, 891 So. 2d 1239, 1244 (La. 2005). The question remains: At what degree of probability does the duty to report arise? Case law has suggested that it arises with less than absolute certainty but more than mere speculation or conjecture. "Actual knowledge is required, but may be inferred from the circumstances when it is apparent that the lawyer must have known of the misconduct." *Board of Overseers of the Bar v. Warren*, 34 A.3d 1103, 1111 (Me. 2011). Case law is also inconsistent from state to state as to what actual knowledge is: It can range from having real facts at hand upon which to make the conclusion that a violation has occurred to reasonable belief based upon the circumstances surrounding the incident. The essence is what a reasonable attorney would presume another would conclude when presented with the same facts and circumstances. This may be tricky ground. A practical approach was espoused:

> [A] lawyer's conduct will be assessed according to a legal standard that assumes a lawyer can "know" the truth of a situation, even if he cannot be absolutely sure. Even the criminal law, after all, does not require absolute certainty; it requires only a conclusion that is beyond a reasonable doubt.

knowledge
The near certainty of belief that a fact is most likely true.

As noted in § 402, the law of lawyering as set forth in the Terminology section of the Rules of Professional Conduct permits a disciplinary authority to "infer from circumstances" that a lawyer knows what a reasonable person would know. More than this, the law takes account of a lawyer's legal training and experience in assessing his or her state of mind. A lawyer is an adult, a man or a woman of the world, not a child. He or she is also better educated than most people, more sophisticated and more sharply sensitized to the legal implications of a situation. The law will make inferences as to a lawyer's knowledge with those considerations in mind.

Attorney U v. Mississippi Bar, 678 So. 2d 963, 971 (Miss. 1996), citing GEOFFREY C. HAZARD, JR., AND W. WILLIAM HODES, THE LAW OF LAWYERING § 404 (1993).

Substantial Question of Fitness to Practice Law

substantial question
A serious doubt as to an attorney's fitness to practice law because his or her actions or inactions reflect negatively on his or her character.

Even more difficult than determining when an attorney or paralegal has reportable knowledge of an incident is deciding when that incident raises a **substantial question** as to the legal professional's honesty, trustworthiness, or fitness to practice. After an attorney or paralegal becomes aware of another's potential violation of the ethics rules or other action that reflects poorly upon the other's capacity to practice law, the legal professional with the knowledge must determine how serious the actions or inactions of the one suspected are and whether they impact the ability to perform legal duties to the standard required. While there are no bright-line rules regarding the reporting obligation, it is clear that criminal activity is grounds to suspect that another legal professional is unfit to practice law. How can an attorney or paralegal claim to uphold and defend the laws when she herself has broken them? These criminal activities do not have to be connected to the practice of law. For example, an attorney was found to be operating a vehicle under the influence and during his arrest, he refused to cooperate with police officers by forbidding them to test his blood for alcohol. "Such conduct, when committed by an officer of the court, constitutes a failure to maintain personal integrity, reflects upon one's fitness to practice law, and brings the bench and the bar into disrepute." *In re Hoare*, 155 F.3d 937, 940 (8th Cir. 1998). Convictions of criminal activity are self-reporting and another legal professional does not necessarily have to worry about his duty to report the violation under this rule. However, where the criminal activity is not known to the authorities, there will be an obligation to report that activity to the ethical tribunal. Behavior that involves lying, cheating, or evasiveness generally rises to the reportable level. This may include questionable billing practices like double-billing and padding and inaccurate record-keeping. It may also be unrelated to the individual's practice of law. Where an attorney acts in a position that can be held by anyone, for example, as the personal representative of an estate, she will still be held to the higher standards of an attorney.

Like the referee, we cannot agree with [the attorney]'s contention that our rules and professional ethics do not apply to an attorney who acts, at some time or another, as a client rather than as an attorney. Conduct while not acting as an attorney can subject one to disciplinary proceedings. As this Court has stated before, "'an attorney is an attorney is an attorney.'" Even in personal transactions and when not acting as an attorney, attorneys must "avoid tarnishing the professional image or damaging the public." We agree with the referee that this claim is simply untenable. The practice of law is a privilege which carries with it responsibilities as well as rights. That an attorney might, as it were, wear different hats at different times does not mean that professional ethics can be "checked at the door" or that unethical or unprofessional conduct by a member of the legal profession can be tolerated.

The Florida Bar v. Brake, 767 So. 2d 1163, 1168 (Fla. 2000), citing *Florida Bar v. Della-Donna*, 583 So. 2d 307, 310 (Fla. 1989).

However, a given interaction with the legal system may not result in a disciplinary action, if that incident does not bring that attorney's honesty or trustworthiness into question. It is always a fact-sensitive inquiry, though, as the same conduct may bring about discipline in one instance and not in another depending upon the surrounding circumstances. For example, failure to pay child support may be due to personal financial difficulties rather than an intentional plan to evade obligations to a former spouse. *See The Florida Bar v. Taylor*, 648 So. 2d 709 (Fla. 1995).

For paralegals certified under one of the state programs or a paralegal association, the duty to refrain from criminal conduct is the same. For example, North Carolina's certification plan contains this statement: "(c) Notwithstanding an applicant's satisfaction of the standards set forth in Rule .0119(a) or (b), no individual may be certified as a paralegal if: [. . .] (3) the individual has been convicted of a criminal act that reflects adversely on the individual's honesty, trustworthiness or fitness as a paralegal." Florida's newly enacted Registered Paralegal Program similarly provides: "The following individuals are ineligible for registration as a Florida Registered Paralegal or for renewal of a registration that was previously granted: [. . .] (2) a person who has been convicted of a felony in any state or jurisdiction and whose civil rights have not been restored."

Reporting Judicial Misconduct

Upholding the dignity of the legal system is also a responsibility of the judges who sit on the bench, not just a duty binding legal practitioners. Therefore, judges are held to professional standards of conduct, and if a member of the judiciary should demonstrate a lack of fitness in her office, an attorney has an

RESEARCH THIS

Find out how to report attorney misconduct to the appropriate authority in your jurisdiction. Make note of the contact information and filing requirements, if any.

obligation to report that misconduct as well. Judges are the figureheads of the legal system and have their own Code of Judicial Conduct that they must follow. Discourteous conduct may be a trait of overly zealous attorneys, but that kind of behavior is not tolerated on the bench. "Thus, the ideal judge is a person who has by habit and practice achieved self-control and acquired the virtue of being able to will and act as a just person ought to act." *Matter of Hocking*, 546 N.W.2d 234, 237 (1996). "It is clear, however, that every graceless, distasteful, or bungled attempt to communicate the reason for a judge's decision cannot serve as the basis for judicial discipline." *Id.* at 12. The true nature of the exchange and the effect it may have upon the administration of justice must be examined. In this case, two separate incidents formed the basis of the judicial complaint. In the first, the attorney accused the judge of rudeness and improper sentencing in a sexual assault case. The judge expressed frustration at the jury's verdict and made improper remarks regarding the victim. The court found that "[t]he comments were tasteless and undoubtedly offensive to the sensibilities of many citizens. They do not display a mindset unable to render fair judgment." *Id.* at 14. In another instance, the court found that the judge "had instigated a confrontational exchange" with the attorney in front of him. He communicated indirectly that he had already made up his mind about the matter and "challenged" the attorney to defend her position. Additionally, the aggressive nature of the exchange, caustic tone, and personal abuse to the attorney was "clearly prejudicial to the administration of justice." *Id.* at 23. In this particular instance, the attorney was in compliance with her ethical obligations to file a report with the grievance commission against the judge. The true test derived from comparing these two incidents in the Hocking matter is the ability of the judge to remain *fair* in handling the parties, the attorneys, and the disposition of the case.

SPOT THE ISSUE

Pat Parkins has worked as a paralegal for the Godwin, Bailey, and Ulmer Law Firm for years and knows a great deal about the practice and the expectations of the firm. Archie, the new associate, is under a tremendous amount of pressure to bill more hours and get more clients. He has begun to binge drink at lunch with potential new clients. One day at lunch, in a loud and drunken voice, he began to complain about a well-known and well-respected judge. Pat was the only employee of the firm that was there to hear this. Three days after that incident, Archie was grumbling about his workload at the local pub with Pat. He claimed that the firm was giving him all the cases in front of this judge just to punish him; after all, the firm had this judge in its "back pocket" and the firm would ultimately win no matter how Archie performed, so this was all just "busy work." Pat knows that other pub patrons heard this comment. What should Pat do? Does Pat have any ethical obligations under your state's rules of professional conduct? What about under the paralegal association's rules of conduct? Is Pat obligated to say anything? If so, to whom?

Confidentiality Exception

The final element of the requirement to report misconduct is the exception for confidentiality. There is a significant, questionable grey area in this situation. Where an attorney or paralegal learns through a client of another's misconduct that rises to the level of a reportable violation of the obligation of honesty and trustworthiness, must the reporting professional obtain the client's consent before he is able to disclose the misconduct of the other professional? The answer is "it depends." It is clear that if an offense that reflects negatively on the attorney's honesty and fitness to practice law is discovered, there is a potentially reportable event. If an attorney came upon this knowledge of another lawyer's embezzlement of client funds in any manner other than a client confidence, there would be no question that ABA Model Rule 8.3 would impose an obligation to report that misconduct. An attorney is under an "absolute" ethical duty to report the misconduct to the appropriate tribunal. *Skolnick v. Altheimer & Gray*, 730 N.E.2d, 4, 13 (Ill. 2014). "Further, the duty, and the certain discipline that flows from a breach of that duty, is animated by a desire to: maintain the integrity of the legal profession, further the ends of justice, and protect the public from unscrupulous attorneys." *Id.* (The defendant law firm was permitted to file a counterclaim under seal, wherein forgery against the plaintiff, a former partner at the defending law firm, was asserted. The Illinois supreme court also modified the protective order to permit the attorney who discovered the ethical breach to report the misconduct to the state ethics and disciplinary commission.) However, if the knowledge of misconduct comes through confidential client communications, the misconduct must also be kept confidential. Compare this scenario: A client sought out another attorney in order to recoup the embezzled funds from the first lawyer. The client withheld consent for the second attorney to disclose the misconduct and therefore, under the rule of confidentiality, the second attorney could not report the misconduct using the client's confidential information that he acquired as a result of the client's representation. The exceptions to the confidentiality rule do not apply in this situation. The disclosure would not be made either to either prevent the client from committing a criminal act or to establish a claim or defense of the lawyer based upon conduct in which the client was involved. *See In re Ethics Advisory Panel Opinion No. 92-1*, 627 A.2d 317 (R.I. 1993).

While the Rhode Island court found that the rules of client confidentiality overruled the rules of reporting misconduct, other courts may take a different view depending on the language and interpretation of the state's code of conduct. The court in *In re Himmel*, 533 N.E.2d 790 (R.I. 1988), came to a different conclusion regarding a client's request not to report a prior attorney's misconduct. It hinged upon the court's definition of "privileged information" received by his client. The court determined that the client had disclosed this same information to third parties and, therefore, did not have an expectation that the information would come under the attorney-client privilege. It is important to note that the court took the narrower view of the confidential nature of the attorney-client communication and held that only evidentiary privilege applied, not the more general rule of confidentiality. This means that only communications made between the attorney and client for purposes of the representation for which no other source of the information existed would exclude the information from being disclosed. The more general rule of confidentiality does not rest upon how the attorney came to know of the information: He may not disclose the information, regardless of the source; it matters only that it pertains to his client. Taking the former, narrow view that privileged information only is excluded from the rule requiring disclosure, the court stated that the attorney having the non-privileged information regarding another lawyer's misconduct must divulge that information to the ethical authority. It is no defense that the client did not give his consent to the disclosure: "A lawyer may not choose to circumvent the rules by simply asserting that his client asked him to do so." *Id.* at 539. This much narrower view is not the one favored by most courts, and the Washington Supreme Court took pains to point out the following: "[We] cannot tolerate for a moment, neither can the profession, neither can the community, any disloyalty on the part of a lawyer to his client. In all things he must be true to that trust, or, failing it, he must leave the profession." *In re Disciplinary Proceeding Against Schafer*, 66 P.3d 1036, 1038 (Wash. 2003) (citing *United States v. Costen*, 38 F. 24, 24 (C.C.D. Colo. 1889)). *See also Weiss v. Lonnquist*, 293 P.3d 1264, 1271 (Wash. App. 2013) ("The bar disciplinary process is an adequate means of promoting the public policy rooted in the rules of professional conduct."). It should be noted that in both the *Schafer* and *Weiss* cases, the reporting attorneys went too far in disclosing the unethical conduct by introducing the material into public forums (newspapers, public officials, and civil complaints, respectively) and therefore were sanctioned for these unnecessarily broad disclosures. Attorneys are obligated to report to their jurisdiction's ethical boards *only*.

Conversely, disclosure where it is not warranted and in violation of the rules requiring the maintenance of confidentiality opens the reporting attorney or paralegal up to sanctions of his own. The attorney, Schafer, not only disclosed

IN-CLASS DISCUSSION

Courtney has filed for divorce from her husband Allen, who is an attorney. He has chosen to represent himself at the divorce proceedings.

At the final court hearing, Allen testifies that he is currently an outpatient in the local hospital's alcohol and drug addiction program. He admits that he has used cocaine recently, but that he has not used it since entering the program two weeks ago. Courtney wins full custody of the children and Allen is required to pay substantial child support.

What duty does Courtney's lawyer have to report Allen's admitted use of cocaine to the appropriate ethical authority? If Allen loses his position at his law firm, he will be unable to pay this support.

N.B. the state ethical opinion that inspired this fact pattern has since been withdrawn.

SURF'S UP

Famous attorneys have famous clients, and somehow the relationship always ends up in the rolls of infamy. Cruise the internet and you will find plenty of attorneys for the rich and famous who set up their own promotional websites to capitalize on their fame. What impact does this have on the integrity of the profession? Do you think this kind of notoriety is good for the reputation of the justice system?

For an example, see http://www.debraopri.com/.

information obtained through his former client to the tribunal; he also published newspaper articles and forwarded investigatory information to the FBI and the IRS regarding the prior questionable business investments of his former client and his former client's business partner, who just happened to presently be a sitting judge with whom the reporting attorney did not get along. The court found that the reporting attorney went too far in disclosing more information than was necessary in order to reveal the misconduct by the judge, and certainly in broadcasting it to too large an audience. Rule 8.3 permits disclosure to the appropriate tribunal, not the world at large in a willful and spiteful exposé. While the court found that the end result, the removal of a corrupt judge, served the public good, the means to bring about that end were not justified, and the attorney was suspended from practice for six months. Viewing these cases as part of the broader picture, it comes down to a case-sensitive balancing act based on the principle of maintaining the integrity of the profession.

THE CATCH-ALL RULE OF CONDUCT

The last rule to be discussed is the "catch-all" for the behavioral control of attorneys. ABA Model Rule 8.4 essentially reiterates and reinforces all the rules that have come before it, and plugs any possible loopholes that a clever attorney might try to find.

The primary mandate of this all-encompassing rule binds an attorney and her agents to all the applicable rules of professional conduct. Not only is an actual violation of the rules a sanctionable offense, so is an attempt to circumvent the obligations under the ethical rules. The rules apply not only to the attorney but to all those who work with him, as he cannot ask a non-attorney to do anything that would violate the rules in order to escape responsibility for the infraction. In a constitutional challenge alleging that ABA Model Rule 8.4(a) is invalid and unconstitutional because it is too vague for the prohibitions to be understood, the court found that argument without merit. Attorneys are well aware of their "shall" and "shall not" obligations under the ethics rules. Any violation, attempted violation, or third-party solicitation to violate the rules on behalf of the attorney is sanctionable. In *Rogers v. Mississippi Bar*, 731 So. 2d 1158, 1166 (Miss. 1999), the court found that the "moonlighting" attorney was improperly taking legal matters from his firm when he worked on them privately after hours, without disclosing this arrangement to the firm. It is under this language as well that paralegals need to be familiar with the ethical rules governing attorneys in their jurisdictions. A paralegal cannot be asked to perform any task that the attorney herself would be prohibited from undertaking under the rules. To do so would be to "knowingly assist or induce another" to violate or attempt to violate the ethical obligations imposed by the relevant code of professional conduct. This is also reflected in NFPA EC 1.3(e). (See Figure 11.2.)

Criminal Activity

Criminal activity is expressly proscribed. To commit an act that is prohibited by the very laws that the attorney has sworn to uphold—to disobey the rule of law before the tribunal of which the attorney is a member—is impermissible and will be sanctioned as professional misconduct, regardless of the fact of conviction or acquittal of the act.

> The lawyer's offense causing disciplinary violation need not be criminal, but rather one that reflects adversely on the profession. The practice of law is an honorable profession and no lawyer should ever do any act or acts that would in any way reflect poorly upon the honorable profession of law. [. . .] Fitness to practice law includes maintaining good moral character. It is a long standing principle that for one to be worthy to practice law, the person must have a good moral character upon entering the profession, and must maintain such character all through his or her professional life. Any act by an attorney that brings the profession or the authority of the courts and administration of the law into disrespect or disregard, such as dishonesty, personal misconduct, questionable moral character, or unprofessional conduct is potential grounds for disbarment. Rather, the public is entitled to rely on an attorney's admission to the practice of law as a certification of the attorney's honesty, high ethical standards, and good moral character.

> *Grigsby v. Kentucky Bar Ass'n*, 181 S.W.3d 40, 42 (Ky. 2005) (citations omitted).

In that matter the attorney, through a plea bargain, was convicted of a misdemeanor offense of possession of a controlled substance. The court looked past the plea bargain arrangement to the actual facts of the situation and found that the original felony charges should form the basis of the sanction. It does not affect the ethical board's sanction power that an attorney has served his criminal time in prison or has otherwise been punished for his conduct. Attorneys are admonished to avoid all illegal conduct and maintain

FIGURE 11.2 ▶
A PARALEGAL'S DUTY TO REFRAIN FROM ASSISTING IN A VIOLATION OF ETHICS RULES.

NFPA EC 1.3(e)

A paralegal shall not knowingly assist any individual with the commission of an act that is in direct violation of the Model Code/Model Rules and/or the rules and/or laws governing the jurisdiction in which the paralegal practices.

only the highest standards in their lives, both professional and personal. "Obedience to the law exemplifies respect for the law." *Toledo Bar Ass'n v. Abood*, 821 N.E.2d 560, 563 (Ohio 2004) (The attorney had failed to pay his federal income taxes due to severe financial difficulties. The fact that he attempted to avoid payment for a period of time aggravated the circumstances and a one-year suspension was warranted.).

Dishonesty, Fraud, or Misrepresentation

The rule further addresses the lack of personal character and integrity, sometimes referred to in a term of art as acts of "moral turpitude." There can be no enumeration of the various and sundry ways in which a person can exhibit a deficiency of the morals and values that are demanded by the legal profession. That is why there is this need for the "catch-all" sections. False notarization and submission of inaccurate bills for reimbursement from public funds are two ways in which a county attorney found himself in trouble and sanctioned by a one-year suspension. He knowingly and selfishly performed these acts of dishonesty and therefore was found unfit to practice. *In re Kraushaar*, 997 P.2d 81 (Kan. 2000). Among other wrongful actions undertaken by an attorney, misrepresentation of the character of practice to induce clients to retain his services and the insertion of a covenant not to sue—including language indicating that documents that could be used as evidence would be destroyed—resulted in an indefinite suspension from the practice of law. *Matter of Holyoak*, 3782 P.3d 1205 (Kan. 2016).

> We rarely see such behavior unaccompanied by any misgivings that reflects so poorly on our profession. We find his conduct, which ultimately evolved into a scheme of bribery and extortion, to be of such a serious magnitude and unconscionable nature that an indefinite period of suspension is warranted. If not fully accepting and appreciating that falsely claiming to the representation of over 50 litigants and offering to destroy all evidence that could be used on their and others' behalf in exchange for wiring $1.9 million to an offshore account is wrongful, nothing short of the action we are taking today will adequately protect the public.

Id. at 1219.

REEL TO REAL

In the classic film-noir *Force of Evil* (1948), attorney Joe Morse (played by John Garfield) wants to use his position and knowledge to consolidate all the small-time numbers racket operators into one big powerful operation, even though his brother, a small-time operator, opposes him. How does this movie embody the maxim "Power corrupts?" Why is legal power so dangerous? Consider what President John Adams had to say on the subject: "Because power corrupts, society's demands for moral authority and character increase as the importance of the position increases."

Conduct Prejudicial to the Administration of Justice

Clearly, the suppression of evidence or otherwise hindering of the process of the legal system is prejudicial to its administration. But less drastic and indirect methods of encumbering the system are sanctionable as well if they are performed by attorneys. As officers of the court, attorneys enjoy a special symbiotic relationship with the justice system and should at all times act in the best interest of its functioning and maintain its dignity. Therefore, the attorney's conduct does not have to affect a singular proceedings in which the attorney is involved; "the 'administration of justice' Rule 8.4(d) seeks to protect from prejudice is much broader than the administration of justice to be effected in any single trial or adjudicatory proceeding. . . . All lawyers, by virtue of their licenses, enjoy the status of officers of the court. That status brings with it the responsibility to refrain from conduct unbecoming such officers . . . [The Rule] encompasses conduct that injures, harms, or disadvantages the justice system generally, regardless of the context in which that conduct occurs or whether it prejudiced a particular proceeding." *In re Kline*, 311 P.3d 321, 340 (Kan. 2013) (internal citations omitted). In preserving the integrity of the system, attorneys uphold the honor of their chosen profession as well. Public commentary regarding unfairness of a particular proceeding should be undertaken with extreme caution.

> Did respondent's mailing of his letter 19 days after his discipline to more than 281 addressees constitute conduct prejudicial to the administration of justice? It did. His minimal research may have supported the existence of certain previous relationships between insurance industry clients and some group of members of the Disciplinary Board; he may truly have realized too late that he should have hired counsel to represent him in his disciplinary proceeding; he may have had previous unpleasant dealings with his own insurance company and suspected an insurance company's involvement in alerting the disciplinary office to his behavior. Even if he was correct in all of these respects, even if his personal animosity toward the insurance industry was somehow justified, his wholesale indictment of the Kansas disciplinary process as "stacked against him" was not. Rule 8.4(d) can be violated by conduct unbecoming an officer of the court, even if a legal proceeding has ended and even if the lawyer stops somewhere short of spreading outright lies.

Members of the Disciplinary Board serve as judges or commissioners in the Kansas disciplinary process. Our society has a substantial interest in protecting them and other actors in the process from unfounded attacks, and it may do so without running afoul of a disciplined attorney's First Amendment rights. There is a line between just and unjust criticism. Respondent crossed it. This is evident from his plainly selfish motive. He displayed no desire to improve the disciplinary system, only to excuse its focus on him.

In re Pyle, 156 P.3d 1231, 1247-1248 (Kan. 2007).

Misuse may not rise to the level of abuse, but the ethical rules make it clear that even small infractions may be significant if they reflect upon the dignity of the tribunal and respect for all the parties involved in the proceedings. Attacking the ability of opposing counsel, threatening to bring disciplinary actions and appeals if the attorney's requests are not met, and other overtly offensive conduct that manifests a disrespect for others are all actions which, while not an express violation of one of the enumerated ethical rules, are a violation of ABA Model Rule 8.4(d). Courts have been warning attorneys through case law to exhibit civility and good manners. Perhaps this statement puts it most eloquently and succinctly: "Care with words and respect for courts and one's adversaries is a necessity, not because lawyers and judges are without fault, but because trial by combat long ago proved unsatisfactory." *In re Converse,* 602 N.W.2d 500, 508 (Neb. 1999) (An applicant seeking to take the State Bar was denied permission to sit for the exam due to his "character deficiencies" in conducting himself as a rather outspoken law student.). Attorneys, like all other people, can be hostile when faced with a stressful situation like litigation, and they will be forgiven the isolated incidents of heated moments of anger or frustration. Extreme reactions will not be tolerated, however. The court in *In re McAlvey,* 354 A.2d 289, 290-291 (N.J. 1976), addressed this overt aggression.

Whatever the remarks were, they caused respondent to fly into a rage. He sprang from his chair screaming, grabbed opposing counsel by the throat and began to choke him. The judge and the law clerk tried to separate the two men who were now locked in combat, and at one point all four persons-the judge, his law clerk and the two attorneys-were rolling on the floor. [. . .] There is no question but that respondent is guilty of a serious violation of our Code. The whole concept of the rule of law is bottomed on respect for the law and the courts and judges who administer it. Attorneys who practice law and appear in the courts are officers of the court. An attorney who exhibits the lack of civility, good manners and common courtesy here displayed tarnishes the entire image of what the bar stands for.

On the other end of the spectrum, coolly calculated attacks are also prohibited. When attorneys have prepared for the insult and have had sufficient time to reflect on the inflammatory nature of their speech or actions, they should be held accountable. These catch-all rules give the court the latitude to discipline them for such outrageous lapses in better judgment that interfere with the proper and rational administration of justice. Discourteous conduct "tears at the fabric of the legal profession, which can expect to have no better reputation for trustworthiness in the community than that of its worst actors." *In re Porter*, 890 P.2d 1377, 1386 (Or. 1995) (The attorney misrepresented his intent to seek a default in the case and therefore, "the accused violated his duty to maintain the standards of personal integrity on which the legal community, and the larger community, rely.").

Improper Influence over the System

Justice can be obtained only where there has been an opportunity for both sides to fairly and equally present their cases before a neutral tribunal. Any interference with the neutrality of the court negatively affects the public perception of the function of the legal system. To suggest that the outcome of the case can be influenced by anything other than the evidence presented and fair deliberation of the merits is to undermine the system. This is the harm that subsection (e) of the ABA Model Rule 8.4 seeks to avoid by making it a sanctionable offense to suggest that an attorney or her agent can influence the outcome of a matter by means other than those permitted. Bribery, a classic example of such impermissible influence, is also considered criminal conduct punishable under subsection (b). Relationships between attorneys and judges may arise as they work in close proximity to each other, sometimes on a fairly regular basis. While there is no prohibition against such associations, they become improper when the judge and the attorney develop a personal, intimate relationship and then must work together. The justice system can work only when a neutral judge is listening to the adversaries before her without personal bias. If there is a personal relationship, a judge may properly recuse herself from the matter in order to preserve the integrity of the pending matter. This is exactly what a judge did in *Disciplinary Counsel v. Cicero*, 678 N.E.2d 517 (Ohio 1997). However, the attorney violated subsection (e) by boasting to opposing counsel and other members of the bar that he was in a sexual relationship with the judge and that any continuances sought in the matter would be denied, as he and the judge would be going away together for the holidays. *Id.* To insinuate that the judge would prefer the attorney's company over the fair administration of justice was entirely unacceptable and warranted a one-year suspension for the attorney from the practice of law. Social media has complicated this issue. For example, lawyers and judges must be very careful to avoid the appearance of intimacy through Facebook "friending." "The issue, however, is not whether the lawyer actually is in a position to influence the judge, but instead whether the proposed conduct, the identification of the lawyer as a 'friend' on the social networking site, conveys the impression that the lawyer is in a position to influence the judge. The Committee concludes that such identification in a public forum of a lawyer who may appear before the judge does convey this impression and therefore is not permitted. Thus, as the Committee recognized, a judge's activity on a social networking site may undermine confidence in the judge's neutrality." *Domville v. State*, 103 So. 3d 184, 185 (Fla. Dist. Ct. App. 2012), citing Fla. JEAC Op. 2009-20. Other jurisdictions have adopted much the same stance—advising caution.

Accessory to Judicial Misconduct

The practice of law is participatory. There are many actors on the justice system's stage, and each one must respect the obligations of the part they play. The last subsection acknowledges that while judges are in a position superior to that of attorneys, they too can be fallible, and an attorney must not assist the members of the bench in committing a violation of the Code of Judicial Conduct. This may be particularly tempting when the violation tends to help the attorney in the matter before the judge, and it may be tempting also where there is little chance of detection or challenge. However, it is to be avoided at all costs; further, as previously discussed, the attorney has a reporting obligation to the relevant ethical board if the attorney knows of the judge's ethical violation. In the case of *In re Wilder*, 764 N.E.2d 617 (Ind. 2002), the town attorney attempted to file a temporary restraining order against the town's commissioners to prohibit them from taking a certain action. The attorney filed the papers and met with the judge ex parte and after 5:00 p.m. to obtain the judge's signature on the order. The signed papers were then served the next morning upon the commissioners. While this may seem to be merely a procedural irregularity, the court found that the judge violated the judicial code by signing the order without finding that there would be irreparable and immediate harm if he did not do so at that moment without notice to the opposing party. The judge was suspended for three days. However, the attorney was also subject to discipline, because he knew that the application for the TRO required notice, and by obtaining the judge's signature without complying with the "exigent circumstances" showing required under the court rules, he was assisting the judge to commit an act of impropriety. As the attorney was found to be equally culpable of the questionable conduct, he was equally sanctioned by a three-day suspension.

PRO BONO ACTIVITIES

In order to maintain the confidence and trust of the public and to better serve the interests of justice, legal professionals should strive to provide **pro bono publico** services in their communities. By doing so, paralegals can provide access to justice and make the difference that the paralegal profession was designed to address. Not only has NFPA incorporated this aspiration to public service in its Model Code, it is deeply committed through its Pro Bono Committee. The association has also incorporated this mission into its ethical code. (See Figure 11.3.) Certified members should aspire to dedicate 24 hours of pro bono service per year in their communities another term. Attorneys are encouraged by ABA Model Rule 6.1 to provide 50 hours of pro bono services. These services can be provided directly to a person of limited means or to charitable, religious, civic, community, governmental, and educational organizations that serve that population. Further qualifying for pro bono service is work for organizations whose goals are to protect civil rights or civil liberties of citizens,

FIGURE 11.3 ▶

A PARALEGAL'S PRO BONO PUBLICO ACTIVITIES

NFPA EC 1.4

1.4   **A paralegal shall serve the public interest by contributing to the improvement of the legal system and delivery of quality legal services, including pro bono publico services and community service.**

Ethical Considerations

EC-1.4 (a)   A paralegal shall be sensitive to the legal needs of the public and shall promote the development and implementation of programs that address those needs.

EC-1.4 (b)   A paralegal shall support efforts to improve the legal system and access thereto and shall assist in making changes.

EC-1.4 (c)   A paralegal shall support and participate in the delivery of *Pro Bono Publico* services directed toward implementing and improving access to justice, the law, the legal system or the paralegal and legal professions.

EC-1.4 (d)   A paralegal should aspire annually to contribute twenty-four (24) hours of *Pro Bono Publico* services under the supervision of an attorney or as authorized by administrative, statutory or court authority to:

1. persons of limited means; or

2. charitable, religious, civic, community, governmental and educational organizations in matters that are designed primarily to address the legal needs of persons with limited means; or

3. individuals, groups or organizations seeking to secure or protect civil rights, civil liberties or public rights.

The twenty-four (24) hours of Pro Bono Publico services contributed annually by a paralegal may consist of such services as detailed in this EC-1.4(d), and/or administrative matters designed to develop and implement the attainment of this aspiration as detailed above in EC-1.4(a), (b), (c), or any combination of the two.

EC-1.4 (e)   A paralegal should aspire to contribute twenty-four (24) hours of Community Service on an annual basis. For purposes of this EC, "Community Service" shall be defined as: volunteer activities that have the effect of providing a valuable service or benefit to a local community, as distinguished from those services which fall within the traditional definition of pro bono publico. By way of example and not limitation, several examples of Community Service may include: working with Habitat for Humanity, volunteering with local women's shelters, volunteering for hurricane relief, serving meals at local soup kitchens or local homeless shelters.

---

pro bono publico
Literally, "for the public good." Describing legal services provided to the public by legal professionals voluntarily and without payment.

either individually or as a whole. All of this work improves the legal profession as well. Further, attorneys are encouraged to make financial contributions to organizations that provide legal services to persons of limited means.

Volunteerism is a noble goal, and professionals are in a unique position to use their special skills to aid those in need. Indeed, one cannot be an advocate for the justice system if one does not act to improve the justice system for all citizens. Legal professionals have a responsibility to promote overall justice and fairness in their communities. The quality of justice should not depend on the ability to pay for legal services.

As attorneys and paralegals are entrusted with matters of great consequence, with their clients' confidence, judges' trust, and societal expectations, they must always seek to act in accordance with those elements. This may place a burden on the profession, but attorneys enjoy a certain status in the justice system which demands such standards. Paralegals are essential in the delivery of these services as well. Their conduct, not just their work product, must support the legal profession as a whole. Failing to comport with these ethical mandates in both personal and professional activities may increase the cynicism of the public in the fair administration of justice. As officers of the court, legal professionals have a duty to project the very characteristics that attorneys must rely upon when they are before the tribunal. The legal profession started as a "gentleman's calling" to serve society, and attempts should be made to preserve the dignity of the system so that every citizen can feel that she will, if need be, get her fair day in court and be treated with courtesy while trying to navigate the system. Further, the system can only operate as well as its least productive or civilized member. It is for these reasons that the legal profession has burdened attorneys with a duty to comport themselves in accordance with the integrity of the profession. This is precisely why the paralegal profession needs to be cognizant of its own development and reputation to ensure its steady and healthy growth. Pre-professional and continuing legal education is vital to the nurturing of the public's perception and confidence in the profession.

Summary

This chapter examined the overarching principles that unify the entire set of ethical rules that bind all legal professionals. Both attorneys and paralegals must comport themselves with strict professional and personal ethical standards. These broad categories of duties to the legal system and administration of justice are as follows:

1. Being honest toward reviewing or admission boards or other legal authorities to maintain the character of the profession

2. Displaying respect for the legal system and its participants

3. Reporting misconduct to the proper authorities, where the legal professional has knowledge of the act or omission that raises a substantial question of fitness to practice law

4. Understanding the code and restraints on judicial conduct and refraining from aiding in judicial misconduct

5. Refraining from criminal, dishonest, or deceitful activities or any other conduct that is prejudicial to the administration of justice

Key Terms

Knowledge   Self-policing
Pro bono publico   Substantial question

Review Questions

MULTIPLE CHOICE

Choose the best answer(s) and please explain *why* you chose the answer(s).

1. A bar candidate must disclose:
   a. All information about herself
   b. Any changes in her situation that are relevant to her application
   c. Nothing that is not specifically asked on the bar application
   d. Only that information that is requested during the oral character and fitness interview

2. If an attorney wants to speak out against a judicial official:
   a. He must first obtain the court's permission
   b. He must file his intended statement with the ethics board in his jurisdiction so they can rule whether he is permitted to say those things
   c. He must remain respectful and truthful but he is free to criticize
   d. All of the above

3. To raise a "substantial question" as to a lawyer's fitness to practice law, the reporting attorney:
   a. Should have independent factual proof of the purported misconduct
   b. Should be reasonably sure that the conduct in question occurred
   c. Has to prove that the lawyer was convicted of a crime of moral turpitude
   d. All of the above

EXPLAIN YOURSELF

All answers should be written in complete sentences. A simple yes or no is insufficient.

1. Explain the concept of a self-policing profession.

2. Describe a situation in which a paralegal should report her supervising attorney's misconduct.

3. Why are paralegals held to the same ethical standards as attorneys?

4. Define acts of "moral turpitude."

FAULTY PHRASES

All of the following statements are *false*. State why they are false and then rewrite each one as a true statement. Do not simply make the statement negative by adding the word "not."

1. An attorney has an obligation to report misconduct only of subordinate lawyers.

2. Before reporting professional misconduct, an attorney must be absolutely sure and have supporting facts relating to his allegations.

3. An attorney has the same free speech protections as other citizens when criticizing the judiciary as a branch of the government.

4. The crime for which the attorney was convicted must relate to dishonesty in order for it to be considered an ethical violation.

5. Judges are held to a slightly lower standard for moral conduct because they are not engaged in the active practice of representing clients.

6. Judges are permitted to conduct themselves as they see fit in their own courtrooms, as long as they can control the attorneys appearing before them.

7. An attorney's duty of confidentiality will always be overtaken by her duty to report misconduct of another attorney.

8. A paralegal's duty to maintain the integrity of the justice system is not as high as that of attorneys and judges.

PORTFOLIO ASSIGNMENT

Write Away

Compose a position statement regarding your views on the future of the paralegal profession. What are the most important characteristics that need to be cultivated in the field? How will this be possible? How do the ethical mandates fit into your position? Do they need to be expanded? Made more specific? Please provide examples or hypotheticals where appropriate.

Cases in Point

CA Eth. Op. 2003-162, 2003 WL 23146201 (Cal. St. Bar Comm. Prof'l Resp.)
Issue: What ethical issues are raised when a California attorney publicly advocates civil disobedience, including violations of law, in furtherance of her personally held political, moral, or religious beliefs, and simultaneously practices law?
Formal Opinion Number 2003-162
2003

DIGEST

While attorneys have rights under the First Amendment to express political, moral, and religious beliefs and to advocate civil disobedience, attorneys must follow their professional responsibility when acting upon their beliefs and when advising clients. At a minimum, attorneys' performance of their professional duties to clients must not be adversely affected by the attorneys' personal beliefs or exercise of First Amendment rights. In selecting areas of legal practice, types of cases and particular clients, attorneys should be cognizant of the possibility that their moral, social, and religious beliefs, and their exercise of their First Amendment rights, could adversely affect the performance of their duties to clients.

AUTHORITIES INTERPRETED

Rules 3-110, 3-210, and 3-310 of the Rules of Professional Conduct of the State Bar of California.

Business and Professions Code sections 6067, 6068, subdivisions (a) and (c), and 6103.

STATEMENT OF FACTS

An attorney (Attorney) maintains a law practice emphasizing business transactional work, estate and tax planning services, and tax controversy matters. She believes sincerely that the entire state and federal tax system is immoral, and has joined an association (Association) that opposes taxation of individuals and family businesses.

She has spoken at Association conferences and advocated resistance to the state and federal tax systems. In these speeches, she has proposed that individuals and small businesses refuse to report to the Franchise Tax Board and the Internal Revenue Service any transaction or event that might lead to the imposition of income, capital gains, or estate taxation, and has advocated that they also refuse to pay taxes.

Attorney has never represented Association, but she receives a substantial number of client referrals from her speeches on behalf of and through her contacts in the organization. While she has publicly advocated civil disobedience, Attorney advises lawful behavior in counseling her clients.

What ethical considerations govern Attorney's activities?

DISCUSSION

I. Is it ethically permissible for Attorney to publicly advocate the refusal to pay taxes?

The facts do not identify the existence of a law prohibiting advocacy of violations of state or federal tax laws. Even if there were such a law, it might well violate the First and Fourteenth Amendments guarantees of free speech and assembly. A state may not forbid or proscribe the advocacy of a violation of law except where such advocacy is directed to inciting or producing imminent lawless action and is likely to incite or produce such action. (*Brandenburg v. Ohio (1969)* 395 U.S. 444 [89 S. Ct. 1827].)

Attorney's status as a lawyer does not change the analysis. To the extent speech is constitutionally protected, Attorney has the First Amendment right to advocate political and social change through the violation of law, even though the First Amendment rights of lawyers are limited in certain respects. (See *Standing Committee on Discipline v. Yagman* (9th Cir. 1995) 55 F.3d 1430, and *In re Palmisano* (7th Cir. 1995) 70 F.3d 483, cert. denied, 116 S. Ct. 1854 (1996) [both dealing with the special problem of discipline for attorneys who publicly criticize judges].)

The Committee notes, however, the distinction between advocating and engaging in violations of law. Attorneys are subject to discipline for illegal conduct even if their conduct occurs outside the practice of law and does not involve moral turpitude. As the California Supreme Court stated in the seminal case of *In re Rohan* (1978) 21 Cal. 3d 195, 203 [145 Cal. Rptr. 855], explaining why discipline was appropriate for an attorney's criminal conviction of willful failure to file tax returns: "An attorney as an officer of the court and counselor at law occupies a unique position in society. His refusal to obey the law, and the bar's failure to discipline him for such refusal, will not only demean the integrity of the profession but will encourage disrespect for and further violations of the law. This is particularly true in the case of revenue law violations by an attorney." (See also *In re Kelley* (1990) 52 Cal. 3d 487 [276 Cal. Rptr. 375] [discipline imposed for two drunk driving convictions, the second while on probation from the first]; *In re Morales* (1983) 35 Cal. 3d 1 [96 Cal. Rptr. 353] [discipline imposed for failure to withhold or pay taxes and unemployment contributions].)

II. Is it ethically permissible for Attorney to advise her clients not to pay taxes that are due under applicable law?

It is important to distinguish between Attorney's exercise of her First Amendment rights and her performance of her duties as a lawyer for clients. By virtue of her participation in and speech on behalf of the Association, Attorney has been retained by clients because of the political and social views she publicly has taken regarding the payment of taxes. Although a lawyer may advocate political and social change through the violation of tax laws, she may not advise a client to violate the law unless she believes reasonably and in good faith that such law is invalid and

there is a good-faith argument for the modification or reversal of that law.[1]

III. Does Attorney have an ethical duty to disclose her relationship with Association and her position on taxation to prospective and existing clients?

An attorney may not accept or continue the representation of a client, if the attorney has any of the several potential or actual conflicts of interest listed in rule 3–310 of the California Rules of Professional Conduct, absent "written disclosure" to and, in many instances, "informed written consent" from, the client or potential client. Together, the written disclosure requirements in paragraphs (B)(1) and (B)(2) of rule 3-310 apply when a lawyer has or had "a legal, business, financial, professional or personal relationship with" a party or witness in the same matter in which the lawyer represents the client.[2] Paragraph (B)(4) of the rule applies when a lawyer "has or had a legal, business, financial, or professional interest in the subject matter of the

---

[1] Rule 3-210 of the California Rules of Professional Conduct prohibits a member from advising a client to violate the law "unless the member believes in good faith that such law . . . is invalid." Similarly, rule 3-200 of the Rules of Professional Conduct prohibits a member from accepting or continuing employment if he or she knows that the client's purpose is "to present a claim or defense in litigation that is not warranted under existing law, unless it can be supported by a good faith argument for an extension, modification, or reversal of such existing law." Further, subdivision (a) of California Business and Professions Code section 6068 requires that California attorneys support the Constitution and laws of the United States and of this state. Subdivision (c) of section 6068 requires that an attorney maintain such actions or proceedings only as they appear to him or her legal or just. Each of these rule and statutory provisions identifies a duty of an attorney; California Business and Professions Code section 6103 in turn provides that an attorney may be disciplined for violation of his or her duties as an attorney.
[2] "Disclosure" is defined as "informing the client . . . of the relevant circumstances and of the actual and reasonably foreseeable adverse consequences to the client. . . ." (Rules Prof. Conduct, rule 3-310(A)(1).) Disclosure permits clients to make knowing and intelligent decisions about their representation when their attorneys have potential or actual conflicts of interest.

representation." As the Association is neither a party or witness in the matters of Attorney's tax clients, no disclosure pursuant to paragraphs (B)(1) or (B)(2) would be required. Similarly, as the Association is not the subject matter of the Attorney's representation of tax clients, no disclosure pursuant to paragraph (B)(4) would be required either.

We recognize that paragraph (B)(3) might appear at first glance to be applicable to Attorney. This part of the rule states that a lawyer shall not accept or continue the representation of a client without providing written "disclosure" to the client or potential client where the attorney has or had a "legal, business, financial, professional, or personal relationship with another person or entity" which the attorney "knows or reasonably should" know would be "substantially affected by resolution of the matter." However, there are no facts that implicate paragraph (B)(3). Whether Attorney "knows or reasonably should know" that the Association would be "substantially affected by the resolution of the matter" depends on the totality of the circumstances. These circumstances might include such things as the scope and object of the client's engagement of Attorney.

IV. Can Attorney competently represent clients in business and taxation matters?

Attorney has publicly advocated that others resist state and federal tax laws by refusing to report transactions and events on which taxation could be imposed, and by refusing to pay taxes. While her constitutional rights of speech and assembly may permit her such advocacy, they do not alter her duties to her clients.

These duties include the obligation to provide competent representation found in rule 3-110 of the California Rules of Professional Conduct.[3] Business

---

[3] Rule 3–110 of the California Rules of Professional Conduct provides:

(A) A member shall not intentionally, recklessly, or repeatedly fail to perform legal services with competence.
(B) For purposes of this rule, "competence" in any legal service shall mean to apply the 1) diligence, 2) learning and skill, and 3) mental, emotional, and physical ability reasonably necessary for the performance of such service.
(C) If a member does not have sufficient learning and skill when the legal service is undertaken, the member may nonetheless perform such services competently by 1) associating with or, where appropriate, professionally consulting another lawyer reasonably believed to be competent, or 2) by acquiring sufficient learning and skill before performance is required.

and Professions Code section 6067 requires that attorneys admitted to practice in California take an oath that includes a promise "faithfully to discharge the duties of an attorney to the best of his [or her] knowledge and ability."

Attorney's personal views and public comments regarding taxation do not necessarily render her unable to competently represent a client in a tax matter. Indeed, it is possible that because of her strong beliefs Attorney has a particularly sophisticated knowledge of the substantive law and the procedures that could be pertinent to her work on tax matters. Despite this possibility, it is important to recognize that the duty of competence includes an emotional component. Rule 3-110 prohibits intentional, reckless or repeated incompetence and defines "competence" as the application of "the 1) diligence, 2) learning and skill, and 3) *mental, emotional and physical ability reasonably necessary for the performance of legal services*." (Italics added.) Thus, if Attorney's mental or emotional state prevents her from performing an objective evaluation of her client's legal position, providing unbiased advice to her client, or performing her legal representation according to her client's directions, then Attorney would violate the duty of competence. (See *Blanton v. Woman Care* (1985) 38 Cal. 3d 396, 407-408 [212 Cal. Rptr. 151]; *Considine v. Shadle, Hunt & Hagar* (1986) 187 Cal. App. 3d 760, 765 [232 Cal. Rptr. 250]; Cal. State Bar Formal Op. No. 1984-77; and L.A. Cty. Bar Ass'n Formal Op. No. 504 (2001).[4]

This opinion is issued by the Standing Committee on Professional Responsibility and Conduct of the State Bar of California. It is advisory only. It is not binding upon the courts, the State Bar of California, its Board of Governors, any persons or tribunals charged with regulatory responsibility or any member of the State Bar.

Source: Reprinted from Westlaw with permission from Thomson Reuters.

---

[4] We express no opinion as to whether or not there may be a duty to communicate to clients the possible impact of her views on taxation, or the knowledge of the taxing authorities of those views, on the outcome of the representation.

65 Cal. 2d 447
Supreme Court of California
Terence HALLINAN, Petitioner,
v.
COMMITTEE OF BAR EXAMINERS of the STATE BAR of CALIFORNIA, Respondent.
S.F. 22295.
Dec. 15, 1966.

Proceeding on petition to review action of committee of bar examiners in refusing to certify applicant to Supreme Court for admission to practice law. The Supreme Court, Peters, J., held that applicant's misdemeanor convictions for unlawful assembly, remaining at place of unlawful assembly, disturbing the peace, trespass to obstruct lawful business, and unlawful entry in connection with peaceful civil rights demonstrations and his beliefs that sit-ins are justified when employers refuse even to talk about hiring Negroes and that a lawyer has duty to disobey some really unconstitutional laws did not warrant refusal to certify him for lack of good moral character.

Certification of petitioner as one qualified to be admitted to practice law ordered.

McComb, J., dissented.

OPINION

Peters, Justice.

Petitioner, Terence Hallinan, seeks review of the action of the Committee of Bar Examiners in refusing to certify him to this court for admission to practice law in California.

Petitioner, now aged 29, graduated from Hastings College of Law and in March 1965 took and passed the bar examination given general applicants. He was not certified for admission, however, pending investigation and hearing into his possession of the "good moral character" requisite for certification for admission. [Footnote omitted.] After lengthy hearings by a three-man subcommittee and a review of the entire record of those hearings and of additional evidence produced before the full Committee of Bar Examiners the latter found that petitioner did not possess the good moral character necessary for admission.

Respondent by letter of April 21, 1966, advised petitioner that this Committee does hereby refuse to certify the applicant to the Supreme Court of California for admission and a license to practice law because said applicant does not satisfy the requirement of Section 6060(c) of the California Business and Professions Code that he "be of good moral character." The letter set forth five grounds upon which this conclusion was based. [Footnote omitted.]

The findings of the Board of Governors of the State Bar or of a committee such as respondent, while given great weight, are not binding upon this court. [Citations omitted.] The burden of showing that the findings are not supported by the evidence or that its decision or action is erroneous or unlawful is upon the petitioner. [Citations omitted.]

In disciplinary proceedings this court examines and weighs the evidence and passes upon its sufficiency. [Citations omitted.] Any reasonable doubts encountered in the making of such an examination should be resolved in favor of the accused. [Citations omitted.] These rules are equally applicable to admission proceedings.

There are some distinctions between admission proceedings and disciplinary proceedings, the essential one being that in the former the burden is upon the applicant to show that he is morally fit, whereas in the latter the burden is upon the State Bar to prove that an attorney is morally unfit. There is early authority for the proposition that the substantive standards and permissible scope of investigation in disciplinary proceedings are distinguishable in some respects from those which apply to an admission proceeding of the type here presented. It has been held, for example, that the inquiry into moral fitness in the admission process may be broader in scope than that in a disbarment proceeding. [Citations omitted.] It was stated in the Wells case, and subsequently reaffirmed in *Spears*, that in a proceeding for admission, "The court may receive any evidence which tends to show (the applicant's) character for honesty, integrity, and general morality, and may no doubt refuse admission upon proofs that might not establish his guilt of any of the acts declared to be causes for disbarment."

Wells and Spears, as well as other California cases approving denial of admission to the bar, have been cited to demonstrate that "good moral character" has traditionally been defined in this state "in terms of an absence of proven conduct or acts which have been historically considered as manifestations of 'moral turpitude." [Footnote omitted.] [Citations omitted.] Since commission of an act constituting "moral turpitude" is a statutory ground for disbarment (Bus. & Prof. Code, § 6106) and is perhaps the most frequent subject of inquiry in disciplinary proceedings, it may readily be seen that, insofar as the scope of inquiry is concerned, the distinction between admission and disciplinary proceedings is today more apparent than real.

Fundamentally, the question involved in both situations is the same—is the applicant for admission or the attorney sought to be disciplined a fit and proper person to be permitted to practice law, and that usually turns upon whether he has committed or is likely to continue to commit acts of moral turpitude. At the time of oral argument the attorney for respondent frankly conceded that the test for admission and for discipline is and should be the same. We agree with this concession. Therefore, in considering the kinds of acts which would justify excluding a candidate for admission we may look to acts which have been relied upon to sustain decisions to disbar or suspend individuals previously admitted to practice.

In order to sustain the burden of proving that he possesses good moral character, petitioner furnished the Committee of Bar Examiners adequate letters of recommendation from members of the State Bar, and introduced before the hearing subcommittee the testimony of other attorneys who knew him.

[. . .]

The findings of the respondent disclose that the conclusion that petitioner 'has a fixed and dominant propensity for lawlessness whenever violation of the law suits his purposes of the particular moment' was predicated on evidence relating to two distinct subjects of inquiry by the hearing committee: first, petitioner's participation in and attempts to justify certain acts of 'civil disobedience' committed for the purpose of vindicating the civil rights of minority groups, particularly Negroes. Petitioner's participation in such acts of civil disobedience has resulted in various admitted and intentional violations of the criminal law for some of which he has been prosecuted and convicted. The second area of inquiry at the hearings concerned petitioner's alleged habitual and continuing resort to fisticuffs to settle personal differences. We discuss these two matters and their legal consequences separately.

First, as to petitioner's activities in connection with civil disobedience. His first arrest in this connection, so far as the record shows, occurred in 1960 while he was in England. At that time he participated in a peace demonstration in London allegedly involving "about a hundred thousand people." Immediately after the demonstration petitioner joined a group of 300 or 400 persons led by Bertrand Russell, a British philosopher, who attempted to deliver a letter of protest to the American Embassy. When the authorities at the embassy refused to accept the letter, the members of Lord Russell's group sat down en masse on a sidewalk on Grosvenor Square near the embassy. All such persons, including petitioner, were arrested. Petitioner was formally charged with "blocking a footpath" and fined one pound on his plea of Nolo contendere.

After returning to the United States, petitioner's growing interest in the civil rights movement caused him to apply for membership in the Student Non-Violent Co-ordinating Committee (SNCC), an organization formed to carry out civil rights activities in the south. As a member of this organization he spent the summer of 1963 assisting in efforts to register Negroes to vote in Mississippi and to desegregate public facilities in that state. During this period, because of these activities, petitioner was twice arrested by local authorities in Mississippi, first for loitering, and subsequently for littering public areas. Neither arrest resulted in a conviction or even a trial. On both occasions petitioner was released from jail after intervention, after the first arrest, by the Attorney General of the United States, and, after the second, by the National Council of Churches.

When petitioner returned to San Francisco from Mississippi he became a member of the Congress of Racial Equality (CORE), the National Association for the Advancement of Colored People (NAACP), the Ad Hoc Committee to End Racial Discrimination, an organization affiliated with the United Freedom Movement, and helped to organize the W.E.B. DuBois

Club, which is composed of young Socialists. As a member of these groups he expanded his participation in activities calculated to obtain civil rights for Negroes by direct action in the form of picketing and "sitting-in" at various business establishments in San Francisco believed to follow discriminatory business or hiring practices. Petitioner was arrested on six occasions by the San Francisco police between September 14, 1963, and April 11, 1964, for demonstrations at a private rental agency, at Mel's Drive-In Restaurant, at the Sheraton Palace Hotel and at an automobile agency located on San Francisco's "auto row." Four of these six arrests were made for petitioner's participation in picketing and 'sit-ins' on separate occasions at the Sheraton Palace and on "auto row." Petitioner was variously charged with violations of Penal Code sections 407 (unlawful assembly), 409 (remaining present at place of unlawful assembly), 415 (disturbing the peace, 602, subdivision (j), (trespass upon land for the purpose of obstructing a lawful business), 602.5 (unlawful entry), and 166, subdivision 4 (willful disobedience of a court order). The charges brought against petitioner for his role in the demonstrations at the rental agency, at Mel's Drive-In and for the picketing of the Sheraton Palace were dismissed. The charges stemming from the "sit-in" at the Sheraton Palace were dismissed on motion of the district attorney after two mistrials.

As a result of petitioner's two arrests on "auto row" he was twice tried and twice convicted on separate charges. He was convicted at the first trial on four counts of violating, respectively, Penal Code sections 407, 409, 415 and 602, subdivision (j), and, at the second trial, of three counts of violating Penal Code sections 407, 409 and 602.5, respectively. At the time of the hearing before the committee an appeal from the latter judgment of conviction was pending.

The so-called "auto row" "sit-ins" were the result of charges by the NAACP that certain automobile dealers adhered to and refused to negotiate about their claimed discriminatory hiring practices. At the first demonstration, on March 14, 1964, the demonstrators, including petitioner, entered the premises of the Cadillac agency, sat down and sang and clapped. The police arrived and the officer in charge read an order to the demonstrators requesting and directing them to leave the building in an orderly manner. Some of the demonstrators, but not petitioner, complied with the order. Those who remained in the building went limp and were carried out by the police and deposited in a patrol wagon. The only resistance offered by these demonstrators was passive. The second "sit-in" at the Cadillac agency occurred on April 11, 1964, after a 'cooling-off' period failed to produce a settlement between the NAACP and the Cadillac dealers. The facts of this demonstration were substantially the same as the preceding one.

Petitioner did not deny his participation in these acts of civil disobedience, but justified his conduct by certain moral and political considerations. In this connection, he was interrogated as great length by members of the subcommittee, often over repeated objections of petitioner's counsel that the questions called for speculative and philosophical answers that were unrelated to the determination whether petitioner possessed "good moral character."

Although the questions varied in form, petitioner was asked on numerous occasions whether, as an Abstract proposition, he ever considered an individual justified in deliberately violating one law in order to force others to comply with another law or overriding constitutional principle. [Footnote omitted.] On one of these occasions, for example, petitioner was asked, "Well, with regard to the overriding consideration (and I understand that you feel that this is an overriding consideration) of civil rights and the United States Constitution, is it your position that you feel it proper to violate a law if this is necessary in order to gain these other ends? To enforce civil rights of other people." Petitioner responded as follows:

"I feel that there are instances where, when you have tried all the other resorts. In other words, I wouldn't think it would be right for us just to go down to the Sheraton-Palace and sit down and say (you know) "we are here to talk about hiring Negro employees"; but when we have tried to negotiate, when we have tried to picket and have tried all the other things and they won't even talk to us, I think then, in those circumstances, that the people are justified in going in and sitting-in. I think that really (and theoretically) they are not breaking the law. That is not a violation of the law. But I think, even if they should nonetheless be instructed and have to go to jail for it if it was me (sic), I would be willing to do it. I mean, I guess I will eventually have to spend some time for what we did there at the Sheraton-Palace and the "Auto Row" and so on; but I feel that because it made so much progress in terms of the civil rights problem in this city, that I'm willing to pay the price for it. Even if it isn't reversed."

Petitioner agreed that the traditional methods of securing changes in the law by instituting legal proceedings or petitioning the Legislature are preferable to attempting to do so through direct action in the form of civil disobedience. He also stated, however, that "Unfortunately part of the progress of moving the legislature to do things has proved to be the necessity for some people committing acts of civil disobedience or sitting-in and picketing and singing and doing whatever you do. That is, without the kind of direct activity and showing of feelings and so on, you won't get the legislature passing the laws. But unless you get the legislature passing the laws and changing the laws, then there is really no objective in all the mass civil disobedience and mass demonstrations and picket lines and everything else."

In response to questions whether, in the event that he were admitted to the practice of law, he would advise others to break the law in order to secure desired changes, petitioner declared that he would not. He stated, in effect, that the would simply inform those who sought his advice whether any of their proposed acts would be violative of the law. He further indicated, however, that he would not interfere in a client's decision to violate intentionally the law for moral reasons after he had been advised as to the illegality of the proposed conduct. Petitioner also admitted that as an attorney he might well take part in a civil rights demonstration "under certain circumstances."

At one point in the hearings a member of the subcommittee read aloud to petitioner portions of an article deploring civil disobedience which appeared in the American Bar Association Journal. Petitioner was asked to comment on the statement in the article that "We must insist upon integrity of the means; we must support and protect the laws, whether we agree with a particular statute or not. We cannot settle for lip service to legality. We cannot be "'sometime' lawyers."

Petitioner stated his disagreement with this statement, "in the sense that I don't think (the author's) conclusion follows from the premises that he first lays out. That is, I don't think you are a 'sometime lawyer' because you won't obey every law to the 'T'. You know. I think, for example, lawyers in Germany during the second world war: It's an unfortunate thing that a

lot more of them, particularly judges, didn't disobey these laws. In fact, they were punished and some of them even killed, for obeying the laws of the Third Reich."

"I think somebody in the southern part of the United States has an obligation—as a lawyer—has a duty, to disobey some of those laws that are really unconstitutional and that persecute people on the basis of their race and everything else. I think that the kind of antithesis that the author of that article draws between the means and the ends is a false one. Certainly nobody would hope to achieve a good end by some brutal means, because you just couldn't do it; but on the other hand, nobody would hope to achieve just a good end without any means. You have to have some means to get at them. And the reasons we have the laws on the books, the reason why today the Civil Rights Act was passed was because of what was happening in Selma—what was happening in Birmingham. And it's only because of the activities, particularly of the Negro people, but a lot of their white supporters too, that a lot of those laws have been passed and that now it is possible to begin, but only to begin, talking about settling these things legally and in court, and not have to demonstrate and so on about it."

Does this type of evidence adequately support the refusal of respondent to certify petitioner for admission? We think not.

Preliminarily, we note that every intentional violation of the law is not, ipso facto, grounds for excluding an individual from membership in the legal profession [citations omitted]. "There is certain conduct involving fraud, perjury, theft, embezzlement, and bribery where there is no question but that moral turpitude is involved. On the other hand, because the law does not always coincide exactly with principles of morality there are cases that are crimes that would not necessarily involve moral turpitude." [Citations omitted.] In such cases, investigation into the circumstances surrounding the commission of the act must reveal some independent act beyond the bare fact of a criminal conviction to show that the act demonstrates moral unfitness and justifies exclusion or other disciplinary action by the bar. [Citations omitted.]

As the United States Supreme Court emphasized in [citations omitted], "A State can require high standards of qualification, such as good moral character or proficiency in its law, before it admits an applicant to the bar,

Chapter 11 Maintaining the Integrity of the Profession **405**

but any qualification must have a rational connection with the applicant's fitness or capacity to practice law. Obviously an applicant could not be excluded merely because he was a Republican or a Negro or a member of a particular church. Even in applying permissible standards, officers of a State cannot exclude an applicant when there is no basis for their finding that he fails to meet these standards, or when their action is invidiously discriminatory." [Citations omitted.]

In addition to an arrest for suspicion of driving a stolen car, the petitioner in Schware had also been arrested at least twice on "suspicion of criminal syndicalism" in connection with a bitter labor dispute in which he participated, and once for violation of the Neutrality Act of 1917, which makes it unlawful for a person within the United States to join or to hire or retain another to join the army of any foreign state. In its evaluation of this evidence, the court first pointed out that Schware had never been indicted or convicted for any of the alleged offenses for which he had been arrested, but then further declared that "the special facts surrounding (Schware's 1934 arrests for criminal syndicalism) are relevant in shedding light on their present significance. Apparently great numbers of strikers were picked up by police in a series of arrests during the strike at San Pedro and many of these were charged with 'criminal syndicalism." [Citations omitted.] The court noted the absence of facts suggesting that Schware was using force or violence in an attempt to overthrow the state or national government. [Citations omitted.]

[. . .]

To the extent that acts of civil disobedience involve violations of the law it is altogether necessary and proper that the violators be punished. But criminal prosecution, not exclusion from the bar, is the appropriate means of punishing such offenders. The purposes of investigation by the bar into an applicant's moral character should be limited to assurance that, if admitted, he will not obstruct the administration of justice or otherwise act unscrupulously in his capacity as an officer of the court. [Citations omitted.] We do not believe that petitioner's participation in the civil disobedience here shown can be characterized as involving moral turpitude. If we were to deny to every person who has engaged in a "sit-in" or other form of nonviolent civil disobedience, and who has been convicted therefor, the right to enter a licensed profession, we would deprive the community of the

services of many highly qualified persons of the highest moral courage. This should not be done.

The crimes with which petitioner has been charged, and in two cases convicted, in connection with his civil disobedience, considered together with the surrounding circumstances, are not analogous to the type of criminal charges or other acts which have been held to justify nonadmission to the bar. [Citations omitted.] The fraudulent acts charged in all of the admission cases just cited, unlike the subject acts committed by petitioner, necessarily impair the basic objects of the legal profession; they demonstrate, in a variety of ways, moral turpitude that is conspicuously absent here. [. . .]

The additional evidence introduced by the State Bar which, it is claimed, tends to establish petitioner's alleged disregard for the law and his propensity for violence, consists of the testimony of various witnesses to nine fist fights in which petitioner was involved during the period from 1953 to 1964. All but three of these altercations occurred before 1959, at least six years prior to petitioner's application for admission, and can be classified as youthful indiscretions. As to the other three we are of the opinion that the explanations given by petitioner and his witnesses should be accepted.

[. . .]

It is of some significance that in its final report to the full Committee of Bar Examiners, in which it was recommended that petitioner not be certified for admission, the subcommittee which conducted all but one of the hearings into petitioner's moral character and which heard and saw the vast majority of the witnesses who testified, disregarded the evidence relating to petitioner's tendency to resort to the use of his fists to settle personal differences. The subcommittee based its recommendation solely on the evidence concerning his participation in acts of civil disobedience and beliefs as to the efficacy of nonviolent civil disobedience. After an independent examination of the record, we are in agreement with the apparent belief of the members of the subcommittee that the evidence of petitioner's intemperate resort to fisticuffs, however censurable, does not support the conclusion that he lacks the good moral character requisite to admission. The question is not whether petitioner's conduct can be condoned. It cannot. The question is whether such conduct demonstrates that he does not presently possess the character to be entitled to practice law. We think that it does not.

[...]

The nature of these acts, moreover, does not bear a direct relationship to petitioner's fitness to practice law. Virtually all of the admission and disciplinary cases in which we have upheld decisions of the State Bar to refuse to admit applicants or to disbar, suspend or otherwise censure members of the bar have involved acts which bear upon the individual's manifest dishonesty and thereby provide a reasonable basis for the conclusion that the applicant or attorney cannot be relied upon to fulfill the moral obligations incumbent upon members of the legal profession. [Citations omitted.] Thus, as was said in State v. Metcalfe, 204 Iowa 123, 214 N.W. 874, 'A quarrelsome disposition, a hasty and ungoverned temper, and even an unwarranted assertion, under provocation, of a claimed right of defense of self or property, are not necessarily incompatible with truthfulness, faithfulness, and integrity.' (Id., 214 N.W. at p. 876.)

[...]

It is also relevant to the issue of petitioner's present propensity for violence to point out that since 1963, when he first became active in the civil rights movement, petitioner has repudiated the use of force as a political principle. In none of the acts of civil disobedience previously described did petitioner resort to violence. His peaceful conduct in situations fraught with tension which might be expected to provoke to violence an individual so predisposed is some indication that petitioner has, in fact, overcome such a propensity.

[...]

Other contentions of respondent so lack merit that no discussion is required.

After reading the entire record, and exercising our independent judgment as to the weight of the evidence, we find that the conclusion of the Committee of Bar Examiners that petitioner does not possess the good moral character required of applicants for admission to the bar is not justified by the record, and to the contrary we find that the record demonstrates that petitioner possesses such character. This being so, being qualified in all respects, petitioner is entitled to be admitted to practice law.

It is ordered that the Committee of Bar Examiners certify petitioner to this court as one qualified to be admitted to practice law.

TRAYNOR, C.J., and TOBRINER, PEEK, MOSK and BURKE, JJ., concur.

McCOMB, Justice (dissenting).

I dissent. An examination of the record and a reading of the majority opinion discloses to me ample evidence to sustain the action of respondent in refusing to certify petitioner to this court for admission to practice law in California.

An attorney's oath requires him "to support the Constitution of the United States and the Constitution of the State of California, and faithfully to discharge the duties of any attorney at law." (Bus. & Prof. Code, § 6067.) It is the duty of an attorney to support the Constitution and laws of the United States and of this State. (Bus. & Prof. Code, § 6068, subd. (a).) At one time petitioner stated that he would take the oath without reservation and would observe it; on the other hand, he stated that everybody has an obligation to uphold the law "to a certain extent," and that there are some laws that are manifestly unjust which he didn't think anybody had an obligation to uphold. The record discloses that petitioner believes and acts upon the belief that it is right to violate the law in order to achieve some end strongly believed by him to be socially or politically desirable.

One of the grounds for respondent's refusal to certify petitioner was that "the record as a whole establishes that he lacks candor and truthfulness." The majority is of the opinion that since petitioner revealed an extensive list of arrests, his failure to make complete disclosure of all the facts called for on his application for permission to take the bar examination must be regarded as *de minimis*. In my opinion, the members of the subcommittee and the Committee of Bar Examiners before whom petitioner appeared were in a better position than we are to pass upon the truthfulness of his testimony, and I agree with their recommendation.

Source: Reprinted from Westlaw with permission from Thomson Reuters.

Appendix A

HOW TO PREPARE THE CASE BRIEF

The paralegal student needs to understand the importance of briefing cases and why this needs to be done properly. After the paralegal has completed collecting the relevant cases through research, the information needs to be summarized and analyzed. A briefed case is the first step in the writing process toward the final trial brief. A case brief is a tool in that it serves as a "cheat sheet"; if a case is briefed properly, no one should have to reread the original case opinion. Some judges have a propensity for verbosity and the use of esoteric language. A paralegal's task is to see through that and simplify and clarify the opinion for future use in the office.

How is the paralegal to accomplish this feat? The following is a relatively standard format for case briefing. Remember to write clearly, use your own words, and be concise.

1. The Facts

- You must identify what the material facts are: what's important. This should read like a story.

    There are two types of facts:
    - Occurrence facts—what happened between the parties that gave rise to the lawsuit.
    - Procedural facts—what happened to the case once it started its journey through the legal system. Most of the time, this involves how/why the case ended up at the appellate level.
- You must learn what is important to a case. For example, the weather conditions are irrelevant in a contract dispute, but they can be vital to a car accident.
    - Pay attention to what the court itself focuses on. These are the facts that make a difference as to how the law is applied in the case.
- Identify the role that each party plays. Are there a buyer and a seller? A realtor and a construction manager? Avoid using the actual names of the parties; it will only confuse and/or annoy the reader.

2. The Issue(s)

▣ This is *not* the guilt or innocence of a party. It doesn't matter what actually happened to the parties; what matters is how their situation was analyzed by the court.

▣ What is the correct legal standard to apply and was it applied properly at the trial level?

▣ You are looking for the reason *why* a certain legal standard was applied in that case, and *how* the result was achieved.

  ☐ In this way, the researcher can determine how that same precedent can or should be applied in the instant case.

▣ It is most helpful to pose the issue as a question. Very frequently starting the question with "Whether . . ." is appropriate and helps to focus the reader.

▣ Break the issue down into its component parts. This may mean that you will have a set of numbered issues.

3. The Holding

▣ Identify the legal standard relied upon by the court.

▣ Identify how the court resolved the legal issue before it. Judges will look for statutory authority first; if there is none, then the judge will apply fundamental ideals of right and wrong (equity).

▣ This should be a short statement; essentially, it answers the question posed in the issue section. Do not try to explain the answer here; that is for the next section.

▣ If you have more than one question posed in the issue section, you should answer each one separately here.

4. Reasoning (the most important part of the brief!)

▣ The court gives the reasons *why* the outcome (holding) is what it has determined. It will explain how the legal standard applies in that case. It is important to always apply the law to the facts. This is essential for you to do, to determine how your case will turn out.

▣ Be sure to mention the relevant law relied upon by the court. Use phrases like "Pursuant to . . .", "In accordance with . . .", etc.

▣ The court may rely on several different theories in making its determination; be sure to discuss all of them. Keep a well-defined format with clear headings to assist the reader in identifying all the pertinent reasoning.

▣ Treat this section as an educational discussion. Remember that you do not want your reader to have to reread the original case.

▣ Also note how the court ultimately treated the case: its "Judgment." Did it affirm, reverse, or remand the case?

An effective case brief should ensure that the reader has all the necessary information without having to refer to the text of the case. Also, please proofread; the spellchecker is not a mind reader.

The following is an example of a case brief based upon *Herbert v. Haytaian*, 292 N.J. Super. 426, 678 A.2d 1183 (1996). The text of the case follows the brief. This case was chosen is to demonstrate the skill of analytical reading as well. The "red herring" issue of sexual harassment may cloud the true ethical issue regarding a conflict of interest if the reader is not careful.

SAMPLE CASE BRIEF
Herbert v. Haytaian, 292 N.J. Super. 426, 678 A.2d 1183 (1996)

Facts

Defendant, the Speaker of the NJ General Assembly, was accused of sexually harassing the Plaintiff, a co-worker at the Office of Legislative Services ("OLS"). Ironically, the Defendant had previously commissioned an investigation of sexual harassment claims by State employees. The Plaintiff, at the direction of the Defendant, contacted outside counsel to undertake this investigation. The Plaintiff discussed the issues involved in the sexual harassment investigation in telephone conversations and letters with the attorney and gave him access to the files of the OLS. The Plaintiff, Defendant and outside counsel considered this material and communications to be confidential. The OLS later concluded that it was not in need of outside counsel and therefore, terminated its "relationship" with the attorney and requested the return of its documents.

Three years later, the Plaintiff contacted the attorney's firm to represent her in an action against the Defendant and State alleging sexual harassment at the OLS. The State moved to disqualify the attorney due to a conflict of interest and appearance of impropriety.

Issues

Whether an attorney who was consulted but never ultimately retained or paid by a first party can later represent a plaintiff in a suit against the first party? When is the attorney-client relationship formed in a "consultation" arrangement? What are the factors to be considered in making that determination?

Holding

The fact of formal employment by signing a retainer letter or receiving payment is not the determinative factor in determining whether the parties have entered into an attorney-client relationship. An attorney-client relationship is created when a party seeks advice or assistance from an attorney and the attorney agrees to render that advice. Further, even if no actual conflict was created the public policy to uphold the integrity of the justice system was compromised due to an "appearance of impropriety" in the later representation.

Reasoning

The court determined that the attorney's access to the confidential information of the Defendant when he consulted with the OLS by and through the Plaintiff created an attorney-client relationship. The Defendant sought the advice of the attorney regarding the identical issue for which the Plaintiff sought to retain the attorney. The OLS and the attorney were ready and willing to enter into a retainer agreement regarding the sexual harassment investigation. The fact that the attorney was not ultimately retained nor paid is of no consequence with regard to his obligation to maintain the confidences of the Defendant, the first party to consult with the attorney in this matter.

> An attorney-client relationship need not rest on an express contract. An attorney-client relationship may be implied 'when (1) a person seeks advice or assistance from an attorney, (2) the advice or assistance sought pertains to matters within the attorney's professional competence, and (3) the attorney expressly or impliedly agrees to give or actually gives the desired advice or assistance.

The attorney acquired sensitive information from the Defendant regarding the subject of the lawsuit now against it. This kind of information was transmitted through the letters, telephone calls and transfer of documents. "Persons who seek legal advice must be assured that the secrets and confidences they repose with their attorney will remain with their attorney, and their attorney alone. Preserving the sanctity of confidentiality of a client's disclosures to his attorney will encourage an open atmosphere of trust, thus enabling the attorney to do the best job he can for the client."

The court argued that even if no actual conflict was found, that the appearance of impropriety would prevent the attorney from taking on the Plaintiff as a subsequent client against this Defendant. "The public display of an attorney representing conflicting interests, regardless of the attorney's good faith, may prevent the prospective client from completely confiding in his attorney. . . . It likewise would tend to erode the public's confidence in the bar."

The attorney was disqualified from representing the Plaintiff.

Superior Court of New Jersey, Appellate Division.
Beth HERBERT, Plaintiff-Appellant,
v.
Garabed HAYTAIAN, Individually and in his official capacity, and The State of New Jersey,
Defendants-Respondents.
Argued May 30, 1996.
Decided July 25, 1996.

HUMPHREYS, J.A.D.

Plaintiff alleges that the defendant Garabed Haytaian ("Haytaian") sexually harassed her from July 1994 to October 1995 while he was Speaker of the New Jersey General Assembly and she was employed in the Assembly Majority Office. She seeks compensatory and punitive damages and other relief from the State and Haytaian.

In March 1993, Neil Mullin ("Mullin"), at the request of Haytaian, agreed to undertake an investigation of alleged sexual harassment of State employees in the bi-partisan State Office of Legislative Services ("OLS"). Judge Ferentz found that this undertaking created an appearance of impropriety and entered an order disqualifying Mullin and his law firm from representing the plaintiff in this action. We granted plaintiff's motion for leave to appeal.

Mullin contends that: (1) he never represented Haytaian or the New Jersey Assembly Majority Office; and (2) during the time of his alleged representation of the State, he did not and "temporally" could not have participated in or acquired confidential information about this case.

After thorough consideration of the record and the arguments of counsel, we conclude that under the Rules of Professional Conduct ("RPC") both an actual conflict of interest and an appearance of a conflict of interest are present. The order of disqualification is affirmed.

I.

In January 1993, defendant Haytaian was the Vice-Chairman of the New Jersey Legislative Services Commission ("Commission") in addition to his position as the Speaker of the New Jersey General Assembly. The Commission is the governing body of the OLS. The OLS is an agency of the Legislature which assists the Legislature in performing its functions. Haytaian also served as Chairman of the Budget and Personnel Committee ("Committee") of the Commission. The Committee has jurisdiction over OLS personnel matters.

In January 1993, Haytaian received an anonymous letter, allegedly from an OLS employee. According to the letter, a supervisory OLS employee was romantically involved with several women in the office resulting in problems for the other employees. The letter writer charged that there was "favoritism" and a "very hostile atmosphere" in the office. The letter writer stated that "someone may be able to sue the Legislature for allowing this to go on."

Barbara S. Hutcheon ("Hutcheon"), Chief Counsel for the New Jersey Assembly Majority Office, states the following in her certification. Haytaian directed her to retain outside counsel to conduct an investigation regarding the charges in the letter. On February 11, 1993, she contacted Mullin with respect to retaining his services as special counsel. She advised Mullin that, before she could discuss the matter with him, he would have to agree that the conversation would be confidential and protected by the attorney-client privilege; and that all "further discussions" between Mullin and her, "or work performed by [Mullin]" would also be privileged. Mullin agreed and also agreed to conduct the investigation.

She told Mullin that he was to conduct an investigation into allegations of a hostile work environment and sexual harassment which had been directed to the attention of Haytaian, and that Mullin was to render legal advice to the Committee in order to safeguard its interests and the interests of Haytaian and the Legislature.

Thereafter she disclosed to Mullin both Haytaian's concerns and the concerns of the Committee regarding "the existence of the allegations and the need to respond to them." She explained to Mullin that Haytaian, who was not an attorney, had particular concerns. Specifically he was very concerned about the consequences of the allegation that a hostile work environment existed and about his duty and that of the Committee. She further disclosed to Mullin the Speaker's concerns regarding the need for outside counsel and the circumstances leading to the decision to hire outside counsel rather than proceeding in a different manner. Legal fees were also discussed.

By letter dated February 12, 1993, she forwarded to Mullin the anonymous letter and the subsequent correspondence between the Legislature and OLS. She also forwarded a copy of the Legislative Services Act of 1978, which established both the Commission and OLS, and a copy of the OLS staff directory. She thanked Mullin in the letter for "undertaking this matter."

She and Mullin discussed by telephone a number of other confidential matters including the specifics of the allegations and her views about their merits. They also discussed: (1) the identities of the parties involved; (2) the reasons why the Commission was hiring special counsel; (3) the proposed strategy devised by Haytaian and the Committee to deal with the matter including the persons involved in devising the strategy and the alternatives that were considered; and (4) the plans regarding how the Committee should handle such allegations including what steps it should take to prepare to handle such matters in the future.

On March 1, 1993, she spoke with Mullin again by telephone and sought his legal advice as to the legal obligations and duties of Haytaian and the Committee to investigate the anonymous allegations. Mullin advised her that, because of the gravity of the matter and the legal consequences of the failure to act, the Committee and Haytaian should conduct an investigation. She and Mullin also discussed "(1) the steps to be taken in starting the investigation, (2) the manner in which the interviews would be handled, and (3) what was to be disclosed regarding the nature of the investigation."

Mullin asked for written confirmation of his retention. A letter dated March 1, 1993 was sent to Mullin. Haytaian signed the letter in his capacity as Chair of the Committee. Haytaian said in the letter:

> This letter will serve to confirm that you have agreed to undertake a matter on behalf of the

Budget and Personnel Committee of the Legislative Services Commission, as previously outlined.

Hutcheon again spoke to Mullin to discuss the specific strategies that should be put in place to carry out the investigation, i.e., the timing of the interviews, the identity and number of witnesses to be interviewed, the preparation and the contents of the report and the results of the work.

Haytaian wrote a second letter to Mullin also dated March 1, 1993 in which Haytaian states: "This letter will serve to confirm that you have agreed to undertake the above-referenced matter on behalf of the Budget and Personnel Committee of the Legislative Services Commission on the following terms and conditions." One of the terms and conditions was that "this arrangement will be ratified by the full Legislative Services Commission at their next regularly scheduled meeting."

Haytaian asked Mullin in the letter to:

> Please confirm your willingness to undertake the engagement of these terms by signing and returning the enclosed copy of this letter.
>
> I am certain you recognize the importance of this matter and can appreciate the Legislature's desire to apply a prudent manage[ment] approach to its use of special counsel.

The following appears on the bottom of the letter, "I hereby agree to the terms and conditions of the above letter." Mullin signed the bottom of the letter and returned it to Haytaian.

Mullin wrote a "PERSONAL AND CONFIDENTIAL" letter to Haytaian dated March 3, 1993, "RE: Investigation of Harassment Allegation." Mullin stated in the letter that "I will proceed as follows, if it meets with your approval."

Mullin then stated at length how he would proceed. The letter contains the following:

> 5. The notes I keep will be attorney work product material. Likewise, I will transmit my report in the capacity of attorney to client, so the report too will be privileged and confidential. If the investigation identifies a substantial problem, I will, at your direction, prepare a final report documented with sworn or verbatim statements that will provide a basis for administrative action.
>
> 6. I will provide a legal framework as well as a factual framework for my conclusions both in the preliminary phase and the final phase. I will cite relevant case law for purposes of evaluating

whether there is any misconduct and whether there is any exposure to the General Assembly as an institution.

Mullin also stated in the letter that, at the conclusion of the investigation, he would "write a preliminary report suggesting whether or not there appears to be unlawful harassment or a polluted work environment." Mullin closed his letter by stating: "Thank you for retaining our firm."

The Commission later decided that special counsel was not needed, and Hutcheon so advised Mullin on March 11, 1993. She asked that he return the documents sent to him previously and he did. She further states:

> In all my conversations and dealings with Mr. Mullin, I engaged him as any client would engage his or her attorney. My understanding was that we had an attorney-client relationship. Thus, I was candid in everything I related to Mr. Mullin about the subject of representation. I understood, and believed that Mr. Mullin understood, that all matters we discussed were and remain privileged and confidential.

Mullin states in his certification that he "never represented, as counsel, the State of New Jersey or Garabed Haytaian." He states he never met Hutcheon or Haytaian and that neither he nor his firm have been paid for any professional services in connection with the matter. He states that he had only four phone calls with Hutcheon "of any substance" and did not receive any confidential information relevant to the current suit. Mullin maintains that his contacts with Hutcheon were "preliminary consultations" and that none of the documents support the passing of any confidences. In addition, plaintiff argues in her brief that Mullin could not have been retained without the approval of the Attorney General and the Governor, see *N.J.S.A.* 52:17A-11 and -13, and the approval was not given.

In January 1996, plaintiff, represented by the Mullin firm, filed this action against the State of New Jersey and Haytaian. Plaintiff alleges in her complaint that from June or July 1994 to October 1995 Haytaian subjected her to "severe and pervasive sexual harassment" and that this "created a hostile, intimidating and offensive working environment."

She also alleges in her complaint that both of the defendants "failed to remediate the sexually hostile work environment"; and that the State of New Jersey is liable under the doctrine of *respondeat superior* because it "delegated to [Haytaian], . . . the authority to control the work environment, was negligent or reckless, intended the conduct or the consequences, or the conduct violated a non-delegable duty."

Plaintiff contends in her complaint that the acts of the defendants constitute sexual harassment in violation of the Law Against Discrimination, *N.J.S.A.* 10:5-1 *et seq.* Plaintiff maintains she sustained "severe mental anguish, humiliation, pain and damage to her career and reputation."

Defendants contend that plaintiff's counsel had a press conference to announce the filing of the complaint. Mullin has been quoted in the newspaper as charging that the State has reacted to plaintiff's allegations with "institutional arrogance."

At oral argument on the State's disqualification motion, Mullin admitted that, in connection with the motion, he had disclosed to plaintiff as much of the information in the anonymous letter as was needed "so [plaintiff] could write a certification to help me defend her." He justified the disclosure because plaintiff "has a right to defend herself."

II.

Mullin contends that because he was not ultimately retained, an attorney client relationship was not created. We disagree. It is indisputable that Mullin was consulted by Hutcheon on conducting an investigation of sexual harassment of employees in a State office, and that he agreed to undertake the investigation. It is reasonable to conclude that, during his telephone conversations with Hutcheon, which took place over a period of a month, Mullin received confidential information and the views and concerns of Hutcheon and Haytaian on the following subjects: (1) sexual harassment of State employees in OLS and perhaps in State government generally; (2) a hostile work environment in OLS and perhaps in State government generally; and (3) how the OLS and perhaps State government generally were responding or had failed to respond to sexual harassment and a hostile work environment. It is also reasonable to conclude that, during these conversations, Mullin expressed his own views and advice on these subjects.

Under these circumstances, an attorney-client relationship was clearly established. The creation of an attorney-client relationship does not rest on whether the client ultimately decides not to retain the lawyer or whether the lawyer submits a bill. When, as here, the prospective client requests the lawyer to undertake the representation, the lawyer agrees to do so and preliminary conversations are held between the attorney and client regarding the case, then an attorney-client relationship is created. In *Bays v. Theran,* 418 *Mass.* 685, 639 *N.E.*2d 720, 723-724 (1994), the court said:

> 'An attorney-client relationship need not rest on an express contract. An attorney-client relationship may be implied 'when (1) a person seeks advice or assistance from an attorney, (2) the advice or assistance sought pertains to matters within the attorney's professional competence, and (3) the attorney expressly or impliedly agrees to give or actually gives the desired advice or assistance.' . . . Such a relationship may be established through preliminary consultations, even though the attorney is never formally retained and the client pays no fee.'

[(Citations omitted).]
[. . .]

The existence of the attorney-client relationship places upon Mullin the responsibilities set forth in RPC. Under RPC 1.9 Mullin cannot represent a party in "a substantially related matter" in which that party's interests are "materially adverse to the interests of the former client" nor can he "use information relating to the representation to the disadvantage of the former client" except when permitted by RPC 1.6 or when the information becomes generally known. *See* RPC 1.9; *see also Reardon v. Marlayne, Inc.,* 83 *N.J.* 460, 474, 416 *A.*2d 852 (1980).

Further:

> Where such substantially related matters are present or when a reasonable perception of impropriety exists, the court will assume that confidential information has passed between attorney and former client, notwithstanding the attorney's declarations to the contrary. The presumption of access to and knowledge of confidences may not be rebutted.
>
> [*Reardon, supra,* 83 *N.J.* at 473, 416 *A.*2d 852.]

In applying these principles, the need to maintain the highest standards of the profession must be balanced against the rights of litigants to freely choose their attorneys. However, "[o]nly in extraordinary cases should a client's right to counsel of his or her choice outweigh the need to maintain the highest standards of the profession." *Dewey v. R.J. Reynolds Tobacco Co.,* 109 *N.J.* 201, 220, 536 *A.*2d 243 (1988); *G.F. Industries v. American Brands,* 245 *N.J. Super.* 8, 15, 583 *A.*2d 765 (App. Div. 1990).

In *Dewey* the Court said:

> We cannot conceive of any situation in which the side-switching attorney or his new firm would be permitted to continue representation if, unlike the situation before us, the attorney had in fact *actually* represented the former client or had acquired confidential information concerning that client's affairs.
>
> [*Dewey, supra,* 109 *N.J.* at 220, 536 *A.*2d 243.]

The Court also said:

> If the court concludes that the side-switching attorney has not represented the former client, then it must determine whether the attorney whose disqualification is sought has 'acquired information protected by *RPC* 1.6 and *RPC* 1.9(a)(2) that is material to the matter.' *RPC* 1.10(b). The burden at that point shifts to that attorney to show that no protected information has been acquired. *See* ABA Model Rule 1.10 comment, G. Hazard and W. Hodes, *The Law of Lawyering, supra,* at 617. Again, a hearing should be held only when it is indispensable to resolution of the issue.
>
> [*Id.* at 222, 536 *A.*2d 243.]

New Jersey strictly construes RPC 1.9. *See G.F. Industries, supra,* 245 *N.J. Super.* at 13, 583 *A.*2d 765. Consequently, "[i]f there be any doubt as to the propriety of an attorney's representation of a client, such doubt must be resolved in favor of disqualification." *Reardon, supra,* 83 *N.J.* at 471, 416 *A.*2d 852.

The two matters here are substantially related. Plaintiff charges in her complaint that a hostile work environment exists in her employment by the State of New Jersey. She seeks compensatory and punitive damages against both defendants. If she proves a hostile work environment, then she may be able to recover from the State more than merely "equitable damages." *See Lehmann v. Toys 'R' Us, Inc.,* 132 *N.J.* 587, 619-620, 626 *A.*2d 445 (1993).

To prove that the State had a hostile work environment, plaintiff will likely attempt to show that the State was negligent in failing to have in place, and to have publicized and enforced: "anti-harassment policies, effective formal and informal complaint structures, training, and/or monitoring mechanisms." *See Lehmann, supra,* 132 *N.J.* at 621, 626 *A.2d* 445.

The Court said in *Lehmann* that an employer may be vicariously liable for compensatory damages "if the employer negligently or recklessly failed to have an explicit policy that bans sexual harassment and that provides an effective procedure for the prompt investigation and remediation of such claims." *Id.* at 624, 626 *A.2d* 445. An employer may also be liable if the employer knows or should know of sexual harassment and "fails to take effective measures to stop it. . . ." *Id.* at 623, 626 *A.2d* 445; *see also Payton v. N.J. Turnpike Auth.,* 292 *N.J. Super.* 36, 46, 678 *A.2d* 279 (App. Div. 1996). The court said in *Payton* that a "core inquiry" is whether the employer had an effective, properly enforced anti-harassment program. *Payton, supra,* 292 *N.J. Super.* at 46, 678 *A.2d* 279. The timeliness of an employer's response to an employee's complaint is an important element in determining the effectiveness of an anti-harassment program. *Ibid.* Further, the employer may be liable for punitive damages where the "'wrongdoer's conduct is especially egregious'" and there is "participation by upper management or willful indifference." *Lehmann, supra,* 132 *N.J.* at 624-625, 626 *A.2d* 445 (citation omitted).

Mullin's conversations with Hutcheon should be helpful to plaintiff in learning: (a) Whether the State had effective anti-harassment policies, structures, training, monitoring, investigatory and remedial procedures in place in 1993, the year before Haytaian's alleged harassment of plaintiff began; (b) If not then in place, did the State afterwards act promptly to put them in place; (c) Did the State know or should it have known of sexual harassment in State offices and fail to take effective measures to stop it; (d) Was there participation by "upper management" or "willful indifference" regarding especially egregious wrongful conduct, in which case punitive damages may be recovered. Thus, Mullin's confidential conversations with Hutcheon should significantly assist plaintiff in establishing the State's potential liability for not just equitable damages but for compensatory and

punitive damages as well. Under these circumstances, Mullin's representation of plaintiff is "materially adverse" to the State. *See RPC* 1.9.

The existence of a conflict is also shown by Mullin's conduct in opposing the disqualification motion. He has admitted that he gave plaintiff confidential information obtained from his former client in order to permit plaintiff to defend herself against the disqualification motion. This was a clear breach of his duty to his former client to preserve the former client's confidences. His conduct shows that, if the interests of his former client and present client conflict, he gives preference to the interests of his present client. This conduct is exactly what the *RPC* were designed to prevent.

Moreover, "the attorney's obligation to preserve the client's confidences" is of "fundamental importance." *Dewey, supra,* 109 *N.J.* at 217, 536 *A.2d* 243. As stated in *Reardon:*

> The ethical obligation of every attorney to preserve the confidences and secrets of a client is basic to the legitimate practice of law. . . . Persons who seek legal advice must be assured that the secrets and confidences they repose with their attorney will remain with their attorney, and their attorney alone. Preserving the sanctity of confidentiality of a client's disclosures to his attorney will encourage an open atmosphere of trust, thus enabling the attorney to do the best job he can for the client.
>
> [*Reardon, supra,* 83 *N.J.* at 470, 416 *A.2d* 852.]

Clearly, an actual conflict of interest is present here.

III.

Aside from the actual conflict, an appearance of impropriety is present. Mullin cannot represent plaintiff if his representation creates an appearance of impropriety, i.e., an "ordinary knowledgeable citizen acquainted with the facts would conclude that the multiple representation poses substantial risk of disservice to either the public interest or the interests of one of the clients." RPC 1.7(c)(2); *see also RPC* 1.9(b).

The appearance of impropriety must be something more than a fanciful possibility. It must have a reasonable basis. The conclusion must be based upon a careful analysis of the record. *See McCarthy v. John T. Henderson, Inc.*, 246 *N.J. Super.* 225, 232-233, 587 *A.2d* 280 (App. Div. 1991). "Under any circumstances the disqualification of an attorney in pending litigation does a great disservice to the affected client." *Dewey, supra,* 109 *N.J.* at 221, 536 *A.2d* 243.

We have carefully analyzed the record and are satisfied that an appearance of impropriety is present. Mullin was asked by Haytaian on behalf of the State to undertake an investigation of sexual harassment in a State office under Haytaian's oversight. Mullin likely received confidential information as to sexual harassment and the possible existence of a hostile work environment in that office. He also likely received confidential information about the knowledge, concerns and views of Haytaian on those subjects. A few years later Mullin represents a plaintiff in an action charging Haytaian and the State with sexual harassment and creating and permitting a hostile work environment. Such a setting is permeated with the appearance of impropriety. The fact that different State offices are involved is not significant. The "average citizen" is not likely to perceive "any distinctions or appreciate the bureaucratic structuring of responsibility." *See In re Petition for Review of Opinion No. 569,* 103 *N.J.* 325, 331, 511 *A.2d* 119 (1986).

Avoiding the appearance of impropriety is extremely important to our legal system. As stated in *Reardon:*

> The public display of an attorney representing conflicting interests, regardless of the attorney's good faith, may prevent the prospective client from completely confiding in his attorney. . . . It likewise would tend to erode the public's confidence in the bar.
>
> [*Reardon, supra,* 83 *N.J.* at 470, 416 *A.2d* 852 (citation omitted).]

The appearance of impropriety here is clear. Mullin would be disqualified for that reason even if no actual conflict existed.

In sum, the facts show both an actual conflict of interest and an appearance of impropriety. Disqualification must follow in order to uphold the high ethical standards of the New Jersey legal system.

Affirmed.

Appendix B

NALA MODEL STANDARDS AND GUIDELINES FOR UTILIZATION OF PARALEGALS

Introduction

The purpose of this annotated version of the NALA, Inc. Model Standards and Guidelines for the Utilization of Paralegals (the "Model," "Standards" and/or the "Guidelines") is to provide references to the existing case law and other authorities where the underlying issues have been considered. The authorities cited will serve as a basis upon which conduct of a paralegal may be analyzed as proper or improper.

The Guidelines represent a statement of how the paralegal may function. The Guidelines are not intended to be a comprehensive or exhaustive list of the proper duties of a paralegal. Rather, they are designed as guides to what may or may not be proper conduct for the paralegal. In formulating the Guidelines, the reasoning and rules of law in many reported decisions of disciplinary cases and unauthorized practice of law cases have been analyzed and considered. In addition, the provisions of the American Bar Association's Model Rules of Professional Conduct, as well as the ethical promulgations of various state courts and bar associations have been considered in the development of the Guidelines.

These Guidelines form a sound basis for the paralegal and the supervising attorney to follow. This Model will serve as a comprehensive resource document and as a definitive, well-reasoned guide to those considering voluntary standards and guidelines for paralegals.

I. Preamble

Proper utilization of the services of paralegals contributes to the delivery of cost-effective, high-quality legal services. Paralegals and the legal profession should be assured that measures exist for identifying paralegals and their role in assisting attorneys in the delivery of legal services. Therefore, NALA, Inc. hereby adopts these Standards and Guidelines as an educational document for the benefit of paralegals and the legal profession.

Comment

The three most frequently raised questions concerning paralegals are (1) How do you define a paralegal; (2) Who is qualified to be identified as a paralegal; and (3) What duties may a paralegal perform? The definition adopted by NALA answers the first question. The Model sets forth minimum education, training and experience through standards which will assure that an individual utilizing the title "legal assistant" or "paralegal" has the qualifications to be held out to the legal community and the public in that capacity. The Guidelines identify those acts which the reported cases hold to be proscribed and give examples of services which the paralegal may perform under the supervision of a licensed attorney.

These Guidelines constitute a statement relating to services performed by paralegals, as defined herein, as approved by court decisions and other sources of authority. The purpose of the Guidelines is not to place limitations or restrictions on the paralegal profession. Rather, the Guidelines are intended to outline for the legal profession an acceptable course of conduct. Voluntary recognition and utilization of the Standards and Guidelines will benefit the entire legal profession and the public it serves.

II. History

NALA adopted this Model in 1984. At the same time the following definition of a legal assistant was adopted:

> Legal assistants, also known as paralegals, are a distinguishable group of persons who assist attorneys in the delivery of legal services. Through formal education, training, and experience, legal assistants have knowledge and expertise regarding the legal system and substantive and procedural law which qualify them to do work of a legal nature under the supervision of an attorney.
>
> Historically, there have been similar definitions adopted by various legal professional organizations. Recognizing the need for one clear definition the NALA membership approved a resolution in July 2001 to adopt the paralegal definition of the American Bar Association. This definition continues to be utilized today.

III. Definition

A paralegal is a person qualified by education, training or work experience who is employed or retained by a lawyer, law office, corporation, governmental agency or other entity who performs specifically delegated substantive legal work for which a lawyer is responsible. (Adopted by the ABA in 1997 and by NALA in 2001.)

Comment

This definition emphasizes the knowledge and expertise of paralegals in substantive and procedural law obtained through education and work experience.

It further defines the paralegal as a professional working under the supervision of an attorney as distinguished from a non-lawyer who delivers services directly to the public without any intervention or review of work product by an attorney. Such unsupervised services, unless authorized by court or agency rules, constitute the unauthorized practice of law.

Statutes, court rules, case law and bar association documents are additional sources for legal assistant or paralegal definitions. In applying the Standards and Guidelines, it is important to remember that they were developed to apply to the paralegal as defined herein. Lawyers should refrain from labeling those as paralegals or legal assistants who do not meet the criteria set forth in this definition and/or the definitions set forth by state rules, guidelines or bar associations. Labeling secretaries and other administrative staff as legal assistants/paralegals is inaccurate.

For billing purposes, the services of a legal secretary are considered part of overhead costs and are not recoverable in fee awards. However, the courts have held that fees for paralegal services are recoverable as long as they are not clerical functions, such as organizing files, copying documents, checking docket, updating files, checking court dates and delivering papers. As established in *Missouri v. Jenkins*, 491 U.S. 274, 109 S. Ct. 2463, 2471, n.10 (1989) tasks performed by legal assistants must be substantive in nature which, absent the legal assistant, the attorney would perform.

There are also case law and Supreme Court Rules addressing the issue of a disbarred attorney serving in the capacity of a paralegal.

IV. Standards

A paralegal should meet certain minimum qualifications.

The following standards may be used to determine an individual's qualifications as a paralegal:

1. Successful completion of the Certified Paralegal (CP) certifying examination of NALA, Inc.;
2. Graduation from an ABA approved program of study for paralegals;
3. Graduation from a course of study for paralegals which is institutionally accredited but not ABA approved, and which requires not less than the equivalent of 60 semester hours of classroom study;
4. Graduation from a course of study for paralegals, other than those set forth in (2) and (3) above, plus not less than six months of in-house training as a paralegal;
5. A baccalaureate degree in any field, plus not less than six months in-house training as a paralegal;
6. A minimum of three years of law-related experience under the supervision of an attorney, including at least six months of in-house training as a paralegal; or
7. Two years of in-house training as a paralegal.

For purposes of these Standards, "in-house training as a paralegal" means attorney education of the employee concerning paralegal duties and these Guidelines. In addition to review and analysis of assignments, the paralegal should receive a reasonable amount of instruction directly related to the duties and obligations of the paralegal.

Comment

The Standards set forth suggest minimum qualifications for a paralegal. These minimum qualifications, as adopted, recognize legal related work backgrounds and formal education backgrounds, both of which provide the paralegal with a broad base in exposure to and knowledge of the legal profession. This background is necessary to assure the public and the legal profession that the employee identified as a paralegal is qualified.

The Certified Paralegal (CP) examination established by NALA in1976 is a voluntary nationwide certification program for paralegals. The CP designation is a statement to the legal profession and the public that the paralegal has met the high levels of knowledge and professionalism required by NALA's certification program. Continuing education requirements, which all certified paralegals must meet, assure that high standards are maintained. The CP designation has been recognized as a means of establishing the qualifications of a paralegal in supreme court rules, state court and bar association standards and utilization guidelines. On April 30, 2014, The National Commission for Certifying Agencies (NCCA) granted accreditation to the NALA Certified Paralegal program for demonstrating compliance with the NCCA Standards for the Accreditation of Certification Programs. NCCA is the accrediting body of the Institute for Credentialing Excellence. The NCCA Standards were created to ensure certification programs adhere to modern standards of practice for the certification industry. The NALA Certified Paralegal program joins an elite group of more than 120 organizations representing over 270 certification programs that have received and maintained NCCA accreditation. The accreditation requires annual reports and renewal every five years to ensure standards.

Certification through NALA is available to all paralegals meeting the educational and experience requirements. Certified Paralegals may also pursue advanced certification in specialty practice areas through the APC, Advanced Paralegal Certification, credentialing program. Paralegals may also pursue certification based on state laws and procedures in California, Florida, Louisiana, North Carolina, and Texas.

V. Guidelines

These Guidelines relating to standards of performance and professional responsibility are intended to aid paralegals and attorneys. The ultimate responsibility rests with an attorney who employs paralegals to educate them with respect to the duties they are assigned and to supervise the manner in which such duties are accomplished.

Comment

In general, a paralegal is allowed to perform any task which is properly delegated and supervised by an attorney, as long as the attorney is ultimately responsible to the client and assumes complete professional responsibility for the work product.

ABA Model Rules of Professional Conduct, Rule 5.3 provides:

> With respect to a non-lawyer employed or retained by or associated with a lawyer:
>
> (a) a partner in a law firm shall make reasonable efforts to ensure that the firm has in effect measures giving reasonable assurance that the person's conduct is compatible with the professional obligations of the lawyer;
> (b) a lawyer having direct supervisory authority over the non-lawyer shall make reasonable efforts to ensure that the person's conduct is compatible with the professional obligations of the lawyer; and
> (c) a lawyer shall be responsible for conduct of such a person that would be a violation of the rules of professional conduct if engaged in by a lawyer if:
>> (1) the lawyer orders or, with the knowledge of the specific conduct ratifies the conduct involved; or
>> (2) the lawyer is a partner in the law firm in which the person is employed, or has direct supervisory authority over the person, and knows of the conduct at a time when its consequences can be avoided or mitigated but fails to take remedial action.

There are many interesting and complex issues involving the use of paralegals. In any discussion of the proper role of a paralegal, attention must be directed to what constitutes the practice of law. Proper delegation to paralegals is further complicated and confused by the lack of an adequate definition of the practice of law.

Kentucky became the first state to adopt a Paralegal Code by Supreme Court Rule. This Code sets forth certain exclusions to the unauthorized practice of law:

> For purposes of this rule, the unauthorized practice of law

> shall not include any service rendered involving legal knowledge or advice, whether representation, counsel or advocacy, in or out of court, rendered in respect to the acts, duties, obligations, liabilities or business relations of the one requiring services where:

>> The client understands that the paralegal is not a lawyer;
>> The lawyer supervises the paralegal in the performance of his or her duties; and
>> The lawyer remains fully responsible for such representation including all actions taken or not taken in connection therewith by the paralegal to the same extent as if such representation had been furnished entirely by the lawyer and all such actions had been taken or not taken directly by the attorney. Paralegal Code, Ky. S. Ct. R 3.700, Sub-Rule 2.

South Dakota Supreme Court Rule 97-25 Utilization Rule a(4) states:

> The attorney remains responsible for the services performed by the legal assistant to the same extent as though such services had been furnished entirely by the attorney and such actions were those of the attorney.

Guideline 1

Paralegals should:

- Disclose their status as paralegals at the outset of any professional relationship with a client, other attorneys, a court or administrative agency or personnel thereof, or members of the general public;
- Preserve the confidences and secrets of all clients; and
- Understand the attorney's Rules of Professional Responsibility and these Guidelines in order to avoid any action which would involve the attorney in a violation of the Rules, or give the appearance of professional impropriety.

Comment

Routine early disclosure of the paralegal's status when dealing with persons outside the attorney's office is necessary to assure that there will be no misunderstanding as to the responsibilities and role of the paralegal. Disclosure may be made in any way that avoids confusion. If the person dealing with the paralegal already knows of his/her status, further disclosure is unnecessary.

If at any time in written or oral communication the paralegal becomes aware that the other person may believe the paralegal is an attorney, immediate disclosure should be made as to the paralegal's status.

The attorney should exercise care that the paralegal preserves and refrains from using any confidence or secrets of a client, and should instruct the paralegal not to disclose or use any such confidences or secrets.

The paralegal must take any and all steps necessary to prevent conflicts of interest and fully disclose such conflicts to the supervising attorney. Failure to do so may jeopardize both the attorney's representation of the client and the case itself.

Guidelines for the Utilization of Legal Assistant Services adopted December 3, 1994 by the Washington State Bar Association Board of Governors states:

> "Guideline 7: A lawyer shall take reasonable measures to prevent conflicts of interest resulting from a legal assistant's other employment or interest insofar as such other employment or interests would present a conflict of interest if it were that of the lawyer."

In Re Complex Asbestos Litigation, 232 Cal. App. 3d 572 (Cal. 1991), addresses the issue wherein a law firm was disqualified due to possession of attorney-client confidences by a legal assistant employee resulting from previous employment by opposing counsel.

In Oklahoma, in an order issued July 12, 2001, in the matter of *Mark A. Hayes, M.D. v. Central States Orthopedic Specialists, Inc.*, a Tulsa County District Court Judge disqualified a law firm from representation of a client on the basis that an ethical screen was an impermissible device to protect from disclosure confidences gained by a non-lawyer employee while employed by another law firm. In applying the same rules that govern attorneys, the court found that the Rules of Professional Conduct pertaining to confidentiality apply to non-lawyers who leave firms with actual knowledge of material, confidential information and a screening device is not an appropriate alternative to the imputed disqualification of an incoming legal assistant who has moved from one firm to another during ongoing litigation and has actual knowledge of material, confidential information. The decision was appealed and the Oklahoma Supreme Court determined that, under certain circumstances, screening is an appropriate management tool for non-lawyer staff.

In 2004 the Nevada Supreme Court also addressed this issue at the urging of the state's paralegals. The Nevada Supreme Court granted a petition to rescind the Court's 1997 ruling in *Ciaffone v. District Court*. In this case, the court clarified the original ruling, stating "mere opportunity to access confidential information does not merit disqualification." The opinion stated instances in which screening may be appropriate, and listed minimum screening requirements. The opinion also set forth guidelines that a district court may use to determine if screening has been or may be effective. These considerations are:

- substantiality of the relationship between the former and current matters
- the time elapsed between the matters
- size of the firm
- number of individuals presumed to have confidential information
- nature of their involvement in the former matter
- timing and features of any measures taken to reduce the danger of disclosure
- whether the old firm and the new firm represent adverse parties in the same proceeding rather than in different proceedings.

The ultimate responsibility for compliance with approved standards of professional conduct rests with the supervising attorney. The burden rests upon the attorney who employs a paralegal to educate the latter with respect to the duties which may be assigned and then to supervise the manner in which the paralegal carries out such duties. However, this does not relieve the paralegal from an independent obligation to refrain from illegal conduct. Additionally, and notwithstanding that the Rules are not binding upon non-lawyers, the very nature of a paralegal's employment imposes an obligation not to engage in conduct which would involve the supervising attorney in a violation of the Rules.

The attorney must make sufficient background investigation of the prior activities and character and integrity of his or her paralegals.

Further, the attorney must take all measures necessary to avoid and fully disclose conflicts of interest due to other employment or interests. Failure to do so may jeopardize both the attorney's representation of the client and the case itself.

Paralegal associations strive to maintain the high level of integrity and competence expected of the legal profession and, further, strive to uphold the high standards of ethics.

NALA's Code of Ethics and Professional Responsibility states "A paralegal's conduct is guided by bar associations' codes of professional responsibility and rules of professional conduct."

Guideline 2

Paralegals should not:

> Establish attorney-client relationships; set legal fees; give legal opinions or advice; or represent a client before a court, unless authorized to do so by said court; nor engage in, encourage, or contribute to any act which could constitute the unauthorized practice law.

Comment

Case law, court rules, codes of ethics and professional responsibilities, as well as bar ethics opinions now hold which acts can and cannot be performed by a paralegal. Generally, the determination of what acts constitute the unauthorized practice of law is made by state supreme courts.

Numerous cases exist relating to the unauthorized practice of law. Courts have gone so far as to prohibit the paralegal from preparation of divorce kits and assisting in preparation of bankruptcy forms and, more specifically, from providing basic information about procedures and requirements, deciding where information should be placed on forms, and responding to questions from debtors regarding the interpretation or definition of terms.

Cases have identified certain areas in which an attorney has a duty to act, but it is interesting to note that none of these cases state that it is improper for an attorney to have the initial work performed by the paralegal. This again points out the importance of adequate supervision by the employing attorney.

An attorney can be found to have aided in the unauthorized practice of law when delegating acts which cannot be performed by a paralegal.

Guideline 3

Paralegals may perform services for an attorney in the representation of a client, provided:

- The services performed by the paralegal do not require the exercise of independent professional legal judgment;
- The attorney maintains a direct relationship with the client and maintains control of all client matters;

- The attorney supervises the paralegal;
- The attorney remains professionally responsible for all work on behalf of the client, including any actions taken or not taken by the paralegal in connection therewith; and
- The services performed supplement, merge with and become the attorney's work product.

Comment

Paralegals, whether employees or independent contractors, perform services for the attorney in the representation of a client. Attorneys should delegate work to paralegals commensurate with their knowledge and experience and provide appropriate instruction and supervision concerning the delegated work, as well as ethical acts of their employment. Ultimate responsibility for the work product of a paralegal rests with the attorney. However, a paralegal must use discretion and professional judgment and must not render independent legal judgment in place of an attorney.

The work product of a paralegal is subject to civil rules governing discovery of materials prepared in anticipation of litigation, whether the paralegal is viewed as an extension of the attorney or as another representative of the party itself. Fed. R. Civ. P. 26(b)(3) and (5).

Guideline 4

In the supervision of a paralegal, consideration should be given to

- Designating work assignments that correspond to the paralegal's abilities, knowledge, training and experience;
- Educating and training the paralegal with respect to professional responsibility, local rules and practices, and firm policies;
- Monitoring the work and professional conduct of the paralegal to ensure that the work is substantively correct and timely performed;
- Providing continuing education for the paralegal in substantive matters through courses, institutes, workshops, seminars and in-house training; and
- Encouraging and supporting membership and active participation in professional organizations.

Comment

Attorneys are responsible for the actions of their employees in both malpractice and disciplinary proceedings. In the vast majority of cases, the courts have not censured attorneys for a particular act delegated to the paralegal, but rather, have been critical of and imposed sanctions against attorneys for failure to adequately supervise the paralegal. The attorney's responsibility for supervision of his or her paralegal must be more than a willingness to accept responsibility and liability for the paralegal's work. Supervision of a paralegal must be offered in both the procedural and substantive legal areas. The attorney must delegate work based upon the education, knowledge and abilities of the paralegal and must monitor the work product and conduct of the paralegal to insure that the work performed is substantively correct and competently performed in a professional manner.

Michigan State Board of Commissioners has adopted Guidelines for the Utilization of Legal Assistants (April 23, 1993). These guidelines, in part, encourage employers to support legal assistant participation in continuing education programs to ensure that the legal assistant remains competent in the fields of practice in which the legal assistant is assigned.

The working relationship between the lawyer and the paralegal should extend to cooperative efforts on public service activities wherever possible. Participation in pro bono activities is encouraged in ABA Guideline 10.

Guideline 5

Except as otherwise provided by statute, court rule or decision, administrative rule or regulation, or the attorney's rules of professional responsibility, and within the preceding parameters and proscriptions, a paralegal may perform any function delegated by an attorney, including, but not limited to the following:

- Conduct client interviews and maintain general contact with the client after the establishment of the attorney-client relationship, so long as the client is aware of the status and function of the paralegal, and the client contact is under the supervision of the attorney.
- Locate and interview witnesses, so long as the witnesses are aware of the status and function of the paralegal.
- Conduct investigations and statistical and documentary research for review by the attorney.
- Conduct legal research for review by the attorney.
- Draft legal documents for review by the attorney.
- Draft correspondence and pleadings for review by and signature of the attorney.
- Summarize depositions, interrogatories and testimony for review by the attorney.
- Attend executions of wills, real estate closings, depositions, court or administrative hearings and trials with the attorney.
- Author and sign letters providing the paralegal's status is clearly indicated and the correspondence does not contain independent legal opinions or legal advice.

Comment

The United States Supreme Court has recognized the variety of tasks being performed by paralegals and has noted that use of paralegals encourages cost-effective delivery of legal services, *Missouri v. Jenkins*, 491 U.S. 274,

109 S. Ct. 2463, 2471, n.10 (1989). In *Jenkins*, the court further held that para-legal time should be included in compensation for attorney fee awards at the market rate of the relevant community to bill paralegal time. Courts have held that paralegal fees are not a part of the overall overhead of a law firm. Paralegal services are billed separately by attorneys, and decrease litigation expenses. Tasks performed by

paralegals must contain substantive legal work under the direction or supervision of an attorney, such that if the paralegal were not present, the work would be performed by the attorney.

In *Taylor v. Chubb*, 874 P.2d 806 (Okla. 1994), the Court ruled that attorney fees awarded should include fees for services performed by paralegals and, further, defined tasks which may be performed by the paralegal under the supervision of an attorney including, among others: interview clients; draft pleadings and other documents; carry on legal research, both conventional and computer aided; research public records; prepare discovery requests and responses; schedule depositions and prepare notices and subpoenas; sum-marize depositions and other discovery responses; coordinate and manage doc-ument production; locate and interview witnesses; organize pleadings, trial exhibits and other documents; prepare witness and exhibit lists; prepare trial notebooks; prepare for the attendance of witnesses at trial; and assist lawyers at trials.

Except for the specific proscription contained in Guideline 1, the reported cases do not limit the duties which may be performed by a paralegal under the supervision of the attorney.

An attorney may not split legal fees with a legal assistant, nor pay a para-legal for the referral of legal business. An attorney may compensate a paralegal based on the quantity and quality of the paralegal's work and value of that work to a law practice.

Conclusion

These Standards and Guidelines were developed from generally accepted prac-tices. Each supervising attorney must be aware of the specific rules, decisions and statutes applicable to paralegals within his/her jurisdiction.

Addendum

For further information, the following cases may be helpful to you:

Duties

Taylor v. Chubb, 874 P.2d 806 (Okla. 1994)
McMackin v. McMackin, 651 A.2d 778 (Del. Fam. Ct. 1993)

Work Product

Fine v. Facet Aerospace Products Co., 133 F.R.D. 439 (S.D.N.Y. 1990)

Unauthorized Practice of Law

Akron Bar Assn. v. Green, 673 N.E.2d 1307 (Ohio 1997)
In re Hessinger & Associates, 192 B.R. 211 (N.D. Cal. 1996)
In the Matter of Bright, 171 B.R. 799 (Bankr. E.D. Mich.)
Louisiana State Bar Assn. v. Edwins, 540 So. 2d 294 (La. 1989)

Attorney/Client Privilege

In re Complex Asbestos Litigation, 232 Cal. App. 3d 572 (Cal. 1991)
Makita Corp. v. U.S., 819 F. Supp. 1099 (CIT 1993)

Conflicts

In re Complex Asbestos Litigation, 232 Cal. App. 3d 572 (Cal. 1991)
Makita Corp. v. U.S., 819 F. Supp. 1099 (CIT 1993)
Phoenix Founders, Inc., v. Marshall, 887 S.W.2d 831 (Tex. 1994)
Smart Industries v. Superior Court, 876 P.2d 1176 (Ariz. App. Div. 1 1994)

Supervision

Matter of Martinez, 754 P.2d 842 (N.M. 1988)
State v. Barrett, 483 P.2d 1106 (Kan. 1971)
Hayes v. Central States Orthopedic Specialists, Inc., 2002 30, 51 P.3d 562
Liebowitz v. Eighth Judicial District Court of Nevada Nev Sup Ct., No 39683,
    November 3, 2003 clarified in part and overruled in part, *Ciaffone v. District
    Court*, 113 Nev. 1165, 945 P.2d 950 (1997)

Fee Awards

In re Bicoastal Corp., 121 B.R. 653 (Bankr. M.D. Fla. 1990)
In re Carter, 101 B.R. 170 (Bankr. D. S.D. 1989)
Taylor v. Chubb, 874 P.2d 806 (Okla. 1994)
Missouri v. Jenkins, 491 U.S. 274, 109 S. Ct. 2463, 105 L. Ed. 2d 229 (1989)
McMackin v. McMackin, Del. Fam. Ct. 651 A.2d 778 (1993)
Miller v. Alamo, 983 F.2d 856 (8th Cir. 1993)
Stewart v. Sullivan, 810 F. Supp. 1102 (D. Haw. 1993)
In re Yankton College, 101 B.R. 151 (Bankr. D. S.D. 1989)
Stacey v. Stroud, 845 F. Supp. 1135 (S.D. W.Va. 1993)

Court Appearances

Louisiana State Bar Assn. v. Edwins, 540 So. 2d 294 (La. 1989)

Appendix C

NFPA MODEL CODE OF ETHICS AND PROFESSIONAL RESPONSIBILITY AND GUIDELINES FOR ENFORCEMENT

Preamble

The National Federation of Paralegal Associations, Inc. ("NFPA") is a professional organization comprised of paralegal associations and individual paralegals throughout the United States and Canada. Members of NFPA have varying backgrounds, experiences, education and job responsibilities that reflect the diversity of the paralegal profession. NFPA promotes the growth, development and recognition of the paralegal profession as an integral partner in the delivery of legal services.

In May 1993 NFPA adopted its Model Code of Ethics and Professional Responsibility ("Model Code") to delineate the principles for ethics and conduct to which every paralegal should aspire.

Many paralegal associations throughout the United States have endorsed the concept and content of NFPA's Model Code through the adoption of their own ethical codes. In doing so, paralegals have confirmed the profession's commitment to increase the quality and efficiency of legal services, as well as recognized its responsibilities to the public, the legal community, and colleagues.

Paralegals have recognized, and will continue to recognize, that the profession must continue to evolve to enhance their roles in the delivery of legal services. With increased levels of responsibility comes the need to define and enforce mandatory rules of professional conduct. Enforcement of codes of paralegal conduct is a logical and necessary step to enhance and ensure the confidence of the legal community and the public in the integrity and professional responsibility of paralegals.

In April 1997 NFPA adopted the Model Disciplinary Rules ("Model Rules") to make possible the enforcement of the Canons and Ethical Considerations contained in the NFPA Model Code. A concurrent determination was made that the Model Code of Ethics and Professional Responsibility, formerly aspirational in nature, should be recognized as setting forth the enforceable obligations of all paralegals.

The Model Code and Model Rules offer a framework for professional discipline, either voluntarily or through formal regulatory programs.

§ 1.	NFPA MODEL DISCIPLINARY RULES AND ETHICAL CONSIDERATIONS
1.1	A PARALEGAL SHALL ACHIEVE AND MAINTAIN A HIGH LEVEL OF COMPETENCE.
	Ethical Considerations
EC-1.1(a)	A paralegal shall achieve competency through education, training, and work experience.
EC-1.1(b)	A paralegal shall aspire to participate in a minimum of twelve (12) hours of continuing legal education, to include at least one (1) hour of ethics education, every two (2) years in order to remain current on developments in the law.
EC-1.1(c)	A paralegal shall perform all assignments promptly and efficiently.
1.2	A PARALEGAL SHALL MAINTAIN A HIGH LEVEL OF PERSONAL AND PROFESSIONAL INTEGRITY.
	Ethical Considerations
EC-1.2(a)	A paralegal shall not engage in any ex parte communications involving the courts or any other adjudicatory body in an attempt to exert undue influence or to obtain advantage or the benefit of only one party.
EC-1.2(b)	A paralegal shall not communicate, or cause another to communicate, with a party the paralegal knows to be represented by a lawyer in a pending matter without the prior consent of the lawyer representing such other party.
EC-1.2(c)	A paralegal shall ensure that all timekeeping and billing records prepared by the paralegal are thorough, accurate, honest, and complete.
EC-1.2(d)	A paralegal shall not knowingly engage in fraudulent billing practices. Such practices may include, but are not limited to: inflation of hours billed to a client or employer; misrepresentation of the nature of tasks performed; and/or submission of fraudulent expense and disbursement documentation.
EC-1.2(e)	A paralegal shall be scrupulous, thorough and honest in the identification and maintenance of all funds, securities, and other assets of a client and shall provide accurate accounting as appropriate.
EC-1.2(f)	A paralegal shall advise the proper authority of non-confidential knowledge of any dishonest or fraudulent acts by any person pertaining to the handling of the funds, securities or other assets of a client. The authority to whom the report is made shall depend on the nature and circumstances of the possible misconduct (e.g., ethics committees of law firms, corporations and/or paralegal associations, local or state bar associations, local prosecutors, administrative agencies, etc.). Failure to report such knowledge is in itself misconduct and shall be treated as such under these rules.

1.3	A PARALEGAL SHALL MAINTAIN A HIGH STANDARD OF PROFESSIONAL CONDUCT.
	Ethical Considerations
EC-1.3(a)	A paralegal shall refrain from engaging in any conduct that offends the dignity and decorum of proceedings before a court or other adjudicatory body and shall be respectful of all rules and procedures.
EC-1.3(b)	A paralegal shall avoid impropriety and the appearance of impropriety and shall not engage in any conduct that would adversely affect his/her fitness to practice. Such conduct may include, but is not limited to: violence, dishonesty, interference with the administration of justice, and/or abuse of a professional position or public office.
EC-1.3(c)	Should a paralegal's fitness to practice be compromised by physical or mental illness, causing that paralegal to commit an act that is in direct violation of the Model Code/Model Rules and/or the rules and/or laws governing the jurisdiction in which the paralegal practices, that paralegal may be protected from sanction upon review of the nature and circumstances of that illness.
EC-1.3(d)	A paralegal shall advise the proper authority of non-confidential knowledge of any action of another legal professional that clearly demonstrates fraud, deceit, dishonesty, or misrepresentation. The authority to whom the report is made shall depend on the nature and circumstances of the possible misconduct, (e.g., ethics committees of law firms, corporations and/or paralegal associations, local or state bar associations, local prosecutors, administrative agencies, etc.). Failure to report such knowledge is in itself misconduct and shall be treated as such under these rules.
EC-1.3(e)	A paralegal shall not knowingly assist any individual with the commission of an act that is in direct violation of the Model Code/ Model Rules and/or the rules and/or laws governing the jurisdiction in which the paralegal practices.
EC-1.3(f)	If a paralegal possesses knowledge of future criminal activity, that knowledge must be reported to the appropriate authority immediately.
1.4	A PARALEGAL SHALL SERVE THE PUBLIC INTEREST BY CONTRIBUTING TO THE IMPROVEMENT OF THE LEGAL SYSTEM AND DELIVERY OF QUALITY LEGAL SERVICES, INCLUDING PRO BONO PUBLICO SERVICES.
	Ethical Considerations
EC-1.4(a)	A paralegal shall be sensitive to the legal needs of the public and shall promote the development and implementation of programs that address those needs.
EC-1.4(b)	A paralegal shall support efforts to improve the legal system and access thereto and shall assist in making changes.

EC-1.4(c)	A paralegal shall support and participate in the delivery of Pro Bono Publico services directed toward implementing and improving access to justice, the law, the legal system or the paralegal and legal professions.
EC-1.4(d)	A paralegal should aspire annually to contribute twenty-four (24) hours of Pro Bono Publico services under the supervision of an attorney or as authorized by administrative, statutory or court authority to: 1. persons of limited means; or 2. charitable, religious, civic, community, governmental and educational organizations in matters that are designed primarily to address the legal needs of persons with limited means; or 3. individuals, groups or organizations seeking to secure or protect civil rights, civil liberties or public rights. The twenty-four (24) hours of Pro Bono Publico services contributed annually by a paralegal may consist of such services as detailed in this EC-1.4(d), and/or administrative matters designed to develop and implement the attainment of this aspiration as detailed above in EC-1.4(a) or (c), or any combination of the two.
1.5	**A PARALEGAL SHALL PRESERVE ALL CONFIDENTIAL INFORMATION PROVIDED BY THE CLIENT OR ACQUIRED FROM OTHER SOURCES BEFORE, DURING, AND AFTER THE COURSE OF THE PROFESSIONAL RELATIONSHIP.**
	Ethical Considerations
EC-1.5(a)	A paralegal shall be aware of and abide by all legal authority governing confidential information in the jurisdiction in which the paralegal practices.
EC-1.5(b)	A paralegal shall not use confidential information to the disadvantage of the client.
EC-1.5(c)	A paralegal shall not use confidential information to the advantage of the paralegal or of a third person.
EC-1.5(d)	A paralegal may reveal confidential information only after full disclosure and with the client's written consent; or, when required by law or court order; or, when necessary to prevent the client from committing an act that could result in death or serious bodily harm.
EC-1.5(e)	A paralegal shall keep those individuals responsible for the legal representation of a client fully informed of any confidential information the paralegal may have pertaining to that client.
EC-1.5(f)	A paralegal shall not engage in any indiscreet communications concerning clients.

1.6	A PARALEGAL SHALL AVOID CONFLICTS OF INTEREST AND SHALL DISCLOSE ANY POSSIBLE CONFLICT TO THE EMPLOYER OR CLIENT, AS WELL AS TO THE PROSPECTIVE EMPLOYERS OR CLIENTS.
	Ethical Considerations
EC-1.6(a)	A paralegal shall act within the bounds of the law, solely for the benefit of the client, and shall be free of compromising influences and loyalties. Neither the paralegal's personal or business interest, nor those of other clients or third persons, should compromise the paralegal's professional judgment and loyalty to the client.
EC-1.6(b)	A paralegal shall avoid conflicts of interest that may arise from previous assignments, whether for a present or past employer or client.
EC-1.6(c)	A paralegal shall avoid conflicts of interest that may arise from family relationships and from personal and business interests.
EC-1.6(d)	In order to be able to determine whether an actual or potential conflict of interest exists a paralegal shall create and maintain an effective recordkeeping system that identifies clients, matters, and parties with which the paralegal has worked.
EC-1.6(e)	A paralegal shall reveal sufficient non-confidential information about a client or former client to reasonably ascertain if an actual or potential conflict of interest exists.
EC-1.6(f)	A paralegal shall not participate in or conduct work on any matter where a conflict of interest has been identified.
EC-1.6(g)	In matters where a conflict of interest has been identified and the client consents to continued representation, a paralegal shall comply fully with the implementation and maintenance of an Ethical Wall.
1.7	**A PARALEGAL'S TITLE SHALL BE FULLY DISCLOSED.**
	Ethical Considerations
EC-1.7(a)	A paralegal's title shall clearly indicate the individual's status and shall be disclosed in all business and professional communications to avoid misunderstandings and misconceptions about the paralegal's role and responsibilities.
EC-1.7(b)	A paralegal's title shall be included if the paralegal's name appears on business cards, letterhead, brochures, directories, and advertisements.
EC-1.7(c)	A paralegal shall not use letterhead, business cards or other promotional materials to create a fraudulent impression of his/her status or ability to practice in the jurisdiction in which the paralegal practices.
EC-1.7(d)	A paralegal shall not practice under color of any record, diploma, or certificate that has been illegally or fraudulently obtained or issued or which is misrepresentative in any way.

EC-1.7(e)	A paralegal shall not participate in the creation, issuance, or dissemination of fraudulent records, diplomas, or certificates.
1.8	**A PARALEGAL SHALL NOT ENGAGE IN THE UNAUTHORIZED PRACTICE OF LAW.**
	Ethical Considerations
EC-1.8(a)	A paralegal shall comply with the applicable legal authority governing the unauthorized practice of law in the jurisdiction in which the paralegal practices.

§ 2.	**NFPA GUIDELINES FOR THE ENFORCEMENT OF THE MODEL CODE OF ETHICS AND PROFESSIONAL RESPONSIBILITY**
2.1	**BASIS FOR DISCIPLINE**
2.1(a)	Disciplinary investigations and proceedings brought under authority of the Rules shall be conducted in accord with obligations imposed on the paralegal professional by the Model Code of Ethics and Professional Responsibility.
2.2	**STRUCTURE OF DISCIPLINARY COMMITTEE**
2.2(a)	The Disciplinary Committee ("Committee") shall be made up of nine (9) members including the Chair.
2.2(b)	Each member of the Committee, including any temporary replacement members, shall have demonstrated working knowledge of ethics/professional responsibility-related issues and activities.
2.2(c)	The Committee shall represent a cross-section of practice areas and work experience. The following recommendations are made regarding the members of the Committee. 1) At least one paralegal with one to three years of law-related work experience. 2) At least one paralegal with five to seven years of law-related work experience. 3) At least one paralegal with over ten years of law-related work experience. 4) One paralegal educator with five to seven years of work experience; preferably in the area of ethics/professional responsibility. 5) One paralegal manager. 6) One lawyer with five to seven years of law-related work experience. 7) One lay member.
2.2(d)	The Chair of the Committee shall be appointed within thirty (30) days of its members' induction. The Chair shall have no fewer than ten (10) years of law-related work experience.

2.2(e)	The terms of all members of the Committee shall be staggered. Of those members initially appointed, a simple majority plus one shall be appointed to a term of one year, and the remaining members shall be appointed to a term of two years. Thereafter, all members of the Committee shall be appointed to terms of two years.
2.2(f)	If for any reason the terms of a majority of the Committee will expire at the same time, members may be appointed to terms of one year to maintain continuity of the Committee.
2.2(g)	The Committee shall organize from its members a three-tiered structure to investigate, prosecute and/or adjudicate charges of misconduct. The members shall be rotated among the tiers.
2.3	**OPERATION OF COMMITTEE**
2.3(a)	The Committee shall meet on an as-needed basis to discuss, investigate, and/or adjudicate alleged violations of the Model Code/ Model Rules.
2.3(b)	A majority of the members of the Committee present at a meeting shall constitute a quorum.
2.3(c)	A Recording Secretary shall be designated to maintain complete and accurate minutes of all Committee meetings. All such minutes shall be kept confidential until a decision has been made that the matter will be set for hearing as set forth in Section 6.1 below.
2.3(d)	If any member of the Committee has a conflict of interest with the Charging Party, the Responding Party, or the allegations of misconduct, that member shall not take part in any hearing or deliberations concerning those allegations. If the absence of that member creates a lack of a quorum for the Committee, then a temporary replacement for the member shall be appointed.
2.3(e)	Either the Charging Party or the Responding Party may request that, for good cause shown, any member of the Committee not participate in a hearing or deliberation. All such requests shall be honored. If the absence of a Committee member under those circumstances creates a lack of a quorum for the Committee, then a temporary replacement for that member shall be appointed.
2.3(f)	All discussions and correspondence of the Committee shall be kept confidential until a decision has been made that the matter will be set for hearing as set forth in Section 6.1 below.
2.3(g)	All correspondence from the Committee to the Responding Party regarding any charge of misconduct and any decisions made regarding the charge shall be mailed certified mail, return receipt requested, to the Responding Party's last known address and shall be clearly marked with a "Confidential" designation.

2.4	PROCEDURE FOR THE REPORTING OF ALLEGED VIOLATIONS OF THE MODEL CODE/DISCIPLINARY RULES
2.4(a)	An individual or entity in possession of non-confidential knowledge or information concerning possible instances of misconduct shall make a confidential written report to the Committee within thirty (30) days of obtaining same. This report shall include all details of the alleged misconduct.
2.4(b)	The Committee so notified shall inform the Responding Party of the allegation(s) of misconduct no later than ten (10) business days after receiving the confidential written report from the Charging Party.
2.4(c)	Notification to the Responding Party shall include the identity of the Charging Party, unless, for good cause shown, the Charging Party requests anonymity.
2.4(d)	The Responding Party shall reply to the allegations within ten (10) business days of notification.
2.5	PROCEDURE FOR THE INVESTIGATION OF A CHARGE OF MISCONDUCT
2.5(a)	Upon receipt of a Charge of Misconduct ("Charge"), or on its own initiative, the Committee shall initiate an investigation.
2.5(b)	If, upon initial or preliminary review, the Committee makes a determination that the charges are either without basis in fact or, if proven, would not constitute professional misconduct, the Committee shall dismiss the allegations of misconduct. If such determination of dismissal cannot be made, a formal investigation shall be initiated.
2.5(c)	Upon the decision to conduct a formal investigation, the Committee shall: 1) mail to the Charging and Responding Parties within three (3) business days of that decision notice of the commencement of a formal investigation. That notification shall be in writing and shall contain a complete explanation of all Charge(s), as well as the reasons for a formal investigation and shall cite the applicable codes and rules; 2) allow the Responding Party thirty (30) days to prepare and submit a confidential response to the Committee, which response shall address each charge specifically and shall be in writing; and 3) upon receipt of the response to the notification, have thirty (30) days to investigate the Charge(s). If an extension of time is deemed necessary, that extension shall not exceed ninety (90) days.
2.5(d)	Upon conclusion of the investigation, the Committee may: 1) dismiss the Charge upon the finding that it has no basis in fact; 2) dismiss the Charge upon the finding that, if proven, the Charge would not constitute Misconduct; 3) refer the matter for hearing by the Tribunal; or 4) in the case of criminal activity, refer the Charge(s) and all investigation results to the appropriate authority.

2.6	PROCEDURE FOR A MISCONDUCT HEARING BEFORE A TRIBUNAL
2.6(a)	Upon the decision by the Committee that a matter should be heard, all parties shall be notified and a hearing date shall be set. The hearing shall take place no more than thirty (30) days from the conclusion of the formal investigation.
2.6(b)	The Responding Party shall have the right to counsel. The parties and the Tribunal shall have the right to call any witnesses and introduce any documentation that they believe will lead to the fair and reasonable resolution of the matter.
2.6(c)	Upon completion of the hearing, the Tribunal shall deliberate and present a written decision to the parties in accordance with procedures as set forth by the Tribunal.
2.6(d)	Notice of the decision of the Tribunal shall be appropriately published.
2.7	SANCTIONS
2.7(a)	Upon a finding of the Tribunal that misconduct has occurred, any of the following sanctions, or others as may be deemed appropriate, may be imposed upon the Responding Party, either singularly or in combination: 1) letter of reprimand to the Responding Party; counseling; 2) attendance at an ethics course approved by the Tribunal; probation; 3) suspension of license/authority to practice; revocation of license/authority to practice; 4) imposition of a fine; assessment of costs; or 5) in the instance of criminal activity, referral to the appropriate authority.
2.7(b)	Upon the expiration of any period of probation, suspension, or revocation, the Responding Party may make application for reinstatement. With the application for reinstatement, the Responding Party must show proof of having complied with all aspects of the sanctions imposed by the Tribunal.
2.8	APPELLATE PROCEDURES
2.8(a)	The parties shall have the right to appeal the decision of the Tribunal in accordance with the procedure as set forth by the Tribunal.

Definitions

"Appellate Body" means a body established to adjudicate an appeal to any decision made by a Tribunal or other decision-making body with respect to formally-heard Charges of Misconduct.

"Charge of Misconduct" means a written submission by any individual or entity to an ethics committee, paralegal association, bar association, law enforcement agency, judicial body, government agency, or other appropriate body or entity, that sets forth non-confidential information regarding any instance of alleged misconduct by an individual paralegal or paralegal entity.

"Charging Party" means any individual or entity who submits a Charge of Misconduct against an individual paralegal or paralegal entity.

"Competency" means the demonstration of: diligence, education, skill, and mental, emotional, and physical fitness reasonably necessary for the performance of paralegal services.

"Confidential Information" means information relating to a client, whatever its source, that is not public knowledge nor available to the public. (**"Non-Confidential Information"** would generally include the name of the client and the identity of the matter for which the paralegal provided services.)

"Disciplinary Hearing" means the confidential proceeding conducted by a committee or other designated body or entity concerning any instance of alleged misconduct by an individual paralegal or paralegal entity.

"Disciplinary Committee" means any committee that has been established by an entity such as a paralegal association, bar association, judicial body, or government agency to: (a) identify, define and investigate general ethical considerations and concerns with respect to paralegal practice; (b) administer and enforce the Model Code and Model Rules; and (c) discipline any individual paralegal or paralegal entity found to be in violation of same.

"Disclose" means communication of information reasonably sufficient to permit identification of the significance of the matter in question.

"Ethical Wall" means the screening method implemented in order to protect a client from a conflict of interest. An Ethical Wall generally includes, but is not limited to, the following elements: (1) prohibit the paralegal from having any connection with the matter; (2) ban discussions with or the transfer of documents to or from the paralegal; (3) restrict access to files; and (4) educate all members of the firm, corporation, or entity as to the separation of the paralegal (both organizationally and physically) from the pending matter. For more information regarding the Ethical Wall, see the NFPA publication entitled "The Ethical Wall—Its Application to Paralegals."

"Ex parte" means actions or communications conducted at the instance and for the benefit of one party only, and without notice to, or contestation by, any person adversely interested.

"Investigation" means the investigation of any charge(s) of misconduct filed against an individual paralegal or paralegal entity by a Committee.

"Letter of Reprimand" means a written notice of formal censure or severe reproof administered to an individual paralegal or paralegal entity for unethical or improper conduct.

"Misconduct" means the knowing or unknowing commission of an act that is in direct violation of those Canons and Ethical Considerations of any and all applicable codes and/or rules of conduct.

"Paralegal" is synonymous with "Legal Assistant" and is defined as a person qualified through education, training, or work experience to perform substantive legal work that requires knowledge of legal concepts and is customarily, but not exclusively performed by a lawyer. This person may be retained or employed by a lawyer, law office, governmental agency, or other entity or may be authorized by administrative, statutory, or court authority to perform this work.

"Pro Bono Publico" means providing or assisting to provide quality legal services in order to enhance access to justice for persons of limited means; charitable, religious, civic, community, governmental and educational organizations in matters that are designed primarily to address the legal needs of persons with limited means; or individuals, groups or organizations seeking to secure or protect civil rights, civil liberties or public rights.

"Proper Authority" means the local paralegal association, the local or state bar association, Committee(s) of the local paralegal or bar association(s), local prosecutor, administrative agency, or other tribunal empowered to investigate or act upon an instance of alleged misconduct.

"Responding Party" means an individual paralegal or paralegal entity against whom a Charge of Misconduct has been submitted.

"Revocation" means the recision of the license, certificate or other authority to practice of an individual paralegal or paralegal entity found in violation of those Canons and Ethical Considerations of any and all applicable codes and/or rules of conduct.

"Suspension" means the suspension of the license, certificate or other authority to practice of an individual paralegal or paralegal entity found in violation of those Canons and Ethical Considerations of any and all applicable codes and/or rules of conduct.

"Tribunal" means the body designated to adjudicate allegations of misconduct.

Source: Reprinted by permission from The National Federation of Paralegal, Associations, Inc., www.paralegals.org.

Glossary

A

access to justice   The full opportunity of all persons to use all the legal resources available to the public, without regard for their ability to pay or knowledge of the legal system or experience in dealing with lawyers.

acquisition of clients   The approaching of people in need of legal services and the obtaining of their consent to represent them in a legal matter; this may be done only by an attorney.

Advanced Paralegal Certification (APC)   NALA's advanced certification that demonstrates a paralegal's mastery of knowledge and skills in specialized practice areas.

adversarial model   The American system of retaining separate independent and oppositional counsel to engage in zealous representation of individual clients.

adverse   Characteristic of a position or interest that is inconsistent or opposite with another, so that they cannot be reconciled without compromising an important element of one or both positions or interests.

advocacy   To engage in the profession of taking on clients to actively support their cause.

alternative fee arrangements   Billing practices that are not tied to time spent on a matter but rather based on the value of the services rendered, such as fixed or capped fees that allocate more risk to the firm.

ambulance chasers   A derogatory term used to describe attorneys that make direct in-person or mailed solicitation to injured persons very shortly after the accident, so that they seem to be waiting at the ambulance door for them.

American Alliance of Paralegals (AAPI)   A national group of paralegals that promote the paralegal profession by focusing on the individual paralegal.

American Association for Paralegal Education (AAfPE)   The nation's largest and continuously operating organization dedicated to promoting quality paralegal and legal studies education.

American Bar Association (ABA)   A national organization of lawyers, providing support and continuing legal education to the profession.

appearance of impropriety   A standard used to evaluate whether actions which are not strictly prohibited are still deemed unethical, because an ordinary citizen would suspect them as inappropriate behavior for a legal professional.

The Association for Legal Professionals, formerly National Association of Legal Secretaries (NALS)   A national organization that serves paralegals, legal secretaries, legal assistants, and all members of the legal support industry.

Association of Legal Administrators (ALA)   A national organization that provides information for legal management issues, resources, and networking opportunities.

attorney-client privilege   The legal relationship established between attorney and client allowing for the free exchange of information without fear of disclosure.

attorney-client relationship   The legal relationship established between an attorney and client. This relationship has many protective and confidential aspects and is unique in the legal context.

B

balance of authority   The balance between the right of the client to choose the desired outcome of the case and the obligation of the attorney to determine the best legal course to obtain that result.

441

billable hour   Time (totaling one hour) spent on a client's matter for which the client is responsible to pay, as the attorney's effort relates to and benefits the client's matter.

boutique firm An attorney or firm that handles only certain types of legal matters that are usually highly detailed and related to each other and that require specialized knowledge and experience.

C

certificated   Describing a person who has completed a certain course of study and thus earned a certificate from the issuing institution.

certification   The recognition of the attainment of a degree of academic and practical knowledge by a professional.

certified specialist An attorney who has been acknowledged to have specialized and demonstrated knowledge in a particular area of law by a bar-recognized legal association.

Certified Paralegal (CP)   These two credentials are interchangeable and are issued by NALA as the entry-level competency credential.

certified specialist   An attorney who has applied for and obtained state or national bar acknowledgement of extensive knowledge and expertise in an area of law through demonstrable evidence of testing scores and experience.

commercial speech   A category of expression that has only limited protection under the United States Constitution because its purpose is not the dissemination of an idea, but rather the garnering of monetary rewards through commerce.

commingling   The mixing of a client's funds with the attorney's personal funds without permission; an ethical violation.

communication   The obligation of an attorney to keep his client informed of the status of the matter, and to respond promptly to the client's requests for information in a candid manner.

competence   The ability to perform legal tasks with the requisite knowledge and skill to obtain a satisfactory result in the relevant field.

confidences   Any communication from the client to the attorney that the client intends to be kept private from everyone else.

conflict check   A procedure used to verify potential adverse interests before accepting a new client.

conflict of interest   A clash between private and professional interests or competing professional interests that makes impartiality difficult and creates an unfair advantage.

conservatorship   *See* guardianship/conservatorship.

constructive discharge   An attorney's cessation of the performance of legal work due to the client's insistence on pursuing unethical or imprudent means to achieve its desired result in the legal matter.

contingency fee   The attorney's fee calculated as a percentage of the final award in a civil case.

continuing legal education (CLE)   Continuing legal education designed to enhance legal services to the public and ensure that the legal professional maintains a certain level of expertise and competence.

Continued legal competence and skills training required of practicing professionals in the legal field. It may take the form of seminars and workshops in either general practice matters or a legal specialty.

controlling jurisdiction   The legal system in which the tribunal sits whose higher courts' opinions are binding authority upon the lower courts.

covenant not to compete   An employment clause that prohibits an employee from leaving his job and going to work for a competitor for a specified period of time in a particular area doing substantially similar work.

customary fee   A rate generally charged in a given locality by lawyers of the same level of expertise and area of practice.

D

diligence   Acting within the legally proscribed time or promptly responding to a client's or party's request.

diminished capacity   A client's incapability to understand legal ramifications of her decisions, as a result of immaturity, or of some mental or physical infirmity.

disbarment Temporary suspension or permanent revocation of an individual's license to practice law.

disclaimer A legal notice that serves to advise the recipient that the disseminator of the information will not be held responsible or liable for the content of the advertising.

disinterested lawyer The standard to which potentially affected attorneys must measure their actions. An attorney must detach himself from any personal interest in the matter and act accordingly.

double-billing Charging two or more clients for the same services and/or same time period.

due process The ensuring of appropriateness and adequacy of government action in circumstances infringing on fundamental individual rights.

Due Process Clause Refers to two aspects of the law: procedural, in which a person is guaranteed fair procedures, and substantive, which protects a person's property from unfair governmental interference or taking

duty of confidentiality An absolute prohibition against the attorney's disclosure of any information gained about his client, regardless of the source of that information. It is much broader than the matter covered under the attorney-client privilege.

E

ethical complaint A report of suspected unethical activity on the part of an attorney to the ethical committee of the state bar association or another appropriate tribunal. The committee may investigate to determine if an ethics violation has indeed occurred.

ethical sanctions Methods of disciplining attorneys who commit a breach of the ethical code of conduct.

ethical wall A set of internal office procedures by which a law firm can isolate or screen attorneys and paralegals who present a conflict with matters in the office and can prevent the disclosure of clients' confidential information.

ethics Standards by which conduct is measured.

ex parte A legal professional's communications regarding the substance of the matter to the tribunal without opposing counsel present.

F

fiduciary One who owes to another the duties of good faith, trust, confidence, and candor.

fiduciary relationship A relationship based on close personal trust that the other party is looking out for the other's best interests using honesty, integrity, and good faith to guide those decisions.

"fishing expedition" A request by an opposing party for potentially damaging information from the attorney, on the premise that the opposing party needs it to prevent harm, but without specific evidence of an actual threat of harm.

freelance paralegal A legal professional who works as an independent contractor under an individual contract with an attorney who provides supervision during a particular time frame or project.

frivolous Having neither factual merit nor legal purpose.

G

gatekeeping function A restriction of entry into a profession to ensure that certain standards are met prior to admission. It serves to protect both the professionals inside and the public at large against unqualified persons performing the tasks associated with that profession.

general practice firm An attorney or firm that will handle almost any type of legal matter that is presented by clients.

good faith An attorney must reasonably believe in the validity of the claim(s) asserted and present them for a proper purpose for adjudication by the tribunal.

guardianship/conservatorship The appointment of a third party who has the legal authority and fiduciary duty to care for a diminished person and/or his property. The individuals are known as either a guardian or a conservator.

I

imputed conflict Applies when one attorney or paralegal in a law office has an individual conflict with a client whom the law office wishes to represent. The conflict is attributed to the whole firm.

in camera **inspection**   A proceeding in the judge's chambers during which the judge can examine the proffered evidence outside of the jury's presence to determine the necessity of disclosure of the confidential information.

independent legal judgment   The attorney's determination of the best course to pursue to obtain the client's objectives, based upon the attorney's obligation to rely upon her own professional assessment of the legal situation, without undue influences from outside forces.

independent paralegals and legal document preparers (LDPs)   Legal professionals who offer services directly to the public. LDPs generally restrict their activities to assisting in preparing legal forms based upon the information obtained from their clients and do not and cannot render legal advice or represent their client in legal matters.

informed consent   Permission that is voluntarily given after having received and understood all relevant information relating to the situation's risks and alternatives.

International Practice Management Association (IPMA, formerly LAMA)   This international organization serves as a resource for information and education on the management of paralegals and other practice support professionals in the global context.

K

knowing   Believing with a reasonable and substantial probability (it is not necessary to be absolutely certain).

L

leading question   The phrasing of an interrogatory so as to suggest the desired answer.

legal advice   Generally, the provision of guidance regarding the meaning or application of the law or the rendering of an opinion on the possible outcome of a legal matter.

legal documents   Papers that are filed in furtherance of a court action or to secure a legal right or grant legal recourse to a party.

legal document preparer (LDP)   A legal professional who offers her services directly to the public. LDPs generally restrict their activities to assisting in preparing legal forms based upon the information obtained from their clients; they do not and cannot render legal advice or represent their clients in legal matters. In jurisdictions where there aren't separate formal designations for the profession of LDP, they are generically called "independent paralegals."

legal malpractice   A civil cause of action wherein a client may sue his attorney for failures in the representation that caused the client actual harm. The client may be entitled to money damages and possibly punitive damages in excess of actual pecuniary loss if the attorney's conduct was egregious.

licensure   A program administered by the appropriate governmental supervisory body that permits the practice in a profession by an individual only by and through its regulations and examinations.

limited license legal technician (LLLT)   Professionals who are licensed by their states to provide a set of legal services to clients directly.

lodestar calculation   A mere guidepost for determining the amount of fee to be charged, by multiplying the time to be spent on the task by the attorney's hourly rate.

M

malfeasance   A wrongful, unethical, or tortious act.

management of law practice   Oversight of the purely business aspects of the law firm, as well as ensuring that the protocols conform to the ethical requirements placed upon the attorneys and support staff.

mandatory withdrawal   Withdrawal of an attorney from representation where that representation will result in a violation of ethical rules, or the attorney is materially impaired, or the attorney is discharged.

material limitation   The inability to render neutral and unbiased services or advice.

materiality   Having a reasonable and recognizable importance in the process of evaluating a situation, such that its omission might affect the determination of fact or law.

materially misleading   Characterized by false information upon which a member of the intended audience would rely in making a decision.

misappropriation   The unlawful and unethical taking of a client's property for the lawyer's own use, regardless of intent or duration of time the property is kept.

misrepresentation   A reckless disregard for the truth in making a statement to another in order to induce a desired action.

mitigating circumstance (mitigating factor)   A fact or situation that does not justify or excuse a wrongful act or offense but that reduces the degree of culpability and thus may reduce the damages in a civil case or the punishment in a criminal case.

mitigating factor   *See* mitigating circumstance.

mitigation   The lessening of the harmful effects of a course of action.

moral turpitude   An act or behavior that gravely violates the sentiment or accepted standard of the community.

multijurisdictional practice   The practice of law by an attorney outside the state in which that attorney was originally licensed, because the clients' interests are interstate or national in scale.

N

National Association of Legal Assistants (NALA)   A legal professional group that lends support and continuing education for legal assistants.

National Federation of Paralegal Associations (NFPA)   National paralegal professional association providing professional career information, support, and information on unauthorized practice of law.

negligent misconduct   Acts that are not done intentionally, but that do not comply with the standard of ordinary care and thought needed to fulfill the relevant ethical obligations.

negotiation and settlement   The alternative means to terminate a legal matter rather than full trial on the merits. As the settlement has the same force as a final adjudication, an attorney must perform the tasks associated with it.

neutral citation   Uniform citation system that contains the name of the case, year of decision, court (postal code) abbreviation, opinion number, and paragraph pinpoint for references.

new law   A novel interpretation of established law.

O

overreaching   Taking unfair commercial advantage of another by going beyond normal and reasonable means to obtain the desired result.

P

PACE   Two-tiered paralegal certification program requiring a bachelor's degree, completion of a paralegal program, and practical experience to qualify for the proficiency examination leading to certification.

paralegal   A person qualified to assist an attorney, under direct supervision, in all substantive legal matters with the exception of appearing in court and rendering legal advice.

paralegal manager   A position in a law firm held by a paralegal who generally recruits, interviews, and hires new paralegals and helps to train them.

paraprofessional   A person with the appropriate education, knowledge, and training to perform specialized work under the supervision of another professional who has the ultimate responsibility for the collaborative work.

perjury   A witness's knowingly false and willful assertion as to a matter of fact, opinion, belief, or knowledge material to an inquiry, made under oath in a judicial proceeding as part of his or her evidence.

permissive withdrawal   The attorney's chosen termination of representation of the client in certain circumstances that comply with the attorney's ethical obligations to the client.

permitted disclosure   The right of an attorney to reveal certain information learned from his client, even without the client's consent, in certain circumstances.

pervasive neglect   Continued disregard for matters pending in the law office, deadlines, and other obligations that seriously impacts clients' interests and indicates an utter lack of diligence.

practical skills   The ability to put theory into practice by performing the tasks necessary to achieve a desired result.

private reprimand   The minimum censure for an attorney who commits an ethical violation; the attorney is informed privately about a potential violation, but no official entry is made.

pro bono publico   Literally, "for the public good." Describing legal services provided to the public by legal professionals voluntarily and without payment.

probation   A court-imposed criminal sentence that, subject to stated conditions, releases a convicted person into the community instead of sending the criminal to prison. Or, in the case of discipline of an attorney for unethical conduct, the monitoring of an attorney's conduct for compliance with ethical rules, sometimes accompanied by additional requirements.

proprietary interest   A definite financial stake in the outcome of a case or matter which may influence the attorney to take a path that is not in the best interest of his client but rather will result in a greater monetary recovery for the attorney.

prospective client   A person who knowingly seeks the advice of an attorney relating to legal matters.

public reprimand   A published censure of an attorney for an ethical violation.

Q

quantum meruit   "As much as is deserved." The reasonable value of services rendered to cover labor and costs where no other specific amount is the subject of an enforceable contract.

R

ratification   The adoption, as one's own, of the words or actions of another person.

reasonable fee   A charge for legal services that accurately reflects the time, effort, and expertise spent on a client matter.

Registered Paralegal (RP)   The credential that a paralegal may use after successful completion of NFPA's Advanced Competency Exam.

representation in court   The right to speak and be heard by the court in a legal matter; a duly licensed attorney is the only person, other than the defendant or plaintiff, who is acknowledged to have this right.

retaliatory discharge   A client's firing of the attorney for the attorney's failure to pursue the client's unethical or imprudent course in handling its legal affairs.

S

self-policing   The profession's practice of relying on its own members to report misconduct by others and to mete out punishment for infractions.

solicitation   An attorney's attempt to gain business, usually directed at a specific individual or group and involving an invitation to consult with the attorney regarding legal matters.

specialist   An attorney who has chosen to practice in a certain area of the law and has developed a concentration in this kind of legal matter.

subordinate attorney   An attorney who must report to a supervising attorney, who then takes ultimate responsibility for the work product's compliance with the firm's ethical practices.

subornation of perjury   Assistance by an attorney in carrying out a witness's offer of false testimony.

substantial gift   A gift from client to attorney large enough to have a significant impact on the attorney's ability to perform services in a neutral and detached manner.

substantial question   A serious doubt as to an attorney's fitness to practice law because his or her actions or inactions reflect negatively on his or her character.

substantive legal tasks   Duties that take legal analysis and application of specialized knowledge, as opposed to clerical duties.

supervising attorney   A partner or manager having ultimate responsibility for the work product of other attorneys and paralegals in the firm.

suspension   The prohibition of an attorney from practicing law for a specified period of time.

T

timesheet   An accurate, daily record of time spent on each task performed by an attorney or paralegal for each client.

trade name   The title of a company that it uses in commerce to identify it and distinguish it from others in the field.

U

unauthorized practice of law (UPL) The performance of certain legal tasks by someone other than an attorney, which can result in civil or criminal penalties.

unbundling of legal services The component parts of a client's legal matter are broken down and the attorney provides representation to only an agreed-upon segment of the client's needs; also known as "limited scope representation."

under the supervision of an attorney A term used to describe the work of a paralegal, which must be assigned, reviewed, and approved by a responsible attorney who takes responsibility for the content of the work.

unintentional disclosure The accidental release of sensitive client information to a third party.

unprotected communications Information that must be disclosed to the opposing party if requested during the discovery phase of litigation.

V

viable claim A claim for which the fact-finder can supply a redress in law by applying the relevant legal standard to the presentable and substantiated facts.

W

waiver of confidentiality Authorization by the client, through his words or actions, of the disclosure of otherwise protected information obtained by his attorney.

work product An attorney's written notes, impressions, charts, diagrams, and other material used by him or her to prepare strategy and tactics for trial.

Index